2
EDITION

Strategic
Corporate
Social
Responsibility

This book is dedicated to:

Thea C. Werther,

who understands the idea of responsibility in all its dimensions

and

チャンドラー 泰子

¼ 長野 ¼ シェフィールド ¼ マイアミ ¼ オースティン

Strategic Corporate Social Responsibility

Stakeholders in a Global Environment

William B. Werther, Jr.
University of Miami

David Chandler
University of Texas at Austin

Los Angeles | London | New Delhi
Singapore | Washington DC

For information:

SAGE Publications, Inc.
2455 Teller Road
Thousand Oaks, California 91320
E-mail: order@sagepub.com

SAGE Publications Ltd.
1 Oliver's Yard
55 City Road
London EC1Y 1SP
United Kingdom

SAGE Publications India Pvt. Ltd.
B 1/I 1 Mohan Cooperative Industrial Area
Mathura Road, New Delhi 110 044
India

SAGE Publications Asia-Pacific Pte. Ltd.
33 Pekin Street #02-01
Far East Square
Singapore 048763

Printed in the United States of America

Library of Congress Cataloging-in-Publication Data

Werther, William B.
Strategic corporate social responsibility: stakeholders in a global environment / William B. Werther, Jr., David Chandler. — 2nd ed.
  p. cm.
Includes bibliographical references and index.
ISBN 978-1-4129-7453-0 (pbk.)
  1. Social responsibility of business. 2. Social responsibility of business—Case studies. I. Chandler, David, 1969- II. Title.

HD60.W46 2011
658.4′08—dc22   2009047305

This book is printed on acid-free paper.

10   11   12   13   14   10   9   8   7   6   5   4   3   2

Acquisitions Editor:	Lisa Cuevas Shaw
Editorial Assistant:	MaryAnn Vail
Production Editor:	Astrid Virding
Copy Editor:	Jacqueline Tasch
Typesetter:	C&M Digitals (P) Ltd.
Proofreader:	Dennis W. Webb
Indexer:	Jean Casalegno
Cover Designer:	Candice Harman
Marketing Manager:	Helen Salmon

CONTENTS

LIST OF FIGURES

GLOSSARY OF TERMS

CORPORATE SOCIAL RESPONSIBILITY TERMS[1]

Consistent definitions, labels, and vocabulary are still emerging and remain hotly debated in the field of CSR. As such, the range of competing terminology that is used can be a source of confusion and disagreement. In our research, for example, we have seen CSR referred to in a number of different ways:

- "Corporate responsibility" or "business responsibility"
- "Corporate citizenship" or "global business citizenship"
- "Corporate community engagement"
- "Community relations"
- "Corporate stewardship"
- "Social responsibility"
- "Strategic philanthropy"

To clarify some of this confusion and provide a consistent vocabulary with which to read this book, brief definitions of the key CSR concepts are detailed below. These concepts and terms are widely discussed in the CSR literature and referred to throughout this book:

CSR—Terminology, Concepts, and Definitions

Accountability: The extent to which a firm attends to the needs and demands of its primary stakeholders (see *Transparency*).

Advocacy advertising: Efforts by firms to communicate their political, social, or business arguments with the intent of positioning themselves favorably in the eyes of the public or of persuading the public of the validity of their point of view.

Business citizenship: Societal-oriented actions by firms designed to demonstrate their role as constructive members of society.

Business ethics: The application of ethics and ethical theory to business decisions.

(Continued)

(Continued)

Cause-related marketing: Efforts to gain or retain customers by tying purchases of the firm's goods or services to a benefit provided by the firm to a nonprofit organization or charity. For example, a proportion of sales may be donated to an identified cause.

Civic engagement: Efforts by employees to improve communities in which the firm operates.

Coalitions: Collections of firms, stakeholders, or individuals that collaborate to achieve common goals.

Community advocacy panels (CAPS): Formal or informal groups of citizens who advise organizations about areas of common interest. Topics range widely but can be collectively defined as specific areas in which the organization's actions affect the local community.

Consumer activism: Efforts by actual or potential customers to have their views represented in organizational decision-making. The overarching collection of consumer activism is also referred to as the consumer movement, which has given rise to consumer rights and laws.

Consumer boycott: Action by consumers to avoid specific industries, firms, or products based on performance metrics that they value.

Consumer buycott: Action by consumers to actively seek to support specific industries, firms, or products through their purchase decisions based on performance metrics that they value.[2]

Corporate citizenship: See *Business citizenship*.

Corporate philanthropy: Contributions by firms that benefit stakeholders and the community, usually through financial or in-kind donations to nonprofit organizations.

Corporate responsibility: A term similar in meaning to corporate social responsibility, but preferred by some companies.

Corporate social performance: The performance benefits to the firm (often measured in traditional financial or accounting metrics) gained from the implementation of its CSR program.

Corporate social responsibility (CSR): A view of the *corporation* and its role in *society* that assumes a *responsibility* among firms to pursue goals in addition to profit maximization and a responsibility among a firm's stakeholders to hold the firm accountable for its actions (see *Strategic corporate social responsibility*).

Corporate social responsiveness: Actions taken by a firm to achieve its CSR goals.

Corporate sustainability: Business operations that can be continued over the long term without degrading the ecological environment (see *Sustainability*).

Enlightened self-interest: The recognition that businesses can operate in a socially conscious manner without forsaking the economic goals that lead to financial success.

Ethics: A guide to moral behavior based on culturally embedded definitions of right and wrong.

Externality: "A side effect or consequence (of an industrial or commercial activity) which affects other parties without this being reflected in the cost of the goods or services involved; a social cost or benefit."[3]

Greenwash: "Green-wash (green'wash', -wôsh') – verb: the act of misleading consumers regarding the environmental practices of a company or the environmental benefits of a product or service."[4]

Iron law of social responsibility: The axiom that suggests that those who use power in ways society deems to be abusive will eventually lose their ability to continue acting in that way.[5]

Nongovernmental organizations (NGOs): Organizations that pursue social good exclusively, rather than profits or the political requirements of government (although many of the activities conducted by an NGO might be government programs or receive government funding). For example, an NGO might help feed the poor after a disaster, although this activity may be seen as a governmental task in other societies or under other conditions (see *Nonprofits*).

Nonprofits: Organizations that exist to meet societal needs rather than seek profits for their owners or the political concerns of government. Nonprofits often differ from NGOs by having a domestic rather than an international focus.

Public policy: Government decisions aimed at establishing rules and guidelines for action with the intent of providing benefit (or preventing harm) to society.

Stakeholders: "A stakeholder in an organization is (by definition) any group or individual who can affect or is affected by the achievement of the organization's objectives."[6]

Strategic corporate social responsibility: The incorporation of a holistic CSR perspective within a firm's strategic planning and core operations so that the firm is managed in the interests of a broad set of stakeholders to achieve maximum economic and social value over the medium to long term.

Sustainability: "Sustainable development is development that meets the needs of the present without compromising the ability of future generations to meet their own needs."[7]

Sweatshops: Operations that employ children or apply working standards with little, if any, respect for human rights. Conditions are deemed to be unsafe and unfair, often in comparison to minimum legal conditions established in more affluent societies.

Transparency: The extent to which organizational decisions and operating procedures are open or visible to outsiders (see *Accountability*).

Triple bottom line: An evaluation of businesses by comprehensively assessing their financial, environmental, and social performance.

Values: Beliefs about appropriate goals, actions, and conditions.

Whistleblower: An insider who alleges organizational misconduct and communicates those allegations of wrongdoing outside the firm to the media, prosecutors, or others.

STRATEGY TERMS

In addition to the CSR terms that are used throughout this book, a number of specialized terms are used to describe a firm's strategy. The intersection between CSR and corporate strategy is central to the argument presented in this book. As such, a glossary and brief definitions of the key concepts associated with a firm's strategic planning and implementation are detailed below:

Corporate Strategy—Terminology, Concepts, and Definitions

Business strategy: The strategy of specific business units within a firm that enable it to differentiate its products from the products of other firms on the basis of low cost or another factor, such as superior technology (see *Differentiation* and *Low cost*).[8]

Capabilities: Actions that a firm can do, such as pay its bills, in ways that add value to the production process.

Competencies: Actions a firm can do very well.

Competitive advantage: Competencies, resources, or skills that enable the firm to differentiate itself from its competitors and succeed over a sustained period of time.

Core competence (or capability): Actions a firm does so well that it is difficult (or at least time-consuming) for other firms to match its performance in this area.[9]

Corporate governance: The structure and systems that officially allocate power within organizations and manage the relationships between the owners (principals) and managers (agents) of a business.[10]

Corporate strategy: The strategy of the firm. Strategy at this level involves decisions that allow the firm to navigate its competitive environment, identifying the businesses in which the firm will compete and deciding whether to enter into partnerships with other firms via joint ventures, mergers, or acquisitions (see *Business strategy*).

Differentiation: A business strategy used by firms to distinguish their products from the products of other firms on the basis of some component other than price (see *Low cost*).

Five forces: A macro-level analysis of the competitive structure of a firm's industry that indicates a firm's potential for profit.[11]

Globalization: The process, facilitated by rapidly improving communication technologies, that allows an organization's operations to transcend national boundaries.

Industry perspective: An external perspective of the firm that identifies the structure of the environment in which the firm operates (in particular, its industry) as the main determinant of competitive advantage.

Low cost: A business strategy used by firms to distinguish their products from the products of other firms on the basis of more efficient operations (see *Differentiation*).

Mission: States what the organization is going to do to achieve its vision. It addresses the types of activities the firm seeks to perform (see *Vision*).

Resources perspective: An internal perspective of the firm that identifies the resources, capabilities, and core competencies of the firm as the main determinant of a sustainable competitive advantage.

Strategy: Determines how the organization is going to undertake its mission. It sets forth the ways it will negotiate its competitive environment to attain a sustainable advantage.

Strategic planning: The process (often annual) whereby firms create or reformulate plans for future time periods.

Supply chain: The linkages formed by relationships among firms that provide a firm with the materials necessary to produce a product (see *Value chain*).

SWOT analysis: A tool used to identify the internal *S*trengths and *W*eaknesses of the firm and the external *O*pportunities and *T*hreats present in the firm's environment. The goal is to match the firm's strengths with its opportunities while strengthening the weaknesses and avoiding any threats.

Tactics: The day-to-day management decisions made to implement the firm's strategy.

Value chain: An analysis of the linkages within the production process that identifies each value-adding stage in the process. This analysis is possible within a firm or among firms.[12]

Vision: A statement designed to answer why the organization exists. It identifies the needs the firm aspires to solve for others (see *Mission*).

FOREWORD TO THE SECOND EDITION

The recent financial crisis brought a new urgency to the question of what is the role of business in society. For a while, it seemed as though there might be a fundamental reappraisal, where the ongoing and accepted belief that the principal role of a business is to maximise shareholder return was seriously questioned, even held to have become part of the problem.

After all it was the need to maximise shareholder return that had started all the problems. Banks were once seen as deeply boring institutions. But new ways emerged to increase profit by increasing risk. Tying the remuneration of top executives to share price performance created incentives to follow the trend towards apparently higher yielding instruments. The drive for higher returns had moved banks into a position where their combined activity threatened the stability of the societies that they served.

In the event, the focus after the crisis broke was distracted by the issue over how much executives got paid, rather than on what basis. This was a shame, because it became about individual greed, rather than how the system of incentives within business should be balanced to achieve socially beneficial outcomes.

A key tenet of Corporate Social Responsibility (CSR) is the unspoken contract between the business and the society within which it operates—the so-called "licence to operate." The financial institutions have discovered how painful it can be when the terms of that licence are called into question. The action taken by governments across the world to penalise those that, having required public money to survive when the crisis broke, went on to offend public sensitivities with lavish bonus schemes would have been unthinkable a couple of years ago. But the world has changed.

This is just the latest illustration of why companies need to undertake a strategic approach to CSR—seeing it as something that goes way beyond the "nice-to-have" extras of corporate philanthropy into rather an integral part of the values and the context within which the company makes its money.

CSR is not only about the programmes to reduce emissions or to invest in a local school—it is about how the company resolves the dilemmas around its core product or service, how that product is produced, how and to whom it is marketed.

For instance, the food industry has found itself under attack for being part of the problem of growing levels of obesity. There is talk of whether marketing to children should be allowed at all. The pharmaceuticals, who have a business model that uses profit to fuel constant innovation on new drugs and treatments have found themselves attacked for daring to make profit from life-saving medicines that people cannot afford. Every industry has its issues—live and emerging—which potentially affect that licence to operate.

CSR is therefore about sustainable wealth creation. Making products and services in a way that can be sustained socially and environmentally, and which will be supported by broader society. Resolving dilemmas when competing interests of stakeholders mean that difficult, often very strategic, decisions need to be taken.

This revised edition of Strategic Corporate Social Responsibility goes a long way towards clearing away the fog. William Werther and David Chandler help us to realise that, once you see CSR in terms of its strategic implications for the core business, you realise that well understood business principles apply.

It is a sign of the immaturity of the CSR movement overall that anyone should think otherwise. We fully accept that marketing campaigns, for example, will achieve their objectives only if the message is right, if the product positioning meets a mood, or a real need. And so it is that skill in execution is an important part of how CSR principles are applied. There is no automatic lever to be pulled, resulting in a surge of goodwill and cash on the bottom line. CSR is about managing the relationships that are central to the future success of the business—and initiatives taken in its name can go disastrously wrong if badly performed. William Werther and David Chandler provide a valuable list of case studies that, unusually for these sorts of works, provide a real focus on those that did badly, and those that have struggled against the odds, not just the (often self-proclaimed) examples of best practice.

The important thing is that expectations in this area can be managed. The qualities that make for good leadership in any conventionally understood sense will serve the business well in how it develops key relationships. Pro-active engagement in emerging issues is the most successful approach. The establishment of understanding and trust during the easy times makes it a lot more likely that people will support you when the inevitable problem occurs.

However, good management is not enough. Strategic CSR demands that the company must take stock of the real fundamentals—what it is in business to achieve. There is no reason to be defensive about a core imperative to make profit. Millions of ordinary citizens depend upon company profits through savings and pension funds—and the wealth that businesses create through goods and services, leading to jobs in the community, make a real contribution to the societies where they operate. Many business leaders get deeply frustrated when the argument is advanced for the more philanthropic activities on the basis that business should "put something back." They see business putting a lot in rather than taking out.

The starting point for any responsible business must be to be profitable. Programmes run in the name of CSR that damage profits, leading to business failure, job losses and worse, are the very opposite of responsible business practice.

But that is not the same as valuing profit above all else. Companies do not exist in order to make profit. They exist in order to make goods and services that people need, and in so doing make a profit. It is perfectly possible to create short term profits whilst eroding the resource base upon which they ultimately depend, or by abusing trust and being careless to the consequences. Even where such an approach may yield short term benefits, it is not a sustainable business model for the future.

There are changing expectations on business that they will manage their overall impact on society—that they will aim to maximise the positive contributions and minimise the negative. And, in addition, that they will act as a genuine corporate citizen, using their skills, resources and other assets to help to resolve common problems, whether they be global issues like climate change, or local ones like crime, or poor education. And they should respond to these expectations, because ultimately it is good for business if these problems can be tackled. As Gandhi said, they are common problems, and there will either be common solutions or no solutions.

That is why the anti-corporate movement is just plain wrong. Environmental sustainability and poverty eradication will not be achieved by the forces of good somehow "defeating" the corporations. In many aspects, the leadership companies are ahead of the politicians and even the NGOs in framing the opportunities inherent in the need to find solutions to problems. Where CSR is healthiest, it is because it has been led by business—with business leaders coming together in partnership with others to make a difference.

But businesses are still more often seen as part of the problem rather than part of the solution, and CSR is still more often seen as a "nice-to-do" add-on. It takes real leadership to take CSR to the strategic level—to frame the purpose of the business as being to create profit by doing good business in every sense of the word. This timely book comes as a welcome boost for all of those who see this as the real challenge of CSR.

–Mallen Baker
Founding Director, Business Respect

PREFACE

WHY CORPORATE SOCIAL RESPONSIBILITY MATTERS

The decision to write the second edition of *Strategic Corporate Social Responsibility: Stakeholders in a Global Environment* was taken in the middle of an economic crisis that was labeled, among other things, "the greatest threat to the international capitalist system since the Great Depression of the 1930s."[13] As a result, this dynamic economic environment undoubtedly shaped our thoughts as we wrote.

In many ways, the dramatic economic events that began toward the end of 2007 brought into focus the comprehensive nature of Corporate Social Responsibility (CSR). The crisis emphasized the many interlocking factors that constitute a modern economy and make CSR so difficult to grasp. At the same time, however, these events also demonstrated how straightforward CSR can be. At its simplest, CSR is not rocket science. It is often common sense combined with an enlightened approach to management and decision making. To look back at some of the decisions taken by key players that contributed to the economic crisis and try to rationalize why they were taken, however, represents an exercise in exasperation. As Thomas Friedman of *The New York Times* notes:

> What do you call giving a worker who makes only $14,000 a year a nothing-down and nothing-to-pay-for-two-years mortgage to buy a $750,000 home, and then bundling that mortgage with 100 others into bonds—which Moody's or Standard & Poors rate AAA—and then selling them to banks and pension funds the world over?[14]

The 2007–2009 economic crisis was driven by three main factors: First, the housing market bubble, which was fueled by low interest rates and easy access to mortgages; second, the underpricing of risk, particularly by investors on Wall Street; and, third, the failure of the regulatory infrastructure to police the increasingly liquid global financial market. All of these decisions were taken within an atmosphere of overdependence on the market as the ultimate arbiter that relieved individual actors of the personal responsibility attached to many of their day-to-day decisions. The evolution of the thoughts of Alan Greenspan, chair of the U.S. Federal Reserve from 1987 to 2006, on the policing role of market forces is instructive:

Greenspan 1963: Writing in Ayn Rand's *Objectivist Newsletter*, Greenspan declared as myth the idea that businessmen "would attempt to sell unsafe food and drugs, fraudulent securities, and shoddy buildings. It is in the self-interest of every businessman to have a reputation for honest dealings and a quality product."

Greenspan 2008: Testifying before the House Committee on Oversight and Government Reform, Greenspan recanted: "Those of us who have looked to the self-interest of lending institutions to protect shareholders' equity, myself included, are in a state of shocked disbelief. . . . This modern [free market] paradigm held sway for decades. The whole intellectual edifice, however, collapsed in the summer of last year."[15]

It is important, therefore, that blame for the crisis can be shared widely—from the individuals who sold mortgages that had attractive commissions but were unlikely to be repaid, to the organizations that allowed these sales to continue because they were passing on the risk, to the regulators who failed to oversee the markets it was their responsibility to monitor, to the investors who developed complex securities and other financial instruments that they knew no one (not even themselves) fully understood, right down to the people who failed to question whether it was wise to apply for 100 percent mortgages on hugely inflated home prices with little or nothing down, purely on the belief that house prices would continue to rise and that, anyway, they would be able to refinance in a couple of years.

The events of the economic crisis focus the debate on the personal ethics of decision makers and on those organizations that foster leaders who are willing to make the best decisions in the long-term interests of their organizations and their stakeholders. It also injects an element of cross-cultural understanding into an online and interconnected global business environment, where decisions taken by firms in one country have implications that can reverberate around the world. As such, the 2007–2009 economic crisis crystallizes a number of questions that strike at the heart of CSR: What does it mean for society when widespread business failure results in broad social and economic harm? How will this affect the environment in which we seek jobs and launch the firms of the future? How will societal expectations of these firms change (if at all), and how should the business community respond? And, what obligations do we have as individuals, organizations, or societies to avoid similar crises in the future?

This book is designed to provide a framework that offers insights into these questions. It provides a foundation that students can take with them into the workforce and wider society and that firms can use to navigate the complex and evolving issue of CSR.

Corporate Social Responsibility

Understanding CSR is important because it represents nothing less than an attempt to define the future of our society. CSR, corporate responsibility, corporate citizenship, and sustainability all matter because they influence all aspects of business. And businesses matter because they create much of the wealth and well-being in society. As such, CSR is increasingly crucial to both business and societal success.

Central to the concept of CSR, therefore, is deciding where companies fit within the social fabric. By addressing business ethics, corporate governance, environmental concerns, and other issues, society creates a dynamic context in which firms operate. The context is dynamic because the ideal mix of business goals and societal expectations is constantly evolving. Along the way, complex questions arise: Why does a business exist? Is the goal simply to maximize profits, or do for-profits serve other goals? Who defines the boundaries between private profits and the public good? What obligations do businesses have to the societies in which they operate? Are these obligations voluntary, or should they be mandated by law? To whom are companies ultimately accountable—their shareholders or also to a broader array of stakeholders? Can the interests of firms, owners, and other stakeholders be aligned, or do they conflict inherently?

While businesses are largely responsible for creating wealth and driving progress within society, they do not act alone. Governments are crucial because they set the rules and parameters within which society and businesses operate. In addition, nonprofits or nongovernmental organizations (NGOs) exist to do social good without seeking profit or fulfilling the duties of a government organization—they reach into areas where politics and profit often do not go. Nevertheless, without the innovation capitalism inspires, social and economic progress declines. Without the great wealth-producing engines of business, the taxes and charity needed to run government and nonprofits fade away, in time reducing our standard of living to some primitive level. A simple thought experiment underscores these points: Look around you and subtract everything that was produced by a business. What is left? Or another example: What is the difference between the poorest nation and the wealthiest nation? Is it not primarily the creativity and productivity of businesses embedded in a societal-defined context?

Businesses produce much of what is good in our society. At the same time, however, they also cause great harm, as pollution, layoffs, industrial accidents, and economic crises amply demonstrate. When these toxic by-products become too onerous to society, nonprofits may emerge to ameliorate the harm; however, their dependence on external funding often limits the effectiveness of these organizations. Alternatively, governments react with regulation to curb the worst excesses of business. Government, however, is often slow to act, and legislation is not always effective. Only after public consensus is reached does political will tend to follow. Yet a successful alignment of dynamic business self-interest and general social benefit creates optimal outcomes, as when a new lifesaving drug emerges from the profit motive.

Between the great good and terrible harm businesses produce, therefore, lies concern about the proper role of corporations in society, especially as globalization and technological innovation expand the reach and potential of multinational corporations. Moreover, this concern has gained renewed attention after the high-level accounting and other scandals that emerged in the early years of the new century, followed by the global economic crisis less than a decade later. As a result, corporate executives face conflict and confusion about societal expectations of their organizations. On the one hand, for example, Milton Friedman, the Nobel Prize–winning economist, argues that "Few trends could so thoroughly undermine the very foundations of our free society as the acceptance by corporate officials of a social responsibility other than to make as much money for their stockholders as possible."[16] On the other hand, however, corporations are increasingly expected to act with a multiple-constituency approach—embracing the needs and concerns of employees, shareholders, lenders, and customers while assuming responsibility for suppliers (throughout their extended supply chain), communities, and the wider environments in which they operate. Which perspective is ideal? Which is right? Are the two positions necessarily mutually exclusive? Perhaps more accurately, what is the best mix of the two that produces a sustainable society and maximizes societal benefit and welfare?

Strategic Corporate Social Responsibility provides a framework within which readers can explore and debate these questions. This book identifies the key issues of CSR, models them around conceptual frameworks, and provides both the means and the (re)sources to investigate this evolving and important topic. Our perspective is the strategic outlook of the firm; we look at the organization's interface with its stakeholders in the larger environment. As this complex web of relationships reveals, however, even simple answers are colored by honest debate, wherein reasonable, honorable, and well-intentioned people disagree, sometimes vehemently.

What makes this exploration exciting and worthy of study is that CSR is as topical as this morning's headlines—jobs and job losses, financial bailouts and record profits, corruption and scientific breakthroughs, pollution and technological innovations, and personal greed and corporate charity all spring from the relentless drive for innovation in the pursuit of profit that we call *business*. As such, CSR can be studied only at the cutting edge, where corporate competencies mold the business strategies that enable firms to compete with each other. And, when they compete in the marketplace, CSR offers a sustainable path between unbridled capitalism, with its mixed consequences, and rigidly regulated economies that are plagued with artificial and stifling limitations. CSR helps businesses optimize both the *ends* of profit and the *means* of execution. And forces are afoot that heighten the importance of optimizing this balance today, which makes CSR considerations even more important tomorrow.

Still, the question remains: What issues matter under the broad heading of CSR? The answer depends on the industry context and the firm's strategy, or how it delivers value to its customers. Because industries and strategies vary widely, however, the appropriate mix of issues will differ from firm-to-firm and change as firms adapt their strategy and execution to their specific business context. The result? It is impossible to prescribe the exact CSR mix to deal with the landscape any single firm is likely to face. Instead, we argue that a strategic lens offers the best viewpoint through which firms should approach CSR because it is through the strategic reformulation process that organizations adapt to their social, cultural, and competitive environments.

Hence, we view strategic CSR from a stakeholder perspective that embraces an external environment made up of many constituent groups, all of whom have a stake in the firm's profit-seeking activities. It demonstrates the value to firms of defining CSR in relation to their operational context and then incorporating a CSR perspective into their strategic planning and all aspects of the organization. The situations change, but the questions remain the same: Who are the primary stakeholders? Which claims are legitimate? What do we say to those stakeholders who will disagree with the decision? What value are we adding and to whom? These and other issues force business thinkers to understand CSR from a stakeholder vantage point that is set against the backdrop of each firm's industry and strategy.

A stakeholder perspective, viewed through a strategic lens, conveys the complexity of balancing competing interests in forming company policy, regardless of whether CSR is taught as a separate course or as a supplement to a capstone corporate strategy or public policy course. Still, two additional constraints remain:

- How should we cover the broad range of topics that fall under the CSR banner without being encyclopedic?
- How should we organize a book to maximize learning and interest within a global society that is increasingly online and connected?

What makes *Strategic Corporate Social Responsibility* a unique tool for this journey is our approach and underlying thesis: Exploration is the best form of learning. We focus on the technological innovation that makes CSR more relevant today than ever before—the Internet. In *Strategic Corporate Social Responsibility,* you will find scores of issues, case studies, and Internet-based resources. Our sense is that students prefer to track down the original sources themselves. By seeking out these Web sites and online documentation, they find it easier to engage and construct informed opinions. For those who like to form their own opinions, then, *Strategic Corporate Social Responsibility* offers a guided tour. It intends first to provoke and then present a road map of questions, examples, case studies, and signposts to guide an Internet-based search for solutions and supporting examples.

In our own search, we have found there are no simple answers and few absolutes. Where simple solutions are prescribed, unintended consequences usually arise. Many answers are relative to a specific industry and to the specific situation in which each company finds itself. Even when answers exist, they inevitably are a result of tradeoffs among competing stakeholder freedoms, with few parties emerging completely satisfied. Rather than provide absolute answers, therefore, we seek to stimulate the *best* questions that consider a broad range of perspectives, provoke vibrant debate, and stimulate further research. As such, this book does not search for solutions to the pressing CSR problems of today. Undoubtedly, such solutions would be generalizations of limited use, quickly outdated by changing societal expectations. Instead, we present a stakeholder perspective as the most effective means of understanding the bigger picture of strategic CSR. To avoid repeating these same mistakes in the future, it is crucial to understand the issues at hand, see the past mistakes made by firms, and possess a structural framework that encourages a holistic perspective.

The journey you are about to undertake will help equip you for a career that is changing at an accelerating rate. CSR is an increasingly important component of this change. Gaining insight into the broad scope of this dynamic topic will increase your understanding and sophistication as a thinker, as a businessperson, and as an informed citizen.

William B. Werther, Jr.
werther@miami.edu

David Chandler
david.chandler@phd.mccombs.utexas.edu

Disclaimer

An important feature of this book is its many Internet-based resources. Relying on such resources, however, presents two specific issues: First, due to the dynamic nature of the Internet, some of the URLs provided will change or disappear over time. One resource for tracking down missing Web sites is the digital library being created by Internet Archive (http://www.archive.org/). Second, to present a balanced and varied selection of resources for further investigation, this book provides links to many organizations. It is not our intention to endorse these organizations or validate their messages in any way but rather to present their voice as part of the ongoing debate relating to each particular issue.

PLAN OF THE BOOK

S*trategic Corporate Social Responsibility* is organized into two distinct parts. Part I of the book highlights the breadth and depth of corporate social responsibility (CSR), while Part II presents a series of real-life issues and case studies, with online resources and questions for further investigation and debate.

Chapters 1 and 2 of Part I lay the foundation for this book by defining CSR and providing a broader understanding of the context from which it emerged. Chapter 1 introduces CSR, providing detail on where this topic originated and how it has evolved over time. In discussing the evolution of this topic, three different arguments for CSR are presented—moral, rational, and economic. This chapter identifies why CSR is a growing concern to students and leaders of business. Businesses are economic entities that exist to meet needs in society and further the financial interests of their owners; we argue that the most effective way to achieve these goals today is by considering the needs and values of a broad range of groups that have a stake in the outcome of the pursuit of profit. These other *nonowner* stakeholders are vital because they can affect the success, even the survival, of the business. Most important, therefore, this chapter defines CSR in light of the global, information, and communications-driven environment that corporations operate within today.

Chapter 2 reflects the importance of a stakeholder perspective to the argument we present in *Strategic CSR*. Throughout this century, as business schools worldwide evolve to account for the changing environment in which firms operate, we believe that CSR will make up an increasingly core component of the curriculum. In addition to being integrated throughout all capstone classes, CSR finds a natural home within corporate strategy. The ideal vehicle for the integration of CSR and strategy is a multistakeholder perspective that enables firms to respond to the dominant trends in society today—globalization and the increasingly free flow of information. In addition to the stakeholder perspective that we weave throughout the book, therefore, this chapter explains why the traditional strategy perspectives (principally the resource-based and industry perspectives) are insufficient tools to help firms craft strategies in today's globalized business environment. We outline a stakeholder model that allows firms to identify and prioritize their key stakeholders, allowing them to respond in the way that maximizes both economic and social value.

The focus of much of the CSR debate (and captured by the term corporate social *responsibility*) is the assumption that firms have a responsibility to pursue goals other than profit maximization. In Chapter 3, we seek to explore this assumption in more detail and examine some of the more contentious elements of the CSR debate. In particular, we propose the idea that the CSR community expects too much of firms; that firms react better than they initiate; and that if, as a society, we decide that firms should act with greater social responsibility, then it is a firm's stakeholders (and their consumers, in particular) that have an equal, if not greater, responsibility to demand this behavior from firms. More important, they need to demonstrate that they will support such behavior. For CSR to be a stakeholder responsibility, however, stakeholders need to care about CSR. The economic argument for CSR presupposes an economic advantage for a company that is a net contributor to society, or at least a belief that there is economic disadvantage for any company that negatively affects key stakeholder groups. Managers, as suggested by advertising campaigns and philanthropic activities, already understand the benefits for businesses that are perceived to make a positive contribution. Although many people say they want responsible companies, however, there are limits to what societies and consumers are willing to pay for the privilege. This willingness to pay for social responsibility is arguable and central to the CSR debate. Without sufficient stakeholder interest in CSR behavior, corporations have less incentive to embrace CSR.

Chapters 4 and 5 conclude Part I of *Strategic CSR* by outlining how firms integrate CSR into day-to-day operations. Chapter 4 places CSR within a strategic context, arguing that CSR exists, or should exist, within the strategic framework of the organization. As the firm matches its capabilities with the opportunities in its competitive environment, it pursues its mission to move the firm toward its aspirations or vision. CSR is an integral part of this strategic process because it serves to filter how businesses interact with their environments and implement their ideas. While strategy seeks competitive success, CSR acts as a screen that helps ensure the profit motive does not harm the firm's long-term viability. Planetwide trends of increased affluence, globalization, the Internet, massive media conglomeration, and branding combine to heighten the strategic importance of CSR today. Moreover, these trends increase the importance of CSR in the future.

Finally, Chapter 5 explores the challenges of integrating CSR into the firm's competitive strategies and its organizational culture. Here, our intent is to identify the factors that strengthen or impede the creation of a strategic CSR orientation at the firm level. Central to this integration process is the commitment of senior management. Strategic direction, mission statements, and day-to-day operating policies must all reinforce this commitment to attaining CSR goals. Ultimately, to integrate CSR into the firm's strategies and its culture, leaders must start an ongoing dialogue within the organization and with key stakeholders about the strategic and operational importance of CSR. This chapter provides a framework for implementing an effective CSR policy throughout the organization.

Part II reflects the range of issues that define CSR in practice, each segmented into one of the three stakeholder groups: organizational, economic, or societal stakeholders. Chapter 6 contains issues primarily involving organizational stakeholders; Chapter 7, economic stakeholders; and Chapter 8, societal stakeholders. Each issue is illustrated with a real-life case study and supporting sources. Differing viewpoints are also available via the Web sites provided. As such, Part II also reveals the unique nature of *Strategic CSR*. We believe that the scope of CSR is a mosaic of issues. Which issues are most important today or tomorrow evolves with changes in society and the competitive environment. Moreover, given individual student and faculty interests, our approach in Part II is to provide a comprehensive introduction to each issue and then provide Internet-accessible source material as a link to further investigation.

Interspersed throughout Parts I and II of the book, we also introduce the reader to the *CSR Newsletters* that are distributed by the authors as a dynamic complement to the text. Taken from the daily reading of the authors, the Newsletters are presented as a value-added library of examples beyond the case studies and online references provided throughout the book. These topical themes, together with access to the complete library of many hundreds of Newsletters on the book's Web site,[17] are designed to represent the breadth of the CSR debate to the reader. This additional resource also helps make this publication an appropriate addition to any professional or business library. Each Newsletter also represents a mini-case study as teaching content related to issues at the cutting edge of the CSR debate, providing stepping stones to help the eager reader delve farther into this complex subject.

In addition to the two parts that constitute *Strategic CSR*, the second edition is accompanied by an interactive Web site (http://www.sagepub.com/StrategicCSR/). This Web site is designed to enhance the content provided in these pages. Primarily, the Web site does this by archiving the CSR Newsletters, which are distributed regularly during the fall and spring academic semesters and provide newspaper articles and commentary on contemporary issues and case studies that characterize current debate within the CSR community. In addition, the Web site archives all the material from the book's first edition (e.g., issues and case studies) that was replaced in writing the second edition. Also, as time goes by and some of the URLs in this edition become inactive, this Web site can also form a means of providing updates or alternative sources of information to keep this edition relevant, even many years following publication. Finally, the Web site will provide instructors with secure access to the *Instructor's Manual* that accompanies this text and other resources of relevant and topical materials that can be used in the classroom. Our goal is for this Web site to provide an additional dimension to *Strategic CSR* that complements its use in the classroom.

NOTES AND REFERENCES

1. For a comprehensive review of the evolution of CSR as an academic discipline see Archie B. Carroll, "Corporate Social Responsibility: Evolution of a Definitional Construct," *Business and Society,* Vol. 38, No. 3 (1999), pp. 268–295. Also, traditional textbooks elaborate on these issues: see Anne T. Lawrence, James Weber, & James E. Post, *Business and Society: Corporate Strategy, Public Policy, Ethics,* 12th edition, McGraw-Hill, 2008. Finally, William C. Frederick, *Corporation Be Good! The Story of Corporate Social Responsibility*, Dog Ear Publishing, 2006, offers a comprehensive timeline and discussion about the evolution of CSR.

2. Amy J. Hebard & Wendy S. Cobrda, "The Corporate Reality of Consumer Perceptions: Bringing the Consumer Perspective to CSR Reporting," *GreenBiz Reports*, February 2009, p. 13.

3. *Oxford English Dictionary,* Second Edition, 1989, http://dictionary.oed.com/cgi/entry/50080908?single=1&query_type=word&queryword=externality&first=1&max_to_show=10

4. "The Six Sins of Greenwashing," *Terrachoice Environmental Marketing*, 2007, http://sinsof-greenwashing.org/findings/greenwashing-report-2009/

5. Keith Davis, "The Case for and Against Business Assumption of Social Responsibilities," *Academy of Management Journal*, Vol. 16, No. 2, 1973, pp. 312–322.

6. R. Edward Freeman, *Strategic Management: A Stakeholder Approach*, Pitman Publishing, Inc., 1984, p. 46.

7. Bill Baue, "Brundtland Report Celebrates 20th Anniversary Since Coining Sustainable Development," *Ethical Corporation Magazine*, June 18, 2007, http://www.ethicalcorp.com/content.asp?ContentID=5175. This definition of *sustainability* was developed by the Brundtland Commission (which got its name from its chair, Gro Harlem Brundtland, the former Prime Minister of Norway). The commission was established by the United Nations in 1983 to address growing concerns about the deteriorating condition of the natural environment. See also: http://www.un-documents.net/wced-ocf.htm

8. Michael E. Porter, *Competitive Strategy*, The Free Press, 1980.

9. C. K. Prahalad & Gary Hamel, "The Core Competence of the Corporation," *Harvard Business Review*, May–June 1990, pp. 79–91; Gary Hamel & C. K. Prahalad, *Competing for the Future*, Harvard Business School Press, 1994.

10. Corporate governance has risen to prominence within the CSR field because of high-profile corporate scandals following the Internet bubble around the turn of this century. Much of the legislative response was an attempt to redress the balance of power between management and stockholders, represented by the board of directors. This issue revisits the fundamental conflict between principals (owners) and their agents (managers), an issue that has plagued limited liability joint stock companies since they were established in the United Kingdom by the Companies Act of 1862 (see John Micklethwait & Adrian Woolridge, *The Company: A Short History of a Revolutionary Idea,* Modern Library, 2003, pp. xvi & xviii).

11. Michael E. Porter, "The Five Competitive Forces That Shape Strategy," *Harvard Business Review*, January 2008, pp. 79–93; Michael E. Porter, *Competitive Strategy*, The Free Press, 1980.

12. Michael E. Porter, *Competitive Advantage*, The Free Press, 1985.

13. Samuel Brittan, "The Key to Keynes," *Financial Times*, August 22–23, 2009, Life and Arts, p. 13.

14. Thomas L. Friedman, "The Great Unraveling," *The New York Times*, December 17, 2008, p. A29.

15. Donald Cohen, "The Education of Alan Greenspan," *The Huffington Post*, October 31, 2008, http://www.alternet.org/workplace/105414/the_education_of_alan_greenspan/

16. Milton Friedman, *Capitalism and Freedom*, University of Chicago Press, 1962, p. 133.

17. http://www.sagepub.com/StrategicCSR/

ACKNOWLEDGMENTS

Although we remain ultimately responsible for the ideas we present in *Strategic Corporate Social Responsibility*, this book would not have been possible without the help of many others.

Crucial to the book's development has been the support of our colleagues at the School of Business Administration at the University of Miami and the McCombs School of Business at the University of Texas at Austin. At the University of Miami, we would particularly like to thank Deans Paul Sugrue and Barbara Kahn for their support. Likewise, the continued encouragement of Linda Neider, Yadong Luo, and Haresh Gurnani as chairs of the Management Department during this revision is much appreciated, as is the early support of Rene Sacasas, chair of the Business Law Department. We would also like to extend our gratitude to Jeff Kerr and John Mezias, professors of strategic management at University of Miami, who provide constant sources of valued insight and friendship.

At the University of Texas, in particular, the second author would like to thank Pamela Haunschild for her support and mentoring. In addition to her workload as Management Department chair, Pam continually finds time to demonstrate what it means to be a top-flight academic researcher—sharing her experience and knowledge gained over many years of producing insightful and valuable organizations research. In addition, the support and advice of Andrew Henderson (University of Texas at Austin), Martin Kilduff (University of Cambridge), Matthew Kraatz (University of Illinois, Urbana-Champaign), Violina Rindova (University of Texas at Austin), and Jim Westphal (University of Michigan) has been invaluable. Their time and commitment to the development of ideas and pursuit of good research continue to be an inspiration.

Without the support of our two business schools, the classroom laboratories where these ideas were tested, and the encouragement of colleagues, *Strategic Corporate Social Responsibility* would not have been possible.

In addition, we express our sincere gratitude to Ken Goodman and Anita Cava, co-directors of the University of Miami Ethics Programs (http://www.miami.edu/ethics/), for creating the opportunity and environment that helped germinate many of the ideas that were the foundation for this book. Their tireless progress and constant innovation, working together with key community activists such as Daniella Levine of the Human Services Coalition of Miami-Dade County (http://www.hscdade.org/), are building an environment in Miami where many of the ideas expressed in this book are becoming reality. We would particularly like to thank Anita Cava of the University of Miami's Business Law Department for her central role in making this project possible.

It is important to recognize that *Strategic CSR* is possible, in large part, because of the prior and ongoing work of many leading scholars in the field of CSR. We would particularly like to acknowledge the pioneering work of Archie B. Carroll of the University of Georgia, Keith Davis of Arizona State University, William C. Frederick of the University of Pittsburgh, Stuart L. Hart of Cornell University, Thomas M. Jones of the University of Washington, Joshua D. Margolis of Harvard Business School, Jim Post of Boston University, C. K. Prahalad of the University of Michigan, and Sandra Waddock of Boston College. Their work, along with the work of many others, has provided the foundation for the field of CSR/Business and Society on which we are able to build.

Dale Fitzgibbons of Illinois State University was an early and enthusiastic supporter of the book. He has been thinking about CSR and teaching the subject in his classrooms for many years. He has a valuable perspective on many of the ideas we present here, and we benefited from his willingness to share his knowledge.

We are also indebted to the ideas and comments offered by the four reviewers of the second edition manuscript: Dale Fitzgibbons of Illinois State University, Warren B. Galbreath of Ohio University, Kathryn Carlson Heler of Springfield College, and Karen Miller Russell of the University of Georgia. Where we were on target, they offered encouragement; where the manuscript could be improved, they pushed us to develop our ideas further. This publication is a better product because of their insights and involvement.

Lisa Cuevas Shaw, MaryAnn Vail, and Eve Oettinger, at Sage Publications have been an incredibly supportive and responsive editorial team, ensuring a timely update of this book. In addition, Astrid Virding and Jacqueline Tasch formed the efficient editing team that converted our manuscript into this finished book. The professionalism of all at Sage who were involved helped make the process of revising this book as painless as possible, while guiding us toward the finish line.

Finally, we would like to thank Leonard Turkel—mentor, community activist, social entrepreneur, and founding co-director of the Center for Nonprofit Management at the University of Miami (http://nonprofit.miami.edu/)—who ceaselessly finds ways to better both his community and the people around him.

Part I

STRATEGIC CORPORATE SOCIAL RESPONSIBILITY

Part I of *Strategic Corporate Social Responsibility* (*Strategic CSR*) highlights the breadth and depth of corporate social responsibility (CSR).

Chapters 1 and 2 lay the foundation for this book by defining CSR and providing a broader understanding of the context from which it emerged and how it has evolved over time. Chapter 1 provides core definitions, identifies three different viewpoints of CSR (moral, rational, and economic), and shows why CSR is of growing concern to business students and leaders. Although businesses exist to further the financial interests of their owners, it should not be their sole, short-term concern. Without the balance of a multi-stakeholder approach, firms can become exploitative, antisocial, and corrupt, losing legitimacy and their ability to pursue the owners' economic goals over the long term.

Chapter 2 reflects the importance of a stakeholder perspective to *Strategic CSR*. All organizations, like organisms, survive or perish depending on how they interact with their environment. Stakeholders are key elements of an organization's environment. In this chapter, we explore in more detail *who* and *what* stakeholders are, as well as how their needs and demands should be of primary concern for firms that are looking to succeed. As such, this chapter explains why a multi-stakeholder perspective best enables firms to craft competitive strategies in today's global business environment.

Chapter 3 examines some of the more contentious elements of the CSR debate. It explores the arguments *against* business involvement with CSR. Expectations about CSR appear in different ways in different cultures and play out on a firm-by-firm, industry-by-industry basis. Businesses that embrace CSR can be a source of pride, retention, and invigoration for employees and are also more likely to engender the support of external stakeholders. Provocatively, however, this chapter contests the assumption that firms have a *responsibility* to pursue goals other than profit maximization. If consumers, for example, demonstrate that they are willing to pay a price premium for CSR behavior (rather than reporting in surveys that they think firms should be more responsible but basing their purchase decisions mainly on price), firms will quickly adapt. If consumers are not willing to pay this premium, however, this chapter asks if it is in society's best interests for firms to bear the burden of producing such products.

Chapters 4 and 5 conclude Part I by outlining how firms integrate CSR into day-to-day operations. Chapter 4 places CSR in a strategic context. Pursuit of the firm's mission must strike a balance between economic ends and socially acceptable means. Restated, strategy seeks competitive success, whereas CSR acts as a filter that helps ensure that profit-directed actions do not harm stakeholders and a firm's viability over the long term.

Finally, Chapter 5 presents a plan to integrate CSR into the firm's competitive strategies and organizational culture. Central to that integration process is a strong and genuine commitment by senior management. Ultimately, if CSR is to be an integral part of the firm's culture and strategies, leaders must start an ongoing dialogue within the organization and with its key stakeholders about the strategic and operational importance of CSR.

CHAPTER 1

WHAT IS CSR?

People create organizations to leverage their collective resources in pursuit of common goals. As organizations pursue these goals, they interact with others inside a larger context called society. Based on their purpose, organizations can be classified as for-profits, governments, or nonprofits. At a minimum, *for-profits* seek gain for their owners; *governments* exist to define the rules and structures of society within which all organizations must operate; and *nonprofits* (sometimes called NGOs—nongovernmental organizations) emerge to do social good when the political will or the profit motive is insufficient to address society's needs. Aggregated across society, each of these different organizations represents a powerful mobilization of resources. In the United States, for example, more than 595,000 social workers are employed largely outside the public sector—many in the nonprofit community and medical organizations—filling needs not met by either government or the private sector.[1]

Society exists, therefore, as a mix of these different organizational forms. Each performs different roles, but each also depends on the others to provide the complete patchwork of exchange interactions (products and services, financial and social capital, etc.) that constitute a well-functioning society. Whether called corporations, companies, businesses, proprietorships, or firms, for example, for-profit organizations also interact with government, trade unions, suppliers, NGOs, and other groups in the communities in which they operate, in both positive and negative ways. Each of these groups or actors, therefore, can claim to have a stake in the operations of the firm. Some benefit more, some are involved more directly, and others can be harmed by the firm's actions, but all are connected in some way to what the firm does on a day-to-day basis.

R. Edward Freeman defined these actors or groups as a firm's *stakeholders*. His definition reflects the broad reach of for-profit activity in our society and includes all those who are related in some way to the firm's goals.[2]

A Firm's Stakeholders

A stakeholder in an organization is (by definition) any group or individual who can affect or is affected by the achievement of the organization's objectives.[3]

Simply put, a firm's stakeholders include those individuals and groups that have a stake in the firm's operations. Such a broad view has not always been the norm, however. Over time, as the impact of business on society has grown, the range of stakeholders whose concerns a company needs to address has fluctuated—from the initial view of the corporation as a legal entity that is granted societal permission to exist by charter, to a narrower focus on the rights of owners, to a broader range of constituents (including employees and customers), and back again and at the end of the 20th century, to a disproportionate focus on shareholders. Increasingly, however, companies are again adopting a broader stakeholder outlook, extending their perspective to include constituents such as the communities in which they operate. Today, companies are more likely to recognize the degree of interdependence between the firm and each of these groups, leaving less room to ignore stakeholders' pressing concerns.

Just because an individual or organization meets this definition of an "interested constituent," however, does not compel a firm (either legally or logically) to comply with every stakeholder demand. Nevertheless, affected parties who are ignored long enough may take action against the firm, such as a product boycott,[4] or they may turn to government for redress. In democratic societies, laws (such as antidiscrimination statutes), rulings by government agencies (such as the Internal Revenue Service's tax-exempt regulations for nonprofits), and judicial interpretations (such as court rulings on the liabilities of board members) provide a minimal framework for business operations that reflects a rough consensus of the governed. Because government cannot anticipate every possible interaction, however, legal action takes time, and a general consensus is often slow to form. As a result, regulatory powers often lag behind the need for action. This is particularly so in complex areas of rapid change, such as information technology and medical research. Thus, we arrive at the discretionary area of decision making that business leaders face on a day-to-day basis, which generates two questions from which the study of CSR springs:

- What is the relationship between a business and the societies within which it operates?
- What responsibilities do businesses owe society to self-regulate their actions in pursuit of profit?

CSR, therefore, is both critical and controversial. It is *critical* because the for-profit sector is the largest and most innovative part of any free society's economy. Companies intertwine with the societies in which they operate in mutually beneficial ways, driving social progress and affluence. In fact, the term *company* comes from a combination of the Latin words *cum* and *panis,* the literal translation of which originally meant "breaking bread together."[5] Today, however, the meaning of a company implies a far greater degree of complexity. Companies create most of the jobs, wealth, and innovations that enable the larger society to prosper. They are the primary delivery system for food, housing, medicines, medical care, and other necessities of life. Without modern day corporations, the jobs, taxes, donations, and other resources that support governments and nonprofits would decline significantly, negatively affecting the wealth and well-being of society as a whole. Businesses are the engines of society that propel us toward a better future.

At the same time, however, CSR remains *controversial.* People who have thought deeply about why businesses exist or what purpose they have within society do not agree on the answers. Do companies have obligations beyond the benefits their economic success already provides? In spite of the rising importance of CSR today for corporate leaders, academics, and bureaucrats alike, many still draw on the views of the Nobel prize–winning economist Milton Friedman, who argued against CSR in the 1960s because it distracted leaders from economic goals. Friedman believed that the only "social responsibility of business is to increase its profits"[6]—that society benefits most when businesses focus on maximizing their financial success.[7] There are others, however, who look to the views of business leaders such as David Packard, a cofounder of Hewlett-Packard:

> I think many people assume, wrongly, that a company exists simply to make money. While this is an important result of a company's existence, we have to go deeper and find the real reasons for our being. As we investigate this, we inevitably conclude that a group of people get together and exist as an institution that we call a company so that they are able to accomplish something collectively that they could not accomplish separately—they make a contribution to society, a phrase which sounds trite but is fundamental.[8]

This book will try to navigate between these competing perspectives to outline a view of CSR that both recognizes its strategic value to firms and incorporates the social value such a perspective also brings to a firm's many stakeholders. The goal is to present a comprehensive perspective of CSR.

CORPORATE SOCIAL RESPONSIBILITY

The entirety of CSR can be discerned from the three words this phrase contains: *corporate, social,* and *responsibility.* CSR covers the relationship between corporations (or other large organizations) and the societies with which they interact. CSR also includes the responsibilities that are inherent on both sides of these relationships. CSR defines *society* in its widest sense and on many levels, to include all stakeholder and constituent groups that maintain an ongoing interest in the organization's operations.

CSR[9]

A view of the *corporation* and its role in *society* that assumes a *responsibility* among firms to pursue goals in addition to profit maximization and a *responsibility* among a firm's stakeholders to hold the firm accountable for its actions.

Stakeholder groups range from clearly defined consumers, employees, suppliers, creditors, and regulating authorities to other more amorphous constituents, such as local communities and even the environment. For the firm, tradeoffs must be made among these competing interests. Issues of legitimacy and accountability exist, with many nonprofit organizations, for example, claiming expertise and demanding representative status, even when it is unclear exactly how many people support their vision or claims. Ultimately, however, each firm must identify those stakeholders that constitute its operating environment and then prioritize their strategic importance to the organization. Increasingly, companies need to incorporate the concerns of stakeholder groups within the organization's strategic outlook or risk losing societal legitimacy. CSR provides a framework that helps firms embrace these decisions and adjust the internal strategic planning process to maximize the long-term viability of the organization. Consider some different viewpoints:

> The notion of companies looking beyond profits to their role in society is generally termed corporate social responsibility (CSR). . . . It refers to a company linking itself with ethical values, transparency, employee relations, compliance with legal requirements and overall respect for the communities in which they operate. It goes beyond the occasional community service action, however, as CSR is a corporate philosophy that drives strategic decision-making, partner selection, hiring practices and, ultimately, brand development. (*South China Morning Post,* 2002)[10]

> CSR is about businesses and other organizations going beyond the legal obligations to manage the impact they have on the environment and society. In particular, this could include how organizations interact with their employees, suppliers, customers, and the communities in which they operate, as well as the extent they attempt to protect the environment. (The Institute of Directors, United Kingdom, 2002)[11]

> The social responsibility of business encompasses the economic, legal, ethical, and discretionary expectations that society has of organizations at a given point in time. (Archie B. Carroll, 1979)[12]

Figure 1.1 elaborates on Archie Carroll's conceptual framework. This useful typology is not rigid, however; issues can and do evolve over time.[13]

Figure 1.1 The Corporate Social Responsibility Hierarchy

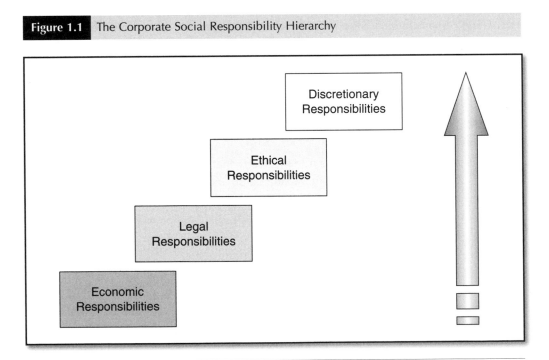

Source: Archie B. Carroll, 'The Pyramid of Corporate Social Responsibility: Toward the Moral Management of Organizational Stakeholders,' *Business Horizons,* July–August, 1991, p. 42.

The Corporate Social Responsibility Hierarchy

Archie Carroll, University of Georgia, was one of the first academics to make a distinction between different kinds of organizational responsibilities. He referred to this distinction as a firm's "pyramid of corporate social responsibility."[14]

- Fundamentally, a firm's *economic responsibility* is to produce an acceptable return on its owners' investment.
- An important component of pursuing economic gain within a law-based society, however, is *legal responsibility*—a duty to act within the legal framework drawn up by the government and judiciary.
- Taken one step further, a firm has an *ethical responsibility* to do no harm to its stakeholders and within its operating environment.
- Finally, firms have a *discretionary responsibility,* which represents more proactive, strategic behaviors that can benefit the firm and society, or both.

One of the central theses of this book is that what was ethical or even discretionary in Carroll's model is becoming increasingly necessary today due to the changing environment within which businesses operate. As such, ethical responsibilities are more likely to equate to economic and legal responsibilities as the foundation for business success. To fulfill its fundamental economic obligations to owners in today's globalizing and wired world, a firm should incorporate a broad stakeholder perspective within its strategic outlook. As societal expectations of the firm rise, so the penalties imposed by stakeholders for perceived CSR lapses will become prohibitive.

CSR, therefore, is a fluid concept. It is both a means and an end. An integral element of the firm's strategy—the way the firm goes about delivering its products or services to markets (*means*)—it is also a way of maintaining the legitimacy of its actions in the larger society by bringing stakeholder concerns to the foreground (*end*). The success of a firm's CSR reflects how well it has been able to navigate stakeholder concerns while implementing its business model. CSR means valuing the interdependent relationships that exist among businesses, their stakeholder groups, the economic system, and the communities within which they exist. CSR is a vehicle for discussing the obligations a business has to its immediate society, a way of proposing policy ideas on how those obligations can be met, and a tool for identifying the mutual benefits for meeting those obligations. Simply put, CSR addresses a company's relationships with its stakeholders.

As such, CSR covers an uneven blend of issues that rise and fall in importance from firm to firm over time. Recently, ethics and corporate governance, for example, have been of growing societal concern. This is a result of the lack of board oversight and poor executive decision making, which led to the accounting-related scandals exposed during the first decade of this century, followed shortly thereafter by the 2007–2009 financial crisis. The corporate response to this heightened concern is evidenced by the rapid growth of the Ethics and Compliance Officers Association (ECOA). Figure 1.2 shows that, since its founding in 1992, the ECOA has grown to more than 1,300 members (http://www.theecoa.org/).[15] In addition, the ECOA

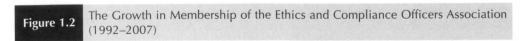

Figure 1.2 The Growth in Membership of the Ethics and Compliance Officers Association (1992–2007)

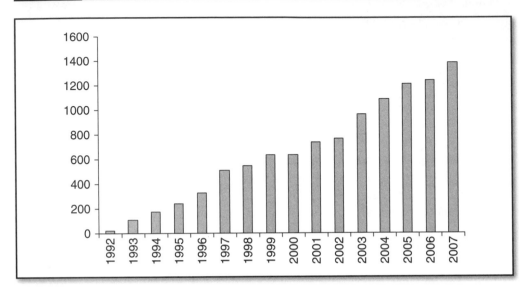

estimates that, in 2008, 85% of the Fortune 500 firms had adopted the ECOA position, with much of that expansion occurring since 2000.

As a result of the blend of academic study and managerial practice, our understanding of CSR and how firms are integrating it is complex and still evolving. And because CSR influences all aspects of a firm's strategic outlook and day-to-day operations, CSR's cutting edge can be controversial, especially among those stakeholders whose interests are not considered primary by decision makers.

CORPORATE STRATEGY AND CSR

CSR, therefore, embraces the range of economic, legal, ethical, and discretionary actions that affect the economic performance of the firm. A significant part of a firm's fundamental responsibilities is complying with the legal or regulatory requirements that relate to day-to-day operations. To break these regulations is to break the law, which does not constitute socially responsible behavior. Clearly, adhering to the law is an important component of any ethical organization. But, legal compliance is merely a minimum condition of CSR.[16] Rather than focus on firms' legal and regulatory obligations, *Strategic CSR* focuses more on the ethical and discretionary concerns that are less precisely defined and for which there is often no clear societal consensus.

CSR is a key element of business strategy. In the words of *The Economist,* it is "just good business."[17] Strategy strives to provide the business with a source of sustainable competitive advantage. For any competitive advantage to be sustainable, however, the strategy must be acceptable to the wider environment in which the firm competes. CSR done incorrectly—or, worse, completely ignored—may threaten whatever comparative advantage the firm holds within its industry. One hundred and twenty years ago, for example, Standard Oil Trust pressured industry suppliers to treat its competitors unfairly in the eyes of society. The result was a series of antitrust laws introduced by government that eventually forced Standard Oil to break into separate companies. Today, activist organizations such as Greenpeace and the Rainforest Action Network target corporate actions they deem to be socially irresponsible. The result of these protests and boycotts can be dramatic shifts in corporate policies and damage to the brand, such as Shell's change of course regarding the breakup of the *Brent Spar* oil platform,[18] or Citigroup's adoption of wide-ranging environmental metrics in the criteria it uses to grant loans—action that ultimately resulted in Citigroup playing a leading role in the creation of the Equator Principles.[19]

However, leaders should address stakeholder concerns like these in ways that carry strategic benefit for the firm. CSR is not about saving the whales or ending poverty or other worthwhile goals that are unrelated to a firm's operations and are better left to government or nonprofits. Instead, CSR is about the economic, legal, ethical, and discretionary issues that stakeholders view as directly related to the firm's plans and actions. The solution to these issues, the overlap where economic and social value intersect, is at the heart of any successful CSR policy. Michael Porter and Mark Kramer outline this approach in defining "strategic corporate philanthropy," but the same approach can be applied to the wider issue of CSR:

> The acid test of good corporate philanthropy is whether the desired social change is so beneficial to the company that the organization would pursue the change even if no one ever knew about it.[20]

Beyond the desired changes, however, are the *approaches* employed to achieve those changes. Too often, the end (building shareholder wealth, for example) has been used to justify the means (polluting the environment). A firm that seeks to implement a *CSR* policy that carries *strategic* benefits is concerned with both the ends of economic viability *and* the means of being socially responsible. As such, the connection between these means and ends is an important component of *strategic* CSR and something that sets it apart from other areas of social responsibility.

This distinction becomes apparent when discussing an issue such as ethics, which is concerned about the honesty, judgment, and integrity with which various stakeholders are treated. There is no debate: Ethical behavior is a prerequisite assumption for strategic CSR. It is hard to see how a firm's actions could be both socially responsible and unethical. Ethics, however, is not the central focus for strategic CSR, except insofar as constituents are affected or society defines a firm's actions as unethical, thus harming the firm's legitimacy and profit potential. Likewise, other socially important issues also exist outside the direct focus of strategic CSR. Concerns over domestic and international income disparity, gender issues, discrimination, human rights, spirituality and workplace religiosity, technological impacts on indigenous populations, and other issues affect societal well-being. Unless firms take actions that directly affect stakeholders in these areas, however, the study of these topics might better fall under ethics, public policy, sociology, or developmental economics courses, which are better suited to explore these complex and socially important topics in greater depth.

THE EVOLUTION OF CSR

The need for social responsibility among businesses is not a new concept. Ancient Chinese, Egyptian, and Sumerian writings often delineated rules for commerce to facilitate trade and ensure that the wider public's interests were considered. Ever since, public concern about the interaction between business and society has grown in proportion to the growth of corporate activity:

> Concerns about the excesses of the East India Company were commonly expressed in the seventeenth century. There has been a tradition of benevolent capitalism in the UK for over 150 years. Quakers, such as Barclays and Cadbury, as well as socialists, such as Engels and Morris, experimented with socially responsible and values-based forms of business. And Victorian philanthropy could be said to be responsible for considerable portions of the urban landscape of older town centres today.[21]

Evidence of social activism in response to organizational actions also stretches back across the centuries, mirroring the legal and commercial development of companies as they established themselves as the driving force of market-based societies:

> The first large-scale consumer boycott? England in the 1790s over slave-harvested sugar.[22]

> Within a few years, more than 300,000 Britons were boycotting sugar, the major product of the British West Indian slave plantations. Nearly 400,000 signed petitions to Parliament demanding an end to the slave trade. . . . In 1792, the House of Commons became the first national legislative body in the world to vote to end the slave trade.[23]

Although wealthy industrialists have long sought to balance the mercantile actions of their firms with personal or corporate philanthropy as a response to social activism or other demands, CSR ultimately originates with leaders who view their role as stewards of resources owned by others (e.g., shareholders, the environment). The words of Ray Anderson, founder and chairman of Interface Carpets, are instructive:

> Can any product be made sustainably? . . . One day early in this journey it dawned on me that the way I had been running Interface is the way of the plunderer, plundering something that is not mine; something that belongs to every creature on earth. And I said to myself, my goodness, the day must come when this is illegal, when plundering is not allowed [and] . . . people like me will end up in jail. The largest institution on earth, the wealthiest, most powerful, the most pervasive, the most influential, is the institution of business and industry—the corporation, which also is the current present day instrument of destruction. It must change.[24]

Leaders such as Anderson[25] face a balancing act that addresses the tradeoffs between the owners (shareholders) that employ them, the society that enables their firms to prosper, and the environment that provides them with the raw materials to produce products and services of value. When specific elements of society view leaders and their firms as failing to meet societal needs, activism results. That is as true of 18th-century England as it is today.

Current examples of social activism in response to a perceived lack of CSR by organizations are in this morning's newspapers, on TV news, and in chat rooms and Web sites all over the Internet. Whether the response is civil disobedience in Seattle, Turin, or Cancun protesting the impact of global corporations on developing societies, consumer boycotts of products that are hazardous to health, or NGO-led campaigns to eradicate sweatshop conditions in the factories of branded-clothing firms, CSR has become an increasingly relevant topic in recent decades in corporate boardrooms, in business school classrooms, online, and in family living rooms.

In addition to public relations fiascos that damage a firm's sales and image, the direct financial impact of CSR failures in a litigious society is never far behind. Widespread, long-term industry practices, which may have previously been deemed discretionary or ethical concerns, can be deemed illegal or socially unacceptable under aggressive legal prosecution or novel social activism. Such violations are less likely in firms with a strong commitment to CSR. For example, the uncovering of the widespread practice of backdating employee stock options by firms, first publicized widely by the *Wall Street Journal,*[26] indicates the dangers of assuming that yesterday's accepted business practices will necessarily be acceptable to others today. Businesses operate against an ever-changing background of what is considered socially responsible. CSR is not a stagnant concept. It is dynamic and continues to evolve as cultural expectations change.

On the one hand, these ever-changing standards and expectations compound the complexity faced by corporate decision makers. Worse, these standards vary from society to society; even among cultures within a given society. Worse still, they also evolve over time. Faced with a kaleidoscopic background of evolving standards, business decision makers must consider a variety of factors on the way to implementation.

In the early history of the United States, for example, the Alien Tort Claims Act "was originally intended to reassure Europe that the fledgling U.S. wouldn't harbor pirates or assassins. It permits foreigners to sue in U.S. courts for violations of the law of 'nations.'"[27] Today, this 1789 law is being used in an attempt to hold U.S. firms accountable for their actions overseas, as well as the actions of their partners (whether other businesses or governments). Thus, what may be legal, or even encouraged, in one country may bring legal repercussions in another. And this is not just an isolated example. Firms such as Citibank, Coca-Cola, IBM, JCPenny, Levi Strauss, Pfizer, Gap, Limited, Texaco, and Unocal have all faced possible suits under this same law, which may extend to hundreds of other national and international firms.[28] Unocal, one of the companies in this list whose case had advanced the furthest in U.S. courts, announced in December 2004, on the eve of having its case heard on appeal, that it would settle for an undisclosed sum:

> Lawsuits filed by 15 villagers from Myanmar . . . said the company "turned a blind eye" to atrocities allegedly committed by soldiers guarding a natural gas pipeline built by the company and its partners in the 1990s. . . . A joint statement by the two sides said Unocal would pay the plaintiffs an unspecified sum and fund programmes to improve living conditions for people living near the pipeline.[29]

In 2008, in the first major case to be brought to trial under the Alien Tort Claims Act, Texaco was cleared of any responsibility for the shooting death of two Nigerian villagers who were protesting on one of the company's oil platforms in 1998. The villagers were killed by police and security officers who were brought in by the firm to diffuse the situation. The Texaco case sets an important precedent for future prosecutions against firms operating in foreign countries to be brought to trial:

> Despite the outcome, . . . the trial was a success for the human rights community because the lawyers succeeded in bringing a case to trial under the Alien Torts law.[30]

Nike, more commonly, reacted to stakeholder criticism of sweatshop conditions in its factories by demanding that its suppliers provide their employees with wages and working conditions that meet the expectations of consumers in developed societies—consumers who might boycott Nike products if they perceive the company to be acting in an unfair or irresponsible manner. Today, media and NGO activists are more likely to criticize the poor treatment of workers in developing economies by holding corporations to standards found in their home markets, especially the United States and the European Union (EU). The result is increased complexity and risk that can harm economic outcomes when CSR is lacking.

On the other hand, however, the pursuit of economic gain remains an absolute necessity. CSR does not repeal the laws of economics under which for-profit organizations must operate (to society's benefit). The example of Malden Mills, below, demonstrates that, unless a firm is economically viable, even the best of intentions will not enable stakeholders to achieve their goals and maximize social value.

Malden Mills[31]

Aaron Feuerstein, CEO of Malden Mills (founded in 1906, family owned), was an excellent man to work for:

Here was a CEO with a unionized plant that was strike-free, a boss who saw his workers as a key to his company's success.[32]

In 1995, however, his approach to business was put to the test when

a fire destroyed Malden Mills' textile plant in Lawrence, an economically depressed town in northeastern Massachusetts. With an insurance settlement of close to $300 million in hand, Feuerstein could have, for example, moved operations to a country with a lower wage base, or he could have retired. Instead, he rebuilt in Lawrence and continued to pay his employees while the new plant was under construction."[33]

As a result, "he was idolized throughout the media. . . . The national attention to Feuerstein's act brought more than the adulation of business ethics professors—it brought increased demand for his product, Polartec, the lightweight fleece the catalogue industry loves to sell."[34]

In addition to full pay, Feuerstein also continued all his employees on full medical benefits and guaranteed them a job when the factory was ready to restart production. In spite of the cost, the decision for Feuerstein was an easy one:

Rebuilding in Lawrence would cost over $300 million while keeping 1,400 laid-off workers on full salaries for a period of up to 3 months would cost an additional $20 million. "I have a responsibility to the worker, both blue-collar and white collar," Feuerstein later said. "I have an equal responsibility to the community. It would have been unconscionable to put 3,000 people on the streets [two weeks before Christmas] and deliver a death blow to the cities of Lawrence and Methuen. Maybe on paper our company is [now] worth less to Wall Street, but I can tell you it's [really] worth more."[35]

But the increased demand for Polartec (http://www.polartec.com/) Feuerstein's actions generated wasn't enough to offset the debt he had built up waiting for the plant to be rebuilt: $100 million.[36] This situation was compounded by the downturn in the market, as well as cheaper fleece alternatives flooding the market. Malden Mills filed for bankruptcy protection in November 2001.[37]

CSR is an important component of a company's strategic and operating perspective; however, alone, it is not enough. It certainly does not replace the need for an effective business model, and no company, whatever the motivation, can or should spend indefinitely money that it does not have. Manufacturing offshore in a low-cost environment, for example, remains a valid strategic decision, particularly in an increasingly globalizing business world. Where CSR considerations play a major role is in how such decisions are made and implemented. And, as *The Economist* notes, there is still plenty of room left for improvement:

> Corporate social responsibility, once a do-gooding sideshow, is now seen as mainstream. But as yet, too few companies are doing it well.[38]

As societies rethink the balance between societal needs and economic progress, CSR will continue to evolve in importance and complexity. And although this complexity muddies the wealth-creating waters, an awareness of these evolving expectations holds the potential for increased competitive advantage. The examples above indicate that the cultural context within which CSR is perceived and evaluated is crucial.

THE CULTURE AND CONTEXT

Firms operate within the context of broader society. The resulting interaction requires a CSR perspective in order for firms to maintain their social legitimacy. Yet, societies differ and so, therefore, does what they consider acceptable. Although differences range from the anthropological and sociological to the historical and demographic, two dimensions consistently influence the visibility of CSR: democracy and economics.

Different societies define the relationship between business and society in different ways. Unique expectations spring from many factors, with wealthy societies having greater resources and, perhaps, more demanding expectations that emerge from the greater options wealth brings. The reasoning is straightforward: In poor democracies, the general social well-being is focused on the necessities of life—food, shelter, transportation, education, medicine, social order, jobs, and the like. Governmental or self-imposed CSR restrictions add costs that poor societies can ill afford. As societies advance, however, expectations change, and the *general social well-being* is redefined. This ongoing redefinition and evolution of societal expectations causes the CSR response also to evolve, as this example of air pollution and public transportation in Chile indicates.

Santiago, Chile

In the 1980s, air pollution in downtown Santiago, Chile, was an important issue, just as it was in Los Angeles, California. The problem, however, was addressed differently in relation to the level of economic development found in these two pollution-retaining basins. Stringent laws went into effect in the Los Angeles basin during the 1980s. At the same time in Chile, necessities (including low-cost transportation) got a higher priority because of widespread poverty. After more than a decade of robust economic growth, however, Chileans eventually used democratic processes to put limitations on the number of cars entering Santiago and required increasingly stringent pollution standards. This shift in priorities reflected their changing societal needs and expectations, along with the growing wealth to afford the new rules and legal actions.

Differences in CSR expectations among rich and poor societies are a matter of priorities. The need for transportation, for example, evolves into a need for nonpolluting forms of transportation as society becomes more affluent. Although poor societies value clean air just as advanced ones do, competing needs may take priority—one of which will be the need for low-cost transportation. As a society prospers economically, new expectations compel producers to make vehicles that pollute less—a shift in emphasis. In time, these expectations may evolve from discretionary to mandatory (legal).

This example reinforces the idea that it is in any organization's best interest (for-profit, nonprofit, or governmental) to anticipate, reflect, and strive to meet the changing needs of its stakeholders to remain successful. In the case of for-profits, the primary stakeholder groups are its owners (its shareholders), customers, and employees, without which the business fails. Other constituents, however, from suppliers to the local community, also matter. Businesses must satisfy the primary groups among these constituents, therefore, if they hope to remain viable over the long term. When the expectations of different stakeholders conflict, CSR enters a gray area, and management has to balance competing interests.

CSR represents an argument for a firm's economic interests, where satisfying stakeholder needs becomes central to retaining societal legitimacy (and, therefore, financial viability) over the long term. Much debate (and criticism) in the CSR community springs from well-meaning parties who argue the same *facts* from different perspectives, breaking down along partisan and ideological lines. Understanding these different perspectives, therefore, is an important component of understanding the breadth and depth of CSR. An introduction to the underlying moral, rational, and economic arguments for CSR follows.

A MORAL ARGUMENT FOR CSR

Although recognizing that profits are necessary for any business to survive, for-profit organizations are able to obtain those profits only because of the society in which they operate. CSR emerges from this interaction and the interdependent relationship between for-profits and society. It is shaped by individual and societal standards of morality, ethics, and values that define contemporary views of human rights and social justice.

Thus, to what extent is a business obliged to repay the debt it owes society for its continued business success? That is, what moral responsibilities do businesses have in return for the benefits society grants? And also, to what extent do the profits the business generates, the jobs it provides, and the taxes it pays already meet those obligations? As an academic study, CSR represents an organized approach to answering these questions. As an applied discipline, it represents the extent to which businesses need to deliver on their societal obligations as defined by society.

A Moral Argument for CSR

CSR broadly represents the relationship between a company and the principles expected by the wider society within which it operates. It assumes businesses recognize that for-profit entities do not exist in a vacuum and that a large part of their success comes as much from actions that are congruent with societal values as from factors internal to the company.

Charles Handy constructs a compelling argument that businesses have a moral obligation to move beyond the goals of maximizing profit and satisfying shareholders above all other stakeholders:

The purpose of a business . . . is not to make a profit, full stop. It is to make a profit so that the business can do something more or better. That "something" becomes the real justification for the business. . . . It is a moral issue. To mistake the means for the end is to be turned in on oneself, which Saint Augustine called one of the greatest sins. . . . It is salutary to ask about any organization, "If it did not exist, would we invent it?" "Only if it could do something better or more useful than anyone else" would have to be the answer, and profit would be the means to that larger end.[39]

A similar sentiment is expressed in a quote attributed to Peter Drucker:

Profit for a company is like oxygen for a person. If you don't have enough of it, you're out of the game. But if you think your life is about breathing, you're really missing something.[40]

At one level, the moral argument for CSR reflects a give-and-take approach, based on a meshing of the firm's values and those of society. Society makes business possible and provides it directly or indirectly with what for-profits need to succeed, ranging from educated and healthy workers to a safe and stable physical and legal infrastructure, not to mention a consumer market for their products. Because society's contributions make businesses possible, those businesses have a reciprocal obligation to society to operate in ways that are deemed socially responsible and beneficial. And because businesses operate within the larger context of society, society has the right and the power to define expectations for those who operate within its boundaries:

Conservatives and Republicans may like to portray "wealth-producing" businesses as precarious affairs that bestow their gifts independently of the society in which they trade. The opposite is the case. The intellectual, human, and physical infrastructure that creates successful companies, alongside their markets, is a social product and that, in turn, is shaped by the character of that society's public conversation and the capacity to build effective social institutions and processes.[41]

At a deeper level, however, societies rest on a cultural heritage that grows out of a confluence of religion, mores, and folkways. This heritage gives rise to a belief system that defines the boundaries of socially and morally acceptable behavior by people and organizations. For many, a focus on money alone is dispiriting—"as vital as profit is, it seems insufficient to give people the fulfillment they crave."[42] Although not always codified into dogma or laws, the cultural heritage leads to an evolving definition of social justice, human rights, and environmental stewardship, the violation of which is deemed morally wrong and socially irresponsible. To violate these implicit moral boundaries can lead to a loss of legitimacy that threatens the long-term viability of the organization.

A RATIONAL ARGUMENT FOR CSR

The loss of societal legitimacy can lead to the countervailing power of social activism, restrictive legislation, or other constraints on the firm's freedom to pursue its economic and other interests. Violations of ethical and discretionary standards are not just inappropriate, they present a rational argument for CSR.

Because societal sanctions (such as laws, fines, prohibitions, boycotts, or social activism) affect the firm's strategic goals, efforts to comply with societal expectations are rational, regardless of moral arguments. When compliance with moral expectations is based on highly subjective values, the rational argument rests on sanction avoidance: It may be more cost-effective, for example, to address issues voluntarily, rather than wait for a mandatory requirement based on government or judicial action. One argument is that businesses can wait for the legally mandated requirements and then react to them.[43] This reactive approach may permit for-profits to ignore their moral obligations and concentrate on maximizing profits or other business goals; however, it also inevitably leads to strictures being imposed that not only force mandatory compliance but often force compliance in ways that are neither preferable nor efficient for the firm. By ignoring the opportunity to influence the debate in the short term through proactive behaviors, an organization is more likely to find its business operations and strategy hampered over the long term. One need only consider the evolution of affirmative action in the United States.

Affirmative Action

Prior to the 1960s, businesses could discriminate against current or potential employees on the basis of race, sex, religion, age, national origin, veteran's status, pregnancy, disability, sexual preference, and other non-merit-based criteria. Putting aside the moral concerns, doing so was a discretionary right that was legal, if far from ethical. Social activism moved these ethical and discretionary decisions into the arena of public debate and, in time, into legal prohibitions. The result for many businesses that were guilty of past or present discrimination meant affirmative action plans to redress racial or other imbalances in their workforce. Those organizations that lagged quickly found themselves the test case in litigation focused on institutionalizing the new legislation.

As Robert Kennedy said during the civil rights movement to those firms that were reluctant to change: "If you won't end discriminatory practices because it's the right thing to do; then do it because it's good for business."[44]

We are not suggesting firms should have been proactive to ensure discrimination remained legal. That would be a moral or ethical lapse and would have involved fighting the evolving societal consensus, risking the societal legitimacy of the firm. Instead, the rational argument advocates self-interest in avoiding the inevitable confrontation. By not adopting a proactive (or at least accommodative) approach to fair treatment, many businesses found their behavior suddenly (and expensively) curtailed through legislation, judicial and agency interpretations, and penalties because of a failure to interpret correctly the evolving social and business environment.

A Rational Argument for CSR

CSR is a rational argument for businesses seeking to maximize their performance by minimizing restrictions on operations. In today's globalizing world, where individuals and activist organizations feel empowered to enact change, CSR represents a means of anticipating and reflecting societal concerns to minimize operational and financial constraints on business.

The rational argument for CSR is summarized by the *iron law of social responsibility,* which states: In a free society, discretionary abuse of societal responsibilities leads, eventually, to mandated solutions.[45] Restated: In a democratic society, power is taken away from those who abuse it. The history of social and political uprisings—from Cromwell in England, to the American and French revolutions, to the overthrow of the shah of Iran or the communist government of the Soviet Union—underscores the conclusion that those who abuse power or privilege sow the seeds for their own destruction.

Parallels exist in the business arena. Financial scandals around the turn of this century at Enron, WorldCom, Adelphia, HealthSouth, and other icons of U.S. business caused discretion-limiting laws and rulings, such as the Sarbanes-Oxley legislation of 2002, that move previously discretionary and ethical issues into the legal arena. Similarly, firms that pay their CEOs and other executives amounts of money that are perceived to be excessive, even following poor performance, face unwelcome oversight from regulatory agencies and politicians who have to answer to their electorates:

Public corporations are political institutions: They depend on the good will of the public to operate successfully. The absence of that good will leaves them open to attacks from Congress, regulators, ambitious attorneys general, pension funds, hedge funds, unions, nongovernmental organizations and just about anyone else who wants a say in a corporation's affairs.[46]

By adopting a rational argument for CSR, however, firms are able to interpret changing societal values and stakeholder expectations and act to avoid future sanctions. Sensing that the tide of public opinion in the United States is moving in favor of regulating carbon emissions, for example, firms have formed groups to lobby the government for change. The group BICEP (Business for Innovative Climate and Energy Policy, http://www.ceres.org/bicep) was established by five firms with proactive CSR track records—Levi Strauss, Nike, Starbucks, Sun Microsystems, and Timberland. Perhaps more surprisingly, however, USCAP (United States Climate Action Partnership, http://www.us-cap.org/), which "supports the introduction of carbon limits and trading. . . . was set up by energy companies and industrial manufacturers" that might otherwise have opposed government action in this area.[47] General Motors, for example, became the first U.S. automobile manufacturer to join USCAP, "which seeks economy-wide greenhouse gas emission reductions of 60 to 80 per cent by 2050."[48] Similar motives result in newspaper headlines, such as, "Exxon CEO Advocates Emissions Tax."[49]

Implementing a rational perspective, these firms realize that it is in their interests to engage with regulators, rather than oppose legislation that is inevitable. As such, acting proactively in a socially responsible manner to avoid unwelcome intrusion or help shape prospective legislation is an act of rational business—particularly so in light of the overwhelming anecdotal evidence that discretionary abuses lead to a loss of decision-making freedoms and financial repercussions for for-profit organizations.

AN ECONOMIC ARGUMENT FOR CSR

Summing the moral and rational arguments for CSR leads to an economic argument. In addition to avoiding moral, legal, and other societal sanctions, incorporating CSR into a firm's operations offers a potential point of differentiation and competitive market advantage on which future success can be built.[50]

An Economic Argument for CSR

CSR is an argument of economic self-interest for business. CSR adds value because it allows companies to reflect the needs and concerns of their various stakeholder groups. By doing so, a company is more likely to retain its societal legitimacy and maximize its financial viability over the medium to long term. Simply put, CSR is a way of matching corporate operations with societal values and expectations that are constantly evolving.

CSR influences all aspects of a business's day-to-day operations. Everything an organization does causes it to interact with one or more of its stakeholder groups. As a result, companies need to build a watertight image with respect to as broad an array of key stakeholders as possible. Whether as an employer, producer, buyer, supplier, or as an investment, a firm's attractiveness and success are increasingly linked to the strengths of its image and brand(s). Concerning socially responsible investments (SRI),[51] for example, "funds that invest with a conscience have more than doubled in size over the last 10 years."[52] Certainly, even for those who believe that the only purpose of a business is to increase the wealth of the owners, being perceived as socially irresponsible risks losing access to an already significant (and growing) segment of investors and their capital. SRI funds amounted to $202 billion in 2007 and, by some measures, outperformed broader market funds, such as the S&P 500.[53] CSR affects operations within a corporation because of the need to consider constituent groups. Each area builds on all the others to create a composite of the corporation in the eyes of its stakeholders. Businesses must satisfy key groups among these constituents if they hope to remain viable over the long term. However,

these messages [firms send to stakeholders] are not incompatible with pursuing shareholder value. Rather, they give the companies a license to operate in order to pursue it.[54]

Strategic CSR expounds the economic argument in favor of CSR. We believe it is the clearest of the three (moral, rational, and economic) arguments supporting CSR and emphasizes the importance of CSR for businesses today. Importantly, however, the economic argument for CSR operates at the intersection of the economic self-interest of the firm and the broader well-being of society. As such, this perspective offers a plan of action that has as its goal the maximization of both economic and social value.

An important distinction is between an effective *business model* and a broader, more sustainable *model for (all) businesses*. The Body Shop, for example, has implemented a successful *business model*, which subscribes to a moral argument for CSR. An activist organization, it is able to draw on support from the small percentage of the population that is aware and sufficiently responsive to a progressive social agenda and translate it into economic success. In contrast, however, an economic argument for CSR speaks to a broad *model for businesses*, which recognizes the limited application of moral activism and, instead, searches for a standard to which all organizations can subscribe. The result is an approach to business that identifies the strategic benefits of a CSR and stakeholder perspective in a way that sustains the firm and maximizes the added total value of its operations.

WHY IS CSR IMPORTANT?

CSR is important, therefore, because it influences all aspects of a company's operations. Increasingly, consumers want to buy products from companies they trust, suppliers want to form business partnerships with companies they can rely on, employees want to work for companies they respect, large investment funds want to support firms that they perceive to be socially responsible, and nonprofits and NGOs want to work together with companies seeking practical solutions to common goals. Satisfying each of these stakeholder groups (and others) allows companies to maximize their commitment to their owners (their ultimate stakeholders), who benefit most when all of these groups' needs are being met. As Carly Fiorina, former chair and chief executive officer of Hewlett-Packard, has argued:

> I honestly believe that the winning companies of this century will be those who prove with their actions that they can be profitable and increase social value—companies that both do well and do good. . . . And, increasingly, shareowners, customers, partners and employees are going to vote with their feet—rewarding those companies that fuel social change through business. . . . This is simply the new reality of business—one that we should and must embrace.[55]

CSR is increasingly crucial to success because it gives companies a mission and strategy around which multiple constituents can rally. The businesses most likely to succeed in today's rapidly evolving global environment will be those best able to balance the often conflicting interests of their multiple stakeholders. Lifestyle brand firms, in particular, need to live the ideals they convey to their consumers.

WHY IS CSR INCREASINGLY RELEVANT TODAY?

CSR as an element of strategy is becoming increasingly relevant for businesses today because of five identifiable trends—trends that seem likely to continue and grow in importance throughout the 21st century.[56]

Growing Affluence

A poor society, in need of work and inward investment, is less likely to enforce strict regulations and penalize organizations that might otherwise take their business and money elsewhere. Consumers in developed societies, on the other hand, can afford to choose the products they buy and, as a consequence, expect more from the companies that make those products. This sense has increased in the wake of the corporate scandals at the turn of this century and the 2007–2009 financial crisis, both of which reduced public trust in corporations and public confidence in the ability of regulatory agencies to control corporate excess. Affluence matters and leads to changing social expectations. Firms operating in affluent societies, therefore, face a higher burden to demonstrate they are socially responsible. As a result, increasing affluence on a global basis will continue to push CSR up the agendas of corporations worldwide.

Ecological Sustainability

An increase in general affluence and changing societal expectations is enhanced by a growing concern for the environment. When the Alaskan pipeline was built in the 1970s, crews could drive on the hardened permafrost 200 days a year. Today, climate changes leave the permafrost solid for only 100 days each year, while NASA photographs reveal that the arctic ice cap "has shrunk more than 20 percent" since 1979[57] and that the rate of decrease is accelerating.[58] Increasing prices for raw materials, rising mutation rates among amphibian populations, and other growing anecdotal evidence all suggest that the Earth has ecological limits. The speed at which we are approaching the Earth's limits and the potential consequences of our actions are complicated issues, about which experts do not agree. What is not in doubt, however, is that human economic activity is depleting the world's resources and causing dramatic changes to the mix of gasses in the Earth's atmosphere—changes that could become irreversible in the near future. As a result, firms that are perceived to be indifferent to their environmental responsibilities are likely to be criticized and penalized. Examples include: court-imposed fines (*Exxon Valdez*),[59] negative publicity (Monsanto's genetically modified foods),[60] or confrontations by activist groups (Friends of the Earth).[61]

Globalization

Increasingly, corporations operate in a global business environment. Operating in multiple countries and cultures magnifies the complexity of business exponentially. Not only are there more laws and regulations to understand, but many more social norms and cultural subtleties to navigate. In addition, the range of stakeholders to whom multinational firms are held accountable increases, as does the potential for conflict among competing stakeholder demands. While globalization has increased the potential for efficiencies gained from production across borders, it has also increased the potential to be exposed to a global audience if a firm's actions fail to meet the needs and expectations of the local community.

The Free Flow of Information

The growing influence of global media conglomerates makes sure that any CSR lapses by companies are brought rapidly to the attention of the worldwide public, often instantaneously. Scandal is news, and yesterday's eyewitnesses are today armed with pocket-size video cameras or pictures taken by mobile phones that provide all the evidence necessary to convict by TV. In addition, the Internet fuels communication among activist groups and like-minded individuals, empowering them to spread their message while giving them the means to coordinate collective action. Such technologies are reaching beyond the control of autocratic governments and allowing people to find new ways to mobilize and protest. Thomas Friedman, for example, explains how this communication revolution is affecting the relationship between the government and people of Iran:

> What is fascinating to me is the degree to which in Iran today—and in Lebanon—the more secular forces of moderation have used technologies like Facebook, Flickr, Twitter, blogging and text-messaging as their virtual mosque, as the place they can now gather, mobilize, plan, inform and energize their supporters, outside the grip of the state.[62]

Google is one company that is increasingly finding new ways to apply these new communication technologies.

CSR Newsletters: Google

The Internet has enormous power to reshape the way information is communicated around the globe. This phenomenon will continue to evolve in ways that we have not yet even begun to imagine (at least, those of us who do not work for Google). As a recent article in the *Wall Street Journal* pointed out, "You can Google to get a hotel, find a flight and buy a book. Now you may be able to use Google to avoid the flu."[63]

The philanthropic arm of the Internet search company (http://www.google.org/) has released a new service (http://www.google.org/flutrends/) that will track Internet search terms related to the flu nationally (e.g., *cough* or *fever*) and use this information to help identify potential outbreaks of the illness:

> It displays the results on a map of the U.S. and shows a chart of changes in flu activity around the country. The data is meaningful because the Google arm that created Flu Trends found a strong correlation between the number of Internet searches related to the flu and the number of people reporting flu symptoms.

This information is powerful because of the speed with which it identifies early trends to which government agencies and health providers can then react:

> Tests of the new Web tool from Google.org, the company's philanthropic unit, suggest that it may be able to detect regional outbreaks of the flu a week to 10 days before they are reported by the Centers for Disease Control and Prevention.

Firms are just beginning to appreciate the ways in which these communication tools will affect their operations and reputations. What seems apparent, however, is that the affect will be dramatic and that firms that are not transparent and accountable to their stakeholders will suffer as a result.

Brands

All of these trends that are driving the importance of CSR overlap in terms of the importance of a firm's reputation and brand. Brands today are often a focal point of corporate success. Companies try to establish popular brands in consumers' minds because it increases any competitive advantage they hold, which then results in higher sales and revenue. In addition, consumers are more likely to pay a premium for a brand they know and trust. Due to growing demands from increasing numbers of stakeholders, however, combined with the increased complexity of business in a global environment and the ability of activists and media organizations to spread missteps instantaneously to a global audience, today, more than ever before, a firm's reputation is precarious—hard to establish and easy to lose. As a result, as *BusinessWeek's* annual brand survey demonstrates,[64] brands are more valuable than ever, and firms need to take ever greater steps to protect an investment that is essential to their continued success.

BEYOND TRENDS

Beyond the trends in CSR that we identify in this chapter, CSR must also work in practice. It must allow firms to prosper as well as act as a conduit for stakeholder concerns. But how are firms supposed to identify their key stakeholders and prioritize among their competing interests? Does CSR matter to stakeholders? Are stakeholders willing to enter the debate and impose their views on corporations? Do they share some of the responsibility for shaping corporate actions? How should firms begin integrating a CSR perspective into their strategic planning and day-to-day operations?

The importance of the stakeholder model to the arguments presented in *Strategic CSR* will be explored further in Chapter 2. Arguments *against* CSR (and the often unintended implications of progressive CSR applications) exist and will be explored in Chapter 3. Chapter 4 puts CSR into strategic perspective and expands on the growing importance of CSR and its impact on corporate strategy. And, issues that influence the implementation of CSR within a strategic decision-making framework provide the basis for Chapter 5, which will conclude Part I of *Strategic Corporate Social Responsibility*.

Questions for Discussion and Review

1. Why do firms exist? What value do businesses serve for society?

2. Define *corporate social responsibility*. What arguments in favor of CSR seem most important to you? How is CSR different from *strategic* CSR?

3. Name the four responsibilities of a firm outlined in Archie Carroll's pyramid of CSR model. Illustrate your definitions of each level with corporate examples.

4. Milton Friedman argued that, "Few trends could so thoroughly undermine the very foundations of our free society as the acceptance by corporate officials of a social responsibility other than to make as much money for their stockholders as possible."[65] Give two arguments in support of Friedman's assertion and two against.

5. Define and discuss briefly the primary moral, rational, and economic arguments for CSR?

6. What five driving forces make CSR more relevant today?

7. Of these five factors, is there any one that you feel is more important than the others? Defend your choice with examples from your own experiences and knowledge.

NOTES AND REFERENCES

1. U.S. Department of Labor, Bureau of Labor Statistics, "Occupational Outlook Handbook, 2008–09 Edition," http://stats.bls.gov/oco/ocos060.htm#emply

2. Post, Preston, and Sachs provide an alternative, narrower, definition of a firm's stakeholder that ties the group or actor more directly to the firm's operations: "The stakeholders in a firm are individuals and constituencies that contribute, either voluntarily or involuntarily, to its wealth-creating capacity and activities, and who are therefore its potential beneficiaries and/or risk bearers." In "Managing the Extended Enterprise: The New Stakeholder View," *California Management Review,* Vol. 45, No.1, Fall 2002, p. 8.

3. R. Edward Freeman, *Strategic Management: A Stakeholder Approach,* Pitman, 1984, p. 46.

4. Libby Brooks, "Power to the People," *The Guardian,* December 20, 2002, http://www.guardian.co.uk/world/2002/dec/20/debtrelief.development

5. John Micklethwait & Adrian Wooldridge, *The Company: A Short History of a Revolutionary Idea,* Modern Library, 2003, p. 8.

6. Milton Friedman, "The Social Responsibility of Business is to Increase its Profits," *New York Times Magazine,* September 13, 1970.

7. Of course, this debate continues today. For one example of a debate that was hosted by a skeptical source but includes different perspectives from the Rainforest Action Network to G.E., see "Corporate Social Responsibility: Good Citizenship or Investor Rip-off?" Big Issues: The Journal Report, *Wall Street Journal,* January 9, 2006, p. R6.

8. Charles Handy, "What's a Business For?" *Harvard Business Review,* December 2002, p. 54.

9. For a comprehensive review of the evolution of CSR as an academic discipline see Archie B. Carroll, "Corporate Social Responsibility: Evolution of a Definitional Construct," *Business and Society,* Vol. 38, No. 3, September 1999, pp. 268–295. Also, traditional textbooks elaborate on these issues: see James E. Post et al., *Business and Society: Corporate Strategy, Public Policy, Ethics,* 10th edition, McGraw-Hill, 2002. Finally, William C. Frederick, *Corporation Be Good! The Story of Corporate Social Responsibility,* Dog Ear Publishing, 2006, offers a comprehensive timeline and discussion about the evolution of CSR.

10. Michael McComb, "Profit to Be Found in Companies That Care," *South China Morning Post,* April 14, 2002, p. 5.

11. Ruth Lea, "Corporate Social Responsibility: IoD Member Opinion Survey," *The Institute of Directors,* UK, November 2002, p. 10.

12. Archie B. Carroll, "A Three-Dimensional Conceptual Model of Corporate Performance," *Academy of Management Review,* Vol. 4, No. 4, 1979, p. 500.

13. See Mark S. Schwartz and Archie B. Carroll, "Corporate Social Responsibility: A Three-domain Approach," *Business Ethics Quarterly,* Vol. 13, 2003, pp. 503–530 for an update on Carroll's pyramid of CSR. Instead of four levels of responsibility, Schwartz and Carroll divide a firm's responsibilities into three domains—economic, legal, and ethical. These three overlapping domains result in seven "CSR categories," or firm profiles, with the appropriate category determined by the firm's orientation (i.e., the different emphases placed on each domain).

14. Archie B. Carroll, "The Pyramid of Corporate Social Responsibility: Toward the Moral Management of Organizational Stakeholders," *Business Horizons,* July–August 1991.

15. In March 2007, the ECOA had 1,388 individual members and approximately 750 organizational members. Individual members are defined by the ECOA as "ethics and compliance professionals."

16. It is worth noting, however, that actions that appear to be legally permissible may still result in lawsuits filed against firms, under obscure treaties and statutes, by innovative activists seeking to right actual or perceived wrongs.

17. "Just Good Business: A Special Report on Corporate Social Responsibility," *The Economist,* January 19, 2008.

18. http://archive.greenpeace.org/comms/brent/brent.html. See also Alex Kirby, "Brent Spar's long saga," *BBC News,* November 25, 1998, http://news.bbc.co.uk/1/hi/sci/tech/218527.stm

19. Marc Gunther, "The Mosquito in the Tent: A Pesky Environmental Group Called the Rainforest Action Network is Getting Under the Skin of Corporate America," *Fortune Magazine,* May 31, 2004, http://money.cnn.com/magazines/fortune/fortune_archive/2004/05/31/370717/index.htm

20. Michael Porter and Mark Kramer, "The Competitive Advantage of Corporate Philanthropy," *Harvard Business Review,* Vol. 80, Issue 12, December 2002, p. 67.

21. Adrian Henriques, "Ten Things You Always Wanted to Know About CSR (But Were Afraid to Ask); Part One: A Brief History of Corporate Social Responsibility (CSR)," *Ethical Corporation Magazine,* May 26, 2003, http://www.ethicalcorp.com/content.asp?ContentID=594

22. Michael Arndt, "An Ode to 'The Money-Spinner,'" *BusinessWeek,* March 24, 2003, pp. 22–23; review of *The Company: A Short History of a Revolutionary Idea,* by John Micklethwait and Adrian Wooldridge, Modern Library, 2003.

23. Adam Hochschild, "How the British Inspired Dr. King's Dream," *New York Times,* January 17, 2005, p. A21.

24. http://www.triplepundit.com/pages/ray-anderson-ex.php. Excerpt from an interview with Ray Anderson that appeared in *The Corporation,* http://www.thecorporation.com/

25. For a video update on Interface's progress toward its "Mission Zero" project (http://www.interfaceflor.eu/internet/web.nsf/webpages/528_EN.html) and goal of "leaving zero footprint, by the year 2020," see http://www.interfaceflor.eu/internet/web.nsf/webpages/58150_EN.html

26. Mark Maremont, "Authorities Probe Improper Backdating of Options—Practice Allows Executives to Bolster Their Stock Gains; A Highly Beneficial Pattern," *Wall Street Journal,* November 11, 2005, p. A1, http://www.biz.uiowa.edu/faculty/elie/wsj1.htm and Charles Forelle and James Bandler, "The Perfect Payday—Some CEOs Reap Millions by Landing Stock Options When They Are Most Valuable; Luck—Or Something Else?" *Wall Street Journal,* March 18–19, 2006, p. A1, http://www.jpl.nasa.gov/news/news.cfm?release=2009-107

27. Paul Magnusson, "Making a Federal Case Out of Overseas Abuses," *BusinessWeek,* November 25, 2002, p. 78.

28. Ibid.

29. Lisa Roner, "Unocal Settles Landmark Human Rights Suits," *Ethical Corporation Magazine,* December 20, 2004, http://www.ethicalcorp.com/content.asp?ContentID=3312

30. Richard C. Paddock, "Chevron Cleared in Nigeria Shootings," *Los Angeles Times,* December 2, 2008, http://articles.latimes.com/2008/dec/02/local/me-chevron2

31. For additional background information on Malden Mills, see Rebecca Leung, "The Mensch of Malden Mills," *60 Minutes,* CBS, July 6, 2003, http://www.cbsnews.com/stories/2003/07/03/60minutes/main561656.shtml. See also Gretchen Morgenson, "GE Capital vs. the Small-Town Folk Hero," *New York Times,* October 24, 2004, p. BU5.

32. Marianne Jennings, "Seek Corporate Balance," *Miami Herald,* September 1, 2002, p11L.

33. Roger Martin, "The Virtue Matrix," *Harvard Business Review,* Vol. 80, No. 3, March 2002, pp. 68–75.

34. Marianne Jennings, "Seek Corporate Balance," *Miami Herald,* September 1, 2002, p. 11L.

35. Manuel G. Velasquez, *Business Ethics: Concepts and Cases,* 5th edition, Prentice Hall, 2002, pp. 122–123.

36. Mitchell Pacelle, "Can Mr. Feuerstein Save His Business One Last Time?" *Wall Street Journal,* May 9, 2003, pp. A1 and A6.

37. In spite of emerging from bankruptcy protection in 2004, the firm continued to struggle and filed for bankruptcy again in 2007. Today, the company continues to make its clothing under the brand name Polartec (http://www.polartec.com/).

38. "Just Good Business: A Special Report on Corporate Social Responsibility," *The Economist,* January 19, 2008, p. 3.

39. Charles Handy, "What's a Business For?" *Harvard Business Review,* December 2002, p. 54.

40. Design Thinking, "Peter Senge's Necessary Revolution," *BusinessWeek,* June 11, 2008, http://www.businessweek.com/innovate/content/jun2008/id20080611_566195.htm

41. Will Hutton, "The Body Politic Lies Bleeding," *The Observer,* May 13, 2001, http://www.guardian.co.uk/politics/2001/may/13/election2001.uk6

42. Michael Skapinker, "How to Fill the Philanthropy-Shaped Hole," *Financial Times,* January 27, 2009, p. 13.

43. Archie B. Carroll, "A Three-Dimensional Conceptual Model of Corporate Performance," *Academy of Management Review,* Vol. 4, No. 4, 1979, p. 500.

44. Eliot Spitzer, "Strong Law Enforcement Is Good for the Economy," *Wall Street Journal,* April 5, 2005, p. A18.

45. Keith Davis and Robert Blomstrom, *Business and Its Environment,* McGraw-Hill, 1966. See also Keith Davis, "The Case for and Against Business Assumption of Social Responsibilities," *Academy of Management Journal,* Vol. 16, Issue 2, 1973, pp. 312–322.

46. Alan Murray, "Twelve Angry CEOs—The Ideal Enron Jury," *Wall Street Journal,* February 15, 2006, p. A2.

47. Jonathan Birchall, "Business Fights for Tougher Rules on Emissions," *Financial Times,* November 20, 2008, p. 4.

48. John Reed, "GM Joins 'Green' Coalition in the US," *Financial Times,* May 9, 2007, p. 18.

49. Russell Gold and Ian Talley, "Exxon CEO Advocates Emissions Tax," *Wall Street Journal,* January 9, 2009, p. B3.

50. Some of the most important research in the business management literature on the relationship between CSR and firm performance is being done by Joshua Margolis of Harvard Business School (see Joshua Margolis and James Walsh, "Misery Loves Companies: Rethinking Social Initiatives by Business," *Administrative Science Quarterly,* Vol. 48, Issue No. 2, 2003, pp. 268–305; Joshua Margolis, Hillary Elfenbein, and James Walsh, "Does It Pay to Be Good? What a Meta-analysis of CSP and CFP Can (and Cannot) Tell Us," *Academy of Management Annual Meeting.* Philadelphia, PA, 2007; and Joshua Margolis and Hillary Elfenbein, "Do Well by Doing Good? Don't Count on It," *Harvard Business Review,* Vol. 86, No. 1, 2008, pp. 19–20). Margolis's main conclusion from his research is that, while there is little evidence that CSR predicts firm performance, there does seem to be evidence of the reverse relationship—firm performance predicting CSR. In other words, while CSR does not increase profits, higher profits lead to greater CSR. One explanation for this failure to establish a conclusive link between CSR and firm performance is that the tools we currently use to measure CSR are not very good. While data and methods are improving all the time, we are yet to identify a sufficiently comprehensive means of establishing a firm's CSR profile. In the absence of such a measure, continuing to research whether or not such activities have positive (or negative) correlations with firm performance (creating a huge black box in the process) seems difficult to justify. Margolis's response is to call on researchers to move beyond investigating the relationship between CSR and firm performance (or vice-versa) and, instead, focus on understanding how and why firms decide to act in relation to CSR—"understanding the mechanisms that connect CFP to CSP, rather than the reverse."

51. Ritchie Lowry, "Capitalism with a Conscience: About Socially Responsible Investing," http://www .goodmoney.com/qna.htm

52. Tara Kalwarski, "Numbers: Do-Good Investments Are Holding up Better,' *BusinessWeek,* July 14 and 21, 2008, p. 15.

53. Ibid.

54. Andrew Likierman, "Stakeholder Dreams and Shareholder Realities," Mastering Financial Management, *Financial Times,* June 16, 2006, p. 10.

55. Carly Fiorina, "A World of Change." Quoted from a speech to the APEC CEO Summit in Shanghai, China, October 19, 2001, http://www.hp.com/hpinfo/execteam/speeches/fiorina/apec_01.html

56. For a more detailed discussion of these trends that are driving the relevance of CSR, see Chapter 5.

57. "Global Warming Puts the Arctic on Thin Ice," Natural Resources Defense Council, November 22, 2005, http://www.nrdc.org/globalwarming/qthinice.asp

58. "New NASA Satellite Survey Reveals Dramatic Arctic Sea Ice Thinning," Jet Propulsion Laboratory, *NASA,* July 7, 2009, http://www.jpl.nasa.gov/news/news.cfm?release=2009–107

59. "Images From the Exxon Valdez Oil Spill," National Oceanic and Atmospheric Administration, March 7, 2001, http://response.restoration.noaa.gov/photos/exxon/exxon.html

60. "Farmers & Consumers Protest at Monsanto's Headquarters in St. Louis," Organic Consumers Association, August 19, 2000, http://www.organicconsumers.org/corp/monprotest.cfm

61. "Corporate Campaigns: Case Studies," http://www.foe.co.uk/campaigns/economy/case_studies/ index.html, and "Success Stories," http://www.foe.co.uk/campaigns/economy/success_stories/index.html

62. Thomas L. Friedman, "The Virtual Mosque," *New York Times,* June 17, 2009, p. A21.

63. Robert A. Guth, "Sniffly Surfing: Google Unveils Flu-Bug Tracker," *Wall Street Journal,* November 12, 2008, pD1, http://sec.online.wsj.com/article/SB122644309498518615.html; Miguel Helft, "Aches, a Sneeze, a Google Search," *New York Times,* November 12, 2008, p. A1, http://www .nytimes.com/2008/11/12/technology/internet/12flu.html

64. Burt Helm, "Best Global Brands," *BusinessWeek,* September 18, 2008, http://www.businessweek .com/magazine/content/08_39/b4101052097769.htm

65. Milton Friedman, *Capitalism and Freedom,* University of Chicago Press, 1962, p. 133.

CHAPTER 2

CORPORATE STRATEGY

A Stakeholder Perspective

All organizations, like organisms, survive or perish depending on how they adapt to their environment. As discussed in Chapter 1, a firm's stakeholders are key elements of its environment. While stakeholders depend on firms to provide the products and services that they demand, companies depend on suppliers, customers, employees, and other stakeholders for the societal legitimacy they need to remain in business. How stakeholders evaluate the firm, therefore, depends not only on *what* the firm does but also on *how* it does it. Strategy seeks a sustainable competitive advantage. Its success rests on matching the organization's internal competencies with the demands of its external competitive environment. Central to that environment are the firm's stakeholders.

Before exploring who and what stakeholders are, we consider the different perspectives of corporate strategy. We argue that, while these perspectives contain important insights into a firm's ability to convert resources into a competitive advantage, a stakeholder perspective is better suited for firms trying to navigate the global business environment of the 21st century. A stakeholder perspective enables firms to identify the multiple constituents in its environment that are affected by the firm's operations, while also allowing them to prioritize among those stakeholders' often competing demands. By integrating a stakeholder/CSR perspective within strategic planning and day-to-day operations, firms are better prepared to respond effectively to their stakeholders' needs. And that responsiveness to its environment helps ensure that the company strategy is effective and durable. Conversely, in today's increasingly global, interconnected world, if key constituencies are ignored, the firm's strategy risks a lack of support, even active resistance, with potentially negative consequences for firm performance and, eventually, its survival.

WHAT IS STRATEGY?

Although businesses exist for many reasons, survival depends on profits. At its simplest, these profits are determined by the extent to which its revenues exceed the costs incurred by the firm during the value creation process. The firm generates its revenues from its customers who are satisfied with the value the firm offers through its employees.[1] The pursuit of profits, however, is so broad a mandate that it offers little guidance about where to begin or what to do. Instead, insight comes from understanding the need in society that the business seeks to meet. That need, toward which the organization strives, forms the basis of its aspirations or *vision*. Ideally, an organization's vision is an ennobling, articulated statement of what it seeks to do and become. A vision that ignores the larger role that a firm plays in society is likely to be neither noble nor sustainable. Vision statements must appeal to multiple stakeholders, including members of the organization (employees), its direct beneficiaries (owners), its economic partners (customers and suppliers), and the larger community in which the organization operates (society, broadly defined). But, to do so, they also must be statements of genuine intent.

From these aspirations, the firm's *mission* identifies what the organization is going to do in order to attain its vision. A food bank, for example, may have a vision of "ending hunger in the community" and a mission to "feed the poor." An automobile company may have a vision of "providing the best personal transportation vehicles to a broad section of society" and a mission of "making affordable, efficient cars." But, here again, the mission must balance both the methods and the results to be considered socially responsible. The vision identifies what the organization is striving toward, while the mission tells us what the organization is going to do to get there. Both these statements are constrained by what the firm's stakeholders and society deem to be acceptable.

A firm's *strategy* explains how the organization intends to achieve its vision and mission. It defines the organization's response to its competitive environment. At the corporate level, a firm's strategy determines which businesses the firm will operate and whether it will enter into partnerships with other firms (via joint ventures, mergers, or acquisitions). Thus, a food bank may have a corporate-level strategy of partnering with a government agency to enhance its access and distribution capabilities, whereas an auto firm may have a corporate-level strategy of securing multiple brands to gain exposure to multiple market segments and minimize risk. At the level of the business unit, a firm's strategy determines how the unit will differentiate its products from the products of its competitors. Thus, the food bank may have a strategy of using a mobile soup kitchen that can transport the food to where the poor live, whereas the auto firm may have a strategy of producing cars with specific technological advantages over its competitors' products.

A firm's *tactics* are the day-to-day management decisions that implement the strategy. Tactics are the actions people in the organization take every day. As a result, tactics are flexible and can be altered more easily to reflect changes in operational context. Ultimately, however, the purpose of these day-to-day tactical actions is to realize the firm's strategy.

A Firm's Vision, Mission, Strategy, and Tactics

- The *vision* answers why the organization exists. It identifies the needs the firm aspires to solve for others.
- The *mission* states what the organization is going to do to achieve its vision. It addresses the types of activities the firm seeks to perform.
- The *strategy* determines how the organization is going to undertake its mission. It sets forth the ways it will negotiate its competitive environment in order to attain a sustainable advantage.
- The *tactics* are the day-to-day management decisions made to implement the firm's strategy.

Aligning its vision, mission, strategy, and tactics gives direction to the firm and focus to its employees. As important, this chain also informs the organization of what it will *not* do. An accounting firm, for example, will not build airplanes without a major revision of its vision, mission, strategy, and tactics. Ultimately, this set of aspirations and policies gives decision makers a template against which decisions can be made and evaluated. The overall goal is to ensure that the strategy and tactics achieve the vision and mission of the firm.

COMPETING STRATEGY PERSPECTIVES

Often, the strategy planning process begins with a SWOT analysis. A SWOT analysis is a tool that allows a firm to identify its internal *Strengths* and *Weaknesses*, while also analyzing the external *Opportunities* and *Threats* that are present in its environment. The goal of a firm's strategy, therefore, is to recognize its strengths and align them with the opportunities that are present in the environment, ensuring that the strategy and tactics remain consistent with its vision and mission. Weaknesses are addressed to the extent that they impair the strategy's effectiveness, while threats in the environment are monitored and evaluated for their disruptive potential.

Building on the foundation of the SWOT analysis, *strategy* is traditionally viewed from two competing perspectives.[2] Although it is not clear that these perspectives enjoy empirical support, they are well established and commonly taught. The two competing perspectives draw on the two sides of the SWOT analysis—the *internal* strengths and weaknesses, and the *external* opportunities and threats. The *resources perspective* is an internal view of the firm, which identifies its unique resources (e.g., highly skilled employees or monopoly access to valuable raw materials) and capabilities (e.g., effective research and development or efficient production processes) as the main determinant of a sustainable competitive advantage. Those firms that have the most valuable resources or most innovative capabilities (collectively called *competencies*) will likely produce the most valued products and services in the most efficient manner. As a result, these firms are able to build and sustain a competitive advantage over the competition.

An alternative view is the *industry perspective*, which focuses instead on the company's immediate operational context. This external perspective of the firm identifies the structure of the environment in which it operates (in particular, its industry) as the main determinant of its competitive advantage. Success in the market, this perspective argues, has less to do with individual differences among firms and more to do with the competitive structure of the firm's industry. To the extent that an industry is structured favorably (as in the case of a monopoly or through favorable government regulation), the companies operating in that industry will enjoy greater profit potential than those firms that operate in a more constrained industry environment.

The tensions between these two perspectives form a central theoretical component of strategy thinking and, as such, merit further elaboration.

THE RESOURCES PERSPECTIVE

The resources perspective is detailed in a 1990 *Harvard Business Review* article[3] by C. K. Prahalad and Gary Hamel, who then expanded on their ideas in a 1994 book.[4] The core idea that Prahalad and Hamel convey is the distinction between a firm that is built around a portfolio of business units and a firm that is built around a portfolio of *core competencies*. While separate business units encourage replication and inefficiencies, core competencies develop efficient systems that can be applied in multiple settings across business units and throughout the firm. Walmart's core competency of efficient distribution, for example, can be applied at all stages of its retail operations. Equally, Google's core competency of writing sophisticated algorithms that allow the firm to pursue its mission to "organize the world's information"[5] can be applied to searching for products, images, academic papers, and many other topics. Moreover, core competencies can be built, given the correct set of circumstances. A firm's set of core competencies will differentiate it from its competition and allow it to sustain a competitive advantage:

> In the short run, a company's competitiveness derives from the price/performance attributes of current products. . . . In the long run, competitiveness derives from an ability to build, at lower cost and more speedily than competitors, the core competencies that spawn unanticipated products. The real sources of advantage are to be found in management's ability to consolidate corporatewide technologies and production skills into competencies that empower individual businesses to adapt quickly to changing opportunities.[6]

Prahalad and Hamel apply three tests that define a core competency: It should be applicable in multiple different markets, it should be valued by the consumer, and it should be difficult for a competitor firm to copy. The resources perspective argues that while different firms have valuable resources and different firms have unique capabilities, it is the combination of the two that leads to a core competency and a sustainable competitive advantage. Southwest Airlines, for example, has a valuable resource in its employees and corporate culture and a unique capability in its ticketing and boarding technologies (in particular, its airplane turnaround times). But, it is the combination of culture and technology that delivers the firm's sustained competitive advantage and profitability. As a result,

> yearend results for 2008 marked Southwest's 36th consecutive year of profitability.[7]

> [Southwest Airlines' profitability is] a record unmatched by any airline in the world.[8]

Limitations of the Resources Perspective

There are two main limitations of the resources perspective. First, by focusing primarily on the internal characteristics of the firm, the resources perspective ignores much of the context in which the firm operates. It is highly likely, however, that this context will influence directly the firm's ability to build core competencies. By not including context in the model, therefore, this perspective provides an incomplete description of the processes that generate the phenomenon (core competencies) that it is seeking to explain.

Second, the resources perspective provides a description of the firm that is very deliberate and rational. The suggestion is that firms are quite capable of identifying potential core competencies and then proceed to gather the necessary resources and design the necessary processes to allow them to flourish. Decades of research on organizations, however, tell us that, even if managers are able to act rationally (which is not clear), a whole host of other factors (ranging from political infighting to events beyond their control) can intervene to prevent the intended goal from being realized.

The combination of these two limitations suggests that, while valuable, the resources perspective alone provides an incomplete understanding of strategy in today's global business environment.

THE INDUSTRY PERSPECTIVE

The industry perspective is grounded theoretically in industrial economics. Its main proponent in the management literature is Michael Porter, whose five-forces model is a staple component of corporate strategy. Porter first outlined his ideas in a 1979 *Harvard Business Review* article.[9] Porter later published two books that expanded on his initial ideas by introducing a distinction between business and corporate-level strategies[10] and the value chain.[11] More recently, in a 2008 *Harvard Business Review* article, Porter updated his five-forces model to account for changes since the initial publication.[12]

The industry perspective focuses on the firm's operating environment (in particular, its industry) as the most important determinant of competitive advantage. There are five competitive forces in Porter's model (Figure 2.1): suppliers, buyers, new entrants, substitutes, and

| Figure 2.1 | Porter's Five Competitive Forces |

Source: Michael E. Porter, "How Competitive Forces Shape Strategy." *Harvard Business Review*, March/April, 1979, p. 141.

industry rivalry. These five forces compete for a fixed pool of resources, and this competition determines the ability of any individual firm to profit in the industry. As such, Porter envisions competition as a zero-sum game between these five forces and the focal firm. The strength of each force is measured relative to the strength of the focal firm. In other words, to the extent that any of the five forces grows in strength, this occurs to the detriment of the focal firm, which becomes relatively weaker. The application of this model can be illustrated effectively by looking at the competitive structure of two specific examples—the carbonated soft drinks-concentrate industry and the airlines industry.

Porter's Five-Forces Model

Examples of two different industries illustrate the value of Porter's model in analyzing a firm's competitive environment:

Carbonated Soft-Drinks Concentrate

This industry is dominated by two firms—Coke and Pepsi.[13]

Power of suppliers: Weak. In this industry, the power of suppliers is weak because the raw materials needed to make the concentrate that Coke and Pepsi sell to their bottlers are cheap. The recipes are tightly held trade secrets, but it is hard to imagine the ingredients are much more than water, corn syrup, and flavorings.

Power of buyers: Weak. The buyers in this industry are not the end consumers of the drinks but the bottlers that Coke and Pepsi have signed up to long-term contracts. In recent years, the bottlers have begun to consolidate somewhat, increasing their power relative to their parents, but they remain relatively weak.[14]

Threat of new entrants: Low. The barriers to entry in terms of distribution networks and brand recognition suggest that Coke and Pepsi are not likely to see any serious competitors in this industry.

Threat of substitutes: High. This is the main weakness in the industry. With rising concerns about obesity and the growth in the noncarbonated drinks industry, this is a threat to the products that still drive a large percentage of Coke's and Pepsi's profits.

Industry rivalry: Low. Although the end consumer sees Coke and Pepsi competing on advertising and price in supermarkets and other retail outlets, the burden of these costs is borne largely by the bottlers (who sell to these outlets), not the concentrate makers. Coke and Pepsi retain significant control over the price they charge bottlers for the concentrate, and each bottler is committed to either Coke or Pepsi.

As a result of this structure, the carbonated soft drinks concentrate industry contains a very favorable competitive structure for Coke and Pepsi. They are well-established competitors in a stable industry.

Airlines

In contrast to the cola concentrate industry, the airlines industry is populated by a large number of firms that are competing furiously.[15]

Power of suppliers: High. There is a great deal of consolidation in the aircraft manufacturing industry, which consists of only two major firms, Boeing and Airbus. As a result, there are not many alternative sources of the airline industry's main input—large airplanes.

Power of buyers: Low. This is one factor that works in the airlines' favor. Buyers (i.e., airline passengers) are diffuse, and invariably there are great discrepancies in the amounts of money paid by different passengers for comparable seats on the same flight. The rise in Internet and Web sites that allow passengers to compare prices, however, has reduced the advantage the airlines hold in this area.

Threat of new entrants: High. In spite of low profits, it is relatively common to read about new airlines entering this industry. In 2007, Virgin America, for example, received approval from the U.S. government to operate a low-cost airline.[16] The danger, in fact, for the established airlines, is that new airlines are competitive because they do not have the legacy costs (e.g., pension and health benefits) and inefficiencies that they are battling.

Threat of substitutes: Low. In the United States, alternative forms of public travel for long distances (such as train) are not well established. As a result, people have little choice but to purchase the services that many airlines offer today.

Industry rivalry: High. Evidence of the high level of competition among airlines lies in the fact that Southwest Airlines' consistent profitability in the industry is the exception, rather than the norm.[17]

As a result of this competitive structure, the airline industry is unfavorable for the different airlines, which operate in an industry with high demand and few alternatives but which seem unable to make sustained profits.

Limitations of the Industry Perspective

There are three main limitations inherent in the industry perspective. First is the presentation of business as a combative pursuit—a zero-sum game of survival. This model teaches firms that their relationship with their different stakeholders is confrontational and that, in order for a firm to survive, it needs to beat its stakeholders in a battle for relative supremacy. In other words, if its customers or suppliers gain an advantage, it is to the disadvantage of the focal firm.

Second, the industry perspective presents a narrow view of the firm's operating environment. Only five forces are included, which cover only three stakeholders—the firm's buyers, suppliers, and competitors. This picture omits numerous stakeholders that have the potential to alter dramatically a company's competitive environment—such as the local community, the government, and other stakeholders.

Third, the industry perspective fails to give sufficient recognition to differences in characteristics among companies, which are likely to be predictive of their ability to thrive in a given environment. A holistic model of the firm in its environment that also recognizes the value of the firm's resources and capabilities would provide a more comprehensive tool that firms can use to analyze their operating context (both internal and external conditions) and plan their strategy accordingly.

While the resources and industry perspectives, therefore, are valuable tools that provide insight into the actions of businesses, the situations in which they operate, and the potential to build a sustained competitive advantage, these two perspectives have their limits. Both are narrow in their application and exclude factors that intuitively contribute to a firm's strategy and, therefore, its success. As such, they limit attention to the components of the larger context facing a company. More relevant to the argument presented in *Strategic CSR* is a broader perspective that incorporates the total mix of influences, expectations, and responsibilities that firms face in their day-to-day operations and that necessarily shape their strategies in response. As students from Generation Y, or the Millennials (people born from about 1980 to 2000), begin to enter business schools, the curriculum will need to account for their more global goals and interests:

> They like personal attention and are used to getting information how they want it, when they want it. They are strong-willed, passionate, optimistic, and eager to work. And . . . they care deeply about the world and its problems.[18]

These students, who will become the executives of the 21st century, require comprehensive tools that allow them to craft strategies that fit a dynamic, globalized business environment. In addition to the two traditional strategy perspectives, therefore, we propose a *stakeholder perspective* as a more complete tool to analyze a firm's operating context and create the most appropriate strategic plan of action.

A STAKEHOLDER PERSPECTIVE

Throughout this century, as businesses worldwide evolve to account for the changing environment in which they operate, CSR will occupy an increasingly core component of the strategic planning process and day-to-day operational decisions of the business. As such, CSR finds a natural home within corporate strategy.[19] The ideal vehicle for the integration of CSR and strategy is a multi-stakeholder perspective that enables firms to respond to the dominant trends in society today—globalization, rapidly evolving communication technologies, and ever-increasing expectations of social goals beyond profit maximization. Although definitions of what constitutes a stakeholder may differ in emphasis, with different groups included,[20] they largely agree in terms of sentiment. Here are two well-known examples:

Definitions of a Stakeholder

A stakeholder in an organization is (by definition) any group or individual who can affect or is affected by the achievement of the organization's objectives.

R. Edward Freeman[21]

The stakeholders in a firm are individuals and constituencies that contribute, either voluntarily or involuntarily, to its wealth-creating capacity and activities, and who are therefore its potential beneficiaries and/or risk bearers.

Post, Preston, and Sachs[22]

A stakeholder, therefore, is a group or individual with an interest in the activities of the firm. In Chapter 1, we outlined why it is in firms' best interests to meet the needs and expectations of as broad an array of stakeholders as possible. The model presented in Figure 2.2 provides a framework that firms can use to identify their key stakeholders.

Figure 2.2 divides a firm's stakeholders into three separate groups: organizational stakeholders (internal to the firm) and economic and societal stakeholders (external to the firm). Together, the three kinds of stakeholders form a concentric set of circles with the firm's organizational stakeholders at the center within a larger circle that signifies the firm's economic stakeholders. Both of these circles sit within the largest outside circle, which represents society and the firm's

Figure 2.2 A Stakeholder Model

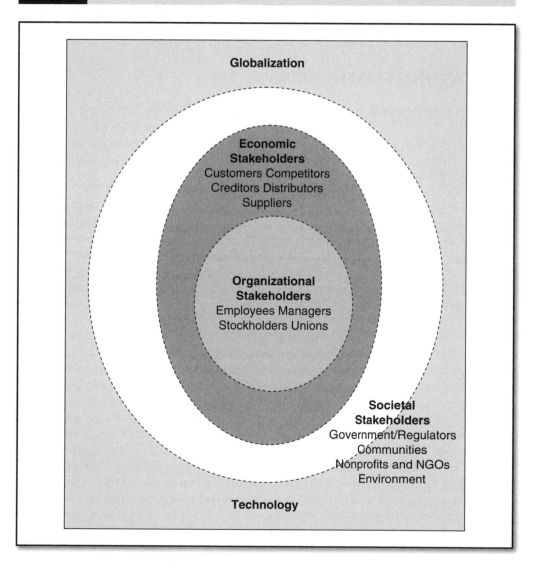

societal stakeholders. A company's employees are, first and foremost, therefore, organizational stakeholders. They are also, however, occasional customers of the company, as well as being members of the society in which the business operates. The government that regulates the firm's industry, however, is only a societal stakeholder and has no economic relationship with the company (beyond the taxes it levies), nor is it a formal part of the organization.

The firm's economic stakeholders represent the interface between the organizational and societal stakeholders. A firm's customers are, first and foremost, therefore, economic stakeholders of the firm. They are not organizational (internal) stakeholders, but they are part of the society within which the firm operates. They are also one of the primary means by which the firm delivers its product and interacts with its society. Without the economic interface, an organization loses its mechanism of accountability and, therefore, its legitimacy over the long term. This is true regardless of whether the organization is a business, government, or nonprofit.

The three layers of a firm's stakeholders all sit within the larger context of a globalizing business environment, driven by revolutionary technology that, together with the other trends identified in Chapter 1, raises the importance of CSR for businesses today.

PRIORITIZING STAKEHOLDERS

An effective stakeholder model, however, must do more than merely identify the company's stakeholders. Equally important, if the model is to be of use to firms in terms of implementation, is the ability to prioritize among these stakeholders. This is particularly important when the interests of these stakeholders conflict, as they often do. The result of this conflict represents a potential threat to the organization:

> Some industries—especially energy . . . have long had to contend with well-organized pressure groups. . . . Many of the world's major pharmaceutical companies have been pushed to sell low-cost drugs to developing countries. Gap and Nike had been attacked for exploiting child labour in the Indian sub-continent. Coca-Cola, Kraft and other food and beverage companies have been accused of contributing to child obesity in the developed world. . . . Companies that do not acknowledge such claims run risks of reputational damage.[23]

The businesses most likely to succeed in today's rapidly evolving global environment will be those best able to adapt to their dynamic environment by balancing the conflicting interests of multiple stakeholders. Integrating a stakeholder perspective into a strategic framework is designed to allow companies to respond to stakeholder demands in ways that maximize both economic and social value. Just because an individual or organization merits inclusion in a firm's list of relevant stakeholders, however, does not compel the firm (either legally or logically) to comply with every demand that stakeholder makes. This would be counterproductive, as the business would spend all its time trying to address these different demands and negotiating among stakeholders with diametrically opposed requests. To operate effectively, therefore, firms need to prioritize among their stakeholders—both in absolute terms and on an issue-by-issue basis.

The concentric circles of organizational, economic, and societal stakeholders presented in Figure 2.2 provide a rough guide to prioritization. By identifying its key stakeholders *within* each category, executives can prioritize the needs and interests of certain groups over others.

In addition, we argue that *among* categories, stakeholders decrease in importance to the firm the further they are removed from core operations. Implicit in our model, therefore, is the idea that organizational stakeholders are a firm's most important constituent groups. Organizational stakeholders are followed in importance by a firm's economic stakeholders, who provide it with the economic capital to survive. Finally, a firm's societal stakeholders deliver the social capital that is central to the firm's legitimacy and long-term validity but are of less immediate importance in terms of the firm's day-to-day operations. Nevertheless, for any given issue, the relative importance of stakeholders can change—sometimes dramatically. Addressing the fluctuating needs of their primary stakeholders and meeting them wherever possible, therefore, is essential for firms to survive in today's global business environment:

Simon Zadek, founder and CEO of AccountAbility (http://www.accountability21.net/), has developed a powerful tool that firms can use to evaluate which stakeholders and issues pose the greatest potential opportunity and danger.[24] First, Zadek identified the five stages of learning that organizations go through "when it comes to developing a sense of corporate responsibility"[25]—defensive (to deny responsibility), compliance (to do the minimum required), managerial (to begin integrating CSR into management practices), strategic (to embed CSR within the strategy planning process), and civil (to promote CSR practices industry-wide). Then, Zadek combined these five stages of learning with four stages of intensity "to measure the maturity of societal issues and the public's expectations around the issues"[26]—latent (awareness among activists only), emerging (awareness seeps into the political and media communities), consolidating (much broader awareness is established), and institutionalized (tangible reaction from powerful stakeholders). The range of possible interactions of these different stages is presented in Figure 2.3.

Figure 2.3	Prioritizing Stakeholder Demands (I)

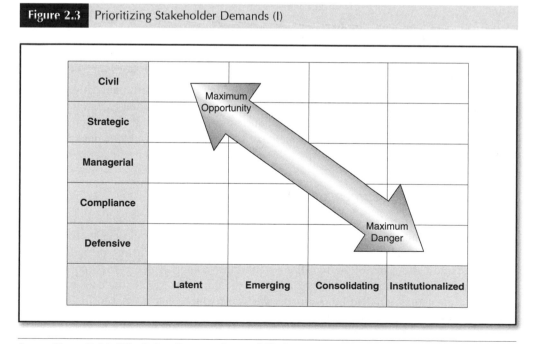

Source: Simon Zadek, "The Path to Corporate Responsibility," *Harvard Business Review*, December 2004, p. 129.

The maximum danger, Zadek argues, is for companies that are in defensive mode when facing an institutionalized issue, as they will be ignoring an issue that poses a potentially significant threat to their business. A firm that continues to deny publicly the existence of climate change, for example, falls into this category. In contrast, those businesses that are promoting industry-wide adoption of standard practices in relation to a newly emerging issue face the maximum opportunity. A firm that introduces a standardized process to measure carbon footprints and report the information on product labels in the retail industry, for example, falls into this category. Such a company stands to gain the maximum economic and social value for its effort.

Although we seek here to provide a guide to prioritizing a firm's stakeholders, we do so with two caveats: First, no organization can afford to ignore consistently the interests of an important stakeholder, even if that group is less important in the firm's relative hierarchy of stakeholders or relatively removed from the firm's day-to-day operations. A good example of this is the government, which is a societal stakeholder in our model and, therefore, in theory, less important to the firm than an organizational or economic stakeholder. It would not be wise, however, for a firm to ignore consistently the government in relation to an important issue that enjoys broad societal support. Given that the government has the power to constrain industries dramatically, it is only rational that firms should adhere to the government's basic needs and requests.[27]

Second, it is important to note that this framework constitutes a general guide as to how firms might prioritize their stakeholders. Inevitably, the relative importance of stakeholders will differ from firm to firm, from issue to issue, and from time to time. What is important, however, is that executives have a means to prioritize their stakeholders' needs and demands for a given issue, so that they can properly account for those expectations in formulating a strategic response.

THE INTEGRATION OF STRATEGY AND CSR

That key proponents of both the resources and industry perspectives implicitly recognize the limitations of their earlier work can be deduced from their more recent publications. In two important respects, both Prahalad and Porter have evolved their positions: first, to integrate both the internal (resources) and external (industry) perspectives into one comprehensive vision, and, second, to incorporate components of CSR and, implicitly, a broader stakeholder perspective.

Combining the Resources and Industry Perspectives

This evolution of their ideas is apparent in Prahalad's recent work detailing the business opportunity for multinational firms in serving the estimated 4 billion people (65% of the world's population) who exist on less than $2,000 per year.[28] This group of people forms the largest and bottom tier of the four-tier pyramid that comprises the world's population—the bottom of the pyramid (BOP). Prahalad views these people as potential consumers who, at present, are largely ignored by multinational firms, which tend instead to focus on consumers in developed economy markets:

It is simply good business strategy to be involved in large, untapped markets that offer new customers, cost-saving opportunities, and access to radical innovation. The business opportunities at the bottom of the pyramid are real, and they are open to any MNC willing to engage and learn.[29]

In Porter's case, the evolution of his ideas is apparent in two *Harvard Business Review* articles that he wrote with Mark Kramer: "The Competitive Advantage of Corporate Philanthropy"[30] and "Strategy & Society":[31]

> For any company, strategy must go beyond best practices. It is about choosing a unique position—doing things differently from competitors in a way that lowers costs or better serves a particular set of customer needs. These principles apply to a company's relationship to society as readily as to its relationship to its customers and rivals.[32]

Both Prahalad and Porter, therefore, talk more expansively in their recent work and, in the process, come much closer to combining the resources and industry perspectives. Prahalad, in discussing the potential opportunity for firms at the BOP, recognizes that a change in environmental context alters the potential of a fixed set of resources and capabilities. In addition, Porter and Kramer incorporate both "inside-out linkages" (a firm-level perspective) and "outside-in linkages" (an environment-level perspective) within one view of the firm and its strategic environment that emphasizes "the interdependence between a company and society."[33]

Integrating CSR

Concerning the integration of CSR into their ideas, there is a strong theme running through all of Prahalad and Porter's recent work. In addition to identifying new markets for multinational corporations, Prahalad is clearly also concerned with the social value that the efficient delivery of products and services can provide to the developing world. In addition, Porter writes equally about the potential social and economic value to the strategic decision-making process in firms:

> Efforts to find shared value in operating practices and in the social dimensions of competitive context have the potential not only to foster economic and social development but to change the way companies and society think about each other.[34]

On the one hand, it is clear that CSR can be thought of as a core competence of the firm. To integrate CSR effectively throughout the organization, a firm needs to draw on resources and capabilities that are valuable, rare, difficult to imitate, and nonsubstitutable.[35] The development of these competencies presents the firm with the potential to differentiate itself from its competitors and build a sustainable competitive advantage.[36] On the other hand, however, CSR is also clearly a means to evaluate a firm's external environment in terms of its primary stakeholder groups—identifying the structural components of that environment that present the firms with a favorable opportunity to succeed.

An important question, however, remains: How do companies define socially responsible action that is strategic? In their work, both Prahalad and Porter are correct to focus on areas of expertise and relevance to organizations. There is a strong connection between the economic competence of firms and the potential for social progress. This is a central component of the concept of strategic CSR—areas of social concern that extend beyond profit maximization, but that are related to the business's core operations. We turn next to this area of firm activity, located at the intersection of strategy, CSR, and a stakeholder perspective.

STRATEGIC CSR

There are four components that are essential to defining *strategic CSR*: First, that firms incorporate a CSR perspective within their strategic planning process; second, that any actions they take are directly related to core operations; third, that they incorporate a stakeholder perspective; and, fourth, that they shift from a short-term perspective to managing the firm's resources and relations with key stakeholders over the medium to long term.

Strategic CSR

The incorporation of a holistic **CSR perspective** within a firm's strategic planning and **core operations** so that the firm is managed in the interests of a broad set of **stakeholders** to achieve maximum economic and social value over the **medium to long term**.

The definition of strategic CSR, therefore, is supported by four key pillars—a CSR perspective, the core operations of the firm, a stakeholder perspective, and medium- to long-term planning. The combination of these four pillars is essential to the integration of CSR within the strategic planning and day-to-day operations of the organization.

A CSR Perspective

Essential to any definition of strategic CSR is that firms incorporate a CSR perspective within their strategic planning process.

In outlining their ideas on how firms can incorporate a social dimension to their strategic decision making, Porter and Kramer provide a three-tiered framework that forms a guide to how organizations can prioritize among their stakeholders and the relevant social issues with which they are expected to deal.[37] The interaction between firms and issues of concern to the societies in which they operate are divided into three levels of interaction:

- Generic social issues (not directly related to a firm's operations)
- Value chain social impacts (the extent to which a firm's operations affect society)
- Social dimensions of competitive context (the extent to which the environment constrains a firm's operations)

In the case of a retail clothing company that outsources most of its production to low-cost environments overseas, for example, the issue of a livable wage (as opposed to a minimum wage) in the United States is a *generic social issue*—an issue that is important and something on which the firm might even take a position but that is not directly relevant to the firm's operations. The issue of a livable wage in a country in which the firm's products are made, however, is a clear example of a *value chain social impact*, an issue in which its operations directly affect the local community. The prospect of legislation on this issue by government represents a *social dimension of competitive context* for the organization, as it has the potential to constrain operations.

Figure 2.4 illustrates how Porter and Kramer use the interactions among social issues, firm operations, and environmental constraints to distinguish between responsive CSR and strategic CSR. *Responsive CSR* occurs when the firm proactively becomes involved in a generic social issue that is not related to operations or when it structures its value chain to avoid any negative social impacts. *Strategic CSR*, however, involves a more proactive integration of a social dimension into the firm's strategic planning. This form of CSR occurs when the organization seeks actively to benefit society as a consequence of its value chain or to influence its competitive context through activities such as strategic philanthropy.[38] Strategic CSR occurs where there is a direct effect of a firm's operations on society and vice versa, allowing it to identify which issues and stakeholders it has the ability to influence. Accounting for CSR as an integrated component of the firm's strategic planning process in this way, therefore, constitutes a good example of strategic CSR in action.

| **Figure 2.4** | Prioritizing Stakeholder Demands (II) |

Source: Michael E. Porter & Mark R. Kramer, "Strategy & Society," *Harvard Business Review*, December 2006, p. 89.

Core Operations

A second component of strategic CSR is that any action a firm takes is directly related to its core operations. In short, the same action will differ in terms of whether it can be classified as strategic CSR, depending on the core expertise of the firm and the relevance of the issue to the firm's vision and mission. Consider the following two questions:

- Does it make sense for a large financial firm to donate money to a group researching the effects of climate change because the CEO believes this is an important issue?
- Does it make sense for an oil firm to donate money to the same group because it perceives climate change as a threat to its business model and wants to mitigate that threat by investigating possible alternatives?

The action is the same—the donation of money from a for-profit firm to a nonprofit organization that is researching the effects of climate change. It is harder for the company in the first example to justify its actions, however, assuming that its operations are not directly related to the environment and the CEO is not an expert on this issue. It is easier to see the relevance of climate change to the second company. It is in this firm's strategic interests to understand an area of debate that is likely to influence its operating environment directly in the foreseeable future.[39]

Along similar lines, it makes a great deal of sense for a computer company like Dell to offer a computer recycling program.[40] It makes much less sense, however, for Dell to offer a "Plant a Tree for Me" program as a way for consumers to offset greenhouse gas emissions produced as a result of the production of their new computer.[41] Dell knows about computers and should know how best to recycle them. Less obvious is Dell's expertise in relation to tree planting—what trees to plant, where to plant them, or whether tree planting is an efficient use of the firm's resources or an effective means of combating climate change.

A Stakeholder Perspective

A third component of strategic CSR is that firms incorporate a stakeholder perspective. A barrier to the implementation of a stakeholder perspective, however, is the primary emphasis currently given by many corporations to the interests of its shareholders.

As discussed above, an issue that is rarely raised in relation to a stakeholder model is the issue of prioritization. It is fine for an organization to be able to identify its different stakeholders and their different interests and demands, but the difficulty comes when those interests and expectations conflict. The most effective means of dealing with stakeholder conflict is prioritization. If a firm has two stakeholder groups whose demands conflict (i.e., the firm is unable to satisfy fully both stakeholders), it makes sense for it to respond more wholeheartedly to the most important of the two, while attempting not to offend the other.

Cynics might point out that this is what firms have been doing all along—it is just that they always give top priority to their shareholders. In reality, however, the choice is not between either a shareholder or stakeholder perspective. A firm's shareholders are one of its organizational stakeholders and, as such, are important to the firm. It is not the case, however, that this automatically ensures their demands are granted the top priority. Anecdotal evidence suggests, in fact, that some of the most successful businesses are those that have considered other stakeholders to be a higher priority than their shareholders.

Johnson & Johnson is an excellent example of a company that has formally prioritized its stakeholders in its famous Credo (http://www.jnj.com/connect/about-jnj/jnj-credo/), which places its customers first and its shareholders (stockholders) last as a "final responsibility." The firm rationalizes that, as long as "we operate according to these principles," with its customers (health practitioners), suppliers and distributors, employees, and communities in which it operates being given a higher priority than its shareholders, then "the stockholders should realize a fair return":

> Small wonder then that, when the Tylenol scare hit in the '80s and seven Chicago residents died after ingesting cyanide-laced capsules, J&J managers knew what they had to do—even without consulting with then-CEO James Burke, who was on a plane as the news broke. By the time Burke had landed and caught up with his top managers, they already had called for all Tylenol products to be pulled off shelves and for production of all Tylenol items to be halted.[42]

Although their policies may not be as formalized as Johnson & Johnson, business leaders as diverse as Herb Kelleher and Colleen Barrett at Southwest,[43] Howard Schulz at Starbucks,[44] and Sam Walton at Walmart[45] all recognized that shareholders are best served when stakeholders that are more immediate to operations (in particular, employees) are motivated, loyal, and committed to serving customers. Amazon has a similar "customers first" approach to business.[46] In addition, Costco routinely rejects investors' calls to reduce the pay and benefits they provide to their employees. In spite of their resistance, Costco's share price has routinely outperformed the share price of its main competitor, Walmart.[47]

None of this, of course, is to argue that shareholder interests do not matter, or that they should never be placed above the interests of other stakeholders. Instead, the important point is that shareholders should not automatically be the primary concern of executives in those instances when the consideration of the interests of a broader set of stakeholders will better serve the long-term interests of the organization.

Medium to Long Term

The final component of strategic CSR is the importance of a shift from a short-term perspective when managing the firm's resources and relations with key stakeholders over the medium to long term.

Businesses must satisfy key groups among their various constituents if they hope to remain viable over the long term. When the expectations of different stakeholders conflict, organizations need to be able to balance the competing interests. An example of such conflict exists among different classes of investors in the business, who might have different definitions of what they consider to be an acceptable level of performance.

The Shareholder Shift—From Investor to Speculator

The evolving role of shareholders has greatly influenced the CSR debate and strengthened the case for adopting a broader stakeholder approach to a business's strategic outlook.

The role of ownership has narrowed considerably over time. Shares today are less and less perceived as a long-term investment in a company and more and more as a stand-alone, short-term investment for personal benefit. A distinction can be drawn, therefore, between investors, who invest in companies with a share price that reflects sound economic fundamentals (e.g., a reasonable price-earnings ratio, profitability, long-term planning) and speculators, who gamble on shares based on whether they think the share price will rise, irrespective of whether it deserves to go up or whether it is valued at a fair price:

> It starts with the fact that the average holding period for stocks has dropped from five years in the mid-1970s to six months today. People aren't investing in your company; they're investing in your stock. That's a huge difference.[48]

This trend was taken to an extreme during the Internet boom when share trading was driven purely by speculation and the desire to maximize investment returns. There was little attempt to establish a company's business worth or potential:

> Amazon's entire float changes hands twice a week. . . . It would take average annual profits of over $1 billion to make sense of Amazon's current $20 billion-odd market value. Yet Amazon's total sales in 1998 were only $600 million. . . . Today's appetite for equities rests on an erroneous belief that they are a one-way bet: that, in the long run, they always pay higher returns than other assets.[49]

In these instances, is it true to say that shareholders actually own the company in which they are investing—in the sense that an owner wants to protect the item being held? Perhaps driven by the preponderance of institutional (versus individual) investors, there is an increasing tendency today to register indifference to the overall health of an organization and seek merely to protect the dollar investment:

> Anglo-Saxon Inc. no longer has any real owners, just a bunch of punters holding betting slips that happen to have its name on them. . . . [Shareholders] have stopped behaving like owners. This is partly because so many shares are now held by institutions, which see their job as managing money, not owning companies. . . . The trick, for success at any size, is to ensure that a company makes the best investment decisions. That is usually done when the deciders are also the owners.[50]

This changing nature of investments and the evolving relationship between companies and owners has seen the importance of shareholders rise to a position that is distracting for businesses. Managers now have to concentrate a disproportionate amount of their time on the short-term considerations of quarterly results,[51] dividend levels, and share price in order to keep demanding shareholders happy, particularly in English-speaking-dominated economies. This short-term perspective often comes at the cost of long-term strategic considerations of the company and its business interests. Many observers see this development as a corruption of the fundamental purpose of a company issuing shares, as well as how those shares are later traded on the stock market. In investment and loyalty terms, the link between shareholder and company has largely disappeared, with a shrinking number of institutional and individual investors today taking the long view:

> It is hard to be influenced by your owners when you do not know who they are. And even if you do, the effect of derivative contracts is to increase the owner's interest in the price of the share, and not on the fundamental value your company is creating.[52]

This transitory element of equity trading is taken to the extreme by the rise of day trading, a phenomenon that emerged in the United States at the height of the Internet boom,[53] but also found its way to other countries such as the United Kingdom.[54] Day trading became possible because of the rise in personal Internet access and developing communications technology. It is often conducted by "quick-triggered amateurs,"[55] with little or no expertise. It can be defined as speculation, "where investors buy shares with the express intent of selling for a quick profit, often within 24 hours."[56] Day trading presents additional compelling evidence that any link investors have with the long-term interests of the company in which they are investing has been largely severed.[57] Short-term profit is the only goal:

> Where "shareholder value" may once have referred to the long term creation of wealth, today's short-term financial investor demands action that can influence the share price even on a daily basis.[58]

And the consequences for not delivering that short-term profit can be severe. As Bill George, the retired CEO of Medtronic, observed,

> They want to know why you didn't make the numbers. . . . You tell them, we're investing in our research programs for the long term. But that doesn't fly. . . .When you [miss stated targets] your stock gets inordinately punished. . . . If your earnings are up 15 percent, but they expected 20 percent, then your stock will go down—not 5 percent, but 25 percent. Then you're vulnerable to a takeover.[59]

> Building and improving a business takes time. You cannot be judged hour by hour on your performance.[60]

(Continued)

(Continued)

> Businesses still have a duty to provide a return for investors. It is central to their economic mission; but the idea that shareholders have the best interests of the firm at heart no longer necessarily holds true. In today's business environment, a broader stakeholder perspective will provide the stability necessary for managers to chart the best course for the company so that it remains a viable entity over the medium to long term. This is in the interests of a company's investors, rather than those of its speculators.

A focus on short-term results, often driven by those investors or other shareholders (such as the firm's executives) who have no interest in the long-term health or viability of the organization, can be hugely damaging to the organization and represents a relatively recent development in Western capitalism. As Alfred Chandler notes, this was not always the case:

> In making administrative decisions, career managers preferred policies that favored the long-term stability and growth of their enterprises to those that maximized current profits.[61]

The development of stock options and other compensation policies designed to solve the principal–agent conflict[62] and align the interests of owners and managers, however, has produced negative consequences. The short-term nature of shareholder investments in firms, combined with the financial incentives executives have had to develop personal wealth at the expense of the long-term health of the firm, have distorted the conditions under which executives are forced to make decisions.[63] The focus is less and less on the underlying value of a business and more and more on the perception of value held by the crowd of investors. John Maynard Keynes perceived this distorting influence of stock exchanges, comparing the process of stock picking to a beauty contest. The object is not to choose the most beautiful face, merely the one that the investor thinks others will find the most beautiful. In other words, for the investor, "It is better … to be conventionally wrong than unconventionally right."[64]

> It is not a case of choosing those [faces] that, to the best of one's judgment, are really the prettiest, nor even those that average opinion genuinely thinks the prettiest. We have reached the third degree where we devote our intelligences to anticipating what average opinion expects the average opinion to be. And there are some, I believe, who practice the fourth, fifth and higher degrees.[65]

As a result, CEOs are increasingly wary of being oversensitive to the needs and demands of short-term investors. Robert C. Goizueta, Coca-Cola's CEO from 1981 to 1997, for example, preferred the term *share owner* to *shareholder* as it implied a greater ownership stake in the firm.[66] Similarly, Wendelin Wiedeking, the CEO of Porsche, has long argued for a broader perspective to strategic planning that shifts executives' attention beyond the short-term demands of investors:

> I have never understood shareholder value as it leaves so many things out. Shareholders give their money just once, whereas the employees work every day.[67]

Similarly, Sumantra Ghoshal, the late professor at the London Business School, argued that the heavy emphasis placed on shareholders does not reflect the relative contributions of different stakeholders to the success of the organization:

> After all, we know that shareholders do not own the company—not in the sense that they own their homes or their cars. They merely own a right to the residual cash flows of the company. . . . They have no ownership rights on the actual assets or businesses of the company, which are owned by the company itself, as a "legal person.". . . Most shareholders can sell their stocks far more easily than most employees can find another job. In every substantive sense, employees of a company carry more risks than do the shareholders. Also, their contributions of knowledge, skills, and entrepreneurship are typically more important than the contributions of capital by shareholders, a pure commodity that is perhaps in excess supply.[68]

In essence, strategic CSR is an enlightened approach to management that retains the focus on creating and adding value that is emphasized by a traditional bottom-line business model, but, in an important difference, it also incorporates a commitment to meeting the needs and demands of key stakeholder groups, broadly defined. Equally important, to implement strategic CSR in a meaningful way, the focus of the firm has to be on maximizing both economic and social value over the long term and acting in areas in which it has expertise (related to core operations). A short-term focus, driven by quarterly earnings guidelines to investors with little long-term interest in the organization, has little value (and is most likely detrimental) to firms committed to implementing strategic CSR. This focus on long-term added value, therefore, is the principal difference between a traditional shareholder-focused business model and a strategic CSR model integrated throughout operations. This shift in perspective (from long to short term) is relatively easy to envision but much more difficult to implement firmwide. Nevertheless, this shift alone brings a firm a lot closer to a CSR perspective. Combining this shift with the integration of a stakeholder perspective into the firm's strategic planning process and a focus on activities that are relevant to the firm's core operations refocuses executives on the implementation of strategic CSR throughout the organization.

A STAKEHOLDER PERSPECTIVE IN ACTION

Beyond the stakeholder model in this chapter, there are a number of contentious areas of debate within the CSR community. These debates lead to confusion regarding possible best-practice standards and difficulties for firms in implementation. As such, Chapter 3 will explore some on the arguments *against* CSR (and the often unintended implications of progressive CSR applications) that are yet to be resolved.

In the final two chapters of Part I, we will outline how firms integrate CSR into day-to-day operations. Chapter 4 puts CSR into strategic perspective and expands on the growing importance of CSR and its impact on corporate strategy. Finally, Chapter 5 discusses the issues that influence the implementation of CSR within a strategic decision-making framework of the firm.

Questions for Discussion and Review

1. Define each of these terms: vision, mission, strategy, and tactics. What is the relationship among them in relation to a firm's strategy planning process?

2. Outline the resources perspective. Identify a firm and its core competency; show how it meets the three tests proposed by Prahalad and Hamel that identify it as a source of sustainable competitive advantage for a firm.

3. Outline the industry perspective. Choose an example industry and conduct an analysis of its competitive structure using Porter's five-forces model.

4. Using a real-life example, list a firm's stakeholders, and use one of the models presented in the chapter to prioritize their importance. What criteria do you think should be used to prioritize competing stakeholder interests?

5. Define strategic CSR in your own words. What are the signs you would look for to indicate that a firm has implemented a strategic CSR perspective?

6. What are the four key components of the definition of strategic CSR? Which of these four do you think will generate the greatest resistance or difficulty for firms?

7. Are shareholders in a firm *investors* or *gamblers*?

NOTES AND REFERENCES

1. Bruce D. Henderson, "The Origin of Strategy," *Harvard Business Review,* November–December 1989, pp. 134–143.

2. An alternative tool to analyze a firm's strategy, one that emphasizes the importance of a comprehensive approach, is the *strategy diamond.* This approach is detailed in an article by Donald C. Hambrick & James W. Fredrickson: "Are You Sure You Have a Strategy?" *Academy of Management Executive*, Vol. 19, No. 4, 2005, pp. 51–62. The strategy diamond contains five elements that cover the range of actions taken by firms to achieve their goals: arenas (the areas in which the firm will compete), vehicles (the ways in which the firm will achieve its goals), differentiators (the means by which the firm will differentiate itself from the competition), staging (the speed and order of implementation), and economic logic (the route to profitability). While the strategy diamond draws on existing knowledge, its value lies in combining this knowledge into a comprehensive tool to analyze a firm's strategy—"an integrated overarching concept of how the business will achieve its objectives" (p. 51).

3. C. K. Prahalad & Gary Hamel, "The Core Competence of the Corporation," *Harvard Business Review*, May–June 1990, pp. 79–91.

4. Gary Hamel & C.K. Prahalad, *Competing for the Future*, Harvard Business School Press, 1994.

5. "Google's Mission Is to Organize the World's Information and Make It Universally Accessible and Useful." http://www.google.com/corporate/

6. C. K. Prahalad & Gary Hamel, "The Core Competence of the Corporation," *Harvard Business Review*, May–June 1990, p. 81.

7. "About the Company," August 27, 2009, http://www.southwest.com/about_swa/press/factsheet.html

8. James L. Heskett, "Southwest Airlines—2002: An Industry Under Siege," *Harvard Business School Press* [9-803-133], March 11, 2003, p. 4.

9. Michael E. Porter, "How Competitive Forces Shape Strategy," *Harvard Business Review*, March/April 1979, pp. 137–145.

10. Michael E. Porter, *Competitive Strategy*, The Free Press, 1980.

11. Ibid.

12. Michael E. Porter, "The Five Competitive Forces That Shape Strategy," *Harvard Business Review*, January 2008, pp. 79–93.

13. David B. Yoffie, "Cola Wars Continue: Coke and Pepsi in 2006," *Harvard Business School Press* [9-706-447], April 2, 2007.

14. In 2009, both Coke and Pepsi announced that they were considering purchasing their main bottlers. While Coke said only that it was open to the idea (Valerie Bauerlein, "Coca-Cola CEO Defends Bottling System," *Wall Street Journal*, April 22, 2009, p. B3), in August 2009, Pepsi paid $7.8 billion to buy its two largest bottlers (Michael J. de la Merced, "PepsiCo to Pay $7.8 Billion to Buy Its Two Top Bottlers," *New York Times*, August 5, 2009, p. B7).

15. James L. Heskett, "Southwest Airlines—2002: An Industry Under Siege," *Harvard Business School Press* [9-803-133], March 11, 2003.

16. Ben Mutzabaugh & Dan Reed, "Virgin America Gets Tentative Approval to Launch U.S. Service," *USAToday*, March 23, 2007, http://www.usatoday.com/travel/flights/2007-03-20-virgin-america-cleared-fly_N.htm

17. "Yearend Results for 2008 Marked Southwest's 36th Consecutive Year of Profitability." http://www.southwest.com/about_swa/press/factsheet.html. "After breaking even less than two years after its founding in 1971, the airline . . . enjoyed 30 consecutive years of profit beginning in 1973, a record unmatched by any airline in the world." "Southwest Airlines—2002: An Industry Under Siege,' *Harvard Business School Press* [9-803-133], 2003.

18. Geoff Gloeckler, "The Millennials Invade the B-Schools," *BusinessWeek*, November 24, 2008, p. 47, http://www.businessweek.com/magazine/content/08_47/b4109046025427.htm

19. For a more complete discussion of the importance of approaching CSR using a strategic lens, see Chapter 5.

20. See Rebecca Tuhus-Dubrow, "US: Sued by the Forest," *The Boston Globe,* July 19, 2009, in CorpWatch, http://www.corpwatch.org/article.php?id=15413 for an interesting discussion about whether the ecological environment is an identifiable stakeholder of the firm with rights that are protected by law.

21. R. Edward Freeman, *Strategic Management: A Stakeholder Approach*, Pitman, 1984, p. 46.

22. James E. Post, Lee E. Preston, & Sybille Sachs, "Managing the Extended Enterprise: The New Stakeholder View," *California Management Review*, Vol. 45, No. 1, Fall 2002, p. 8.

23. Andrew Likierman, "Stakeholder Dreams and Shareholder Realities," Mastering Financial Management, *Financial Times*, June 16, 2006, p. 10.

24. Simon Zadek, "The Path to Corporate Responsibility," *Harvard Business Review*, December, 2004, pp. 125–132.

25. Ibid., p. 127.

26. Ibid., p. 128.

27. See the discussion around "A Rational Argument for CSR" in Chapter 1.

28. C. K. Prahalad & Allen Hammond, "Serving the World's Poor, Profitably," *Harvard Business Review,* September 2002, Vol. 80, No. 9, pp. 48–58; C. K. Prahalad, "The Fortune at the Bottom of the Pyramid: Eradicating Poverty Through Profits," *Wharton School Publishing*, 2006.

29. C. K. Prahalad & Allen Hammond, "Serving the World's Poor, Profitably," *Harvard Business Review,* September 2002, Vol. 80, No. 9, pp. 48–58.

30. Michael E. Porter & Mark R. Kramer, "The Competitive Advantage of Corporate Philanthropy," *Harvard Business Review*, December 2002, pp. 57–68.

31. Michael E. Porter & Mark R. Kramer, "Strategy & Society," *Harvard Business Review*, December 2006, pp. 78–92.

32. Ibid., p. 88.

33. Ibid., p. 84.

34. Ibid., p. 92.

35. For a detailed explanation of the characteristics of valuable, rare, imperfectly imitable, and non-substitutable resources that lead to a "sustained competitive advantage" for the firm, see Jay Barney, "Firm Resources and Sustained Competitive Advantage," *Journal of Management*, Vol. 17, No. 1, 1991, pp. 99–120.

36. The authors would like to thank Marta White of Georgia State University for introducing this idea to us and allowing us to build on it for inclusion in this chapter of *Strategic CSR*.

37. Michael E. Porter & Mark R. Kramer, "Strategy & Society," *Harvard Business Review*, December 2006, p. 85.

38. Michael E. Porter & Mark R. Kramer, "The Competitive Advantage of Corporate Philanthropy," *Harvard Business Review*, December 2002, pp. 57–68.

39. Notwithstanding this logic, however, at its 2008 AGM, Exxon rejected a shareholder motion that was instigated by the Rockefeller family (politically influential shareholders of the firm) to force Exxon to take the issue of climate change and the search of alternative sources of energy more seriously. "A survey carried out by the UK's Royal Society found that in 2005 ExxonMobil distributed $2.9m to 39 groups that the society said 'misrepresented the science of climate change by outright denial of the evidence.'" In David Adam, "Exxon to Cut Funding to Climate Change Denial Groups," *The Guardian*, May 28, 2008, http://www.guardian.co.uk/environment/2008/may/28/climatechange.fossilfuels. The primary motion proposed that the CEO and chair positions at Exxon be split to better account for potential shifts in Exxon's operating environment that pose a threat to its core areas of profit generation (oil exploration, refining, and distribution). The motion received 39.5% share of the vote and was reported as a strong rebuke to Exxon's management. See Stephen Foley, "Rockefeller's Descendants Tell Exxon to Face the Reality of Climate Change," *The Independent*, May 1, 2008, http://www.independent.co.uk/news/business/news/818778.html, and Andrew Clark, "Exxon Facing Shareholder Revolt Over Approach to Climate Change," *The Guardian*, May 19, 2008, http://www.guardian.co.uk/business/2008/may/19/exxonmobil.oil

40. http://www.dell.com/recycling/. See also "Dell Will Offer Free Recycling for Its Computer Equipment," *Wall Street Journal*, June 29, 2006, p. D3.

41. http://www.dell.com/content/topics/global.aspx/about_dell/values/environment/tree?c=us&l=en&s=corp. See also: "Dell Unveils 'Plant a Tree for Me,'" *Financial Times*, January 10, 2007, p. 17.

42. Heesun Wee, "Corporate Ethics: Right Makes Might," *BusinessWeek*, April 11, 2002, http://www.businessweek.com/bwdaily/dnflash/apr2002/nf20020411_6350.htm

43. James L. Heskett, "Southwest Airlines—2002: An Industry Under Siege," *Harvard Business School Press* [9-803-133], March 11, 2003.

44. "Starbucks Corporation: Building a Sustainable Supply Chain," *Stanford Graduate School of Business* [GS-54], May 2007.

45. Stephen P. Bradley & Pankaj Ghemwat, "Wal-Mart Stores, Inc.," *Harvard Business School Press* [9-794-024], November 6, 2002.

46. Joe Nocera, "Putting Customers First? What an Amazonian Concept," *New York Times*, January 5, 2008, p. B1.

47. Steven Greenhouse, "How Costco Became the Anti-Wal-Mart," *New York Times*, July 17, 2005, http://www.nytimes.com/2005/07/17/business/yourmoney/17costco.html. See also John Helyar, "COSTCO: The Only Company Wal-Mart Fears," *Fortune,* November 10, 2003, http://money.cnn.com/magazines/fortune/fortune_archive/2003/11/24/353755/index.htm

48. Bill George, retired CEO of Medtronic, speaking to Marjorie Kelly, "Conversations With the Masters," *Business Ethics,* Spring 2004, pp. 4–5.

49. *The Economist,* Editorial, January 30, 1999, pp. 17–18.

50. "Punters or Proprietors? A Survey of Capitalism," *The Economist,* May 5–11, 1990, pp. 21–23.

51. Candace Browning, "Companies Should Drop Quarterly Earnings Guidance," *Financial Times*, March 20, 2006, p. 13.

52. Mark Goyder, "Who Is Paying the Piper?" *Ethical Corporation Magazine*, June 2006, p. 48.

53. The numbers of day traders "swelled to more than 100,000 in the late 1990s." Ianthe Jeanne Dugan, "For Day Traders, German Index Is Overnight Sensation," *Wall Street Journal,* October 19, 2004, p. A1.

54. At the height of the Internet boom in 1999, there were estimated to be 40,000 online share-trading accounts in the United Kingdom. This figure was expected to "grow to 700,000 within four years," according to Fletcher Research. "Day Trading: Gambling on the Edge," *The Independent,* July 31, 1999, p. 21.

55. Ianthe Jeanne Dugan, "For Day Traders, German Index Is Overnight Sensation," *Wall Street Journal,* October 19, 2004, p. A1.

56. "Day Trading: Gambling on the Edge," *The Independent,* July 31, 1999, p. 21.

57. In a legislative reaction to the presence of growing numbers of day traders, "new Federal rules in 2001 required that people trading stocks more than four times a week keep $25,000 in their accounts at all times." Ianthe Jeanne Dugan, "For Day Traders, German Index Is Overnight Sensation," *Wall Street Journal,* October 19, 2004, p. A1.

58. Stefan Stern, "The Short-Term Shareholders Changing the Face of Capitalism," *Financial Times*, March 28, 2006, p. 11.

59. Marjorie Kelly, "Conversations With the Masters," *Business Ethics,* Spring 2004, pp. 4–5.

60. Stefan Stern, "Short-Term Owners Who Leave the C-suite Bitter," *Financial Times*, June 24, 2008, p. 14.

61. Alfred D. Chandler, *The Visible Hand: The Managerial Revolution in American Business*, Harvard University Press, 1977, p. 10.

62. See the Executive Compensation Issue in Chapter 6.

63. Michael Skapinker, "Every Fool Knows It Is a Job for Government," *Financial Times*, November 18, 2008, p. 13.

64. John Kay, "Beauty in Markets Is Best Judged by the Beholder," *Financial Times*, June 10, 2009, p. 9.

65. John Maynard Keynes, *The General Theory of Employment, Interest and Money*, Harcourt Brace and Co., 1936, p. 156.

66. Roberto C. Goizueta, "You Are Tomorrow's Leaders," Remarks at Emory University's Business School graduation ceremony, May 13, 1996, http://www.goizueta.emory.edu/aboutgoizueta/quotes/calling_full.html

67. Richard Milne, "The Jovial Locust Killer," *Financial Times*, November 1/November 2, 2008, p. 7.

68. Sumantra Ghoshal, 'Bad Management Theories Are Destroying Good Management Practices,' *Academy of Management Learning & Education*, Vol. 4, No. 1, March, 2005, pp. 79–80.

CHAPTER 3

HOW MUCH DOES CSR MATTER?

Whose responsibility is CSR? The term *corporate social responsibility* suggests that such behavior is the responsibility of corporations. But, where does the motivation for socially responsible behavior come from?

Should corporations act responsibly because they are convinced of the moral argument for doing so (irrespective of the financial implications of their actions), or should they act responsibly because it is in their self-interest? What is the point of a firm acting socially responsibly if its key stakeholders do not care or do not want to pay the price premium that is often associated with such actions? As the Malden Mills example in Chapter 1 indicates, the best intentions do not help a firm's stakeholders if the firm is bankrupt. The economic argument for CSR assumes that firms act most effectively when they are incentivized to do so. It assumes that organizations are conservative—that they are more responsive to external stimuli and are less willing to initiate change proactively when there is little evidence that their actions will be rewarded in the marketplace. It assumes that CSR maximizes both economic and social value when the firm's goals and society's expectations are aligned.

Chapters 1 and 2 present compelling strategic reasons for firms to integrate a CSR perspective throughout the organization. Nevertheless, unprincipled behavior, even outright disregard for CSR, does not always have a direct and immediate impact. Sometimes stakeholders are willing to overlook socially irresponsible behavior because other issues are more pressing. A firm with unacceptable employment practices that are despised by employees, for example, may not reap the negative consequences of its actions if the jobs are vital to the well-being of the local community, and there are no good alternatives. Should firms interpret the lack of pushback against their actions as an invitation to uphold the status quo without consideration for broader societal concerns about their operations?

A more difficult question arises when a CSR perspective fails to align the firm's interests with those of its stakeholders. What happens when stakeholders demand non-socially responsible behavior? What happens, for example, if consumers want to purchase a product that is not only bad for them (e.g., tobacco, alcohol, or fast food) but also bad for society (e.g., has greater health or resource implications)? What happens when consumers' primary concern is the lowest price, to the exclusion of all other concerns, such as the conditions in the factories where the product is made? If firms can be successful without implementing a CSR perspective, does this mean that CSR does not matter, or at least does not matter all of the time?

The focus of much of the dialogue around CSR has been to urge firms to act proactively out of a social or moral duty. The label *CSR* itself talks about the *social responsibility* of corporations, without understanding that, often, there are no meaningful consequences for firms that do not act *responsibly* and that, in contrast, they are often rewarded economically for *not* pursuing CSR. Unless their business suffers as a result of their actions, should firms be expected to change?

Discussion around the issue of CSR almost exclusively focuses on the responsibilities of business, while ignoring the responsibilities of stakeholders (consumers, in particular) to demand action from firms. There is anecdotal evidence to suggest, however, that consumers want the highest quality products at the lowest possible prices. If those products happen to coincide with an ethical message, then that is great, but consumers (on the whole) are willing to plead ignorance if it means getting their sneakers for $10 less:

> In the United Kingdom, ethical consumerism data show that although most consumers are concerned about environmental or social issues, with 83 percent of consumers *intending* to act ethically on a regular basis, only 18 percent of people act ethically occasionally, while fewer than 5 percent of consumers show consistent ethical and green purchasing behaviors.[1]

If, on the other hand, consumers began demanding specific minimum standards from firms and took their custom elsewhere if they failed to comply, firms would be forced to change their practices and change them quickly. How can we expect businesses to act socially responsible when doing so means they have to try and interpret what consumers say they want—opinions that often contradict the criteria those same consumers use to make their purchase decisions?

Just because stakeholders do not react immediately, however, does not mean that CSR is unimportant or is something that can be ignored for too long. Socially irresponsible behavior without immediate consequences does not mean that the behavior is, or should be, condoned. Equally, business practices that are profitable today may not necessarily be profitable tomorrow. Short-term success simply means that other issues take precedence . . . for now. As circumstances or societal expectations evolve, the lack of CSR may alter the firm's prospects. A vivid example comes from the 2007–2009 economic crisis:

The 2007–2009 Economic Crisis

In pursuit of process fees, brokers sold adjustable mortgages to those who could not afford them. These loans were then packaged and sold to investors (in pursuit of annual bonuses), who didn't understand them or appreciate the associated risks. Given the AAA rating these securities were assigned by the credit-rating agencies (in pursuit of corporate fees), the mortgages continued to be sold to a growing percentage of the population. With insufficient oversight by regulators, these socially irresponsible actions were repeated for years. When housing prices declined and mortgage defaults soared, however, the lack of social responsibility by brokers, bankers, credit-rating agencies, and Wall Street resulted in dire consequences and bankruptcies for many firms that did not practice CSR.

The title of this chapter, "How Much Does CSR Matter?" reflects an important debate within the CSR community: Can firms safely ignore calls for reform as long as they are profitable? By definition, profitability means that a firm is adding value (perceived or real) for key stakeholder groups, even if those needs have broader, negative consequences? This chapter is designed to address these questions within the larger framework of strategic CSR constructed in Chapters 1 and 2. A central question is: Whose responsibility is it to bring about socially responsible behavior among firms? We examine why stakeholders may not always care about CSR or, even when they do care, why they may not evidence that concern with action. We propose not only that CSR matters in its own right, but that the failure to be perceived as socially responsible by stakeholders will at some point carry moral, rational, and economic repercussions for any firm—as the 2007–2009 economic crisis revealed.

CSR: A CORPORATE RESPONSIBILITY?

The focus of much of the CSR debate (and captured by the term corporate social *responsibility*) is the assumption that firms have a *responsibility* to pursue goals other than profit maximization. This chapter explores this assumption in more detail. In particular, we propose the idea that the CSR community expects too much of firms; that firms *react* to change better than they *initiate* change and that, if society decides it wants greater social responsibility from firms, then perhaps it is a firm's stakeholders (and their consumers, in particular) that have an equal, if not greater *responsibility* to demand this behavior. More important, stakeholders need to demonstrate that they will support such behavior. Firms that provide services that are not demanded by consumers will quickly go out of business. With CSR, as with many aspects of business, it does not pay firms to be too far ahead of the curve. If consumers, for example, demonstrate that they are willing to pay a price premium for CSR behavior (rather than reporting in surveys that they think firms should be more responsible, but basing their purchase decisions mainly on price), firms will quickly adapt. If consumers are not willing to pay this premium, however, is it really in society's best interests for firms to bear the burden of producing such products?

Milton Friedman Versus Charles Handy

Two important articles on CSR frame this debate about the responsibility that a firm has to be socially responsible. The first article was published in the *New York Times Magazine* in 1970 by the Nobel prize–winning economist, Milton Friedman—"The Social Responsibility of Business Is to Increase Its Profits."[2] In the article, Friedman argues that profit, as a result of the actions of the firm, is an end in itself. He believes strongly that a firm need not have any additional justification for existing and that, in fact, social value is maximized when a firm focuses solely on pursuing its self-interest in attempting to maximize profit:

> I share Adam Smith's skepticism about the benefits that can be expected from "those who affected to trade for the public good." . . . in a free society, . . . "there is one and only one social responsibility of business—to use its resources and engage in activities designed to increase its profits."[3]

The second article is a 2002 *Harvard Business Review* article by the influential British management author and commentator, Charles Handy.[4] In contrast to Friedman, Handy presents a much broader view of the role of business in society. For Handy, it is not sufficient to justify a firm's profits as an end in itself. For Handy, a business has to have a motivation other than merely making a profit in order to justify its existence—profit is merely a means to achieve a larger end. A firm should remain in existence not just because it is profitable, but because it is meeting a need that society *as a whole* values:

> It is salutary to ask about any organization, "If it did not exist, would we invent it?" "Only if it could do something better or more useful than anyone else" would have to be the answer, and profit would be the means to that larger end.[5]

On the surface, the positions taken by Friedman and Handy would appear to be irreconcilable. Indeed, Friedman appears to go out of his way to antagonize CSR advocates by arguing that socially responsible behavior is a waste of the firm's resources, which legally do not belong to the firm's executives but to the firm's owners, its shareholders:

> That is why, in my book *Capitalism and Freedom,* I have called [social responsibility] a "fundamentally subversive doctrine" in a free society.[6]

But, on closer analysis, how different are the articles, really? Incorporating a strategic CSR perspective closes the gap between these two commentators considerably. As outlined in Chapter 2, there are four important components of strategic CSR: First, that firms incorporate a CSR perspective within their strategic planning process; second, that any actions they take are directly related to core operations; third, that they incorporate a stakeholder perspective; and, fourth, that they shift from a short-term perspective to managing the firm's resources and relations with key stakeholders over the medium to long term. Consider again the following two questions:

- Does it make sense for a large financial firm to donate money to a group researching the effects of climate change because the CEO believes this is an important issue?
- Does it make sense for an oil firm to donate money to the same group because it perceives climate change as a threat to its business model and wants to mitigate that threat by investigating possible alternatives?

The action—a large for-profit firm donating money to a nonprofit group—is the same. The difference is the relevance of the nonprofit's activities to the firm's core operations. Most level-headed CSR advocates would consider the first a waste of money (incorporating Friedman's argument that the actions represent an inefficient allocation of resources in an area in which the firm has no expertise), while the second is a strategic recognition by the firm that it needs to address issues that are important to key stakeholder groups in the firm's operating environment. Taking the positions of Friedman and Handy in their entirety, a more insightful interpretation of their arguments is that, to the extent that it is in a firm's interests to meet the needs of its key stakeholders, strategy should incorporate all four levels of Carroll's CSR pyramid.[7] From Handy's perspective, this point is easy to argue, but Friedman also recognizes this. He qualifies his statement that a manager's direct responsibility is to the owners of the enterprise, who seek "to make as much money as possible," by noting that this pursuit must be tempered:

> While conforming to the basic rules of the society, *both those embodied in law and those embodied in ethical custom. . . .* [A firm's actions are acceptable, only as long as it] engages in open and free competitors *without deception or fraud.*[8] (Emphasis added)

CSR: A STAKEHOLDER RESPONSIBILITY?

How much does CSR matter? What responsibility do firms have to initiate CSR? These questions raise the issue of whether stakeholders care about CSR. In particular, do stakeholders have an obligation to help ensure the business community adopts a CSR perspective?

Underlying much of the CSR debate (and captured by the term corporate social *responsibility*) is the assumption that firms have the primary *responsibility* to pursue goals other than profit maximization. This chapter explores this assumption in more detail. In particular, we examine the idea that the CSR community expects too much of firms; that firms *react* to change better than they *initiate* change and whether stakeholders also have a *responsibility* to demand CSR behavior from firms. Should investors, regulators, and other stakeholders, for example, demand greater care in the issuing of loans from the finance industry? Should consumers demand higher wages for employees in the retail industry? The point is not to argue *yes* or *no* here, but to examine whether stakeholders have an obligation to help design the society in which they want to live and work. If society decides that financial bubbles and crises should be avoided, then it is fair to acknowledge they have a role in realizing this outcome. Similarly, if society decides that it does not want all of its jobs outsourced to low-cost environments, then it needs to pay the higher prices that will result from keeping domestic jobs. The responsibility is not solely with one group or another, but it is important to acknowledge that "we live in the house we all build."[9]

CSR Newsletters: Earthshare

Consider a full-page advertisement that appeared in the *New York Times* for the environmental activist group Earthshare.org (http://www.earthshare.org/). A graphic of the ad can be viewed at: http://www.earthshare.org/psa/earthshare_printpsa_2008.pdf:

> Every decision we make has consequences. We choose what we put into our lakes and rivers. We choose what we release into the air we breathe. We choose what we put into our bodies, and where we let our children run and play. We choose the world we live in, so make the right choices. Learn what you can do to care for our water, our air, our land and yourself at earthshare.org.

(Continued)

(Continued)

What is attractive about the ad is the emphasis it places on individual responsibility, rather than merely haranguing firms for polluting too much. The headline of the ad (including capital letters and bold) captures the tone exactly:

WE **LIVE** IN THE HOUSE WE ALL **BUILD**

This emphasis is often absent from the CSR debate. Firms act much more quickly in response to key stakeholder demands (consumers, in particular) than they do when expected to initiate action that has no demonstrated support in the marketplace. In other words, if consumers stop buying a certain product because they disapprove of the way it was produced or some other action by the firm that produced it, that firm will quickly adapt or fail. In other words, stakeholders are as responsible for the corporations that survive and thrive in our society as the organizations themselves. It is not a perfect solution for the problems in our capitalist system, and firms are not absolved of all responsibility (and those firms that are able to differentiate themselves in relation to CSR will be more successful in the long term); it is just that more would be achieved that much faster in terms of CSR advocacy if an equal emphasis were placed on *stakeholder responsibility* (e.g., consumer education) as on *corporate responsibility*.

Do Stakeholders Care?

In order for CSR to be a stakeholder responsibility, however, stakeholders need to care sufficiently to warrant corporate action. The argument in favor of CSR presupposes that there are benefits for a company being perceived as a net contributor to the society in which it is based. At the very least, there should be economic disadvantages for firms that act contrary to the expectations of key stakeholders. Managers already understand the benefits of being perceived as an important and positive influence within a local community, as suggested by existing advertising campaign strategies and levels of corporate philanthropy. The extent to which that perceived image differs from societal expectations represents the potential for a *CSR deficit,* as depicted in Figure 3.1. The CSR deficit suggests a gap between the expectations of the firm's stakeholders (both internal and external) and what the firm delivers.

A firm that is successfully implementing a *strategic CSR* perspective (represented by the 45-degree line in Figure 3.1) is able to align the *economic value* its internal stakeholders seek with the broader *social value* that is sought by its various external stakeholders. Typically, the economic value sought is growing profits, which benefit organizational stakeholders such as shareholders and employees. To be considered legitimate over the medium to long term, however, the firm's pursuit of economic value should also provide social value to the firm's external stakeholders, such as the local community in the form of preserving local jobs or producing products that are safe to consume.

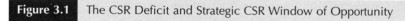

Figure 3.1   The CSR Deficit and Strategic CSR Window of Opportunity

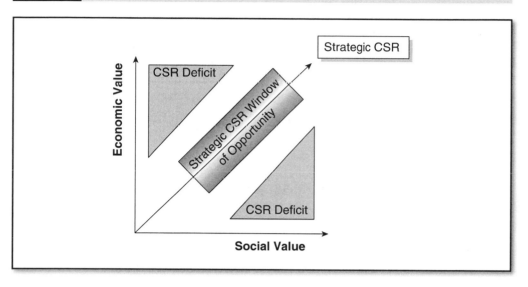

   The range of firm behavior that generates both economic and social value in sufficient quantities is termed the *Strategic CSR Window of Opportunity.* As such, the Strategic CSR Window of Opportunity suggests the need for balance. An unchecked, unbridled pursuit of economic value, without regard to the social consequences (e.g., such as a manufacturing process that generates excessive pollution), creates a CSR deficit for the society in which the firm operates. Likewise, a firm that pursues social value too aggressively (e.g., Malden Mills in Chapter 1) may diminish its ability to generate economic value—causing a CSR deficit in the form of slowed economic activity and lower returns to the owners. Simply put, when either social or economic value is deficient to some degree, stakeholders have a basis on which to question the legitimacy of the firm as a member of society. Consider these two examples where a CSR deficit of social value resulted in stakeholder reactions against business.

The CSR Deficit

Prior to the Equal Pay Act of 1963, many employers paid their employees less than what was thought to be an *acceptable* (if not ethical) amount. When business pay discrimination continued for too long, falling short of evolving societal expectations, these ethical and moral concerns became embodied in the 1963 law that constrained firms' flexibility to operate.

   Similarly, Walmart's focused pursuit of economic benefits via its low-cost model can devastate smaller, less efficient retailers in the local community. As a result, many city and county governments have responded to Walmart's perceived CSR deficit by limiting Walmart's growth through zoning restrictions—also a constraint on business.

While actions that focus solely on profit maximization (economic) or philanthropic activity unrelated to the firm's core operations (social) add value, they do so in ways that fail to support a strategic CSR perspective. The alignment of economic and social value represents the implementation of a strategic approach to CSR throughout the organization. Restated, organizations must act in ways that are valued by their multiple stakeholders—not just their owners, employees, or any other single constituent. For the Strategic CSR Window of Opportunity to apply in practice, however, it is important that stakeholders evaluate firm actions and act to correct a CSR deficit when they perceive one. Anecdotal evidence, however, questions whether stakeholders, in general, and consumers, in particular, care sufficiently about CSR to make significant short-term sacrifices in the name of a larger social cause:[10]

CSR Newsletters: Ethical Consumers

A recent article[11] questions the assumption of many CSR advocates that consumers care sufficiently about business ethics and CSR to sustain a fundamental shift in the dominant economic model. In essence, consumers will say one thing in response to survey questions about ethics or CSR, then turn around and make their purchase decisions based on different principles:

> For most people to choose an "ethical" product over a regular product, that product must not cost any more than an ordinary one, it must come from a reputed brand, require no special effort to buy or use, and it must be at least as good as its alternative.

In spite of a rise in availability of ethical products and producers willing to sell them:

> For the majority of consumers, cheap products of decent quality remain the popular choice.

If true, then:

> What incentives do businesses have in maintaining responsible or ethical standards?

While the article addresses the issue of reputation risk for firms, it also argues that the threat of regulation represents the strongest incentive for firms to reform ahead of consumer demands that they do so. Because consumers are unlikely to voluntarily sacrifice their current standard of living for a future, uncertain benefit (the article argues), governments will eventually be forced to act on their behalf:

> Because the future will have to be one in which governments and regulators will have to take a much tougher line on the way externalities are priced by business.

The rational argument for CSR is not the most forceful (or uplifting) argument for sustainable change, but it might be the best one that we have!

Although many people say they want responsible companies, there is a limit to how much society and stakeholders are willing to impose their views. How many stakeholders are willing or able to pay for socially responsible behavior—and how much—is debatable. Consider consumers as one stakeholder group, for example. Although it appears that the numbers of socially concerned are growing (the Co-operative Bank's ninth annual report into green spending estimated that "the overall ethical market in the UK was worth £35.5 billion in 2007, up 15 per cent from £31 billion in the previous 12 months"),[12] a large component of consumer-driven economic pressure still demands that companies compete in terms of price or other, more traditional characteristics, such as quality. To what extent are investors, suppliers, and other stakeholders willing to sacrifice some value in the name of CSR? Are employees, creditors, regulators, and other key stakeholders always willing to exert influence when they enjoy some degree of leverage?

As a collective, consumers have the power to shape the society they say they want. This is particularly true for a group of consumers as large as those that shop at Walmart every week:

> Does [Wal-Mart's operating practice] matter? Only if consumers say it does, . . . Wal-Mart listens to "voters." If shoppers say they won't buy [a product] until Wal-Mart insists on higher standards from suppliers, then Wal-Mart will make those demands.[13]

Many CSR advocates have relied on the moral argument for their cause, which boils down to the notion that businesses *should* act in a socially responsible manner because it is the *right* thing to do; however, values, such as judgments of right and wrong, are subjective and can be subordinated within organizations to profit, sales, or other bottom-line considerations. Companies may wish or intend to act in a socially responsible manner for a variety of reasons, but they are more likely to commit consistently and wholeheartedly to CSR business practices if they are convinced of the rational or economic benefits of doing so. Stakeholder concerns become more evident and measurable for firms when key groups are willing to support their words with actions.

Stakeholder Advocacy

Stakeholders encourage strategic CSR behavior when they represent rational or economic motives for the firm. Although this advocacy often comes from customers, investors, or other external activists, internal advocates (including founders, leaders, and employees) can also push a CSR agenda. Proponents of an economic argument for CSR believe that the most efficient means of maximizing profits is to ensure that companies meet the expectations of the widest possible range of these stakeholders. Although firms have motives to respond to stakeholder concerns, however, stakeholders also carry a responsibility to educate themselves about a firm's activities and respond appropriately. Do stakeholders care *enough* to push their own agenda and be the fuel that drives corporations to become increasingly responsive in the 21st century?

If stakeholders do care, then firms need to ensure their actions do not run counter to the prevailing consensus; otherwise, they run the risk of negatively affecting the bottom line. If stakeholders do not care, then there is little economic incentive for firms to incorporate a CSR perspective within the organization *today* (even though there may be moral or rational reasons for doing so).

The revolution in communications technology, which fueled the growth of the Internet and global media industry, has presented stakeholders with the opportunity to mobilize effectively and convey their collective message to corporations. They now have previously unimaginable abilities to monitor corporate operations and widely and quickly disseminate any actions or information they feel do not represent their best interests. In this manner, the communications revolution has been a great leveler of corporate power.

As Figure 3.2 illustrates, globalization has facilitated a great expansion in corporate influence. Today, global companies span national boundaries, outsourcing large elements of operations offshore, incorporating supply chain efficiencies, cutting costs, and growing their brands into cultural icons that span the globe: Think of Coke, Nike, or McDonald's as examples, all of which regularly feature in surveys of the world's most important brands.[14]

Phase II of globalization, however, has been marked by countervailing pressures from stakeholders with access to increased sources of information about firms and to increased

Figure 3.2   The Two Phases of Globalization

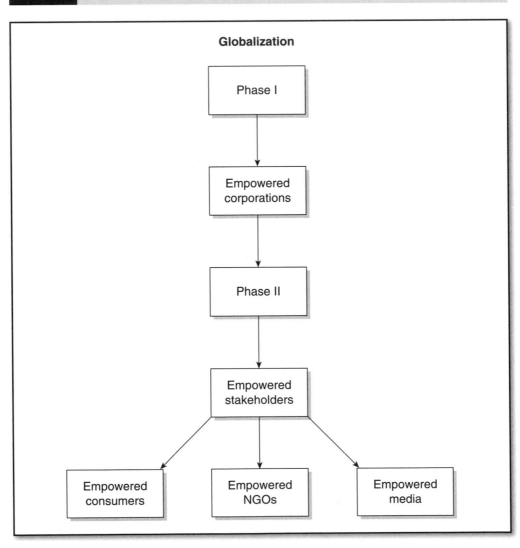

means of acting on that information. Thomas Friedman, with greater historical perspective, refers to this as the:

> era of "Globalization 3.0," following Globalization 1.0, which ran from 1492 until 1800 and was driven by countries' sheer brawn, and Globalization 2.0, in which the "key agent of change, the dynamic force of driving global integration, was multinational companies" driven to look abroad for markets and labor. . . . That epoch ended around 2000, replaced by one in which individuals are the main agents doing the globalizing, pushed by . . . software [and a] global fiber-optic network that has made us all next-door neighbors.[15]

Globalization relies on powerful tools that stakeholders can use to represent their best interests—that is, if they are willing to take advantage of the opportunity and if they really care.

Intention Versus Reality

To the extent that they indicate which issues are on the minds of stakeholders, opinion surveys can serve as a useful tool. The message polls send, however, may not always be clear. The *USA Today/Gallup* Annual Honesty and Ethics Poll, which rates "the honesty and ethics of workers in 21 different professions," for example, reveals that the public's perception of business executives is not very high. Figure 3.3 indicates that a review of the results from

Figure 3.3   The Honesty and Ethics of Business Executives (1992–2008)

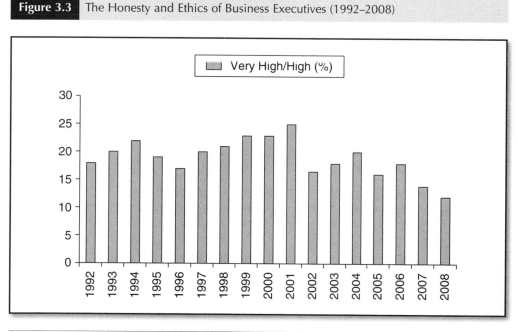

Source: USA Today (USAToday/GallupPoll,http://www.usatoday.com/news/polls/tables/live/2006-12-11-ethics.htm) and *Gallup* (Jeffrey M. Jones, "Lobbyists Debut at Bottom of Honesty and Ethics List," *Gallup*, December 10, 2007, http://www.gallup.com/poll/103123/Lobbyists-Debut-Bottom-Honesty-Ethics-List.aspx; Lydia Saad, "Nurses Shine, Bankers Slump in Ethics Ratings," *Gallup*, November 24, 2008, http://www.gallup.com/ poll/112264/Nurses-Shine-While-Bankers-Slump-Ethics-Ratings.aspx) Web sites.

1992 to 2008 shows the percentage of the U.S. public surveyed who rated business executives' ethics as high or very high never rises above 25% and is trending downward.[16]

The implicit accusation is that the current performance of executives is unacceptable and people would rather it were better. While people say they disapprove of unethical behavior, however, there appears to be a disconnect between perception and personal practice. A survey of MBA students by Donald McCabe, a professor at Rutgers University, for example, shows that "56 percent of MBA students admitted to cheating and, according to McCabe, they were doing it to 'get ahead.' "[17] This figure is little changed from a 2002 survey of 1,100 undergraduate students on 27 university campuses in the United States by the nonprofit organization SIFE (Students in Free Enterprise, which aims to teach ethical business practices to students, http://www.sife.org/), which identified a similar discrepancy between ideals and application:

> Some 59% [of college students polled] admit cheating on a test (66% of men, 54% of women). And only 19% say they would report a classmate who cheated (23% of men, but 15% of women).[18]

The pessimistic (or realistic, depending on your perspective) view of human nature held by Dov Charney, America Apparel's CEO, is that "to get what you want, you must appeal to people's self-interest, not to their mercy." Charney's approach to business, at least in relation to the teenage market segment to which American Apparel appeals, lies in understanding this gap between people's stated intentions and actual practice:

> A whopping majority of American shoppers may consider themselves environmentalists, but, according to the *Journal of Industrial Ecology,* only 10% to 12% "actually go out of their way to purchase environmentally sound products." Similarly, *Brandweek* reported on a survey that found that even among consumers who called themselves "environmentally conscious," more than half could not name a single green brand.[19]

An indicator of hope for a future in which CSR becomes more prominent, therefore, is the degree to which individual and corporate responsibility is being integrated with the education of future business leaders: To what extent are ethics and CSR classes entering the business school curriculum?

The *Beyond Grey Pinstripes* (http://www.beyondgreypinstripes.org/) biennial survey by the Aspen Institute is designed to measure progress in this area: "Our mission is to spotlight innovative full-time MBA programs that are integrating issues of social and environmental stewardship into curricula and research." The organization's 2007/2008 report, which assesses schools in four areas: student opportunity, student exposure, course content, and faculty research, reported that "the percentage of schools surveyed that require students to take a course dedicated to business and society issues has increased dramatically over time, from 34% in 2001 to 63% in 2007."[20]

Net Impact (http://www.netimpact.org/) is another example of progress. The organization, originally founded as Students for Responsible Business in 1993, boasts a growing membership of "MBAs, graduate students, and professionals." The group's goal is "to make a positive impact on society by growing and strengthening a community of leaders who use business to improve the world."

A growing awareness and acceptance of CSR and related ethical issues is a significant development. The extent to which future business leaders are aware of the importance of this issue will increase the likelihood of its acceptance in a corporate setting. More important from a corporate perspective, however, is the extent to which a growing awareness of CSR affects the business bottom line. If the market rewards CSR-sensitive companies and punishes CSR-insensitive companies, that will provide the greatest incentives for leaders to integrate CSR policies into their strategic perspective and day-to-day operations.

Public opinion, expressed through surveys, is one way to measure a society's attitudes toward CSR.[21] To what extent, however, do people tell pollsters their true feelings rather than merely what they think they should say or what they think the pollster wants to hear? Undoubtedly, most people would agree that some degree of responsibility among firms is a desirable trait; however, does self-interest outweigh one's sense of responsibility to society? Will customers, for example, continue buying the cheapest product on the shelf while failing to ask the necessary questions to determine whether a company is socially responsible? Will other stakeholders question whether pronouncements of social responsibility are merely superficial public relations attempts to raise the company's profile?

In the next section of this chapter, an extended case study examines the perspectives of multiple stakeholders and how they influence Walmart's approach to CSR. Besides being the largest for-profit organization in the world, Walmart embodies the full range of domestic and international CSR concerns as it expands globally. As such, this extended example illustrates the interconnections among corporate actions and consequences, from the perspective of customers, communities, shareholders, and other stakeholders, and demonstrates that CSR-related actions can release a cascade of effects that are tempered by economic, cultural, and other realities. The intent is not to praise or condemn, merely to highlight the breadth and depth of CSR, as seen from the perspective of this important firm.

THE WALMART CONUNDRUM

Walmart, as the world's largest company, is a test case for CSR:

> Walmart is the world's largest retailer with $401 billion in sales for the fiscal year ending Jan. 31, 2009. In the U.S., Wal-Mart Stores, Inc. operates more than 4,200 facilities. . . . Internationally, Walmart operates 3,600 additional facilities in 16 markets worldwide. . . . Walmart employs more than 2 million associates worldwide, including more than 1.4 million in the United States.[22]

Walmart, whose total annual revenue represents "a sum greater than the economies of all but 30 of the world's nations"[23] and is growing faster than any of them, is an extremely successful and influential company. At the foundation of the company's success, however, is its business strategy of minimizing costs, which relies on many policies and decisions that affect stakeholders in different ways.

The argument *against* CSR offers up Walmart as its main case in point. Walmart has suffered considerable criticism about its alleged insensitivity to local communities, employees, and other constituents. If this criticism is true, while sales continue to grow, does this suggest that the majority of stakeholders do not really care about CSR? Would Walmart be as successful, today, if they did care? Would it be more successful? Yet, in spite of the criticism it attracts, it is also clear that Walmart also delivers great value to tens of millions of customers every week. These competing views of the firm explain why whenever Walmart enters a new market, some greet it like a liberating force, while others see it as a conquering imperialist.

Wal-Mart Invades, and Mexico Gladly Surrenders.[24]

Walmart Invades India—Who's Next?[25]

A brief survey of article headlines indicates the negative feelings the company generates and concerns about its long-term influence:

Is Wal-Mart Too Powerful?[26]

The Wal-Martization of America[27]

Is Wal-Mart Good for America?[28]

The paradox that surrounds Walmart and the controversy generated by its success suggest why the company is a case study in so many different business disciplines. Overall, does the company provide a net positive or net negative impact on the societies in which it operates? As one writer observed, "Wal-Mart might well be both America's most admired and most hated company."[29] And does the fact that consumers continue to shop at the store (on average, 15 to 20 million customers pass through Walmart's doors every day)[30] critically undermine the argument in favor of CSR?

IS WALMART GOOD FOR SOCIETY?

Is it healthy for an economy to have companies with the size and power of Walmart? Proponents of the pro-Walmart case credit the company with directly saving U.S. consumers $20 billion because of the downward pressure it exerts on prices and another $80 billion due to the price reductions it forces on competitors, on an annual basis:[31]

The giant retailer is at least partly responsible for the low rate of U.S. inflation, and a McKinsey & Co. study concluded that about 12% of the economy's productivity gains in the second half of the 1990s could be traced to Wal-Mart alone.[32]

Walmart gives consumers what they indicate (with their shopping practices) they want—low prices. Yet, the methods by which Walmart achieves these cost savings and low prices are also having a lasting impact, often negative, in the eyes of other stakeholders. The Walmart conundrum is magnified when the long-term impact of the company's policies are extrapolated. We suspect that the same people who are complaining today about the number of U.S. jobs being exported overseas, particularly manufacturing jobs, also form a significant percentage of Walmart consumers, to whom the company's low prices are so attractive:

"Wal-Mart is a double-edged sword, and both edges are quite sharp," Bernstein of the Economic Policy Institute said. "On the price side, consumers wouldn't flood Wal-Mart if there wasn't something there they liked, the low prices. On the other hand, by sticking solidly to the low-wage path, they create tons of low-quality jobs that dampen wage and income growth, not just for those who work in Wal-Mart but for surrounding communities as well."[33]

The potential dangers for Walmart are many. What if consumers begin to worry about the impact the company is having on the economy and society more than they welcome the lower prices the company brings? Communities that worry about a megastore's impact on rural downtowns have already restricted Walmart's growth.[34] Will employees continue to apply for positions at Walmart if better paid alternatives exist? As the company continues to expand, will the government begin to fear the monopolistic characteristics of such a huge market influence? Suppliers are stakeholders who both relish Walmart's market scale and scope and fear their pricing pressures. How will these various stakeholder reactions affect Walmart's business strategy over the longer term? What is the outlook for the company from a CSR perspective?

Before elaborating on the salient characteristics of Walmart's operations, consider the following snapshot:

Is Walmart Good for Society? Yes!

☺ Lower prices for consumers (lower inflation).

☺ Good jobs in economically deprived regions.

☺ Wide range of products.

☺ Redefinition of supply chain management (SCM) and general pursuit of technologically driven efficiencies.

☺ Increased productivity.

Is Walmart Good for Society? No!

☹ Loss of jobs to overseas suppliers.

☹ Strong opposition against collective representation of workforce.

☹ Relatively low employee wages and benefits.

☹ Competitors (and sometimes suppliers) go out of business, reducing competition and, ultimately, consumer choice.

☹ Litigation against the company on issues of alleged discrimination, employment of illegal immigrants, refusal to pay employee overtime, and so forth.

We consider the impact of Walmart's business decisions on its various stakeholders from five different perspectives: prices, suppliers, jobs, competitors, and quality and variety.

Prices

First, Walmart has grown to such an influential point that it now dominates any industry it enters by driving down prices and imposing punishing margins on its competitors. Walmart accounts for about 30% of household goods sold in the United States (predicted to rise to 50% by 2010), including 32% of disposable diapers, 30% of hair care products, 26% of toothpaste sales, 20% of pet food, and 13% of home textiles. In addition, the company accounts for 15–20% of CD, video, and DVD sales; for 15% of all single-copy magazine sales;[35] and for 21% of toy sales.[36]

Walmart arrives at its low prices by reducing costs through two separate strategies. First, it has revolutionized the management of supply chains and inventory within the retail industry. Now, thanks to Walmart's innovations, many firms are better able to manage the flow of goods and materials that form an interconnected chain from providers (such as subcontractors and suppliers), through the firm, to the customer. The company uses information technology to track products—from the supplier to the warehouse to the shelf to the cash register—and ensure, as soon as they are sold, that replacements are back on the shelf waiting for the next customer. And, with this greater refinement in managing the flow from suppliers around the world, it has become easier for firms like Walmart and others to outsource supplies globally. In turn, due to Walmart buying on a global basis, this trend of outsourcing has caused higher-cost domestic producers to lose their supplying relationship to Walmart, sometimes with disastrous results for the suppliers, including bankruptcy. The company's commitment to integrate radio frequency identification (RFID) technology throughout their distribution systems further pushes the technological boundaries of supply chain management.[37] Walmart's innovations have created savings across the board. And it passes these savings on to customers in the form of lower prices.

Second, however, Walmart also seeks to cut costs in other areas by pursuing activities that impose specific outcomes. Examples include paying some of the lowest wages in the retail sector and making specific demands on suppliers. It achieves this advantage by virtue of its size and importance within the economies in which it operates:

> Wal-Mart wields its power for just one purpose: to bring the lowest possible prices to its customers. At Wal-Mart, that goal is never reached. The retailer has a clear policy for suppliers: On basic products that don't change, the price Wal-Mart will pay, and will charge shoppers, must drop year after year.[38]

And, Walmart's impact is always industry-wide. It was accused of causing great dislocation within the toy industry during the 2003 holiday season (leading to the bankruptcies of both F.A.O. Schwarz and KB Toys) and reducing the margins of all the other major industry retailers, in particular Toys R Us:

> The toy war is merely the most recent manifestation of what is known as the Wal-Mart effect. To the company's critics, Wal-Mart points the way to a grim Darwinian world of bankrupt competitors, low wages, meager health benefits, jobs lost to imports, and devastated downtowns and rural areas across America.[39]

This relentless driving down of costs above all else is good in the short term for consumers. In the long term, however, competition and quality are diminished, as all elements of the production process become potential cost savings that need to be made to compete, from research and development (R&D) to the components used to make the product.

Suppliers

Second, Walmart's size increases its importance for any of its 61,000 U.S. suppliers[40] *lucky* enough to have the company as a client, and the company's growing influence among certain brands is astounding. In 2008, it was reported that 28% of total sales for Dial were made from Walmart stores.[41] Similar figures are true for Del Monte, Clorox, and Revlon, among others.

This growing dependence, however, can be a double-edged sword for stakeholders who find themselves out of favor for whatever reason. From the point of view either of governmental or supplier stakeholders, overdependence on one company can cause societal harm or supplier collapse. More important, it also presents the company with disproportionate negotiating power and an advantage over suppliers when times are good:

> Wal-Mart is legendary for forcing its suppliers to redesign everything from their packaging to their computer systems. It is also legendary for quite straightforwardly telling them what it will pay for their goods.[42]

Walmart is able to dictate the cost at which goods should be supplied and enforces its demands by sourcing elsewhere, leaving the supplier unable to plug the gap such an important client leaves behind.

Jobs

Third, often in rural areas, Walmart is the only large employer in town, which gives the company additional clout:

> Wal-Mart's reputation for bringing a wide variety of goods to small towns and rural communities gives the company leverage over town councils and planning boards, which are often asked to grant zoning concessions or relax environmental standards. And, Wal-Mart's frequent position as the only big employer in town allows it leeway to hire workers at low wages.[43]

Walmart, however, vehemently denies that it creates only low-paying jobs.[44] Walmart is known for promoting from within, and the firm emphasizes the high percentage of senior managers who have risen through the firm's ranks. What is not in doubt is the number of people who apply for a job at Walmart when one is offered. If Walmart is as low-paying as it is reported to be, it would not continue to attract so much interest from potential employees:

> If Wal-Mart were as greedy as its detractors say, it would never have attracted 8,000 job applicants for 525 places at a new store in Glendale, Ariz., or 3,000 applicants for 300 jobs in outlying Los Angeles.[45]

For instance, when we opened a store just outside of Chicago in 2006, 25,000 people applied for 325 jobs.[46]

Nevertheless, alleged poor employment policies may well indicate some of the CSR-related dangers facing the company down the road. When employees do have a choice, they may start choosing not to work for Walmart. A reputation as a poor employer leads to low morale, which reduces productivity, and high turnover rates, which raise costs and disrupt service as new employees retrain. The operating practices that create such a reputation do not make good business sense in the long term as, in any given year, Walmart estimates that "about 44% of its 1.4 million employees will leave,"[47] which means the firm has to hire hundreds of thousands of new employees to replace them. And where an employer's bad practices become inherent to the way the company conducts business, the fallout can have even more expensive repercussions. Walmart faces a growing number of lawsuits from disgruntled employees alleging illegal overtime pay rates, sexual discrimination in promotion policies,[48] and the hiring of illegal immigrants at even lower wage levels:[49]

[There are] questions over whether the retailer's relentless drive to cut costs is causing it to stray too close to the boundary of legality. . . . Many powerful businesses eventually run into issues that threaten to hold back their progress. . . . Could labor issues become the kind of thorn in the side for Wal-Mart that antitrust probes became for Microsoft?[50]

In December 2008, for example, Walmart agreed to pay "at least $352 million, and possibly far more" to settle allegations that the firm forced employees to work unpaid overtime. The decision to settle, which was reported to have been prompted by the change in CEO from Lee Scott to Michael T. Duke, was described by lawyers "as the largest settlement ever for violations of wage-and-hour laws."[51]

Competitors

Fourth, another area of criticism that has been leveled against Walmart is in terms of the intense pressure its competitors face once a Walmart comes to town. The devastating impact the presence of a Walmart Supercenter is likely to have on existing mom-and-pop stores is often cited in protests opposing the opening of a new store. While a new Walmart undoubtedly causes some small businesses to go out of business, this has to be weighed against the jobs that become available at the new store. These are often jobs that offer greater potential for advancement and a stable career. There is also evidence to suggest that the net jobs total following the opening of a Walmart store is positive. While some businesses close, they create space for other businesses to open:

Creative destruction occurs when the introduction of a new idea or product results in the obsolescence of other products. New inventions, for instance, often result in the business failures of products supplanted by now-outdated technologies. This is unfortunate for the old businesses, but it benefits consumers and it frees money and resources that can then give rise to new businesses and further advancements.[52]

It is also worth keeping in mind that Walmart is successful only because consumers choose to shop there and choose not to shop at smaller vendors:

Critics are wrong when they say that Wal-Mart puts little people out of business. We (consumers) put little people out of business. . . . We vote with our wallets, and we're the ones who choose Wal-Mart over local stores.[53]

Quality and Variety

Finally, an important component of Walmart's pricing strategy that enables it to lower prices is its policy of stocking the most profitable top tier of products in an industry—the top 10% of best-selling toys from the biggest brands, for example. Walmart can afford to market these best sellers at lower margins (or even as loss leaders) because of the volume and extra business they generate for the store. The concern for product quality and variety in the long term, however, is related to future research and development (R&D). By cherry-picking today's most profitable products and selling them at low margins, Walmart is taking away the profits that other industry-focused companies use to fund current and future R&D. Without these profits to finance the innovation that drives product development, creates choice, and produces the hits of the next generation, consumers may be ensuring future quality and variety will be diminished. Is Walmart also hurting its own future business strategy by narrowing the number of best-seller products it is able to market at low margins over time?

WALMART IS NO. 1 . . . TODAY

In 2002, Walmart became the No. 1 firm on the Fortune 500[54] and has remained as either No. 1 or No. 2 ever since.[55] In 2003 and 2004, Walmart also was named Fortune's "Most Admired Company in America."[56] It is the largest for-profit organization in the world and, as the discussion above indicates, generates both passion and loathing.

None of the issues mentioned above, however, deal with the paradox that Walmart's promise to produce "everyday low prices" appeals to the very workers who cannot afford to pay more. Many of these workers have had their wages driven down and their job security threatened because of Walmart's pursuit of ever lower costs, whether they work for the company itself, a supplier, a competitor, or another company in the affected labor pool.

A CSR perspective, however, argues that Walmart's business model will remain viable only as long as its attractions offset the consequences of its actions. In the end, a strategy of lower prices that alienates increasing numbers of stakeholders will gradually erode the innovation, choice, and support of needed constituents. For a number of years from the 1990s into the 2000s, coalitions of unions, environmentalists, community organizations, state lawmakers, and academics planned coordinated attacks on Walmart to force it to change its methods.[57] Walmart's actions in some communities were restricted, leading Walmart to mount large-scale media campaigns to influence the public's perception of its actions.[58] It held its "first-ever media event," to defend its policies and actions[59] and opened a lobbying office in Washington, D.C.[60]

CSR is an argument about business today in conjunction with an ability to understand what business will be about tomorrow. Today, Walmart is No.1. But to sustain its dominant market position, stakeholder theory argues that a CSR perspective should be integrated into the organization's strategic planning processes and throughout day-to-day operations. Absent this perspective, CSR theory suggests that Walmart will eventually lose societal legitimacy, particularly among the key constituents (such as local community zoning boards) that are crucial to its growth mandate. There are some indications that Walmart understands this and has moved to change its perception among specific stakeholder groups.

WALMART AND SUSTAINABILITY

A key focus of Chapter 3 is what we refer to as "the Walmart question." If CSR is central to a firm's competitiveness in a global business environment, how is it that a firm like Walmart can apparently ignore calls for greater social responsibility from key stakeholders? The answer is that perhaps it cannot. This is increasingly evident because Walmart's position regarding CSR has evolved drastically since the publication of the first edition of *Strategic CSR*. Ultimately, Walmart recognized that the

> "constant barrage of negatives" in the US over everything from Wal-Mart's low wage business model to alleged discrimination against women could threaten the company's ability to grow.[61]

Particularly in relation to environmental and sustainability issues, the firm is now considered by many to be a market leader.[62] Walmart has even employed Adam Werbach, past president of the Sierra Club, as an environmental consultant to the firm:

> I wholeheartedly believe in what Wal-Mart's doing. . . . Our goal . . . is to have Wall Street look at Wal-Mart's green performance, and say, "Wow, do more of that."[63]

An early indication of the firm's dramatic change in policy and practice occurred when Walmart announced a $35 million campaign in partnership with the National Fish and Wildlife Foundation "to offset the amount of land [Walmart] develops to use for its stores and other facilities" over the next 10 years by purchasing 138,000 acres "of land in sensitive habitats" for conservation.[64]

But the real shift came in a speech given by then-CEO Lee Scott, titled "Wal-Mart: Twenty First-Century Leadership."[65] The speech followed shortly after the devastation of Hurricane Katrina in and around New Orleans in August 2005. In the immediate aftermath of the storm, Walmart was the first source of relief for residents. The firm had the distribution infrastructure to restock its stores with those supplies that were in demand with an efficiency that the federal and state governments were unable to match.[66] The experience was reported to have been a personal revelation for Scott.[67] This sense of "a key personal moment"[68] was conveyed in the speech he subsequently delivered approximately two months later in October 2005.

In retrospect, this speech by Scott appears designed to achieve two goals. First, it served to reinforce Walmart's key core competence—identifying inefficiencies in the value chain and eliminating them to minimize costs. In this sense, this speech and Walmart's focus on sustainability reinforce their existing business model. Second, however, the speech was also intended to reposition Walmart, both the firm and its operations, in the eyes of its various external stakeholders:

To better understand our critics and Wal-Mart's impact on the world and society, [our top executives] spent a year meeting with and listening to customers, Associates, citizen groups, government leaders, non-profits and non-government organizations, and other individuals. . . . most of our vocal critics do not want us to stop doing business, but they feel business needs to change, not just our company, but all companies.[69]

In particular, Scott used the speech to commit Walmart to an overarching framework of three environmental goals.

Walmart's Environmental Goals[70]

1. To be supplied 100% by renewable energy.

2. To create zero waste.

3. To sell products that sustain our resources and environment.

As an initial step toward reaching these goals, Scott announced a number of specific quantifiable policy targets, such as "reducing greenhouse gases at our existing [stores] . . . by 20 percent over the next 7 years," "increasing our fleet efficiency by 25 percent in the next 3 years," "reducing our solid waste from U.S. [stores] by 25 percent in the next 3 years," and "working with suppliers to create less packaging overall, increase product-packaging recycling and increase use of post-consumer material." Taken together, these commitments constitute a comprehensive sustainability policy about which Walmart appears to be both serious and sincere:

[Hurricane] Katrina asked this critical question, and I want to ask it of you: What would it take for Wal-Mart to be that company, at our best, all the time? What if we used our size and resources to make this country and this earth an even better place for all of us: customers, Associates, our children, and generations unborn?[71]

In essence, Walmart's consumers make short-term purchase decisions based on price, with less emphasis placed on the longer term, broader societal consequences of those decisions. Implementing a stakeholder perspective reveals to Walmart that it must pay attention to a broader set of stakeholders if it wants to remain viable over the long term. It is insufficient merely to be profitable in the short term. However, as Walmart exposes itself to different ideas, it is discovering that responding to its stakeholders' demands need not diminish the firm's business model and may even enhance it. The turnaround has been dramatic:

After years of running afoul of the United States government on labor and environmental issues, Wal-Mart now aspires to be *like* the government, bursting through political logjams and offering big-picture solutions to intractable problems.[72]

An indication of Walmart's willingness to engage in a new start with its stakeholders was the introduction of a new logo and slogan in July 2008.

CSR Newsletters: Save Money, Live Better

A recent article[73] discusses the meaning behind Walmart's new logo:

> Something's up at Wal-Mart. Visitors to walmart.com will notice that the logo consumers have become accustomed to over the past 17 years is gone. . . . In its place: a new logo made up of rounded, lowercase characters. The hyphen has disappeared. And in place of the star is a symbol that resembles a sunburst or flower.

The article argues that the logo is an attempt by Walmart to capitalize on its increasing reputation for progressive action in relation to environmental sustainability. The introduction of the new logo (changing from "Everyday low prices" to "Save money. Live better.")

> coincides with CEO H. Lee Scott's goal of transforming Wal-Mart . . . into a more environmentally friendly corporation.

The article contains quotes, however, that suggest the design will fall short of its intentions:

> [Marty Neumeier, president of Neutron, a branding firm in San Francisco] adds that the image lacks the distinctive power of the most successful logos, such as Target's (TGT) bull's eye . . . . [Walmart's new logo] "is designed so simply that there's no ownership to it" . . . it could be used by almost any corporation.

One area where Walmart has the potential to deliver massive social value is in terms of stakeholder education. To care about CSR, first and foremost, stakeholders have to be aware of the issues and their ability to do something about them.

Michael Moore

Interviewed in the movie, *The Corporation*[74]

I said to my wife. We are both sons and daughters of autoworkers in Flint, Michigan. There isn't a single one of us back in Flint, any of us, including us, who ever stopped to think . . . this thing we do for a living, the building of automobiles, is probably the single biggest reason the polar ice-caps are going to melt and end civilization as we know it. There is no connect between "I am just an assembler on an assembly line, building a car," which is good for society, it moves [people] around, but never stop to think about the larger picture and the larger responsibility of what we are doing. Ultimately, we have to, as individuals, accept responsibility for our collective action and the larger harm it causes in our world.

Simply because of the scale and scope of Walmart's operations—not only the number of consumers it interacts with on a weekly basis, but also the huge numbers of suppliers that make the products the firm sells in its stores—Walmart merely has to dip its toes in the water for it to make an immediate, meaningful impact.

CSR Newsletters: Solar Power

Whenever it does something, Walmart immediately makes an impact due to its immense scale of operations:

> It may be now on the way to adding another, as it takes the first steps towards becoming the US's largest user of solar power.

A recent article[75] demonstrates the firm's influence in relation to the economies of scale that can be achieved with solar energy:

> Wal-Mart is about to embark upon the most substantial private sector commitment yet to solar power. It could be at least 50 times bigger than anything anyone has done so far.

By following the lead of other firms (the article gives the examples of Staples and Whole Foods) and by virtue of the scale on which Walmart operates, the consensus of the people quoted in this article is that Walmart's entry into this market immediately changes the economics for everyone involved:

> Just as they've brought low prices to consumer goods, they could bring everyday low costs to renewables by using their scale to push the technology and bring down price.

[Mike Duke, Wal-Mart's CEO since February 2009] has gone on record saying that "Wal-Mart and our supplier partners must operate in a more socially and environmentally responsible way wherever we do business . . . we at Wal-Mart are also committed to being a leader on sustainability." Using its vast size to influence entire supply chains to its advantage—the very practice that skeptics criticize as "bullying"—Wal-Mart is now leveraging this muscle to shift markets toward greener practices.[76]

A good example of Walmart's reach and influence is the firm's commitment to greatly reduce the waste packaging that is processed through its stores. The policy change had an immediate effect within Walmart:

Our packaging team, for example, worked with our packaging supplier to reduce excessive packaging on some of our private-label Kid Connection toy products. By making the packaging just a little bit smaller on one private brand of toys, we will use 497 fewer containers and generate freight savings of more than $2.4 million per year. Additionally, we'll save more than 38-hundred trees and more than a thousand barrels of oil. Again, think about this with Wal-Mart's scale in mind: this represents ONE relatively simple package change on ONE private toy brand.[77]

Importantly, however, it also had dramatic ramifications for all the firms with whom Walmart does business:

[Wal-Mart's] decision in 2006 to stock only double concentrate liquid laundry detergent led to the entire US detergent industry shifting to smaller, lighter bottlers by the start of [2008], saving millions of dollars in fuel costs.[78]

And Walmart's ambition is growing. In July 2009, for example, Walmart's CEO announced a commitment

to create a global, industry-wide sustainable product index. The ambitious plan . . . aims to establish a sustainability rating system for each item on Wal-Mart's shelves. This will help shoppers understand the social and environmental impact of products. It should also drive innovation among suppliers.[79]

Literally, Walmart has the ability to change the world. For 2007, for example, the firm announced a goal to sell 100 million compact fluorescent light bulbs (CFL)—a doubling of the market for CFLs over the previous year's sales:

Wal-Mart wants to change energy consumption in the United States, and energy consciousness, too. It also aims to change its own reputation, to use swirls to make clear how seriously Wal-Mart takes its new positioning as an environmental activist.[80]

Walmart reached its goal by the end of September;[81] in total, selling

137 million bulbs in 2007. . . . As of June 2009, Walmart and Sam's Club in the U.S. have sold more than 260 million CFLs. We estimate during the life of these CFL bulbs, our customers will save more than 7 billion dollars on their electric bills.[82]

So, is Walmart acting because of a belief in the moral, rational, or economic arguments for CSR? In our assessment, Walmart realizes that, even if specific stakeholders do not care or think about CSR in the short term, there are *moral* arguments for acting that win it support in particular circles. In addition, there are very *rational* arguments for pursuing a course of action that limits potential future constraints on the firm's business goals and interests. Finally, Walmart also recognizes that implementing a CSR perspective assists the firm in its overall *economic* goal of providing goods to consumers as efficiently as possible—that waste is an inefficiency that drives up the cost of business. As a result, the combination of the three arguments—the moral, rational, and economic arguments for CSR—has resulted in Walmart's sustainability vision:

[In October, 2008] Scott told analysts that Wal-Mart had shifted its position in the political spectrum so that it was able to "no longer be the whipping post for what is happening out there, but to take a leadership role."[83]

SO HOW MUCH DOES CSR MATTER?

The central question of this chapter is this: How much does CSR matter?

Central to answering this question is an understanding of who is responsible for CSR and whether stakeholders care sufficiently to warrant corporate action. These are not easy questions, but they are central to the CSR debate. The goal of this extended case study on Walmart was to convey the complexity of these issues. Walmart is an essential part of the global economy today. Whether you love the store or refuse to shop there, understanding what Walmart does and why it does it (particularly in relation to CSR) is an important component of understanding the role of CSR in business today.

This case study provides insight into a firm's (sometimes fraught) relations with its stakeholders, particularly its customers and shareholders. What should have been apparent is that different stakeholders have different perspectives and that these different perspectives often lead to conflict. In other examples, corporate actions may be seen as less ambiguous with more direct consequences. Think of Bhopal, India, where a Union Carbide plant accident killed thousands;[84] Enron's self-destruction due to the lack of social responsibility among its leaders, which resulted in lost jobs and shareholder value (as well as criminal indictments); or the 2007–2009 financial crisis that was fueled by irresponsible selling of subprime mortgages to people with little chance of repaying the loans, resulting in record foreclosures and evictions. In these examples, among many others presented in this book, a lack of strategic CSR has led to uniform and universal condemnation, along with significant legal and market penalties.

In general, firms that ignore societal tradeoffs face limits, as suggested by the "iron law of social responsibility" (Chapter 1). The stakeholder backlash to a firm's indifference to CSR, however, is not necessarily felt immediately—the tobacco and fast-food industries stand as prime examples. Nevertheless, a company that fails to reflect the evolving interests of its stakeholders is ultimately putting itself, its reputation, and its brand at risk. Companies understand this today, which is why they go to such strenuous efforts to avoid the negative publicity CSR lapses bring.

Many consumers cannot afford the luxury of the choice between economic and social issues. On that basis, the low-wage jobs offered by Walmart may well be a cause for praise: Most people would agree that a low-paying job is better than no job at all. This does not, however, negate the central idea of *Strategic CSR:* The long-term interests of a company depend on it implementing a broad stakeholder perspective. The anecdotes presented in this chapter indicate that Walmart appreciates this sentiment more today than before. Due to Walmart's cherry-picking approach to CSR, however, the firm remains a conundrum that is central to the issues raised in this chapter. Walmart has made great strides since the first edition of *Strategic CSR,* but the firm retains a relatively narrow CSR perspective. Walmart focuses its efforts almost exclusively on environmental sustainability as a means of doing what it does best—reducing costs and passing those savings on to customers in the form of lower prices. Because of its continued selectivity in relation to the larger issues of social responsibility, however, the jury is still out in relation to its broader CSR activities. There is little evidence to suggest, for example, that Walmart would choose the socially responsible option in any situation where that decision would lead to an increase in costs.

Central to the argument presented in this chapter is the idea that when short-term perspectives allow economic necessity to take precedence over social concerns, the consequences will eventually catch up with the perpetrators. But as the examples of the tobacco and fast-food companies illustrate, it is fair to say that firms in certain industries can delay the CSR day of reckoning for a significant period of time. This is because the threshold of concern varies for each stakeholder and within each industry.

Stakeholders' CSR concerns depend on a unique mix of individual priorities and available options, both of which change over time. They also reflect the interwoven battle among conflicting constituent interests. In the short run, even a flagrant disregard for CSR may be ignored by some, or even all, stakeholders. On the other hand, reaction may be swift and unequivocal. Mostly, however, reactions will be mixed. Eventually, it is clear that firms suffer the consequences of stakeholder disillusionment for a perceived lack of commitment to CSR. Walmart has had its requests for zoning variations denied because its operations were deemed contrary to community interest, for example. Growing unionization efforts within the company's stores in the United States, Canada, and most dramatically in China[85] seem at least partially attributable to revolt against its human resource policies.

So, finally, do stakeholders care about CSR? Although a decisive answer must be hedged by the tradeoffs between stakeholder groups—as when company profits compete with paying a living wage to foreign factory workers—and differences between industries and cultures, it is apparent that firms need to work proactively and not merely react to what their stakeholders are telling them today. Stakeholder and broader societal concerns are fluid. What is *acceptable* today can become *unacceptable* very quickly. To some extent, therefore, whether stakeholders *care* today is a red herring. Yes, firms need to understand their stakeholders' needs today and meet those needs, but they should also seek to exceed those needs in relation to CSR and anticipate how those needs will evolve tomorrow. If stakeholders today do not care about CSR, companies that seek to meet non-CSR needs have to balance the moral and ethical arguments for and against doing so. What is clear, however, is that they cannot rely on those needs remaining stable (or even legal) over time.

CSR is not a short-term issue. As indicated in the definition of strategic CSR in Chapter 2, the focus of a firm's motivation for integrating CSR in its strategic planning and day-to-day operations needs to be on managing the firm's resources and relations with key stakeholders over the medium to long term. The job for boards of directors is to choose leaders who are able to anticipate shifting stakeholder concerns, respond, and aim their firm toward a more successful future. In an increasingly globalizing business environment, this future-oriented vision offers benefits for all stakeholders, particularly stockholders.

A broader consideration of the question, "How much does CSR matter?" therefore, leads to the conclusion that, irrespective of whether stakeholders *care,* firms are best served by implementing a stakeholder perspective that attempts to meet the expectations of their stakeholders, today and tomorrow. In other words, whether a specific group (i.e., consumers) *cares,* or even thinks about, CSR in the short term is irrelevant and a distraction for a firm (even though this might be a source of short-term profitability). Rest assured that they will care at some point in the future. And whenever that is, the companies that survive will be those that remain one step ahead of these evolving standards. A holistic view of the firm and its interests (only possible with a stakeholder perspective combined with the goal of medium- to long-term viability), therefore, dictates that CSR should be central to a business's strategic planning and implemented throughout operations.

CSR IN IMPLEMENTATION

Of course, the answer to the questions raised by Walmart cannot be resolved definitively at this point. Much will depend on the decisions made by the company's 15 to 20 million daily customers. Nevertheless, it does seem that CSR concerns raised by Walmart's previous actions are altering the way the firm perceives its relations with its various stakeholders. As such, this case study also provides insight into how firms integrate CSR into their strategic planning process and implement CSR throughout operations. Next, Chapters 4 and 5 investigate these issues in greater detail. Chapter 4 puts CSR into strategic perspective and expands on the growing importance of CSR and its impact on corporate strategy. Finally, Chapter 5 will conclude Part I with a discussion of the issues that influence the implementation of CSR by firms.

Questions for Discussion and Review

1. Who is *responsible* for CSR—firms or their stakeholders? Why?

2. What is meant by *stakeholder advocacy?* Do stakeholders care about CSR?

3. Would you report a classmate you suspected of cheating at school? Why? Why not?

4. If you were a member of Walmart's top management, what arguments would you make to a community group that is trying to stop the building of a Walmart in their community? If you were the leader of the community group resisting Walmart's expansion into your community, what arguments would you make to oppose the development?

5. Walmart argues that it provides valuable jobs to small communities and should be allowed to grow. Critics argue that these jobs are often low paying, with few benefits. What is your position? Is a low-paying job better than no job at all?

6. Would you ever consider boycotting a certain brand or store because of the parent company's actions or stance on a particular issue? Illustrate with an example.

7. Compare Walmart's new and old logos:

| Old logo | New logo |

Which do you prefer? What is your impression of Walmart's new logo and slogan?[86] Do you get the sense that Walmart is genuine in its commitment to sustainability issues, or is it just an example of corporate *greenwash?*

NOTES AND REFERENCES

1. Deborah Doane, "The Myth of CSR: The Problem With Assuming That Companies Can Do Well While Also Doing Good Is That Markets Don't Really Work That Way," *Stanford Social Innovation Review,* Fall 2005, p. 26.

2. Milton Friedman, "The Social Responsibility of Business Is to Increase Its Profits," *New York Times Magazine,* September 13, 1970, http://www.colorado.edu/studentgroups/libertarians/issues/friedman-soc-resp-business.html

3. Ibid.

4. Charles Handy, "What's a Business For?" *Harvard Business Review,* December 2002, pp. 49–55.

5. Ibid., p. 52.

6. Milton Friedman, "The Social Responsibility of Business Is to Increase Its Profits," *New York Times Magazine,* September 13, 1970, http://www.colorado.edu/studentgroups/libertarians/issues/friedman-soc-resp-business.html

7. See Figure 1.1, Chapter 1, and Archie B. Carroll, "The Pyramid of Corporate Social Responsibility: Toward the Moral Management of Organizational Stakeholders," *Business Horizons,* July–August 1991.

8. Milton Friedman, "The Social Responsibility of Business Is to Increase Its Profits," *New York Times Magazine,* September 13, 1970, http://www.colorado.edu/studentgroups/libertarians/issues/friedman-soc-resp-business.html

9. Earthshare, Summer 2008, http://www.earthshare.org/psa/earthshare_printpsa_2008.pdf

10. For an argument that humans are innately focused on the short term, see Peter Wilby, "Humanity Must Recognise Our Entire Way of Life Is Chronically Short-Termist," *The Guardian,* June 1, 2007, p. 33, http://www.guardian.co.uk/commentisfree/2007/jun/01/comment.comment

11. Chandran Nair, "Ethical Consumers—Cop-out at the Checkout," *Ethical Corporation,* September 8, 2008, http://www.ethicalcorp.com/content.asp?ContentID=6074

12. "Economic Downturn Will Not Stop Rise in Ethical Consumerism," *Ethical Consumer,* November 28, 2008, http://www.ethicalconsumer.org/Default.aspx?tabid=62&EntryID=252. The 2007 figure represents a significant increase on the 2002 figure of £19.9 billion, although the article also notes that "overall ethical spend at £35.5 billion is still a small proportion of the total annual consumer spend of more than £600 billion."

13. Kathleen Parker, "Attention, Wal-Mart Shoppers: You Have a Say," *Orlando Sentinel* (reprinted in the *Austin American Statesman*), January 30, 2006, p. A9.

14. "Best Global Brands," *Interbrand,* September 2009, http://www.interbrand.com/best_global_brands.aspx

15. Warren Bass, "A Brave New World in 9/11 Aftermath," *Miami Herald,* April 10, 2005, p. 7M. Review of *The World Is Flat: A Brief History of the Twenty-First Century,* by Thomas L. Friedman, Farrar Straus Giroux, 2005.

16. Data compiled from the *USAToday* (USAToday/Gallup Poll, http://www.usatoday.com/news/polls/tables/live/2006-12-11-ethics.htm) and *Gallup* (Jeffrey M. Jones, "Lobbyists Debut at Bottom of Honesty and Ethics List," *Gallup,* December 10, 2007, http://www.gallup.com/poll/103123/Lobbyists-Debut-Bottom-Honesty-Ethics-List.aspx; Lydia Saad, "Nurses Shine, Bankers Slump in Ethics Ratings," *Gallup,* November 24, 2008, http://www.gallup.com/poll/112264/Nurses-Shine-While-Bankers-Slump-Ethics-Ratings.aspx) Web sites.

17. Archie Carroll, "Survey Says Not Many Think Highly of Executives' Ethics," *Athens Banner-Herald,* January 7, 2007, http://www.onlineathens.com/stories/010707/business_20070107012.shtml

18. "You Mean Cheating Is Wrong?" *BusinessWeek,* December 9, 2002, p. 8.

19. Rob Walker, "Sex vs. Ethics," *Fast Company Magazine,* Issue 124, April 2008, pp. 54–56, http://www.fastcompany.com/magazine/126/sex-vs-ethics.html

20. The Aspen Institute Centre for Business Education, "Beyond Grey Pinstripes 2007–2008: Preparing MBAs for Social and Environmental Stewardship," http://www.beyondgreypinstripes.org/rankings/bgp_2007_2008.pdf

21. For an analysis of the awareness and importance of CSR to the public and other corporate stakeholders, see Jenny Dawkins and Stewart Lewis, "CSR in Stakeholder Expectations and Their Implication for Company Strategy," *Journal of Business Ethics,* Vol. 44, May 2003, pp. 185–193: "Over ten years of research at MORI has shown the increasing prominence of corporate responsibility for a wide range of stakeholders, from consumers and employees to legislators and investors. . . . Traditionally, the factors that mattered most to consumers when forming an opinion of a company were product quality, value for money, and financial performance. Now, across a worldwide sample of the public, the most commonly mentioned factors relate to corporate responsibility (e.g., treatment of employees, community involvement, ethical and environmental issues)."

22. Corporate Fact Sheet—"Corporate Facts: Walmart by the Numbers," August, 2009, http://walmartstores.com/FactsNews/FactSheets/. For more "facts" about Walmart, see the company's Web site: http://walmartstores.com/FactsNews/

23. Tim Weiner, "Wal-Mart Invades, and Mexico Gladly Surrenders," *New York Times,* December 6, 2003, p. A1, http://www.nytimes.com/2003/12/06/world/wal-mart-invades-and-mexico-gladly-surrenders.html

24. Anthony Bianco and Wendy Zellner, "Is Wal-Mart Too Powerful?" *BusinessWeek,* October 6, 2003, pp. 100–110.

25. Phil Butler, "Walmart Invades India—Who's Next?" *profy,* February 20, 2007, http://profy.com/2007/02/20/walmart-invades/

26. Anthony Bianco and Wendy Zellner, "Is Wal-Mart Too Powerful?" *BusinessWeek,* October 6, 2003, pp. 100–110.

27. Editorial, "The Wal-Martization of America," *New York Times,* November 15, 2003, p. A12, http://www.nytimes.com/2003/11/15/opinion/the-wal-martization-of-america.html

28. Steve Lohr, "Is Wal-Mart Good for America?" *New York Times, ,* 2003, Section 4, p. 1.

29. Anthony Bianco & Wendy Zellner, "Is Wal-Mart Too Powerful?" *BusinessWeek,* October 6, 2003, pp. 100–110.

30. "More than 176 million customers visit Wal-Mart stores around the globe each week." In "December 7Wal-Mart's Merchandise Reflects Our "Store of the Community" Philosophy,' Merchandising Fact Sheet, September 2009, http://walmartstores.com/FactsNews/FactSheets/

31. Anthony Bianco & Wendy Zellner, "Is Wal-Mart Too Powerful?" *BusinessWeek,* October 6, 2003, pp. 100–110.

32. Charles Fishman, "The Wal-Mart You Don't Know," *Fast Company Magazine,* November 15, 2008, http://www.fastcompany.com/magazine/77/walmart.html

33. Constance L. Hays, "When Wages Are Low, Discounters Have Pull," *New York Times,* December 23, 2003, pp. C1 and C4.

34. For example, see John M. Broder, "Stymied by Politicians, Wal-Mart Turns to Voters," *New York Times,* April 5, 2004, p. A12; Steven Malanga, "The War on Wal-Mart," *Wall Street Journal,* April 7, 2004, p. A18; Ann Zimmerman, "Wal-Mart Loses Supercenter Vote," *Wall Street Journal,* April 8, 2004, p. B7; and, providing some degree of balance in the coverage, George F. Will, "Waging War on Wal-Mart," *Newsweek,* July 5, 2004, p. 64.

35. Anthony Bianco & Wendy Zellner, "Is Wal-Mart Too Powerful?" *BusinessWeek,* October 6, 2003, pp. 100–110.

36. Daren Fonda, "Will Wal-Mart Steal Christmas?" *Time,* December 1, 2003, http://www.time.com/time/magazine/article/0,9171,1101031208-552147,00.html

37. *RFid Gazette,* http://www.rfidgazette.org/walmart/

38. Charles Fishman, "The Wal-Mart You Don't Know," *Fast Company Magazine,* November 15, 2008, http://www.fastcompany.com/magazine/77/walmart.html

39. Steve Lohr, "Is Wal-Mart Good for America?" *New York Times,* December 7, 2003, Section 4, p. 1.

40. "Wal-Mart's Merchandise Reflects Our `Store of the Community' Philosophy," Merchandising Fact Sheet, September 2009, http://walmartstores.com/FactsNews/FactSheets/

41. Charles Fishman, "The Wal-Mart You Don't Know," *Fast Company Magazine,* November 15, 2008, http://www.fastcompany.com/magazine/77/walmart.html

42. Ibid.

43. Sharon Zukin, "We Are Where We Shop," *New York Times,* November 28, 2003, p. A31.

44. Wal-Mart reports "our average, full-time hourly wage for Walmart stores is $11.24 and is even higher in urban areas. The average full-time hourly wage is $11.66 in Atlanta, $12.55 in Boston, $11.61 in Chicago, $11.25 in Dallas, $11.43 in San Francisco and $11.50 in New York City." In "Corporate Facts: Walmart by the Numbers," Corporate Fact Sheet, September 2009, http://walmartstores.com/FactsNews/FactSheets/

45. Steven Greenhouse, "Can't Wal-Mart, a Retail Behemoth, Pay More?" *New York Times,* May 4, 2005, http://wakeupwalmart.com/news/20050504-nyt.html

46. "Sustainability Progress to Date 2007–2008," http://walmartstores.com/sites/sustainabilityreport/2007/communityJobs.html

47. Anthony Bianco and Wendy Zellner, "Is Wal-Mart Too Powerful?" *BusinessWeek,* October 6, 2003, pp. 100–110.

48. The largest lawsuit facing Wal-Mart was allowed to proceed as a class-action suit in June 2004. This court decision, involving a lawsuit initially filed by six former employees who felt they were not treated equally to male employees, presents "the world's largest retailer with the prospect of fighting a lengthy legal battle or potentially paying a multibillion-dollar settlement. . . . [involving] as many as 1.6 million current and former female U.S. employees" (Ann Zimmerman, "Judge Certifies Wal-Mart Suit as Class Action," *Wall Street Journal,* June 23, 2004, pp. A1 & A6). See the Web site (http://www.walmartclass.com/) for information about this lawsuit. Information about the "current status of the case" is provided at: http://www.walmartclass.com/walmartclass_case developments.html

49. In March 2005, Wal-Mart agreed "to pay $11 million to settle a federal investigation into allegations it knowingly hired floor-cleaning contractors who employed undocumented workers." The settlement was "about four times as large as any other single payment received by the government in an illegal-alien employment case." Ann Zimmerman, "Wal-Mart Settles Immigration Case," *Wall Street Journal,* March 21, 2005, p. B3.

50. "Labor Issues a Thorn at Wal-Mart," *Financial Times,* in *Miami Herald,* November 22, 2003, p. 2C.

51. Steven Greenhouse & Stephanie Rosenbloom, "Wal-Mart to Settle Suits Over Pay for $352 million," *New York Times,* December 24, 2008, p. B1.

52. Andrea M. Dean & Russell S. Sobel, "Has Wal-Mart Buried Mom and Pop?" *Regulation,* Spring 2008, p. 40, http://www.cato.org/pubs/regulation/regv31n1/v31n1-1.pdf

53. Kathleen Parker, "Attention, Wal-Mart Shoppers: You Have a Say," *Orlando Sentinel* (reprinted in the *Austin American Statesman*), January 30, 2006, p. A9.

54. The Fortune 500 is ranked according to the revenues of the firm.

55. In 2006, Exxon was named No. 1; Wal-Mart returned to the top spot in 2007 and 2008; but Exxon retook the top spot in 2009 based on higher oil prices, with Wal-Mart at No. 2.

56. "Corporate Facts: Walmart by the Numbers," Corporate Fact Sheet, September, 2009, http://walmartstores.com/FactsNews/FactSheets/

57. Steven Greenhouse, "Opponents of Wal-Mart to Coordinate Efforts," *New York Times,* April 13, 2005, p. 16.

58. For example, Emily Kaiser, "Wal-Mart Goes on PR Offensive to Repair Image," *Reuters,* February 2, 2004.

59. "Wal-Mart CEO Defends Wages, Health Benefits," *Wall Street Journal,* April 6, 2005, p. A6.

60. Jeanne Cummings, "Wal-Mart Opens for Business in Tough Market: Washington," *Wall Street Journal,* March 24, 2004, p. A1, http://online.wsj.com/article/SB108008903615163648.html

61. Jonathan Birchall, "Duke Faces Test of His Political Aptitude," *Financial Times,* November 22/23, 2008, p. 9.

62. For example, Erica L. Plambeck and Lyn Denend, "The Greening of Wal-Mart," *Stanford Social Innovation Review,* Spring 2008, pp. 53–59; "Wal-Mart Celebrates Thanksgiving by Sourcing Local Food, Supporting Hunger-Relief, and Buying Wind Power," *CSRWire,* November 26, 2008, http://www.renewacycle.com/2008/11/wal-mart-celebrates-thanksgiving-by.html; and Danielle Sacks, "Working With the Enemy," *Fast Company Magazine,* Issue 118, September 2007, http://www.fastcompany.com/magazine/118/working-with-the-enemy.html

63. Danielle Sacks, "Working With the Enemy," *Fast Company Magazine,* September 2007, p. 77.

64. Ryan Chittum, "Wal-Mart to Give $35 Million for Wildlife Areas," *Wall Street Journal,* April 13, 2005, p. B4; and Stephanie Strom, "Wal-Mart Donates $35 Million for Conservation and Will Be Partner With Wildlife Group," *New York Times,* April 13, 2005, p. A16.

65. Lee Scott, "Wal-Mart: Twenty First-Century Leadership," October 24, 2005, http://walmartwatch.com/img/documents/21st_Century_Leadership.pdf

66. Editorial, "Private FEMA: In Katrina's Wake, Wal-Mart and Home Depot Came to the Rescue," *Wall Street Journal,* September 10, 2005, http://www.opinionjournal.com/editorial/feature.html?id=110007238; Michael Barbaro and Justin Gillis, "Wal-Mart at Forefront of Hurricane Relief," *Washington Post,* September 6, 2005, p. D1, http://www.washingtonpost.com/wp-dyn/content/article/2005/09/05/AR2005090501598.html

67. "Message From Lee Scott," http://walmartfacts.com/reports/2006/sustainability/company Message.html

68. Lisa Roner, "Wal-Mart—An Environmental Epiphany?" December 7, 2005, http://www.climatechangecorp.com/content.asp?ContentID=4009

69. Ibid.

70. Ibid.

71. Ibid.

72. Michael Barbaro, "Wal-Mart: The New Washington," *New York Times,* February 3, 2008, http://www.nytimes.com/2008/02/03/weekinreview/03barb.html

73. Reena Jana, "Wal-Mart Gets a Facelift," *BusinessWeek,* July 3, 2008, http://newsletters.businessweek.com/c.asp?713736&c55a2ee820194f0f&14

74. Mark Achbar, Jennifer Abbott, and Joel Bakan, "The Corporation," http://www.thecorporation.com/

75. Jonathan Birchall, "Sun Rises Over Wal-Mart's Power Policy," *Financial Times,* January 22, 2007, p. 11, http://us.ft.com/ftgateway/superpage.ft?news_id=fto012120071012471507

76. "Wal-Mart Celebrates Thanksgiving by Sourcing Local Food, Supporting Hunger-Relief, and Buying Wind Power," *CSRWire,* November 26, 2008, http://www.renewacycle.com/2008/11/wal-mart-celebrates-thanksgiving-by.html

77. Lee Scott, "Wal-Mart: Twenty First-Century Leadership," October 24, 2005, http://walmartwatch.com/img/documents/21st_Century_Leadership.pdf

78. Jonathan Birchall, "Big Box Looks to Small Packages,' *Financial Times,* November 4, 2008, p. 16.

79. Rajesh Chhabara, "Wal-Mart—Thinking Outside the Big Box," *Ethical Corporation,* September 7, 2009, http://www.ethicalcorp.com/content.asp?ContentID=6583

80. Charles Fishman, "How Many Lightbulbs Does it Take to Change the World? One. And You're Looking at It," *Fast Company Magazine,* September 2006, http://www.fastcompany.com/magazine/108/open_lightbulbs.html

81. "Wal-Mart Reaches 100-Million CFL Goal Three Months Early," *Sustainable Life Media,* October 3, 2007, http://www.sustainablelifemedia.com/content/story/strategy/10032007

82. "Saving Money and Energy with CFLs," Fact Sheets, August 29, 2009, http://walmartstores.com/FactsNews/FactSheets/

83. Jonathan Birchall, "Duke Faces Test of His Political Aptitude," *Financial Times,* November 22/23, 2008, p. 9.

84. Mallen Baker, "Bhopal: 25 Years Later the Echoes Are Still Loud," *Ethical Corporation,* August 20, 2009, http://www.ethicalcorp.com/content.asp?ContentID=6562

85. "Wal-Mart Approves Unions in China," *BBC News,* November 24, 2004, http://news.bbc.co.uk/2/hi/business/4037423.stm; Harold Meyerson, "Wal-Mart Loves Unions (in China)," *Washington Post,* December 1, 2004, http://www.washingtonpost.com/wp-dyn/articles/A23725-2004Nov30.html

86. "Walmart U.S. Refreshes Stores' Logo," June 30, 2008, http://walmartstores.com/FactsNews/NewsRoom/8411.aspx

CHAPTER 4

THE STRATEGIC CONTEXT OF CSR

There are three kinds of organizations: nonprofit, governmental, and for-profit. Each exists to meet different needs in society. Those needs may be altruistic, such as feeding the poor, in the case of a nonprofit; they may be civic, such as providing for the safety and security of the public, in the case of government agencies; or they may be primarily economic, such as organizing resources in ways that yield a surplus for the owners, called profit. In a free society, all organizations exist to meet societal needs in some form, or they eventually go away. Restated, no publicly traded company, government, or nonprofit initially sets out to do harm. Yet, as demonstrated in the first three chapters of *Strategic CSR,* organizations can create undesired consequences. These often unintended consequences spring not from the organization's goals themselves but from the methods or strategies deployed to pursue these goals. As a result, it is important to understand the strategic context of CSR.

In fulfilling their mission and vision, organizations face constraints on their methods and results. The economics of survival, for example, requires each entity to produce the *results* that generate the sources of income they require to operate—donations for nonprofits, taxes for governments, or profits for firms. At the same time, these results must be attained by *methods* that are acceptable to the larger society. Leaders of all organizations constantly grapple with the tradeoffs between methods and results. When these issues involve for-profits, CSR helps firms balance the methods they use and the results they seek. It does this by ensuring that profit-seeking businesses plan and operate from the perspective of multiple stakeholders.

The problem that decision makers face is straightforward: Which stakeholders and what issues *matter* under the broad heading of corporate social responsibility as it pertains to our organization? The simple answer depends on the for-profit's strategy. And because these strategies vary widely, the right mix will differ from firm to firm and industry to industry. The answer will also evolve over time as firms adapt both their strategy and its execution to increasingly turbulent operational environments. As a result, the exact issues that any firm is likely to face at any given time are impossible to predict. What is a constant and can be applied by any firm in any situation, however, is that a strategic lens offers the best viewpoint through which to study CSR.

CSR THROUGH A STRATEGIC LENS

Effective strategy results in providing businesses with a source of sustainable, competitive advantage. For any competitive advantage to be sustainable, however, the tactics used to implement a firm's strategy must be acceptable to the societies in which they are deployed. If they are not, social, legal, and other forces may conspire against the firm, as when legal and regulatory sanctions are levied against a manufacturer for polluting the air and water.

Both CSR and strategy are primarily concerned with the firm's relationship to the societal context in which it operates. Whereas *strategy* addresses how the firm competes in the marketplace (its operational context), *CSR* considers the firm's impact on relevant stakeholders (its societal context). *Strategic CSR* represents the intersection of the two. Thus, in order to implement a strategic CSR perspective throughout operations, it is essential that executives understand the interdependent relationships among a firm, its strategy, and its stakeholders that define the firm's operating environment and constrain its capacity to act.

As illustrated in Figure 4.1, a firm's vision, mission, strategy, and tactics are limited by three kinds of constraints—resource constraints, internal policy constraints, and environmental constraints.[1] First, a significant limitation on the firm's ability to act is its access to resources and capabilities—the human, social, and financial capital that determine what the firm is able to do. A second constraint is the firm's internal policies, which shape the culture of the organization by requiring and forbidding specific actions. These policies, however, are internally enforced and can be changed relatively easily by management (a flexibility that is indicated in Figure 4.1 by the dashed line). Finally, an organization's environmental constraints are generated by a complex interaction of sociocultural, legal, and stakeholder factors, together

Figure 4.1 Strategic Constraint and the CSR Filter

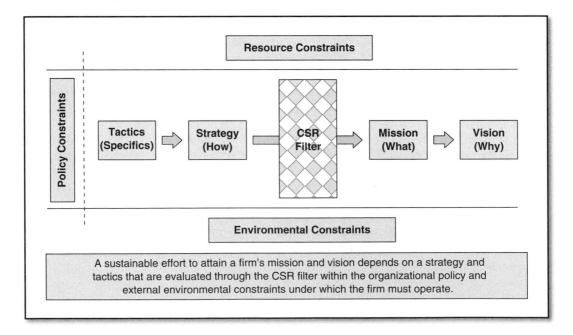

A sustainable effort to attain a firm's mission and vision depends on a strategy and tactics that are evaluated through the CSR filter within the organizational policy and external environmental constraints under which the firm must operate.

with the influence of markets and technology. These forces further limit the firm's freedom to act by shaping the context in which the firm implements tactics to pursue its strategic goals, which, in turn, enable it to perform its mission and strive toward its vision. Compounding the complexity of integrating CSR into the vision-mission-strategy-tactics linkages, therefore, is the ever-changing expectations of society.

As a result of this complexity, a sole focus on the linkage among vision, mission, strategy, and tactics is insufficient to achieve the firm's goals. Not only is such a narrow focus insufficient, however; it also represents potential danger. Tactical and strategic actions necessary to achieve the mission (and, thus, the vision) must be evaluated by first passing through a *CSR filter.* The CSR filter assesses management's planned actions by considering the impact of day-to-day tactical decisions and longer term strategies on the organization's constituents. A tactical or strategic decision that runs counter to stakeholder interests can undermine the firm's sustainable competitive advantage. At the extreme, such violations may even force the firm into bankruptcy—as happened to Malden Mills and Enron, albeit for very different reasons.

FIRM STRATEGY AND THE CSR FILTER

Strategy formulation links the firm's strengths with opportunities in its environment. The strategic decision-making process faces limitations, however, which are presented in Figure 4.2.

First, a feasible strategy is limited by the firm's vision and mission, which are determined by the leadership. A plane manufacturer, such as Boeing or Airbus, is unlikely to make cars and trucks because these activities do not achieve its vision and mission, which is to make jet-powered commercial planes. Second, the strategy is further limited by a firm's competencies—competitive actions that the firm does well. Boeing and Airbus, for example, which undoubtedly could make cars and trucks if they wanted, lack other competencies, such as the network of sales and distribution dealers necessary to sell cars and trucks nationwide. Third, whatever strategy the firm develops, it is constrained by the CSR filter, which identifies the range of strategies that are acceptable to constituents. Above all, Boeing and Airbus must make safe planes in ways that do not harm the key constituents in their environment—their communities, employees, flyers, and other stakeholders. In other words, before a competency-based strategy can be deployed in the firm's environment, the strategy must be evaluated through a CSR filter to assess its impact on the organization's stakeholders.

There is an iterative relationship between the resulting strategy and organizational design. While strategy shapes design, it is also true that the firm's structure, roles, and reporting relationships should be configured to facilitate strategy. The *correct* organizational structure is a design that best supports the execution of strategy. For most organizations, that means a departmental structure organized into a hierarchy. In terms of implementing a CSR perspective throughout strategy and operations, therefore, the organizational structure presents an additional opportunity to instill decisions made at the top (with a CSR filter) throughout the organization.

The connection among a firm's internal strengths and its external opportunities is driven by the strategic axiom that success depends on a position of competing from strengths. For the strategist to connect strengths with opportunities in a globalizing business environment requires an intimate understanding of both. To remain competitive, therefore, it is essential for firms to employ a CSR filter in formulating and implementing their strategy. Figure 4.2 demonstrates how the CSR filter fits between a

Figure 4.2 Firm Strategy and the CSR Filter

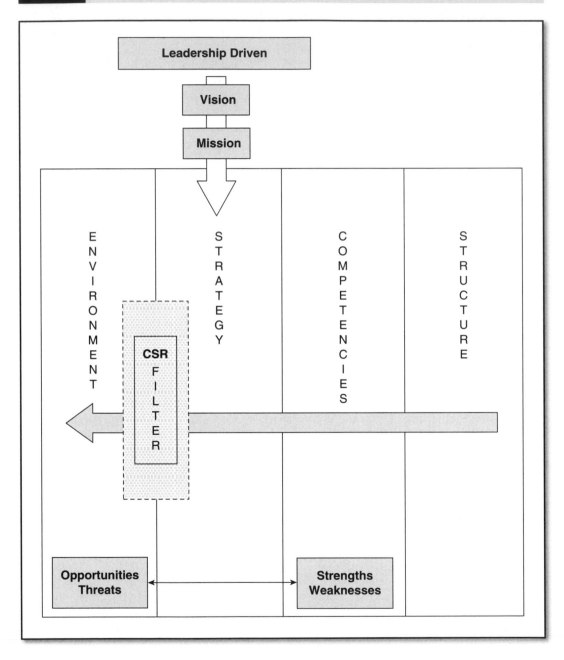

firm's strategy and the environment in which it operates. In order to better understand the role of the CSR filter in a firm's strategic success, however, it is important to investigate the complex interplay among a firm's competencies, strategy, and structure in relation to its operating environment.

Competencies

For a firm to compete from strength, it must identify its strengths. They represent the critical factors that determine how the firm will compete in its operating environment. To facilitate an understanding of strengths, a clear distinction among *capabilities, competencies,* and *core competencies* is required.

> • Capabilities are actions that a firm can do, such as pay its bills, in ways that add value to the production process.
>
> • Competencies are actions a firm can do very well.
>
> • Core competencies are actions a firm does in such a superior way that it is difficult (or at least time consuming) for other firms to match its performance in this area.

Thus, a firm's core competencies combine its valuable resources (such as its people, capital, and technology) with its unique capabilities. Consider how Walmart is able to manage the flow of goods from suppliers through its stores and on to its customers, often referred to as *supply chain management.*

Walmart's Supply Chain Management

Walmart has a capability of hiring employees; it has a competency to locate stores where they will be successful; and it has a core competency of maintaining and distributing its inventory throughout the supply chain. In fact, Walmart is so very good at managing its supply chain that it minimizes both the amount of inventory it carries and the number of times items are out-of-stock in its stores. Other firms have the capability to maintain their inventory; some even have a competency at doing that, but none of Walmart's competitors appear to match its core competency of supply chain management.

Strategy

Walmart's *vision* is to offer the best customer value in retailing, which gives rise to a *mission* of delivering groceries and other consumer products efficiently. That vision and mission are attained by a *strategy* of passing on cost savings to customers by continually seeking to roll back their "everyday low prices." In turn, that strategy is built upon *competencies* and *core competencies,* which are Walmart's competitive weapons. How Walmart folds its competencies into a strategy and then how it deploys that strategy vis-à-vis stakeholders determines how society views the degree to which Walmart is socially responsible.

Certainly, a firm like Walmart must advertise and do hundreds, even thousands of other activities. But its competitive advantage comes from its network of store locations, backed by an unmatched ability to manage and deliver its inventory in optimal ways. These competencies interact, reinforcing each other. Without its exceptionally efficient and effective supply chain management competencies, it would not be a low-cost provider of groceries and other goods. But with these competencies supporting its strategy, it creates a *virtuous cycle* in which Walmart's lower prices attract more customers. More customers, in turn, mean greater volumes, which lead to increased economies of scale in operations and greater power in demanding price reductions from its suppliers. The result is even lower costs, which allow the firm to reduce prices further, which, in turn, continues the virtuous cycle by attracting still more customers. The increased economies of scale in distribution and purchasing perpetuate the cycle of still lower costs. Thus, the firm's strategy rests upon its competencies and supports its mission and vision. Although not all firms are able to create a virtuous cycle like Walmart, all successful strategies ultimately rest upon a firm's competencies . . . until the competitive environment changes.

When the competitive environment demands a different strategy, the existing capabilities or competencies of the firm may no longer be sufficient. If Walmart is seen as exploiting its low-paid workers, for example, the accompanying negative publicity may eventually harm its image. This can cause customers to shop elsewhere or cause communities to deny Walmart's applications for zoning variances needed to build or remodel stores. Evolving societal expectations force changes in Walmart's competitive environment (as with all firms), requiring new competencies in public relations, advertising, and human resource management.

When environmental changes like these or others occur, leaders face a *make-or-buy* decision. Should the needed competencies be developed internally (*make*) or acquired from others outside the firm (*buy*)? Historically, many large firms like Walmart have had the resources to develop the needed competencies internally through hiring and training. Today, the external environment is changing so rapidly that firms often buy the needed skills from others because the speed of execution is critical. If the decision makers decide to buy the necessary capabilities or competencies, leaders then face a second decision— whether to bring the needed capabilities under the control of the organization structure or to outsource those activities via contractual relationships with suppliers. When the activity is seen as a core competency (managing inventory at Walmart, for example, or product design at firms like Apple[2] or Nike[3]), most firms capture that activity within the structure of the firm to strengthen this vital component of their strategic advantage. If the activity is seen as peripheral, such as calculating and printing payroll checks or manufacturing sneakers, the firm will often outsource the activity if it is cheaper or faster to do so.

A Firm's Business-Level Strategy[4]

Business strategy: The strategy of a specific business unit within a firm that enables it to differentiate its products from the products of other firms on the basis of price or other factors (such as superior technology).[5]

Walmart employs a *low-cost* business strategy in order to compete. Mercedes-Benz, on the other hand, does not seek to produce the lowest-priced cars. Instead, it competes based on a *differentiation* business strategy. By making its products superior along the lines of safety, prestige, and durability, Mercedes-Benz (and other luxury goods producers) can charge a premium for the differentiation (real or perceived) that consumers receive. Apple is another firm that seeks to differentiate its products on the basis of some factor other than price—product design. For The Body Shop, their point of differentiation is not product quality so much as the social agenda and campaigns that the firm pursues. Consumers of The Body Shop's products gain value from this social agenda and by associating themselves with values to which they aspire, in addition to the functional value they gain from the firm's products.

McDonald's, by contrast, strives for a focused strategy that embraces both low costs and product differentiation. Relatively low costs result from its high volume and standardization, leading to economies of scale; however, McDonald's also differentiates the product it offers by providing fast service, putting it in the fast-food segment of the restaurant industry.

Firms that are able to establish a point of differentiation are then able to build a brand. Brands are valuable because they instill customer loyalty and enable the firm to charge an additional price premium for their product and further increase their potential profits. Whether that point of distinction is fashion, lifestyle, design, technical quality, product functionality, or social responsibility, a business level strategy of differentiation can be valuable for a firm. Companies that differentiate their products on the basis of low cost, however, may perceive CSR-related efforts as adding costs and, therefore, be less proactive regarding CSR.

Whether firms compete on cost, differentiation, or a focused strategy that embraces either cost or differentiation (or both), strategy strives to add customer-focused value as a means of gaining a competitive advantage.

Structure

The structure (the organizational design) exists to support the strategy of the firm. What architects say of a building, organization designers say of the firm's structure form follows function. Thus, the *right* structure is the one that best supports the strategy. When low-cost strategies are pursued, expertise is often concentrated into a *functional* organization design, in which site location, store construction oversight, information systems, warehousing, distribution, store operations, and other similar activities are grouped together by their common functions into specialized departments. This functional grouping takes advantage of specialization and is scalable as the firm grows. The result is called a functional organization design.

In the case of Walmart, different parts of the company might pursue different structural designs. Support activities like accounting or finance, for example, may be grouped by function at corporate headquarters. At the same time, because Walmart is spread across many geographical areas, the store management oversight and distribution systems may be organized along geographical lines, such as a northeastern warehouse division or overseas store operations. At Nike, CSR is such an important function that it is built into the firm's structure in the form of a separate Corporate Responsibility department, headed by a vice president.[6]

The optimal organization design is the one that best supports the firm's strategy, giving attention to key functions. Organization structure varies from industry to industry, therefore, as well as from company to company within an industry.

The CSR Filter

Competencies molded into a strategy and supported by an efficient structure are necessary minimum conditions for success—but, increasingly, more is required. It is vital that firms also consider the societal and stakeholder implications of their strategy and operations. The *CSR filter* is a conceptual screen through which strategic and tactical decisions are evaluated for their impact on the firm's various stakeholders. Here, the intent is to take a viable strategy and make it *optimal* for the stakeholder environment in which the strategy must be executed. Although CSR is only one part of the strategic big picture, even clever strategies can fail if they are perceived as socially *irresponsible*. The CSR filter injects multiple considerations into the decision mix beyond the profit maximization goals that are central to the firm's survival. The application of these societal-based considerations screens strategies for their impact on the firm's multiple constituents. Together, these stakeholders form the larger societal environment in which the firm operates and seeks to implement its tactics, strategy, mission, and vision. Consider the example of Nike.

The CSR Filter: Nike

Nike is a well-managed firm with an extremely valuable brand. Nike exploits its brand value to great effect in selling its lines of shoes, apparel, and other products. Each of its product lines, however, faces strong, high-quality competition from companies such as Adidas, Puma, and New Balance. If Nike's strategy of off-shore contract production leads to employer abuse in its factories (perceived or actual), consumers may shift their buying preferences to the firm's competitors. Even if Nike does not own or manage its overseas contract factories, unfavorable publicity—such as a video clip or unfavorable report from a nongovernmental organization (NGO) highlighting human rights abuses—represents danger to Nike's otherwise effective business strategy of product differentiation. Thus, Nike's offshore sourcing strategy must be constantly scrutinized through a CSR filter.

Part II of this book identifies some of the scores of issues embedded in the CSR filter. Beyond this, Part II also provides company-specific case studies that outline the practical impact of these considerations, as well as online resources for further exploration. But before turning to the specific issues that make CSR an intellectually challenging and operationally vital subject, we examine the changing societal expectations that underscore the growing importance of CSR for firms and, therefore, represent a significant influence on a firm's strategy.

A FIRM'S ENVIRONMENTAL CONTEXT

Customers, competitors, economics, technology, government, sociocultural factors, and other forces all drive changes in the firm's operating environment. Often, these changes are gradual and imperceptible to all but the keenest observers. But, over time, their cumulative effect redefines the competitive environment and determines what organizational strategies and actions are deemed socially acceptable. As Professor Archie Carroll observed,[7] this evolution of what is socially expected of organizations typically migrates from discretionary to ethical to mandatory (legal and economic).

Equal Pay

Over time, actions that were previously considered discretionary or ethical can be codified as laws or government rulings and, finally, as economic components of operations—in other words, minimum standards to which a firm needs to adhere in order to remain competitive. Many firms in the United States, for example, once blatantly paid women less than men for the same work. In spite of whatever justifications were applied, this behavior was within the discretionary decision-making authority of businesses.

Gradually, such discrimination was seen to be unfair, even unethical. Then, in 1963, the federal government enacted the Equal Pay Act, which outlawed discrimination in pay based solely on an employee's gender. This legislation immediately served to limit this once discretionary area of management decision making. Today, diversity in the workplace is viewed as an economic imperative that enables firms to respond effectively to their consumers' needs.

Once society determines that a particular form of behavior has become unacceptable, the perceived abuse can lead to a legally mandated correction, such as the Equal Pay Act. Consequently, the range of socially acceptable employment policies used to facilitate competitive strategies has changed greatly in the last half century as societies evolve.[8] Changes can be identified with regard to environmental pollution, product safety standards, financial record-keeping, and scores of other previously discretionary behaviors. Once discretionary issues evolve into legal constraints, meeting societal expectations becomes an absolute requirement that is enforced by criminal or civil sanctions.

More difficult to identify are issues not yet subject to legal mandates, but which may still affect the firm. If leaders exercise discretionary authority to attain economic ends, but the actions are perceived to be socially irresponsible (even though they are legally permissible), the consequences may damage the firm. Such damage becomes evident in terms of lower sales, diminished employee recruitment and retention, evaporating financial support from investors and markets, and a host of other important relationships. What should a company do?

At one extreme is the view that CSR-related issues are a distraction from the firm's profit-seeking and wealth-creating functions. Proponents of this position argue that, as long as a company is profitable, it is providing value for some segment of society and should be entitled to remain in operation because it provides jobs and taxes for society, as well as a return on investment for shareholders. At the other extreme, however, lies the argument that society has the right, even the obligation, to restrain the negative excesses of businesses. This position states that, just as societies rely on the commerce and industry that businesses create, companies unarguably rely on the resources of the societies in which they are based. No organization exists in isolation, and businesses, without exception, have an obligation to contribute to the communities on which they rely so heavily for employees and financial or other resources. If these firms are unwilling to accede voluntarily to society's demands, then they should be forced to do so.

Strategic CSR bridges both of these positions. Ultimately, stakeholders have the right and the power to determine what is acceptable corporate behavior. It is also true that societies benefit greatly from the innovation that firms create in pursuit of profits. Nevertheless, in today's global environment, businesses are expected to pursue their strategies in ways that, at a minimum, do not harm others and, increasingly, address and solve social problems.[9] What makes this calculation so difficult for firms is that, as societies become more affluent and interconnected, the definition of *social harm* changes constantly.

As such, in terms of CSR, we argue that very little is discretionary any more. Past perspectives that viewed businesses narrowly as profit engines have been altered beyond recognition both by globalization and growing social affluence. Highly interconnected societies have more knowledge and more choice, while wealthier societies have the resources to demand greater social responsibility from their firms. Developed economies around the world, for example, uniformly demand that car producers make safer and less polluting cars because they understand the implications of unsafe and polluting cars and can afford to pay extra for technological improvements.

In today's globalizing world, *shareholder* value can be maximized over the long term only if the firm addresses the needs of its primary *stakeholder* groups. Satisfying stakeholders is often most efficiently achieved by adopting a CSR perspective as part of strategic planning, especially within informed and affluent societies.

THE FIVE DRIVING FORCES OF CSR

As outlined in Chapter 1, there are five environmental forces that are driving CSR to the fore-front of corporate strategic thinking: growing affluence, ecological sustainability, globalization, communications technologies, and brands. Any one of these drivers might be ignored by managers not convinced of the strategic benefits to the firm of CSR. Collectively, however, they are reshaping the business environment by empowering stakeholder groups. And, because each of these trends interacts with the others, the reinforcing effects mean that the environmental context will not only change, but change at an increasingly rapid rate—often in ways not foreseen by today's best strategists. Although each of these forces is discussed separately, their interactive effects heighten the importance of the *CSR filter* for corporate strategists.

CSR and Growing Affluence

CSR issues tend to gain a foothold in societies that are more affluent—societies where people have jobs, savings, and security and can afford the luxury of choosing between, for example, low-cost cars that pollute and high-cost hybrids that do not. As public opinion evolves and government regulation races to catch up, however, actions previously thought of as discretionary often become legal obligations.

Externalities

The *Oxford English Dictionary* defines an externality as:

A side-effect or consequence (of an industrial or commercial activity) which affects other parties without this being reflected in the cost of the goods or services involved; a social cost or benefit.[10]

In the past, manufacturers have often been able to externalize some of their production costs to the larger society by polluting the environment. When the majority of people are desperately focused on the need for jobs to feed their families, pollution seems of limited concern. When most members of a society are desperately seeking food, shelter, and other necessities of life, CSR seems a luxury of little relevance. As societies become increasingly affluent, however, the collective understanding of social issues like pollution grows, as does the ability of society to afford solutions.

As a result, the greatest attention to CSR is found in developed economies; however, it would be shortsighted to assume that CSR is only applicable where there is affluence. Increasingly, multinational corporations are being held to high standards for their overseas activities in developing countries. Nike, for example, typically requires its subcontractors in developing nations to provide wages and working conditions above the local norms.[11] Even so, activists continue to take Nike to task,[12] criticizing the pay and working conditions of its subcontractors because local standards often are well below those that prevail in Nike's home country, the United States. Other high-profile firms, such as Apple, can also present an easy target to campaigners.

CSR Newsletters: Apple

A recent article[13] provides insight into the tactics sometimes used by interest groups to pressure high-profile companies that the interest group suspects of committing social harm:

> Greenpeace is bringing the rhetorical hammer down on Apple for what it considers environmental offenses, namely for not moving fast enough to eliminate nasty chemicals from its products. Its latest headline-grabbing maneuver: pressure on ex-Vice-President and current Apple director Al Gore. . . . Publicly pressuring Gore, the thinking goes, improves the chances that Apple's board will amply consider two eco-friendly shareholder proposals.

In this case, however, it is hard to escape the conclusion that Greenpeace is picking on a high-profile brand, rather than focusing on meaningful reform. As the article notes, Greenpeace seems to be applying double standards in this case and unfairly targeting Apple for what it has failed to say, rather than what it has actually done:

> As of now, neither Apple nor Dell—nor Hewlett-Packard (HPQ) for that matter—is selling a single PVC- or BFR-free computer. . . . And while it's one thing to call attention to a problem that an entire industry needs to address, Greenpeace's methodologies, in this particular case, don't paint an accurate picture.

Similarly, protests against pollution, deforestation, and civil disruption by international petroleum companies have occurred when the companies' operating standards have been construed as harmful to host countries' societal interests. In Nigeria, for example, residents in the Niger Delta continue to attack oil workers and sabotage equipment because they believe the central Nigerian government is not distributing the oil wealth. Although Shell and other companies comply with Nigerian law, they are being attacked by those who believe they are being harmed. The obvious conclusion is that firms' competitive strategies must consider the ever shifting pattern of societal expectations that become emboldened by the greater choices affluence affords societies.

CSR and Ecological Sustainability

The effects of growing affluence and the changes in societal expectations that accompany it are enhanced by a growing concern for the environment.[14] This is an issue that has gained a great deal of visibility in recent years due to two events, in particular. First, the Stern Report, which was published by the United Kingdom in 2006,[15] focused attention on the financial and economic consequences of deferring action today and waiting to see how bad things get. Second, the movie documentary, *The Inconvenient Truth,* essentially a souped-up PowerPoint presentation by former U.S. Vice President Al Gore, brought climate change to the attention of a global audience.[16] The movie was awarded the 2007 Nobel Peace Prize as well as, perhaps more important for its mass public exposure, an Oscar for Best Documentary Feature.

CSR Newsletters: The Stern Report

For those interested in a point of view that challenges aspects of the Stern Report (issued on behalf of the British government), a recent article[17] presents a different perspective.

There does seem to be a great deal more confusion than suggested by the popular, sensationalized press coverage of climate change. In general, any suggestion that human economic behavior can be so dramatically shifted as easily as the Stern Report suggests (spending 1% of global GDP today) seems an overly simplistic solution to a massive, systemic problem. In the article quoted here, Bjorn Lomborg raises a surprisingly large number of important questions concerning the methodology used to generate the headline figures from the Stern Report:

The Stern review's cornerstone argument for immediate and strong action now is based on the suggestion that doing nothing about climate change costs 20% of GDP now, and doing something only costs 1%. However, this argument hinges on three very problematic assumptions. First, it assumes that if we act, we will not still have to pay. Second, it requires the cost of action to be as cheap as he tells us—and on this front his numbers are at best overly optimistic. Third, and most importantly, it requires the cost of doing nothing to be a realistic assumption.

Important methodological concerns are raised in the article that suggest that a more accurate estimate of the cost of climate change is "climate change will cost us 0% now and 3% of GDP in 2100," as suggested by an opinion piece in the *Financial Times.*[18] Stern's response to the criticisms is contained in this second article.[19]

Although experts disagree about the speed of climate change and the likely extent of corrective action we will need to take, what is not in doubt is that human economic activity is depleting the world's resources and causing dramatic changes to the mix of gasses in the Earth's atmosphere—changes that could become irreversible in the near future:

CSR Newsletters: The Most Terrifying Video You'll Ever See

The video in the url below condenses the convoluted, passionate, and often partisan debate about climate change into a straightforward argument:

http://video.stumbleupon.com/#p=p6o08udcmw[20]

The goal of the presentation is to remove the conflict over the science behind climate change and global warming from the debate and instead, reduce the argument to one of risk management. In other words, whether you believe in the science or not, the dangers of not acting far outweigh any dangers associated with acting.

Despite the video's title, it is probably not the "most terrifying video" you'll ever see, but the presenter makes his case very well, and the most important message is to focus on "the columns" rather than "the rows" (you'll have to watch the video to find out!).

What is also clear is that internalizing the nature of the problem and the extent of action necessary to effect meaningful change has implications for our entire economic system:

CSR Newsletters: The Story of Stuff

The video in this url is a 20 minute video that focuses on sustainability. It is more polemical than it is objective and scientific, but it is entertaining and educational, and it makes some very important points:

http://www.storyofstuff.com/index.html

The most effective way of achieving the overarching goal of the video (how to make a linear system more sustainable) lies in maintaining a focus on CSR in its broadest interpretation. It is only by focusing on the system as a whole that meaningful and lasting change can occur.

Because waste is inherent to economic growth—our economic growth models prefer us to replace our cars every 3 years rather than every 10 and to buy disposable products rather than ones we can reuse—and because resources are finite, it is essential that we learn to recycle more effectively in order for our current economic system to remain sustainable in the long run.[21] Some CSR advocates see this fault in our economic model and call for a revolution. *Strategic CSR,* on the other hand, seeks to reform the system we have so that capitalism works to maximize both economic and social progress by integrating a CSR perspective into firm strategy and throughout operations.

As a result of the growing realization of the ecological changes that are occurring, firms that are seen as indifferent to their environmental responsibilities are likely to be criticized and penalized by stakeholders. Firms increasingly recognize this shift. As illustrated in Chapter 3, Walmart has become a market leader in terms of issues surrounding sustainability.[22] In addition, firms as diverse as General Electric, with its *Ecoimagination* program,[23] and products like Toyota's Prius hybrid car[24] demonstrate the extent to which firms are responding to this growing and evolving issue.

A significant degree of innovation on this issue has taken place in the United Kingdom, with firms competing on metrics such as food miles,[25] carbon footprints,[26] and recycling programs.[27] Indeed, the supermarket Tesco now claims that its UK stores send zero waste to landfills:

> The United Kingdom's largest retailer says 100 percent of its waste from stores, offices and distribution centers across the country are now diverted from landfill—the result of aggressive recycling and treatment programs that include turning as much as 5,000 tonnes of old meat into heat and electricity each year.[28]

While there is much progress still to be made, where stakeholder awareness of environmental sustainability issues is high, progressive firms in this area can secure market share by being early innovators and adopters.

CSR and Globalization

Globalization is yet another force propelling the strategic use of CSR. Increasingly, corporations operate in a global business environment. The Internet, which drives this global environment, is a powerful enabling tool for communication and education; however, it also depersonalizes relations between individuals and reduces our sense of an immediate community. This, in turn, affects a business's sense of self-interest and can loosen the self-regulating incentive to maintain strong local ties. As Dr. Peter Whybrow[29] observes

> Historically, . . . built-in social brakes reined in our acquisitive instincts. In the capitalist utopia envisioned by Adam Smith in the 18th century, self-interest was tempered by the competing demands of the marketplace and community. But with globalization, the idea of doing business with neighbors one must face the next day is a quaint memory, and all bets are off.[30]

In Adam Smith's[31] view of the world during the 18th century, all competition was local—the vast majority of products were produced and consumed within the same community. As a result, Smith reasoned, it would be in producers' self-interest to be honest because, to do otherwise would threaten the reputations and goodwill on which they depend to continue trading in their community. As firms grew in size, they began selling to ever more distant markets and dividing operations between geographic locations in order to minimize costs and maximize profits; Smith's fundamental assumption broke down. Firms were free to be bad employers in Vietnam or polluters in China because they sold their products in the United States or Europe, and there was no way for Western consumers to know the conditions under which the products they were buying were produced. Disgruntled employees in Vietnam and local villagers in China were no threat to this business model, especially when even the worst jobs in the factories of multinational firms were often the best jobs available, and these firms were generating much-needed local economic progress. As globalization progresses, information is communicated more efficiently, and the world grows ever smaller, however; societies are again approaching the conditions under which Smith first suggested self-interest will effectively regulate action. Once again, all business is local, with the Internet allowing any individual with a cell phone to broadcast what he or she witnesses to anyone interested worldwide.

These ideas are expressed graphically in Figure 4.3 in terms of the three phases of control over stakeholder access to information—from industrialization, to international trade, to globalization. Adam Smith lived in a simpler time, when all information was local, and that kept firms honest. Due to the benefits of globalization, however, a similar access to information at a micro level is returning. As communication technology continues to innovate and power over its control is increasingly devolved to individuals, the ability of firms to manipulate stakeholder perceptions of their activities will decrease.

Globalization, therefore, transforms the CSR debate and magnifies its importance exponentially. A domestic context is not the only lens through which the issue of CSR should be viewed. Today, no multinational company can afford to ignore CSR, even if local employees or consumers appear not to care. European consumers, for example, are just as likely to look to a company's operations in the United States, or elsewhere in the world, when judging to what extent a U.S. company's actions are acceptable and whether they are going to buy the company's products. This is a lesson that the British bank, Barclays, learned when it continued to do business in an apartheid-plagued South Africa[32] and a lesson that the oil multinational, Shell, learned through its involvement with the Nigerian regime that executed Ken Saro-wiwa.[33] Differences in cultures across the globe lead to widely varying expectations of workers, customers, governments, and citizens. Actions that may be acceptable, even required, in one culture may be prohibited in another.

| Figure 4.3 | The Three Phases of Control Over Stakeholder Access to Information |

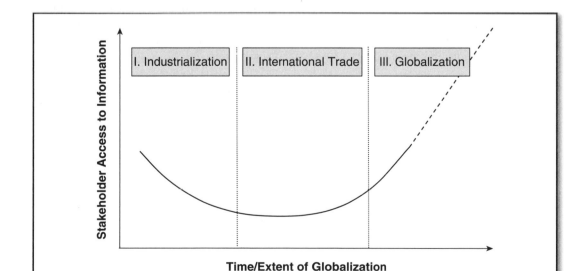

Discrimination

Discrimination based on gender is generally prohibited in developed societies, albeit with varying degrees of enforcement; however, in some cultures, like Saudi Arabia, women are segregated from male workers and encounter gender-based limitations on the type of work available to them.[34] A firm operating in Europe and Arabia may well be considered socially irresponsible and culturally insensitive if it applies the same human resource policies across all operating locations. Yet, if women are treated differently in Saudi Arabia, criticisms may arise in Europe or elsewhere. Ignoring inconsistencies in company practices can place multinational firms in very awkward positions. On the one hand, they must adapt their strategies to local expectations; but, on the other hand, strategies based on varying standards can leave the firm open to negative publicity, lawsuits, or other harmful outcomes at home.

CSR is more relevant today than ever before because of globalization. In terms of the relationship between corporations and their various stakeholders, this process of globalization appears to be progressing through two phases, as suggested by Figure 3.2 in Chapter 3.

Phase I of globalization greatly empowered corporations, enabling them to expand operations on a worldwide basis, shift manufacturing offshore, reform supply chain management, and develop powerful global brands. Merger and acquisition activities blossomed (because it was a quick way for companies to grow) and, as they grew, their power increased significantly. Many commentators today claim one consequence of this growth is that corporations now have greater economic power than most nation-states:

> Of the world's 100 largest economies, 49 of them are countries and 51 are companies. General Motors has greater annual sales than the gross national products of Denmark, Thailand, Turkey, South Africa, or Saudi Arabia. Wal-Mart's economy is larger than that of Poland, Ukraine, Portugal, Israel, or Greece. Because of the size and influence of modern corporations, business ethics take on special significance.[35]

As globalization transcends the control of nation-states, the power of global firms expands further. Companies today are free to incorporate offshore to avoid paying higher tax rates in their home country. They are also increasingly able to move their manufacturing operations or production processes to lower cost environments, often in countries with less rigorous labor and environmental regulations. In addition, corporations benefit from establishing global brands because of greater sales and worldwide customer loyalty. The brand's value proposition may entice consumers with price, reliable quality, status, or other features not available elsewhere. Even regulating authorities may fear losing jobs, tax revenues, or public support by fighting back against a corporate power. Imagine, for example, if the European Union banned Microsoft products because of unfair or monopolistic operating practices.[36] Microsoft's leverage over both consumers and regulating authorities may be too strong for such an outcome to be politically or economically feasible.

Globalization, however, creates countervailing forces that are capable of curtailing corporations' expanding power (as depicted in Phase II of Figure 3.2 in Chapter 3). Corporations are losing control over the flow of information that empowers NGOs and consumer activists to communicate and mobilize. A growing list of examples suggests that companies are no longer able to dictate the quality and quantity of information about their company and how that information affects the social debate. Nike,[37] GAP,[38] Coca-Cola,[39] and Google[40] are just a few examples of companies that have been damaged at some point by global information flows. Companies may be well advised to try to anticipate stakeholder needs and begin promoting operations from a CSR perspective, rather than fight against the free flow of information:

> Thanks to instant communications, whistle-blowers and inquisitive media, citizens and communities routinely put firms under the microscope. And the Internet is a central focus and organizing force for all these activities. . . . Transparency is on the rise, not just for legal or purely ethical reasons but increasingly because it makes economic sense. Firms that exhibit openness and candor have discovered that they can better compete and profit.[41]

This self-feeding cycle of globalization, triggering reactions that are met with reformulated strategies and CSR policies, may well be leading to what Malcolm Gladwell refers to as "the tipping point"[42]—the point of critical mass after which an idea or social trend spreads wildly (like an epidemic) and becomes generally accepted and widely implemented. CSR may well have reached its tipping point largely because of globalization and will increasingly become a mainstay of strategic thinking for businesses, especially global corporations.

The CSR tipping point is reinforced by the gradual institutionalization of CSR in society. This institutionalization is evidenced by the numerous publications, references, and articles related to CSR found in the endnotes of each chapter of this book. A Google search of the term *corporate social responsibility* (in quotation marks) reveals 3,530,000 hits, and the number is growing daily.[43] Perhaps more relevant to CSR professionals, the institutionalization of the field is documented by the growing number of organized CSR-related consultancies, think tanks, and advocacy groups, which continue to lobby firms and governments to continue the adoption of CSR policies and legislation.

CSR and the Free Flow of Information

As presented in Figure 3.2 (Chapter 3), Phase II of globalization suggests a shift in the balance of power concerning control over the flow of information back toward stakeholders in general and three important constituent groups in particular. First, the Internet has greatly empowered consumers because of the access it provides to greater amounts of information, particularly when an issue achieves a critical mass in the media. Second, globalization has increased the influence of NGOs and other activist groups because they, too, are benefiting from easily accessible and affordable communications technologies. These tools empower NGOs by enabling them to inform, attract, and mobilize geographically dispersed individuals and consumer segments, which helps to ensure that socially nefarious corporate activities achieve visibility worldwide. And third, new tools of communication and the demand for instantaneous information have enhanced the power of media conglomerates. Media companies have responded by increasing both their size and scope of operations, which ensures corporations today are unable to hide behind the fig leaves of superficial public relations campaigns:

> We are approaching a theoretical state of absolute informational transparency. . . . As individuals steadily lose degrees of privacy, so, too, do corporations and states. . . . It is

becoming unprecedentedly difficult for anyone, anyone at all, to keep a secret. In the age of the leak and the blog, of evidence extraction and link discovery, truths will either out or be outed. This is something I would bring to the attention of every diplomat, politician and corporate leader: the future, eventually, will find you out. . . . In the end, you will be seen to have done that which you did.[44]

The new kind of activism this technology is stimulating among consumers and NGOs, combined with the insatiable demand of the always-on global media conglomerates, is increasingly extending CSR concerns and awareness. And globalization is continuing to enhance the power of the Internet. Developing economies will enjoy increasing access via wireless technology (mobile phones and text messaging),[45] for example, rather than via the desktop computers and land telephone lines that were the foundation of the Internet in the developed economies. The result is an ever widening, free flow of information in a globalizing world, as suggested by Figure 4.4.

This technology is spreading and is increasingly being turned toward corporate targets. It is only a matter of time. Whether it is via flash mobs[46] (http://www.flashmob.com/), moblogs[47] (using mobile camera phones to construct blog-type diary Web sites), or simply playing Pac-Manhattan[48] (adapting the computer game Pac-Man to the streets of Manhattan using mobile phones and global positioning system [GPS] technology), the power of information technology to mobilize strangers and unite them under a common agenda is growing daily. Harnessing this power and directing it at a corporate target has the potential to inflict significant damage to any firm's product, brand, or reputation.

Figure 4.4   The Free Flow of Information in a Globalizing World

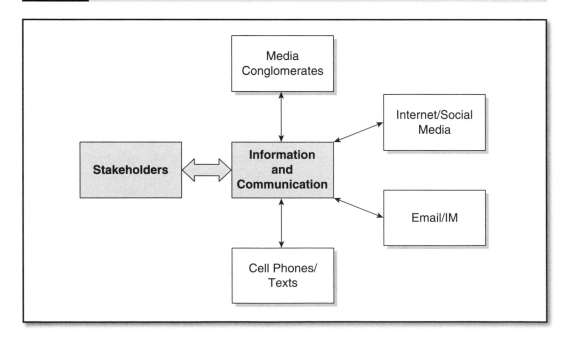

The relationship between stakeholders and the growing pool of information and communication is iterative (Figure 4.4). As stakeholders gain access to larger amounts of information and communicate this information among each other, so they build campaigns attacking corporations that become media events themselves that other stakeholders feed off.

This trend is already becoming apparent with the rapid growth in user-generated content Web sites such as YouTube (http://www.youtube.com/), MySpace (http://www.myspace.com/), and Flickr (http://www.flickr.com/). It is taken a step further with Web sites that allow users to rate and review the products and services firms provide. Online retailers, like Amazon (http://www.amazon.com/), and auction Web sites, such as eBay (http://www.ebay.com/), were early movers in this field, allowing consumers to rate those who sold products to them. This medium has now been advanced by Web sites such as Yelp (local businesses in different U.S. cities, http://www.yelp.com/), TripAdvisor (travel and hotels, http://www.tripadvisor.com/), and Urbanspoon (food and restaurants, http://www.urbanspoon.com/), all of which allow consumers to rate the different products and services they have purchased. Blogs that are dedicated to specific firms and their products, such as those dedicated to Apple (e.g., TheAppleBlog, http://theappleblog.com/ and The Unofficial Apple Weblog, TUAW, http://www.tuaw.com/), and Starbucks (e.g., Starbucks Gossip, http://starbucksgossip.com/) take this level of interaction between a firm and its stakeholders to another level—for good and for bad, depending on the firm and the extent to which it attempts to respond to the needs and demands of key stakeholder groups. The result is that more and more consumers are researching firms and products online before they make their purchase decisions. They are informed, and they are willing to share their horror stories with millions of others.[49] Consequently, firms have an even more precarious hold on their reputations and need to be more responsive to stakeholders' concerns in order to protect them:

> Businesses spend millions to cultivate their reputations; now consumer evaluations can make or break them instantly. "The conventional wisdom is that a satisfied customer will tell one person and an unhappy person will tell 10, . . . That's now been upped by orders of magnitude.[50]

Success today assumes companies reflect accurately the values and aspirations of a broad range of stakeholder groups. For companies that promote lifestyle brands, such as Nike or Apple, this rule is even more significant. Corporations moving to take the initiative and meet stakeholder expectations (while avoiding confrontation) need to put in place clear and open channels of communication that allow stakeholder concerns to find their way through to the strategy and decision-making table.

A key component of this dialog can be partnering with NGOs (and other nonprofits) to pursue talks or projects in areas of common concern. Both NGOs and consumers use the free flow of information, with the help of the media, to spread knowledge and build coalitions. These coalitions can occur spontaneously or as part of coordinated campaigns. One consistent factor, however, is their fluidity, encouraged by an ever-expanding technical capability, with groups bonding together for a particular issue then disbanding and joining other partners for a different issue. Besides avoiding conflict, developing a dialog with stakeholders offers potential benefit for firms. NGOs and nonprofits can help companies understand the rapidly evolving markets in which they operate, help them stay

Examples: The Free Flow of Information

Simply put, "The Internet makes it possible to organize a global community around a certain issue in a split second."[51] Consider two brief examples:

- *Media conglomerates—the CNN test. A few giant media companies control large percentages of the information we receive across a wide range of media.*
  The CNN test has been a criterion that causes CSR-sensitive decision makers to ask, "How will this be viewed by watchers of CNN when broadcast around the world?" Even U.S. military commanders used this test to select bombing targets during the second Iraq war in 2003. This test shows the influence of the media in shaping government policy as well as public opinion today and why the CNN test is part of the CSR filter for some organizations.
- *Internet—knowledge. The Internet conveys information rapidly to large numbers of people.* Barack Obama's use of a broad base of low dollar donations in the 2008 Democratic primaries and presidential election to raise record amounts of money is another example of how the Internet can drive social change:

New numbers show that Barack Obama's presidential campaign shattered fundraising records. According to reports filed with the Federal Election Commission, the campaign raised $104 million in the weeks around Election Day. Overall, Obama raised nearly $750 million.[52]

in touch with their target consumers, and contribute in areas such as product development.

In general, the firms most progressive in terms of CSR will be the ones that take external pressure for more responsible behavior, ethics, transparency, and social involvement and use it to revamp their strategic approach to business. Those firms best able to implement a strategic CSR perspective more genuinely throughout operations will be those firms best placed to operate in a global business environment in which they no longer control the flow of information. In short, for companies to enjoy sustained success, CSR will increasingly form a central component of strategy and operations, particularly in relation to a firm's reputation and brand management.

CSR and Brands

Brands today are often a focal point of corporate success and should be protected by integrating a strategic CSR perspective throughout the firm. Companies try to establish popular brands in consumers' minds because it increases their competitive advantage. We have identified three benefits of CSR to brands: positive brand building, brand insurance, and crisis management.

Positive Brand Building

The Body Shop: Anita Roddick long championed the power of an influential global brand to enact meaningful social change. In doing so, she helped distinguish her firm in the minds of consumers, gaining a strategic advantage. Whether you agree with the stance that The Body Shop adopts on a number of fair trade and other social issues,[53] many consumers are drawn to purchase the company's products because of the positions it takes. Its fair trade stance helps differentiate the firm's offerings and stands out in the minds of consumers. Similarly, Benetton has also set itself apart through advertising, using its voice to comment on the social issues that it thinks are relevant to its consumers.[54] Ben & Jerry's is another activist-alternative brand that pursues a similar strategy,[55] although its cult-like status has faded somewhat since the company was bought by Unilever in 2000.[56]

BP: With a $200 million rebranding exercise, BP (the giant British Petroleum company) has repositioned itself as the most environmentally and socially responsible of the integrated petroleum companies. The firm stands in stark contrast to ExxonMobil, which faces ongoing NGO attacks, consumer boycotts, and activist-led litigation because of its decision to oppose the environmental movement.[57] Shell has also done a good, if less high-profile, job of rebranding itself in a similar way to BP, although it was tainted by a scandal concerning the reporting of proven oil reserves in 2004.

Positive brand building alone, however, is insufficient. A firm has to be genuine in its statements and committed to implementing CSR throughout operations in order for the full benefits to be realized. BP's recent troubles in relation to CSR, such as lethal accidents at key U.S. refineries and criticism about the extent of its investment in alternative energy sources,[58] have undermined the firm's significant investment in building a positive brand image.

Brand Insurance[59]

Nike: Today, this company is one of the most progressive global corporations in terms of CSR. We argue that a significant reason for this is the firm's past mistakes and attacks by NGOs that continue to this day.[60] Those attacks focused largely on the working conditions in Nike factories in Southeast Asia, which, as Phil Knight, Nike's founder and CEO, admitted, "produced considerable pain" for the firm in the late 1990s.[61] Although, initially, Nike was reluctant to reform,[62] today, the firm has become more proactive in arguing the positive impact of its operations and products worldwide. Nike has created a vice president for corporate responsibility and publishes CSR reports to institutionalize a commitment to CSR in its corporate structure and operations as well as help protect the company's brand against future CSR lapses.

CSR Newsletters: Nike

It is characteristic of the media that good news takes a back seat to scandal, but this recent article[63] is worth highlighting as an example of how far Nike has come regarding CSR. The article, buried deep in the sports pages of a local paper, reports Nike's voluntary disclosure of the mistreatment of workers at the factory of a Nike subcontractor in Malaysia:

> including squalid living conditions, garnished wages and withheld passports of foreign workers.

Nike's response is impressive:

> Nike said all workers are being transferred to Nike-inspected and approved housing . . . All workers will be reimbursed for any fees and going forward, the fees will be paid by the factory. All workers will have immediate access to their passports and any worker who wishes to return home will be provided return airfare.

Those executives that remain unconvinced of the value of CSR, however, are likely to remain skeptical as long as such proactive behavior remains unrecognized, while the slightest transgression is plastered all over the front pages.

Merck & Co.: Reflecting a socially responsible stance, George W. Merck, son of the pharmaceutical company's founder, announced, "Medicine is for the patients, not for the profits." This radical corporate vision translates into an often cited example of the company donating the medicine Mectizan to combat the devastating disease, river blindness:[64]

> Twenty-two years ago, Merck started giving away a drug to treat river blindness, a devastating infectious disease endemic to certain countries in Africa and Latin America. The company has donated 2.5 billion tablets at a total cost of $3.75 billion over that time. Merck manages the program with the World Health Organization and other groups, and the effort is widely cited as a model of successful public-private partnerships. [In 2009], WHO announced for the first time that it sees evidence the disease will be eliminated in Africa with Merck's drug.[65]

It could be argued that Merck's actions bought a degree of insurance against attacks by social activists because of the company's up-front commitment to such a worthwhile, unselfish, and unprofitable cause. Perhaps this socially responsible viewpoint has enabled Merck to enjoy a relatively free run from the activist criticism visited on other pharmaceutical companies. The reputation it gained from this act has also been cited as a significant reason for the company's success in entering new markets, most notably Japan, where its socially responsible reputation preceded it. Yet even Merck's proactive CSR efforts may not save it from the economic and legal implications of Vioxx, a Merck product voluntarily withdrawn from the market in 2004 after a growing number of heart-related health problems among users.[66]

Crisis Management

Johnson & Johnson: Johnson & Johnson's transparent handling of the Tylenol crisis in 1982 is widely heralded as the model case in the area of crisis management. J&J went beyond what had previously been expected of corporations in such situations, instigating a $100 million recall of 31 million bottles of the drug following a suspected poisoning incident. In acting the way it did, J&J saved the Tylenol brand, enabling it to remain a strong revenue earner for the company to this day:

> The cost [of the re-call] was a high one. In addition to the impact on the company's share price when the crisis first hit, the lost production and destroyed goods as a result of the recall were considerable. However, the company won praise for its quick and appropriate action. . . . Within five months of the disaster, the company had recovered 70% of its market share for the drug. The fact this went on to improve over time showed that the company had succeeded in preserving the long-term value of the brand. Companies such as Perrier, who had been criticised for less adept handling of a crisis, found their reputation damaged for as long as five years after an incident. In fact, there is some evidence that it was rewarded by consumers who were so reassured by the steps taken that they switched from other painkillers to Tylenol.[67]

Brand value is critical to firms, whether on the local or global stage. Today, the value of the intangible brand may even exceed the value of the firm's tangible assets. The Coca-Cola brand, for example, is worth significantly more than half of the company's total market capitalization.[68] And CSR is important to brands within a globalizing world because of the way brands are built: on perceptions, ideals, and concepts that usually appeal to higher values. CSR is a means of matching corporate operations with stakeholder values at a time when these values are constantly evolving. Thus, given the large amount of time, money, and effort companies invest in creating them, a good CSR policy has become a vital component of a successful corporate brand—an effective means of maximizing its market appeal while protecting the firm's investment over the long term.

Companies today need to build a watertight brand with respect to all stakeholders. The attractiveness of a company—whether as an employer, producer, buyer, supplier, or investment—is directly linked to the strength of its brand. CSR affects all aspects of operations within a corporation because of the need to consider the needs of constituent groups. Each area builds on all the others to create a composite image of the corporation and its brand in the eyes of its stakeholder groups, which has great value for the firm.

THE MARKET FOR SOCIAL RESPONSIBILITY

Central to the economic argument for CSR, therefore, is the notion that firms that best reflect the current needs of their stakeholders and anticipate how those needs will evolve over time will be more successful in the marketplace over the medium to long term.

The CSR Price Premium

As demonstrated in Chapter 3, Walmart has found that adopting specific aspects of CSR (environmental sustainability, in particular) need not undermine the firm's business model and might even enhance it. What Chapter 3 also demonstrates, however, is that Walmart is still taking the path of least resistance in the early stages of CSR implementation:

"There is a substantial opportunity to make green pay," [Rand Waddoups, Wal-Mart's senior director of corporate strategy and sustainability] said. "We haven't even gotten to the low-hanging fruit yet. We are still picking up $1,000 bills off the floor."[69]

Walmart's business strategy relies on a core competence of minimizing costs and passing those savings on to customers. As such, there is little evidence to suggest that Walmart would choose the socially responsible option in any situation where that decision would lead to an increase in costs. This would threaten to undermine the laser-like focus on costs that Walmart executives have spent decades instilling in the firm's employees. What happens, however, when CSR increases costs and firms are forced to pass those costs increases on to their customers in the form of higher prices?

As indicated earlier in this chapter, firms that seek to differentiate their products on some feature other than low cost often charge a price premium for that product. Integrating a long-term stakeholder perspective throughout the firm can lead to an increase in costs and a reduction in short-term returns. Those firms that are genuine in their approach to CSR, therefore, should ensure CSR becomes a point of differentiation for their firm—a distinction that has value in the marketplace:

Ethical products are premium brands, insofar as consumers willingly pay more for them. A report published last year by Packaged Facts, a research company, revealed that half of Americans aged 18 to 29 would spend more for products labelled organic, environmentally friendly or fair trade.[70]

An important distinction here, therefore, is between those firms that perceive CSR to be a cost and those that perceive it to be an opportunity.[71] Until firms perceive CSR to be an opportunity, they have little chance of successfully implementing CSR throughout operations.

Greenwashing—Abuse of the Market for CSR

The market for CSR is complicated by the potential for abuse. Stakeholders, in general, and consumers, in particular, need to be vigilant. There is a gap between the information about a product that is known to the firm and the information that the consumer is willing and able to access about that product—in other words, there is an

information asymmetry between manufacturers and the buying public about the real social, health, and environmental impacts of consumer goods.[72]

As the number of groups and individuals interested in CSR grows, so does the amount of information that is distributed by firms seeking to take advantage of consumer trends and sympathies. Some of this information will be accurate, while some will be misleading; some of the misleading information will be mistakenly so, while some will be deliberate. Whether deliberate or accidental, as CSR becomes more profitable, the potential for *greenwash* increases:

Greenwash

Green-wash (green'wash,' -wôsh')—verb: the act of misleading consumers regarding the environmental practices of a company or the environmental benefits of a product or service.[73]

Greenwash measures the extent to which firms are willing to jump on the CSR bandwagon and mislead consumers in the hope of financial gain. Marketing research suggests that a significant percentage of CSR product marketing claims are false or misleading. In 2007, for example, the environmental marketing organization, Terrachoice, tested the veracity of the environmental claims made on the labels of 1,018 consumer products:

All but one made claims that are demonstrably false or that risk misleading intended audiences.[74]

The report identifies "six sins"[75] that firms engage in when marketing the CSR components of their products. These sins include the Sin of the Hidden Trade-off, the Sin of No Proof, the Sin of Vagueness, the Sin of Irrelevance, the Sin of Fibbing, and Sin of the Lesser of Two Evils and, taken together, they indicate

both that the individual consumer has been misled and that the potential environmental benefit of his or her purchase has been squandered.[76]

The accusation is that firms might say the *correct* things, while not fundamentally altering the way they do business:

McDonald's may support sustainable fisheries, but its core business is still selling Big Macs. Big oil companies can talk all they want about reducing greenhouse emissions but they are still drilling for hydrocarbons. And Ford Motor, well, think for a minute about the predicament that company is in.[77]

Moreover, as different groups push their own agendas and seek to have their CSR ranking, or their fair trade certification, or their environmental sustainability policy established as the standard, so CSR comes to mean different things to different people. While the market for CSR information and practices takes time to sort out which ideas will emerge as the standard, the potential for confusion grows. Consumers, in particular, stand to be confused as different self-proclaimed experts bombard them with more information.

CSR Newsletters: Green Noise

A recent article[78] introduces the concept of "green noise":

"green noise"—static caused by urgent, sometimes vexing or even contradictory information [about the environment] played at too high a volume for too long.

The idea of "green noise" adds value to the debate. While terms like "greenwashing" describe the conduct of firms, "green noise" presents a consumer perspective on the exponential growth in information on issues related to the environment and climate change that is often contradictory. The overall effect is to obfuscate, rather than clarify, whether deliberately or with good intentions:

An environmentally conscientious consumer is left to wonder: are low-energy compact fluorescent bulbs better than standard incandescents, even if they contain traces of mercury? Which salad is more earth-friendly, the one made with organic mixed greens trucked from thousands of miles away, or the one with lettuce raised on nearby industrial farms? Should they support nuclear power as a clean alternative to coal?

In outlining the concept of "green noise," the article also highlights the effect of this information overload on consumer behavior:

Consumers surveyed in 2007 were between 22 and 55 percent less likely to buy a wide range of green products than in 2006. The slipping economy had an effect, but message overload appeared to be a major factor as well.

There is an interesting relationship between the amount of information and effective decision making—the idea that more information is better, but too much leads to paralysis and, consequently, bad or non decisions. Information overload in relation to the environment or sustainability issues is likely to result in backlash from consumers.

To a certain extent, this confusion is unavoidable. Here, the CSR field is a victim of its own success. If CSR wasn't growing in popularity and acceptance, the issue of increasing amounts of contradictory information would neither exist nor matter. The goal, however, should be to avoid the accusation that:

CSR is often just a new bottle into which the old wine of philanthropy is decanted.[79]

STRATEGIC CSR

The Strategic CSR Model, Figure 4.5, visually summarizes the relationship between CSR and strategy.

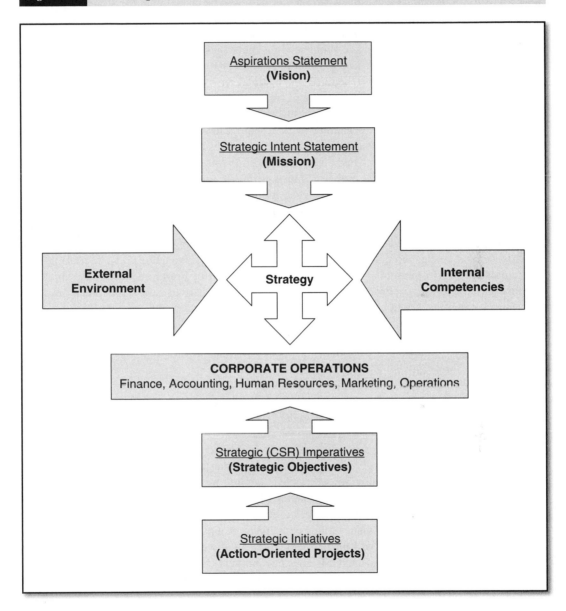

Figure 4.5 The Strategic CSR Model

Corporate success assumes that *strategy* matches *internal competencies* with the *external environment* (stakeholder expectations), within the constraints of *mission* and *vision*. The implementation of strategy, however, rests upon *corporate operations* being successful. Finance, accounting, human resources, and other operational aspects must be executed effectively if the strategy is to be successful at matching competencies to opportunities in the environment. To improve overall performance, therefore, leaders create *strategic objectives* that aim to strengthen these corporate operations. To ensure sufficient financial resources, for example, strategic objectives may be set for the accounting department to accelerate the collection of accounts receivables. Or, marketing might be tasked with the strategic objective of gaining 5% market share. These strategic objectives, however, must be viewed as strategic (must do) imperatives that enhance the firm's CSR goals; otherwise, the tactics and strategies may cause resistance among stakeholders. To achieve these strategic objectives that meet the firm's strategic imperatives, key players must undertake strategic initiatives in the form of *action-oriented projects.* The head of accounting, for example, might create a task force charged with a project that identifies and tracks clients who are slow to pay their bills. A similar action-oriented task force might also be created in marketing to evaluate the firm's advertising as a first step to gaining market share. However these actor-oriented projects perform, they must do so by achieving strategic objectives in ways that are consistent with the firm's strategic CSR imperatives; otherwise, larger threats to the firm's viability arise.

As societies in general become more affluent, societal expectations evolve, and communication technologies become even more widespread, greater and greater demands for CSR will result—undoubtedly prompting more action-oriented projects intended to achieve strategic CSR imperatives. Certainly, moral and rational arguments exist for companies to act in a socially responsible manner; however, a strong economic incentive also exists to be perceived as a net contributor within a society. CSR, therefore, is a competitive differentiator for a firm, as well as a form of brand insurance, in which the brand represents the perception of the company by each of its key stakeholder groups.[80] This economic argument surfaces daily in firms' advertising and public relations campaigns and is, perhaps, the strongest reason for the implementation of CSR to ensure the long-term viability of the organization. The sophisticated level to which the crisis management industry has evolved in advanced economies further demonstrates the value of reputation. In addition, increasingly, investors

are willing to give higher valuations to companies that are deemed good citizens. Put another way, investors give some companies with good track records the benefit of the doubt.[81]

Companies understand the value of being perceived as friendly neighbors and good corporate citizens. Until now, however, managers have largely confined this concern to public relations departments because they were able to control the information that shaped the public face of the corporation. Figure 3.2 (Chapter 3) and Figures 4.3 and 4.4 illustrate why this situation is changing as the momentum, in terms of information control, swings away from multinationals and toward their various constituent groups. As globalization progresses, the Internet and global media will further democratize and feed the exchange of information in all free societies. Thus, strategic CSR goes beyond public relations. It represents substantive actions—good or bad—that can flash around the world through electronic technologies and the global media.

Firms need to reflect the concerns of society through substantive actions, especially regarding the consumer base of their target market. Ideally, progressive companies seek to stay ahead of these evolving values and are able to meet new stakeholder demands as they arise. Significantly, core constituent groups are increasingly acquiring the information necessary to see past superficial advertising campaigns, as well as the means to communicate their message and mobilize where necessary. The balance of power and influence is transferring from corporations to their stakeholders because of this shift in control of the flow of information. An effective and genuine CSR perspective, communicated broadly to stakeholders, allows firms to take advantage of these changes and maximize their economic performance in an increasingly globalizing world.

Central to the practical impact of CSR, therefore, is the ability to persuade business leaders that CSR offers strategic and, therefore, economic benefits. Firms can maximize *shareholder* value in a globalizing world only by utilizing strategies that address the needs of key *stakeholders.* CSR, driven by stakeholder theory, delivers these results. It is a means of allowing firms to analyze the total business environment and formulate appropriate organizational strategies. It can protect the firm and its assets, while also offering a point of competitive differentiation. When the business community perceives CSR as more of an opportunity than a threat,[82] CSR will receive greater attention from 21st-century leaders.

IMPLEMENTING CSR

This chapter outlines in more detail the relationship between a firm's strategy and CSR. Viewing CSR through a strategic lens offers firms the most effective means of navigating an increasingly complex, global business environment. In order for firms to receive the benefit of a CSR perspective, however, there also needs to be a focus on implementation. Without comprehensive and effective implementation, combined with support from the highest levels of the organization, the best-laid plans will fall short of their potential. Chapter 5 offers guidance for firms on this issue by discussing the factors that influence the implementation of CSR by firms. It provides insight in terms of the short-, medium-, and long-term aspects of implementation and concludes Part I of *Strategic CSR*.

Questions for Discussion and Review

1. Why is it important to view CSR from a strategic context?

2. Why are large multinational firms more likely to be concerned about CSR?

3. How do competencies, strategy, structure, and the external environment combine to create a successful organization?

4. Why are lifestyle brands more susceptible to CSR than companies that seek to differentiate their products with a business-level strategy of low cost?

5. What advantages does a *CSR filter* give to a company? If you were CEO of a firm, how would you go about implementing the CSR filter—what form might it take? Can you think of a company that is successfully utilizing a CSR filter today?

6. What are the five environmental forces propelling greater interest in CSR? Explain using real-life examples to illustrate your points. Do you see emerging forces that may reshape CSR in the future?

7. Why does *greenwash* present a danger to CSR? Have a look at Terrachoice's 2009 report, *The Seven Sins of Greenwashing.* Which of the seven sins do you think is the most important (http://sinsofgreenwashing.org/findings/the-seven-sins/)? Think of a firm that is committing that sin—what is misleading about the firm's actions?

NOTES AND REFERENCES

1. The flip side of each of these "constraints" is an opportunity for the firm to build a sustainable competitive advantage.

2. http://www.theyshoulddothat.com/2007/08/post_3.html

3. http://www.computerweekly.com/galleries/237328-4/The-Nike-Trash-Talk-Award-winning-product-design-of-2009.htm

4. To learn more, see Michael E. Porter, *Competitive Strategy,* The Free Press, 1980.

5. A firm's business-level strategy stands in contrast to its corporate-level strategy, which is the strategy of the firm as a whole. Strategy at this level involves decisions such as the businesses in which the firm will compete and whether or not to enter into partnerships with other firms via joint ventures, mergers, or acquisitions.

6. http://www.nikebiz.com/responsibility/; http://www.nikeresponsibility.com/

7. Archie B. Carroll, "A Three-Dimensional Conceptual Model of Corporate Performance," *Academy of Management Review,* Vol. 4, No. 4, 1979, pp. 497–505.

8. Same-sex partner employee benefits will likely be the next form of discrimination to be corrected by legal mandate. Many progressive firms today are proactively implementing such policies so as to avoid being forcefully sanctioned by litigation as the tide of social acceptability turns. See Kathryn Kranhold, "Groups for Gay Employees Are Gaining Traction," *Wall Street Journal,* April 3, 2006, p. B3.

9. Michael E. Porter & Mark R. Kramer, "Strategy & Society," *Harvard Business Review,* December 2006, pp. 78–92.

10. *Oxford English Dictionary,* Second Edition, 1989, http://dictionary.oed.com/cgi/entry/50080908?single=1&query_type=word&queryword=externality&first=1&max_to_show=10

11. Aaron Bernstein, "Nike's New Game Plan for Sweatshops," *BusinessWeek,* September 20, 2004, http://www.businessweek.com/magazine/content/04_38/b3900011_mz001.htm

12. For an overview, see "Nike Campaign," *Center for Communication & Civic Engagement,* http://depts.washington.edu/ccce/polcommcampaigns/Nike.htm. For a current example of an anti-Nike campaign, see "Sweatfree Communities," *Global Exchange,* http://www.globalexchange.org/campaigns/sweatshops/nike/

13. Arik Hesseldahl, "Is Greenpeace off the Mark on Apple?" *BusinessWeek,* March 31, 2007, http://newsletters.businessweek.com/c.asp?653539&c55a2ee820194f0f&51

14. For more detailed discussion of issues related to the environment, see the "Environmental Sustainability" in Chapter 8.

15. http://www.sternreview.org.uk/ or http://www.occ.gov.uk/activities/stern.htm

16. http://www.climatecrisis.net/

17. Bjorn Lomborg, "Stern Review," *Wall Street Journal,* November 2, 2006, p. A12, http://www.opinionjournal.com/extra/?id=110009182

18. Max Wilkinson, "Stern's Report Is Based on Flawed Figures," *Financial Times,* November 3, 2006, http://www.ft.com/cms/s/0/48bf3b58-6ae0-11db-83d9-0000779e2340.html

19. Nicholas Stern, "Gains From Greenhouse Action Outweigh the Costs," *Financial Times,* November 8, 2006, p. 19, http://www.ft.com/cms/s/0/7b257b5a-6ecf-11db-b5c4-0000779e2340.html

20. This video is also available at http://www.youtube.com/watch?v=zORv8wwiadQ

21. See the following two articles for interesting discussions about the central role of continuous growth in our economic models: Andrew Marr, "Charles: Right or Wrong About Science?" *The Observer,* May 21, 2000, http://www.guardian.co.uk/theobserver/2000/may/21/focus.news; and Steven Stoll, "Fear of Fallowing: The Specter of a No-Growth World," *Harper's Magazine,* March 2008, pp. 88–94, http://www.harpers.org/archive/2008/03/0081958

22. Lee Scott, "Wal-Mart: Twenty First Century Leadership," October 24, 2005, http://walmartwatch.com/img/documents/21st_Century_Leadership.pdf

23. http://ge.ecomagination.com/

24. http://www.toyota.com/prius-hybrid/

25. Joanna Blythman, "Food Miles: The True Cost of Putting Imported Food on Your Plate," *The Independent,* May 31, 2007, http://www.independent.co.uk/environment/green-living/food-miles-the-true-cost-of-putting-imported-food-on-your-plate-451139.html

26. http://www.walkerscarbonfootprint.co.uk/

27. See http://www.recycle.co.uk/ or http://www.recycle-more.co.uk/

28. "Tesco Gets Rid of Garbage: Zero Waste Goes to Landfill in UK," *Reuters,* August 11, 2009, http://uk.reuters.com/article/idUK302721664320090811

29. Peter Whybrow is the director of the Semel Institute of Neuroscience and Human Behavior at the University of California at Los Angeles.

30. Summarized by Irene Lacher, "In New Book, Professor Sees a 'Mania' in U.S. for Possessions and Status," *New York Times,* March 12, 2005, p. A21.

31. For more information about Adam Smith, as well as examples of his work (in particular, *The Theory of Moral Sentiments*), see http://www.adamsmith.org/adam-smith/

32. Margaret Ackrill & Leslie Hannah, *Barclays: The Business of Banking, 1690–1996,* Cambridge University Press, 2001.

33. "Royal Dutch/Shell in Nigeria (A)," *Harvard Business School Press* [9–399–126], August 10, 2006.

34. For information on the development of CSR in countries like Saudi Arabia, see "First Study on Corporate Saudi Arabia and CSR," *CSRWire.com,* March 29, 2007, http://www.csrwire.com/press/press_release/15949-First-Study-on-Corporate-Saudi-Arabia-and-CSR

35. O. Lee Reed, Peter Shedd, Jere Morehead, & Marisa Pagnattaro, *The Legal and Regulatory Environment of Business,* 12th edition, McGraw-Hill, 2002, p. 133.

36. "Microsoft Loses Anti-Trust Appeal," *BBC News,* September 17, 2007, http://news.bbc.co.uk/2/hi/business/6998272.stm

37. Debora L. Spar, "Hitting the Wall: Nike and International Labor Practices," *Harvard Business School Press* [9–700–047], September 6, 2002.

38. "GAP Hit by 'Sweatshop' Protests," *BBC News,* November 21, 2002, http://news.bbc.co.uk/2/hi/business/2497957.stm

39. "'Killer Coke' or Innocent Abroad?" *BusinessWeek,* January 23, 2006, http://www.businessweek.com/magazine/content/06_04/b3968074.htm; Nandlal Master, Lok Samiti, & Amit Srivastava, "India: Major Protest Demands Coca-Cola Shut Down Plant," *GlobalResearch.ca,* April 8, 2008, http://www.globalresearch.ca/index.php?context=va&aid=8591

40. "Google Censors Itself For China," BBC News, January 25, 2006, http://news.bbc.co.uk/2/hi/technology/4645596.stm

41. Don Tapscott & David Ticoll, "The Naked Corporation," *Wall Street Journal,* October 14, 2003, p. B2. Tapscott and Ticoll are coauthors of *The Naked Corporation: How the Age of Transparency Will Revolutionize Business,* Free Press, 2003.

42. Malcolm Gladwell, *The Tipping Point: How Little Things Can Make a Big Difference,* Little Brown, 2000, http://www.gladwell.com/. See also Malcolm Gladwell, "The Tipping Point," *The New Yorker Magazine,* June 3, 1996, http://www.gladwell.com/pdf/tipping.pdf

43. Search performed in August 2009 at http://www.google.com/. Note: This number has increased significantly from the search conducted for the first edition of *Strategic CSR* in May 2005, which generated 1,430,000 hits.

44. William Gibson, "The Road to Oceania," *New York Times,* June 25, 2003, p. A27.

45. Grameen Telecom (GTC) was established in 1995 as a not-for-profit company established by Dr. Muhammad Yunus for improving the standard of living and eradication of poverty from rural Bangladesh with the help of Grameen Bank, http://www.grameentelecom.net.bd/

46. Daniel Chang, "Flash Mobs Come (Late) to South Florida," *Miami Herald,* August 30, 2003, p. 1E; Wanda J. DeMarzo, "Dollars, and Jaws, Drop as `Flash Mob' Fad Hits S. Florida," *Miami Herald,* August 31, 2003, p. 4A.

47. Ann Grimes, "Moblog for the Masses," *Wall Street Journal,* April 29, 2004, p. B4.

48. Warren St. John, "Quick, After Him: Pac-Man Went Thataway," *New York Times,* May 9, 2004, Section 9, p. 1.

49. For examples of stakeholders creating Web sites to criticize the firms they particularly dislike, see http://walmartsucksorg.blogspot.com/, http://ibmsucks.org/ or http://targetsucks.blogspot.com/

50. Anya Kamenetz, "On the Internet, Everyone Knows You're a Dog," *Fast Company Magazine,* December 2008/January 2009, pp. 53–55.

51. Michael Elliott, "Embracing the Enemy Is Good Business," *Time,* August 13, 2001, p. 29.

52. Peter Overby & Renee Montagne, "Obama Campaign Shatters Fundraising Records," National Public Radio, December 5, 2008, http://www.npr.org/templates/story/story.php?storyId=97843649

53. "Our Values & Campaigns," http://www.thebodyshop.com/_en/_ww/values-campaigns/index.aspx

54. http://www.benettongroup.com/en/whatwesay/campaigns.htm

55. http://www.benjerry.com/activism/mission-statement/

56. James Austin & James Quinn, "Ben & Jerry's: Preserving Mission and Brand Within Unilever," *Harvard Business School Press* [9–306–037], January 18, 2007.

57. "A survey carried out by the UK's Royal Society found that in 2005 ExxonMobil distributed $2.9m to 39 groups that the society said 'misrepresented the science of climate change by outright denial of the evidence.'" In David Adam, "Exxon to Cut Funding to Climate Change Denial Groups," *The Guardian,* May 28, 2008, http://www.guardian.co.uk/environment/2008/may/28/climatechange.fossilfuels

58. Mallen Baker, "Companies in the News: BP," October, 2007, http://www.mallenbaker.net/csr/CSRfiles/bp.html

59. William B. Werther & David Chandler, "Strategic Corporate Social Responsibility as Global Brand Insurance," *Business Horizons,* Vol. 48, No. 4, July 2005, pp. 317–324.

60. "Sweatfree Communities," http://www.globalexchange.org/campaigns/sweatshops/nike/; "Don't Do It," http://www.dontdoitarmy.com/home.php

61. Debora L. Spar, "Hitting the Wall: Nike and International Labor Practices," *Harvard Business School Press* [9–700–047], September 6, 2002, p. 11.

62. Derrick Daye & Brad VanAuken, "Social Responsibility: The Nike Story," July 25, 2008, http://www.brandingstrategyinsider.com/2008/07/social-responsi.html

63. Sarah Skidmore, "Nike Finds Major Violations at Malaysian Factory," *Associated Press,* August 1, 2008, http://www.newsvine.com/_news/2008/08/01/1713691-nike-finds-major-violations-at-malaysian-factory

64. http://www.merck.com/corporate-responsibility/access/access-developing-emerging/mectizan-donation-riverblindness/

65. Arlene Weintraub, "Will Pfizer's Giveaway Drugs Polish Its Public Image?" *BusinessWeek,* August 3, 2009, p. 13, http://www.businessweek.com/managing/management_innovation/blog/archives/2009/07/drugs_1.html

66. http://www.merck.com/newsroom/vioxx/

67. Mallen Baker, "Companies in Crisis: What to Do When It All Goes Wrong," *CSR Case Studies in Crisis Management: Johnson & Johnson*, http://www.mallenbaker.net/csr/CSRfiles/crisis02.html

68. Coca-Cola's brand is consistently ranked No. 1 in value in *BusinessWeek's* annual brand survey. In 2008, the brand was estimated to be worth $66.667 billion and was ranked No. 1 for the eighth straight year, http://images.businessweek.com/ss/08/09/0918_best_brands/2.htm; Burt Helm, "Best Global Brands," *BusinessWeek,* September 18, 2008, http://www.businessweek.com/magazine/content/08_39/b4101052097769.htm

69. Cathryn Creno, "Wal-Mart's Sustainability Efforts Draw Praise," *The Arizona Republic,* May 26, 2008, http://www.azcentral.com/business/articles/2008/05/26/20080526biz-greenretailers0526-ON.html

70. Rikki Stancich, "Recession Ethics: CSR in a Downturn—Recession-proof Ethics Can Weather the Storm," *Ethical Corporation Magazine,* March 5, 2008, http://www.ethicalcorp.com/content .asp?ContentID=5751

71. David Grayson & Adrian Hodges, *Corporate Social Opportunity!,* Greenleaf Publications, 2004, http://www.greenleaf-publishing.com/productdetail.kmod?productid=63

72. Karen K. Nathan, "Behind the Label: The Case for Eco-disclosure," *Barron's,* August 3, 2009, p. 32. Review of the book by Daniel Goleman, *Ecological Intelligence: How Knowing the Hidden Impacts of What We Buy Can Change Everything,* Broadway Business, 2009.

73. *Terrachoice,* http://sinsofgreenwashing.org/

74. "The Six Sins of Greenwashing," *Terrachoice,* 2007, p. 1.

75. In 2009, the organization added the "seventh sin," the "sin of worshipping false labels," which it defines as "a product that, through either words or images, gives the impression of third-party endorsement where no such endorsement exists; fake labels, in other words." This definition, along with definitions for the other six sins, can be found at: http://sinsofgreenwashing.org/findings/the-seven-sins/

76. Dan Mitchell, "Being Skeptical of Green," *New York Times,* November 24, 2007, p. 5. http://www.nytimes.com/2007/11/24/technology/24online.html

77. Joe Nocera, "The Paradoxes of Businesses as Do-Gooders," *New York Times,* November 11, 2006, p. B1.

78. Alex William, "That Buzz in Your Ear May Be Green Noise," *New York Times,* June 15, 2008, http://www.nytimes.com/2008/06/15/fashion/15green.html

79. Jonathan Guthrie, "Ethics, Enterprise and Expediency," *Financial Times,* June 15, 2006, p. 13.

80. William B. Werther & David Chandler, "Strategic Corporate Social Responsibility as Global Brand Insurance," *Business Horizons,* Vol. 48, No. 4, July 2005, pp. 317–324.

81. Paul J. Lim, "Gauging That Other Company Asset: Its Reputation," *New York Times,* April 10, 2004, p. A18.

82. David Grayson & Adrian Hodges, *Corporate Social Opportunity!,* Greenleaf Publications, 2004, http://www.greenleaf-publishing.com/productdetail.kmod?productid=63

CHAPTER 5

IMPLEMENTATION

The Integration of CSR Into Strategy and Culture

The first four chapters of this book set out the case for CSR, addressed the anti-CSR argument, and analyzed CSR's strategic importance within the global economy. This chapter provides insights as to what a firm must do to integrate strategic CSR into its culture, strategy, and everyday operations. That is, *when* and *how* does a company become more socially responsible? When should a company begin adopting CSR as a strategic driving factor, for example? Is there a standard point of organizational evolution at which this should occur, or does it differ from company to company and among industries? How should management construct CSR policies that can then filter down throughout the organization? How will stakeholders distinguish between a genuine CSR strategy and a cynical attempt to create positive public relations or, worse, misleading *greenwash*?

We address the *when* by focusing on the *CSR threshold*, a tipping point that triggers firms to move toward strategic CSR. Then, we turn to the *how* by outlining the design, timing, and implementation of strategic CSR, introducing the necessary corporate infrastructure and key policy ideas in the form of a comprehensive plan of action for a firm seeking to implement CSR throughout operations.

THE CSR THRESHOLD

The decision of *when* to implement a CSR policy is compounded by *why, where*, and *how* it should be implemented, not to mention *who* should oversee the process. The industry context complicates things further because of the varied stages of acceptance of CSR by different competitors. Another level of complexity, differences among countries and cultures, ensures different firms will approach CSR in vastly different ways. Although the value of an effective CSR policy within specific industries and firms is becoming increasingly accepted, the point at which such a policy becomes ripe for implementation (or unavoidable to those unconvinced of the benefits) varies. Thus, *when* depends on many factors, which include the CEO's attitude toward CSR, the firm's industry and actions of competitors, and the cultural environment in which the firm is operating.

Companies can pursue an effective CSR policy of either offense ("corporate social opportunity")[1] or defense (CSR as "brand insurance").[2] The innovative, proactive CEO who is convinced of the intrinsic value of CSR sees it as an opportunity to maximize company capabilities and identify new competitive advantages.[3] Examples abound: From Nike's sustainable Air Jordan XX3 athletic shoe, which is made with "the near absence of chemical-based glues and an outsole made of recycled material,"[4] to the wide range of products licensed under Bono's Product (RED) brand,[5] to Anheuser-Busch's efficient recycling policies,[6] firms seeking CSR innovations find lots of good ideas with which to work and plenty of good reasons to put them into practice. Companies with a progressive and innovative mind-set see benefits that range from being an attractive employer (helping retention and recruitment), to greater acceptance among government agencies (such as needed zoning and tax relief), to better relations with social activists (such as Greenpeace). In short, an effective and innovative CSR program improves a firm's relations with both its external and internal stakeholders. Timberland, for example, believes that its Path of Service program, which grants "40 hours of annual paid time off to work on service projects in [employees'] communities,"[7] raises morale and increases retention, therefore lowering training costs while inducing new skills and stoking corporate pride.[8]

In terms of defense, CSR still has value by avoiding criticism and other attacks on the firm or its offerings. In this instance, CSR is a rational choice that acts like a brand insurance policy, minimizing or offsetting stakeholder disillusionment in response to perceived lapses in CSR.[9] A good example of this approach is the USCAP (United States Climate Action Partnership, http://www.us-cap.org/), formed by a group of energy and manufacturing firms, which "supports the introduction of carbon limits and trading" as a means of mitigating federal legislation designed to control carbon emissions.[10]

Either approach (offense or defense) assumes an up-front investment in creating CSR policies; *when* to introduce CSR into the strategic process, however, depends on the driving force behind its implementation. For those managers convinced of CSR's strategic potential, there is no time like the present. Innovative ideas and policies that maximize market opportunities, minimize costs, and increase productivity can produce immediate benefits. For managers yet to be persuaded by the CSR argument, however, the temptation exists to delay as long as possible. Worse, cynical managers might see CSR as merely a public relations exercise or, worse still, postpone hard CSR choices by assuming they can avoid the expense altogether. Perhaps this is analogous to someone who imagines that, as long as they remain healthy, they will be able to avoid outlays for health insurance.

Nevertheless, a crisis point can arise. Once reached and stakeholder backlash becomes sufficient to warrant the introduction of a reactionary CSR policy, however, it may be too late. As mentioned in Chapter 3, Walmart announced that it would donate $35 million to the National Fish and Wildlife Foundation in April 2005. Although commendable, this action took place "barely a week after environmentalists forged a broad alliance with organized labor and community groups to attack Wal-Mart and its business practices."[11] Complicating matters further, this threshold of when to act ebbs and flows with public perceptions and media spin, which can change with the next news cycle. Even more confounding is the variability that exists among industries, cultures, and nations, as well as among companies within the same industry.

In summary, firms introduce CSR for different reasons. Implementing CSR proactively throughout the firm can generate multiple business advantages and may yield additional benefits associated with first-mover status. In addition, the genuine implementation of CSR, whether for offensive or defensive reasons, generates insurance-like benefits that render CSR lapses less damaging if committed due to factors outside the firm's control. Whatever the motivation, however, there is a *CSR threshold* in every industry that acts as a CSR point of no return. The sooner CSR is introduced, the less likely a firm is to cross this "tipping point,"[12] which varies for each company (depending on whether it is the market leader or a smaller player) and within each industry (some industries are more susceptible to stakeholder backlash than others). The variable nature of this CSR threshold suggests why some companies perceive CSR to be of greater or lesser importance to their particular organization at different points in time. Still, why is it that different companies and industries have different CSR thresholds for different reasons? An important part of the answer comes from the business-level strategy a company pursues.

Variation Among Companies

Analyzing a company's business-level strategy reveals how it distinguishes its products in the marketplace. Its value proposition is captured in its strategy and attracts stakeholder groups, particularly customers. In turn, the firm's strategy has a direct impact on the CSR threshold for that company within its industry.

Consider these comparisons in light of Figure 5.1. Walmart's strategy, for example, probably raises the company's CSR threshold; that is, it has more CSR leeway and can "get away

Figure 5.1   The Business-Level CSR Threshold

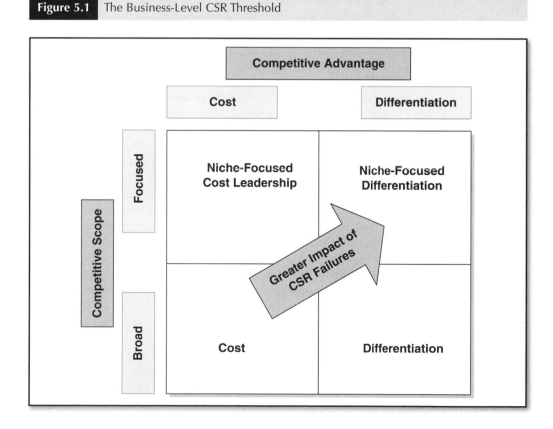

with" more because its value proposition is based on a business-level strategy of low cost. Thus, a Walmart shopper is unlikely to be surprised to discover that the company favors products manufactured overseas in low-cost environments, rather than higher cost products made by U.S. employees. For a company like The Body Shop, however, which has built its reputation and customer base largely on the social justice issues it chooses to advocate (such as no animal testing and fair trade), the CSR threshold at which customers, media, and society react may have a much lower tipping point. Thus, The Body Shop's stakeholders are more likely to have a lower threshold of tolerance for perceived CSR violations. Restated, The Body Shop consumers would expect the company to live up to the values that attracted them in the first place, which translates into a correspondingly lower CSR threshold for the firm. For example, one CSR error by The Body Shop may well be equal, in terms of stakeholder perception, to multiple CSR oversights by Walmart.

As suggested by Figure 5.1, business-level strategies can be divided into those that pursue low costs and those that pursue differentiation (see Chapter 2). The low-cost approach suggests an ability to deliver products or services at a price below that of competitors. The products that Walmart sells, for example, are not fundamentally different from those of its competitors. As a result, the firm gains its competitive advantage from its "everyday low prices," which enable its customers to "Save money. Live better." Walmart is able to generate its low prices because of its laser-like focus on minimizing costs throughout the value chain. Differentiation strategies, however, offer the customer something unique, such as a luxury car from Rolls Royce, for which there is often an associated price premium.

These low-cost and differentiation strategies can be further categorized as either broad (e.g., targeting a broad market segment, such as the automobile market) or narrowly focused (e.g., targeting only consumers seeking to purchase high-end cars, but not SUVs, station wagons, or pickup trucks). As a result, Walmart has a scope of business that can be labeled *broad,* while Rolls Royce's products are *focused.* Overall, therefore, Rolls Royce's business strategy offers a *differentiated* product, focused on the *niche* market of high-end cars, whereas Walmart's strategy pursues *cost leadership* (low costs) across a *broad* base of customers.[13] An alternative strategy is pursued by a firm like McDonald's, which seeks a focused strategy of low cost (cheap food) *and* differentiation (fast service).[14]

Whether a company pursues a cost- or differentiation-based strategy shapes the firm's CSR threshold—the point at which CSR becomes obviously critical to strategic success. The most vulnerable strategy will be focused differentiation, particularly for those products dependent on lifestyle segmentation—products that are targeted at specific customers based on their personal values. Nike, for example, makes a determined effort to associate its products (athletic wear and shoes) with people who have a positive and physically active lifestyle. If, however, Nike is seen as socially irresponsible by its target customers, they are less likely to want to associate their lifestyle with these products. Market segments, or niches, such as lifestyle brands are especially valuable to a company because they often rest more heavily on subjective impressions tied up within shifting social trends, rather than objective price and quality comparisons. As such, customers who associate the brand's appeal with their lifestyle are often willing to pay a greater premium for the product. Yet, paradoxically, those able to pay this premium are precisely those with the widest range of alternatives, backed by the resources to make different choices. The subjective base on which lifestyle brand allegiance lies, therefore, also presents a danger to these firms. A CSR-related failure that might inflict limited harm on a firm relying on a broad, cost-based strategy could prove significantly damaging to one reliant on a strategy of focused differentiation.

The petroleum industry, where consumers draw less distinction between similar gasolines from different companies, offers a good example. The nature of this industry allows ExxonMobil to adopt a lower CSR profile than either BP or Shell without penalty.[15] This implies a higher CSR threshold for ExxonMobil because it has both lower visibility among environmentalists and because it is difficult to differentiate its products (in terms of technical quality and performance) from those of either BP or Shell.

As different companies move across the chart in Figure 5.1 (in the direction of the shaded arrow) from cost- to differentiation-based strategies, the CSR threshold that they face is likely to fall. That is, a business-level strategy of differentiation is likely to make those firms more susceptible to stakeholder backlash. This increases the importance of an effective and well-implemented CSR policy within the firm. A similar tendency is visible when analyzing the industries within which these firms operate.

Variation Among Industries

Different industries also evoke different stakeholder emotions. Although there are likely to be differences within the apparel industry, for example, between a firm that sells unbranded clothing based on low costs (a higher threshold) and a firm using a focused differentiation strategy that offers a "lifestyle brand" (a lower threshold), the industry as a whole (with its reputation for sweatshop labor in developing countries) may have a lower threshold than industries where the connection between product, brand, and customer aspirations is weaker.

In the financial or banking industry (with its strategy of broad differentiation), for example, the CSR threshold may be relatively higher than for apparel. Here it may be harder for consumers to identify a victim or accurately quantify the degree of harm caused by any CSR violation. For example, the U.S. mutual fund scandals in 2003—"one of the biggest financial scandals in U.S. history, which has so far implicated 15 mutual funds, 12 brokerage firms, 4 banks, and dozens of individuals"[16]—suggests that when it comes to personal finance, the average American is more willing to separate ethics from personal benefit:[17]

> There's little evidence that scandal is hurting mutual fund sales. In October [2003], net inflows to equity funds hit an estimated $31 billion. . . . A strong stock market trumps some funds' bad behavior.[18]

While firms benefit from striving to meet the needs and demands of their stakeholders, in general, and their customers, in particular, this relationship is more easily open to abuse for those firms that profit by selling products that their consumers do not fully understand. In the case of the financial and banking industries, "the logic of the industry rewards complexity."[19] And, even when they perceive a bank to be acting in a way they do not support, consumers are sometimes relatively powerless to act. When the First National Bank of Chicago decided to charge all customers $3 for every transaction they conducted that was not online, for example, there was significant stakeholder backlash. The result?

The bank lost a percentage of its customers, but its profits went up by 28 per cent. Why? There was indeed a big move to cheaper electronic transactions, and the customers they lost were generally the unprofitable ones they were only too happy to gift to their competitors. So what about the right of those customers to get a decent service? What about the social role that banking provides and their public duty?[20]

The issues that determine the CSR threshold for an industry are more complicated than those for individual companies, with specific industries being more vulnerable than others. Indeed, a number of industries have already passed through their CSR threshold, causing companies that operate within those industries to take significant corrective action. One example is the fast-food industry and its relatively recent conversion to the benefits of health foods.[21] Another example, the tobacco industry, passed through its CSR threshold long ago. To see Philip Morris on its Web site warning against the dangers of smoking, the health consequences of consuming their products, and recommending tips on how to give up smoking[22] is to know that the industry long ago passed the point of no return in terms of its CSR threshold.

Variation Among Cultures

CSR thresholds driven by different cultural expectations further complicate the environmental context for firms. Even among developed economies, there are stark differences. For example, it was legal action in the United States that determined the CSR thresholds for the tobacco, fast food, and asbestos industries. In Europe, by contrast, instead of litigation-driven activism, NGO and nonprofit activism has largely driven the CSR agenda. Again, examples abound and include Greenpeace's campaigns against Shell's operations in Nigeria,[23] Friends of the Earth's campaigns against Monsanto and genetically modified foods,[24] and Oxfam's work (both with and against) Starbucks and its fair trade coffee program.[25]

In much of the developing world, however, the perception of CSR has traditionally revolved around issues of corporate philanthropy, an issue that consumes only a fraction of the CSR debate in developed economies.[26] This is slowly changing, however, as C. K. Prahalad's work on the value of bottom-of-the-pyramid consumers to multinational corporations[27] and Muhammad Yunus's work with Grameen Bank (for which he and the bank were jointly awarded the Nobel Prize for Peace in 2006) have transformed perceptions of the developing economies among multinational firms, as well as perceptions of CSR within the developing economies.[28]

Although these differences among cultures are real and have consequences for firms, globalization and the free flow of information help drive down CSR thresholds across the board (reducing stakeholder tolerance and increasing the chance of backlash). As the news media and blogosphere continue to expose corporate CSR lapses and people are better able to compare conditions across cultures, societal tolerance for socially irresponsible behavior is lowered. Consider the results of a survey among 138 companies in eight East Asian countries that reviewed their corporate governance, social, and environmental performance:

"On the whole the East-West difference is rather overblown and for a long time used by governments and ultra-nationals to defend the status quo" on corporate social and environmental performance, Mr. Choo (a researcher in the area of socially responsible investing) said. "I personally believe almost all [Socially Responsible Investing] issues are universal and are not culturally based—it doesn't matter if Asians consider tobacco industries unethical or not, they are just plain bad and it doesn't take a Ph.D. to understand this."[29]

This greater availability of information helps forge a more recognizable link between stakeholders and the company or product. Furthermore, as levels of affluence and living standards rise generally, and it becomes apparent that problems like climate change are transnational, the CSR threshold is likely to become lower still as issues of societal necessity evolve into greater social choice and demands for change.

Just reporting on corruption among different countries, for example, highlights environments where CSR lapses are more likely and suggests areas where even greater controls are needed. Transparency International's annual Corruption Perceptions Index,[30] which was first published in 1995 and "highlights the fatal link between poverty, failed institutions and graft,"[31] is the best guide to how different countries perform in terms of corruption:

The Transparency International CPI measures the perceived levels of public-sector corruption in a given country and is a composite index, drawing on different expert and business surveys. The 2008 CPI scores 180 countries . . . on a scale from zero (highly corrupt) to ten (highly clean). Denmark, New Zealand and Sweden share the highest score at 9.3, followed immediately by Singapore at 9.2. Bringing up the rear is Somalia at 1.0, slightly trailing Iraq and Myanmar at 1.3 and Haiti at 1.4.[32]

The combination of globalization, rising living standards, and media applications of first-world standards to developing-world operations suggests that an effective CSR policy is increasingly advisable for all firms and will grow in importance as these trends continue into the future. The CSR threshold model presented here argues that the different points at which CSR jumps onto the radar screens of leaders in different industries and cultures and between different companies varies based on a host of strategic and stakeholder factors. Best practice in response to the uncertainty suggests a proactive CSR policy that provides business benefit to the firm, as well as a means of avoiding, or at least minimizing, negative publicity and societal backlash.

CSR—AN INTEGRAL ASPECT OF THE FIRM?

A research sample of 515 firms studied by the Center for Corporate Citizenship at Boston College (http://www.bcccc.net/) emphasizes the potential business value of CSR to small, medium, and large corporations:

Like financial controls and human resource management, corporate citizenship is integral to keeping a business healthy. Most accept the notion that businesses have responsibilities that go beyond the traditional making money, providing jobs, and paying taxes. Most respondents report that their commitment is rooted in tradition and values; eight of ten say corporate citizenship helps the bottom line; and more than half indicate it is important to their customers. The attitude about and commitment to corporate citizenship by small- and medium-sized business leaders are just as strong as they are in the largest corporations.[33]

The study also found that good corporate citizenship was driven by a variety of internal and external forces. Traditions and values, reputation or image, and business strategy were internal forces, with consumers forming the most significant external pressures and cited by more than 50% of the respondents. Lack of resources and a lack of top-management commitment, however, were perceived to be the greatest barriers to good corporate citizenship. Encouragingly, only 9% of the respondents reported seeing no benefit to the firm for good corporate citizenship.[34]

These research findings are supported by anecdotal evidence from a variety of top firms. Companies such as Nike,[35] Starbucks,[36] Ford,[37] Microsoft,[38] Timberland,[39] and others have grouped CSR-related activities into CSR, Corporate Responsibility, Sustainability, or Ethics and Compliance departments. Those that are most successful are led by senior executives in the firm, such as Nike's vice president of corporate responsibility.[40] Although not all firms have interwoven CSR into their operations to this extent, these kinds of internal organizational structures are likely to be increasingly common as CSR grows in importance.

In spite of progress by individual firms, however, there is still great room for improvement. *The Economist*, in a special report on CSR, notes that in spite of the increased profile of CSR in recent years, firms are still slow to grasp the full implications of what it means for day-to-day operations:

> Since there is so much CSR about, you might think that big companies would by now be getting rather good at it. A few are, but most are struggling.[41]

As we begin to understand more about how firms react to emerging issues, such as CSR, we understand more about their learning stages and how they translate that learning into action. Simon Zadek, the founder and CEO of AccountAbility,[42] has made an important contribution in this effort by identifying the five stages of learning that organizations go through "when it comes to developing a sense of corporate responsibility."[43]

The Five Stages of CSR Learning

1. Defensive (to deny responsibility)

2. Compliance (to do the minimum required)

3. Managerial (to begin integrating CSR into management practices)

4. Strategic (to embed CSR within the strategy planning process)

5. Civil (to promote CSR practices industry-wide)[44]

It is relatively easy to map this taxonomy onto the *CSR threshold* model outlined above. While an industry or culture might be approaching its threshold (the point at which CSR becomes a strategic imperative), there is still likely to be variance among firms in terms of individual executives' attitudes to these ideas. While some firms will long ago have recognized the benefits that a CSR perspective can generate for the firm and be safely in the strategic or civil stages, there will be others that lag behind in either the defensive or compliance stages.

Assuming that a firm has decided to implement CSR, therefore, how does it actually go about becoming socially responsible?

IMPLEMENTATION: SHORT TO MEDIUM TERM

The urgency with which CSR policies are implemented depends on the perceived CSR threshold and the priority the issue holds for the firm's leaders. Implementation is about common-sense policies that represent a means to integrate a stakeholder perspective throughout operations, thus protecting the often huge investments corporations make in their public image, investor confidence, and brands. The eventual goal should be for CSR to form an integral component of a business's culture, as reflected in its day-to-day operations. The challenge is to move to a position at which all employees approach their work using a *CSR filter* (see Figure 4.2).

The following steps offer an overview of how any corporation can further the integration of CSR into its operating practices and organizational culture over the short to medium term.

From the Top Down

The CEO must actively sponsor CSR. This executive *ownership* is the foundation of an effective CSR policy and is central to ensuring that CSR is institutionalized as a core component of day-to-day operating practice. Ideally, the CEO will consider himself or herself the chief CSR officer.[45] At a minimum, the CEO must remain in touch with the effectiveness of the company's CSR policy by receiving regular updates, while granting a clear line of access to the top for the CSR officer. This commitment from senior management is crucial for effective implementation. Executives must exhibit leadership to infuse a stakeholder perspective. Otherwise, any CSR policy or statement will quickly become a hollow public relations gesture.

Look at this list of corporate values: Communication. Respect. Integrity. Excellence. They sound good don't they? Strong, concise, meaningful. Maybe they even resemble your own company's values, the ones you spent so much time writing, debating, and revising. If so, you should be nervous. These are the corporate values of Enron, as stated in the company's 2000 annual report. And as events have shown, they're not meaningful; they're meaningless.[46]

Top-Down Support for CSR at Enron—
How It Should Not Be Done!

A perfect example of a firm that, on the surface, had all the components of an effective ethics program in place, but failed to implement it effectively throughout the organization, is Enron—a firm that went bankrupt because of fraudulent financial practices on a massive scale. Consider its "award-winning" Code of Ethics:[47]

> As officers and employees of Enron Corp., its subsidiaries, and its affiliated companies . . . . we are responsible for conducting the business affairs of the Company in accordance with all applicable laws and in a moral and honest manner.[48]

> Enron stands on the foundation of its Vision and Values. Every employee is educated about the Company's Vision and Values and is expected to conduct business with other employees, partners, contractors, suppliers, vendors and customers keeping in mind respect, integrity, communication and excellence. Everything we do evolves from Enron's Vision and Values statements.[49]

> Employees of Enron Corp., its subsidiaries, and its affiliated companies (collectively the "Company") are charged with conducting their business affairs in accordance with the highest ethical standards. An employee shall not conduct himself or herself in a manner that directly or indirectly would be detrimental to the best interests of the Company or in a manner that would bring to the employee financial gain separately derived as a direct consequence of his or her employment with the Company. Moral as well as legal obligations will be fulfilled openly, promptly, and in a manner which will reflect pride on the Company's name.[50]

Language is important and its ability to shape behavior should not be underestimated. Clearly, however, a well-crafted position statement is not enough; neither is senior management's less than complete support. Ostensibly, CSR and ethics at Enron had top management support: CEO Kenneth Lay signed off on all the documents. The point is not only that the move to inject a CSR perspective must be supported by top management, but that the commitment must be genuine and enforced in practice on a day-to-day basis to avoid accusations of "empty rhetoric."[51] In spite of its market-leading position on CSR today, for example, early on, Nike was also reluctant to embrace CSR:

> Initially, the Nike response was a textbook example of how not to handle corporate social responsibility (CSR). In the 1997 documentary *The Big One,* Michael Moore raised the issue of underage workers with a clearly uncomfortable Phil Knight. "Tell it to the United Nations," was his response.[52]

Consider, however, that

A well-led organisation will always seek to create the optimal value in all its relationships. In a way, that is simply good leadership. The most impressive corporate leaders have always been those whose vision of a successful business stretches beyond the product and the profits to their positive impact on the world around them.[53]

CSR Officer[54]

Top-management support must be translated into tangible action. As *The Economist* notes,

It has become almost obligatory for executives to claim that CSR is "connected to the core" of corporate strategy, or that is has become "part of the DNA."[55]

To be effective, however, CSR needs both visibility and sponsorship within the organization. Backing by the CEO equals sponsorship, and the creation of a CSR officer position, staffed by a company executive with a direct reporting relationship to the board of directors, creates visibility. Influencing the corporate culture toward greater CSR requires time, effort, and details. Given other demands, CEOs are forced to delegate their efforts to a CSR officer. This CSR executive needs to formulate the direction that the company will pursue in terms of CSR. Thus, the champion must have access to the highest levels of decision making to ensure a CSR perspective is part of the strategic direction of the company. Starbucks[56] and Nike[57] provide good examples of this approach:

[Since the position was established in 1998, Nike's vice president for corporate responsibility has] overall responsibility for managing Nike's global corporate responsibility function, including labor compliance, global community affairs, stakeholder engagement and corporate responsibility strategic planning and business integration. She will report to Nike['s] Brand President.[58]

The CSR officer defines, implements, and audits the company's CSR policies. This includes assisting with legal and regulatory compliance, as well as compliance with discretionary certifications, such as the ISO (International Organization for Standardization) standards, which include ISO 9000 standards for quality management and ISO 14000 standards for environmental management,[59] as well as ISO 26000 guidelines for social responsibility.[60] It will undoubtedly also include responding to the numerous requests firms receive to complete surveys tied to "the proliferation of non-financial performance metrics,"[61] such as social responsibility and sustainability rankings.[62] As activist organizations increasingly hold firms accountable for their operations,

managers at major U.S. employers receive literally thousands of pages of surveys each year on their social, environmental, governance, and ethics policies.[63]

Perhaps the most famous of these is *Fortune Magazine*'s Most Admired Firm rankings,[64] although many others, such as the *CRO Magazine's* 100 Best Corporate Citizens,[65] the Global

Reporting Initiative,[66] and indexes produced by social responsibility research firms such as KLD Research & Analytics[67] are also becoming established within the CSR field. The rankings constitute signals to external constituents about the work that the firm is doing in relation to CSR. Although the surveys are no doubt tedious and repetitive, performing well in these rankings may well be of strategic advantage to the firm.

In addition, a CSR officer may lead innovations—such as the introduction of a Stakeholder Relations Department in place of the existing Investor Relations Department—to actively demonstrate the CSR commitment of the firm. Most important, however, the position must focus on contributing to strategy formulation. This aspect of company policy is where the CSR officer can hope to make the most progress in terms of fully integrating CSR throughout all aspects of operation.

All these policies need an organization-wide perspective to ensure effective implementation and dissemination of benefits and goals. Ideally, the CSR officer must create awareness with a blend of rewards, as well as penalties for organizational members who act in contrary ways. Thus, the CSR position is all encompassing. In particular, the CSR officer should be part risk manager, part ethics officer, part crisis manager, part brand builder and insurer, and part beacon bearer. In addition, the CSR officer will need to develop contingency plans for any unexpected CSR emergencies.

Ideally, the long term goal for all departments within the firm is to grow a CSR perspective:

> Ultimately, whilst we are professionalizing corporate social responsibility, adding new impenetrable jargon and making it a place fit for experts, we are missing the real deal. This is not a specialist part of business per se, it is business as usual.[68]

In the short term, however, this effort must begin with a focal point in the form of a corporate officer whose contribution to the strategic decision-making process starts from a CSR perspective. Over time, CSR will become more ingrained throughout the organization. But, initially at least, focused leadership, supported by the CEO, is vital to strengthening the CSR perspective within the organization's culture.

CSR Vision

Equally important for the company's CSR direction is a CSR position statement. Cadbury's CSR vision statement, for example, is displayed prominently on its Web site and in its CSR reports:

> Cadbury Schweppes is committed to growing responsibly. We believe responsible business comes from listening and learning, and having in place a clear CSR vision and strategy. It also comes from having the processes and systems to follow through and an embedded commitment to living our values.[69]

All stakeholders (internal and external) need to understand the firm's CSR position and how that stance affects them. The value of a statement outlining the vision and mission for the organization is part of this awareness process, as detailed in Chapter 2. These same benefits apply to specific aspects of a firm's policies. Most relevant to this discussion is the firm's CSR vision statement:

The CSR Vision Statement

The development of an effective CSR position statement:

- *Engages* the organization's key stakeholders to determine their perspectives
- *Helps* map out a conflict resolution process that seeks mutually beneficial solutions
- *Involves* the CEO's necessary endorsement and active support
- *Reinforces* the importance of CSR through rewards and sanctions
- *Provides* policies on how CSR is to be implemented on a day-to-day basis

Measurement and Rewards

Collectively, top-management support, the creation of a senior executive CSR position, and the elaboration of the firm's CSR vision in a position statement address a critical element in implementing CSR— awareness. Although the intent of CSR may be noble, however, people tend to focus on "what is inspected not expected." Many CSR violations arise from decision makers at different levels of the organization who were sincerely trying to make good decisions for the organization but had not been given the tools or incentives to make the *most appropriate* decision. Faced with a choice between a minor violation of company rules about pollution, for example, or meeting a key performance deadline, a decision maker at any level of the firm might make a tradeoff that results in a CSR backlash. Why? Because, in most firms, rewards (pay, promotions, and bonuses) are based on performance results, not CSR compliance. If an incentive is tied to meeting a goal and CSR is neither measured nor rewarded, reasonable people inside the firm may conclude that CSR is of secondary importance.

Nike's Subcontractors

Third-world subcontractors to Nike must comply with company employment standards that dictate pay, rest breaks, and other terms and working conditions. These standards are enforced by inspections. Those subcontractors who perpetuate sweatshop conditions that are contrary to Nike's requirements risk the penalty of losing their production contracts, even if these firms are in full compliance with local human resource laws and practices.

For a long time, however, Nike's production demands contradicted the employment conditions outlined in its code of conduct for suppliers. It is ineffective to stipulate specific low cost and high production targets, if, at the same time, a firm is asking its suppliers to restrict employee overtime and pay living wages. Given the choice, many suppliers chose to meet Nike's production demands in order to keep their contracts with the firm. Often, this choice was made at the expense of working conditions in their factories.

Once Nike realized the counterproductive effects of this contradiction, however, the firm worked to ensure its incentive scheme for subcontractors more accurately reflected and supported its corporate responsibility goals.[70]

Rewards and measures serve a fundamental role in shaping the organizational culture. The creation of rewards and measures, particularly if those who apply the CSR standards are the same people who develop them, increases awareness of CSR and its profile within the firm. Then, the reporting of CSR measures and assignment of rewards further reinforce CSR as an integral part of the firm's strategy. These measures become part of the basis for auditing the firm's CSR performance.

CSR Audit and Report

A genuine organization-wide CSR audit, with published results, furthers awareness among both internal and external stakeholders about the firm's CSR activities. Environmental audits, for example, are now widely conducted and documented in the annual report because consumers and the public began demanding greater accountability for the environmental consequences of businesses' actions:

> Currently, 81 per cent of FTSE 100 companies [the largest 100 firms in the United Kingdom based on market capitalization] are producing stand-alone reports on corporate responsibility, sustainability, environment or similar. And 56 per cent of companies listed in the FTSE All World Developed Index, representing 77 per cent of its total value, have adopted clear environmental policies.
>
> Those percentages may seem impressive, but the bigger picture is less inspiring. Of the millions of companies operating around the globe, only 2,380 are producing these non-financial reports.[71]

In general, poor countries often put economic needs ahead of environmental controls. That is, poorer countries are more likely to permit firms to externalize environmental, safety, or other costs onto society—a tradeoff made to gain or retain jobs. The poorer a country, the more desperate it is likely to be for jobs and the more willing it may be to allow firms to avoid costs such as pollution cleanup or worker safety. As societies develop and consumer and employee choices increase, however, the willingness to accommodate undesirable behavior decreases. Although many companies recognize the importance of being held publicly accountable for the consequences of operations, this realization does not always permeate the countless tactical decisions made by employees throughout the firm. The result can be lapses in a firm's CSR—the avoidable Exxon Valdez accident in 1989 provides a well-known example, as individual and corporate poor judgment resulted in a shipwreck and massive oil spill in Alaska's pristine waters.[72]

Figure 5.2 suggests the entirety of the CSR auditing process. A firm that wants to be transparent and accountable to all stakeholders should expand the scope of its annual report to incorporate the *triple bottom line,*[73] which measures a company's financial, environmental, and social performance. More and more firms are incorporating a CSR audit and the triple bottom line into their reporting process. Since 1999 in the Netherlands and 2002 in France, for example, an evaluation of social and environmental risks, as related to operations, is legally mandated as part of a company's financial reports.[74]

An example of an effective CSR audit and its implications comes from the Gap. The 2003 launch of Gap's *Social Responsibility Report,*[75] which was well received by NGOs monitoring the industry,[76] shows the extent to which CSR has advanced for apparel companies. Imagine the

| Figure 5.2 | A Broader Perspective: The Triple Bottom Line |

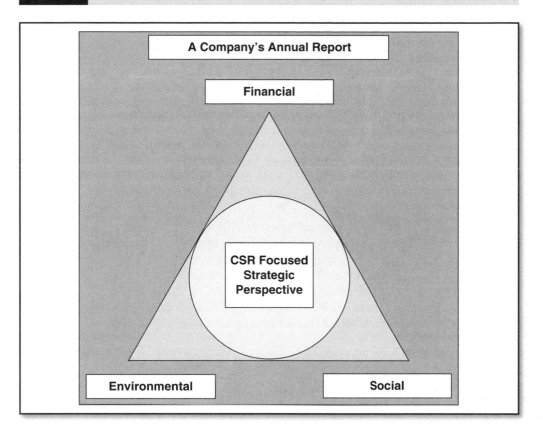

likelihood of strongly enforced, CSR-related human resource policies among Gap's employees and subcontractors if they knew there would be no audit or social responsibility report.

Gap: Social Responsibility Report

Key findings from Gap's first *Social Responsibility Report*:

- 3,000—Number of factories worldwide that contract with Gap
- 8,500—Number of visits by Gap compliance officers to factories
- 90—Percentage of factories that fail initial inspection
- 136—Number of factories with severe enough violations that Gap pulled out[77]

Another good example of a company leading the way in CSR auditing and reports is Shell. Shell was prompted to reanalyze its business practices in 1995 following two separate NGO-orchestrated campaigns that attacked, first, the company's decision to sink the *Brent Spar* oil platform in the ocean and, second, the firm's failure to prevent the execution by the Nigerian government of an environmental activist, Ken Saro-Wiwa, who had been campaigning against Shell's operations in Nigeria. The stakeholder backlash against the company over these two issues threatened its underlying business model.[78] Following the intense international criticism Shell received for its reactions to these two high-profile events, "the company decided it needed to become a better global citizen."[79] One component of the drive to change the corporate culture and increase awareness of CSR at Shell was the *Shell Report:*

> The report has become famous for disclosing Shell's successes and failures in human rights and environmentalism, including oil spills and community protests, as well as the profits and losses of its multibillion-dollar business. . . . "I don't know any American oil company that produces anything as comprehensive and candid about its global social responsibility programs as the Shell Report," said Frank Vogl, co-founder of Transparency International, a European watchdog group that tracks corruption around the world. ". . . there is a tremendous level of sincerity behind what [the company] is trying to do."[80]

Other progressive companies are initiating product life-cycle assessments, using recent innovations to measure the carbon footprint (the total amount of carbon emitted during the life cycle of a product, from production to consumption) for each of their products. Examples include Walkers in the United Kingdom[81] and Pepsi in the United States.[82] The advantages for these firms are clear—in addition to understanding their value chain more completely and highlighting potential CSR transgressions before they read about them in the media, such analyses also identify waste, which carries the potential for cost savings. Such tools, for example,

> helped companies discover that vendors consume as much as 80% of the energy, water, and other resources used by a supply chain, and that they must be a priority in the drive to create sustainable operations.[83]

Another positive step (vital for validity) is to have an audit conducted, or at least verified, by an independent third party in the same way that an independent auditor verifies a company's financial reports.[84] Some form of objective verification lends credence to the information included. The sooner industry standards can be agreed upon and applied, the more meaningful CSR audits and reports will become. As one research study concluded,

> Of the 56 NGOs surveyed . . . . 79 percent find CSR reports "very" or "fairly" useful, but only 44 percent consider the reports "believable." . . . According to the survey, companies can gain credibility for their reports by disclosing poor sustainability performance, or significant challenges, or noncompliance with social or environmental laws or regulations. Other factors that boost confidence in CSR reporting include comprehensive performance metrics, third-party certification, and standardization of reporting.[85]

Organizations such as Ceres (http://www.ceres.org/)[86] and the Global Reporting Initiative (http://www.globalreporting.org/) are leading the push for international standards in the area of CSR and sustainability reporting. The GRI's push for standardization has drawn criticism, however, by those who think some of the context is being lost in the process. Producing a CSR report is one thing; ensuring it is accurate, that it enables external observers to understand the extent of a firm's CSR activities,[87] and that firm performance is comparable across organizations[88] represents another level of transparency altogether.

Code of Conduct

One way to encourage the desired CSR behavior throughout the firm is to record expectations and the boundaries of acceptable behavior in a Code of Conduct. Similar to a vision or mission statement for the firm, a Code of Conduct must by genuine to be meaningful. As the Enron example demonstrated, it is easy to say one thing (the *right* thing), yet do something different:

> By adopting its own code, a company can clarify for all parties, internal and external, the standards that govern its conduct and can thereby convey its commitment to responsible practice wherever it operates.[89]

In addition to a CSR audit and Code of Conduct for their own operations, firms are also increasingly being held to account for the actions of their partners throughout the value chain. The business operations of suppliers, in particular, are a potential risk to a firm, especially when key elements of the production process are outsourced to low-cost business environments. As discussed previously, Nike experienced firsthand the potential for danger to the brand when it ignored unacceptable working conditions in its supply chain.[90] Other firms have also had to respond to accusations (fairly or unfairly) that they are insufficiently aware of the conditions under which their products are being made:

CSR Newsletters: Gap's Supply Chain

A recent article[91] reports on Gap's response to a piece of investigative journalism by the UK newspaper *The Observer*, which uncovered evidence of under-age children making Gap clothes. The story is interesting on two levels. First, the speed and extent of Gap's response, which appears to be genuine:

> Gap said it would refine its procedures to ensure that items made in textile workshops in India were not being produced by children. It also announced a grant of $200,000 to improve working conditions. . . . the children who were found to be embroidering decorations on blouses for toddlers for Gap would be paid until they were of working age and then offered employment.

Second, the extent to which Gap could have (or should have) been expected to avoid this problem. It appears that Gap's vendor had subcontracted the embroidery work to a rural community center that had, in turn, subcontracted the work to a smaller workshop in Delhi:

> While auditing in factories is relatively straightforward, checking conditions in the informal workshops where hand embroidery is done is harder because large contracts are often divided up among dozens of small workshops.

It is one thing for a firm to be held responsible for the business practices of an immediate supplier. It seems to be another thing altogether to expect Gap to know about a subcontractor (a rural community center) that had again contracted out this order to a Delhi factory—three steps removed from the initial order by Gap. The extent to which a firm is responsible for the actions of its suppliers throughout its supply chain (as well as how that responsibility should be enforced) is an issue on which a consensus within the CSR community is yet to arise.

What is unclear from these examples is the extent of a firm's responsibility throughout its supply chain. Should firms be responsible for absolutely everything that occurs in their supplier firms, irrespective of how far removed that action is from any employee of the focal firm? Should Gap, for example, be held responsible for the actions of the subcontractor of the subcontractor of the firm's main subcontractor in India (even though the number of these sub-sub-subcontractors is in the tens of thousands)? What about the factories that process the cotton that is used by Gap's suppliers? What about the farmers who grow the cotton and the numerous hands through which the cotton passes before it even reaches a factory that subcontracts to Gap? This is an evolving area of debate within the CSR community. While it is generally agreed that a firm should be responsible for its immediate suppliers, it is less clear how far responsibility extends beyond this initial relationship. At present, the profile of the brand seems to be the most likely predictor of media exposure in the event of an *issue* in this area, rather than the nature of the supposed offense (see the *CSR threshold*).

CSR Ombudsman

A key component of the continuous internal reinforcement necessary for a CSR policy to remain effective is an anonymous feedback, complaint, or whistle-blowing procedure. This process should be available via a third party or CSR ombudsman. This requirement in the United States was a key component of the Sarbanes-Oxley (SOX) Act of 2002.[92] In relation to business ethics, a notable component of the legislation compelled firms to establish a confidential reporting procedure (e.g., a toll-free telephone number or e-mail helpline) for employees to report ethics transgressions within the organization.[93] As a result, a number of independent companies have emerged offering to provide this service (often online) to firms wishing to contract it out:

> Shareholder.com[94] is typical of online services. Employees of a company that hires Shareholder.com can file their complaints with the . . . firm. The complaints then are forwarded electronically to the appropriate people back at the company—but only after all identifying information is stripped away.[95]

An independent third party performing this job is ideal because it better guarantees the protection of employees' identities, which prevents retaliation from within the organization. The online provision conveys the sense of an additional degree of anonymity. This infrastructure encourages the reporting of any breeches of policy, particularly in terms of ethics compliance, that would affect the company's stated CSR position. It should also encourage positive feedback in the form of ideas from employees, who are often best placed to evaluate the organization's CSR policies in action.

Organizational Structure

In order for all these CSR elements to coalesce into an effective CSR policy that represents stakeholder interests within the strategic decision-making process of the firm, an organizational CSR framework is essential. The CSR effort must have visibility. Ideally, the day-to-day operationalization of CSR demands the direct involvement of top management with board commitment and oversight. Evidence among firms of the growing importance of CSR will be found when the board of directors puts CSR on the same level as other key corporate governance issues, such as the integrity of the firm's financial information. Furthermore, the access of the CSR officer to the CEO, with a direct reporting relationship to the board of directors, suggests further operational support for CSR. The danger is, of course, that many firms will lag in terms of instituting the necessary structural support for CSR. Other firms may well establish structural positions, such as the CSR officer, but then fail to give them the substantive support necessary to do their job.

The Ethics and Compliance Officers Association, for example, estimates that 85% of the Fortune 500 firms have adopted the ethics and compliance officer (ECO) position.[96] Anecdotal evidence has surfaced in the media, however, that many of these positions are considered to be "trendy" and serve mainly as "window dressing,"[97] that ECOs receive insufficient resources to do their jobs effectively,[98] and that

> Many ECOs are set up for failure due to deficient resources, inadequate preparation, or insufficient authority.[99]

Although board-level support is rare and may seem like overkill, especially in otherwise well-run, ethical, and socially responsible firms, tangible visibility for CSR within the organizational structure demonstrates the firm's genuine commitment in ways that mere memos, posters, hollow speeches, or press releases fail to do.

IMPLEMENTATION: MEDIUM TO LONG TERM

Beyond minimum start-up conditions for CSR, the organization must also seek to institutionalize and externalize the substance of its CSR policies. Over the medium to long term, the organization should communicate its perspective, while seeking feedback from stakeholder groups to make them feel both informed and involved.

Stakeholder Involvement

All large, publicly held corporations have well-developed investor relations departments. They have become the norm because of the primacy shareholders have typically enjoyed as a company's main stakeholder, particularly in English-speaking economies. As a company's share price has become the key indicator of corporate and management success, keeping investors happy has become central to a CEO's ability to retain his or her job.

As part of moving CSR to the center of a company's strategic outlook, this two-way avenue of communication should be expanded to include a firm's broader set of stakeholders. One approach would be to change the focus of the investor relations department to become the "stakeholder relations department." Although the scope and skills of these two departments will vary, the expansion of the investor relations department would be a far more substantive move than merely changing the title on the door. The goal should be to develop relationships with all stakeholder interests, including employees, governments, the communities in which the firm operates, and the NGOs that seek to reform the firm's practices:

> NGOs—nongovernmental organizations—have won significant influence over global companies. . . . [It is] a trend that—mostly quietly and behind the scenes—is defining our

age. From companies like the coffee shop giant Starbucks (attacked for the treatment of workers on plantations and the price it pays for coffee), to Big Oil (a perennial target for environmentalists), to tuna canners (think dolphins), companies are increasingly changing their business practices when pressured by activists.[100]

As Paul Tebo, DuPont's corporate vice president for safety, health, and environment and "an advocate for social responsibility," more succinctly put it: "The closer [Dupont] can align with social values . . . the faster we will grow."[101]

Manage the Message

Strategic CSR that is genuine and substantive needs to be communicated to the firm's stakeholders. As such, a firm's PR department is an important medium through which the firm can communicate its CSR progress.[102] But firms need to be careful as this is a sensitive area. Excessive self-promotion soon comes to be interpreted as a cynical effort of going through the CSR motions only to receive the public relations benefits and raises the specter of *greenwash*. Avoiding the impression of spin is crucial; however, it is also essential to let stakeholders know that the company values their input and interests. More important, firms do not want their identity defined by others via the media. The aim, therefore, is to meet stakeholder expectations by matching promises with reality.

Examples of companies that have failed to take the lead in determining the public perception of their organization are many. Often, the perception of a company in the public mind, once created, is difficult to shift. For example, in spite of the company's recent progressive CSR work, Nike's initial failure to anticipate the reaction by its stakeholders to manufacturing offshore in low-cost environments and the failure to work closely with NGOs in this area has tagged it with an image that still prevails in many eyes. As noted at the time by the humorist Dave Barry

In May . . . Nike signs a $90 million endorsement deal with 18-year-old basketball player and Humvee owner LeBron James Incorporated. To pay for this, Nike raises the average price of a pair of its sneakers to $385, which includes $1.52 for materials, and 17 cents for labor.[103]

Go to Nike's corporate Web site[104] today, however, and it soon becomes apparent that the company has redefined the way it conducts its operations in relation to CSR and presents its corporate message to the outside world. Due to its early lapses, however, the company continually finds itself having to play catch-up, with some stakeholders refusing to grant the company any concessions at all.

Corporate Governance[105]

Corporate governance matters and is central to a firm's CSR activities.[106] In a study of 1,500 firms, researchers concluded that "there is a premium associated with good governance."[107] In another study of 3,220 global firms by GovernanceMetrics International, which was designed to evaluate the effectiveness of corporate governance, the 1% of firms that scored best had superior financial returns.[108] The importance of corporate governance has grown in recent years, even leading to the formation of the International Corporate Governance Network (http://icgn.org/) to exchange information about corporate governance and raise governance standards generally.

Transparency and *accountability* have become the watchwords of effective corporate governance, which has also become a vital aspect of effective CSR. Increased legal requirements reinforce this change in sentiment for all but the most narrow-sighted of corporate boards; however, equally important is the ability to move ahead of today's legal requirements and anticipate the legal expectations of tomorrow. Shareholder activism is increasing and is driving reform in this area of corporate law. Ensuring a company's policies and procedures are transparent, that its managers are accountable to the company's owners, and that the process by which these policies are created and board members appointed is democratic are all crucial to ensuring the traditional conflict between principal and agent is minimized.

Corporate governance will increasingly become the target of reforms prompted by insufficient attention to CSR. Following the financial scandals early in this century, where Enron and other firms failed because of unethical practices, Sarbanes-Oxley became law. In short, it places increased reporting requirements on firms, for which firms need to maintain additional records and issue additional reports. And while it was only a few irresponsible firms that caused the scandals, the law was applied to all publicly traded companies. More recently, the 2007–2009 economic crisis revealed new scandals and Ponzi schemes that resulted in a near total collapse of the world financial system. Driven by individual and corporate greed, the result was increased scrutiny of corporate finance and investments.

These two waves of scandals in the first decade of the new century would have been less likely if CSR had been more widely practiced. As such, these waves illustrate the *Iron Law of Social Responsibility* (see Chapter 1)—the result is greater constraints on how corporations are governed.

Corporate Activism

Both The Body Shop and Ben & Jerry's found that activism alone is insufficient to remain viable in the long run. In both cases, the founders were forced to cede operational control to professional managers as their organizations grew in complexity. Activism of any sort, particularly CSR-related efforts, must support an economically viable business strategy. CSR-focused organizations benefit few if they are stuck in bankruptcy court. Economic viability and operating within society's legal parameters are minimum conditions for business survival. Activism does not preserve an operation if basic economical, legal, or other business fundamentals are missing.

That said, however, a sincere CSR focus throughout the firm helps further its viability over the long term by solidifying its relationships with its various stakeholders. Corporate activism matters because in cases like the Gap, Nike, and other lifestyle brands, activism helps align the firm's actions with the values of customers who care. It may also serve as a potential defense, especially in more ambiguous circumstances, such as the Gap's problems with the sub-sub-contractors of its primary subcontractors in India. Beyond customer relations, corporate activism is more likely to win the firm the support of other stakeholders—from employees, local communities, and government agencies. Corporate activism, however, must extend from the boardroom and senior executives, through CSR professionals, throughout the organizational culture.

An overview of the different components of the implementation of CSR throughout an organization is presented in Figure 5.3.[109] Together, these different steps and policies represent a comprehensive plan of action for a firm seeking to implement a CSR perspective.

Figure 5.3	A Firm's CSR Plan of Implementation

Time Frame	Action	Summary
Short to Medium Term	From the Top Down	The CEO must establish the necessary components of an effective CSR policy and ensure that CSR is institutionalized within the firm as a core component of day-to-day operating practice.
	CSR Officer	CSR needs both visibility and sponsorship within the organization. Backing by the CEO equals sponsorship, while the creation of a CSR officer position staffed by a company executive (and with a direct reporting relationship to the board of directors) creates visibility.
	CSR Vision	A CSR vision statement allows stakeholders (internal and external) to understand the firm's CSR position and how that stance affects them.
	Measurement and Rewards	The creation of rewards and measures that align the firm's production and corporate responsibility goals increases awareness of CSR and its profile within the firm.
	CSR Audit and Report	A genuine organization-wide CSR audit, with published results, furthers awareness among both internal and external stakeholders about the firm's CSR activities.
	Code of Conduct	One way to encourage CSR throughout the firm and its supply chain is to record expectations and the boundaries of acceptable behavior in a Code of Conduct for employees and suppliers.
	CSR Ombudsman	A key component of the continuous internal reinforcement necessary for a CSR policy to remain effective is an anonymous whistle-blowing procedure that is available via a CSR ombudsman.
	Organizational Structure	In order for all these CSR elements to coalesce into an effective CSR policy, tangible support for CSR within the organizational structure demonstrates the firm's genuine commitment.
Medium to Long Term	Stakeholder Involvement	As part of moving CSR to the center of a company's strategic outlook, a two-way avenue of communication should be opened with a firm's broader set of stakeholders.
	Manage the Message	Strategic CSR that is genuine and substantive needs to be communicated to the firm's stakeholders via a firm's PR department.
	Corporate Governance	*Transparency* and *accountability* have become the watchwords of effective corporate governance, which has also become a vital aspect of an effective CSR policy.
	Corporate Activism	While no substitute for business fundamentals, corporate activism helps further the firm's viability over the long term by solidifying its relationships with its various stakeholders.

IMPLEMENTATION: BUILDING CSR INTO THE ORGANIZATIONAL CULTURE

The primary CSR responsibility of the CEO is to actively support the integration of CSR into the culture of the firm through the activities of the CSR officer. The CSR officer's role is to hold the company accountable to its own CSR vision. The main method of achieving this is to conduct a substantive annual CSR audit of the company, as well as remain accountable for the actions of the firm's subcontractors. And although few firms have their CSR audit independently verified, such verification may become necessary for firms that have lost credibility because of past actions. The final report, released to all stakeholders (including investors), forms an integral and prominent aspect of the company's triple bottom line annual report, along with information detailing the company's environmental and financial performance. The overall job perspective of the CSR officer is to ensure congruity among the firm's CSR goals and its actions.

Other stakeholders can be expected to hold the organization accountable to the standards it has set for itself—especially when the firm articulates a set of companywide standards, informed from values, such as Johnson & Johnson's credo[110] and Hewlett Packard's HP Way.[111] Emboldened by technology and growing expectations for CSR, stakeholders will grow increasingly assertive in ensuring their best interests are represented. And stakeholder activism may be the final piece of the CSR jigsaw puzzle that pushes CEOs and legislatures past the CSR threshold, ushering in a greater commitment to CSR. The real question is: Will that commitment by firms be proactive or reactive?

From a Strategic Perspective: Planning

Although CSR involves the firm's overall direction and day-to-day activities, its implementation begins with the annual planning process. Most firms sufficiently large and sophisticated to implement a CSR perspective undertake some form of strategic planning, usually on an annual basis. The planning process seeks to identify targeted goals, strategies to attain those goals, and an allocation of financial, human, and other resources in pursuit of those goals.

Typically, long-range planning and goal setting begin early in the calendar (or fiscal) year of the firm. *Long range,* however, has vastly different meanings from one industry to another. For electricity utilities, for example, the planning horizon might stretch 10, 15, or more years into the future (given the complexity of estimating future electricity demand; designing, permitting, and building a base-load power plant; and connecting long distribution lines from facilities to users, with often contentious regulatory and hearing requirements coupled with a not-in-my-backyard mentality). In a consumer products firm, however, the long term might be measured in months, from idea to product introduction and obsolescence. A firm like Zara, the Spanish clothes retailer, for example, has constructed an efficient value chain that allows them to move from design to production to display "in as little as two weeks."[112] Their production cycle is significantly faster than the industry average of several "months to bring new merchandise to market"[113] and has led to the invention of a new term, "Fast Fashion."[114]

Nevertheless, the goal of long-range planning is to agree on the future objectives the firm will seek. In turn, business goals (growth rates, market share, and the like) must be translated into realizable objectives for each business unit and within these units for operating and support groups—from production to finance to human resource departments. Broad, overarching goals form the basis for specific strategies. An example in terms of CSR might include the goal of being the most widely admired firm in the industry because of the firm's CSR profile. Although such a goal might not lead to immediate financial gains, it may be indispensable to hiring hard-to-find employees with unique skills. In fact, the ability to hire and retain key players may be a necessity for survival (especially as the huge baby boomer generation retires and is replaced in the workplace by the Millennials or Generation Y), further justifying the allocation of time and resources toward socially responsible goals.

Long-term goals and their strategies for attainment must then be translated into more specific, short-term objectives. Ideally, short-term objectives are SMART, that is, Specific, Measurable, Attainable, Relevant, and Time-bound. Then, the resources necessary to implement these objectives are allocated. The unifying approach to the allocation of resources to future objectives is the budgeting process. Usually done near the end of the fiscal or calendar year, the budgeting process allocates money and resources (and, through salaries and capital budgets, people and investments) for the upcoming year.

Because this approach traditionally focuses on business investments selected on some objective basis (such as the payback period or return on investment), hard-to-measure objectives such as social responsibility may fail to register. And because most firms seek multiple objectives, the relative importance of goals must be weighed by a correspondingly appropriate allocation of resources and rewards. CSR can fall through the cracks without an appropriate mandate from senior management or the board of directors and a dedicated CSR officer.

The ease with which CSR can be overlooked in this planning process, therefore, only further emphasizes the importance of adopting a methodical approach to ensuring uniform implementation throughout the organization. The integration of CSR within the strategic decision-making process and organizational culture along the lines outlined in this chapter goes a long way to ensuring CSR achieves the position of prominence within the organization that is increasingly necessary in today's global business environment.

From a Firm Perspective: Action

At the firm level, CSR plans are meaningless unless they are translated into action. Public relations releases to the media, speeches to employees or trade groups, or assertions of CSR in annual reports are not the end goal of CSR. Necessary as these activities may be to raise awareness about CSR within the firm and the firm's broader stakeholder environment, CSR must be operationally integrated into the firm's day-to-day activities. For CSR to become integrated in this way requires a CSR filter to be applied to the vision, mission, strategy, and tactics of the firm (see Figure 4.1). Granted, in a capitalist system, for-profit firms face an absolute economic imperative. Businesses do not exist merely to be nice to constituents; they exist to meet needs in society, and this value is demonstrated via the profit the firm is able to generate. Increasingly, however, these societal needs include expectations beyond profit maximization. Ultimately, the viability of the firm—its ability to grow, make shareholders wealthy, and meet the needs of customers and other stakeholders—presupposes both an external and internal environment that is conducive to success.

With the primacy of economics, however, other components of the firm's activities can easily be relegated to a distant concern. The result may be a hostile environment that impairs the firm's economic performance, even its long-term viability. A CSR perspective, integrated throughout the organization, offers an alternative business approach, one that is more likely to provide the long-term stability companies require. To achieve this, however, top-management support, a dedicated CSR officer (at least until CSR is fully integrated into the processes and culture of the firm), a well-defined CSR position statement, awareness built through measurements and rewards, a CSR audit and public report to relevant stakeholders, a code of conduct for employees and suppliers, an internal or external ombudsman, and a structure that institutionalizes these elements are merely a beginning. Ideally, stakeholder involvement will include all affected constituencies to as great a degree as possible. Inclusion is more than just an attempt to co-opt relevant constituents. Whether internal or external, inclusion means giving stakeholders a voice and requires leaders that are both receptive and proactive to stakeholder concerns. Admittedly, the message must be managed, if for no other reason than to assure the firm's efforts are communicated and recognized. How else can stakeholders react and become involved in the process? With transparency and corporate activism added to the mix, a firm has the basic ingredients for the successful integration of a CSR perspective throughout operations.

The ultimate test of a firm's CSR, therefore, is its actions. And for those actions to rise above mere window dressing,[115] CSR must form part of the firm's larger strategic plan. Here, concern must focus not only on the results, but also on the methods used. This focus must also be recalibrated to accommodate, as much as possible, the differing perspectives of the relevant constituents that the firm touches. Initially, both short- and long-term objectives are translated into action through the planning process. Then, plans are converted into budgets, which directly allocate financial and other resources. The way these actions are received by those most affected by them indicates the success of the process by which the socially responsible organization matches plans and intentions to actions and results.

The varied stakeholder issues that define CSR are the focus of Part II of *Strategic CSR*. Taking advantage of the Internet, which is reshaping the role of CSR within the competitive business landscape, current CSR issues are identified and discussed. Throughout, relevant Web sites provide both the specifics and implications of these issues, as well as forming jumping-off points to deeper individual research and investigation.

Questions for Discussion and Review

1. What is meant by the phrase "CSR as brand insurance?" Can you think of a firm that has benefited from CSR in this way?

2. Why do some firms, industries, and cultures have different CSR thresholds than others? Illustrate your answer with examples for all three categories.

3. What role do stakeholders play in establishing the level of the CSR threshold for a particular firm or within a particular industry? Think of an example firm and/or industry; what event do you think would push that firm or industry over its CSR threshold?

4. Why is top-management support for CSR so critical? Can CSR be delegated? If so, why and to whom?

5. List four of the eight components of a firm's plan of action necessary to implement CSR over the short to medium term. What examples from business can you think of where firms have performed these actions successfully?

6. How does a firm avoid the perception that its CSR report is *greenwash*? Does it matter whether the reasons behind an action are genuine or cynical if the outcome is the same?

7. Use Figure 5.3 to develop a CSR plan for a firm of your choice. Then, evaluate the firm against your plan. How is the firm doing in terms of implementing CSR? How could it improve?

NOTES AND REFERENCES

1. David Grayson & Adrian Hodges, *Corporate Social Opportunity! Seven Steps to Make Corporate Social Responsibility Work for Your Business*, Greenleaf Publications, 2004, http://www.greenleaf-publishing.com/productdetail.kmod?productid=63

2. William B. Werther & David Chandler, "Strategic Corporate Social Responsibility as Global Brand Insurance," *Business Horizons*, Vol. 48, No. 4, July 2005, pp. 317–324.

3. David Grayson & Adrian Hodges, *Corporate Social Opportunity! Seven Steps to Make Corporate Social Responsibility Work for Your Business*, Greenleaf Publications, 2004, http://www.greenleaf-publishing.com/productdetail.kmod?productid=63

4. Nicholas Casey, "New Nike Sneaker Targets Jocks, Greens, Wall Street," *Wall Street Journal*, February 15, 2008, p. B1, http://online.wsj.com/article/SB120303911940170393.html

5. Alan Beattie, "Spend, Spend, Spend. Save, Save, Save," *Financial Times*, January 27, 2007, p. 18, http://www.ft.com/cms/s/e96ffa6e-aaa6-11db-b5db-0000779e2340.html and Marc Gunther, "Better (Red) Than Dead," *CSRWire*, August 5, 2008, http://greenbiz.com/blog/2008/08/03/better-red-dead

6. Lisa Roner, "Anheuser-Busch Reports Recycling 97% of Solid Waste," *Ethical Corporation Magazine,* June 21, 2004, http://www.ethicalcorp.com/content.asp?ContentID=2228

7. http://www.timberland.com/corp/index.jsp?page=csr_civic_engagement

8. For more details on this program, see "Employee Relations" Issue in Chapter 6.

9. William Werther & David Chandler, "Strategic Corporate Social Responsibility as Global Brand Insurance," *Business Horizons,* Vol. 48, No. 4, 2005. pp. 317–324.

10. Jonathan Birchall, "Business Fights for Tougher Rules on Emissions," *Financial Times*, November 20, 2008, p. 4.

11. Stephanie Strom, "Wal-Mart Donates $35 Million for Conservation and Will Be Partner With Wildlife Group," *New York Times,* April 13, 2005, p. A16.

12. Malcolm Gladwell, *The Tipping Point: How Little Things Can Make a Big Difference*, Back Bay Books, 2002.

13. Although there are disagreements as to which categorization best fits different business models, what all these firms have in common is that their strategies seek to provide their customers with superior value.

14. In drawing these distinctions among firms, it is important to stress that the distinction between low cost and differentiation and between broad and narrow refers to a firm's *business-level* strategies. As such, it is possible for a firm to have different strategies across its different business units. Apple's range of computers, for example, (for which the firm willingly exchanges high margins for continued low market share), targets a narrow segment of the total computer market, while its i-Pods and other consumer electronic devices (such as the i-Phone) have a broader scope.

15. In July 2008, ExxonMobil announced the largest ever quarterly profit for a publicly traded U.S. company: "The company's income for the second quarter rose 14 percent, to $11.68 billion, compared to the same period a year ago. That beat the previous record of $11.66 billion set by Exxon in the last three months of 2007. Exxon's profits were nearly $90,000 a minute over the quarter, . . . (The company calculates that it pays $274,000 a minute in taxes and spends $884,000 a minute to run the business.)." Clifford Krauss, "Exxon's Second-Quarter Earnings Set a Record," *New York Times*, August 1, 2008, http://www.nytimes.com/2008/08/01/business/01oil.html

16. Paula Dwyer, "Breach of Trust," *BusinessWeek,* December 15, 2003, pp. 98–108.

17. Jesse Eisinger, "Year of the (Shrugged Off) Scandal," *Wall Street Journal,* January 2, 2004, p. R3.

18. Strategic Insight, a New York fund–research firm, in "Mutual Funds," *BusinessWeek,* December 8, 2003, p. 116.

19. Mallen Baker, "Financial Services: Will Banks Ever Treat Customers Fairly?" *Ethical Corporation*, April 1, 2008, http://www.ethicalcorp.com/content.asp?ContentID=5807

20. Ibid.

21. Richard Gibson, "McDonald's Seeks Ways to Pitch Healthy Living," *Wall Street Journal,* May 27, 2004, p. D7.

22. http://www.philipmorrisusa.com/en/cms/Products/Cigarettes/Health_Issues/default.aspx

23. http://archive.greenpeace.org/comms/brent/brent.html and http://archive.greenpeace.org/comms/ken/

24. "Who Benefits From GM Crops? An Analysis of the Global Performance of GM Crops (1996–2006)," Friends of the Earth, January 2007, http://www.foei.org/en/publications/pdfs/gmcrops2007execsummary.pdf; "Monsanto Moves to Force-Feed Europe Genetically Engineered Corn," Friends of the Earth, January 10, 2006, http://www.organicconsumers.org/ge/europecorn011106.cfm

25. Lisa Roner, "Starbucks and Oxfam Team Up on Ethiopian Development Programme," *Ethical Corporation Magazine,* October 18, 2004, http://www.ethicalcorp.com/content.asp?ContentID=2961; and Alison Maitland, "Starbucks Tastes Oxfam's Brew," *Financial Times* (U.S. Edition), October 14, 2004, p. 9.

26. See Andrew Wilson, "CSR in Emerging Economies: Lessons From the Davos Philanthropic Roundtable," January 31, 2008, http://www.eurasia.org/documents/davosoped.pdf; "First Study on Corporate Saudi Arabia and CSR," *CSRWire.com*, March 29, 2007, http://www.csrwire.com/press/press_release/15949-First-Study-on-Corporate-Saudi-Arabia-and-CSR

27. C. K. Prahalad, *The Fortune at the Bottom of the Pyramid: Eradicating Poverty Through Profits,* Wharton School Publishing, 2006; C. K. Prahalad & Allen Hammond, "Serving the World's Poor, Profitably," *Harvard Business Review,* September 2002, Vol. 80, No. 9, pp. 48–58.

28. Also see Michael Hopkins, *Corporate Social Responsibility and International Development: Is Business the Solution?* Earthscan, 2007.

29. William Baue, "Corporate Social and Environmental Performance Varies Widely Across Far-East Asia," *Social Funds,* March 19, 2004, http://www.socialfunds.com/news/article.cgi/1372.html

30. http://www.transparency.org/policy_research/surveys_indices/cpi

31. http://www.transparency.org/news_room/latest_news/press_releases/2008/2008_09_23_cpi_2008_en

32. Ibid.

33. "The 2005 State of Corporate Citizenship," May 2005, http://www.bcccc.net/index.cfm?fuseaction=Page.viewPage&pageId=694&node%20ID%20=1&parentID=473

34. Ibid.

35. http://www.nikeresponsibility.com/

36. http://www.starbucks.com/aboutus/csr.asp

37. http://www.ford.com/about-ford/company-information/corporate-sustainability

38. http://www.microsoft.com/about/corporatecitizenship/

39. http://www.timberland.com/corp/index.jsp?page=csr_civic_engagement

40. http://www.nikebiz.com/responsibility/cr_governance.html

41. "Just Good Business: A Special Report on Corporate Social Responsibility," *The Economist*, January 19, 2008, p. 4.

42. http://www.accountability21.net/

43. Simon Zadek, "The Path to Corporate Responsibility," *Harvard Business Review*, December 2004, pp. 125–132.

44. Ibid.

45. The Ethics and Compliance Officer Association in the United States (http://www.theecoa.org/) believes the CEO acronym should also stand for "chief ethics officer."

46. Patrick M. Lencioni, "Make Your Values Mean Something," *Harvard Business Review,* Vol. 80, No. 7, July 2002, pp. 113–117.

47. For example, "In 2000, Enron received six environmental awards. It had progressive policies on climate change, human rights, and anti-corruption" (David Gebler, "Culture of Compliance," *CRO Magazine*, http://www.thecro.com/node/68).

48. Memorandum from Kenneth Lay to All Employees, Subject: Code of Ethics, July 1, 2000.

49. Enron Corp's Code of Ethics, p. 5.

50. Ibid, p. 12.

51. John Kay, "Weasel Words Have the Teeth to Kill Great Ventures," *Financial Times*, January 14, 2009, p. 9.

52. Derrick Daye & Brad VanAuken, "Social Responsibility: The Nike Story," July 25, 2008, http://www.brandingstrategyinsider.com/2008/07/social-responsi.html

53. A quote from Mark Goyder, "Redefining CSR: From the Rhetoric of Accountability to the Reality of Earning Trust," in Mallen Baker, "'Redefining CSR' report by Tomorrow's Company," *Ethical Corporation Magazine*, August 1, 2003, http://www.ethicalcorp.com/content.asp?ContentID=900. The full report by Goyder can be accessed at: http://www.tomorrowscompany.com/uploads/Redef_CSRintro.pdf

54. The title of this position will vary considerably across firms and including corporate responsibility officers, sustainability officers, and ethics and compliance officers. The important point is that a position is created and that it has the substantive support of the CEO.

55. Daniel Franklin, "'The Year of Unsustainability,' The World in 2009," *The Economist*, November 19, 2008, p. 20, http://www.economist.com/theworldin/displayStory.cfm?story_id=12494427&d=2009

56. "What Does It Mean to Be VP of CSR? A Conversation with Sandra Taylor of Starbucks," *Business Ethics Magazine,* Summer 2004, p. 4.

57. Lisa Roner, "Ethics Cited in Choice of New Nike Chief Executive," *Ethical Corporation Magazine,* November 24, 2004, http://www.ethicalcorp.com/content.asp?ContentID=3248

58. "Nike Names New VP of Corporate Responsibility," Nike press release, October 20, 2004, http://www.csrwire.com/News/3154.html

59. http://www.iso.org/iso/management_standards.htm

60. http://www.iso.org/sr

61. Aaron Chatterji & David Levine, "Breaking Down the Wall of Codes: Evaluating Non-financial Performance Measurement," *California Management Review*, Vol. 48, No. 2, 2006, p. 35.

62. Charles J. Fombrun, "List of Lists: A Compilation of International Corporate Reputation Ratings," *Corporate Reputation Review*, Vol. 10, No. 2, 2007, pp. 144–153.

63. Aaron Chatterji & David Levine, "Breaking Down the Wall of Codes: Evaluating Non-financial Performance Measurement," *California Management Review*, Vol. 48, Issue 2, 2006, p. 29.

64. http://money.cnn.com/magazines/fortune/mostadmired/2008/index.html

65. http://www.thecro.com/node/615

66. http://www.globalreporting.org/

67. http://www.kld.com/

68. Mallen Baker, "Corporate Social Responsibility: When the Competent Become the Enemy of the Good," *Ethical Corporation*, February 25, 2008, http://www.ethicalcorp.com/content.asp?ContentID=5735

69. Cadbury Schweppes CSR Report 2006, http://www.cadbury.com/SiteCollectionDocuments/2006CorporateSocialResponsibilityReport.pdf

70. See Simon Zadek, "The Path to Corporate Responsibility," *Harvard Business Review*, December 2004, pp. 125–132, for a detailed discussion of how Nike aligned its incentive scheme for subcontractors with its corporate responsibility goals..

71. Rikki Stancich, "Recession Ethics: CSR in a Downturn—Recession-proof Ethics Can Weather the Storm," *Ethical Corporation Magazine*, March 5, 2008, http://www.ethicalcorp.com/content.asp?ContentID=5751

72. The National Oceanic and Atmospheric Administration's Web site provides details of the *Exxon Valdez* oil spill at http://response.restoration.noaa.gov/spotlight/spotlight.html and images from the event at http://response.restoration.noaa.gov/photos/exxon/exxon.html. Another authoritative Web site is administered by the Exxon Valdez Oil Spill Trustee Council at http://www.evostc.state.ak.us/

73. The phrase *triple bottom line* was first introduced in 1994 by John Elkington of SustainAbility (http://www.sustainability.com/) "to describe social, environmental, and financial accounting." The term was used in conjunction with the launch of SustainAbility's "first survey benchmarking non-financial reporting." William Baue, "Sustainability Reporting Improves, but Falls Short on Linking to Financial Performance," *Social Funds*, November 5, 2004, http://www.socialfunds.com/news/article.cgi/article1565.html

74. Deborah Doane, "Mandated Risk Reporting Begins in UK," *Business Ethics Magazine,* Spring 2005, p. 13.

75. Gap Inc., Social responsibility report, http://ccbn.mobular.net/ccbn/7/645/696/index.html

76. Matthew Gitsham, "Book and Publication Reviews: Gap's 2003 Social Responsibility Report," *Ethical Corporation Magazine,* June 21, 2004, http://www.ethicalcorp.com/content.asp?ContentID=2231

77. Amy Merrick, "In Candid Report, Gap Details Violations in Its Factories," *Wall Street Journal,* May 12, 2004, p. A9.

78. Elizabeth Becker, "At Shell, Grades for Citizenship," *New York Times,* November 30, 2003, Section 3, p. 2.

79. Ibid.

80. Ibid.

81. http://www.walkerscarbonfootprint.co.uk/

82. See Andrew Martin, "How Green Is My Orange?" *New York Times*, January 21, 2009, http://www.nytimes.com/2009/01/22/business/22pepsi.html

83. Ram Nidumolu, C. K. Prahalad, & M.R. Rangaswami, "Why Sustainability Is Now the Key Driver of Innovation," *Harvard Business Review*, September 2009, p. 59.

84. Verité (http://www.verite.org/) is a good example of a firm that provides this verification service: "At Verité, we are committed to ensuring that people worldwide work under safe, fair and legal conditions. In over 60 countries around the world we provide governments, corporations, investors, factories, NGOs and workers with information on global working conditions and innovative programs to improve them."

85. William Baue, "Survey Says: NGOs Believe Corporate Social Responsibility Reports That Reveal Faults," *Social Funds,* November 14, 2003, http://www.socialfunds.com/news/article.cgi/1268.html

86. For example, see Eric Marx, "Ceres—Serious About reporting," *Ethical Corporation*, June 12, 2009, http://www.ethicalcorp.com/content.asp?ContentID=6499

87. Mark Goyder, "Redefining CSR: From the Rhetoric of Accountability to the Reality of Earning Trust," *Tomorrow's Company*, 2003, http://www.tomorrowscompany.com/uploads/Redef_CSRintro.pdf; Mallen Baker, "'Redefining CSR' report by Tomorrow's Company," *Ethical Corporation Magazine*, August 1, 2003, http://www.ethicalcorp.com/content.asp?ContentID=900

88. Jon Entine, "Reporting Contradictions," *Ethical Corporation*, June 7, 2009, http://www.ethicalcorp.com/content.asp?ContentID=6492

89. Lynn Paine, Rohit Deshpandé, Joshua D. Margolis, & Kim Eric Bettcher, "Up to Code: Does Your Company's Conduct Meet World-Class Standards?" *Harvard Business Review*, December 2005, p. 123.

90. Debora L. Spar, "Hitting the Wall: Nike and International Labor Practices," *Harvard Business School Press* [9-700-047], September 6, 2002.

91. Amelia Gentleman, "Gap Vows to Combat Child Labor at Suppliers," *New York Times*, November 16, 2007, p. 6, http://www.nytimes.com/2007/11/16/business/worldbusiness/16gap.html

92. Also in 2002, both the NYSE and NASDAQ altered their listing requirements, compelling firms listed on the exchange to adopt and disclose both corporate governance guidelines and a code of business conduct and ethics for all employees, following SEC approval of standards for such reports.

93. Section 301.4b (2002: 776), http://www.404.gov/about/laws/soa2002.pdf

94. http://www.shareholder.com/. Another company providing a similar service is EthicsPoint Inc. (http://www.ethicspoint.com/), where "about 78% of the complaints channeled through [the company] had arrived via the Web," Phyllis Plitch, "Making It Easier to Complain," in the supplement, Corporate Governance: The Journal Report, *Wall Street Journal,* June 21, 2004, p. R6.

95. Ibid.

96. Personal correspondence with authors.

97. Hannah Clark, "Chief Ethics Officers: Who Needs Them?" *Forbes Magazine*, October 23, 2006, http://www.forbes.com/2006/10/23/leadership-ethics-hp-lead-govern-cx_hc_1023ethics.html

98. Lisa Roner, "Ethics Officers—Positions That Need Power," *Ethical Corporate Magazine*, October 4, 2007, http://www.ethicalcorp.com/content.asp?ContentID=5411

99. "Leading Corporate Integrity: Defining the Role of the Chief Ethics & Compliance Officer (CECO)," *Ethics Resource Center*, 2007, http://www.ethics.org/resource/ceco

100. Michael Elliott, "Embracing the Enemy Is Good Business," *Time,* August 13, 2001, p. 29.

101. Marc Gunther, "Tree Huggers, Soy Lovers, and Profits," *Fortune,* June 23, 2003, pp. 98–104.

102. For a useful list of dos and don'ts in relation to green marketing, see "How to Look Good Green," *Ethical Corp*, January 21, 2009, http://www.ethicalcorp.com/content.asp?ContentID=6298

103. Dave Barry, "2003: A Dave Odyssey," *Miami Herald,* December 28, 2003, pp. 1M, 5M–7M.

104. http://www.nikebiz.com/

105. See the "Corporate Governance" Issue in Chapter 6.

106. Michael Hopkins, *The Planetary Bargain: Corporate Social Responsibility Matters*, Earthscan, 2003.

107. Paul J. Lim, "Gauging That Other Company Asset: Its Reputation," *New York Times,* April 10, 2004, p. A18.

108. Ibid.

109. For additional ideas regarding a comprehensive plan of implementation, it might also be helpful to read: Susan Graff, "Six Steps to Sustainability," *CRO Magazine*, June 2007, http://www.thecro.com/node/520

110. See "Our Credo Values," http://www.jnj.com/connect/about-jnj/jnj-credo/

111. See: "HP Corporate Objectives and Shared Values," http://www.hp.com/hpinfo/abouthp/corpobj.html and "The HP Way," http://www.hpalumni.org/hp_way.htm

112. Kerry Capell, "Zara's Fast Track to Fashion," *BusinessWeek*, June 2008, http://images.businessweek.com/ss/06/08/zara/index_01.htm

113. Ibid.

114. Andrew McAfee, Anders Sjoman, & Vincent Dessain, "Zara: IT for Fast Fashion," *Harvard Business School Press* [9-604-081], September 6, 2007; "Store Wars: Fast Fashion," *BBC News*, June 9, 2004, http://news.bbc.co.uk/2/hi/business/3086669.stm

115. Hannah Clark, "Chief Ethics Officers: Who Needs Them?" *Forbes Magazine*, October 23, 2006, http://www.forbes.com/2006/10/23/leadership-ethics-hp-lead-govern-cx_hc_1023ethics.html

Part II

CSR

Issues and Case Studies

Part II reveals the unique nature of *Strategic Corporate Social Responsibility*. Chapters 6, 7, and 8 explore the breadth and depth of corporate social responsibility (CSR) through 24 issues and case studies, each of which serves as a practical introduction to a broader component of the CSR debate. Collectively, these issues and case studies form a basis for discussion and explanation that is enriched by online resources for further investigation.

The case studies in Part II represent issues that range from corporate governance and accountability to product safety and economic crisis; from environmental sustainability and fair trade to microfinance and religion. They represent a selection of some of the many issues that firms need to anticipate and react to every day. As such, they illustrate the direct impact of CSR on corporate behavior and strategic planning—decisions and actions that are made in a complex, ever-evolving economic and social operating environment. A glimpse of this complexity is revealed by the World Clock.

World Clock

To get a sense of the complex economic and social context within which firms make decisions, consider the World Clock:

http://www.peterrussell.com/Odds/WorldClock.php

Most clocks are happy just to tell us what time it is. But there are different ways of showing elapsed time, and they are not all chronological. This Web site, which

(Continued)

(Continued)

keeps track of nearly every measurement of human progression, is a prime example. If you're a student of statistics, you will have your fill, from the number of traffic accidents since the beginning of [the year], to the number of marriages or divorces for the same period. What makes this site so interesting is that you can see it change before your eyes. Some figures, such as the world population, are in a state of constant change, while others show a much slower increase. Other categories include the number of barrels of oil pumped, cars and computers produced, and the variable temperature of the earth shown in billionths of a degree. If you wish to break down the information into shorter periods, you can view the figures broken down monthly, weekly, daily, and even now (where the counts will start from the moment you click on it).[1]

The CSR issues presented in Part II can benefit or detract from the bottom line. They shape stakeholder relationships with the firm via perceptions of the corporate brand, product, or behavior. For firms, the cumulative effect of these issues directly influences their chances of survival and, as such, they cannot be avoided by any organization that aims to be successful over the medium to long term.

To grasp the spectrum of CSR issues that affect corporate behavior, consider Figure II.1. We use this model to classify broadly the 24 issues of Part II into the three stakeholder groups that we initially presented in Chapter 2: Chapter 6 contains issues and case studies primarily involving organizational stakeholders; Chapter 7, economic stakeholders; and Chapter 8, societal stakeholders.

Chapter 6: Organizational Stakeholders. First, stakeholders exist within the organization. Examples of organizational stakeholders include shareholders, employees, and managers. Taken together, these internal stakeholders constitute the organization as a whole and, therefore, should be its primary concern. In this chapter, the business functions and practices that affect organizational stakeholders are presented from a CSR perspective.

Chapter 7: Economic Stakeholders. Second are economic stakeholders, examples of which include consumers, creditors, and competitors. The interactions that these stakeholders have with the firm are driven primarily by economic concerns. As such, these stakeholders fulfill an important role as the interface between the organization and its larger social environment. The issues in this section not only affect the financial/economic aspects of the organization, but also create bonds of accountability between the firm and its operating context.

Chapter 8: Societal Stakeholders. Third are those stakeholders that constitute the broader business and social environment in which the firm operates. Examples of societal stakeholders include government agencies and regulators, communities, and the environment itself. These societal stakeholders are essential for the organization in terms of providing the legitimacy necessary for it to survive over the medium to long term. Without the general consensus that it is *valued* by its broader society, no organization can expect to survive indefinitely.

Globalization and Technology. Finally, the twin forces of globalization and technology frame this bull's-eye model of concentric circles. A central argument of *Strategic CSR* is that the

Figure II.1   A Stakeholder Model

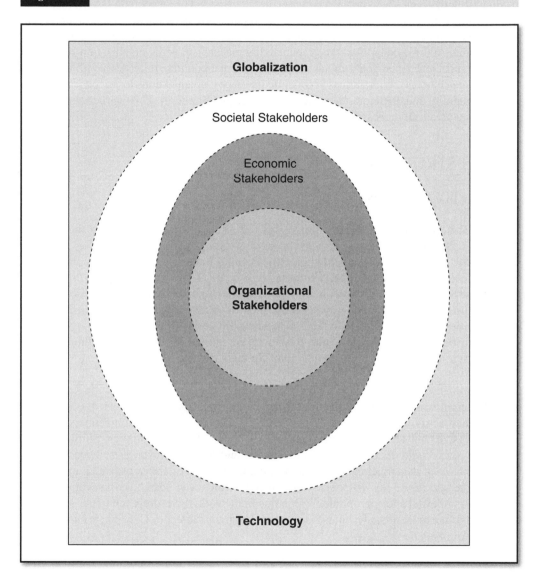

emergence of these two forces in recent years has changed the rules of the game for corporations—they have led directly to a shift in control over the free flow of information from firms to their stakeholders (see Chapter 4). As such, these two forces provide the overall context within which CSR and stakeholder theory have become essential components of the strategic and operating business environment for corporations today.

This model is not limited to for-profit organizations and can be applied equally to governments and nonprofits. Economic stakeholders, for example, serve as the accountability interface between any organization and the society within which it operates. Among businesses, the accountability mechanism is profit and loss—if a company fails to make a profit over the medium to long term, it will be unable to remain in business. For democratic governments, the accountability mechanism is twofold—it is a combination of campaign contributions that finance the democratic process and the support of individual voters (taxpayers) that determine the outcome. And for nonprofits, the accountability mechanism is the organization's ability to generate sufficient operational funds by justifying its continued existence to economic stakeholders (funders). Without these economic interfaces, organizations lose their mechanism of accountability and, therefore, their legitimacy over the long term. This is true regardless of whether the organization is a business, government, or nonprofit.

PART II STRUCTURE

Each issue in the three chapters of Part II is divided into five sections:

- **CSR Connection:** A brief summary of the issue and its relevance to the broader CSR debate.
- **Issue:** A detailed discussion that identifies central issues and recent developments that make it a current topic of CSR interest.
- **Case Study:** An illustration of the issue via a real-life context and corporate action or reaction.
- **Online Resources:** Links to the Web sites of organizations and other information sources that relate directly to the issue and case study.
- **Questions for Discussion and Review:** Five questions that provide guidance for further investigation and a starting point for class discussion.

As demonstrated in Part I of *Strategic CSR*, CSR is a multifaceted, dynamic subject. As such, the eight *issues* for each of the three stakeholder groups presented in Part II (24 in total) are designed as introductions to a variety of CSR-related topics and are not intended to be comprehensive analyses of the subjects covered, many of which are complex. Similarly, each supporting *case study* is intended to be illustrative and does not cover every aspect of each issue within each demarcation. With this in mind, the *online resources* provided are there to support the *questions for discussion and review,* which can lead to whatever depth of discovery is relevant and appropriate. Within this framework, therefore, each issue is designed as a stand-alone topic of study, but is also part of the larger subject of CSR that is summarized in the *CSR connection.*

ISSUES AND CASE STUDIES

The issues selected for inclusion in Part II illustrate CSR's practical and wide-reaching effects. As topical as today's newspaper headlines, they form the basis for active discussion and further inquiry using the online resources provided. Many of the issues are broad, stretching across organizational, economic, and societal boundaries. As such, our goal here is to classify each issue in terms of its primary impact. Separately, these issues and case studies are key elements of the contemporary CSR debate. Together, however, they represent the depth, breadth, and importance of CSR for firms today:

ORGANIZATIONAL ISSUES

Issues

Corporate charters
Corporate governance
Employee relations
Executive compensation
Shareholder activism
Social entrepreneurship
The corporation
Wages

Case Studies

Federalization
Split CEO/Chair
Timberland
Stock Options
SRI Funds
The Body Shop
Primark vs. Marks & Spencer
McDonald's

ECONOMIC ISSUES

Issues

Fair trade
Finance
Financial crisis
Microfinance
Patents
Product safety
Profit
Supply chain

Case Studies

Starbucks
Citigroup
Countrywide
Grameen Bank
AIDs
Monsanto
One Laptop Per Child (OLPC)
Nike

SOCIETAL ISSUES

Issues

Accountability
Compliance
Environmental sustainability
Ethics
Media
Nongovernmental organizations (NGOs)
Religion
Stakeholder Relations

Case Studies

ISO 26000
Paper vs. Plastic
e-waste
Ethics and Compliance Officers
CNN
Product (RED)
Islamic Finance
Ben & Jerry's

CHAPTER 6

ORGANIZATIONAL ISSUES AND CASE STUDIES

CORPORATE CHARTERS

 CSR CONNECTION: This issue analyzes a company's *public purpose*— its responsibilities and obligations as determined by corporate law and founding charters.

Issue

What responsibilities and obligations do corporations have, as determined by their founding charters?

The corporation, as created by law, compels executives to prioritize the interests of their companies and shareholders above all others. The law forbids any other motivations for company actions, whether to assist workers, improve the environment, or help consumers save money. Corporate social responsibility is thus illegal—at least when it is genuine.[2]

This shareholder perspective was enshrined in the United States in a Michigan Supreme Court case, *Dodge v. Ford Motor Company*,[3] in which two brothers, John Francis Dodge and Horace Elgin Dodge (who, together, owned 10% of Ford's shares), sued Henry Ford because of his decision to distribute surplus profit to customers in the form of lower prices for his cars, rather than to shareholders in the form of a dividend. In deciding in the Dodge brothers' favor, the judge in the case

reinstated the dividend and rebuked Ford—who had said in open court that "business is a service, not a bonanza" and that corporations should be run only "incidentally to make money"—for forgetting that "a business corporation is organized and carried on primarily for the profit of the stockholders"; it could not be run "for the merely incidental benefit of shareholders and for the primary purpose of benefiting others." *Dodge v. Ford* still stands for the legal principle that managers and directors have a legal duty to put shareholders' interests above all others and no legal authority to serve any other interests—what has come to be known as "the best interests of the corporation" principle.[4]

This approach of shareholder supremacy, however, is not written in stone but has evolved over time in accordance with the values we choose to espouse as a society. Today, courts give corporate leaders greater flexibility to meet shareholders' expectations. Ironically, *public purpose* was once required. The legislation that removed the public purpose provision of a corporation's charter (or its articles of incorporation) was designed to root out the corruption that had become inherent in the political power to award charters:

> The earliest, recognisably modern business corporation was the famous—or infamous— East India Company. Chartered on 31 December, 1600, its public purpose—"the advancement of trade"—was in fact nothing more glorious than the making of money for its proprietors.[5]

In working to treat "the corporation as simply another business form, available to all—just as a partnership or an unincorporated company" in the United States in the first half of the 19th century, President Andrew Jackson deliberately eliminated

> determinations of a "public purpose" that warranted granting special privileges to a particular business organization. Theoretically, all corporations would receive the same privileges and immunities.[6]

The status quo, however, is a social construction that has evolved over time. It can be changed if, as a society, we decide it should be different. The state government in Vermont, for example, is famous for passing the "Ben & Jerry's law," which

> permitted a company's directors to reject a takeover bid if "they deem it to be not in the best interests of employees, suppliers, and the economy of the state." Thus, even when a company was offered a financial premium in a buyout situation, its directors were permitted to reject the offer based on the best interests of the State of Vermont.[7]

What is the best approach, from a CSR perspective, to determine the responsibilities and obligations firms seek to fulfill? What prevents a firm from operating in the best interests of a broad array of stakeholders, rather than a narrow section of shareholders, who can only loosely be referred to as owners?

> Owners carry responsibility. If I own a dog, and it bites a child, I am legally responsible. Shareholders provide capital to the business and acquire a right to a percentage of the profits of the business. They should get a fair return. But capital is not the only asset the business should value—it must protect its staff, its reputation and the continued favor of its customers.[8]

What should a corporate charter look like and what is the most appropriate authority (federal vs. state government) to regulate this area of corporate law?

Case Study   Federalization

Issues of corporate governance in the United States are currently regulated under state rather than federal law. Those who support this system argue that it encourages competition between states (to entice corporations to incorporate within their state) and, therefore, produces effective and efficient legislation. Critics of this system, however, rebut the benefits of interstate competition because the result is a race to the bottom as states bend over backward to craft legislation that appeases corporations. States want firms to incorporate within their jurisdiction because of the lucrative fees they receive for each company that registers there, wherever the company is actually headquartered:

> Corporations don't have to incorporate where a firm is headquartered, or even where it employs the most people. Managers can go jurisdiction-shopping, looking for the most advantageous set of laws, since getting a corporate charter is easier than getting a driver's license. As a result, some 60 percent of the Fortune 500 is incorporated in Delaware, which is most protective of managerial interests.[9]

Delaware is perceived as having the most advantageous system of regulation for companies, which translates as having the least regulation. The state, "whose more than 600,000 registered companies compare with an estimated 865,000 inhabitants,"[10] also advertises additional benefits:

> Delaware company agents advertise the state as allowing even greater secrecy than offshore tax havens.[11]

In terms of oversight, liability, responsibility, and regulation, Delaware has "long been reluctant to disturb the decisions of corporate boards."[12] As such, other states feel compelled to reproduce Delaware's lax environment, simply to keep companies currently headquartered there from moving to Delaware:

> If another state wants to be more aggressive in fighting corporate crime or protecting shareholders, employees, or communities, it runs the risk that its companies will simply re-incorporate in Delaware. So most states end up mimicking Delaware law.[13]

There is a growing belief that meaningful reform in the area of governing corporations can take place only if the federal government takes control of the process. This would allow either Congress or the Securities and Exchange Commission (SEC) to raise the bar for all corporations without having to worry that companies would simply flee in protest to the state with the weakest rules, although here the risk would be that firms would incorporate overseas in such places as Bermuda, for example, with its favorable tax treatment.[14]

(Continued)

(Continued)

A starting point for the federal government would be a law stating that corporations have to incorporate where they have the largest presence—that is, where their true headquarters are, where they employ the most people, or where they have the greatest percentage of operations. This would make corporations more directly accountable for their actions to the community within which they actually operate. By introducing these changes, the government would also go a long way toward closing the loophole in the tax code that allows corporations to incorporate offshore (again, irrespective of where their headquarters are) to avoid paying the higher rates of corporation tax levied in the United States.

As a first step in this campaign toward federalization, various attempts have been made to introduce a Code for Corporate Responsibility at the state level, which would reform the law with regard to directors' duties:

For public corporations, the corporate purpose of maximizing returns for shareholders is now held in place by the state law of director's duties, which in all states say that directors must act in the best interests of the corporation and its shareholders. Attorney Robert Hinkley has drafted a model Code for Corporate Responsibility which would change this to say, in effect, directors may not pursue shareholder gain at the expense of employees, the community, and the environment. If these parties can demonstrate harm, they would have a right to sue under the proposed law.[15]

The potential impact of this simple but far-reaching change to the law would be significant. The entire purpose of the corporation would necessarily shift and the new law would give stakeholders a tool with which to hold corporations accountable for their actions and policies. Forcing this multiconstituency approach would result in U.S. firms increasingly acting like European ones, as well as firms in Asian countries such as Japan, which tend to define their stakeholders more broadly and actively. Groups in both Minnesota and California have begun to campaign for this change, with states such as Maine and Massachusetts also showing interest.[16] Legislation has been introduced in California to put the new code into effect:[17]

In California—where the state legislature is controlled by Democrats—corporate purpose legislation was introduced . . . by Senate Majority Whip Richard Alarcon (D-San Fernando Valley). While current law says directors must maximize profits for shareholders, Alarcon's Good Corporate Citizen bill (SB 917) says companies may not do so at the expense of the environment, human rights, the public health, the community, or the dignity of employees. The attorney general could bring civil action against violators. Under certain conditions, directors would be personally liable.[18]

In February 2009, Minnesota Senator John Marty and Representative Bill Hilty introduced a Bill for Socially Responsible Corporations into the Senate[19] and House,[20] respectively. According to the Citizens for Corporate Redesign Web site:

The bill creates a new section of law for an alternative kind of corporation, the SR (socially responsible) corporation:

1. Directors will have an affirmative duty to all stakeholders,

2. Employees and representatives of the public interest will be on the Board of Directors,

3. Directors will be protected from shareholder suits when they choose to consider other stakeholders and the public interest,

4. Socially Responsible investors and consumers will know where to invest their money, and

5. Socially Responsible Companies will be protected from hostile takeover.[21]

There are legitimate issues relating to the implementation of these proposed laws. For example, "What happens if a company moves a plant to a more environmentally friendly facility, thereby helping the environment but harming the employees and community of the previous locality?"[22] What would be the consequences if investors sell their stock under these anti-investor policies in favor of firms in more investor-friendly countries? Also, what would be the proposed penalties for directors that fail the new test? Would they be individually liable? Nevertheless, the idea that modern corporations should be compelled to register a public purpose that reflects a broader set of social responsibilities is receiving growing support.

A New "Best Interests of the Corporation" Principle?

A *BusinessWeek*/Harris Poll asked which of the following options was preferable:

"Corporations should have only one purpose—to make the most profit for their shareholders—and pursuit of that goal will be best for America in the long run."

—or—

"Corporations should have more than one purpose. They also owe something to their workers and the communities in which they operate, and they should sometimes sacrifice some profit for the sake of making things better for their workers and communities."

An overwhelming 95 percent of Americans chose the second proposition. . . . When 95 percent of the public supports a proposition, enacting that proposition into law should not be impossible.[23]

Online Resources

- Background information and a copy of the Code for Corporate Responsibility, press cuttings, examples of existing state laws, reports of attempts to reform state laws, and other resources can be found at Citizen Works (founded by Ralph Nader), http://www.citizenworks.org/enron/corp_code.php

"According to Corporate Law, Corporations make decisions based only on maximizing profits and increasing stock prices. The Code for Corporate Responsibility seeks to add protections for the environment, human rights, public health and safety, the welfare of our communities and the corporate employees."

- Code for Corporate Responsibility activity in Minnesota, http://www.c4cr.org/

  "Vision Statement: C4CR envisions a world in which corporations work for a just, peaceful and sustainable global society. Mission Statement: To transform the legal purpose of corporations to include responsibility to employees, communities and the environment."

- Code for Corporate Responsibility activity in California, http://groups.yahoo.com/group/c4cr_california/

For information concerning Bill SB 917 and an update on its progress, see http://info.sen.ca.gov/cgi-bin/postquery?bill_number=sb_917&sess=PREV&house=B&site=sen

- Common Dreams NewsCenter, http://www.commondreams.org/about-us

- Corporation 20/20, http://www.corporation2020.org/

  "What would a corporation look like that was designed to seamlessly integrate both social and financial purpose? Corporation 20/20 is a new multi-stakeholder initiative that seeks to answer this question."

- Robert Hinkley, "How Corporate Law Inhibits Social Responsibility: A Corporate Attorney Proposes a 'Code for Corporate Citizenship' in State Law," published in the January/February 2002 issue of *Business Ethics: Corporate Social Responsibility Report.*

- Tomorrow's Company, http://www.tomorrowscompany.com/

  "Tomorrow's Company is a not-for-profit research and agenda-setting organisation committed to creating a future for business which makes equal sense to staff, shareholders and society."

Questions for Discussion and Review

1. What is your opinion of the verdict delivered in *Dodge v. Ford Motor Company?* Was the judge correct to rule the way he did? If the case came before the court today, would the outcome be any different?

2. What is the argument for having corporate governance issues regulated at the federal rather than state level? Do you agree?

3. Do you agree with the vision and mission statements of the Code for Corporate Responsibility (http://www.c4cr.org/)? If yes, why? If no, can you write alternative statements that are *better?*

4. Develop an argument against the Code for Corporate Responsibility—is it persuasive?

5. Do you agree with the statement that "corporations should have only one purpose—to make the most profit for their shareholders," or do you agree with the statement that

corporations "have more than one purpose. They also owe something to their workers and the communities in which they operate, and they should sometimes sacrifice some profit for the sake of making things better for their workers and communities"? Which of these two positions from the *BusinessWeek*/Harris Poll do you support? Why?

CORPORATE GOVERNANCE

 CSR CONNECTION: This issue reflects the growing importance of evaluating the effectiveness of boards of directors within the field of corporate governance.

Issue

The duties of a board of directors are twofold:

- *Strategic advice:* First, the board exists to provide the CEO and executive team with assistance in shaping the firm's medium- to long-term strategy. Thus, a board filled with experienced officers from a variety of different firms and industries provides the firm's executives with a variety of knowledge on which to draw.

- *Oversight:* Second, the board exists to represent shareholders. In this function, directors pursue the best interests of the firm's owners by monitoring the actions and performance of the CEO and executive team. The theory is that, to the extent that the interests of the shareholders and executives are aligned, the business will be managed in a way that best serves the shareholders. Given that shareholders are unable or unwilling to manage the firm on a day-to-day basis, the board serves to ensure that the capital they have invested in the firm is well-managed on their behalf.

While it is difficult to evaluate the extent to which a board's strategic advice is sought and adhered to by the executive team (and even harder to know whether it changed fundamentally the fortunes of the firm), it is easier to know when a board has failed in its oversight role. The result of such a failure is often a transgression of some kind that receives widespread media attention.

Scrutiny of the performance (and independence) of corporate boards has increased as a result of the corporate scandals in the early years of the 21st century. Scandals at Enron (2001), WorldCom (2002), Tyco (2002), HealthSouth (2003), and others showed the damage that can occur when a weak board fails in its duty of oversight. These scandals raised the profile of corporate governance as an effective tool to limit executive excess. As a result of the public outcry at the corrupt practices brought to light by these corporate scandals, the U.S. legislature stepped in to regulate further the area of corporate governance. One result was the Sarbanes-Oxley Act of 2002, a key provision of which is greater responsibilities for executive officers, holding them personally accountable for the actions of the organization:

Under new federal sentencing guidelines after the Sarbanes-Oxley Act, corporate crooks can get life in prison if crimes involve some combination of the following: over 250 victims, a loss of at least $400 million, involvement of a public company, or threat to a financial institution's solvency.[24]

The Act requires audit committee members

to be entirely composed of outside directors and chief executives to certify personally that a company's financial reports accurately reflect its financial condition.[25]

Rather than being a theoretical ideal to which lip service is paid but not acted on, the ability of the board to hold a firm's executive team accountable for the firm's actions is now a key investment criterion in terms of evaluating corporations and establishing confidence. Publications such as *BusinessWeek's* ranking of the best and worst boards reflect this change in attitude toward the issue of corporate governance in the United States:

Bad boards, in particular, have made extraordinary strides in confronting [difficult corporate governance issues]. Spurred in many cases by scandal, crisis, or a plummeting stock price, former laggards have become ardent believers in good governance.[26]

Principles of Good Governance[27]

BusinessWeek ranks corporate boards according to four principles of good governance:

Independence: The number of directors who were previously company executives or have existing business relationships with the company (e.g., consulting contracts).

Stock ownership: The amount of stock each member of the board owns in the company, therefore aligning personal interests directly with shareholder interests. *BusinessWeek* has stipulated an ideal minimum of $150,000 per director (excluding stock options).

Director quality: Directors should have experience in the same industry of the company's core business, as well as management experience of a similar-sized organization. "Fully employed directors should sit on no more than four boards, retirees no more than seven. Each director should attend at least 75% of all meetings."[28]

Board activism: Boards should meet regularly, should also meet without management present, and should show restraint in areas such as executive compensation.

The consequences for firms with good or bad boards can be significant:

The stocks of companies with the best boards outperformed those with the worst by 2 to 1. [In addition, during economic recessions] the Best Boards companies retained much more of their value, returning 51.7%, vs. −12.9% for the Worst Boards companies.[29]

As a result, calls for corporate governance reform reflect the importance of the board's oversight function. The Financial Services Authority in the United Kingdom, for example, has been critical of the failure of boards to help avert the collapses of Northern Rock and the Royal Bank of Scotland in 2008/2009:

> The Financial Services Authority started examining the quality of boards and demanding change "where the caliber/expertise/skills of non-executive directors [is] not good enough."[30]

Debates about the relative value of the different corporate governance rules and structures in the United States and the United Kingdom continue.[31] These differences between the two systems become apparent in relation to the separate roles of the CEO and the chair of the board.

Case Study   Split CEO/Chair

One of the biggest factors regarding the operational effectiveness of corporate boards is the issue of whether the jobs of CEO and chair of the board should be legally separated. Traditionally, in the United States, power is concentrated in one person who both chairs the board and is the top employee of the company, the CEO. In Canada, Britain, and continental Europe, however, the separation of these two jobs is standard practice. For corporate governance to be effective within an organization, the performance of the board of directors is crucial. And for this performance to be effective, the board's independence from management is important. Many in the United States are now arguing that the board cannot effectively monitor the CEO in terms of day-to-day operations if that same person is also the chair of the board:

> Andrew S. Grove, who is chairman of Intel Corp., while Craig R. Barrett is its CEO, made the point . . . this way: "The separation of the two jobs goes to the heart of the conception of a corporation. . . . If [the CEO is] an

employee, he needs a boss, and that boss is the board. The chairman runs the board. How can the CEO be his own boss?" In a recent survey of board members from 500 large U.S. companies, McKinsey & Co. found similar views. Nearly 70% of respondents said a CEO should not run the board.[32]

The oversight role played by the board is growing in importance as investors (who rely on boards to protect their investments) are required to monitor and evaluate multinational organizations that produce increasingly complex financial statements. The position of chair of the board, as chief representative of investors, therefore, is also growing in importance. Add in the different skills required by both positions and the difficulty in having one person in both roles becomes more apparent:

> [Before 2003], the share of companies separating the two jobs was rising about 2% annually. [In 2003], the share of companies whose CEOs didn't also hold the chairman's reins increased to 25% of the S&P 500 from 21% in 2002.[33]

(Continued)

(Continued)

As shareholders become aware of the conflict of interest inherent in one person holding both positions, the backlash against companies that ignore calls for reform is also increasing. Within the pharmaceutical industry,[34] shareholder resolutions tabled in 2005 garnered support for dividing the two roles and appointing an independent director chair of the board at Wyeth (39%), Eli Lilly & Co. (25%), Abbott Laboratories (17%), Merck & Co. (46.5%), and Pfizer Inc. (42.1%).[35] At Disney's 2004 annual general meeting, 43% of shareholders voted in favor of a no-confidence motion against Michael Eisner. In response, the board removed him as chairman of the company, allowing him to retain his position as CEO. In spite of the growing support for the idea of splitting the CEO and chair positions, however, many corporations in the United States maintain unified responsibilities:

Of the 30 large companies that make up the Dow Jones Industrial Average [in 2002], only eight have split functions.[36]

One compromise that has grown in popularity as a result of the Sarbanes-Oxley legislation is the appointment of an independent lead director of the board. This position is given to one of the board's independent directors (i.e., a director who is not an executive of the firm), who is expected to chair the board whenever there is a conflict of interest that requires the CEO to excuse him- or herself from the conversation. It satisfies governance reformers because, in theory, it encourages greater independent oversight of the CEO on sensitive issues such as executive compensation, while CEOs favor this compromise because it allows them to retain both the CEO and chair titles:

The percentage of S&P 500 companies appointing a lead or presiding director more than doubled [in 2003] to 53% from 26% [in 2002]. . . . The proportion of companies that divide the CEO and chairman's position also accelerated [in 2003], but at a slower pace, with the overall numbers still trailing the companies opting for a lead director structure.[37]

A 2005 survey, "including most of the nation's largest companies" and released by the Business Roundtable, reported that this trend is continuing:

Seventy-one percent [of responding companies] said they now hold executive sessions ["without company managers present"] at every board meeting, up from 68% [in 2004] and 55% [in 2003]. Moreover, 83% of the companies said they now have an independent chairman, a lead director or a presiding director—up 12 percentage points from [2004].[38]

It is important to remember, however, that independence from the organization does not automatically mean effectiveness:

The Sarbanes-Oxley Act requires public companies to have a majority of independent directors. . . . But the SEC still allows director nominations to be closely controlled by management. So as James McRitchie of Corp.Gov.net put it, independent directors "can still be the CEO's golfing buddies." Enron, we might recall, had 12 out of 14 independent directors.[39]

Given this, some are skeptical as to whether independence in itself, or even split CEO and chair functions, will guarantee the kind of objective oversight that is sought:

> The nostrum widely recommended today is more "independent directors"— yet firms like Enron and WorldCom had many prominent outside directors, and still routinely rubber-stamped management schemes that impoverished employees, communities and shareholders alike.[40]

Much more important than split CEO/chair positions, some advocates argue, is the ability for shareholders to directly nominate and vote for board members:[41]

> "I don't give a damn about separation of the two positions," says Neil Minnow, editor of The Corporate Library, a research firm that specializes in corporate governance. "In the US, it's never been proven that it's better. There's only one thing that matters, and that's who gets to decide who sits on the board."[42]

Although not primarily a corporate governance issue, the 2007–2009 financial crisis indicated that executives are still making decisions that place their firms in precarious positions. In some cases, boards were aware of these decisions and fully supported the firm's executives; in other cases, they were left in the dark. In either case, however, boards were unwilling or unable to prevent what turned out to be highly damaging decisions.[43] In spite of the realization that further reform is necessary, the concern is that the desire to enact meaningful reform will fade as the attention of regulators, investors, and the public to these issues ebbs and flows in cycles:

> There is a sense that if the capital markets simply recover and the stock market goes up, this whole focus on governance will lose steam.[44]

Nevertheless, some look to recent developments as a sign of positive change. One of the fallouts from the 2007–2009 financial crisis, for example, was strong public reaction to specific practices (such as high executive compensation) in the firms that received government financial assistance. In the case of Bank of America, one consequence of this stakeholder reaction resulted in Ken Lewis, the firm's CEO, being forced out of his job as chair of the board:

> The vote . . . was a stunning rebuke of Mr Lewis' authority at the bank. . . . But it was also seen as a watershed moment for the US corporate governance movement, a sign that the European-style separation of the chairman and chief executive positions was gaining traction in North America.[45]

Online Resources

- CorpGov.net, http://www.corpgov.net/

"Since 1995 the Corporate Governance site at CorpGov.net has facilitated the ability of institutional and individual shareowners to better govern corporations, enhancing both corporate accountability and the creation of wealth."

For a comprehensive list of corporate governance Web sites, see: http://www.corpgov.net/links/links.html

- Global Corporate Governance Forum (OECD & World Bank), http://www.gcgf.org/

  "The Forum aims to promote the private sector as an engine of growth, reduce the vulnerability of developing and transition economies to financial crisis, and provide incentives for corporations to invest and perform efficiently in a socially responsible manner."

- GovernanceMetrics International, http://governancemetrics.com/

  " . . . the world's first global corporate governance ratings agency."

- International Corporate Governance Network, http://www.icgn.org/

  "The ICGN is a global membership organisation of around 450 leaders in corporate governance based in 45 countries with a mission to raise standards of corporate governance worldwide."

- PIRC (Pensions & Investment Research Consultants Ltd.), http://www.pirc.co.uk/

  "PIRC is the UKs' leading independent research and advisory consultancy providing services to institutional investors on corporate governance and corporate social responsibility."

- PricewaterhouseCoopers, http://www.pwc.com/us/en/sarbanes-oxley/index.jhtml

  "The following collection of content [on SOX] aims to give you a deeper understanding of this monumental legislation, and its impact on public companies."

- Public Company Accounting Oversight Board, http://www.pcaobus.org/

  "The PCAOB is a private-sector, nonprofit corporation, created by the Sarbanes-Oxley Act of 2002, to oversee the auditors of public companies in order to protect the interests of investors and further the public interest in the preparation of informative, fair, and independent audit reports."

- Sarbanes-Oxley, http://www.sarbanes-oxley.com/

  "Sarbanes-Oxley provides a complete cross-referenced index of SEC filers, audit firms, offices, CPAs, services, fees, compliance/enforcement actions and other critical disclosure information."

- The Corporate Library, http://www.thecorporatelibrary.com/

  "The Corporate Library's mission is to provide independent corporate governance research and analysis to enable our clients to enhance value."

- The OECD's initiative to strengthen Corporate Governance, http://www.oecd.org/topic/0,2686,en_2649_37439_1_1_1_1_37439,00.html

The OECD Principles of Corporate Governance, http://www.oecd.org/department/
0,2688,en_2649_34813_1_1_1_1_1,00.html

- U.S. Securities and Exchange Commission, http://www.sec.gov/spotlight/
sarbanes-oxley.htm

Questions for Discussion and Review

1. What is the job of a corporation's board of directors? Whose interests *should* they serve? Whose interests *do* they serve? Which of their two main responsibilities do you think is the most important? Why?

2. Many CEOs complain that the result of the Sarbanes-Oxley legislation has been to complicate further the auditing process and push up fees that the auditing companies charge corporations. Do you think that this is an area of law that can be left to market forces, or do you think that, if corporations cannot regulate their own behavior, then it is the duty of government to step into the void?

3. Look at the four principles of good governance used by *BusinessWeek's* ranking in "The Best & Worst Boards." Which of these do you think is the most important? Why?

4. Are "independent" board members truly independent? What would you do to ensure the greater independence of board members?

5. What is your opinion regarding the issue of splitting the roles of CEO and chair of the board? Justify your position.

EMPLOYEE RELATIONS

> **CSR CONNECTION:** This issue argues that a firm benefits when it meets the needs of one of its key stakeholders, its employees. Volunteer programs, effectively implemented, are an established means of increasing employee productivity and retention, while decreasing costs.

Issue

Employees are a central stakeholder of the firm. To the extent that the organization fosters a feeling of commitment and loyalty within its workforce, the firm benefits. Employees are proud to work for organizations with an ethical reputation,[46] a sense that carries over into the quality of work that is produced:

Evidence from the Sunday Times' "100 best companies to work for" list shows that the share prices of the quoted companies on the list outperform the FTSE All Share Index by between 10% and 15%, a result that is seen in every country that produces a list.[47]

The Benefits of Motivated Employees

There are many causal-related benefits for companies that ensure their employees remain happy and healthy at work:

- Employee retention reduces costs associated with advertising for and training new staff, as well as lost productivity as the staff gain experience in their new positions:

Workers are six times more likely to stay in their jobs when they believe their company acts with integrity, according to Walker Information, a research company that measures employee satisfaction and loyalty at the workplace. But when workers mistrust their bosses' decisions and feel ashamed of their firm's behavior, four out of five workers feel trapped at work and say they are likely to leave their jobs soon.[48]

- Increased employee safety leads to reduced amounts of lost time and productivity due to injuries. Intel's approach to this issue makes both moral and business sense:

At Intel (No. 3), based in Santa Clara, Calif., good citizenship . . . includes careful attention to employee safety—so much that CEO Craig Barrett insists he be sent an e-mail report within 24 hours any time one of his firm's 80,000 employees loses a single day of work to injury. . . . In 2000, Intel's worldwide injury rate was just .27 injuries per 100 employees, compared to an industry average of 6.7.[49]

- An effective employee share-ownership scheme ensures that the workers,' managers,' and owners' interests are more closely aligned and that employees will feel more committed to generating positive outcomes for the company as a whole. In spite of the criticism leveled at stock options—and their debatable impact on performance for top management—companies that distribute ownership of the company throughout the organization do see notable improvements in job motivation and satisfaction:

Evidence suggests that smart use of options and other compensation do boost performance. Companies that spread ownership throughout a large portion of their workforce, through any form—options, Employee Stock Ownership Plans, or other means—deliver total shareholder returns that are two percentage points higher than at similar companies. . . . Better stock performance isn't the only benefit. Companies with significant employee ownership do better on a wide range of performance metrics, including productivity, profit margins, and return on equity, according to the studies.[50]

William Greider argues in his book, *The Soul of Capitalism,* that positively motivated employees are central to the goal of altering "the basic operating values of American capitalism so that the priorities of society [over the narrow financial priorities of stockholders] become dominant":

Most Americans, in current life, go to work daily and submit to what is essentially a master-servant relationship inherited from feudalism. . . . The solution is for workers to own their work. The forms for doing so—employee-owned firms, partnerships, cooperatives and other hybrids—are alive and growing. To be effective, they must incorporate not only employee ownership but collaborative decision making as well.[51]

Case Study   Timberland[52]

When companies ask for a "bottom line" benefit for implementing a comprehensive CSR perspective, employee volunteer programs deliver:

> Today, more corporations are turning to hands-on volunteer projects to get their people motivated and working as a team. In many cases, participants say such activities help them forge bonds that remain even after they return to the office.[53]

In terms of employee loyalty and retention, employee volunteer programs revitalize employees. Such programs expose employees to a new environment away from their everyday position, allowing them to feel pride in their company and its standing within the community while also leading to the development of new skill sets:

> Marc Benioff, CEO of Salesforce.com, promotes what he calls "the 1 percent solution": 1 percent of the company's equity, 1 percent of its profits, and 1 percent of its employees' paid work hours are devoted to philanthropy.
>
> U.S. software maker SAS, which for six years has been among the Top 20 in

Fortune's annual list of the 100 best companies to work for, offers a volunteer initiative that lets employees use flexible schedules to take paid time off for projects in the community, or even work in teams with their managers on a volunteer effort during business hours.[54]

Employee Volunteer Programs

Increasingly, firms are recognizing the benefits of employee volunteer programs and are prepared to dedicate increasing amounts of resources to ensure their success:

- **Accenture**—Loans employees to non-profits at discount rates.
- **Cisco Systems**—Places employees with education-related organizations for a year, at full salary.
- **Bain & Co.**—Supports employees who volunteer with local organizations, and pays for their time on full-time consulting projects.
- **Pfizer**—Pairs employees with health-related organizations to help with research and training.
- **Wells Fargo**—Pays employees to work with a school for as many as four months.[55]

(Continued)

(Continued)

In addition, AstraZeneca, HSBC, and KPMG all have dedicated employee volunteer programs in partnership with the United Kingdom's Volunteer Service Overseas (VSO) organization.[56] And, in response to the growing popularity of volunteer programs in the United Kingdom,[57] the British government (Home Office) designated 2005 as the Year of the Volunteer.[58]

Timberland is committed to its *Community Engagement* employee volunteer program[59] and reports the program's results along with the quarterly financial reports it releases in its annual Corporate Social Responsibility Report. The company's CEO, Jeffrey Swartz, inspired the volunteer program.[60] Swartz saw the power the company possessed to evoke social change and also had the foresight to see the potential benefits this activism would bring:

Timberland launched an in-house volunteer program in 1992, the Path of Service.[61] . . . Due to strong employee participation, the program expanded to . . . forty hours in 1997, where it remains today. Workers . . . choose their own volunteer activities. Service can range from serving meals in a homeless shelter to coaching a Little League baseball team. Above all, the company wants to make it as easy as possible for workers to find a service program that matches their interests. It's effective: more than 90 percent of Timberland workers take part in the Path of Service. The company added . . . a service sabbatical program. Up to four employees each year are awarded three to six months of leave to work full time with a nonprofit organization of their choosing. The sabbatical comes with full pay and benefits, and participating employees return to their same job after completing their assignment. Although community well-being ranks high on Timberland's agenda, the Path of Service is first and foremost an avenue for employee enrichment. "We believe that investing in our community begins by investing in our employees," declares Swartz.[62]

In response to a survey conducted by Timberland to learn more about the reception of the plan among employees:

79 percent of employees agree with the statement: "Timberland's commitment to community is genuine and not a public relations vehicle." The survey . . . also reveals that 89 percent of employees say community service is valuable to them, while 50 percent report that Timberland's volunteer programs influenced their decision to work for the company.[63]

In general, research indicates that volunteerism at the workplace is a key driver for positive worker attitudes. One study finds that individuals who participate in employer-sponsored community activities are 30% more likely to want to continue working for that company and to help make it a success:[64]

Accenture's program quickly became a draw for some employees. Hundreds applied, and those accepted now must wait weeks or months for an assignment. The program makes Accenture "more attractive as an employer," says Jill Smart, senior managing director of human resources.[65]

For the Midcounties Co-operative, the second-largest cooperative in the United Kingdom:

Total staff turnover for the year [2008] was 31.29% and in colleagues that have participated in volunteering these figures drop dramatically to 3.4%, showing a direct link between the retention of colleagues and participation in community activity.[66]

And, for Accenture, its program is not even one that will cost it any money:

Accenture is in effect running a social enterprise unit within the organization—and one that is meant to break even financially. The company contributes, the employees contribute (via a cut in pay when they are doing it) and the client will pay a fee—although it is a fraction of the market cost.[67]

In return, Accenture benefits from greater employee loyalty, additional employee training, and improved relations with its community stakeholders.

Online Resources

- Fair Labor Association, http://www.fairlabor.org/

"[The FLA is] a nonprofit organization dedicated to ending sweatshop conditions in factories worldwide."

- Salesforce.com, http://www.salesforce.com/foundation

"The Salesforce.com Foundation was created to apply the core strengths of salesforce.com to help organizations further their social mission, deepen their impact, and better the lives of those in need."

- SAS, http://www.sas.com/corporate/community/index.html

"SAS supports education in our communities through four programs: educational initiatives, charitable donations, in-kind donations and employee volunteerism."

- SERVEnet, http://www.servenet.org/

"Launched in 1996, servenet.org is a website that mobilizes and empowers the volunteer service community to tackle some of the toughest challenges facing local communities."

- Timberland's Community Engagement, http://www.timberland.com/corp/index.jsp?page=csr_civic_engagement

"In over 35 countries around the world, employees use their Path of Service™ program benefit of 40 hours of annual paid time off to work on service projects in their communities."

- Volunteer Service Overseas (VSO), http://www.vso.org.uk/

  "VSO is the world's leading independent, international development charity that works through volunteers to fight poverty in developing countries."

- Work Foundation, http://www.theworkfoundation.com/

  "The Work Foundation is the leading independent authority on work and its future."

Questions for Discussion and Review

1. What are some of the benefits to companies that operate a volunteer employee program stated in the case study? Do you agree that these benefits are likely to come from a volunteer program?

2. What would your reaction be if a firm you worked for had a volunteer program? Would you consider participating? Would it change your feelings about working for the firm?

3. How can companies encourage employees to participate in volunteer programs and avoid having employees feel that "by volunteering, they are potentially derailing their chances for a promotion because of the time they'll spend out of the office"?[68]

4. Go to Timberland's main Web site (http://www.timberland.com/) and also the company's volunteer Web site (http://www.timberland.com/corp/index.jsp?page=csr_civic_engagement). Do you get the sense that Timberland is genuine in its commitment to CSR? Does that create a good impression of the company or not make much difference in your perception of It?

5. Find another employee benefit program to compare to Timberland's. Which is better? Why?

EXECUTIVE COMPENSATION

 CSR CONNECTION: This issue reflects the central role of the conflict between a company's *principals* (shareholders) and *agents* (managers) in understanding the stakeholder approach to CSR.

Issue

Principal/agent theory describes the inherent tension that exists between the owners of an organization (collectively, the *principals,* which include the shareholders and their representatives, the board of directors) and the managers (the *agents*), whom the owners (the principals) appoint to operate the business and protect their investment.

The conflict of interest that arises between these two groups is a problem that has plagued limited liability joint stock companies ever since they were established in the Companies Act of 1862.[69] The concept of *limited liability* contained within the legislation allowed people to invest in companies but *limit* their *liability* to the amount of that investment, thus avoiding any additional liability for the firm's debts. We take this for granted today, but at the time, it was revolutionary and provoked considerable resistance.[70] As such, limited liability corporations encouraged the emergence of a class of investors who had the money to support various ventures but did not have the time or expertise to become involved in day-to-day management. What emerged in their place was a class of professional managers who managed the investors' money on their behalf. Almost immediately, however, the issue arose of how best to ensure the managers were managing the investors' money with the investors' best interests in mind—how best to protect "shareholder value":[71]

> [Adam] Smith, in his 1776 classic, *The Wealth of Nations,* said he was troubled by the fact that corporations' owners, their shareholders, did not run their own businesses but delegated that task to professional managers. The latter could not be trusted to apply the same "anxious vigilance" to manage "other people's money" as they would their own, he wrote, and "negligence and profusion therefore must prevail, more or less, in the management of such a company."[72]

One of the safeguards put in place was the appointment of a board of representatives with the power to oversee managers' actions, as well as provide advice wherever possible (the board of directors). Over time, however, relations between the principals' representatives (the board) and their agents shifted from one that was paternal to one that became fraternal. As a result, lines of interest became blurred. Compounding this tension was the relatively recent shift in emphasis of corporate outlook—from managing the relationships between the organization and its many stakeholder groups over the medium to long term to focusing on short-term measures of success above all else (for example, emphasizing quarterly earnings reports to bolster a company's share price):

> Before the 1980s one tenet of corporate governance was that company management served several constituencies: shareholders, yes, but also employees, customers, and perhaps others too. . . . But the shareholder-value crowd insisted that the only clientele that mattered was stockholders. If they were rewarded, then all other players would reap benefits as a byproduct of an even higher stock price. This mantra of shareholder value, however, could be taken to an extreme and perverted—you can see how this bit of dogma could become a handy all-purpose justification for mass firings, shoddy products, and the dumping of chemicals into rivers.[73]

As such, in its modern reincarnation, this conflict between principal and agent eventually resulted in the corporate scandals that peppered the business world around the turn of this century:

> The Enron scandal—and those at WorldCom, Tyco, Adelphia and others—exposed a glaring flaw in the oversight of America's top executives. . . . In the textbooks, capitalism works because corporate managers are kept in check by shareholders, who operate through

directors they elect. The truth, however, is that many American directors are handpicked and handsomely compensated by the very executives they oversee.[74]

The central question of this issue, therefore, remains the same: What is the best way to align the interests of the owners of the organization (the principals) with those of the agents entrusted to operate the organization on the owners' behalf? In the 1990s, stock options became the new Holy Grail: By awarding executives options, the theory held that they would have a direct interest in the performance of the company. If the company performed well, stock prices would rise and the executives would benefit personally; however, this theory was quickly shown to be flawed, as some executives saw the short-term stock price as their most important focus (maximizing personal benefit) rather than the long-term health of the organization.

Case Study   Stock Options

A key focus of the principal/agent conflict is the issue of executive compensation. A significant assumption inherent in the granting of stock options is that executives' interests are best served in paying them as much as possible. The reasoning goes that both shareholders and executives seek to maximize personal financial gain—shareholders via a higher share price and executives via higher levels of compensation. If executives can be paid in a way that meets their needs, while also meeting the needs of shareholders, then the two sets of interests will be aligned. One solution that became popular in the early to mid 1990s was stock options. The result of this shift in executive compensation was an explosion in the amounts of money paid to *top* CEOs:

In 2007, S&P 500 CEOs averaged $10.5 million (some 344 times the pay of typical American workers). The top 50 hedge-fund and private-equity fund managers averaged $588 million each (19,000 times the pay of typical workers). In 2007, the five biggest Wall Street firms paid bonuses of a staggering $39 billion—huge payments to the executives who investments banks have since been bailed out by American taxpayers.[75]

Ironically, this growth in popularity of stock options emerged from congressional attempts to limit executive pay:

The $1 million limitation on [the tax] deductibility of senior executive compensation, which became law in 1993, resulted in many companies *increasing* CEO salaries to $1 million.[76]

Rather than a ceiling for pay, as Congress had intended, the $1 million became the floor and de facto standard by which a CEO was judged. The differentiator then became the amount of the executive's compensation that was tied to *performance*. And stock options, which grant employees the right to purchase company stock at a fixed price at a future point in time, became the method of choice. Firms could afford to pay CEOs ever-increasing amounts of this form of *performance-related pay* because they were viewed as having minimal impact on a firm's accounts:

In recent years, especially during the halcyon days of the technology boom, stock options were handed out liberally with no direct impact on companies' bottom lines, because most of these options, which critics contend impose a real economic cost on companies, weren't booked as expenses. They simply were referenced in footnotes in annual reports.[77]

Attempts to expense stock options following the ethics scandals of the turn of the century (forcing companies to attribute a value to the options and treat that value as an expense that counts against earnings) met with resistance by corporate interests. Small technology firms, in particular, argued that they need options to attract talent—they are generally younger organizations and less likely to have the established cash flows necessary to pay higher salaries or other traditional forms of compensation. In addition, there are a number of technical difficulties with expensing stock options. These principally involve what value to assign to them, as it is unknown when and at what price and future date they will be vested. Having initially attempted to introduce this reform in 1991, however, the Financial Accounting Standards Board (FASB) eventually implemented a rule for firms to expense stock options given to all employees in 2005.[78] In spite of the change, however, stock options remained a popular means of providing executives with high levels of compensation.

Initially, the idea behind options-based compensation was that by aligning CEO and top management interests more closely with the interests of the firm's shareholders (via the company's share price), management would have an incentive to maximize company performance. This, in turn, would lead to maximum sustainable growth for the company and share price over time. In practice, however, many CEOs did whatever they could to raise the company's share price in the short term, sometimes irrespective of the legality or honesty of their actions or the long-term impact on the interests of the company:

These huge [compensation packages] bolster a system in which executives have incentives to manage the numbers for short-term gain and personal payout, and not manage their businesses for long-term growth and shareholder value. Exorbitant compensation feeds the worst instincts and egos of powerful CEOs, fueled by their desire to win at all costs and resulting, too often, in the cutting of ethical corners.[79]

Another component of this desire to maximize personal gain without regard for the firm's well-being emerged in the 2006 stock options backdating scandal, where firms agreed to executives' demands to backdate the issuing of stock options to a point when the share price was at its lowest:

A key purpose of stock options is to give recipients an incentive to improve their employer's performance, including its stock price. No stock gain, no profit on the options. Backdating them so they carry a lower price would run counter to this goal by giving the recipient a paper gain right from the start.[80]

(Continued)

(Continued)

As a result of these different distortions of the main purpose behind stock options, their value essentially fell out of correlation with company performance:

Executive Compensation and Firm Performance

People who report and comment on business practices have found evidence that high executive compensation does not necessarily produce correspondingly good results.

Compensation researcher Equilar studied 450 companies in the Standard & Poor's 500 and found something curious: The worst-performing companies in 2002 were those that gave their chief executives the biggest option grants in 2001. The median grant for those CEOs was $9.4 million. Median shareholder return the next year: −50%. CEOs with the best performances received much smaller grants—the median size was $3.7 million—and delivered returns of 17%.[81]

In the past decade, companies that granted 90% of all options to CEOs and a few top managers performed worse than those that distributed options more evenly and fairly among employees. There is no justification for increasing the compensation of CEOs from 40 times that of the average employee in the 1960s to nearly 600 times today.[82]

Consider: If you had invested $10,000 in the stock market (as represented by the Standard & Poor's average of 500 stocks), you would have more than doubled your money over 10 years, accumulating

$22,170 by the end of 2002, despite the bear market. . . . But if you were investing in the companies with the highest-paid executives over the same period of time, the value of your investment would have fallen 71 percent to $2,899."[83]

How a company approaches the issue of stock options as a component of executive compensation, therefore, is an important indicator of that company's approach to transparency, corporate governance, and reporting financial statements and company information.[84] In short, it speaks to the firm's approach to communicating with its stakeholders. Many of the scandals that have plagued corporate America resulted from a lack of these characteristics. Many of the problems revolved around violating the spirit, if not the letter (although that happened, too), of the law and deceiving investors for personal, self-motivated corporate gain:

Pay isn't just about recruitment and retention. It's also a form of communication about a company's culture and value, which can impact a company's relationship with its employees, its brand reputation, and ultimately its share value.[85]

Moving forward, the goal for those seeking reform of executive compensation should be to refocus incentives on the long-term health of the company and find ways to best encourage workers throughout the organization to work toward that goal. Some companies have stopped giving out earnings estimates to investors as one way of reducing pressure on the short-term share price:

Critics worry that a lack of guidance could lead to more earnings surprises, greater stock volatility, or even less vigorous oversight of management. In fact, it's a great leap forward. Successful strategies are not executed in three-month time slots. By refusing to play the quarterly guessing game, companies reduce the focus on short-term performance. That lessens incentives for accounting shenanigans aimed only at juicing the numbers.[86]

The 2007–2009 financial crisis further highlighted the large compensation packages paid to the CEOs and senior executives of large firms and the failure of stock options to resolve the principal/agent conflict. As such, the mood shifted against stock options as the preferred performance-related component of executive pay. From the severance package "worth roughly $210 million" of Robert Nardelli, who resigned as CEO of Home Depot in January 2007,[87] to the 59.42% shareholder defeat of Shell's 2009 executive pay plan,[88] to the "outrageous" bonuses of $165 million (later revised up to $218 million)[89] paid to the financial services group at the insurance giant AIG during the height of the 2007–2009 financial crisis,[90] the public perception was that executives were being paid for failure:

A major reason for public outrage [is] the outlandish $165 million in bonuses that were paid to a few hundred executives at AIG—in a division of the company that lost $100 billion! That's the teetering industrial giant into which taxpayers have poured about $170 billion in aid with another $30 billion to come. One can only wonder whether they would have received bigger bonuses if they lost $200 billion.[91]

Today, reform movements are pushing for executive compensation packages that highlight numerous reforms that will hopefully close the gap between the interests of agents and a broader set of principals. As Shell's CEO admitted as he called for reform of executive compensation in response to the "shareholder revolt" against his controversial 2009 proposed pay increase:

You have to realise: if I had been paid 50 per cent more, I would not have done it better. If I had been paid 50 per cent less, then I would not have done it worse.[92]

Executive Compensation Reform

Possible reforms include, but should not be limited to:

- Full and clear disclosure of the compensation of senior executives in a firm.[93]
- A salary cap for cash compensation. Whole Foods, for example, has a cap of "19 times the average pay [in the firm]," which it considers sufficient "to make the compensation to our executives more competitive in the marketplace."[94]
- Packages that include a range of incentives that encourage short-, medium-, and long-term performance.

(Continued)

(Continued)

- Capping of potential payouts of total compensation to limit excessive risk taking.
- Compensation committees that possess the ability to revise packages according to new circumstances as they arise.
- Encouragement of long-term executive ownership with restricted stock versus options with short-term vesting periods.
- Clawback[95] policies that allow a percentage of compensation to be recovered in the event that a firm is forced to restate earnings at a future date:

More than 64% of the Fortune 100 companies have clawback policies. If a company doesn't perform as well as originally believed, then why pay executives as if it did?[96]

- Shareholder voting on compensation packages—required in the United Kingdom since 2002.[97] As a result of the legislation, "The typical British CEO earns a little more than half what his or her U.S. counterpart makes."[98]

- Shareholder voting rules that allow for directors to be replaced easily, particularly those that sit on the compensation committee of the board.[99]

There is hope that a better form of executive compensation is emerging from all the damage since 2000:[100]

According to Equilar Inc. . . . roughly 70% of total compensation for S&P 500 CEOs [is] in the form of long-term incentives, typically earned over three years or more and predominantly tied to shareholder return.[101]

In 2006, only 18% of the 100 largest U.S. companies by revenue had clawback policies, but that increased to 64% by 2008.[102]

Similarly, by 2009, an increasing number of firms were announcing plans to hold "say on pay" votes at their annual general meetings, "when investors vote their proxy ballots on shareowner resolutions and other business,"[103] in response to increasing shareholder[104] and public[105] anger at the level of CEO compensation packages and the unresponsiveness of firms on this issue.

Online Resources

- 2009 Executive PayWatch, http://www.aflcio.org/corporatewatch/paywatch/

"In Executive PayWatch, you can find CEO compensation data for some of the country's largest companies, compare your pay to the CEOs, learn more about executives enjoying job and retirement security . . . and play a satisfying online game: Boot the CEO."

- Cato Institute, http://www.cato.org/

  "The Cato Institute was founded in 1977 by Edward H. Crane. It is a nonprofit public policy research foundation headquartered in Washington, D.C."

  Alan Reynolds, "Expensing Stock Options is a Faddish Fraud," July 18, 2002, http://www.cato.org/research/articles/reynolds-020718.html

- Center on Executive Compensation, http://www.execcomp.org/

  "The Center on Executive Compensation is dedicated to developing and promoting principled pay and governance practices and advocating compensation policies that serve the best interests of shareholders and other corporate stakeholders."

- Citizen Works—Expense Stock Options, http://www.citizenworks.org/corp/options/options-main.php

  "CEO greed and stock options. Stop the stock options con game."

- Financial Accounting Standards Board, http://www.fasb.org/

  "Since 1973, the Financial Accounting Standards Board (FASB) has been the designated organization in the private sector for establishing standards of financial accounting."

- How do stock options work? http://money.howstuffworks.com/personal-finance/financial-planning/stock-options.htm

  "What are stock options? Why are companies offering them? Are employees guaranteed a profit just because they have stock options? The answers to these questions will give you a much better idea about this increasingly popular movement."

- International Accounting Standards Board, http://www.iasb.org/

  "Our mission is to develop, in the public interest, a single set of high quality, understandable and international financial reporting standards (IFRSs) for general purpose financial statements."

- myStockOptions.com, http://www.mystockoptions.com/

  "We publish the best and most comprehensive personal-finance website on stock compensation for the millions of people who participate in stock plans."

Questions for Discussion and Review

1. What is your opinion about the current level of executive compensation? Do you agree with the statement: "Pay peanuts, get monkeys. Pay obscenely huge amounts, get obscenely greedy monkeys"?[106] Are executives being paid the "market rate," or is some factor distorting the market for top executives?

2. What is the issue at the core of the principal/agent conflict? Are stock options a good form of employee or manager compensation? Do they begin to heal the inherent conflict that exists between principals and agents?

3. Refer to the Corporate Governance issue earlier in this chapter; what is the role of the board of directors in setting the level of executive compensation?

4. Look at some of the Web sites listed in the subsection, Online Resources. Is expensing stock options a good idea?

5. Some companies award stock options to all employees. Starbucks is a good example of the loyal employees and good press coverage such a policy can generate. Have a look at some information about the company's Bean Stock program written in a case study at http://www.mhhe.com/business/management/thompson/ 11e/case/starbucks-1.html (under the heading "Schultz's Strategy to Make Starbucks a Great Place to Work"). Would such a policy encourage you to join one company over another, or is salary level still the most important determining factor in deciding between compensation packages?

SHAREHOLDER ACTIVISM

CSR CONNECTION: This issue reflects the significant rise in shareholder activism in recent years. It is a growing, if controversial, area within CSR, to which firms will face increasing pressure to respond. To what extent are investors willing to discriminate among companies and sacrifice short-term returns in order to pursue socially responsible investing strategies?

Issue

There are two types of *shareholder activists:*

• Institutional investors—professional investors who manage large blocks of shares, such as hedge, pension, or mutual funds, and who are driven largely by concerns of maximizing shareholder price. A good example of an institutional investor is Carl Icahn, whose fights with the management of firms such as General Motors or Time Warner make front page news;[107] and,

• NGOs, other socially concerned groups, and individual shareholders—social activists who usually hold smaller blocks of a firm's shares but who attempt to influence corporate action on specific issues that reflect the social values that are important to them and their members. Some good examples of such groups include TIAA-CREF (http://www.tiaa-cref.org/), the teachers' and college professors' pension fund; the Interfaith Center on Corporate Responsibility (http://www.iccr.org/); and groups such as Investors Against Genocide (http://www.investorsagainstgenocide.org/).[108]

While, from a CSR perspective, the second group has traditionally been the more relevant group of activist investors, as risk management becomes a more mainstream area of concern for firms and socially responsible mutual funds grow in importance (in terms of dollar amounts), the distinction between these two groups has blurred. As a result, on specific issues in relation to specific firms, both groups can easily find themselves seeking the same change in firm behavior.

Consequently, it is interesting to investigate instances where these two groups see overlapping interests. It is not clear, for example, whether demands for greater management transparency and accountability from these groups (on issues such as corporate governance, executive pay, and greenhouse gas emissions) lead necessarily to changes in corporate behavior. In addition, what opportunities exist for individual investors who seek to make investments that are consistent with their values? What is clear is that both groups are increasingly becoming more vocal in their public criticism of executives and the actions they take on behalf of their firms.[109]

This increased activity is apparent from the rise in shareholder resolutions related to the environment that are tabled at firms' annual general meetings (AGMs) and voted on by both institutional investors and social activists. For example, in 2007, "43 climate-related shareholder resolutions were filed with US companies, of which 15 led to positive actions by companies."[110] This number continued to rise in 2008, when a total of 54 resolutions were filed, "an increase of approximately 25% on 2007 and nearly doubling the number filed [in 2006]."[111] In addition,

A total of 61 mainstream mutual funds voted for climate change-related shareholder proposals an average of 23.6 per cent of the time during the 2008 proxy season—up from 13.6 per cent the previous year. . . . That does not include socially responsible investing funds, which voted for these types of resolutions 100 per cent of the time.[112]

This rise in the number of shareholder resolutions being filed, which is prevalent across a broad range of issues, signals what the *Financial Times* refers to as

the trend towards investor activism amid a crisis of confidence in corporate America . . . investors are no longer content merely to make money, but want to ensure they are doing so responsibly.[113]

The SEC stipulates a threshold of only 3% of shareholder votes for a proposition to be deemed to have sufficient shareholder support for it to be resubmitted for a vote the following year.[114] This is due to the disproportionate weight of individual shareholder votes:

Institutional investors hold more than 50% of all listed corporate stock in the United States (about 60% in the largest 1,000 corporations).[115] The largest 25 pension funds accounted for 42% of the foreign equity held by all U.S. investors.[116]

Institutional votes, therefore, constitute the majority of votes cast at AGMs. As such, they are highly influential, and these investors have traditionally tended to vote with the company's management. This is changing, however, as individual shareholders become increasingly strident in expressing their opposition to the excesses in corporate management that appeared early this century. Alternative shareholder resolutions that seek directly to counter board recommendations, as well as votes of 20% and up in support of those resolutions, are becoming increasingly common. As pressure increases on institutional investors to ensure corporate governance reflects general shareholder and public values, the number of votes approaching and exceeding the 50% barrier looks set to increase.

One example of shareholder pressure resulting in policy change occurred when Dell Computer announced the launch of a recycling campaign ("asset recovery" program) to help customers dispose of their computers. Correct dismantling ensures the toxic chemicals they contain do not end up in landfill waste sites. Dell announced plans to charge customers $49 per computer for this service. The company was pressured into this move by a proxy-session campaign to improve recycling efforts by all the major computer manufactures instigated by

> a group of activist shareholders led by Calvert Group and the As You Sow Foundation. . . . Dell, which has been blasted for not taking a lead role in keeping toxic-laden PCs from ending up in landfills, will set specific recycling targets, disclose its progress to the public, and make sure its recycled goods are handled properly. Dell also pledged to study how to use its direct distribution model to lower the cost of recycling tech waste.[117]

In general, however, a firm is usually not bound by the result of a shareholder vote, even if the vote is a majority of total shareholder voters. Legislation in place in the United Kingdom since 2002, for example, requires companies to produce a remuneration report every year, which then must be voted on at the AGM. This produces a great deal more information for shareholders and investors on issues surrounding various elements of a corporation's remuneration package, such as contract terms, takeover clauses, and pension arrangements, as well as clauses inserted into CEO contracts that result in large payments in the event that the company is taken over. Such information has previously been very difficult for interested parties to discover; however,

> while voting on it is mandatory, the company is not obliged to make any changes even if the report is rejected, and no heads will roll.[118]

In the United States, where shareholder democracy has traditionally been less of a concern for regulators than in countries such as the United Kingdom,[119] a recognition that fundamental shareholder powers can assist in the oversight of firms has led to institutional support in the prevailing atmosphere of tighter control over corporate governance:

> Under current rules, companies can ignore votes on resolutions proposed by share-holders. But the Securities and Exchange Commission has instituted a review of the proxy system. . . . If it makes shareholder votes mandatory the effect could be dramatic.[120]

In addition:

> The SEC is revisiting the fundamental question of how directors of publicly traded corporations are elected. Until recently, those elections were Stalinesque: Only one slate of candidates was on the ballot, and while shareholders could withhold their support, withheld votes didn't count. As long as one shareholder supported each director, those directors prevailed.[121]

In general, it is true that:

> Companies cannot be properly accountable to their shareholders unless the latter can express their opinion in proportion to the capital they have at risk. If companies are not accountable to their owners, they will need more regulation.[122]

As a result of current practices, however, almost invariably, management's slate of directors is elected.[123] In one round of elections of board directors that took place, for example:

> The Institutional Shareholder Services, a proxy advisory firm, says only 14 out of 14,000 board candidates were rejected by a majority of votes cast in elections.[124]

Nevertheless, it is also true that firms are beginning to see that listening and talking with concerned stakeholders offers the path of least resistance regarding sensitive issues. Firms, for example, are increasingly consulting with shareholders ahead of votes, surveying their opinion to gauge what package structure would be most acceptable:

> In its [2009] proxy, Amgen, . . . directed shareholders to a 10-question online survey [about the firm's compensation plan]. Queries include whether the plan is based on performance and whether the performance goals are understandable. . . . Prudential Financial Inc. [in 2009] created a link on its Web site so investors could comment on its compensation plan. . . . Shareholders at roughly 400 companies that accepted federal aid will conduct advisory votes [in 2009] on those companies' compensation plans.[125]

One way in which investors can hold firms accountable and impose their wishes on management is by investing in tailored funds that reflect the interests they value. In terms of CSR, socially responsible investment (SRI) funds seek to achieve this.

Case Study   SRI Funds

To what extent are investors limiting their investments to companies deemed to be operating in an ethical and socially responsible manner? Such investments are often referred to as socially responsible investment (SRI) funds.

An important debate that speaks to the potential for SRI funds to influence firm behavior is the question of whether SRI funds are any more or less successful than regular investment funds. Critics claim SRI funds are ineffective and that ethical or virtuous stocks do not outperform either regular mutual funds or so-called *sin* stocks. Those who support SRI funds, however, are beginning to find hope in numbers that appear to support their case. In the aftermath of the corporate scandals that occurred following the tech boom in the early years of this century,

> while investors pulled $10.5 billion out of U.S. diversified equity funds, they added $1.5 billion to socially responsible mutual funds.[126]

Although still a relatively small fraction of total investments, the assets invested in

(Continued)

(Continued)

SRI funds are growing rapidly, as are mutual funds claiming to be socially or environmentally responsible:

> Assets of so-called socially responsible funds grew five times faster than those of other mutual funds in the past three decades. . . . Socially and environmentally responsible mutual fund assets had reached a record $103 billion by mid-2001, up from $150 million in 1971—a growth rate of more than 68 times. The assets of all other mutual funds have grown by an average of about 13.5 times. . . . In 1971, Pax World had the category to itself. But today, there are 192 such funds, representing an increase of 9,500 percent. . . . This compares with a 4,074 percent increase for all other funds.[127]

CSR Newsletters: SRI Funds

A recent article[128] and corresponding graphics provide some interesting statistics regarding the recent performance of SRI mutual funds:

> Socially responsible investing, such as avoiding tobacco, defense, or other stocks for ethical reasons, is increasing in popularity among individual investors. The assets of these funds hit $202 billion in 2007. In the recent downturn, their returns have declined less than the broader market's.

> According to the Activism vs. the Market graph in the article, while SRI funds did not perform as well as the S&P 500 in a rising market (3–5 years ago), they have held their value better than the S&P 500 in the more recent declining market. Such lower volatility is something that should appeal to investors and, perhaps, indicates more fundamentally sound organizational management.

Other figures support the sentiment that SRI funds are growing in number, size, and influence:

> SRI funds . . . are on the rise, according to fund tracker Lipper Inc. Assets in SRI funds have increased 74 percent over the last five years, while assets in non-SRI funds have grown only 36 percent.[129]

> Over the past 20 years, the total dollars invested in SRI [have] grown exponentially, as has the number of institutional, professional, and individual investors involved in the field. Between 1995 and 2007, total dollars under professional management in SRI grew from $639 billion to $2.71 trillion, outpacing the overall market.[130]

This growth is continuing in the United States:

> The trend [in SRI fund growth] has seen assets in SRI mutual funds grow almost 50 per cent in less than four years, from $23.3bn [billion] (£11.2bn, €16.1bn) at the start of 2004 to $34.6bn as of September 30 [2007], according to figures from Lipper.[131]

> Strong SRI growth is also evident in Europe, where:

Total sales for the SRI sector for December, 2008, were €999.4m ($1.3 bn [billion]) to take its overall value to €35.4bn. Significantly, total SRI fund sales came out at 10% of the total European equity fund sales figure of just over €10bn in December, which suggests SRI fund sales are holding up well and increasing in comparison to their mainstream peers during the current economic market crisis.[132]

In the United Kingdom, funds invested with a socially responsible focus have grown from £1bn to £746bn ($1,260bn, €897bn) in 12 years.[133]

CSR Newsletters: Pros and Cons of SRI Funds

A recent article[134] discusses the pros and cons of SRI. The general overview is that, while SRI might not always outperform the market, and rarely is able to change the world, it is often able to mirror the market. This means that:

It looks possible to screen out morally-questionable investments and still match the market. . . . So it need not hurt your wallet.

What is most interesting is the use of "social screens" by funds that rule out investments in certain types of firms, such as tobacco firms, arms manufacturers, and so on. When such categories of firms are automatically excluded, however, it invariably hurts the performance of these investment funds:

The Domini 400 social index, maintained the Boston index group KLD, is the clearest expression of this philosophy. It applies social screens, but tries to match the S&P 500 after making its exclusions. Since early 2005, when tobacco began to rebound, it has underperformed the S&P significantly, but for several years earlier this decade the two indices tracked each other closely.

Notably:

In the US, the charmingly named Vice Fund specialises in four sectors: alcohol, tobacco, arms and gambling. Since its launch in September 2002, it has grown at a rate of 20 per cent, eclipsing the S&P 500's growth rate of 16 per cent per year.

While different products have different social benefits and consequences, some of which we should aim to avoid, it is unhelpful to use such a blunt instrument to brand a firm either totally good or bad in terms of CSR. Almost all firms that remain profitable are providing some degree of social benefit. Tobacco firms, for example, employ people, pay taxes, and support the local economy, above and beyond whatever harm their product does.

It is OK for someone trying to evaluate a firm's overall CSR score to add up the pros and the cons and declare that the cons outweigh the pros, but it is less rational not even to consider the pros by declaring a firm's product the be-all-and-end-all of its contribution to

(Continued)

(Continued)

society. If a more holistic approach is adopted, it is likely that there will be some tobacco firms that are more or less socially responsible than others, which is a degree of subtlety that the CSR evaluation debate is far away from at present.

In reaction to the growth of SRI funds and a doubt that they make a difference, some analysts have begun leading a backlash against ethical or environmental investment funds. As one consequence of this, sin funds have been developed (focusing on companies in the tobacco, alcohol, gambling, defense, and oil extraction industries) that aim to improve returns to investors:

> [Mutuals.com's] new Vice Fund went on sale to the public in [2002], advertising itself as a "socially irresponsible fund" that will invest clients' assets in tobacco, gambling, liquor, in addition to defence. . . . According to the fund's prospectus, only tobacco stocks under-performed the Standard & Poor's 500 index over the last five years. The largest gainer was alcoholic-beverage stocks. They gained 62.57% over the five years, compared with an 11.8% gain for the S&P 500.[135]

From its shaky beginnings,[136] the Vice Fund has grown into a serious attempt to rival the reach and impact of SRI funds:

> We're pleased to report that as of December 31, 2008, in the multi-cap core funds category, based on total return, Lipper ranks the Vice Fund:
>
> • Top 2% among 455 funds over the past five years;
> • Top 5% among 640 funds over the past three years;
> • 75% percentile among 787 funds for the one year period.[137]

Anecdotal evidence suggests that there is an empirical justification for investing in sin stocks:

> Only three Standard & Poor's 500 stock index subindustries posted an increase in average price performance during the 11 market declines associated with recessions since World War II: Alcoholic Beverages, Household Products, and Tobacco. I guess that's the reason for the old Wall Street saying "When the going gets tough, the tough go eating, smoking and drinking."[138]

More objective research suggests that, at the very least, while there may not be a significantly advantageous financial return from SRI funds, there is no disadvantage to investing in funds that employ a CSR filter:

> Researchers at Maastricht University in the Netherlands recently found that, in the long run, there's no statistical difference in performance between SRI and non-SRI funds in the U.S. or abroad.[139]

Other commentators, however, argue that the level of return is not the issue. What is more misleading is the idea that investing in an SRI fund advances the CSR causes in which the investor believes:

> Socially responsible investing oversimplifies the world, and in doing so distorts reality. It allows investors to believe that their money is only being invested in "good companies," and they take foolish comfort in that belief. Rare is the company, after all, that is either all good

or all bad. To put it another way, socially responsible investing creates the illusion that the world is black and white, when its real color is gray.[140]

Pax World Funds' 2006 announcement that it will stop avoiding whole industries in making its investment decisions and, instead, "selectively invest in these industries based on a company's `entire social-responsibility profile'"[141] is a step in the right direction, which allows Pax funds to invest in a best-practice firm from a sin industry that other SRI funds using blunter industry or product screens automatically avoid. Overall, however, the question of how good measures of social responsibility SRI funds really are remains a valid critique of the SRI industry. It is also debatable whether they have any impact in terms of encouraging more socially responsible behavior in corporations:

There is not one iota of data that supports the idea that investing in these companies makes the world a better place.[142]

Online Resources

- Calvert Social Investment Fund, http://www.calvertgroup.com/sri.html

  "As a leader in sustainable and responsible investing (SRI), Calvert offers a range of SRI strategies."

- Dow Jones Sustainability Indexes, http://www.sustainability-index.com/

  "Launched in 1999, the Dow Jones Sustainability Indexes are the first global indexes tracking the financial performance of the leading sustainability-driven companies worldwide."

- Ethical Investment Research Service, http://www.eiris.org/

  "EIRIS is the leading global provider of independent research into the social, environmental and ethical performance of companies."

- FTSE 4 Good, http://www.ftse4good.com/

  "The FTSE4Good Index Series has been designed to measure the performance of companies that meet globally recognised corporate responsibility standards, and to facilitate investment in those companies."

- Interfaith Center on Corporate Responsibility, http://www.iccr.org/

  "For thirty-eight years the Interfaith Center on Corporate Responsibility (ICCR) has been a leader of the corporate social responsibility movement."

- Investors Against Genocide, http://www.investorsagainstgenocide.org/

  "The goal of Investors Against Genocide is to convince financial institutions to make a commitment that they will not invest in genocide."

- New Alternatives Fund, http://www.newalternativesfund.com/

  "New Alternatives Fund is a Socially Responsible Mutual Fund Emphasizing Alternative Energy and the Environment."

- Pax World Funds (http://www.paxworld.com/) ("oversees the oldest, and among the largest, socially responsible funds.")[143]

  "Launched on August 10, 1971, with $101,000 in assets, [the Pax World Fund] was the first broadly-diversified, publicly-available mutual fund to use social as well as financial criteria in the investment decision-making process."

- Principles for Responsible Investment, http://www.unpri.org/

  "An investor initiative in partnership with UNEP Finance Initiative and the UN Global Compact."

- SocialFunds.com, http://www.socialfunds.com/

  "SocialFunds.com features over 10,000 pages of information on SRI mutual funds, community investments, corporate research, shareowner actions, and daily social investment news."

- Social Investment Forum's Advocacy and Public Policy Program, http://www .socialinvest.org/projects/advocacy/

  "The purpose of the Advocacy and Public Policy Program is to . . . provide a platform for Social Investment Forum members and colleagues to share information and collaborate on shareholder proposals, social investing and corporate social responsibility issues."

- SRI World Group, http://www.sriworld.com/

  "The Internet's most comprehensive personal finance site devoted to socially responsible investing including complete coverage of social mutual funds, community investment, and shareowner action."

- USAMutuals Vice Fund, http://www.vicefund.com/vicefund/abt.aspx

  "Our rigorous focus on aerospace/defense, gaming, tobacco and alcoholic beverages has given us experience navigating within them, and provides our investors with maximum exposure to these sectors."

Questions for Discussion and Review

1. Do you own any shares of a company? If so, do you vote at the company's annual general meeting (either in person or by proxy)? Is it important for shareholders to be actively involved with the company they own? Why, or why not?

2. What are your thoughts about the UK legislation (outlined above) that requires companies to produce a remuneration report every year, which then must be voted on at the AGM? Is it a good idea or unnecessary interference in the day-to-day management of the firm? Should the votes be binding?

3. When considering an investment in a mutual fund, would you consider the social responsibility of the companies in which the fund invested? What about SRI funds? Why, or why not?

4. Would you think twice about investing in a *sin fund* if historical returns showed greater growth potential than SRI funds? What is the justification for your decision?

5. Choose any one of the social investment fund companies listed in the *Online Resources* subsection. What is your opinion of its home page and its stated mission and values? Is the company a force for *good,* or is it merely lulling gullible investors into a false sense of security by allowing them to think they are investing with a conscience?

SOCIAL ENTREPRENEURSHIP

> **CSR CONNECTION:** This issue covers those firms that overtly combine the profit motive with a social mission. It also highlights the difficulties that can arise when the founder retires or when ownership is transferred to a larger firm with competing priorities.

Issue

Social entrepreneurs fashion themselves as capitalists with a heart. They form organizations that are guided by considerations other than profit. They see their mission of solving a social problem as a point of differentiation in the market—something that consumers will support because they value the mission that the entrepreneur has outlined. Famous examples of firms with strong social missions include: Tom's of Maine (http://www.tomsofmaine.com/), "a company with a conscience;"[144] Nau (http://www.nau.com/), "The ideas Nau promotes are as important as the clothes it sells;"[145] Patagonia (http://www.patagonia.com/) "an environmentally responsible and socially innovative company;"[146] and many more.[147] Social entrepreneurs (like all entrepreneurs) see themselves as revolutionaries—challenging the status quo; only social entrepreneurs also see their success as a means for "taking on the world's social problems."[148] As Nau CEO, Chris Van Dyke, puts it:

> We're challenging the nature of capitalism. . . . We started with a clean whiteboard . . . [and] believed every single operational element in our business was an opportunity to turn traditional business notions inside out, integrating environmental, social, and economic factors. Nau represents a new form of activism: business activism.[149]

Social entrepreneurs, who claim to be the founders of "a whole new, distinct fourth sector" of organizations,[150] however, face two issues that remain unresolved within CSR. First, is there a market for *compassion?* Will consumers prefer a *social* product over its *market* equivalent in sufficient numbers to sustain the organization? In other words, will consumers pay a *CSR premium* for a product? Second, how can such organizations retain their mission and operating practices when the founder leaves or ownership is transferred to a for-profit parent that might not pursue the same goals with the same set of priorities? Issues of relevance and legacy are central to the discussion about social entrepreneurs.

The first issue facing social entrepreneurs relates to the size of the market for CSR goods. While this is definitely growing, it is still not very big. In addition, while successful social entrepreneurs attract a lot of attention and there is a lot of activity in this area,[151] the overall influence of the group of social entrepreneurs, in terms of market share, is not very large. It is relatively easy to have high percentage growth if the base amount is small. In 2007, for example, the Co-operative Bank's Ethical Consumerism Report stated that:

> The overall ethical market in the UK was worth £35.5 billion in 2007, up 15 percent from £31 billion in the previous 12 months. . . . However, overall ethical spend at £35.5 billion is still a small proportion of the total annual consumer spend of more than £600 billion.[152]

Reflecting the limited size of the market for CSR goods is the idea that consumers are not uniform in their goals or willingness to support a social cause with their purchase decisions, but, in fact, can be broken down into several subgroups. One study, conducted in the United Kingdom, divides the market into four different types of consumers:

> The first, about 8 per cent of the total, are committed cause-driven purchasers. A second group, accounting for 30–35 per cent, want to purchase ethically but are not really sure how and are looking to retailers to help them. The third group, also about 30–35 per cent, feel the same, but doubt that their individual purchases can make much difference. The fourth group, the remainder, are completely uninterested, often because they are too poor to think about much more than putting food on the table for their families.[153]

Supporters of social entrepreneurship argue that it is the only way that certain intractable social problems can be addressed. They contend that social entrepreneurs fill the gap between problems that the market has avoided and philanthropy has been unable to solve:

> Social enterprise is proving one of the most interesting, if disparate, ways of tackling disease, poverty and environmental damage.[154]

Critics, however, remain unconvinced that social entrepreneurs are adding any more social value than regular for-profit firms with traditional for-profit motivations. They argue

> Businesses that have wrapped themselves in a social cloak—such as Body Shop, the cosmetics retailer, or the growing number of organizations offering carbon offsets for air travelers—simply salve the consciences of customers who would do more for the environment by reducing their overall consumption.[155]

The second issue facing social entrepreneurs relates to the threat to the organization's social mission following a decision to sell the firm or for the founder to retire—"the legacy problem":[156]

Stewardship means a sense of responsibility for that which you own and handle every day. . . . With the separation of ownership from control in the listed company, stewardship does not disappear, but it does erode.[157]

In essence, many social entrepreneurs who build firms around social missions that enjoy consumer support are victims of their own success:

> Pret a Manger . . . agreed to sell a third of its business to McDonald's; Pepsi swallowed P&J Smoothies . . . ; Cadbury Schweppes bought Green & Black's organic chocolate . . . ; Go Organic and Ben & Jerry's are now owned by Unilever—and the list goes on.[158]

In spite of promises made at the time of acquisition, the acquired firm and its founders (who are often replaced by professional managers as part of the purchase) have very little leverage if situations change at some future point. Essentially, in agreeing to sell the firm, the social entrepreneur loses the power to control its character and the values by which it operates. That's why Gary Erickson, CEO and founder of Clif's Bars, turned down a "generous buyout offer" for his firm:

> Erickson walked away from millions not because he had dreams of taking Clif public, or because he thought he could command a higher price. Rather, he decided that a corporate parent would ultimately destroy the company. . . . Unilever gobbled up the famously iconoclastic Ben & Jerry's. Coca-Cola owns juice purist Odwella. Dean Foods runs soy milk pioneer White Wave and dairy brand Horizon Organic. But [Clif founder Gary] Erickson aspires to be a market leader while remaining private and staying true to ideals of corporate social responsibility.[159]

A good example of some of the issues that can arise is Unilever's hostile takeover of Ben & Jerry's:

> [Ben] Cohen had been estranged from the company he co-founded after losing the business to European packaged goods giant Unilever in a $326 million hostile takeover in 2000.[160]

Others, however, while recognizing the risks, contend that the fears are overblown:

> Such is the emotion invested in small ethical brands. Body Shop, Ben & Jerry's, Green & Blacks—these are the darlings of corporate responsibility. One by one, bigger brands have swallowed them up. But each time, concerns over their future seem to have been exaggerated.[161]

Threats to the integrity of an organization's social mission, however, do not come only from an acquisition or founder retirement. Accusations of a *sell-out* also occur when an organization with a social mission lends its name and reputation to a for-profit firm for a marketing campaign. Pleasing grassroots members, many of whom are diehard believers in the organization's mission and less willing to compromise with organizations that they perceive to be *the enemy,* can be challenging at the best of times.

CSR Newsletters: Clorox and The Sierra Club

A recent article[162] analyzes the partnership between Clorox and the Sierra Club, which places the Sierra Club's logo on all of the products in Clorox's new line of cleaning products—Green Works. In exchange, the Sierra Club will receive a percentage of the profits from sales. Although Clorox has benefited handsomely from "one of the most successful launches of a new cleaning brand in recent memory":

> Within the Sierra Club, the reaction to the deal has been contentious, with emails flying back and forth and charges that [Sierra Club Executive Director] Pope's executive committee has sold out . . . the awkward pairing with Clorox underlines both the huge potential upside for major brands discovering green and the danger for nonprofit environmental groups plunging headlong into the for-profit world.

On the face of it, the Sierra Club seems to have the most at risk in forming this relationship with a firm whose core product many environmentalists believe to be fundamentally opposed to their conception of sustainability. The article notes that Clorox had been working on sustainable ingredients "for nearly a decade." Even after improvements in cost and availability, however, the firm still faces a difficult challenge in persuading environmentalists that their products really can be green.

While difficult, however, the Sierra Club's attitude when approached by Clorox is the attitude that many NGOs need to have if they are truly invested in realizable change. While there will always be a role for antagonists and idealism is fine, reality inevitably means incremental progress. That is not to say, however, that the Sierra Club is handling everything as well as it should:

> With no independent scientific assessment of Green Works products, and with an undisclosed amount of money changing hands, what does that Sierra Club seal on the back of the bottle really mean?

Ultimately:

> For Clorox, it's nothing but upside. For the Sierra Club, it's risking—if not undermining—its most valuable asset: its independent reputation.

This skeptical tone is continued in this second article:[163]

> Transparency and accountability are double-edged. Embedded in an organisation's culture they can burnish credibility and encourage progressive innovation. But if the promise does not match the practice, the greenwashing backlash can cause considerable brand damage.

Case Study   The Body Shop

In addition to the two central issues facing social entrepreneurship outlined above, a third issue arises for those organizations with particularly zealous founders: To what extent can companies that claim to be ethically conscious and socially responsible live up to the high standards they claim or hold to others?

The Body Shop, with its high-profile founder, Anita Roddick, became a global retailing force on the back of its image as a progressive, conscience-driven, campaigning corporation. Many of its consumers are drawn to the company because of its activism as much as the quality and range of its products:

A growing number of companies such as The Body Shop, a global skin- and hair-care retailer, make corporate virtue part of their value proposition: Buy one of our products, The Body Shop tells its customers, and you improve the lives of women in developing countries, promote animal rights, protect the environment, and otherwise increase the supply of social responsibility.[164]

As the ever provocative Roddick, who once described corporate executives as "F---ing robber barons,"[165] puts it:

Today's CSR movement doesn't explain how to put its ideas into practice and ignores a truth that nobody wants to discuss: if it gets in the way of profit, businesses are not going to do anything about it. When we are measured by a financial bottom line that does include human rights, social justice and workers' justice, then something will change.[166]

One of the first issues the company focused on, and became famous for campaigning against, was the issue of using animals for the testing of human cosmetic products:

The use of animals to test cosmetics and toiletries products and ingredients continues around the world today. It is estimated that over 35,000 animals are used in cosmetics tests every year throughout the European Union alone. In some cases the tests can cause suffering and even death. The Body Shop believes cosmetics testing on animals is unethical, unnecessary and should be banned.[167]

PETA[168]

Although not a company, PETA is still an organization that should strive to remain transparent and accountable to as many of its stakeholders as possible. Any organization that fails to meet consistently the needs and goals of a significant proportion of its stakeholders is unlikely to remain viable over the long term:

People for the Ethical Treatment of Animals (PETA) is the largest animal rights group in the world. We have more than 700,000 members around the globe. . . . We work to help people

(Continued)

(Continued)

understand that the things they do every day either help or hurt animals—animals in our lives, like the dogs and cats who live with us, and animals we never see, like cows, chickens, and pigs killed for food. PETA believes that animals are not ours to eat, wear, experiment on, or use for entertainment.[169]

Not many people would argue with most of PETA's goals. Many, however, take issue with the extent to which the organization takes its point of view (elevating the rights of animals to a status that is equal, or sometimes above, those of humans) and also the methods by which it attempts to convey its message and achieve its goals (direct, often violent action). Accusations have also been made that, while trying to improve its own public face, PETA finances other much more radical operations:

The FBI lists the group and its counterpart, the Animal Liberation Front [ALF], as domestic terrorists. The government has said the two groups are responsible for more than 600 cases of ecoterrorism around the country, such as spray-painting buildings, breaking windows, and burning fur farms.[170]

The organization is a relatively powerful fund-raising operation, gathering $13 million in direct donations and fundraisers in 2000. Some of the donations the organization has made with these funds have raised eyebrows:

Notwithstanding claims by PETA leader Ingrid Newkirk that her organization is not violent, her defense of ALF is not merely rhetorical: It included $45,000 for the legal defense of an ALF arsonist accused (and ultimately convicted) of torching a Michigan State research lab.[171]

[One accuser] cites a $1,500 contribution PETA made in April 2001 to the North American Earth Liberation Front, a violent activists group that has taken responsibility for setting fire to buildings and businesses. Most recently, the group claimed responsibility for burning Ford vehicles at a large dealership in Pennsylvania.[172]

A significant section of The Body Shop's customers are loyal to the organization because of the ethical stand it adopts. There is evidence, however, to suggest that there may be a degree of public relations gloss covering much of the company's ethical position in its history and perhaps not quite as much substance as many customers believe:

Is the Body Shop's social conscience just a sham?[173]

The Body Shop's official position on animal testing, for example, is outlined in its 2005 "Values Report:"

The company refuses to buy any ingredient that has been tested on animals for cosmetic purposes after 31 December 1990, but points out that most of the ingredients used in cosmetic and toiletry products have been animal tested for some purpose at some time in their history so it would be near impossible to sell products whose ingredients had never been tested on animals.[174]

Although The Body Shop may not itself use ingredients that have been tested on animals, it is clearly benefiting from the knowledge gained by others who have previously used animals to test the same ingredients and ensure they are safe for human use:

> During 1989, The Body Shop switched from "not tested on animals" to "against animal testing" labeling after a lawsuit by the German government. The lawsuit claimed that Body Shop labeling was misleading, since their products' ingredients may have been tested on animals.[175]

While, as a cosmetics company, it would be irresponsible for The Body Shop to do any differently, the company's claims of innocence in this regard are disingenuous at a minimum and probably misleading to a significant percentage of its customers:

> Helping animals?—Although the Body Shop maintains that they are against animal testing, they do not always make clear that many of the ingredients in their products have been tested on animals by other companies, causing much pain and suffering to those animals. . . . Also, some Body Shop items contain animal products such as gelatine (crushed bone).[176]

In addition, its claim relating to animal testing is only one of several issues that have been raised by various campaigning and interested parties:

> Beyond balance-sheet woes, the company that likes to insist it puts principles before profits has been buffeted for [years] by allegations, which Roddick angrily denies, that it has misled the public about everything from its stand against animal testing to the ingredients of elderflower eye gel.[177]

The wide-ranging criticisms of Roddick, who claims "the stories were all fabrications,"[178] continued after her decision to sell The Body Shop to L'Oreal in 2006 for £652 million and her death in 2007. In relation to social entrepreneurship, they serve to indicate the double-edged sword of a holier-than-thou approach to business:

> What is Roddick's real legacy? . . . She will be remembered as a one-of-a-kind innovator, but when the solemnity subsides and the history books are finally written, she is not likely to be remembered as the world's most socially responsible executive.[179]

Online Resources

- *Animal People:* "Body Shop Animal Testing Policy Alleged 'a Sham,'" http://www.animalpeoplenews.org/94/8/body_shop.html

"*Animal People* is the leading independent newspaper providing original investigative coverage of animal protection worldwide. Founded in 1992, *Animal People* has no alignment or affiliation with any other entity."

- McSpotlight (beyond McDonald's), http://www.mcspotlight.org/beyond/companies/bs_ref.html

  "What's Wrong with the Body Shop? A criticism of 'green' consumerism."

- A reply by The Body Shop to McSpotlight's accusations is posted at: http://www.mcspotlight.org/beyond/companies/bs_reply.html

- PBS—What is Social Entrepreneurship? http://www.pbs.org/opb/thenewheroes/whatis/

  "A social entrepreneur identifies and solves social problems on a large scale."

- PETA—People for the Ethical Treatment of Animals, http://www.peta.org/

  "People for the Ethical Treatment of Animals (PETA), with more than 2.0 million members and supporters, is the largest animal rights organization in the world."

- The Body Shop, http://www.thebodyshop.com/

  "The Body Shop . . . strives to protect this beautiful planet and the people who depend on it—not because it's fashionable, but based on the belief that it's the only way to do business."

- The Humane Society of the United States, http://www.hsus.org/

  "Established in 1954, The HSUS seeks a humane and sustainable world for all animals—a world that will also benefit people."

Questions for Discussion and Review

1. What is your definition of a *social entrepreneur?* How is it different from a *regular* entrepreneur? Is this something that you see yourself becoming?

2. Is *social entrepreneurship* the future of business or a phenomenon that, ultimately, must give way to "the supremacy of the profit motive"?

3. What are the two main issues with social entrepreneurship ? Which do you think is the most dangerous to the case for social entrepreneurship? Why?

4. Think of an example of a corporation that you feel has been hypocritical in terms of its ethical or CSR stance. What is your reaction to the company's actions? Would you consider boycotting the products of a company that you felt had acted in a socially irresponsible way? How about one you felt had acted in a hypocritical way?

5. Read the essay titled, "Body Shop Animal Testing Policy Alleged 'a Sham'" (http://www.animalpeoplenews.org/94/8/body_shop.html). Then compare it with The Body Shop's Web site dealing with the same issue (http://www.thebodyshop-usa.com/beauty/against-animal-testing). Which of the two accounts do you believe? Does The Body Shop's stance on this issue matter?

THE CORPORATION

 CSR CONNECTION: This issue analyzes the entity that is the focus of this book—the corporation. To what extent is the firm a part of the problem versus part of the solution?

Issue

The corporation is the focus of much of the critical attention of CSR advocates. It is the organization blamed for many of the ills created by globalization and free trade. The attention reflects the high profile of the corporation in modern society:

> One hundred and fifty years ago, the corporation was a relatively insignificant entity. Today, it is a vivid, dramatic and pervasive presence in all our lives. Like the Church, the Monarchy and the Communist Party in other times and places, the corporation is today's dominant institution. But history humbles dominant institutions. All have been crushed, belittled or absorbed into some new order. The corporation is unlikely to be the first to defy history.[180]

In contrast to this bleak outlook, *Fortune* magazine heralds the corporation as one of "the most significant innovations of the past 50 years":

> Without [corporations] and their proven ability to marshal and allocate resources, organize and harness the ingenuity of people, respond to commercial and social environments, and meet the ever more elaborate challenge of producing and distributing goods and providing services on a global scale, we would have far less innovation—and less wealth.[181]

This perspective is shared by Micklethwait and Wooldridge in their book, *The Company: A Short History of a Revolutionary Idea:*

> Hegel predicted that the basic unit of modern society would be the state, Marx that it would be the commune, Lenin and Hitler that it would be the political party. Before that, a succession of saints and sages claimed the same for the parish church, the feudal manor, and the monarchy. The big contention of this small book is that they have all been proved wrong. The most important organization in the world is the company: the basis of the prosperity of the West and the best hope for the future of the rest of the world. Indeed, for most of us, the company's only real rival for our time and energy is the one that is taken for granted—the family.[182]

Bill Gates is even more effusive:

> "[The] modern corporation is one of the most effective means to allocate resources we've ever seen. It transforms great ideas into customer benefits on an unimaginably large scale."

Drucker and Collins, likewise, think [all organizations] would benefit if they learned to behave more like corporations. . . . Whether or not the ever-evolving modern corporation can be a panacea for the ills and dysfunctions of other kinds of institutions, there's no question that it is peerless at creating wealth and providing meaningful employment for tens of millions of people.[183]

When a corporation attempts to implement a CSR perspective, it is important to remember that, merely by existing—by providing a return on investment to shareholders, by providing jobs for employees and suppliers, by providing value to customers, and by paying taxes to government—the corporation is benefiting society. If you add to that mix the constant product innovation necessary to maintain sales and profits (in general, only products that are in demand are purchased), then the corporation, as a concept, can be considered a positive and productive component of a healthy society. As Todd Stitzer, CEO of Cadbury Schweppes, proclaims:

Remember Adam Smith's invisible hand? It is one of the most repeated phrases in the business world. But business has allowed society to forget a very simple fact: the hand that connects markets and balances supply and demand is ours. We are the people who put food on plates, books on shelves, music in people's ears and information online. We are the distributors and we are the creators of wealth.[184]

The corporation, however, can also do harm to the societies in which it operates. Doing all of the above does not ensure an organization's long-term viability and does not replace the need for an effective CSR policy implemented throughout the organization. Our discussion of Walmart in Chapter 3, for example, shows that a company that is successful and producing products in demand can still be accused of behavior that is harmful to society as a whole. As a result, the positive aspects of Walmart's operations[185] are often lost among all the negative publicity the company receives.[186]

To what extent, therefore, is the corporation a positive factor in the CSR debate? To what extent is business essential to achieve the social agenda sought by CSR advocates? And how can a corporation's contribution to the wider good be measured and evaluated?

Case Study   Primark Versus Marks & Spencer

A central component of the argument presented in this book is the recognition that corporations exist because their products are in demand and that, in general, it is in society's best interests to encourage healthy and wealthy corporations because they bring many benefits. An equally important component of our argument, however, is that, while demand for a product might be sufficient for short-term gain, it is insufficient for survival over the medium to long term. On top of a healthy foundation of an efficient organization and a profitable product, therefore, is the construction of an integrated, effective CSR policy that seeks to maximize stakeholder benefit over the medium to long term.

The Center for Corporate Citizenship at Boston College and the U.S. Chamber of Commerce's Center for Corporate Citizenship analyzed the level of CSR awareness within the modern U.S. corporation. The subsequent report (*The State of Corporate Citizenship in the U.S.: A View From Inside*), a survey of 515 business leaders from firms across the U.S. business landscape,

> concludes that regardless of company size, business executives see corporate citizenship as a fundamental part of business and central to good business practice. Eighty-two per cent of respondents say good corporate citizenship helped the bottom line and 59% feel these practices improve company image and reputation. Fifty-three per cent report corporate citizenship is important to their customers. More than half of the executives surveyed say corporate citizenship is part of their business strategy.[187]

We, as a society, benefit if we are progressing. Corporations help us progress and generate much of the wealth on which we measure that progress. The business world is society's most important stakeholder and is the key to future progress. CSR helps corporations understand the environment in which they operate and helps them chart a more sustainable path forward. CSR helps corporations maximize their potential and benefit for the widest number of constituent groups.

One way of assessing the value a corporation can add, over and above its legal obligations, is to compare how two different corporations are reacting to the increased demands that arise from operating in a global, constantly wired, and increasingly complex business environment. Primark (http://www.primark.co.uk) and Marks & Spencer (http://www.marksandspencer.com) are both UK retailers. While Primark produces low-cost clothes to compete with firms such as Walmart (Asda in the United Kingdom), however, Marks & Spencer seeks to differentiate its products based on quality and charges a corresponding price premium to reflect the different market segment it targets. How these two companies are approaching the issue of CSR is indicative of the pattern of CSR adoption outlined in the CSR threshold (Chapter 5).

In 2007, Marks & Spencer launched Plan A[188] (http://plana.marksandspencer.com/). The plan was named *Plan A* because there is no Plan B—i.e., no alternative to implementing a CSR perspective throughout all aspects of operations:

> We're doing this because it's what you want us to do. It's also the right thing to do. We're calling it Plan A because we believe it's now the only way to do business.[189]

Plan A consists of a 100-point plan, spread over five commitment areas, that the firm has pledged to achieve by 2012 and that "promises to 'change beyond recognition' the way M&S operates:"

Initiatives within the 100-point plan include transforming the 460-strong chain into a carbon neutral operation; banning group waste from landfill dumps; using unsold out-of-date food as a source of recyclable energy and making polyester clothing from recycled plastic bottles.[190]

(Continued)

(Continued)

In spite of an initial plan to spend £200 million over the five years of Plan A,[191] by the first half of 2009, M&S claimed that Plan A remained "cost-neutral."[192] More important, based on progress during the first half of the plan's five years,

three broad conclusions can be drawn. Corporate responsibility guidance and the Plan A commitment have systematically embedded themselves into the company's management platform; clear package labels and effective outreach to third-party stakeholders are changing consumer behavior; and steady progress is being made towards fulfilling Plan A's five commitment areas of carbon emissions, waste, sustainable sourcing, ethical trading, and healthy lifestyles. So far, 20 of the plan's 100 commitments have been completed and a further 75 are under way.[193]

The favorable coverage Marks & Spencer has received for its Plan A (as well as the business benefits it has gained from implementing the plan) can be compared with media coverage Primark received in 2009 concerning issues that emerged in its supply chain:

[In January, 2009] One of Primark's UK suppliers was found to be employing illegal workers and paying staff less than the minimum wage. . . . Primark is having to explain itself to the Ethical Trading Initiative (ETI), the UK body set up to improve supply chain working conditions, which it joined in 2006. The incident came just months after it

emerged that Primark clothes were being made in India by factories using child labour.

Marks & Spencer was quick to point out the apparent differences between the two firms' approaches to CSR, in general, and the supply chain, in particular:

[Stuart Rose, CEO of Marks & Spencer] takes a swipe, seemingly at Primark, the low-cost retailer that has often been accused of unwittingly using cheap labour in its supply chain, . . . "How can you sell a T-shirt for £2 and pay the rents and pay the rates and pay the buyer and pay the poor boy or girl who [is] making it a living wage? You can't".[194]

A central goal of Strategic CSR is to try and restore faith in the corporation. For all its faults, it is clear to us that the corporation is uniquely placed to achieve many of the goals CSR advocates support. While the government and nonprofit organizations also fill valuable social roles, it is the corporation that has the ability to allocate valuable and scarce resources in ways that encourage innovation and, therefore, maximize social value. Those corporations that embrace CSR at all levels of operations, seeking to engage stakeholders to meet their needs and expectations, will be much better placed to survive and thrive over the medium to long term. In spite of what Marks & Spencer says, there is a Plan B; it is just not in anyone's interests to have firms pursue it.

Online Resources

- Bakan, Joel, *The Corporation: The Pathological Pursuit of Profit and Power,* Free Press, 2004, http://www.thecorporation.com/

- Corporation 20/20, http://www.corporation2020.org/

  "Creating the vision and charting the course for the Future Corporation."

- GoodCorporation, http://www.goodcorporation.com/

  "GoodCorporation is a for-profit company owned by a group of private individuals interested in responsible business management."

- The Center for Corporate Citizenship at Boston College, http://www.bcccc.net/

  "[The Center for Corporate Citizenship at Boston College is] committed to helping business leverage its social, economic and human assets to ensure both its success and a more just and sustainable world."

- *The Corporation,* http://www.thecorporation.com/

  "THE CORPORATION explores the nature and spectacular rise of the dominant institution of our time."

- Tomorrow's Company, http://www.tomorrowscompany.com/

  "Tomorrow's Company is a not-for-profit research and agenda-setting organizations committed to creating a future for business which makes equal sense to staff, shareholders and society."

Questions for Discussion and Review

1. Make the case for the corporation as a force for good in society today.

2. Can you imagine a world without corporations? What would we lose? What would we gain?

3. Go to the Web site for the movie documentary, *The Corporation* (http://www .thecorporation.com/). Have a look at the trailer posted on the site.[195] Is this kind of commentary helpful to those promoting CSR? Do you agree with the message it is conveying? Why, or why not?

4. Look at Marks & Spencer's Plan A Web site (http://plana.marksandspencer.com/). What are your impressions? Do you get the sense that this is a genuine effort, or is it window dressing?

5. Primark is a low-cost retailer, while Marks & Spencer seeks to differentiate its products based on quality. Is there a causal link between these two different business-level strategies and the firm's respective CSR performance? What does this say for the future of the business case for CSR?

WAGES

 CSR CONNECTION: This issue reflects the importance of wages as a highly visible component of a firm's relationship with one of its key organizational stakeholders, its employees.

Issue

One of the concerns expressed with capitalism is that, in spite of all its efficiencies in creating innovation and opportunity,

> what it's not good at is distributing the fruits, because the logic in the boardroom . . . . is always cut your labor costs to improve your quarterly [numbers] and your profit margins for shareholder value.[196]

Employees, in particular, are sometimes treated as a means to an end, rather than being a valued partner in the process:

> Layoffs. Downsizing. Rightsizing. Job cuts. Separations. Terminations. Workforce reductions. Off-shoring. Outsourcing. Whatever the term, getting rid of employees can be a necessary and beneficial strategic move for companies to make.[197]

By reducing those labor costs (by minimizing wage levels, outsourcing, and/or cutting labor positions within an organization), however, are companies also reducing the overall health of the communities within which they are based and hope to sell their products? In other words, by cutting costs in the short term, is a firm undermining the market on which it depends for its long term survival?

> The same workers who've been let go are the same people who have consumed the goods and services. . . . They are not just a factor in the means of production. They're not only the consumers, they're the shareholders. So when you [sack] them . . . you slowly lose the purchasing power to empty inventories and long-term savings in the form of institutional pension funds to invest in the stocks and bonds of these companies.[198]

Equally, however, if a firm fails to cut its costs in the short term, might that not jeopardize the entire enterprise anyway? The effort to minimize the cost of production is a legitimate business strategy. But a major corporation must also come to terms with the fact that the employees whose wages it squeezes can also be the customers on whom it relies for sales.

In addition, firms need also to consider the possible reputation costs incurred from cutting jobs, as well as the damage to morale of those remaining employees who are left wondering, "Will I be next"? In March 2007, for example, Circuit City was roundly criticized for cutting 3,400 jobs (7% of the firm's workforce). The rationale behind the "wage management

Ford[199]

Nearly a century ago, Henry Ford drew no distinction between his employees and his customers. Challenging the conventional wisdom that the best way to maximize profits was to tailor your product to the wealthiest segment of society, Ford decided to market his black Model T as "America's Everyman car."[200]

For Ford, mass production went hand in hand with mass consumption. His benchmark for worker compensation was whether his own workers could afford to buy the product they were making. He offered a $5-a-day minimum wage for *all* his workers (crashing through the race barriers of the day[201])—twice the prevailing automobile industry average.

In doing so, Ford created a *virtuous circle.* Workers flocked to his factory to apply for positions. If they managed to secure one of Ford's coveted jobs, then in time they too would be able to afford one of his cars. The company flourished based on the twin pillars of a desirable product and a highly motivated employee base. "By the time production ceased for the Model T in 1927, more than 15 million cars had been sold—or half the world's output."[202]

initiative" was that the fired employees were being overpaid, so the firm immediately re-advertised their jobs at a lower wage:

> The company did not disclose specifics, but *The Baltimore Sun* reported that the laid-off workers, known as "associates," made 51 cents more per hour above what the company had set as market wages. . . . The company said, however, that the people who lost their jobs received severance packages and could reapply for their old jobs, at lower pay, but had to wait 10 weeks to do so.[203]

What was the result of Circuit City's "series of changes to improve financial performance largely by realigning [the company's] cost and expense structure"?[204] The firm filed for bankruptcy in October 2008 and liquidated its remaining stores and inventory in January 2009.[205]

An alternative corporate perspective argues that in spite of accounting convention, employees should be treated as an *asset,* rather than a *cost.* In this view, employees, as with any asset, will grow and improve with investment. In other words, there is a strong business argument for ensuring that a firm's employees are respected as an asset that can assist the firm achieve its goals, rather than a potential barrier that might prevent the firm from achieving these goals. An analysis of the relationship between the "dollars spent on employee skills" and firm performance supports the value of this approach:

> The results were unambiguous: firms that made large investments in employee development subsequently outperformed the stock market. Indeed, training and development

expenditures per employee proved to be an important leading indicator of future stock prices.[206]

This view of employees as an asset, rather than a cost, is supported by firms such as Costco, the warehouse membership-based retailer:

"From day one, we've run the company with the philosophy that if we pay better than average, provide a salary people can live on, have a positive environment and good benefits, we'll be able to hire better people, they'll stay longer and be more efficient," says Richard Galanti, Costco's chief financial officer.[207]

There are a number of other firms that share Costco's willingness to invest in their employees, believing that the motivation and loyalty such policies generate outweigh the potential cost savings gained by lower wages. At Zappos, an online retailer of shoes and handbags, for example, customer service is the firm's No. 1 priority. As such, the firm makes sure that its employees are highly motivated and share the firm's values:

After a few weeks of intensive training, new call-center employees are offered $1,000 on top of what they have already earned to that point if they want to quit. The theory . . . is that the people who take the money "obviously don't have the sense of commitment" Zappos requires from its employees. The company says about 10 percent of its trainees take the offer.[208]

At WL Gore, the creator of Gore-Tex fabric, the firm seeks to create a nonadversarial environment where innovation is encouraged through consensus. As such, the firm has worked hard to create a very flat hierarchical structure:

No one gets to tell anybody else what to do. Decisions are reached by agreement, not diktat. Leaders emerge through a democratic process rather than being appointed from the top, and peer appraisal is crucial to both salary levels and career advancement.[209]

Similarly, Whole Foods, the organic supermarket that is consistently ranked as one of Fortune Magazine's 100 Best Companies to Work For, has[210]

an open, relatively non-hierarchical organization. The pay of every employee is known, and even senior executives receive no more than 19 times the average wage. New recruits are voted in through a process of peer appraisal after a four-week probationary period.[211]

In the absence of a firm's progressive approach to wage levels, it is clear that the significant drop in trade union membership in recent years has contributed to workers' loss of bargaining power that might otherwise protect the wages they receive:[212]

In the UK, trade union membership has halved over the past quarter of a century. . . . fewer than one in five private sector employees belongs to a union. In the US, the decline has been even steeper. There, only one in ten private sector employees belongs to a union.[213]

What is an acceptable wage rate to pay employees that balances the need to maintain efficient operations and also helps create a consumer base that supports sales? Different people and ideologies suggest different solutions:

- The minimum wage (determined by the government),
- The average wage for the job and industry (determined by the market), or
- A living wage[214] (determined by nonprofits and NGOs).

An example of the discrepancies that these three different calculations can create is seen when the federal hourly minimum wage in the United States ($7.25 per hour)[215] is compared with living wage campaigners' estimates of the "poverty line" wage for a family of four ($8.85 per hour for a 40-hour work week).[216] It is also surprising to see the extent to which state minimum wages in the United States differ from the federal minimum and also vary among themselves. Washington state, for example, has a minimum wage of $8.55 per hour, Connecticut's minimum wage is $8.25 per hour, and Massachusetts' minimum wage is $8 per hour, while Wyoming has a minimum wage of only $5.15 per hour.[217]

A history of the changes in the federal minimum wage in the United States, since its introduction at $0.25 in 1938, is presented in Figure 6.1.[218]

| **Figure 6.1** | The Federal Hourly Minimum Wage in the United States (1938–2009) |

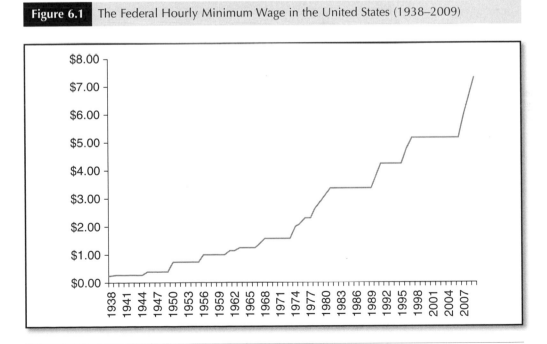

Source: "Federal Minimum Wage Increase for 2007, 2008, & 2009," *Labor Law Center*, July 24, 2009, http://www .laborlawcenter.com/t-federal-minimum-wage.aspx

Case Study · McDonald's

Mc.Job \m¶k-'jäb\ n (1986): a low-paying job that requires little skill and provides little opportunity for advancement.[219]

CSR Newsletters: McJob

Two recent articles frame a valiant attempt by McDonald's in the United Kingdom to banish the term *McJob* from the dictionary:

a term the Oxford English Dictionary describes as "an unstimulating, low-paid job with few prospects, esp. one created by the expansion of the service sector."[220]

McDonald's position, it turns out, deserves some sympathy:

In the UK at least, McDonald's has established a pretty solid reputation as a decent employer. It has featured regularly in most of the main "good employer" league tables, and recently won Caterer and Hotelkeeper magazine's "Best place to work in hospitality" award. . . . Eighty per cent of McDonald's UK branch managers joined the company as hourly paid "crew members," as did half the company's executive team. Compared with some other companies in the service sector, McDonald's is serious about training and development. It is also more "female-friendly" than most: 40 per cent of managers and 25 per cent of the company's executives are women.[221]

Given McDonald's trials and errors in the past with efforts to change its image in the court of public opinion, however, perhaps the firm should have learned its lesson by now.

The relative purchasing power of a McDonald's wage is instructive. A study, conducted by Asian Labor Update[222] aimed to compare the relative value of the wages paid to McDonald's employees[223] in various Asian countries, as well as Australia and New Zealand. How long would each individual need to work to be able to buy a Big Mac sandwich at the McDonald's that employed him or her?

The responses we received show quite clearly that the target consumer group varies from country to country. Taking extreme examples, an Australian cleaner could buy three Big Macs after working for one hour, whereas a Pakistani cleaner would have to work for more than fourteen hours to buy the same burger.[224]

In Australia, where McDonald's staff work for A$10.61 (US$5.60) per hour, it costs A$3.00 (US$1.58) to purchase a Big Mac. In Pakistan, however, where the company's staff work for PR13 (US$0.22) per hour, a Big Mac costs PR185 (US$3.08). The difference between wage rates and the cost of a Big Mac produces the difference in purchase parity.

The countries covered in the report included Australia, China, Hong Kong, India, Malaysia, New Zealand, Pakistan, Philippines, South Korea, Sri Lanka, and Thailand. Significant differences were identified. Wage rates ranged from a staff member who works for IRs5.60 (US$0.11) per hour in India to the higher wages paid to McDonald's Australian employees: A$10.61 (US$5.60) per hour. In terms of the cost of burgers, Big Mac prices ranged from MR4.30 (US$1.13) in Malaysia, to NZ$3.95 (US$1.72) in New Zealand.

These differences reflect the different stages of economic development of the varied countries throughout the Asian continent, and a similar study conducted today would, no doubt, produce different results. In addition, the differences in purchase parity—how long each worker would have to work to purchase a burger—reflect the different perceptions of a McDonald's meal within each country. In a developed country like Australia, McDonald's food is considered low-cost fast food. In a developing country, like India, however, McDonald's is more exotic and, therefore, relatively more expensive. Nevertheless, the results are instructive in terms of the value of the same workers in different countries and cultures. The study also puts a new twist on Henry Ford's benchmark for worker compensation—whether his own workers could afford to buy the product they were making!

The issue of relative value is important in an age when Western consumers often judge a multinational corporation's operations in a developing country by their own standards, rather than the standards facing the company in that developing country. The result is often very difficult for the company that believes it faces a no-win situation. Nike, for example, has to manage a global network of over 700 independent supplier factories. To what degree is the company responsible for what happens within the operations of those organizations?

The relationship is delicate. . . . NGOs have berated firms such as Nike for failing to ensure that workers are paid a "living wage." But that can be hard, even in America. . . . In developing countries, the dilemma may be even greater: "In Vietnam, [Nike's] workers are paid more than doctors. What's the social cost if a doctor leaves his practice and goes to work for [Nike]? That's starting to happen."[225]

Even within countries, the value of a particular job can change according to the job and context:

It's seldom possible to classify a job as good or bad in isolation. Economic conditions matter. Job seekers might sneer at jobs at fast-food franchises in fast-growing Las Vegas, for example, where they can land lucrative positions as waiters in casinos. But they might covet them in a struggling textile town in the Carolinas.[226]

Another relative measure of wage levels for company employees, and an equally important indicator of the health of an organization, is the amount that is paid to corporate executives. What is an acceptable rate to pay top management? It seems that pay scales are relative and arbitrary:

Just how much do you have to pay a guy to run an outfit with 170,000 employees that's critical to our national defense? If he's the CEO of Boeing (which actually has 167,000 employees), the answer is $4 million plus lots of incentive compensation. If he's the Commandant of the U.S. Marine Corps (which actually has 174,000 employees), the answer is $169,860. Even Boeing's chief financial officer makes 10 times that much.[227]

(Continued)

(Continued)

Ironically, a study found that

chief executives of companies that had the largest layoffs and most underfunded pensions and that moved operations off-shore to avoid U.S. taxes were rewarded with the biggest pay hikes.[228]

As Peter Drucker wrote, somewhat hopefully, in a 1977 article for the *Wall Street Journal* criticizing "excessive" executive pay:

It is a business responsibility, but also a business self-interest, to develop a sensible executive compensation structure that portrays economic reality and asserts and codifies the achievement of U.S. business in this century: the steady narrowing of the income gap between the "boss man" and the "working man."[229]

The argument for a *fair* pay structure could be made on behalf of all of a firm's employees—as indicated by a *Wall Street Journal* headline:

Happy Workers Are the Best Workers.[230]

Online Resources

- Asia Monitor Resource Center (AMRC), *Asian labor update,* http://www.amrc.org.hk/

  "Asia Monitor Resource Center (AMRC) is an independent non-government organization (NGO) which focuses on Asian labour concerns."

- Fairness Initiative on Low-wage Work, http://www.lowwagework.org/

  "Today, more than 30 million men and women in this country work in jobs that pay poverty wages and provide few if any benefits."

- Green America, http://www.coopamerica.org/programs/sweatshops/

  "Green America provides the information you need to help stop sweatshop labor and promote fair treatment of workers everywhere."

- Labor Law Center, http://www.laborlawcenter.com/

  "Since 1999, LaborLawCenter has been providing compliance solutions to small, medium, and large businesses nationwide."

- McDonald's Careers, http://www.mcdonalds.com/usa/work.html

  "Careers @ McDonald's: It's not just a job, it's a career."

- McSpotlight, What's Wrong with McDonald's? http://www.mcspotlight.org/campaigns/translations/trans_uk.html

  "McDonald's spends over $2 billion a year broadcasting their glossy image to the world. This is a small space for alternatives to be heard."

- The Foundation of Economic Trends, http://www.foet.org/

  "The Foundation examines the economic, environmental, social and cultural impacts of new technologies introduced into the global economy."

- U.S. Department of Labor, Wage and Hour Division, http://www.dol.gov/whd/flsa/index.htm

  "To promote and achieve compliance with labor standards to protect and enhance the welfare of the nation's workforce."

- United for a Fair Economy, http://www.faireconomy.org/

  "UFE raises awareness that concentrated wealth and power undermine the economy, corrupt democracy, deepen the racial divide, and tear communities apart."

Questions for Discussion and Review

1. Is any job (at any wage) better than no job? Does your answer change if you apply the question to a worker in a developing, rather than developed country?

2. What is a fair wage? What does *fair* mean? What is the lowest hourly wage for which you would be willing to work?

3. Is there a maximum absolute amount that a CEO should earn? Is $1 million a year OK? What about $10 million? $100 million? Is it OK to pay a CEO any amount, as long as the net benefit the CEO brings to the organization exceeds her or his compensation?

4. Is it a good idea for companies to apply a pay-scale ratio whereby the highest and lowest wage levels within an organization are kept within a certain ratio (such as in the Whole Foods example illustrated above)?

5. Where would you rather shop—Walmart/Sam's Club or Costco? If you answered Walmart based on the price of its products, would you be willing to pay a higher price if you knew that the extra money would go directly to the firm's employees? Think of some of the jobs you have done—would you work harder if your pay had been higher?

NOTES AND REFERENCES

1. This quote was taken from a circular e-mail received by the authors that described the purpose of the World Clock.

2. Joel Bakan, *The Corporation: The Pathological Pursuit of Profit and Power*, Free Press, 2004. Quoted in *Business Ethics Magazine*, Spring 2004, p. 6.

3. *Dodge v. Ford Motor Company*, 204 Mich. 459, 170 N.W. 668 (1919).

4. Joel Bakan, *The Corporation: The Pathological Pursuit of Profit and Power*, Free Press, 2004, p. 36.

5. Peter Kinder, "Public Purpose—Corporate History's Lesson for Companies Now," *Ethical Corporation*, October 3, 2007, http://www.ethicalcorp.com/content.asp?ContentID=5406

6. Ibid.

7. James E. Austin & James Quinn, "Ben & Jerry's: Preserving Mission and Brand within Unilever," *Harvard Business School* [Case # 9–306–037], December 8, 2005, p. 5. See also "Ben & Jerry's Takes a Licking," *Eurofood*, February 3, 2000, http://findarticles.com/p/articles/mi_m0DQA/is _2000_Feb_3/ai_59544165/

8. Mallen Baker, "Remuneration—Value Society, Mr President," *Ethical Corporation*, March 11, 2009, http://www.ethicalcorp.com/content.asp?ContentID=6391

9. Kent Greenfield, "It's Time to Federalize Corporate Charters," *Business Ethics Magazine*, Fall 2002, p. 6.

10. Michael Peel, "Delaware: America's Own Home to Corporate Anonymity," *Financial Times*, December 1, 2008, p. 11.

11. Kent Greenfield, "It's Time to Federalize Corporate Charters," *Business Ethics Magazine*, Fall 2002, p. 6.

12. Ibid.

13. Ibid.

14. See, for example: Vanessa Houlder, "The Tax Avoidance Story as a Morality Tale," *Financial Times*, November 22, 2004, p. 7; Roger Cowe, "Special Report: Corporate Responsibility and Tax," *Ethical Corporation*, January 3, 2005, http://www.ethicalcorp.com/content.asp?ContentID=3341; and Mallen Baker, "In Search of the Business Case for Responsible Tax," *Ethical Corporation*, March 27, 2006, http://www.ethicalcorp.com/content.asp?ContentID=4168

15. Kent Greenfield, "State Chartering Initiatives," *Business Ethics Magazine*, Fall 2002, p. 6.

16. http://www.citizenworks.org/corp/fact/code.pdf

17. http://www.c4cr.org/article12.html

18. Marjorie Kelly, "Despairing Globally, Hoping Locally," *Business Ethics Magazine*, Spring 2003, p. 4.

19. Senate File 0510, https://www.revisor.leg.state.mn.us/revisor/pages/search_status/status _detail.php?b=Senate&f=SF0510&ssn=0&y=2009

20. House File 0398, https://www.revisor.leg.state.mn.us/revisor/pages/search_status/status_detail .php?b=House&f=HF0398&ssn=0&y=0&ls=86

21. Citizens for Corporate Redesign, http://www.c4cr.org/

22. Susan Wennemyr, "Code for Corporate Responsibility Considered by Two State Legislatures," *BizEthics Buzz*, e-mail newsletter, March 2004, http://groups.yahoo.com/group/Babel/message/7873?var=1

23. Robert Hinkley, "How Corporate Law Inhibits Social Responsibility," *Business Ethics Magazine*, Spring 2002, http://www.commondreams.org/views02/0119-04.htm

24. "Quick Takes," *Business Ethics Magazine*, Summer 2003, p. 8.

25. Gary S. Becker, "What the Scandals Reveal: A Strong Economy," *BusinessWeek*, December 30, 2002, p. 30.

26. Louis Lavelle, "Special Report: The Best and Worst Boards," *BusinessWeek*, October 7, 2002, pp. 104–114, http://www.businessweek.com/magazine/content/02_40/b3802001.htm

27. "Principles of Good Governance," *BusinessWeek*, October 7, 2002, http://www.businessweek .com/magazine/content/02_40/b3802005.htm

28. Ibid.

29. Louis Lavelle, "Special Report: The Best and Worst Boards," *BusinessWeek*, October 7, 2002, pp. 104–114, http://www.businessweek.com/magazine/content/02_40/b3802001.htm

30. Kate Burgess, "Criticism of Board Intensifies," *Financial Times*, January 20, 2009, p. 21.

31. Tony Chapelle, "Which Set of Company Rules Are OK? US-Style or UK?" *Financial Times Special Report: Corporate Governance*, June 18, 2009, p. 1.

32. "Don't Let the CEO Run the Board, Too," *BusinessWeek*, November 11, 2002, p. 28.

33. Phyllis Plitch, "Post of Lead Director Catches On, Letting CEOs Remain Chairmen," *Wall Street Journal*, July 7, 2003, p. B2B.

34. Paul Davies, "Drug Firms Urged to Split Top Jobs," *Wall Street Journal*, April 22, 2005, p. C3.

35. Interfaith Center on Corporate Responsibility, http://www.iccr.org/shareholder/proxy_book05/05statuschart.php

36. "Survey: U.S. Directors Favor Splitting CEO, Chairman Roles," *Daily Yomiuri,* May 30, 2002, p. 17.

37. Phyllis Plitch, "Post of Lead Director Catches On, Letting CEOs Remain Chairmen," *Wall Street Journal,* July 7, 2003, p. B2B.

38. Alan Murray, "Emboldened Boards Tackle Imperial CEOs," *Wall Street Journal,* March 16, 2005, p. A2.

39. Marjorie Kelly, "Eureka: An Opening for Economic Democracy," *Business Ethics Magazine,* Summer 2003, p. 4.

40. John Logue, Executive Director of the Ohio Employee Ownership Center, quoted in *BizEthics Buzz,* December 2002.

41. For discussions of this issue, see Floyd Norris, "Greater Say on Boards Holds Risks," *New York Times,* May 22, 2009, p. B1; "A Much Needed Shareholder Victory," *Financial Times Editorial,* May 22, 2009, p. 8; and "Creating 'a Bigger Mess?' Battle Lines Are Drawn on the Proxy Access Rule," *Knowledge@Wharton,* September 2, 2009, http://knowledge.wharton.upenn.edu/article.cfm?articleid=2331

42. Greg Farrell, "Separation of Functions Still Has a Way to Go," *Financial Times Special Report: Corporate Governance,* June 18, 2009, p. 3.

43. Justin Baer, "Executives Face up to Inevitable Changes," *Financial Times Special Report: Corporate Governance,* June 18, 2009, p. 1.

44. Christopher Davies, portfolio manager at David Advisors. Quoted in Nanette Byrnes, David Henry, Emily Thornton, & Paula Dwyer, "Reform: Who's Making the Grade," *BusinessWeek,* September 22, 2003, pp. 80–84.

45. Greg Farrell, "Separation of Functions Still Has a Way to Go," *Financial Times Special Report: Corporate Governance,* June 18, 2009, p. 3.

46. "Business Ethics: Doing Well by Doing Good," *The Economist,* April 22, 2000, pp. 65–68.

47. Newsdesk, "The Great Company Contribution," *Ethical Corporation,* October 5, 2004, http://www.ethicalcorp.com/content.asp?ContentID=2884

48. David Batstone, *Saving the Corporate Soul—and (Who Knows?) Maybe Your Own,* Jossey-Bass, 2003, p. 3.

49. Peter Asmus, "100 Best Corporate Citizens of 2003," *Business Ethics Magazine,* Spring 2003, pp. 6–10.

50. Nanette Byrnes et al., "Beyond Options," *BusinessWeek,* July 28, 2003, pp. 36–37.

51. William Greider, "Beyond Scarcity: A New Story of American Capitalism," *Business Ethics Magazine,* Fall 2003, pp. 9–11.

52. In *Fortune* magazine's list of 'The 100 Best Companies to Work For' in 2003, Timberland placed number 50. "[Timberland] gives employees up to 40 hours a year of paid time off for community service. 'Businesses should do more than just make money,' says planning analyst Anthony Gow, and his does: Last year Timberland granted him a six-month sabbatical to help a local food pantry." Christopher Tkaczyk, "The 100 Best Companies to Work For," *Fortune,* January 12, 2004, p. 68.

53. Martha C. White, "Doing Good on Company Time," *New York Times,* May 8, 2007, p. C6.

54. Richard Pound & Karl Moore, "Volunteering to Be a Better Manager," *Strategy + Business e-news,* April 29, 2004, http://www.strategy-business.com/article/04217

55. Loretta Chao, "Theory & Practice: Sabbaticals Can Offer Dividends for Employers," *Wall Street Journal,* July 17, 2006, p. B5.

56. Rhymer Rigby, "Time Out to Help Less Fortunate Is Its Own Reward," *Financial Times,* July 21, 2009, p. 10.

57. "[The UK's Home Office] estimates that the number of Britons engaged in 'active community participation' rose from 18.8 million to 20.3 million between 2001 and 2003." Simon Kuper, "Office Angels," *FT Weekend,* December 31, 2004, to January 2, 2005, p. W2.

58. http://www.yearofthevolunteer.org/

59. http://www.timberland.com/corp/index.jsp?page=csr_civic_engagement

60. For a detailed history of the origins of Timberland's volunteer program, see: Avery Yale Kamila, "Timberland Goes Beyond Philanthropy: Building Value for Community and Brand With Volunteers," *Ethical Corporation,* February 13, 2004, http://www.ethicalcorp.com/content.asp?ContentID=1659

61. Note: The Path of Service program has been renamed timberlandserve.com.

62. David Batstone, *Saving the Corporate Soul—and (Who Knows?) Maybe Your Own,* Jossey-Bass, 2003, p. 83.

63. For a detailed history of the origins of Timberland's volunteer program, see Avery Yale Kamila, "Timberland Goes Beyond Philanthropy: Building Value for Community and Brand With Volunteers," *Ethical Corporation,* February 13, 2004, http://www.ethicalcorp.com/content.asp?ContentID=1659

64. David Batstone, *Saving the Corporate Soul—and (Who Knows?) Maybe Your Own,* Jossey-Bass, 2003, p. 87.

65. Loretta Chao, "Theory & Practice: Sabbaticals Can Offer Dividends for Employers," *Wall Street Journal,* July 17, 2006, p. B5.

66. "The Co-operative 2009 Social Responsibility Report," *The Midcounties Co-operative,* 2009, p. 19.

67. Rhymer Rigby, "Time Out to Help Less Fortunate Is Its Own Reward," *Financial Times,* July 21, 2009, p. 10.

68. Richard Pound & Karl Moore, "Volunteering to Be a Better Manager," *Strategy + Business e-news,* April 29, 2004, http://www.strategy-business.com/article/04217

69. John Micklethwait & Adrian Wooldridge, *The Company: A Short History of a Revolutionary Idea,* Modern Library, 2003. pp. xvi & xviii.

70. Ibid.

71. The term *shareholder value* was introduced in a 1981 *Harvard Business Review* article by an accounting professor, Alfred Rappaport, who designed an index "to determine the value-creating prospects for alternative strategies at the business unit and corporate levels." In Alfred Rappaport, "Selecting Strategies That Create Shareholder Value," *Harvard Business Review,* Vol. 59, No. 3, 1981, pp. 139–149.

72. Joel Bakan, *The Corporation: The Pathological Pursuit of Profit and Power,* Free Press, 2004, p. 37.

73. Andy Serwer, "Wall Street Comes to Main Street," *Fortune,* May 3, 2004, pp. 132–146.

74. Alan Murray, "Political Capital: CEO Responsibility Might Be Right Cure for Corporate World," *Wall Street Journal,* July 13, 2004, p. A4.

75. Kevin Rudd, Australian Prime Minister, "The Global Financial Crisis," *The Monthly,* No. 42, February, 2009, http://www.themonthly.com.au/monthly-essays-kevin-rudd-global-financial-crisis--1421

76. Richard R. Floersch, "The Right Way to Determine Executive Pay," *Wall Street Journal,* March 5, 2009, p. A15.

77. Gene Colter, "Stock Options Lose Appeal as an Option," *Wall Street Journal,* October 12, 2004, p. C3.

78. "How New Accounting Rules Are Changing the Way CEOs Get Paid," *Knowledge@Wharton,* May 2006, http://knowledge.wharton.upenn.edu/index.cfm?fa=printArticle&ID=1465

79. Arthur Levitt Jr., "Money, Money, Money," *Wall Street Journal,* November 22, 2004, Op-ed page.

80. Charles Forelle & James Bandler, "The Perfect Payday," *Wall Street Journal,* March 18–19, 2006, p. A1.

81. Louis Lavelle, "Wretched Excess: Mega Options, Mega Losses," *BusinessWeek,* June 23, 2003, p. 14.

82. Editorial, "What We Learned in 2002," *BusinessWeek,* December 30, 2002, p. 170.

83. Kathy Kristof, "Shareholders Should Look for Signs of Excessive Exec Pay," *Miami Herald,* June 22, 2003, p. 6E.

84. For example, see Kate Burgess and Richard Milne, "Floored Boards," *Financial Times,* June 2, 2009, p. 12; Josh Martin, "Committees Strive to Achieve the Right Mix," *Financial Times Special Report: Corporate Governance,* June 18, 2009, p. 3.

85. Richard R. Floersch, "The Right Way to Determine Executive Pay," *Wall Street Journal,* March 5, 2009, p. A15.

86. Nanette Byrnes, "Earnings Guidance: Silence Is Golden," *BusinessWeek,* May 5, 2003, p. 87.

87. "Home Depot CEO Nardelli Quits," *Associated Press,* January 3, 2007, http://msnbc.msn.com/id/16451112/

88. Robin Pagnamenta & Helen Power, "Shell's Pay Committee Bears the Brunt of Growing Investor Anger," *The Times,* May 20, 2009, p. 38.

89. "AIG Bonus Payments \$218 Million," *Reuters,* http://www.reuters.com/article/idUSTRE52K19L20090321

90. Alan Beattie, "Summers' 'Outrage' at AIG Bonuses," *Financial Times,* March 15, 2009, http://www.ft.com/cms/s/0/31bafc52-1192-11de-87b1-0000779fd2ac.html

91. Clarence Page, "Is the Honeymoon Over?" *Chicago Tribune,* in the *Daily Yomiuri,* March 31, 2009, p. 17.

92. Carola Hoyos & Michael Steen, "Outgoing Shell Chief Calls for Executive Pay Reform," *Financial Times,* June 9, 2009, p. 1.

93. Kara Scannell & Joann S. Lublin, "SEC Asks Firms to Detail Top Executives' Pay," *Wall Street Journal,* August 1, 2007, p. B1.

94. John McKay, CEO of Whole Foods, "Final Word: `I No Longer Want to Work for Money,'" *Fast Company,* February 2007, p. 112.

95. In July 2009, the U.S. Securities and Exchange Commission extended its use of the clawback law to include executives who had benefitted from fraud or misstated earnings in their firm, even if they were not personally involved: Joanna Chung, "SEC Toughens Stance With First 'Clawback' Move," *Financial Times,* July 29, 2009, p. 3.

96. Richard R. Floersch, "The Right Way to Determine Executive Pay," *Wall Street Journal,* March 5, 2009, p. A15.

97. Jesse Eisinger, "Long & Short: 'No Excessive Pay, We're British,'" *Wall Street Journal,* February 8, 2006, p. C1.

98. Joanna L. Ossinger, "Poorer Relations: When It Comes to CEO Pay, Why Are the British So Different?" *Wall Street Journal,* April 10, 2006, p. R6.

99. Carol Hymowitz, "Sky-High Payouts to Top Executives Prove Hard to Curb," *Wall Street Journal,* June 26, 2006, p. B1.

100. For an example of one CEO's compensation package that "wins praise from compensation critics," see Joann S. Lublin, "Valeant CEO's Pay Package Draws Praise as a Model," *Wall Street Journal,* August 24, 2009, p. B4.

101. Richard R. Floersch, "The Right Way to Determine Executive Pay," *Wall Street Journal,* March 5, 2009, p. A15.

102. David Bogoslaw, "Shareholder Value: Time for a Longer View?" *BusinessWeek,* March 17, 2009, http://www.businessweek.com/investor/content/mar2009/pi20090317_247202.htm

103. See Bill Baue, "This Proxy Season, Shareowners Getting a `Say,'" *CSRWire.com,* May 20, 2009, http://www.csrwire.com/press/press_release/26990-The-Latest-Corporate-Social-Responsibility-News-This-Proxy-Season-Shareowners-Getting-a-Say-

104. Phred Dvorak, "As 'Say on Pay' Votes Start, Investors Diverge," *Wall Street Journal,* April 14, 2009, p. B1.

105. See Richard Milne, "Sharp Divide in Public Opinion on Bonus Culture," and "How Business Turned Into the Bogeyman," *Financial Times,* April 14, 2009, p. 6; David Bolchover, "Business as Usual on Executive Pay?" *Financial Times,* June 9, 2009, p. 12.

106. Mallen Baker, "Remuneration—Value Society, Mr. President," *Ethical Corporation,* March 11, 2009, http://www.ethicalcorp.com/content.asp?ContentID=6391

107. Gene G. Marcial, "Carl Icahn's Cure for Corporate America," *BusinessWeek,* November 18, 2005, http://www.businessweek.com/bwdaily/dnflash/nov2005/nf20051118_0496.htm

108. Bill Baue, "Investing in . . . Genocide?" *CSRwire.com,* March 31, 2009, http://www.csrwire.com/News/14977.html

109. For example, see Kate Burgess, "Investors Are Taking a Share in Revolution," *Financial Times,* May 6, 2009, p. 15.

110. "43 Climate-Related Shareholder Resolutions Filed This Year," *Environmental Leader,* August 14, 2007, http://www.environmentalleader.com/2007/08/14/43-climate-related-shareholder-resolutions-filed-this-year/

111. "Investors File 54 Global Warming-Related Shareholder Resolutions," *Environmental Leader,* March 9, 2008, http://www.environmentalleader.com/2008/03/09/investors-file-54-global-warming-related-shareholder-resolutions/

112. Kristin Gribben, "Mutual Funds Take Their Stand on Climate Change," *Financial Times FT fm,* June 1, 2009, p. 8.

113. Sheila McNulty, "Shareholder Activists Hijack Exxon's AGM," *Financial Times,* May 9, 2003, p. 17.

114. Quoted by an officer from the Investor Responsibility Research Center on *The NewsHour With Jim Lehrer,* PBS, June 10, 2003.

115. http://www.corpgov.net/forums/commentary/S7-10-03.html

116. http://corpgov.net/news/archives/archived996.html

117. Andrew Park, "Dell Gets Greener," *BusinessWeek,* May 5, 2003, p. 89.

118. Heather Connon, "Investors in Revolt Against Bosses' Feeding Frenzy," *The Observer*, May 25, 2003, http://www.observer.co.uk/business/story/0,6903,962775,00.html

119. John Gapper, "The Votes of Investors Should Count," *Financial Times,* April 17, 2006, p. 13.

120. Heather Connon, "Investors in Revolt Against Bosses' Feeding Frenzy," *The Observer*, May 25, 2003, http://www.observer.co.uk/business/story/0,6903,962775,00.html

121. Alan Murray, "Pivotal Fight Looms for Shareholder Democracy," *Wall Street Journal,* November 22, 2006, p. A2.

122. Peter Montagnon & Roderick Munsters, "One Share, One Vote Is the Way to a Fairer Market," *Financial Times,* August 14, 2006, p. 11.

123. The proxy review by the SEC continues, but progress is being made. For one example concerning shareholders' ability to nominate directors, see Deborah Brewster, "Investors in Boardroom Victory," *Financial Times,* May 21, 2009, p. 15; Stephen Labaton, "S.E.C. Proposes to Widen Investors' Say on Boards," *New York Times,* May 21, 2009, p. B3.

124. Dennis K. Berman, "Boardroom Defenestration," *Wall Street Journal,* March 16, 2006, p. B1.

125. Phred Dvorak, "Companies Seek Shareholder Input on Pay Practices," *Wall Street Journal,* April 6, 2009, p. B4.

126. Patrick McVeigh, "Most Valuable Players: Annual SRI Mutual Fund Review for 2002," *Business Ethics Magazine,* Spring 2003, p. 18.

127. Tania Padgett, "Socially Responsible Funds' Popular, Although Some Express Skepticism," *The Japan Times,* August 16, 2001.

128. Tara Kalwarski, "Do-good Investments Are Holding Up Better," *BusinessWeek,* July 14, 2008, p. 15, http://images.businessweek.com/ss/08/07/0703_numbers/index.htm

129. Barbara Kiviat, "Heart on One's Sleeve, Eye on Bottom Line," *Miami Herald,* January 19, 2003, p. 3E.

130. "Performance and Socially Responsible Investments," *Social Investment Forum,* 2007, http://www.socialinvest.org/resources/performance.cfm

131. Sam Mamudi, "FT Report—Fund Management: The Rise of the Activist Shareholder in the US Boost Socially Responsible Investment," *Financial Times,* November 6, 2007, http://www.ftchinese.com/story/001016607/en

132. "SRI Fund Sales Hit 1 Billion Euro Mark in December 2008," *NaturalChoices.co.uk,* February 26, 2009, http://www.naturalchoices.co.uk/SRI-fund-sales-hit-1-billion-euro?id_mot=1

133. Chip Feiss, "Social Enterprise—the Fledgling Fourth Sector," *Financial Times,* June 15, 2009, p. 11.

134. John Authers, "There Are Clear Arguments for a Clear Conscience," *Financial Times,* July 28, 2007, p. 16, http://www.ft.com/cms/s/1/80690410-3c2e-11dc-b067-0000779fd2ac.html

135. Jem Bendell, "Have You Seen My Business Case?" *Ethical Corporation,* November 2, 2002, http://www.ethicalcorp.com/content.asp?ContentID=264

136. "The Vice fund is tiny, with assets of $6.6m. Institutions have steered clear. But it is growing fast." In "Socially Irresponsible Investment: Virtues of Vice," *The Economist,* November 1, 2003, pp. 71–72.

137. http://www.usamutuals.com/vicefund/fund_perf.aspx

138. Sam Stovall, "Tobacco Stocks: A Classic Defensive Play," *BusinessWeek,* January 29, 2008, http://www.businessweek.com/investor/content/jan2008/pi20080129_262388.htm

139. Barbara Kiviat, "Heart on One's Sleeve, Eye on Bottom Line," *Miami Herald,* January 19, 2003, p. 3E.

140. Joe Nocera, "Well-Meaning but Misguided Stock Screens," *New York Times,* April 7, 2007, p. B1.

141. Diya Gullapalli, "Pax May Bless Some 'Sin' Stocks," *Wall Street Journal,* September 1, 2006, p. C1.

142. Jon Entine, quoted in Tania Padgett, "Socially Responsible Funds' Popular, Although Some Express Skepticism," *The Japan Times,* August 16, 2001; Newsday, Inc., August 9, 2001, p. A51.

143. Ibid.

144. Sean Donahue, "Tom's of Mainstream," *Business 2.0,* December 2004, p. 72.

145. Polly LaBarre, "Leap of Faith," *Fast Company Magazine,* June 2007, p. 98.

146. "Leadership, Patagonia-style: Changing the Criteria for Success," *Knowledge@Wharton,* October 31, 2007, http://knowledge.wharton.upenn.edu/article.cfm?articleid=1829

147. Stephanie Strom, "Make Money, Save the World," *New York Times,* May 6, 2007, p. BU1.

148. Steve Hamm, "Capitalism With a Human Face," *BusinessWeek,* December 8, 2008, p. 49.

149. Polly LaBarre, "Leap of Faith," *Fast Company Magazine,* June 2007, p. 98.

150. Chip Feiss, "Social Enterprise—the Fledgling Fourth Sector," *Financial Times,* June 15, 2009, p. 11.

151. "[UK] government estimates put the number of social enterprises in the UK at 55,000, with a turnover of £27 billion, contributing about £8 billion to the UK's gross domestic product and employing more than 500,000 people." In Steve Coomber, "New Business Is Modeled on Old-Fashioned Mutual Interest," *The Times,* July 24, 2007, p. 6.

152. Co-operative Bank's Ninth Annual Ethical Consumerism Report, November 28, 2008, http://www.goodwithmoney.co.uk/ethicalconsumerismreport/

153. Michael Skapinker, "There Is a Good Trade in Ethical Retailing," *Financial Times,* September 10, 2007, http://www.ft.com/cms/352205cc-5fc6-11dc-b0fe-0000779fd2ac.html

154. Andrew Jack, "Beyond Charity? A New Generation Enters the Business of Doing Good," *Financial Times,* April 5, 2007, p. 11.

155. Ibid.

156. Marjorie Kelly, "Cover Story: The Legacy Problem," *Business Ethics Magazine,* Summer, 2003, http://www.esopbuilders.com/articles/the-legacy-problem.pdf

157. Mark Goyder, "Ownership and Sustainability—Are Listed Companies More Responsible?" *Ethical Corporation,* July 14, 2008, http://www.ethicalcorp.com/content.asp?ContentID=6004

158. "Virgin, Ben & Jerry's, 02, BP, Starbucks to Discuss How They Brand Their Values," *Ethical Corporation* Press Release, *CSRwire.com,* September 27, 2005, http://www.csrwire.com/press/press_release/22741-Virgin-Ben-Jerry-s-O2-BP-Starbucks-to-Discuss-How-They-Brand-Their-Values

159. Melanie Warner, "Solo Climb," *Business 2.0,* December 2004, p. 152.

160. Christopher Palmeri, "From Ice Cream to Nuclear Freeze," *BusinessWeek,* August 24, 2006, http://www.businessweek.com/investor/content/aug2006/pi20060824_523626.htm

161. John Russell, "Body Shop Takeover—Ethical Business as Usual," *Ethical Corporation,* March 11, 2007, http://www.ethicalcorp.com/content.asp?ContentID=4936

162. Anya Kamenetz, "Cleaning Solution," *Fast Company Magazine,* September 2008, pp. 120–125, http://www.fastcompany.com/magazine/128/cleaning-solution.html

163. Jon Entine, "Sell-out at the Sierra Club," *Ethical Corporation,* September 1, 2008, http://www.ethicalcorp.com/content.asp?ContentID=6055

164. Roger Martin, "The Virtue Matrix," *Harvard Business Review,* March 2002, Vol. 80, No. 3, pp. 68–75.

165. Jon Entine, "Queen of Green Roddick's 'Unfair Trade' Started When She Copied Body Shop's Formula," *The Mail on Sunday,* September 15, 2007, http://www.dailymail.co.uk/femail/article-482012/Queen-Green-Roddicks-unfair-trade-started-copied-Body-Shop-formula.html

166. Tony Dawe, "Business Takes on Board the Need for Social Responsibility," *The Times,* July 24, 2007, p. 3.

167. The Body Shop's Web site, http://www.thebodyshop.com/bodyshop/index.jsp, December 2002.

168. http://www.peta.org/

169. PETA's Web site, http://www.peta.org/, February 2003.

170. Emily Gersema, "PETA Denies Accusation of Supporting Violence," *Miami Herald,* February 16, 2003, p. 26A.

171. "Review and Outlook: Fair or Fowl?" *Wall Street Journal,* July 16, 2004, p. W11.

172. Emily Gersema, "PETA Denies Accusation of Supporting Violence," *Miami Herald,* February 16, 2003, p. 26A.

173. Saulo Petean, "Broken Promises," December 1996, http://www.brazzil.com/p16dec96.htm

174. Matthew Gitsham, "The Body Shop's 2005 Values Report—Cleaner, But Not Sparkling," *Ethical Corporation,* December 6, 2005, http://www.ethicalcorp.com/content.asp?ContentID=4006

175. Aisha Ikramuddin, "The Cosmetic Mask: Decoding Cruelty-Free," June 30, 2007, http://healthychild.org/blog/comments/the_cosmetic_mask_decoding_cruelty_free

176. "What's Wrong With The Body Shop?-A Criticism of 'Green Consumerism,'" London Greenpeace, March 1998, http://www.mcspotlight.org/beyond/companies/bodyshop.html

177. Charles Wallace, "Can the Body Shop Shape Up?," *Fortune,* April 1996, http://money.cnn.com/magazines/fortune/fortune_archive/1996/04/15/211474/index.htm

178. Jon Entine, "Queen of Green Roddick's 'Unfair Trade' Started When She Copied Body Shop's Formula," *The Mail on Sunday,* September 15, 2007, http://www.dailymail.co.uk/femail/article-482012/Queen-Green-Roddicks-unfair-trade-started-copied-Body-Shop-formula.html

179. Ibid.

180. *The Corporation,* Movie-documentary, http://www.thecorporation.com/. The documentary is summarized in the *Wall Street Journal* ("The Corporation," July 9, 2004, p. W2) as "a documentary that functions as a 2½-hour provocation in the ongoing debate about corporate conduct and governance."

181. Brent Schlender, "The New Soul of a Wealth Machine," *Fortune,* April 5, 2004, pp. 102–110.

182. John Micklethwait & Adrian Wooldridge, *The Company: A Short History of a Revolutionary Idea,* Modern Library, 2003, pp. xiv–xv.

183. Brent Schlender, "The New Soul of a Wealth Machine," *Fortune,* April 5, 2004, pp. 102–110.

184. Todd Stitzer, "Business Must Loudly Proclaim What It Stands for," *Financial Times,* June 1, 2006, p. 11.

185. "Wal-Mart, the most prodigious job creator in the history of the private sector in this galaxy, has almost as many employees (1.3 million) as the U.S. military has uniformed personnel. A McKinsey company study concluded that Wal-Mart accounted for 13 percent of the nation's productivity gains in the second half of the 1990s, which probably made Wal-Mart about as important as the Federal Reserve in holding down inflation. By lowering consumer prices, Wal-Mart costs about 50 retail jobs among competitors *for*

every 100 jobs Wal-Mart creates. Wal-Mart and its effects save shoppers more than $200 billion a year, dwarfing such government programs as food stamps ($28.6 billion) and the earned-income tax credit ($34.6 billion)." In George F. Will, "Democrats vs. Wal-Mart," *The Washington Post,* September 14, 2006, p. A21, http://www.washingtonpost.com/wp-dyn/content/article/2006/09/13/AR2006091301573.html

186. For example, http://walmartwatch.com

187. Lisa Roner, "More Than Half of U.S. Executives Surveyed Say Corporate Citizenship Is Part of Their Business Strategy," *Ethical Corporation,* July 12, 2004, http://www.ethicalcorp.com/content.asp?ContentID=2363

188. For more detail about Marks & Spencer's Plan A and its value for the firm, see David E. Bell, Nitin Sanghavi, & Laura Winig, "Marks and Spencer: Plan A," *Harvard Business School* [Case # 9–509–029], January 5, 2009.

189. http://plana.marksandspencer.com/about/

190. Simon Bowers, "M&S Promises Radical Change With £200m Environmental Action Plan," *The Guardian,* January 15, 2007, http://www.guardian.co.uk/business/2007/jan/15/marksspencer.retail

191. Ibid.

192. Michael Skapinker, "Why Corporate Responsibility Is A Survivor," *Financial Times,* April 21, 2009, p. 11.

193. EC Newsdesk, "Marks and Spencer—A-Grade Progress," *Ethical Corporation,* March 2, 2009, http://www.ethicalcorp.com/content.asp?ContentID=6363

194. James Hall, "Sir Stuart Rose on the Ethical Spirit of Marks & Spencer," *The Daily Telegraph,* February 6, 2009, http://www.telegraph.co.uk/finance/4425524/Sir-Stuart-Rose-on-the-ethical-spirit-of-Marks-and-Spencer.html

195. http://www.thecorporation.com/index.cfm?page_id=46 also on YouTube: http://www.youtube.com/watch?v=xa3wyaEe9vE

196. Interview of Jeremy Rifkin by David Batstone, "The Future of Work," first published in *Business 2.0 Magazine,* reprinted by Right Reality Inc., February 10, 2004, http://www.jobpostings.net/articleDetail.cfm?id=286/

197. "Short-Circuited: Cutting Jobs as Corporate Strategy," *Knowledge@Wharton,* April 4, 2007, http://knowledge.wharton.upenn.edu/article.cfm?articleid=1703

198. Interview of Jeremy Rifkin by David Batstone, "The Future of Work," first published in *Business 2.0 Magazine,* reprinted by Right Reality Inc., February 10, 2004, http://www.jobpostings.net/articleDetail.cfm?id=286

199. Quoted from David Batstone & David Chandler, "Ford's Success Formula Not Followed to a T," *Atlanta Journal-Constitution,* December 17, 2004, http://www.sojo.net/index.cfm?action=sojomail.display&issue=041216

200. Lee Iacocca, "Henry Ford," *Time 100,* http://www.time.com/time/magazine/article/0,9171,989769-1,00.html

201. "In 1913, One Ad Changed the Face of America's Middle Class," Ford ad in *Fortune,* February 9, 2004.

202. Lee Iacocca, "Henry Ford," *Time 100,* http://www.time.com/time/magazine/article/0,9171,989769-1,00.html

203. "Short-Circuited: Cutting Jobs as Corporate Strategy," *Knowledge@Wharton,* April 4, 2007, http://knowledge.wharton.upenn.edu/article.cfm?articleid=1703

204. Ibid.

205. Parija B. Kavilanz, "Circuit City to Shut Down," *CNNMoney.com,* January 16, 2009, http://money.cnn.com/2009/01/16/news/companies/circuit_city/

206. Lauri Bassi & Daniel McMurrer, "Are Employee Skills a Cost or an Asset," *Business Ethics Magazine,* Fall 2004, p. 20.

207. Ann Zimmerman, "Costco's Dilemma: Be Kind to Its Workers, or Wall Street?" *Wall Street Journal,* March 26, 2004, p. B1.

208. "What's Online: Shoe Seller's Secret of Success," *New York Times,* May 24, 2008, p. B5.

209. Stefan Stern & Peter Marsh, "The Chaos Theory of Leadership," *Financial Times,* December 2, 2008, p. 10.

210. *Fortune Magazine,* http://money.cnn.com/magazines/fortune/bestcompanies/

211. Stefan Stern, "Authoritarian Boss Belongs in the Past," *Financial Times,* September 13, 2007, p. 12.

212. See also Steven Greenhouse, "Low-Wage Workers Are Often Cheated, Study Says," *New York Times,* September 2, 2009, p. A11.

213. Stefan Stern, "Managers Will Come to Miss the Voice of the Proletariat," *Financial Times,* September 5, 2006, p. 10.

214. For more information about a "living wage," see Rajesh Chhabara, "Wages—Working for a Living," *Ethical Corporation,* June 30, 2009, http://www.ethicalcorp.com/content.asp?ContentID=6519

215. U.S. Department of Labor, September, 2009, http://www.dol.gov/dol/topic/wages/minimum wage.htm

216. The Living Wage Campaign, March, 2009, http://livingwagecampaign.org/index.php?id=1954

217. "Minimum Wage Laws in the States," U.S. Department of Labor, July 24, 2009, http://www .dol.gov/esa/minwage/america.htm. A table showing how states' minimum wages have changed over time is at http://www.dol.gov/whd/state/stateMinWageHis.htm. Additional commentary and data are available at Anthony Balderrama, "Could You Survive on Minimum Wage?" *CareerBuilder.com,* April 6, 2009, http://www.careerbuilder.com/Article/CB-1174-The-Workplace-Could-You-Survive-on-Minimum-Wage/

218. For additional data, see Tara Kalwarski & David Foster, "The Minimum Wage Rises—And Is Outpacing Inflation," *BusinessWeek,* August 3, 2009, p. 15, http://images.businessweek.com/ss/09/07/0723_numbers/index.htm

219. This definition is from the *Oxford English Dictionary.* "[The] new entry for 'McJob' in the 11th edition of [Merriam-Webster's] collegiate dictionary, which . . . defines the term as a dead-end occupation." Quoted in "Review & Outlook: Thinking Outside the Bun," *Wall Street Journal,* November 14, 2003, p. W15.

220. Stefan Stern & Jenny Wiggins, "New Definition Would Be Just the Job for McDonald's," *Financial Times,* March 20, 2007, p1, http://www.ft.com/cms/s/2065c45e-d65d-11db-99b7-000b5df 10621.html

221. Stefan Stern, "McJob: n., Slang, C20, a Fulfilling Role With Great Prospects," *Financial Times,* March 20, 2007, p. 10, http://www.ft.com/cms/s/fc6a318a-d688-11db-99b7-000b5df10621.html

222. "How Long McDonald's Cleaners Must Work to Buy a Big Mac," *Asian Labour Update,* No. 42, January–March 2002, http://www.amrc.org.hk/alu_article/wages/how_long_mcdonalds_cleaners_ must_work_to_buy_a_bigmac

223. Specifically, cleaners, or the nearest equivalent worker for which the necessary data were available.

224. "How Long McDonald's Cleaners Must Work to Buy a Big Mac," *Asian Labour Update,* No. 42, January–March 2002, http://www.amrc.org.hk/alu_article/wages/how_long_mcdonalds_cleaners_ must_work_to_buy_a_bigmac

225. "Doing Well by Doing Good," *The Economist,* April 22, 2000, http://www.mindfully.org/Industry/Business-Ethics-Oxymoron.htm

226. "Are Franchises Bad Employers? A Closer Look at Burger Flippers and Other Low-paid Jobs," *Knowledge@Wharton,* September 5, 2007, http://knowledge.wharton.upenn.edu/article.cfm?articleid=1801

227. Andrew Tobias, "How Much Is Fair?" *Miami Herald,* Parade Magazine, March 2, 2003, p. 10.

228. Kathy Kristof, "Study Ties Biggest CEO Raises to Largest Layoffs," *Miami Herald,* August 30, 2003, p. 1C.

229. Peter Drucker, "An American Sage," *Wall Street Journal,* November 14, 2005, p. A22.

230. Steven Kent, "Happy Workers Are the Best Workers," *Wall Street Journal,* September 6, 2005, p. A20.

CHAPTER 7

ECONOMIC ISSUES AND CASE STUDIES

FAIR TRADE

CSR CONNECTION: This issue reflects the growing support among consumers in developed economies, particularly Europe, for companies that are perceived to have healthy supply chains. *Fair trade* allows firms to secure stable supplies of quality raw materials, while signaling that commitment to consumers.

Issue

Although much of CSR enables firms to operate more efficiently and, therefore, reduce costs,[1] other aspects of CSR cost firms money. To operate in a socially responsible manner means to do things the *right* way, which is not always the easiest or the cheapest way. As such, an important debate within the CSR movement is the extent to which consumers are willing to pay a price premium for CSR. While consumers often say they want to purchase from firms that are ethical and socially responsible,[2] to what extent do their purchase decisions support these statements?

Related to this question, to what extent do companies have an interest in operating an ethical supply chain? Is there any added value to purchasing products from suppliers at prices that are *fair,* therefore ensuring their suppliers' well-being, rather than at prices that are dictated by the market? What is the extent of the market in the developed economies for products with ingredients that have been purchased in this way?

Products like coffee, tea and chocolate that we in the north have come to depend on, are produced in the warmer climates of the south. The prices paid for these commodities have not risen in real terms over the last forty years, whilst the value of fertilisers, pesticides and machinery (imported from the rich countries) has increased substantially. Consequently many of the people who grow these crops are having to work harder and longer for less money. On top of this the market price of commodities frequently drops below the cost of producing them.[3]

Unstable commodity prices affect a wide range of raw materials. One product that Western consumers use daily and is readily associated with the fair trade movement is coffee. The *Fairtrade* label first appeared on coffee packets in Europe toward the end of the 1980s:[4]

In 2007 the Fairtrade logo adorned £117m of coffee sold in the UK.[5]

In response to the question, "What is Fairtrade?" the Fairtrade Foundation writes that

Fairtrade is about better prices, decent working conditions, local sustainability, and fair terms of trade for farmers and workers in the developing world. By requiring companies to pay sustainable prices (which must never fall lower than the market price), Fairtrade addresses the injustices of conventional trade, which traditionally discriminates against the poorest, weakest producers. It enables them to improve their position and have more control over their lives.[6]

The Fairtrade Foundation also reports that, to date, it "has licensed over 3,000 Fairtrade certified products for sale through retail and catering outlets in the UK." In addition, the market for fair trade and other socially responsible products is growing:

The UK market is doubling in value every 2 years, and in 2007 reached an estimated retail value of £493 million. The UK is one of the world's leading Fairtrade markets, with more products and more awareness of Fairtrade than anywhere else. Around 20% of roast and ground coffee, and 20% of bananas sold in the UK are now Fairtrade.[7]

Fair trade, therefore, is not just about coffee but encompasses a growing range of consumer products, such as sugar,[8] fruit,[9] cotton,[10] palm oil,[11] and chocolate:

Figures from the Fairtrade Foundation show that Britain ate just over 1,000 tonnes of their chocolate in 2003, up from 82 tonnes in 1998—a 12-fold increase in five years, albeit from a very low base. . . . Most British supermarkets now offer some sort of "fair trade" chocolate.[12]

CSR Newsletters: Ethical Retailing

A recent article[13] reviews the extent of the market for *ethical retailing*. In spite of the common perception among executives that consumers do not make purchase decisions based on their best intentions, the author argues this is now changing:

Worldwide sales of Fairtrade-certified products, for example, grew 42 per cent last year, although at Pounds 1.1bn [billion] (Dollars 2.2bn) they are still equivalent to only 2.6 per cent of Tesco's revenues and 0.6 per cent of Wal-Mart's.

In general, the author portrays the UK's ethical retail market as being relatively mature and divided into four separate categories:

The first, about 8 per cent of the total, are committed, cause-driven purchasers. A second group, accounting for 30–35 per cent, want to purchase ethically but are not really sure how. . . . The third group, also about 30–35 per cent, feels the same, but doubt that their individual purchases can make much difference. The fourth group, the remainder, are completely uninterested.

In using this evidence to make his case, however, the author only serves to highlight the limitations of this market. These category numbers mean that the "completely uninterested" group is at least twice the size of the "committed, cause-driven consumers," possibly three times as big. At the end of the day, there is nowhere near a majority of consumers who are willing to place social responsibility concerns above more traditional considerations in arriving at their purchase decisions. The overwhelming sense, despite the author's enthusiasm, is that any gains made are still largely superficial and are more about relieving first-world consumer guilt than re-shaping the underlying business model to instill a permanent strategic CSR perspective:

By publicising their initiatives the supermarkets help consumers feel they have done the world a good deed.

The final quote in this article, however, is most interesting and demonstrates the danger for firms that are too progressive on this issue:

A smart retailer is half a step ahead of the consumer. Ten steps ahead and you're out of business.

In spite of the speed at which the market for fair trade goods has grown, it is important to remember that the overall market segment to which such goods appeal is limited. To what extent fair trade has mass market appeal remains an open question. In general

Purchasing levels of green and ethically-produced goods are linked to levels of affluence. For the majority of consumers, price overrides ethical considerations as the key factor in their decision-making.[14]

Beyond a limited market, there are three main criticisms of fair trade. The first of these is that fair trade encourages inefficiency:

The economist's automatic critique is that paying above the market price encourages farmers to stay in unprofitable sectors, inducing over-supply and pushing down prices for everyone else.[15]

The main counterpoint to this argument is that the world market prices for many commodities are not set on an open and free market, with many Western producers benefiting from large government quotas and subsidies. In terms of cotton, for example,

Eleven million growers raise cotton today [in West Africa]. . . . those millions of black farmers are undercut by the 35,000-or-so mainly white farmers in the former slave states of Texas and the American south. Some $4bn [billion] dollars a year in federal government handouts encourages high-cost American farmers to dump subsidized cotton on the world market, depressing its price.[16]

As such, the ultimate argument against fair trade is an argument in favor of free trade, which proponents believe would have a wider, quicker, and longer lasting impact in favor of farmers worldwide than any artificial designation of what may or may not constitute *fair:*

Poor people are poor because they do not participate sufficiently in the world international trading system. They are not poor because they are unjustly treated when they do.[17]

Advocates often use the words of Adam Smith to justify their arguments, noting that developed economies could do much more for farmers in developing countries by dropping all barriers to trade and extensive support provided by governments to domestic producers:

What is prudence in the conduct of every family can scarce be folly in that of a great kingdom. If a foreign country can supply us with a commodity cheaper than we ourselves can make it, better buy it of them with some part of the produce of our own industry, employed in a way in which we have some advantage.[18]

Trade subsidies and quotas prevent farmers from the developing world from competing on a level playing field. As such, action to reduce these market inefficiencies would have a much greater impact than any artificial fair trade market, which is dismissed as a phenomenon created to appease consumer consciences:

[The Fair Trade movement is] part of a broader movement to make shoppers feel good about themselves and the food they are buying.[19]

The second criticism of fair trade is that, because it appeals to consumers' better instincts, it is open to abuse by organizations that want to appear more socially responsible than they actually are.[20] These accusations are made against supermarkets and other Western retailers, suggesting they use fair trade to gain additional revenue for themselves, while passing on only small amounts to the farmers who produced the raw materials:[21]

Probably only about 9 cents of the $3.10 cost of an average fairly traded 100g bar of chocolate goes to Africa or a poor country.[22]

In response, some progressive retailers "realize the danger to their brand of being perceived as Fairtrade profiteers"[23] and have pledged not to increase margins on fair trade products. They also point out that one cause of the higher prices of fair trade products is the initial costs involved in establishing a fair trade supply chain:

The [Marks & Spencer] Fairtrade cotton T-shirt, for example, retails at £8, a pound more than a conventional equivalent. But a lot of the difference reflects limited availability of Fairtrade cotton and the cost of running small batches of cotton through the supply chain—problems that M&S expects to shrink as the volume of Fairtrade cotton buying increases.[24]

There is a growing belief that *equitrade* is an effective response to this criticism because it offers a more equitable distribution of the economic benefits of ethical retailing:

Whereas Fairtrade provides help to a relatively small (though growing) number of farmers, Equitrade tries to raise the quality of life for the majority of poor people by carrying out the processing operations, where most of the profits are made, in the poor countries themselves. Malagasy Foods, for example, has . . . started harvesting and processing chocolate in Madagascar. It thereby ensures that 40 per cent of its income stays in Madagascar, with an extra 11 per cent benefiting the country through tax.[25]

Both models have advantages and disadvantages. Fairtrade demonstrably helps the groups of people whom it targets, and works through cooperatives that guarantee environmental and social standards and that demand democratic decision-making over how the extra money earned is distributed. Equitrade stimulates the wider economy, but is less accountable and assumes that the manufacturer treats the cocoa bean growers or other farmers and suppliers fairly.[26]

Finally, the third criticism of fair trade is that, for consumers who want to support CSR companies and causes and for whom issues such as "food miles"[27] are important, buying a local product is more ethical and sustainable than sourcing one from thousands of miles away. While there is some truth to this point, making the *best* choice becomes a matter of choosing among priorities. Whether, for example, a consumer's support for local farmers in the West adds more or less social value than the same support for poor farmers in Africa is a personal judgment.

For an increasing number of firms, however, the positives of fair trade outweigh any real or perceived negatives. These firms increasingly see fair trade as more of a good business decision than an act of charity. Beyond improved consumer perceptions of the firm and its products, fair trade is a means by which firms can build long-term relationships with suppliers and guarantee a more stable supply of higher quality products.

The UK company Cadbury is one such company. In 2009, in partnership with the Fairtrade Foundation, Cadbury made an important decision to supply all of the cocoa beans it uses to make chocolate from Fairtrade sources:[28]

Fairtrade is growing fast—UK sales were up 43 per cent [in 2008]—but adding the Cadbury products will give it a boost. Sales of all Fairtrade products last year, from bananas to T-shirts, totaled £700m ($987m, €780m). Sales of Cadbury's Dairy Milk [the firm's most famous chocolate bar] in the UK and Ireland are worth £200m.[29]

The next goal for many activists, such as the International Labor Rights Forum (ILRF) and Global Exchange, is to secure the support for fair trade chocolate from a major U.S. manufacturer.

[They] have been campaigning for years to convince major US chocolate companies such as Nestlé, Mars, and Hershey's to purchase Fairtrade cocoa to counter the worst forms of child labor and trafficked labor, both widespread problems on cocoa farms in West Africa. They support the Commitment to Ethical Cocoa Sourcing, a set of guidelines supported by over 60 chocolate companies (such as Equal Exchange) and nonprofits (such as Green America).[30]

Ultimately, "Cadbury has decided its interest lies in long-term relationships with suppliers who earn a decent living."[31] This is a message that is increasingly resonating with firms as fair trade becomes an established way to source ethically and is demanded by consumers.

Starbucks is another firm that believes in the market value of fair trade.

Case Study   Starbucks

As the statistics above suggest, the issue of fair trade affects many industries in many countries. Fair trade campaigns have often focused on coffee to catch the attention of consumers and corporations in the developed world.[32]

As one of the top five coffee buyers in the world,[33] Starbucks' actions have significant influence over the industry as a whole and have been a source of negative publicity for the company in the past. Among other things, the company has been accused of profiting at the expense of others:

> While company profits have tripled since 1997, to $181 million in fiscal 2000, many of the world's coffee farmers have been devastated by historically low prices. Coffee is now priced around 50¢ per pound, while production costs are around 80¢ per pound.[34]

Although not totally at fault, Starbucks has made a big effort to improve its image in this area.[35] The company is involved

> with various programs aimed at hiking the wages of farmers and improving the local environment. Starbucks recently unveiled guidelines that will pay farmers a premium price if they meet certain environmental, labor, and quality standards. [In 2001] the company joined TransFair, an organization that guarantees that farmers will receive most of the $1.26 per pound that coffee roasters pay for high-quality beans.[36]

There is still more, however, that activists would like the company to do: Starbucks buys less than 10% of the 1.8 million pounds of fair trade coffee that activists would like it to buy.[37] As such, the brand remains a target for some. A campaign organized by the Organic Consumers Association (OCA), for example, has the goal to, among other things, "improve working conditions for coffee plantation workers, and brew and seriously promote fair trade coffee in all of their cafes."[38] Another, "Protest Starbuck$," states that

> While Starbucks has slowly bought more certified Fair Trade coffee, it represents only a very small percentage of their total coffee (about 3.7%). Starbucks rarely offers certified Fair Trade coffee as their coffee of the day, nor has it followed its own policy of brewing Fair Trade coffee, on demand.[39]

The coffee company Green Mountain Coffee is attracting positive attention with its attempts to address this issue. Its progressive approach is one of the main reasons the company ranked No. 1 in *Business Ethics Magazine's* 2006 and 2007 list of 100 Best Corporate Citizens:[40]

> Today, with suppliers at small farmer cooperatives in Peru, Mexico, and Sumatra, Green Mountain pays Fair Trade prices for coffee beans—not the market price of 24 to 50 cents per pound, but a

minimum of $1.26 per pound for conventional coffee and $1.41 for organically grown. In 2002, these Fair Trade purchases represented 8 percent of sales. Green Mountain also has a "farm direct" program that cuts out middlemen to deliver higher prices to farmers. Roughly a quarter of its coffee purchases are farm direct.[41]

CSR Newsletters: Fair Trade

What is interesting about one recent article[42] is *not* that the fair trade coffee company (AMT) lost its license to operate coffee kiosks at London railway stations to a competitor that doesn't stock any fair trade coffee. What is interesting is that the reason the firm lost its license relates back to a strategic decision not to pass on its higher supply chain costs to its customers, which has a direct impact on the firm's profits. It is not clear whether this is due to a managerial misstep, or whether the firm has no confidence that UK consumers are willing to pay the price premium associated with Fair trade coffee. Either way, it is not good news for AMT and potentially has implications for the fundamental CSR business model.

For example, it is fine for AMT to say

> We can sleep at night knowing that the people picking our beans that go in our cups are being looked after—unlike the high street guys who are trying to take over the world.

But, the reality is that

> The closures slashed a hefty £6 million off AMT's £15 million revenue in one fell swoop.

Firms that differentiate their products on some aspect other than price (i.e., quality, technology, design, etc.) charge a corresponding price premium because, in general, the products are more expensive to produce and the consumers who buy such products are less price sensitive than consumers who make their purchase decisions based primarily on price. The same laws of economics apply to firms that want to differentiate their products based primarily on socially responsibility, which often incurs a higher cost structure.

Due to the awareness surrounding the Fair Trade brand in the United Kingdom ("Four-fifths of UK consumers now recognise the Fair Trade brand, according to the Department for Environment, Food and Rural Affairs") and the likely small increase in price per cup involved, it seems fair to assume that UK consumers place a higher importance on CSR issues than most and would be willing to pay the difference. But, that will not help AMT if the firm goes out of business without testing to see whether or not this is true.

Due to high-profile NGO campaigns and firm responses, public awareness about fair trade issues is growing. In addition to the growing popularity of fair trade products in

(Continued)

(Continued)

Europe, for example, according to the National Coffee Association (NCA), awareness about fair trade is also growing among U.S. consumers:

> Awareness of fair-trade coffee among U.S. coffee drinkers aged 18 and over has risen to 12% [in 2004] up from 7% in 2003 and purchases among those aware have risen to 45% from 38%.[43]

More recently:

> In 2006, 27 percent of Americans said they were aware of the [Fair Trade] certification, up from 12 percent in 2004.[44]

Starbucks has been at the vanguard of raising the profile of fair trade in the United States, working closely with suppliers to help them convert to sustainable practices and offering them long-term contracts as an incentive to do so. This approach helps the company meet the needs of the fair trade industry, as well as increase the quality of the product they buy and then resell in their stores.

In response, Starbucks launched the Coffee Agronomy Company. It is based in Costa Rica and positioned as "the flagship vehicle for Starbucks' sustainable supply chain commitment." Soon after, the company also launched its Coffee and Farmer Equity (CAFE) Practices guidelines, which "spell out Starbucks' expectations for its suppliers on economic, social and environmental issues."[45]

Starbucks's CAFÉ Practices[46]

When Starbucks implemented C.A.F.E. Practices, it had six objectives in mind:

1. Increase economic, social, and environmental sustainability in the specialty coffee industry, including conservation and biodiversity.

2. Encourage Starbucks suppliers to implement C.A.F.E. Practices through economic incentives and preferential buying status.

3. Purchase the majority of Starbucks coffee under C.A.F.E. Practices guidelines by 2007.

4. Negotiate mutually beneficial long-term contracts with suppliers to support Starbucks growth.

5. Build mutually beneficial and increasingly direct relationship with suppliers.

6. Promote transparency and economic fairness within the coffee supply chain.

Starbucks developed CAFÉ in conjunction with the environmental charity Conservation International. The goal for suppliers in conforming to the guidelines (Starbucks wants the majority of suppliers compliant within five years) is to be certified as a Starbucks preferred supplier, which contains specific price guarantees by Starbucks over and above current market prices.[47] The internal logic behind Starbucks's action made it a clear operational and strategic decision:

> To support [its] high growth rate, it was clear that an integral part of the company's future success would come from meeting increased demand through a secure supply of high-quality coffee beans. Coffee beans constituted the bread and butter of Starbucks' business—the company had to ensure a sustainable supply of this key commodity.[48]

In the broader picture, the business case for fair trade throughout the coffee industry is convincing:

> Sure, by creating a healthier supply chain, [Starbucks] might end up helping some of [their] competitors. . . . But in the end, it helps the industry. And a healthier industry is better for us, better for the consumer, for the environment, for everyone.[49]

These results have been repeated elsewhere, particularly in Europe, where growth in this area is stronger. In September 2004, Marks & Spencer, the well-known UK retailer, announced it would source all of the coffee it serves in its coffee shops from fair trade sources. The move doubled the amount of fair trade coffee on sale in UK coffee shops. Significantly, it announced it would do this without raising prices. The Co-operative Group has also been a strong example of the bottom-line benefits of fair trade goods:

> Since making all their own brands of coffee and chocolate Fairtrade they have seen sales soar. Chocolate sales volumes were up 24% in the 12 months following conversion to Fairtrade and a further 46% in the first half of [2004]. In both periods, sales of other more established brands have stayed static.[50]

In recent years, Starbucks has faced a rapidly evolving competitive market and wildly fluctuating commodity prices.[51] Starbucks has always faced competition on price (people could always buy coffee cheaper elsewhere), but now the firm is also facing real competition on quality as fast-food U.S. firms such as McDonald's and Dunkin' Donuts seek to eat into Starbucks's core target market,[52]

including fair trade coffee.[53] In response, Howard Schultz, Starbucks CEO, states,

> It is vitally important that we maintain our commitment to the basic fundamental value of what Starbucks stands for . . . I take great personal pride in the fact we are now the largest buyer of Fair Trade coffee in the world.[54]

This competition strikes at the heart of Starbucks's business model and is spreading beyond the United States,[55] where Nestlé's Nespresso "premium coffee brand . . . has pledged to source 80% of its beans from farms meeting strict social and environmental standards by 2013."[56] What is Starbucks's product? Is it *quality coffee* or the *coffeehouse experience* that Howard Schultz (Starbucks's CEO) tried to bring back to the United States from a 1983 trip to Milan, Italy? When there is deterioration in the economy, can Starbucks justify the price premium it charges based on experience alone (if competitors are catching up in terms of quality, yet offering products at a cheaper price)? Either way, the company is increasingly being pushed to innovate and fair trade coffee is seen as an area where Starbucks can continue to push industry best practice:

> [In September, 2009] Starbucks stores in the UK and Ireland . . . began serving 100% Fairtrade Certified and Starbucks Shared Planet verified coffee in all of their espresso-based beverages. Every one of the two million visitors per week can walk away with a Fairtrade Certified Cappuccino, Latte or Mocha and help support small-scale farmers and their communities in developing countries around the world.[57]

Online Resources

- Commitment to Ethical Cocoa Sourcing, http://www.laborrights.org/stop-child-labor/cocoa-campaign/

  "Almost 60 organizations and fair trade chocolate companies have endorsed a joint statement [that] outlines how the chocolate industry can embrace a more ethical cocoa supply chain."

- Common Code for the Coffee Community, http://www.sustainable-coffee.net/

  "A global association aiming at social, environmental and economic sustainability in the mainstream coffee sector."

- Conservation International, http://www.conservation.org/

  "Conservation International is committed to helping societies adopt a more sustainable approach to development—one that considers and values nature at every turn."

- Ethical Trading Initiative (ETI), http://www.ethicaltrade.org/

  "The Ethical Trading Initiative is a ground-breaking alliance of companies, trade unions and voluntary organisations. We work in partnership to improve the working lives of people across the globe who make or grow consumer goods."

- Fairtrade Foundation, http://www.fairtrade.org.uk/

  "The Fairtrade Foundation is the independent non-profit organisation that licenses use of the FAIRTRADE Mark on products in the UK in accordance with internationally agreed Fairtrade standards."

- Fair Trade Labeling Organization (FLO), http://www.fairtrade.net/

  "We are 24 organizations working to secure a better deal for producers. We own the FAIRTRADE Mark—the product label that certifies international Fairtrade standards have been met."

- International Cocoa Initiative, http://www.cocoainitiative.org/

  "Founded in 2002, the International Cocoa Initiative (ICI) is dedicated to ending child and forced labour in cocoa-growing."

- International Labor Rights Forum (ILRF), http://www.laborrights.org/

  "ILRF is an advocacy organization dedicated to achieving just and humane treatment for workers worldwide."

- Kuapa Kokoo,[58] http://kuapakokoogh.com/kuapa/

  "KUAPA KOKOO is a cocoa farmers co-operative that works to improve the lot of their members. It was established in 1993."

- National Coffee Association (NCA), http://www.ncausa.org/

  "We serve the public and our members by championing the well being of the coffee industry within the context of the global coffee community."

- Organic Consumers Association, http://www.organicconsumers.org/

  "The Organic Consumers Association (OCA) is an online and grassroots non-profit 501(c)3 public interest organization campaigning for health, justice, and sustainability."

- U.S. Fair Labor Association, http://www.fairlabor.org/

  "The Fair Labor Association (FLA), a nonprofit organization dedicated to ending sweatshop conditions in factories worldwide."

Questions for Discussion and Review

1. Do you believe in *fair trade?* Why, or why not? What does *fair* mean?

2. Are you happy to pay a price premium for CSR products?

3. What do you think explains the fact that, in Europe, "the market for Fair Trade Certified products is three times larger in dollar sales than it is in the U.S."?[59]

4. Do you know what the Fairtrade symbol looks like? Can you name a Fairtrade product that you have bought recently? Why did you buy that product?

5. Did you know about Starbucks's involvement in this issue and the Fairtrade products the company sells? Do you think this is something the company should publicize? Is there any downside to doing so?

FINANCE

CSR CONNECTION: This issue reflects the increasing pressure being placed on financial institutions by NGOs to ensure that money that is loaned to organizations (including governments), particularly in developing economies, is not used to support socially irresponsible projects.

Issue

To what extent do financial institutions, whose financing is necessary to fund projects and operations in countries around the world, share responsibility for the use to which their funds are put?

[In 2004] the website of Friends of the Earth UK invites activists to submit pro forma emails to the Chairman of both HSBC and the Royal Bank of Scotland to dissuade the banks from financing the Baku-Tbilisi-Ceyhan pipeline because of environmental concerns about the project. . . . For all this, however, private sector banking institutions have not received the sustained and broad-based scrutiny experienced by their clients, or by the international finance institutions (IFIs) and export credit agencies (ECAs) that lend in parallel to major projects.[60]

The banks ABN AMRO and Citigroup, in consultation with NGOs, are recognized as taking a prominent role in developing progressive policies in this area.

Case Study   Citigroup

As Sandy Weill, former CEO of Citigroup, stated in a memo to employees:

> One of our foremost goals, wherever Citigroup has a presence, is to make the community better because we are there. As a global institution with a presence in 100 countries, that responsibility extends throughout the world and includes appropriate sensitivity to sustainable development and environmental impacts.[61]

In 2000, Citigroup became the target of a campaign by the NGO, Rainforest Action Network (RAN). RAN has been accused of using extreme measures to pursue a fringe agenda that largely focuses on environmental issues. "Others have accused the group of coercion, blackmail, even terrorism."[62] Their tactics may be controversial; however, what is not in doubt is that they have been extremely successful in forcing policy changes by some of the largest corporations in the United States:

> This green coalition has in recent years persuaded dozens of companies, including Home Depot, Lowe's, Staples, Office Depot, and homebuilders Centex and Kaufman & Broad, to alter their conduct to protect forests, their species, and the people who live in them.[63]

RAN began targeting Citigroup in an effort to stop the bank lending money to finance projects that they believed involved harm to the environment and the indigenous people living in the vicinity of those projects. In response to the bank ignoring their request, RAN slowly ratcheted up its campaign against Citigroup. Its tactics included protests at branches, high-profile media stunts, TV advertising, and personal hounding of Weill (Citigroup CEO at the time), both on bank business and on vacation. Citigroup's tarnished image in the wake of the corporate scandals around the turn of the century only encouraged RAN to turn up the heat on the firm.

The campaign eventually forced Citigroup to the negotiating table, where the company agreed to a wide review of its policies toward lending in the areas RAN had highlighted. The review resulted in the publication of industry-leading standards in terms of Citigroup's lending and investment policies, as well as related environmental issues such as the company's recognition of the problem of global warming. The bank, in conjunction with RAN, did not stop there:

Shortly after RAN and Citi declared their cease-fire, ten global banks, including Citi, adopted the Equator Principles, a voluntary set of guidelines they developed to manage the social and environmental impact of capital projects that cost $50 million or more in the developing world. Citi's more recent environmental policy goes further.[64]

Details defining the Equator Principles (launched in 2003 and based on the International Finance Corporation's, IFC, "environmental and social guidelines for funding projects in developing countries"),[65] the goals of the pact, and means to achieve these goals are introduced by the Web site http://www.equator-principles.com/:

> The Equator Principles are a framework for financial institutions to manage environmental and social issues in project financing. . . . [The Principles represent] an industry approach for financial institutions in determining, assessing and managing environmental and social risk in project financing.[66]

The bank describes its involvement with the Equator Principles on the company's Web site:

> On June 4, 2003, Citigroup joined nine other banks from around the world to adopt the "Equator Principles," a voluntary set of guidelines developed by the banks for managing social and environmental issues related to the financing of development projects in all industries, including mining, oil and gas, and forestry. The Equator Principles are based on the policies and guidelines of the World Bank and International Finance Corporation (the private-sector investment arm of the World

Bank), which provided extensive advice and guidance in drafting the new project finance principles for the banks.[67]

Many see the Equator Principles as providing the platform for developing international standards that can be used by lending institutions to ensure all are operating on a level playing field; however, there are others that doubt the potential for real and lasting change. According to a report that aimed to establish the effectiveness of the Equator Principles one year after implementation, there is a large degree of uncertainty as to the effectiveness of the initiative:

> According to a report by BankTrack, the Equator Principles are having little impact. . . . "Many controversial projects have gone ahead virtually unaltered by the existence of the Principles . . ." said Michelle Chan-Fishel of BankTrack/Friends of the Earth U.S. . . . "If the Equator banks continue to finance controversial deals, pursue an anti-environmental lobbying agenda and cloak themselves in secrecy and unaccountability, public confidence will be irretrievably lost."[68]

Others worry about the extent of the impact activist groups such as RAN will have on companies that are unable to fight back because of successive years of corporate scandals and declining public trust:

> Over time, politicization of bank lending hurts not only the banks, but also the future of the economy. . . . Denying loans for oil drilling and timber cutting will hurt poor nations desperately trying to pull themselves out of poverty.[69]

(Continued)

(Continued)

In spite of these concerns, the popularity of the Equator Principles has grown with time. In June 2007, the Equator Principles had

> 51 signatories that account for nearly 90 per cent of emerging market project finance—about $28bn [billion] in 2006.[70]

In August 2009, Fortis Bank Nederland became the 68th financial institution to adopt the Equator Principles:

> In adopting the Principles, Fortis Bank Nederland joins 67 other financial institutions worldwide, representing >85% of project finance transactions.[71]

Importantly, the financial institutions that are signatories to the principles have also altered their perception of the principles' value. They have evolved from an initial defensive mechanism against growing NGO criticism, into a broader system for managing external risk and, increasingly, are "being used to create and market products to meet growing demand for ethical investment opportunities."[72] A reflection of this shift came in the decision by the banks to introduce Equator II, in 2006, to account for the revised IFC guidelines for financing projects in developing countries:[73]

> The principles were revamped in 2006, to make them more transparent and to increase scrutiny of social issues such as safety and security, pollution prevention and community health. The threshold for deals covered by the principles has been lowered from $50m to $10m.[74]

While organizations such as the Bank Information Centre still express concerns about how the guidelines are implemented in practice,[75] the IFC reports indicate that the banks' reactions to the voluntary guidelines have been genuine and significant:

> It is no longer a question of why banks should adopt social and environmental standards, but how.[76]

In short,

> The Equator Principles have, in only a few years, changed the way projects are financed.[77]

CSR Newsletters: Citigroup

A recent article[78] provides a good example of how firms that pursue their own economic self-interest, while keeping half an eye on their stakeholders' concerns and their own reputation, can generate socially beneficial outcomes:

> Citigroup is rolling out a network of biometric automatic cash machines aimed at illiterate Indian slum dwellers, using the latest technology to woo the millions of "unbanked" poor. The machines will recognise account holders' thumbprints, eliminating the need for a personal identification number, and will have colour-coded screen instructions and voiceovers to guide them through transactions.

The article highlights the primarily economic focus of Citigroup's experiment and "the enormous market potential of India's lower income groups." Learning from the high-profile successes of the micro-finance schemes, Western banks are beginning to recognize that such developing country consumers might be less of a risk than initially believed and a potentially huge opportunity:

> Though India's population exceeds 1bn [billion], Citigroup estimates that there are only about 300m bank accounts in the country. However, loan repayment rates among the poorest borrowers in micro-finance schemes are about 98 per cent—among the highest in the banking sector.

In addition to its involvement with the Equator Principles, Citigroup appears to be committed to the broader concept of *sustainable banking*.[79] For all the firm's PR problems and complicity in the 2007–2009 financial crisis,[80] Citigroup continues to set high standards to which it is willing to commit itself publicly. In February 2008, for example, together with JPMorgan and Morgan Stanley, Citigroup announced a new set of Carbon Principles.[81] The set of principles are designed to govern financial institutions that advise and lend money to U.S. power companies and were initiated

> in anticipation of the government capping GHG [green house gas] emissions in the coming years. . . . The new standards are the result of nine months of negotiations among the banks, environmental groups, and large utilities.[82]

> Although the Carbon Principles do not preclude financing coal power plants that

attempt to minimize their green house gas emissions (by, for example, capturing their carbon dioxide emissions and reinjecting them underground), they commit signatory institutions to placing a higher priority on renewable alternatives.

More detail about the Carbon Principles, including its goals and means by which banks will be held to account for their commitments can be found at the Web site, http://www.carbonprinciples.com/:

> The Carbon Principles provide a consistent approach for banks and their U.S. power clients to evaluate and address carbon risks in the financing of electric power projects. The Principles and the accompanying Enhanced Environmental Diligence Process strive to create industry best practice for evaluating options to meet the electric power needs of the United States in an environmentally responsible and cost effective manner in an uncertain policy environment.[83]

Online Resources

- ABN AMRO, http://www.abnamro.com/about/about.cfm

"Protecting, sustaining and enhancing human, natural, and financial capital for the future."

- BankTrack, http://www.banktrack.org/

  "BankTrack is a global network of civil society organisations and individuals tracking the operations of the private financial sector (commercial banks, investors, insurance companies, pension funds) and its effect on people and the planet."

- Carbon Principles, http://www.carbonprinciples.com/

  "The Carbon Principles provide a consistent approach for banks and their U.S. power clients to evaluate and address carbon risks in the financing of electric power projects."

- Citigroup Corporate Citizenship, http://www.citigroup.com/citigroup/citizen/index.htm

  "As a global financial institution and industry leader, Citi takes pride in its citizenship efforts."

- Equator Principles, http://www.equator-principles.com/

  "The Equator Principles have become the project finance industry standard for addressing environmental and social issues in project financing globally."

- International Finance Corporation, http://www.ifc.org/

  "IFC fosters sustainable economic growth in developing countries by financing private sector investment, mobilizing capital in the international financial markets, and providing advisory services to businesses and governments."

- Rainforest Action Network (RAN), http://www.ran.org/

  "We believe that a sustainable world can be created in our lifetime, and that aggressive action must be taken immediately to leave a safe and secure world for our children."

- UN Principles for Responsible Investment, http://www.unpri.org/

  "The Principles are voluntary and aspirational. They are not prescriptive, but instead provide a menu of possible actions for incorporating environmental, social and corporate governance (ESG) issues into mainstream investment decision-making and ownership practices."

Questions for Discussion and Review

1. From a CSR perspective, what is your impression of Citigroup? Should it share responsibility for the projects for which its funds are used?

2. From the same CSR perspective, what is your impression of the Rainforest Action Network (RAN)? What do you think of the organization's tactics to bring about changes that it thinks are correct?

3. How did you choose where to open your main bank account? Would you ever choose a bank based on its CSR performance? Alternatively, would you avoid a bank that received negative press coverage because of an ethical or CSR transgression?

4. Go to the Equator Principles Web site (http://www.equator-principles.com/). Is it naive to expect huge financial organizations to aspire and adhere to the values and principles contained within the document? Why or why not?

5. What is your impression of the Carbon Principles? Are they an improvement on the Equator Principles or just a means of avoiding or weakening anticipated government legislation?

FINANCIAL CRISIS

CSR CONNECTION: This issue views the global economic system through the eyes of the 2007–2009 economic crisis. What challenges does the crisis present to the global economy and capitalist system? What is the role of CSR in the crisis? And, what changes should the CSR movement advocate?

Issue

In many ways, the economic events that began toward the end of 2007,[84] which have widely been reported as producing "the most serious financial crisis since the Great Crash of 1929"[85] with a total cost to the global economy estimated by the IMF to be $4,100 billion,[86] brought into focus the comprehensive nature of CSR. From individual greed and the abdication of responsibility, to organizational fraud and the mismanagement of resources, to governmental failure to monitor and adequately regulate the financial system, the crisis emphasized the many interlocking factors that make CSR such a complex issue. At the same time, however, and with the benefit of hindsight, these events also demonstrated how much common sense is integral to a CSR perspective. Essentially, the crisis resulted from the cumulative effects of multiple bad decisions by individuals who had lost their sense of perspective:[87]

> the current financial crisis—how [could] so many people . . . be so stupid, incompetent and self-destructive all at once.[88]

> The scale of stupidity and greed at the big banks defies belief.[89]

> That's how we got here—a near total breakdown of responsibility at every link in our financial chain, and now we either bail out the people who brought us here or risk a total systemic crash.[90]

> How could the people who sold these [products] have been so short-sightedly greedy? . . . how could the people who bought them have been so foolish?[91]

At various stages, key actors suspected the *system* was unsustainable, but they had no self-interest in advocating for change. As Citibank's Chuck Prince said in 2007, shortly before his ouster as CEO later that year:

> As long as the music is playing, you've got to get up and dance. We're still dancing.[92]

Essentially, the 2007–2009 economic crisis was driven by three main factors: First, the housing market bubble that was fueled by low interest rates and easy access to mortgages; second, the underpricing of risk, particularly by investors on Wall Street; and, third, the failure of the regulatory infrastructure to police the increasingly liquid global financial market. All of these decisions were taken within an atmosphere of overdependence on the *market* as the ultimate arbiter that relieved individual actors of the personal responsibility attached to many of their day-to-day decisions. The crisis was inherently an invention of the U.S. financial markets, but for it to have the global reach that it did required the buy-in of the rest of the global financial system. Everyone was happy to play along while the market was going up. The resulting backlash against the status quo following the crash, however, represents a challenge to the spread of globalization shaped largely by U.S. liberal capitalism (e.g., deregulation, free international money flows, self-correcting markets, and the efficient pursuit of profit in the form of shareholder returns):

> The fall of the Berlin Wall was held to mark the triumph of [the] Washington consensus. The collapse of Lehman Brothers [in the autumn of 2008] marked its demise.[93]

What is emerging is a post-liberal model that better meets the needs and values of the other economic systems:

> This suspicion of Anglo-Saxon economic liberalism cut across the usual political boundaries. Right wing industrialists disliked it, but so did left-wing labor unions. Chinese communists felt threatened, but so did Green Party activists in Germany. . . . The critique of U.S. liberalism . . . is shared by a diverse group that includes French President Nicolas Sarkozy, German Chancellor Angela Merkel, Chinese Prime Minister Wen Jibao and Russian President Dmitry Medvedev.[94]

Along with this shift in economic ideology comes a corresponding shift in global political power. The dominant feature of the U.S. economic model prior to the crisis was an inherently unstable combination of excessively low savings and excessively high borrowing. This surplus of credit was being used to finance an unsustainable level of consumption—unsustainable because the United States was consistently spending more than it saved. That money had to come from somewhere, and most of it came from China. As such, the only real, long-term solution to the crisis is a rebalancing of demand and supply within the global economy, which represents a shift in influence from the borrower to the lender:[95]

> [The crisis] is not only a crisis of capitalism or of a particular form of capitalism after all, it's one of U.S. economic and global power as well. . . . the fact that [the meeting to discuss a global response to the crisis] is one of the G-20 rather than the Group of Seven—and that its most important meetings are between Obama and Chinese President Hu Jintao—is a symbol of the decline of U.S. economic power exposed by the crisis.[96]

The sense is that the times have changed and U.S. capitalism, as the driving force behind globalization, will have to change with them:

> When mass protests exploded on the streets of Seattle in 1999 against the kind of globalization embodied in the World Trade Organization, their anticapitalist message was

widely portrayed as utopian. A decade on, as anticapitalist demonstrators vent their fury [at the 2008 meeting in London of the G20 to discuss solutions to the crisis] on the social and ecological vandals of the City [the financial center of London] . . . it looks more like common sense.[97]

Even a newspaper as inherently pro-business as [*The Economist*] has to admit that there was something rotten in finance. The basic capitalist bargain, under which genuine risk-takers are allowed to garner huge rewards, seems a poor one if taxpayers are landed with a huge bill for it.[98]

The debate that has emerged within the CSR community regarding the future shape of capitalism reflects this shift in the content and tone of discussions about the global economy. Bill Baue, contributing editor of *CSRwire.com,* for example, highlights the intersection of the economic and environmental crises:

The economic meltdown of 2008 mirrors the simultaneous environmental meltdown fueled by the climate calamity—both share common roots, and many in the Corporate Social Responsibility (CSR) community believe they share a common salvation. At the most basic level, the global economy is melting down because the belief in perpetual growth, propped up by deregulation and outright fraud, has smacked up against the finite nature of reality. Likewise, our atmosphere is literally melting our ecosystems, primarily because of the growth curve of fossil fuel emissions and carbon concentrations. . . . The most likely savior scenario likewise entwines economy and environment: a "green" recovery promises to create good jobs and strong companies while transitioning to a low-carbon energy infrastructure powered by renewable resources such as wind and solar.[99]

A similar argument was presented to a much larger audience by Thomas Friedman in the *New York Times:*

What if the crisis of 2008 represents something much more fundamental than a deep recession? What if it's telling us that the whole growth model we created over the last 50 years is simply unsustainable economically and ecologically and that 2008 was when we hit the wall—when Mother Nature and the market both said: "No more."?[100]

Bradley K. Googins, executive director of the Boston College Center for Corporate Citizenship, presented an equally strong critique in an article titled "Time for Capitalism to Adapt or Depart":

The freeing of markets has unleashed many unintended consequences not envisioned by the architects of global capitalism. Key issues ranging from the growing inequality gap, persistent and negative consequences of loose regulation to environmental degradation and chronic corruption are increasing the call for a re-examination of the current state of capitalism and challenging us to create a version that can better address these issues and build in different trade-offs. . . . There are in effect a series of cracks appearing in the foundation of capitalism, cracks that need to be seriously examined.[101]

In early 2009, articles with titles such as "Is Capitalism Working?"[102] "The End,"[103] and "The End of the Financial World As We Know It"[104] began to appear. This sense of seismic change was reinforced by a major series of articles in the *Financial Times* about the crisis and its consequences for the global economic order. The goal of the series, which was titled the "Future of Capitalism" and had contributions from the newspaper's top economic columnists as well as invited articles by experts such as Paul Kennedy, Nigel Lawson, and Amartya Sen, was to assess the consequences of the crisis, given that "Assumptions that prevailed since the 1980s embrace of the market now lie in shreds. The scope of government is again widening and the era of free-wheeling finance is over." Representative of the debate was this comment by Martin Wolf in the opening article in the series:

> It is impossible at such a turning point to know where we are going. . . . Yet the combination of a financial collapse with a huge recession, if not something worse, will surely change the world. The legitimacy of the market will weaken. The credibility of the US will be damaged. The authority of China will rise. Globalisation itself may founder. . . . The era of financial liberalization has ended. Yet, unlike the 1930s, no credible alternative to the market economy exists. . . . Where we end up, after this financial tornado, is for us to seek and determine.[105]

Combined with Bill Gates's call for "creative capitalism"[106] and Muhammad Yunus's book, *Creating a World Without Poverty*,[107] the sense is that we are at a point of "inflection"[108] in the economic history of our planet and, whatever shape globalization takes moving forward, it will be different than what it was prior to the crisis.[109]

CSR Newsletters: Moral Hazard

Two recent articles touch indirectly on issues related to social responsibility within the global financial system. In particular, they focus on the decline in global stock markets and discuss possible causes of the impending recession that analysts are projecting. In the first article,[110] George Soros uses the presence of moral hazard to highlight the failure of a pure market ideology:

> [Market] Fundamentalists believe that markets tend towards equilibrium and the common interest is best served by allowing participants to pursue their self-interest. It is an obvious misconception, because it was the intervention of the authorities that prevented financial markets from breaking down, not the markets themselves.

The article accuses governments of creating a system that is, ultimately, unsustainable. In order to avoid the damage to the broader economy that would result from undermining the positions of traders in the global financial system, Soros notes that governments and central banks averted their eyes from the moral hazard that is an inherent part of the global financial system:

Every time the credit expansion ran into trouble the financial authorities intervened, injecting liquidity and finding other ways to stimulate the economy. That created a system of asymmetric incentives also known as moral hazard, which encouraged ever greater credit expansion.

The second article, by Martin Wolf,[111] paints an even more complicated interaction of causes that range from a "fundamentally defective financial system," "rational responses to incentives," "the short-sightedness of human beings," overly loose US monetary policy, and "the massive flows of surplus capital" around the global financial system. The article also highlights the role of governments in sustaining a system that has become too important to fail and the advantages traders gain by knowing this. Unfortunately, he concludes that politicians, with all their human weaknesses (primarily the short-term driver of self-preservation), are unlikely to change anything any time soon:

Those who emphasise rationality can readily point to the incentives for the financial sector to take undue risk. This is the result of the interaction of "asymmetric information"— the fact that insiders know more than anybody else what is going on—with "moral hazard"—the perception that the government will rescue financial institutions if enough of them fall into difficulty at the same time. There is evident truth in both propositions: if, for example, the UK government feels obliged to rescue a modest-sized mortgage bank, such as Northern Rock, moral hazard is rife.

The evolution of the thoughts of Alan Greenspan, chair of the U.S. Federal Reserve from 1987 to 2006, on the policing role of market forces is instructive. In 1963, Greenspan wrote that it would be self-defeating (and, therefore, highly unlikely) for firms "to sell unsafe food and drugs, fraudulent securities, and shoddy buildings. It is in the self-interest of every businessman to have a reputation for honest dealings and a quality product." By 2008, in testimony to the U.S. Congress's House Committee on Oversight and Government Reform, however, Greenspan admitted the error in this line of thought:

Those of us who have looked to the self-interest of lending institutions to protect shareholders' equity, myself included, are in a state of shocked disbelief. . . . This modern [free market] paradigm held sway for decades. The whole intellectual edifice, however, collapsed in the summer of last year.[112]

Greenspan's shift demonstrates the limits of the free market approach (the "efficient market hypothesis")[113] in the face of incentives that significantly distort the checks and balances that are theoretically in place. As the *Financial Times* summarized,

The intellectual impact of the crisis has already been colossal. The "Greenspanist" doctrine in monetary policy is in retreat. . . . Finance has already changed irrevocably.[114]

As such, the economic crisis focuses the debate back onto the personal ethics of decision makers and those organizations that foster leaders willing to make the best decisions in the long-term interests of their organizations and their stakeholders. Together with the debate about what the crisis holds for the global political power balance and the form of capitalism that will drive globalization forward, the crisis also injects an element of cross-cultural under-standing. In an increasingly online and interconnected global business environment, the deci-sions of firms in the West have important implications for their counterparts in countries around the world. As such, this crisis crystallizes a number of questions that strike at the importance of CSR for firms today.

Case Study   Countrywide

Countrywide is a good example of how bad things had become prior to the downturn:

> More than any other lending institution, Countrywide has become synonymous with the excesses that led to the housing bubble.[115]

Countrywide, founded in 1969 by Angelo Mozilo and David Loeb, was a mortgage lender that aggressively sought to expand its market share by "promoting homeownership for as many Americans as possible."[116] As the firm became more successful, however, particularly in the early 1990s, external pres-sures to maintain that success led to the search for growing numbers of customers and increasing amounts of money to loan them. As this search became more difficult, the temptation to compromise Countrywide's loan qualification standards became too great. It proved to be a short step from granting mortgages to customers who met standard qualifications, to a more liberal interpretation of those standards, to the development of riskier financial products that would expand the potential pool of applicants:

> When the great refinancing wave of 2003 came to a close, [Countrywide] scrambled to maintain volume by offering riskier

types of loans and encouraging Americans to pull the equity out of their house and spend the proceeds.[117]

At the height of the boom, the subprime mortgage industry in the U.S. had clearly lost all sense of proportion:

> In Bakersfield, Calif., a Mexican strawberry picker with an income of $14,000 and no English was lent every penny he needed to buy a house for $720,000.[118]

> Between 2005 and 2007, which was the peak of sub-prime lending, the top 25 subprime originators made almost $1,000bn [billion] in loans to more than 5m borrowers, many of whom have [since] had their homes repossessed.[119]

In Countrywide's case, the pursuit of growing profits without consideration for the societal implications, led to the rapid growth in Alt A and subprime mortgages (both home mortgages given to less than fully qualified people) that tipped off the financial crisis. Individual mortgage brokers, however, were responding to incentives that had been devised to encourage short-term revenue maximization, rather than a longer term focus on sustainable profit:

Countrywide, determined to gain market share, kept making high-risk loans well into 2007 as the housing market began to crumble. . . . The managers also believed that their bonuses would rise indefinitely, or at least as long as the company continued to expand. . . . Greed and wishful thinking prevailed.[120]

Mallen Baker argues that, within the financial industry, the potential for this kind of abuse is higher. While firms benefit from striving to meet the needs and demands of their customers, he suggests that this relationship is weaker for those firms that sell products that their consumers do not necessarily need and do not fully understand:

If someone wants a tin of beans from a supermarket, they can immediately see whether that retailer has the product actually in stock, and they can pretty easily compare the price of that tin of beans with identical products being sold elsewhere. But, if you could fleece the customer and knowingly sell products that don't wholly meet their needs, but are immensely profitable, would you do it?[121]

Baker's accusation is that the underlying logic of the financial sector is confusion (of the consumer), combined with a fundamental legitimacy (people know, in principle, that it is important to save and invest money):

Many banks in different countries will offer a basic deposit account to put your money into which is free if you stay in credit. They will also provide a number of outlets for you to withdraw cash for free as well. . . . Beyond that, the logic of the industry rewards complexity.[122]

The result of this short-term focus and rapid expansion of the mortgage market was a service that undermined trust and proved to be very costly for Countrywide. It was disastrous, however, when extrapolated to the level of the national and global economic system:

It took Fannie [Mae] and Freddie [Mac] over three decades to acquire $2 trillion in mortgages and mortgage-backed securities. Together, they held $2.1 trillion in 2000. By 2005, the two [Government-sponsored Enterprises] GSEs held $4 trillion, up 92% in just five years. By 2008, they'd grown another 24%, to nearly $5 trillion. . . . [Critics estimate that] $1 trillion of this debt was subprime and "liar loans," almost all bought between 2005 and 2007.[123]

In terms of the U.S. housing market, large numbers of excessive mortgages loaned to people who were unable to repay the loans or keep up payments resulted in large numbers of foreclosures and repossessions. The recession that followed the bursting of the housing bubble exacerbated this problem:

The severe recession has transformed the situation into an outright foreclosure crisis, with 1 million owners [by early 2009] having lost homes since 2006 and 5.9 million more expected to do so over the next four years.[124]

(Continued)

(Continued)

While Countrywide became the face of the mortgage-fueled asset bubble in the United States, therefore, it was by no means the only transgressor. In addition to the role played by Fannie Mae and Freddie Mac, who, in 2008, owned "almost half of all American mortgages,"[125] Washington Mutual faced similar accusations of improper lending practices, with equally devastating consequences:

> At WaMu, getting the job done meant lending money to nearly anyone who asked for it—the force behind the bank's meteoric rise and its precipitous collapse [in 2008] in the biggest bank failure in American history. On a financial landscape littered with wreckage, WaMu . . . stands out as a singularly brazen case of lax lending. By the first half of [2008], the value of its bad loans had reached $11.5 billion, nearly tripling from $4.2 billion a year earlier.[126]

A similar fate occurred at the mortgage lender Northern Rock, which became the face of the financial crisis in the United Kingdom. Northern Rock's collapse and eventual nationalization prompted the first run on a British bank since 1866. The mortgage lender was eventually nationalized in February 2008[127] with a large capital injection by the British government:

> [Northern Rock] had seen its debt to the government balloon to £29.6bn [billion] at the end of 2007 as it struggled to survive, while its savings deposits, decimated by the run on the bank by anxious customers, shrank by almost £14bn in six months to £10.5bn.[128]

All of this, in spite of early warning signs by prominent, independent observers:

> As early as 1993, the Interfaith Center on Corporate Responsibility was filing shareholder resolutions raising red flags on predatory subprime lending.[129]

The industry, as a whole, experienced all the signs of a bubble, the aftermath of which generated dramatic headlines such as "Sex, Lies, and Mortgage Deals."[130] Primarily, however, the mortgage-fueled asset bubble and the corresponding financial crisis highlight the central role of CSR in today's global business environment. When organizations lack a CSR perspective they endanger themselves, but they can also cause great harm to society. Countrywide Financial and Merrill Lynch, for example, the biggest firms in their market space, are gone because of the socially *irresponsible* manner in which these firms were run. A short-term profit maximization mind-set, without socially oriented guiding principles (without CSR), is a moral issue for individual employees and an issue of survival for the organization:

> The price was attractive. There was money to make on the deal. Was it responsible? Irrelevant. It was legal, and others were making money that way. And the consequences for the banking system if everybody did it? Not our problem. Now we are paying the price in trillions of dollars for that imprudent attitude. . . . Responsibility means awareness of the system consequences of our actions. It is not a luxury, it is the cornerstone of prudence.[131]

Unscrupulous individual decision making, combined with executives' abdication of their fiduciary responsibilities to protect the long-term interests of shareholders add up to irresponsible levels of risk that, ultimately, threatened the existence of many firms:

> On June 25, 2008 California Attorney [General] Jerry Brown Jr. sued Countrywide Financial, CEO Angelo Mozilo, and president David Sambol, for "engaging in deceptive advertising and unfair competition by pushing homeowners into mass-produced, risky loans for the sole purpose of reselling the mortgages on the secondary market." . . . [and used specific schemes] to mislead and deceive borrowers into taking out risky, costly and complex subprime and adjustable rate mortgage (ARM) loans that were inappropriate for most homeowners.[132]

> On July 1, 2008, Bank of America announced that it completed a full takeover of Countrywide after receiving approval from the Federal Reserve's Board of Directors on June 5. On October 16, 2008, Countrywide announced it would delist its stock.[133]

Bank of America's purchase of Countrywide, together with assumption of responsibility for Countrywide's bad debts, contributed toward Bank of America's $1.79 billion loss in the fourth quarter of 2008—the bank's first quarterly loss in 17 years,[134] as well as adding $20 billion to the $25 billion in bailout money the firm had already received from the U.S. government.[135]

On April 27, 2009, Bank of America "quietly retired" the Countrywide brand:

> BofA bought Countrywide in [2008] in a deal valued at $4.1bn [billion] after the biggest US mortgage lender ran aground on multi-billion-dollar losses. The bank is renaming Countrywide's operations as part of Bank of America Home Loans, ending four decades of a brand established by Angelo Mozilo, former chief executive.[136]

> In June 2009, the U.S. Securities and Exchange Commission charged Mozilo and his top two executives with fraud, "alleging that they misled investors about the financial condition of the mortgage company in the months leading up to its sale to Bank of America."[137]

Online Resources

- B Corporation, http://www.bcorporation.net/

  "B Corporations are a new type of corporation which uses the power of business to solve social and environmental problems."

- Countrywide Watch, Center for Responsible Lending, http://www.responsible lending.org/

  "The Center for Responsible Lending is a nonprofit, nonpartisan research and policy organization dedicated to protecting homeownership and family wealth by working to eliminate abusive financial practices."

- Federal Reserve Bank of St. Louis, http://timeline.stlouisfed.org/

  "The Financial Crisis—A Timeline of Events and Policy Actions."

- International Monetary Fund—Financial Crisis, https://www.imf.org/external/np/exr/key/finstab.htm

- Mallen Baker's Web site, http://www.mallenbaker.net/csr/

  "This site is the personal website of Mallen Baker, a writer, speaker and strategic advisor on corporate social responsibility and the founding director of Business Respect."

- Martin Wolf's blog at the *Financial Times,* http://blogs.ft.com/economistsforum/

  "Leading economists discuss issues raised by Martin Wolf and others."

- Mortgage Bankers Association, http://www.mbaa.org/

  "The Mortgage Bankers Association (MBA) is the national association representing the real estate finance industry, an industry that employs more than 280,000 people in virtually every community in the country."

- Summit on the Future of the Corporation, http://www.summit2020.org/

  "Join leaders from business, civil society, labor, law and the media in a dynamic forum to debate one of the most pressing issues of our time: how can financial markets be returned to their rightful role as servant to, rather than master of, the real economy?"

- World Bank—Financial Crisis, http://www.worldbank.org/financialcrisis/

Questions for Discussion and Review

1. In your view, what were the main causes of the 2007–2009 financial crisis?

2. Given your answer to Question 1, what are the main solutions? What form of global economic system should we be striving to create?

3. What role does CSR play in the crisis—what were the CSR lapses that helped cause the crisis and how does CSR help us find a solution? View Bill Gates's speech at 2008 World Economic Forum at Davos at: http://www.youtube.com/watch?v=Ql-Mtlx31e8. What do you think?

4. What reforms would you recommend to a mortgage lender in terms of its employee incentives to ensure it avoids the mistakes of Countrywide? In general, how do you incentivize salespeople who work on commission (as the majority of mortgage brokers did in the run-up to the 2007–2009 financial crisis)? How can a company encourage them to sell products that are in their customers,' rather than their own, interests?

5. How many credit cards do you carry? Do you think that reform of the credit-fueled economic model in the U.S. is essential for a more equitable global economy? In general, to what extent is it *fair* to ask the U.S. to make any sacrifices in its standard of living for the benefit of the rest of the world?

MICROFINANCE

> **CSR CONNECTION:** This issue reinforces the idea that finance and personal loans on a smaller scale can act as a force for encouraging socially positive outcomes. It also demonstrates that the microfinance business model is profitable.

Issue

One of the biggest barriers to development in any area of the world is access to finance. This barrier is even greater in developing economies and in poorer communities in the developed world. This lack of provision is a result of large financial institutions that ignore poorer economic regions and consumers at "the bottom of the pyramid"[138] who, traditionally, have not been thought of as a good or profitable target market. Why is this so? Are poorer people more of a credit risk? Does the bureaucracy involved in administering loans for smaller amounts offer lower and less attractive margins for the lenders? Is there a business case and a market for companies willing to loan in smaller amounts to more-difficult-to-reach customers and markets around the world?

One solution to the provision of finance in poorer economic regions is *microfinance.*[139] Microfinance is a broad term that encompasses the range of personal financial services (e.g., loans, savings, insurance, and money transfers), but provided on a smaller scale to meet the specific needs of poorer consumers. Microcredit, or microloans, therefore, are sub-components of microfinance, in which financial institutions provide small amounts of money as a loan, "without any collateral and often without any written contract,"[140] to finance specific entrepreneurial projects. In practice, however, *microfinance* has become the general term that is applied to those financial services provided to consumers that have traditionally been ignored by mainstream financial institutions.

Microfinance by the Numbers[141]

Some statistics that reflect the growing reach and scale of microfinance:

- By 2010, investors will put an estimated $20bn [billion] into microfinance institutions worldwide.
- The volume of microfinance loans grew from $4bn in 2001 to $25bn in 2006.
- Since 2004, foreign funding of microfinance has doubled to $4.4bn.
- Estimated funding gap—the extra amount needed to make microfinance services available to the world's three billion poor: $250bn.
- Estimated number of microcredit borrowers worldwide: 152 million.
- Worldwide there are more than seven savings accounts for each loan account.

Case Study | Grameen Bank

The microfinance industry is synonymous with the name Muhammad Yunus and his Grameen Bank:[142]

> The movement began [in the 1970s] with Muhammad Yunus, founder and managing director of Grameen Bank in Bangladesh, which so far has provided $5 billion in loans to four million people. . . . [In total] more than 500 microfinance institutions around the world have loaned $7 billion to about 30 million small-business people.[143]

CSR Newsletters: Muhammad Yunus

A recent article[144] reports an interview in the *New York Times* with Muhammad Yunus, winner of the 2006 Nobel Peace Prize. The interview provides interesting background information on how Grameen Bank's microcredit system works, the impact it has had on the societies in which it operates, as well as Yunus's philosophy regarding the value of social entrepreneurship over charity and philanthropy:

> **Q.** Can you talk a little about the relative merits of nonprofit microcredit versus it as a business model and whether that is more sustainable, perhaps?
>
> **A.** First of all, I'm not in favor of nonprofit things. These are charities. I'm not involved in that. I don't particularly get excited about it. I'm talking about the business part of it where you do things so that you get your money back. . . . So one is a profit-maximizing business. The other is a social business. I'm on the social business side of it. If somebody wants to run it as a profit-maximizing business, welcome. This is competition. My mission is to get the person out of poverty rather than how much money I'm making out of it."

Another interview[145] with Yunus, this time in the *Financial Times,* also provides some amazing facts and figures that reveal the huge social impact Yunus's work has had in his native Bangladesh:

> Thanks in large part to the widespread availability of micro-credit, 90 per cent of families in Bangladesh now have access to some form of finance. . . . Grameen started in 1976 with a $27 loan that Yunus made to furniture-makers in the village of Jobra. . . . Today, lending about $800m a year, with an average loan size of almost $130, the bank has 6.7 million borrowers—97 per cent of them women—and an unmatched 99 per cent loan-repayment rate.

This interview also provides some insight into the next Grameen project, which is already proving to help combat poverty in significant ways:

> Grameen has also diversified into telecommunications, developing the concept of the "telephone lady," who borrows money from the bank to buy a mobile phone from

Grameen Telecom, a not-for-profit company, and then sells airtime to villagers. On average, each of the nearly 200,000 Grameen telephone ladies earns a profit equivalent to twice the national average income.

Microfinance is being used to help foster capitalist activity within the poorer regions of the world. The healthier an economy becomes, the greater the likelihood of loan repayments and need for future loans. Microloans, usually defined as beginning at $50, have had a huge impact in those parts of the developing world where they have taken off:

> Hundreds of thousands of enterprises started with microloans have helped generate 5%-a-year economic growth for the past decade.[146]

The aim behind microfinance is to "foster sustainable economic activity at the grassroots":

> In Uganda . . . 245,000 families have borrowed from village banks run by international and local agencies. The money has been used to start everything from rabbit farms to grocery stores. Microlenders "are reaching more people than Uganda's entire commercial banking sector." . . . A bank started by FINCA [Foundation for International Community Assistance, which runs a global network of microcredit banks] . . . has 36,000 clients borrowing an average of $137—and boasts an 11% return on equity.[147]

In an attempt to raise the profile of microfinance and encourage greater provision of this service to the poorer regions of the world, the United Nations declared 2005 to be the International Year of Microcredit.[148]

This recognition grew when the 2006 Nobel Peace Prize was awarded jointly to Grameen Bank and Yunus,[149] while annual awards such as the *Financial Times'* Sustainable Banking Awards, highlight industry best practice.[150] The main barrier to a more rapid expansion of microfinance, however, has historically been the high interest rates associated with such loans. These are caused by the lack of financers competing to make loans available to poorer clients and also by the high transaction costs associated with making many smaller loans. This is beginning to change, however, as the early success of microfinance, increasingly efficient systems to manage the numerous loans, and relatively low risk associated with such high rates of repayment are beginning to attract interest from more mainstream financial institutions.[151] Accion,[152] one of the leading nonprofit organizations operating in the field of microfinance, for example, consistently achieves exceptionally high repayment rates on its microloans. Accion International, which was founded in 1961,

> made its first small loans in Recife, Brazil, in 1973. Since then, Accion International has made $4.6 billion in loans averaging $590 to more than 2.7 million microenterprises with a 97 percent repayment rate.[153]

Accion's network, operating in 23 countries, boasts a repayment rate of 97% on some $7.6 billion of loans to more than 4.7 million people.[154]

(Continued)

(Continued)

In contrast, for example, "U.S. credit card issuers typically charge off around 5% of outstanding balances."[155] It is interesting, therefore, that even in the United States, Accion has enjoyed exceptional success:

Accion USA was founded in 1991 as an affiliate of Accion nternational.... Over the last dozen years [to 2003], Accion USA has made more than $66.9 million in loans averaging about $4,600 to more than 8,000 small business with a repayment rate somewhere between 94 and 95 percent.[156]

As a result of such high repayment rates, the opportunity to lend to a large and underserved percentage of the world's population represents an extremely viable business model:

Returns to [microfinance institutions] rival those of commercial banks. Studies conducted in India, Kenya and the Philippines found that the average annual return on investments by microbusinesses ranged from 117% to 847%, according to the United Nations.[157]

Other, more conservative estimates report returns of "about 6% a year, with the best-performing funds returning three or four times that amount."[158]

Accion (1998–2008)[159]

- Total number of clients served: 7.7 million.

- Total amount of finance disbursed (excluding the U.S.): $23.4 billion.
- Historical repayment rate: 97 percent.
- Women borrowers: 61 percent.

This empirical evidence demonstrating the attractiveness of the microfinance business model is supported by other companies that work in poorer economic regions in the developed economies. An article on *Socialfunds.com's* Web site by William Baue,[160] outlines in detail the benefits of another form of loans to atypical finance customers: community investing.[161] Similar to microfinance, community investing seeks to advance capital to poorer areas of the developed world. In the United States, the community investment industry is "a thriving and growing field with overall assets of . . . $7.6 billion."[162]

Throughout the United States, there are many examples of the social value community investing can add:

Community-based financial institutions have helped low-wage workers in North Carolina purchase homes, have assisted battered women in Texas in opening a shelter, and have renovated a crime-ridden neighborhood in Kentucky.[163]

In addition, in January 2008, Yunus started Grameen America in New York. Within two months, the organization had "lent out a total of $145,000, with interest rates at around 15% on the declining loan balance."[164]

CSR Newsletters: Microfinance in the United States

A recent article[165] addresses the often overlooked microfinance industry that operates in the United States, making small loans to consumers who would not qualify for a traditional loan from a more *mainstream* financial institution:

A typical example: the $3,300 it lent Teresa Ceja, a 37-year-old mother of five who two years ago needed a van for a home day-care service she was opening. . . . On average, loan recipients see a 33% increase in income in the two years after a loan is made.

The columnist uses this example to introduce a broader debate about the role of social entrepreneurs that seek to make a profit from a social cause and whether it is morally OK for these business people to "do well while also doing good." The problem is that most venture capitalists expect an operation to make a profit before they will consider injecting the funds microlenders in the United States need. While microfinance operations overseas do generate profits, there are valid reasons why it is more difficult to do so in the United States:

One of the reasons is that interest rates at overseas microlenders are higher—running to double and even triple digits. [These high rates] . . . couldn't be levied in the U.S., if only on account of usury laws. What's more, overseas microlending operations have minimal marketing or administrative expenses. Lenders can just show up in a village or densely populated urban neighborhood and find plenty of qualified applicants to borrow all of the bank's loan reserves.

The author finishes with a compelling quote on the benefits of these loans from the microlender featured in the article:

"If markets can solve poverty, why haven't they?" Mr. Weaver asks. "Poverty is getting worse in this country. Don't forget that Bill Gates doesn't expect his health-care programs around the world to make any money."

Traditionally, microfinance institutions have relied on aid and government lending to finance their activities. Due to the success of Grameen Bank, however, private mainstream banks are beginning to see the potential commercial opportunity of operating in microfinance and are expanding the areas in which they are willing to invest. This is ironic, since it was the ignoring of this market segment (i.e., very small loans to poorer borrowers) that led to the gap in provision that Yunus sought to fill initially.[166] In particular, funds for microfinance-backed projects are increasingly available via socially responsible investment funds,[167] venture capital,[168] and multinational banks:[169]

Emerging markets bank Standard Charter, for example, in May [2008] had an outstanding microfinance portfolio of $180m. . . . In early October, New York-based Citigroup announced the opening of two micro-credit firms in China's Hubei province. . . . London headquartered HSBC and Standard Chartered entered the Chinese microfinance sector last year.[170]

Multinational corporations also benefit indirectly from microfinance. By taking out small loans from microfinance institutions, local businesswomen form networks of intermediaries, selling products in hard-to-reach

(Continued)

(Continued)

rural areas for firms such as Unilever and its Indian subsidiary, Hindustan Lever:

> Today, about 13,000 poor women [many of whom received start-up microloans] are selling Unilever's products in about 50,000 villages in India's 12 states and account for about 15% of the company's rural sales in those states. Overall, rural markets account for about 30% of Hindustan Lever's revenue.[171]

And, Yunus claims, it is microfinance's reliance on this *real* economy that insulated it from the 2007–2009 financial crisis:

> The simple reason is because we are rooted to the real economy—we are not paper-based, paper-chasing banking. When we give a loan of $100, behind the $100 there are chickens, there are cows. It is not something imaginary.[172]

Increased innovation, aided especially by the spread of mobile phones, is allowing institutions to expand their potential customer base. Studies suggest that, in the near future, "mobile phone payment systems could be available to 15 per cent of the world's 3bn [billion] unbanked people."[173] In South Africa, for example, "Less than half of South Africans have bank accounts, but nine out of 10 own a mobile phone."[174]

> Mobile technology has the potential to offer cheap no-frills banking, at low risk, because transactions are monitored in real-time, on widely-used, high-quality infrastructure.[175]

The potential for economic gain, tied to social progress, is great. As *The Economist* notes:

> In a typical developing country, a rise of ten mobile phones per 100 people boosts GDP growth by 0.6 percentage points.[176]

In spite of all this activity, however, there is evidence that the potential demand for microfinance far outstrips available supply:

> Microfinance funding has been relatively concentrated with 89 per cent of foreign investment going to 148 institutions as of mid-2004, of which 87 per cent were in Latin America and central and eastern Europe. At the end of 2004, the World Bank estimated that the global supply of microfinance was about $12bn while the demand was $300bn.[177]

The situation since 2004, although improved, is still inconsistent from country to country. In 2009, according to the International Finance Corporation (part of the World Bank Group),

> Penetration of microfinance in Brazil and Argentina is about 3 per cent. This means that for every 100 microenterprises that would be eligible for microfinance products, only three are currently being served. However, the rate in Paraguay, Chile and Peru is between 25 and 35 per cent. In Bolivia, . . . the IFC says penetration is more than 160 per cent.[178]

The danger, however, is that as more and more for-profit institutions enter the market, they will distort the business model as they pursue economic over social value at ever-higher rates of interest:

A credit crisis is brewing in "microfinance," the business of making the tiniest loans in the world. . . ." We fear a bubble, . . . Too much money is chasing too few good candidates." . . . In India, microloans outstanding grew 72% in the year ended March 31, 2008, totaling $1.24 billion, according to Sa-Dhan, an industry association in New Delhi.[179]

Online Resources

- Association for Enterprise Opportunity, http://www.microenterpriseworks.org/

  "Founded in 1991, AEO is the only national membership association committed to microenterprise development as an effective economic development strategy and a powerful poverty alleviation tool."

- Community Investing Center, http://www.communityinvest.org/

  "Community Investing provides resources and opportunities for lower-income communities, along with competitive financial returns."

See also: The 1% or More in Community Investing Campaign, http://www.community invest.org/investors/campaign.cfm

- Community Reinvestment Act, http://www.ffiec.gov/cra/

  "The Community Reinvestment Act (CRA), enacted by Congress in 1977 (12 U.S.C. 2901) and implemented by Regulations 12 CFR parts 25, 228, 345, and 563e, is intended to encourage depository institutions to help meet the credit needs of the communities in which they operate."

- Consultative Group to Assist the Poor (CGAP), http://cgap.org/

  "CGAP is an independent policy and research center dedicated to advancing financial access for the world's poor."

- FINCA, http://www.villagebanking.org/

  "FINCA International provides financial services to the world's lowest-income entrepreneurs so they can create jobs, build assets and improve their standard of living."

- Hand in Hand,[180] http://www.hihseed.org/

  "Hand in Hand is a Public Charitable Trust registered in the year 2002 with an initial focus on child labour elimination, education, and the empowerment of women."

- Microbanking Bulletin, http://www.themix.org/

  "The World's Leading Business Information Provider for the Microfinance Industry."

- Microfinace Gateway, http://www.microfinancegateway.org/

  "The Microfinance Gateway is the most comprehensive online resource for the global microfinance community."

- Socialfunds.com, http://www.socialfunds.com/

  "SocialFunds.com features over 10,000 pages of information on SRI mutual funds, community investments, corporate research, shareowner actions, and daily social investment news."

- Women's World Banking Network, http://www.swwb.org/

  "Women's World Banking seeks to alleviate global poverty by expanding the economic assets, participation and power of the poor, especially women."

Questions for Discussion and Review

1. Why do you think more companies are not involved in either microfinance or community investing? Are these valid reasons?

2. Visit the Accion International Web site at http://www.accion.org/. What are your impressions and thoughts regarding the work this organization is doing?

3. Have a look at the article "Community Investing Pays"[181] on the Socialfunds.com Web site (http://www.socialfunds.com/news/article.cgi/article945.html). Does the author make a convincing case that low-income borrowers represent a lower default risk than conventional borrowers? What do you think about the CDFI Fund, establish in 1994?

4. To what extent do you think there is a business model for microfinance in the developed economies?

5. What is your opinion of the Community Reinvestment Act (see Online Resources)? Is it a good piece of legislation? Do you think it played a role in the credit crisis that led to the 2007–2009 economic crisis?

PATENTS

CSR CONNECTION: This issue captures the value of a firm's intellectual property. It also reflects the criticism faced by some companies that seek to own the sole rights to a technology or a process that they have invented, for a limited period of time, in the face of a general public interest in more widespread distribution.

Issue

What is the best way to encourage the innovation that results in social progress? How do we incentivize firms to invest in developing the technologies of the future? What rights should they have to the knowledge (processes and products) that they discover? How do these rights change when the innovations involve public goods, such as natural resources, food, or the environment? In short, who should own intellectual property when the greater public interest is at stake?

In 1910, [the Diamond Match Company] obtained a patent for the first nonpoisonous match. That product was so critical to the public's health that President Taft made a plea to the company to voluntarily surrender its patent rights. Despite the enormous moneymaking potential of the idea, Diamond Match did so. It even sent employees to other matchmaking factories to show them the process.[182]

CSR Newsletters: Patents

When does a patent application stifle innovation and the social benefit that competition brings, and when is it an incentive that encourages and rewards entrepreneurial enterprise? A recent article[183] highlights this debate and the extent to which patent applications are being abused in the United States (e.g., crustless peanut and jelly sandwiches!) in an interesting U.S. Supreme Court case.

A workable patent system is essential to a vibrant economy to encourage firms to innovate and profit from their innovation without fear that their ideas will be stolen by free-riders. It is also true, however, that

Countries that issue too many obvious patents hurt innovation by giving lazy inventors a monopoly in areas that ought to be open to competition.

The arguments on both sides are complex, but speak to the social benefit that arises from competition and the innovative nature of for-profit firms that seek to maximize profits by pursuing their self-interest. On the one hand:

"The patenting of obvious extensions of existing technologies has high social costs and is contrary to the constitutional purpose of the patent system"—to foster innovation by balancing property rights for inventors against the creative potential of the public domain. [On the other hand, firms] . . . including DuPont, Procter & Gamble and others—say the federal patent court's standard helps prevent the problem of "hindsight bias": the natural human tendency to think that, once something has been invented, it was always obvious that it would be.

There are social benefit and, potentially, great costs at stake, depending on which way the Court decides:

Tinkering with the standard now could unleash a "blizzard of litigation," says Teleflex, and jeopardise millions of patents representing an underlying investment of "many tens of billions of dollars."

At what point does a need to encourage corporations to invest in the research and development necessary to stimulate new discoveries by allowing them to profit from their inventions become an abuse of an unfair monopoly position?

The research-based pharmaceutical industry . . . currently spends upwards of $33 billion annually on R&D, investing a far greater percentage of sales (17.7%) in research and development than any other industrial sector, including electronics (6%), telecommunications (5.1%) and aerospace (3.7%).[184]

Developing medicines is inherently costly and risky. Firms have to invest huge amounts of money knowing there is very little chance that any one drug will become successful:

Only one in every 5,000 products screened is ultimately approved as a new medicine; the others drop out because of concerns about safety, efficacy or profitability. And only three in 10 of the drugs that are approved and marketed ultimately produce revenues that recoup their R&D costs.[185]

Consequently, when pharmaceutical firms develop a hit, they seek to exploit it. It is the profits from the few hits that generate the working capital that they need to invest in future R&D. Firms are willing to undertake the cost and effort of producing the drugs from which society benefits, but there is a quid pro quo inherent to the relationship between the private sector and regulatory agencies. Ultimately, pharmaceutical companies

typically spend $1 billion on research and development to bring a drug to market, with an 11% success rate on average. But they endure that burden on the understanding that FDA approval [in the United States] will give them a period to sell that drug with patent protection.[186]

How can we expect pharmaceutical firms to develop products for poor-country diseases (such as malaria and tuberculosis) where, even with patent protection, the inability of patients to buy the drugs means that the potential for a profit is slim?[187] What about the sale of generic copies of profitable drugs to developing economy markets where the prospects for profit are greatly reduced? Is it acceptable for pharmaceutical companies to oppose cheaper generic alternatives of their medications in countries where the majority of people who require that medication cannot afford to pay the full retail price? How about opposing the export of generic drugs to countries that do not have the capability to produce those drugs themselves—regulation supported by the EU?[188] Is it acceptable for a company to patent the DNA of a naturally occurring plant or food (that some argue should be available for the benefit of all), simply because they were the first to submit the patent application? Does that answer change if that process or knowledge has existed in local folklore or custom for many generations? The costs of development and the rewards for commercial success lead corporations to push for the maximum possible gain:

Battling against "unfair" intellectual property rights on plant varieties is a mainstay in [Rural Advancement Foundation International's] workload. Recently, the group forced a private research institute in Australia to drop two patents on cowpeas because RAFI discovered that the germ plasma originated from a public trust gene bank. The discovery led to the reversal of the patents and the investigation of a subsequent 147 similar patents.[189]

The challenging aspect of this issue, however, is that it is often in the public interest that pharmaceutical firms pursue their self-interest. It is the potential profits from new drugs that incentivize firms to innovate and, in turn, lead to the rapid advances in public health and well-being from which society as a whole benefits. Governments are often happy to secure the public health benefits of private sector innovation but are more reluctant to allow pharmaceuticals to profit from those gains. It is not easy to separate the public gain from private profit. At the World Trade Organization (WTO) meeting in Doha, Qatar, in November 2001, member states agreed that

> patent protection—though imperative to the development of new, life-prolonging drugs—
> "should not prevent member [states] from taking measures to protect public health." In
> other words, when weighing public health against property rights, public health should
> always be a bit heavier.[190]

Initially, poor countries would be allowed to manufacture generic drugs, under certain emergency circumstances, as long as they produced and distributed them only domestically. This agreement, however, was effectively meaningless because most countries lack the necessary technology and expertise to manufacture the drugs. The WTO member states gave themselves a deadline of 12 months to reach a further detailed agreement outlining the production and sale (including exports) of generic drugs to the poorest countries of the world. This had not occurred by December 2002, and the blame for that failure was placed largely on the U.S. government and the U.S. pharmaceutical industry:[191]

> The United States was the lone holdout on an agreement that would have permitted companies in the developing world to copy patented drugs and sell them at low prices to the poorest nations of Africa and Asia.[192]

After a further 9 months of negotiation and debate (and some say stalling by the pharmaceutical industry),[193] an agreement was finally reached by the WTO in Geneva in August 2003. The delay came from U.S. pharmaceutical companies' legitimate concerns regarding the smuggling of generic drugs from developing countries back into developed ones (particularly Europe and North America) as well as the production of counterfeit drugs:[194]

> The World Health Organization determined global sales of counterfeit drugs to be $32 billion in 2003—10% of all medicines sold worldwide.[195]

There were also worries that developing countries will invoke the "emergency circumstances" rule too leniently, allowing generic producers to generate profits at the expense of U.S. pharmaceutical companies. Both of these issues affect the profit-related incentives companies need to continue developing ground-breaking medicines. As Novartis's CEO puts it

> If you want to make production sustainable, you have to create financial incentives.[196]

From a public policy perspective, however, these concerns

> pale in comparison to the concerns of Third World inhabitants who suffer from deadly diseases.[197]

Case Study AIDS

The treatment of AIDS is central to the debate over the sale of generic drugs in developing countries:

> According to UNAids, the United Nations HIV/Aids programme, there are 40 million people in the world who are HIV positive, of whom 25.8 million are in sub-Saharan Africa. Three million people died from Aids in 2005 [8,000 each day].[198]

CSR Newsletters: Generic Drugs

A recent article[199] profiles Yusuf Hamied, the CEO and largest shareholder of Cipla, a firm in India that breaks pharmaceutical patents by copying drugs and selling them at vastly reduced prices. This business model has turned Cipla into one of India's largest firms and "the largest supplier of antiretroviral drugs in the world":

> To his supporters, Hamied has saved countless lives by making medicines affordable. But to his critics—above all the large western pharmaceuticals who first developed the drugs—he is a "pirate," an opportunist who has exploited others' intellectual property to swell his own profits.

The business model is extended across the board to hundreds of different kinds of drugs, leading to claims by Hamied that the firm has "more products than any (drug) company in the world." Rather than a threat to the large Western pharmaceutical firms, however, Hamied argues that he wants to collaborate with them to broaden the markets to which they can supply and for which there is overwhelming demand for pharmaceutical products:

> Hamied argues that western drug companies should—at best in exchange for modest royalties—allow generic producers to compete by making their medicines available immediately at the lowest possible cost.

Needless to say, Cipla has run into significant resistance from those with most to gain from the status quo:

> Richard Sykes, head of Glaxo, denounced Hamied as a "pirate" and described the quality of Indian generic drugs as "iffy." Hamied fired back, saying that the company was a "global serial killer" for charging such high prices.

In addition to the public health implications of the spread of AIDS, the disease also directly affects the economic vitality of the countries in which it takes root. Firms with significant numbers of employees with AIDS are finding that their ability to operate is limited if employees, or their relatives, are forced to take time off frequently to cope with the disease. This is a problem, however, that firms have often ignored in the past:

According to a [2004] report by the World Economic Forum, two-thirds of 1,620 companies operating in Africa expect AIDS to affect their profits over the next five years, but only 12% have an AIDS policy. A U.N. survey found that just 21 of 100 large multinationals have AIDS programs.[200]

The number of firms who are addressing this problem, however, is increasing. Heineken (http://www.heinekeninternational.com/), for example, was one of the early innovators.

Heineken operates in Africa because it is profitable for the company to do so. The continent presents many operational challenges, however, one of which is the spread of AIDS among the workforce. In response, the firm has begun fighting the disease and protecting its workers (thereby protecting the company's investment in personnel and training):

The $9 billion (sales) Dutch giant has guaranteed anti-retroviral drug coverage not only to its staff of 6,000 in Africa but also to their immediate dependents.[201]

The company's reaction to the disease has been termed "extraordinary" and is recognized as a leading effort among multinationals working in Africa:

Over the past year Heineken has been treating employees in Rwanda and neighboring Burundi, where one in eight people is infected with HIV. The company is rolling out the program in four other countries—the two Congos, Nigeria and Ghana. . . . In all, Heineken—which had net profits of $1.2 billion in its latest fiscal year— expects to spend $2 million a year treating workers in Africa.[202]

The bottom-line return for Heineken makes good business sense, as it does for other companies operating in Africa (such as the mining company Anglo American) that have introduced similar programs for employees:

[Anglo American] expects to treat 3,000 people [in 2004], up from 223 in 2003. In a report delivered to the International AIDS Conference held in Bangkok in July [2004], the company said the treatment costs were "offset by the sharp decline in mortality— from 30% to 3.4% in the first year—and in absenteeism due to illness."[203]

Other firms that are also acting proactively with respect to helping their employees deal with AIDS include De Beers and Eskom, both of which "have seen AIDS decimate their workforce and affect productivity and profits."[204] SAB Miller is another large company "to have implemented a far-reaching programme."[205] And, there are also calls for small and medium sized companies to develop similar policies.[206] Although there is a human element driving these firms to act, it is also clear that they now realize the business cost of inaction:

Gold Fields, a mining company, has estimated the cost of HIV at $5 for every ounce of gold produced in South Africa. Economists at Anglo American, the London-listed mining group, have estimated that, with absenteeism, early retirement, treating AIDS-related conditions,

(Continued)

(Continued)

death benefits and recruiting replacements, the overall cost of failing to provide an AIDS-infected employee with antiretroviral drugs (ARVs) is about $32,000 per person.[207]

Firms weigh these costs against the ever-reducing costs of treatment:

In the late 1990s, the cost of treating an employee infected with HIV was as much as $15,000 a year. But by 2001 treatment costs had dropped to between $1,200 and $1,500. [In 2006] antiretroviral drugs cost as little as $700-$800, with laboratory costs adding a further $200. That means the cost of treating an infected employee is now as little as $3 a day.[208]

Pharmaceutical firms that have the technical knowledge of how to treat AIDS (i.e., they produce the necessary life-saving medication), therefore, face both moral and economic pressures to make those drugs widely available. But, where is the line drawn between allowing those firms to protect their intellectual property and recoup the massive investments they made in developing these drugs, and the issue of public health in countries that have a large proportion of their population suffering from AIDS? What rights do patients have to access the drugs and what rights do governments have to manufacture the generics that could be used to treat AIDS in developing countries?

The average AIDS patient in the United States takes a combination of drugs that costs about $14,000 per patient each year. . . . Generic drugs would cost a fraction of that figure.[209]

Needless to say, the U.S. pharmaceutical industry paints a positive picture of its role

in alleviating pain and suffering and heralds the 2003 Geneva WTO agreement as a success. Pfizer, which played a prominent role in the negotiations, posted this statement on its Web site:

Pfizer has stepped forward in partnership with governments and non-governmental organizations to develop a series of initiatives to address the HIV/AIDS crisis in the U.S. and abroad. Pfizer's strategy is to partner with effective organizations already in place to offer results-oriented programs that will have a significant impact in preventing the spread of the disease and easing the health burdens of those who have been infected by the virus. This comprehensive, team-based approach combines the distribution of critical medicines with training, education, mentoring and the building of sound medical infrastructures.[210]

Although all the major pharmaceutical companies have reduced the prices of their AIDS drugs, many still face pressure to reduce their prices further.[211] Nevertheless, critics of the U.S. pharmaceuticals are still pushing for further concessions. They complain that there are still too many restrictions preventing the timely manufacture and purchase of sufficient quantities of generic drug alternatives at reasonable prices:

In poor places like Guatemala, the price difference between branded and generics are crucial. A cocktail of AIDS-fighting brand drugs that cost $10,000 a year in 2000 now costs $700 because of generic competition. [Médecins Sans Frontières, MSF] says that the generic equivalent is $400, and [it] can get generics from India for $300.[212]

And, demand for the drugs continues to rise:

> Even with all these savings, in a country where the average worker earns under $100 a month . . . only 1,500 of the 67,000 HIV-positive patients in Guatemala are being treated.[213]

In response to widespread criticism that the private sector is not doing enough to balance its desire to profit from its innovations, combined with the moral obligation many feel the industry has to distribute life-saving medicines to those who need them, irrespective of their ability to pay, pharmaceutical firms are beginning to expand their philanthropic role.[214] In addition, the criticism is being heeded by interested parties such as the Pharmaceutical Shareowners Group (PSG), a group of institutional investors with significant pharmaceutical holdings who argue that the public perception of the industry is vital to maintaining the "social contract" necessary for continued acceptance and success.[215] As with many debates, there is truth and fault on both sides, and the reality lies somewhere in-between the extremes. Yet, a compromise position appears to be emerging:

> Industry best practice seems to be differential pricing in different countries based on ability to pay, with technology transfer and voluntary licences issued to a range of generic suppliers to make their medicines in bulk at the lowest cost. That must be balanced by safeguards to ensure no "diversion" of these generic versions into higher priced markets, which would undermine the revenues required for future innovation.[216]

There is also evidence that multinational pharmaceuticals are beginning to grant licenses to small, local drugs companies to manufacture generic copies of branded drugs for limited distribution within specific countries.[217] Others are agreeing to shorten the life of patents on specific drugs, in exchange for a guaranteed period of uninterrupted distribution.[218] The result, however, is still inadequate access to medications for those who need them the most:

> Pushing down the cost of drugs is only the first challenge in scaling up treatment to the estimated 10m HIV-positive people who will need it by the end of the decade.[219]

As a result of ongoing criticism, in 2009, GlaxoSmithKline (GSK) announced plans that promised real progress. In a speech at Harvard medical school, Andrew Witty, GSK's CEO committed his firm to reduce prices on a wide range of medicines, share patents in a "patent pool" to combat "neglected diseases such as tuberculosis, malaria and leprosy"[220] as well as AIDS,[221] and increase its investment in health infrastructure:

> In the world's 50 least developed countries, GSK will cap prices for its drugs at 25% of their cost to rich nations. . . . The move builds on the company's existing philanthropic efforts. To date, GSK has donated more than one billion albendazole treatments to stop the transmission of lymphatic filariasis in 48 countries. It has also committed to donate 50m doses of pre-pandemic H5N1 flu vaccine to the WHO's planned stockpile facility. In 2008, the company valued its donation programmes (calculated according to industrialised

(Continued)

retail price), in-cash social investments and other charitable projects at £124m.[222]

It remains to be seen whether these announcements, designed to promote GSK as "a catalyst for change" will have any effect on the public's perceptions of the pharmaceutical industry. In spite of the widespread social value of the products they produce, it seems that the widespread perception of the pharmaceutical industry remains negative. Newspaper articles with headlines such as "Drug firm blocks cheap blindness cure"[223] and "HIV/AIDS victims in India protest over drug patent"[224] continue to outweigh the positive work that these firms do:

Despite its successes in treating disease and extending longevity, soaring health-care costs and bumper profits mean that big drug firms are widely viewed as exploitative, and regarded almost as unfavorably as tobacco and oil firms.[225]

Ultimately, the drug companies may well be in a no-win situation and will always be portrayed as "the companies everyone loves to hate":

Good health is seen as a basic human right, and the idea that a corporation would charge you for your rights, let alone deny them to you because you can't afford its product, is seen as morally reprehensible.[226]

Online Resources

- Doctors Without Borders (Médecins Sans Frontières, MSF), http://www.msf.org/

  "Médecins Sans Frontières (MSF) is an international humanitarian aid organisation that provides emergency medical assistance to populations in danger in more than 70 countries."

- European Patent Office, http://www.epo.org/index.html

  "The European Patent Office (EPO) provides a uniform application procedure for individual inventors and companies seeking patent protection in up to 38 European countries."

- Generic Pharmaceutical Association, http://www.gphaonline.org/

  "The Generic Pharmaceutical Association (GPhA) represents the manufacturers and distributors of finished generic pharmaceutical products, manufacturers and distributors of bulk active pharmaceutical chemicals, and suppliers of other goods and services to the generic pharmaceutical industry."

- Global Business Coalition on HIV/AIDS (GBC), http://www.businessfightsaids.org/

  "We apply the private sector's special capabilities to the fight against HIV/AIDS, tuberculosis and malaria."

- Heineken's HIV/AIDS Policy, http://www.smartwork.org/resources/heineken.shtml

  "We believe that public health is primarily the responsibility of natural [sic] governments. However, we have to face the facts that in some areas of the world governments fail to fill their primary public health duties. In such areas, Heineken accepts, under certain conditions, a supplementary role in the organization of health care."

- PharmAccess International (PAI), http://www.pharmaccess.org/

  "PharmAccess Foundation (PharmAccess) is a Dutch not-for-profit organization dedicated to the strengthening of health systems in sub-Saharan Africa."

- Pharmaceutical Research and Manufacturers of America, http://www.phrma.org/

  "PhRMA represents the country's leading research-based pharmaceutical and biotechnology companies."

- World Intellectual Property Organization, http://www.wipo.int/

  "The World Intellectual Property Organization (WIPO) is a specialized agency of the United Nations. It is dedicated to developing a balanced and accessible international intellectual property (IP) system, which rewards creativity, stimulates innovation and contributes to economic development while safeguarding the public interest."

Questions for Discussion and Review

1. Is the patent process an effective way of incentivizing companies to innovate?

2. Is it acceptable for pharmaceutical companies to oppose cheaper generic alternatives of their medication in countries where the majority of people who require that medication cannot afford to pay for it? In general, is it acceptable that the same drugs cost vastly different amounts in different countries—even within the developed world?

3. Is it acceptable for a company to patent the DNA of a naturally occurring plant or food (that some argue should be available for the benefit of all) simply because they were the first to make the patent application? Does that answer change if that process or piece of knowledge has existed in local folklore or customs for many generations?

4. Look at Heineken's HIV/AIDS policy (detailed at http://www.smartwork.org/resources/heineken.shtml and summarized at http://www.smartwork.org/resources/policies.shtml). Why is it in Heineken's self-interest to develop this policy?

5. What are the arguments against Heineken and other firms instituting this sort of policy? Do you think it is a wise investment of the firm?

PRODUCT SAFETY

> 🌐 **CSR CONNECTION:** This issue looks at the tension firms experience between adequate research into the safety of a product and the pressure to minimize development costs and bring the product to market as soon as possible.

Issue

Some companies today are accused of rushing products to market before they have been adequately tested or enough is known about the products' uses and any side effects that may result from their use. Consumer activists argue that a company should bear the burden of proving that a product is safe before releasing it, rather than assume it is safe as long as there is no evidence to the contrary.

This reasoning, together with popular pressure stemming from Upton Sinclair's *The Jungle*,[227] gave rise to the Food and Drug Administration (FDA), which came into existence in the United States in 1906 as part of the Food and Drugs Act. The agency evolved slowly as ideological opposition to the idea of government regulation faded in the wake of several deaths and other disasters caused by products that had not been adequately tested. It was not until 1938, however, that substantial progress was enacted:

> It took 107 deaths from a liquid antibiotic preparation using highly toxic diethylene glycol (a common ingredient in today's antifreeze) to get Congress to pass a landmark 1938 law. At last, before a product could be sold, a company would have to submit data proving that it was safe. Similarly, the thalidomide tragedy of the early 1960s . . . [allowed the Kennedy Administration] to push through the then startling idea—bitterly opposed by the American Medical Association as well as conservatives—that drugs should be tested to see if they actually work before they can be sold.[228]

Nestlé[229]

S. Prakash Sethi highlighted the controversy surrounding the distribution of infant formula throughout LDCs (less developed countries) as a good example of the problems faced by corporations when consumer expectations exceed existing legal obligations.[230]

In the late 1960s, debate around this issue began to surface, culminating in 1974 with the publication of a pamphlet by Mike Muller titled, *The Baby Killer*. Nestlé, inadvertently feeding the fire, sued the public action group that produced the pamphlet:

> Thus, between 1974 and mid-1976 when the case was decided, the issue received considerable international media coverage.[231]

The ultimate result was to connect the controversy permanently in the public's mind with Nestlé, although at the time there were a number of firms involved. As awareness about the issue spread, the reaction of these different corporations was continually called into question and the problem ballooned:

Some public interest groups launched a campaign to boycott Nestlé products in the United States. At the LDC level, the government of Papua New Guinea passed a law declaring baby bottles, nipples, and pacifiers health hazards and their sale restricted through prescription only. The objective was to discourage indiscriminate promotion, sale, and consumption of infant food formulas.[232]

In an attempt to appease consumer criticism, the International Council of Infant Food Industries (ICIFI),[233] a corporation-led industry forum, was established and a code of practice introduced; however, it was criticized as being too weak from an early stage, and those companies committed to improving the situation withdrew and introduced their own, more restrictive, policy practices.

Nestlé's response to the problem continues today in the form of a page on its company Web site (http://www.nestle.com/CSV/Compliance/InfantHealthAndNutrition/Introduction .htm) that is dedicated to promoting its "responsible" promotion of its infant formula in developing countries. It also provides a link to another site (http://www.babymilk .nestle.com/) dedicated to the "facts." The controversy, however, and opposition to Nestlé as an organization continues (e.g., http://www.babymilkaction.org/). The company is involved in a claim for compensation that it is making against the Ethiopian government (and there-fore the Ethiopian people, too) for $6 million. As a result, it finds itself the target of a cam-paign waged by Oxfam in the United Kingdom, which, although not dismissing the legality of the claim, finds it morally reprehensible that the company can be claiming that amount of money from a country that is so poor and has 11 million people facing famine.

Oxfam is drawing on public support to make sure their criticism of Nestlé is heard loud and clear and claims to have had some success. The NGO reports that "nearly 50,000" e-mails were sent to the Web site and that "after just a week Nestlé retreated,"[234] backing off from the figure of $6 million (to offer a lower figure of $1.5 million) and also stating that any money received will be reinvested within Ethiopia (a commitment Oxfam claims had not previously been made by the company).[235]

In spite of the best initial intentions of the FDA, however, many products still reach mar-ket today without passing through any significant testing procedures. In general, a product must be proven unsafe before it is banned, rather than the company having to prove the prod-uct is safe before it is released:

In the United States, industrial chemicals are presumed safe until proven otherwise. As a result, the vast majority of the 80,000 chemicals registered to be used in products have never undergone a government safety review. Companies are left largely to police themselves.[236]

Existing laws [in the EU in 2004] allow most chemical-based products to be introduced without prior assurances by the company of their safety. The result is that 99% of the total chemicals sold in Europe have not passed through any environmental and health testing process.[237]

The paucity of government oversight and focus on product safety can be seen in the emerging and rapidly expanding area of nanotechnology. While the technology is hugely promising, there is much that we do not know about it, and the issues that scientists are tackling are challenging. In spite of the fact that the nanotechnology industry is

> fraught with an unusual number of potential ethical, and therefore PR, landmines. . . . many nanotechnology companies are simply not interested in safety testing in the first place. Of the companies surveyed in Europe, only 6% have studied the effects of nanoparticles on living organisms; only 20% investigated whether their nanotechnology products could be toxic, and 25% did not know if toxicity tests had been conducted.[238]

In the United States, the Environmental Protection Agency (EPA) is the other government agency (in addition to the FDA) with jurisdiction in this area. The EPA was granted authority to regulate industrial chemicals as part of the 1976 Toxic Substances Act, but it needs to overcome a high threshold of evidence to act. Essentially, the EPA must prove that a chemical is unsafe and that the risks posed by it outweigh the economic benefits from its existence in the market. In addition, the law "grandfathered in about 62,000 chemicals then in commercial use,"[239] effectively exempting them from closer inspection and only required firms to "report toxicity information to the government,"[240] rather than submit to safety testing. As a result, and in spite of Congress's attempts to give the EPA more powers to screen industrial chemicals under the 1996 Food Quality Protection Act,

> Nine years after the 1999 deadline, the agency has yet to screen a single chemical.[241]

It is not clear, however, that more effective screening would improve the level of vigilance concerning issues of product safety. After all, even after evidence begins to mount that an existing product might not be safe, regulators are still reluctant to issue a recall:

> The United States has a long tradition of keeping harmful substances—lead, DDT, tobacco, PCBs—on the market for decades after scientists find adverse effects.[242]

The Price of Safety[243]

Safety, like CSR, often comes at a price. Whether the price is worth paying—whether it provides a sufficient return on investment—is crucial to the argument for or against:

> How efficient are safety regulations? To decide, economists estimate how many lives a regulation saves, then compare that with the cost of implementing the rule. By this measure, the labeling of trans-fat content in foods is a clear winner.[244]

The AEI-Brookings Joint Center for Regulatory Studies reports that the cost of including the trans fat content on food labels is only $3,000 for each life this action saves. This can be compared with the cost of $300,000 for each life saved by insulating airplane cabins to protect against fire.

> Automobile safety regulations tend to be more expensive: It is estimated that state seat belt laws cost $500,000 for each life saved, whereas one life is saved for every $1.1 million spent on reinforcing car side doors.
>
> The most expensive regulation highlighted, however, was reducing the exposure of factory workers to asbestos. This move was estimated to cost $5.5 million for each life the regulation saves.

In an attempt to alter this balance between profit and safety, the EU Commission proposed regulation that is built around the concept of "the precautionary principle":

> [The proposed directive] would force companies to prove chemical products introduced into the marketplace are safe before being granted permission to market them . . . [and represents] a radical new approach to science and technology based on the principle of sustainable development and global stewardship of the Earth's environment.[245]

The proposal was termed the REACH directive, which stands for the Registration, Evaluation, Authorization, and restriction of CHemicals.[246] At the time, it angered the U.S. chemical industry, which saw it as a threat to the more than $20 billion of chemicals it sells in Europe every year. Companies would be required to register and test the safety of up to 30,000 chemicals at an estimated cost of approximately €6 billion.[247] The companies had support in their resistance from the U.S. government. In spite of the EU amending the proposed regulation in the face of strong lobbying from U.S. firms backed by Washington,

> still, the U.S. government fears $150 billion of its exports could be affected, and the American Chemistry Council estimates the proposal could cost U.S. companies $8 billion during the next decade.[248]

The REACH legislation was passed in the EU in December 2006[249] and, in 2008, the EU reinforced the legislation, announcing

> new restrictions on makers of chemicals linked to cancer and other health problems.[250]

As such, the REACH legislation marks an important shift in the modern-day regulation of product safety. Its emphasis on risk prevention, rather than risk taking, is gaining support, especially as the penalties for mistakes seem to become higher by the day:

> From its crackdown on antitrust practices in the computer industry to its rigorous protection of consumer privacy, the European Union has adopted a regulatory philosophy that emphasizes the consumer. Its approach to managing chemical risks . . . is part of a European focus on caution when it comes to health and the environment.[251]

In the United States, also, there are encouraging signs that the global reach of the REACH legislation is forcing manufacturers to search "for safer alternatives to chemicals used to make thousands of consumer goods, from bike helmets to shower curtains."[252] They are being forced to adapt because of the necessity of competing in the EU, the world's second-largest consumer market of 27 countries and approximately 500 million consumers. In addition, in May 2008, Senator Frank Lautenberg introduced the Kid-Safe Chemical Act, which attempts to move the regulatory environment in the same direction as the EU legislation:

[The legislation] would reverse the burden of proof on chemicals, requiring manufacturers to demonstrate their safety in order to keep them in commerce. The E.U. passed a similar law in 2006, as did Canada in 1999.[253]

Product Safety Legislation

The following list contains some of the most important product safety laws passed in the United States:

- 1906—Food and Drugs Act
- 1938—Food, Drugs, and Cosmetic Act
- 1962—Kefauver-Harris Amendments
- 1976—Toxic Substances Control Act
- 1996—Food Quality Protection Act
- 2008—Kid-Safe Chemical Act

Case Study   Monsanto

Companies that launch a product just because there is no reason *not* to do so see only their good intentions and the product's benefits and tend to ignore the position of the consumers they are attempting to service. Consumer fear—often expressed through product boycotts or large-scale protests, but more commonly expressed through lower sales—can be the result. Following a 2006 salmonella scare caused by Cadbury's delay in informing government inspectors about the presence of salmonella in some of its chocolate bars and resulting in the firm losing 1.1% of its total market share in a month, for example, the firm protested that it had relied on science to judge whether or not its products were safe for consumption:

Cadbury said that in the absence of government guidelines on quality assurance, it had chosen its own protocol, based on scientific evidence about the likelihood of small levels of contamination causing people to become ill. Consultants, however, say that Cadbury was wrong to rely on science, and should have been thinking about how its brand would be perceived with consumers.[254]

Today, a good example of consumer uncertainty and concern surrounds the rapidly expanding production of genetically modified (GM) foods:

Worried about falling behind its global competition, much of Asia is rushing forward with the development and cultivation of genetically modified crops. . . . Critics of genetically modified crops say these moves in Asia could leave consumers around the world with little choice but to accept them. . . . But in the absence of any solid evidence that genetically modified crops are harmful to humans, scientists in Asia are experimenting on everything from genetically modified corn, potatoes and papaya to biotech mustard and chili peppers.[255]

While GM crops were introduced with much less concern in North America and much of Asia, European consumers reacted with horror to what Greenpeace and the British tabloids labeled "Frankenfood."[256] Greenpeace's deliberate tactic is to raise fears about a science that is little understood but can easily be interpreted as human subversion of nature. Short of securing a complete halt of all GM crops, a favored

campaign target is the introduction of food labels that would provide consumers with information about the levels of GM foods in the products they were buying.

Transparency in food labeling was the goal of an Oregon initiative (Measure 27) slated for elections in 2002. The initiative sought to "require food companies to clearly label any product sold or produced in the state that contains GM ingredients."[257] The campaigners, officially, were not taking a stance for or against GM foods but, instead, arguing that consumers had a right to know exactly what is contained within the food they are buying. The food and biotech industries fought the initiative, out of concern that

such labeling could cause consumers to reject genetically modified food. . . . That's shortsighted. The food industry would be better off educating the public about the safety and benefits of genetic modification. Their fear of a labeling law only means they have done a lousy job so far. . . . By blocking grassroots attempts to put advisory labels on food, the food and biotech industries look as if they have something to hide.[258]

The tactic, however, may well have paid off in the short term. The initiative was soundly defeated, with only 27% of voters supporting the move and 73% rejecting it. In Europe, in contrast, campaigners had greater success:

Around the world, 19 countries require such labeling, and the European Union has banned the sale of any newly

(Continued)

(Continued)

engineered products since 1988. . . . In U.S., such labeling isn't required. About a dozen varieties of soybeans, corn and tomatoes genetically altered to resist pests, frost and weed killers have been approved for human consumption and are common ingredients in processed food.[259]

In response to consumer fears about GM foods, the EU introduced legislation making it harder for GM crops to be approved:

While genetically modified foods have gained favor around the world, Europe has resisted. The 25-nation EU refused to approve new types between 1998 and 2004, and only in Spain are such crops grown on a commercial scale. Many grocery stores won't stock genetically modified food.[260]

A chief proponent of GM foods worldwide is Monsanto, which initially pitched genetically modified food as a large part of the solution to third-world poverty and starvation. By adapting foods to grow in severe conditions, crops could be produced in many more places than is currently possible:

In the second half of the 1990s Monsanto dramatically failed to walk the talk on sustainability as it launched genetically modified crops onto the market and it was met with a global campaign that coined the powerful term "Frankenfood." Ongoing fallout has included the breakup of the company, serious damage to the whole life-sciences sector, threats to the U.S.-style industrialized food system and the rapid growth of a vibrant organic farming industry.[261]

In spite of the company's PR battle failures, however, perhaps the war is being won:

The planting of genetically modified crops increased in 2002 despite lingering concern in some countries about their safety and environmental effects.[262]

[In 2005], roughly 75% of U.S. processed foods . . . contain some genetically modified, or GM, ingredients. . . . More than 80% of the soy and 40% of the corn raised in [the U.S.] is a GM variety. Global plantings of biotech crops . . . grew to about 200 million acres [in 2004], about two-thirds of it in the U.S.[263]

CSR Newsletters: The Meatrix

A series of videos presents a disturbing view on factory farming from inside the Meatrix (http://www.themeatrix.com/):

Want to know more about problems with factory farming while finding healthier food for you and your family? Learn, discuss, get involved—inside The Meatrix.

If we are able to place our fear of the unknown aside and put in place a rigorous system of testing that works in the interests of consumers, rather than business, it is easy to argue that Monsanto has a point. Given that world food prices are becoming increasingly unstable[264] and the paradox that we live in a world containing "the simultaneous existence of nearly 1 billion who are malnourished and nearly 1 billion who are overweight,"[265] a comprehensive assessment of where we get our food and how best to grow sufficient amounts to satisfy an expanding global population is essential.

To put it another way, if the current agribusiness model, with its overuse of pesticides and overproduction of meat,[266] is indeed unsustainable and even damaging to our health,[267] it would be irresponsible *not* to investigate further Monsanto's GM technology. The range of organic food that is sold in high-priced supermarkets such as Whole Foods (http://www.wholefoodsmarket.com/) and, now, even Walmart,[268] together with local farmers markets and the *locavore* ("the noun that became the *Oxford American Dictionary*'s word of the year for 2007")[269] and slow food (http://www.slowfood.com/) movements, are surely luxuries of the developed world. Even in the United States, where organic food is a rapidly growing and successful industry, organics constitute only "2.5% of America's half-trillion-dollar food economy."[270] The fact that organic food is still a long way from providing the United States with the food it needs suggests that it would also be an unsustainable model for food production elsewhere. The large areas of the world that are deficient in water and nutritious soil suggest any measure that can increase yields and produce crops more consistently should be welcome.

In addition, even if organic or locally grown alternative food sources were able to generate sufficient food for all, it is not clear whether they contribute a net positive or net negative social value. Organically fed cows, for example,

eat a higher proportion of grass and hay than conventionally fed cows. As a result, the burps of organically fed cows contain larger quantities of methane, a greenhouse gas that is at least 20 times more toxic than carbon dioxide (interestingly, cattle are thought to be responsible for almost half the world's methane emissions).

Equally, locally grown produce is often favored over crops grown overseas in efforts to reduce food miles:[271]

But a better option might be to buy snow peas from Zimbabwe, where if even a small percentage of the retail price goes to growers, it can significantly boost their annual income.[272]

For all of its troubles, Monsanto is beginning to convince the world that it can be a force for good:

During the 12 months preceding [the current CEO] Grant's elevation, Monsanto's stock price fell nearly 50% to $8 a share. In 2002, the prior fiscal year, the company lost $1.7 billion. . . . Fewer than five years later, Monsanto is thriving. The St. Louis company's net income leaped 44% last year, to $993 million, on $8.5 billion in revenue. Monsanto shares, which closed at $104.81 on Dec. 5, have risen more than 1,000% during Grant's tenure.[273]

The main reason for the firm's recovery is its decision to switch away from straight-to-market consumer GM foods to the seeds that are used to grow key food ingredients

(Continued)

(Continued)

for agribusiness, such as animal feed, ethanol, and corn syrup. Monsanto's retreat from foods more likely to stoke consumer fears about the science behind genetic modification has enabled the firm to steer clear of the focus of activist groups and build a commanding market share:

Today, more than 90% of the genetically modified seeds in the world are sold either by Monsanto or by competitors that license Monsanto genes in their own seeds.[274]

The larger, more fundamental debate raised by the issues surrounding Monsanto centers around questions such as how do we grow and raise, distribute and sell, prepare and eat food? And how do our patterns of doing these things affect the rest of the world (and vice versa)?[275]

While issues remain around its methods (not to mention the agri-business industry as a whole), and it is hard to look past parts of the firm's history,[276] it is arguable that the products Monsanto is producing and selling, in some form, are part of the solution. In response to the threat of increasing water scarcity, for example, Monsanto is targeting "2012 as the launch date for the drought-tolerant corn seed it is developing in partnership with BASF."[277]

Online Resources

- Association for Science in the Public Interest, http://www.public-science.org/

  "The Association for Science in the Public Interest (ASIPI) is a professional society dedicated to fostering the participation of scientists in public processes, the conduct of community research and the promotion of scientific work that supports the public good."

- Food and Drug Administration, http://www.fda.gov/

  "FDA is the federal agency responsible for ensuring that foods are safe, wholesome and sanitary; human and veterinary drugs, biological products, and medical devices are safe and effective; cosmetics are safe; and electronic products that emit radiation are safe. FDA also ensures that these products are honestly, accurately and informatively represented to the public."

- Greenpeace on Genetic Engineering, http://www.greenpeace.org/international/campaigns/genetic-engineering

  "While scientific progress on molecular biology has a great potential to increase our understanding of nature and provide new medical tools, it should not be used as justification to turn the environment into a giant genetic experiment by commercial interests."

- Monsanto, http://www.monsanto.com/

  "Monsanto is an agricultural company. We apply innovation and technology to help farmers around the world produce more while conserving more."

- Organic Consumers Association, http://www.organicconsumers.org/

  "We are the only organization in the US focused exclusively on promoting the views and interests of the nation's estimated 50 million organic and socially responsible consumers."

- The True Food Network, http://truefoodnow.org/

  "The Center for Food Safety is a national, non-profit, membership organization dedicated to protecting human health and the environment by curbing the use of harmful food production technologies and by promoting organic and other forms of sustainable agriculture."

Questions for Discussion and Review

1. Do you support the motives behind the EU's "precautionary principle"?

2. Do you eat GM foods? Do you eat organic food? Do you actively shop for food based on its source? Would you support a move to label the quantities of GM ingredients in all food products?

3. Look at the videos that take you inside the Meatrix (http://www.themeatrix.com/). Do they change your views of the agri-business model that produces the vast majority of our food supplies? If so, how?

4. Have a look at this video about GM foods and a Greenpeace protest against the spread of GM foods in Canada: http://archives.cbc.ca/environment/environmental_protection/clips/5012/. Which side of the debate do you support? Why?

5. Read Monsanto's pledge outlining the firm's approach to its business on its Web site: http://www.monsanto.com/monsanto/layout/our_pledge/default.asp. What is your impression of the firm from reading this? Does it match the opinion you had before reading it?

PROFIT

> **CSR CONNECTION:** This issue forms an essential component of the CSR debate. The best of intentions aside, a bankrupt company does not benefit any of its stakeholders. Any CSR argument that does not allow the company to pursue profits is ill-conceived and fighting against the tide of economic theory and human history.

Issue

By definition, profit is what drives all *for-profit* organizations. This pursuit of profit underwrites market-based economies and forces companies constantly to stimulate innovation and progress to meet society's developmental needs. Profit is also cited by business leaders as a reason for not being able to pursue CSR behavior; that is, a corporation has a duty to be as profitable as possible in order to ensure it remains in business and maximizes returns for investors.

The merging of the pursuit of profit and integration of CSR within corporate strategy renders a *short* term, profit-only approach increasingly untenable. Combined with the increasing pressure placed on companies today to perform consistently, over the *medium* to *longer* term, managers need to be as innovative and broad-minded as possible in seeking to implement the organization's vision, mission, strategy, and tactics:

> [For business] doing good does not necessarily rule out making a reasonable profit. You can . . . make money by serving the poor as well as the rich. . . . There is a huge neglected market in the billions of poor in the developing world. Companies like Unilever and Citicorp are beginning to adapt their technologies to enter this market. Unilever can now deliver ice cream in India for just two cents a portion because it has rethought the technology of refrigeration. Citicorp can now provide financial services to people, also in India, who have only $25 to invest, again through rethinking technology. In both cases the companies make money, but the driving force is the need to serve neglected consumers. Profit often comes from progress.[278]

Is it OK for firms to profit from poverty? Where is the dividing line between a social mission and a valid market opportunity in an emerging market that also produces social progress? Is there any value in attempting to draw such a distinction? Today, is it more helpful to think of all firms as having a social mission, but delivering varying degrees of added value?

CSR Newsletters: Intel

A recent article[279] contains a case study of Intel's attempt to build its market presence in the developing world. Due to declining revenue in the United States and Europe, Intel has launched its World Ahead Program ("a fine example of enlightened self-interest") to explore market opportunities in the developing world. The scale of the potential markets in these economies underlies their importance to firms:

> Half of the global middle class lives in the developing world today. Within 25 years, that figure will be 90%, according to the World Bank's latest forecast. That will more than double, to 1 billion, the number of potential buyers for products that today are considered luxuries, including not only cars and refrigerators but also computers.

Equally interesting, however, is Intel's strategic approach to these markets:

> Intel is pursuing not the so-called bottom of the pyramid, or BOP—the billions of people who live on a few dollars a day or less—but the next billion, consumers who rank economically just below those it serves today.

This strategy differs from the BOP focus that drives much of the CSR debate on this issue. Intel seeks to deliver social value to those economies best able to afford its products over the short to medium term. As Intel's chairman, Craig Barrett, bluntly points out in the article:

We're not a charitable organization, . . . We're trying to foster the continued growth of our products.

It is estimated that "the richest 2 per cent of adults own more than 50 per cent of global assets, while the poorest half of the population holds only 1 per cent of wealth."[280] This means that 65% of the world's population, or 4 billion people, exist on less than $2,000 per year.[281] This section of the world forms Tier 4—the largest and bottom of the four-tier pyramid that comprises the world's population—the bottom of the pyramid (BOP). As such, these people represent a huge market segment that needs the help of the developed world, but they also can pay their way in terms of buying essential and reasonably priced products:

Individually, the purchasing power of Tier 4 is limited. . . . But together it adds up to trillions. [Their] general wants and needs are familiar: securing better lives for their children, getting the best price for their labor, staying healthy, and having fun.[282]

This "huge potential market,"[283] however, remains largely ignored by many companies. What is required is an innovative approach by firms to deliver their products to places previously thought to be inaccessible, at prices previously thought to be unprofitable:

But to be profitable, firms cannot simply edge down market, fine-tuning the products they already sell to rich customers. Instead, they must thoroughly re-engineer products to reflect the very different economics of BOP: small unit packages, low margin per unit, high volume. Big business needs to swap its usual incremental approach for an entrepreneurial mindset, because BOP markets need to be built not simply entered.[284]

Certainly, succeeding in BOP markets requires multinationals to think creatively. The biggest change though, has to come in the attitudes and practices of executives. . . . Perhaps MNCs should create the equivalent of the Peace Corps: Having young managers spend a couple of formative years in BOP markets would open their eyes to the promise and the realities of doing business there.[285]

Progressive multinationals have begun to explore new ways to serve these markets:

Hindustan Lever, the Indian consumer goods company 51% owned by Unilever for example, knew that many Indians could not afford to buy a big bottle of shampoo. . . . So it created single-use packets (in three sizes, according to hair length) that go for a few cents—and now sells 4.5 billion of them a year.[286]

Another multinational that has done a lot of work in this area of "progressive profit" is Hewlett-Packard, which created e-Inclusion,[287] a business unit dedicated to creating market-based solutions to problems in developing economies using IT products:[288]

When Hewlett-Packard launched its e-Inclusion division, which concentrates on rural markets, it established a branch of its famed HP Labs in India charged with developing products and services explicitly for this market. . . . For example, 16 researchers are looking into things like speech interfaces for the Internet, solar applications, and cheap devices that can connect with the web. HP made e-Inclusion a business venture rather than a philanthropic one because it believes only systems that can sustain themselves economically can address the scale of the need—and in that scale is a business opportunity.[289]

For C. K. Prahalad (professor at the University of Michigan Business School and "perhaps the most visible proponent of the view that the globe's poor are a huge—and hugely untapped—market"),[290] the business opportunity is clear.[291] It requires effort and commitment on the part of multinational corporations (MNCs), but there are benefits in terms of top-line growth, reduced costs, and inspired innovation:

If we stop thinking of the poor as victims or as a burden and start recognizing them as resilient and creative entrepreneurs and value-conscious consumers, a whole new world of opportunity will open up.[292]

It is simply good business strategy to be involved in large, untapped markets that offer new customers, cost-saving opportunities, and access to radical innovation. The business opportunities at the bottom of the pyramid are real, and they are open to any MNC willing to engage and learn.[293]

It is important to note that Prahalad has his critics[294] who question the size of the market at the bottom of the pyramid, as well as the ability (and willingness) of MNCs to provide products that add significant social value:

Much of the profitable business with lower income markets involves products such as mobile phones, not the provision of basic nutrition, sanitation, education and shelter. . . . In addition, . . . claims about empowering people by providing means for them to consume cannot be taken at face value. The environmental impacts of changing consumption patterns also need to be looked at. . . . And we need to assess, if more foreign companies do come to serve lower income markets, might they not displace local companies and increase the resource drain from local economies?[295]

Nevertheless, it is also clear that Prahalad has had a significant influence on how firms perceive the developing world that has had a material impact (for better or worse) on the lives of consumers there.[296] As a result, reports of for-profit firms, such as P&G,[297] Nestlé,[298] and Unilever,[299] operating in emerging economies are now much more common. As the case below indicates, however, it is not always easy for firms to adapt to those projects that have a primary social mission.

Case Study	One Laptop Per Child (OLPC)

In 2004, Nicolas Negroponte, founder of MIT's Media Lab, announced that he intended to build and market a $100 laptop for children in the developing world. The goal of the project was

> to create rugged, Internet- and multi-media-capable laptop computers at a cost of $100 apiece.[300]

Negroponte was driven by the trans-formative potential of a computer in some of the poorest homes in the world.[301] In many cases, such homes did not even have electricity. As Negroponte explained, both kids and their parents benefit:

> When the kids bring them home and open them up, it's the brightest light source in the home. . . . Parents love it. . . . It is a way of having children be the agents of change. . . . They bring the device home and the parents look over their shoulder.[302]

To develop, manufacture, and market his $100 laptop, Negroponte established the One Laptop Per Child (OLPC) organization (http://laptop.org/en/). The OLPC project faced numerous constraints in order to "place the laptops in the hands of 100 to 150 million students," yet keep the price under a $100.[303] Major components, such as a screen that was affordable and would not drain the battery, were a major early problem. Ensuring a reliable Internet connection was another. Software was also a challenge, with the project also being constrained by

ideology. Apple, for example, offered to put its OS X software on the laptop for free, but OLPC declined because they wanted any software on the machine to be open source.[304] Early reports outlined solutions to many of the laptop's challenges:

> To get the price down, an eight inch diagonal screen . . . will run in two modes, with a high-resolution monochrome mode for word processing and a lower-resolution color mode for Internet surfing. It will be powered by both a power adapter, if electricity is available, or through a wind-up mechanism. The device will have wireless capabilities and can network with other units even without Internet access.[305]

While interest in Negroponte's idea was high from the beginning, he also had to face questions such as whether the Internet connection would be prohibitively expensive, or whether a mobile phone device would provide a more realistic means of reaching the project's goals. Critics with alternative ideas included people such as Bill Gates and Craig R. Barrett (chair of Intel).[306] Negroponte's response was to emphasize the educational benefit of a computer for each child and continue to make announcements:

> Quanta Computer would be manufacturing the device, based on a chip from Advanced Micro Devices and the Linux operating system. Quanta, a Taiwan company, makes about 30 percent of the world's laptops, so its involvement lends considerable credibility to the project.[307]

(Continued)

(Continued)

In spite of the criticism, it seems clear that Negroponte's work and ideas stimulated others into action, which brought OLPC into direct competition with the private sector:

It turns out there are lots of efforts under way right now to get computers and Internet connectivity to the poor regions of the world. Advanced Micro Devices has a program called 50x15— it hopes to have 50 percent of the world connected to the Internet by 2015. Microsoft has a bunch of programs. So does Intel. . . . [These] two companies, along with Dell, will introduce a new low-cost notebook device that the three companies hope will be suitable—and desirable—in the developing world.[308]

[In 2007] Dell, the world's number two computer company, launched a desktop computer in China . . . that sells for as little as $336. . . . Quanta computer, the world's largest contract manufacturer of notebook computers, says [in 2008] it will start making laptops that will sell for only $200 [as well as making the OLPC laptop].[309]

CSR Newsletters: One Laptop Per Child Software

A recent *BusinessWeek* article[310] provides an update on the progress of the $100 laptop. The article demonstrates the innovation that can emerge from social entrepreneurship:

Sugar [the new user interface for the OLPC computer] offers a brand new approach to computing. . . . It's the first complete rethinking of the computer user interface in more than 30 years.

The concept "now officially called XO" is nearing mass production:

About 2,500 beta test machines ran off assembly lines in Taiwan in February and are now being shipped to participating countries so they can kick the tires on the technology. The final version is supposed to be ready by August.

The project's goal is all the more amazing for its scope:

The audience [Negroponte] and his colleagues have in mind is the hundreds of millions of poor kids all over the world. Negroponte came up with the nonprofit "one laptop per child" idea when he was chairman of the MIT Media Lab and observed the failure of standard attempts to use computers in education to improve the lives of underprivileged children.

In 2007, as the laptop neared production, reviews (from neutral sources) were positive:

The truth is, the XO laptop [now called XO because if you turn XO 90 degrees, it looks like a child] . . . is absolutely amazing, and in my limited tests, a total kid magnet. Both the hardware and the software exhibit breakthrough after breakthrough—some of them not available on any other laptop, for $400 or $4,000.[311]

The hand-crank, wind-up mechanism that featured in the initial model was replaced with a "pull-cord charger, . . . a $12 solar panel that . . . provides enough power to recharge or power the machine," and a new battery technology that "runs at one-tenth the temperature of a standard laptop battery, costs $10 to replace, and is good for 2,000 charges—versus 500 on a regular laptop battery."[312] In addition, the screen was bright and readable in direct sunlight, as well as being a low power drain, which elongated the battery life. New antennas aided connection to the Internet and among computers, while the software was innovative and user-friendly:

Despite all the obstacles and doubters, OLPC has come up with a laptop that's tough and simple enough for hot, humid, dusty locales; cool enough to keep young minds engaged . . . ; and open, flexible and collaborative enough to support a million different teaching and learning styles.[313]

For Christmas, 2007, in the United States, OLPC announced a plan for consumers in the developed world to buy the computers for $399 (Give 1 Get 1, http://laptop.org/g1g1)—keep one for themselves and have one donated to a child in the developing world. As indicated above, however, the success and attention the OLPC was receiving did not go unnoticed by the private sector. Intel, in particular, seemed to draw the ire of Negroponte.

CSR Newsletters: One Laptop Per Child

A recent article[314] provides an update on the One Laptop Per Child (OLPC) computer that is being developed by Nicholas Negroponte (http://laptop.org/en/) and details Intel's decision to abandon the project. The acrimonious split comes after a troubled relationship that saw Intel publicly supporting OLPC, while also commercially producing its own competing low-cost computer:

After several years of publicly attacking the XO, Intel reversed itself over the summer and joined the organization's board, agreeing to make an $18 million contribution and begin developing an Intel-based version of the computer. Although Intel made an initial $6 million payment to One Laptop, the partnership was troubled from the outset as Intel sales representatives in the field competed actively against the $200 One Laptop machine by trying to sell a rival computer, a more costly Classmate PC. The Classmate sells for about $350 with an installed version of Microsoft Office, and Intel is selling the machine through an array of sales organizations outside the United States.

It is hard to know what Intel hopes to achieve by competing with Negroponte, whose actions are purely philanthropic. Even if there is a compelling business case to be made for selling low-cost computers in developing countries, Negroponte's goals largely involve sales to governments in order to provide laptops to the neediest children—not an obvious market foundation on which Intel can build a strong market presence. In such a fight, Intel

(Continued)

(Continued)

is always going to lose out in the media arena. This would apply even against someone who is not nearly as media-savvy as Negroponte, who, for example, frames Intel's actions as

a little bit like McDonald's competing with the World Food Program.

Any time the headline of an article that features a firm is along the lines of "Intel Quits Effort to Get Computers to Children," that firm is losing the PR battle.

The OLPC project continues to promote progress and innovation. In February 2009, the Indian government announced its support for an Indian-made $20 computer that would "be commercially available in six months."[315]

Online Resources

- Advanced Micro Devices, 50 × 15 Program, http://50x15.amd.com/en-us/

  "The 50 × 15 mission is to enable affordable, accessible Internet connectivity and computing capabilities for 50 percent of the world's population by the year 2015."

- HP Global Citizenship, http://www.hp.com/hpinfo/globalcitizenship/

  "Global citizenship encompasses our commitment to align our business goals with our impacts on society and the planet. It is one of our seven corporate objectives, rooted in HP's founding values and key to our success."

- Executives Without Borders, http://www.executiveswithoutborders.org/

  "OUR MISSION: To accelerate the accomplishment of the UN Millennium Development Goals by leveraging the same skill set that has made business successful."

- Intel's Classmate computer, http://www.classmatepc.com/

  "Intel's vision is to connect people to a world of opportunity by driving adoption of technology in education."

- MIT Media Lab, http://www.media.mit.edu/

  "The MIT Media Lab applies an unorthodox research approach to envision the impact of emerging technologies on everyday life—technologies that promise to fundamentally transform our most basic notions of human capabilities."

- NextBillion.net[316]—Development Through Enterprise, http://www.nextbillion.net/

  "NextBillion.net is a website and blog bringing together the community of business leaders, social entrepreneurs, NGOs, policy makers and academics who want to explore the connection between development and enterprise."

- One Laptop Per Child, http://laptop.org/

  "Mission Statement: To create educational opportunities for the world's poorest children by providing each child with a rugged, low-cost, low-power, connected laptop with content and software designed for collaborative, joyful, self-empowered learning."

- World Resources Institute, http://www.wri.org/

    "WRI is an environmental think tank that goes beyond research to find practical ways to protect the earth and improve people's lives."

Questions for Discussion and Review

1. Is it OK for a firm to profit from poverty?

2. Outline the opportunity for corporations that exists at the base of the pyramid. Can you think of a company and an existing product and how it can be modified to become profitable in the developing world?

3. Assuming a firm found a profitable niche in serving the fourth tier (the 4 billion people at the bottom of the economic pyramid), how might such a breakthrough benefit the firm in selling to the developed world at the top of the economic pyramid?

4. Was Intel *wrong* to compete with the OLPC project or was it just bad PR? Justify your position by referring to another firm that has acted in a similar (or different) way when faced with a similar situation.

5. Have a look at this article by Timothy Ogden (http://www.miller-mccune.com/business_economics/computer-error-1390).[317] What are some of the criticisms of OLPC? Do you think it is an effective way of improving the education of children in developing countries?

SUPPLY CHAIN

CSR CONNECTION: This issue highlights the complexities of CSR when dealing with conflicting values in different cultures. This is a particular problem for multinational corporations that source their products in many different countries, but are expected to please all stakeholders.

Issue

To what extent do business practices contribute to the community in which the organization is based and operating? Increasingly, firms are becoming more global. One consequence is that companies are relocating their operations offshore as part of a cost minimization strategy. This often means that jobs are lost at home and gained by the low-cost environments overseas to which the companies relocate. The upside of this component of globalization is that firms are increasingly able to locate operations in the region of the world that makes the most sense. It results, for example, in situations where a Ford Mustang is assembled using parts largely manufactured abroad, while a Toyota Sienna is assembled in Indiana with 90% of its parts originating in the United States and Canada.[318] Another outcome is that

a shirt imported to the US from Hong Kong includes tasks of workers from as many as 10 countries.[319]

The downside of this movement of operations affects the component of production that is often least portable—a firm's employees. And abuse overseas, where it occurs, seems to fall disproportionately on those least able to defend themselves:

The International Labour Organization (ILO) estimates that there are 122m economically active five to 14-year-olds in the Asia-Pacific region, with 44m of them in India, giving it the largest child workforce in the world.[320]

As such, while advocates of offshoring or outsourcing often point to the benefits the process brings to the workers in developing countries who now have jobs, ultimately, it is not clear whether these foreign employees benefit (from the jobs created)[321] or suffer (from the conditions in which they are forced to work),[322] or even whether better quality products and services are delivered at home.[323] From blue-collar factory jobs in China and Southeast Asia to white-collar call-center and computer-programming jobs in India, many U.S. citizens are experiencing globalization up close and personal:

By some estimates, roughly 1.3 million manufacturing jobs have moved abroad since the beginning of 1992, the bulk in the past three years to Mexico and East Asia.[324]

Forrester Research Inc. predicts that American employers will move about 3.3 million white-collar service jobs and $136 billion in wages overseas in the next 15 years.[325]

Although some of these jobs would have been lost to automation anyway, to what extent does operating in a foreign environment, with different cultural values and norms, render the corporation vulnerable to cultural conflict? What role does outsourcing play for firms seeking to implement CSR throughout the supply chain? To what extent can a firm's total ethical supply chain, "from ethical purchasing through to proper disposal of the end product,"[326] become a force for positive change?[327]

CSR Newsletters: Supply Chain

This recent newspaper advice column[328] addresses the issue of a firm's responsibility for its extended supply chain. It cites two recent examples in the United Kingdom (Primark and Tesco) where evidence suggests a systematic abuse of human (child laborers) and employment (low pay) rights in factories that supply both firms. The column then asks for advice from four different perspectives in response to the following questions:

Is it ever possible for companies with suppliers in developing economies to guarantee that their goods have been produced in ethically acceptable conditions? And what kind of audit system could provide consumers with such a guarantee?

In relation to the first question, it was encouraging to see the position taken that consumers should not be surprised when they pay such relatively low prices for clothes and it then emerges that the clothes did not cost much to produce:

Consumers massage their consciences, crying crocodile tears when an abused producer is found by an intrepid journalist, but show their true colours shopping for underwear.

In addressing the second question, the general response was also refreshing (in terms of its perceptiveness), suggesting that (a) firms should not be surprised that suppliers in developing countries try and deceive auditors and (b) that they only have themselves to blame because, while firms might say that they want their suppliers to adhere to certain standards, they incentivize them to minimize costs. Until firms are serious about providing financial incentives for suppliers to adhere to their codes of conduct and punish transgressors, they are unlikely to see the kind of behavior they say they seek:

That means engaging the supply chain in good corporate social responsibility practices rather than relying on spot checks. It means getting suppliers to recognise that adhering to sound employment practices is in their own interests and helping suppliers develop policies and practices that will make them a trusted supplier and build a long-term relationship.

The absence of a choice for many workers in the developing world is also a point well made:

Poor parents in India, Pakistan or Vietnam cannot choose between sending their children to a school or a factory. The real choice is between eating or going hungry.

The upshot is that the column does not provide many specific answers, but at least everyone is realistic in terms of the situation on the ground.

To what extent is this conflict a CSR issue and how might firms deal with it? Also, what is the potential damage of a perceived abuse for the company in its home market, where observers and consumers do not judge the company by the standards of the foreign culture?[329] It is also worth asking: Are sweatshops necessarily bad?

We in the West mostly despise sweatshops as exploiters of the poor, while the poor themselves tend to see sweatshops as opportunities.[330]

The argument in favor of *sweatshops* is that, in comparison to the alternatives facing many people living in developing economies, a factory job with a Western multinational represents the opportunity for advancement:

[Proponents of] labor standards in trade agreements mean well, for they intend to fight back at oppressive sweatshops abroad. But, while it shocks Americans to hear it, the central challenge in the poorest countries is not that sweatshops exploit too many people, but that they don't exploit enough. Talk to those families [who live and scavenge in a garbage] dump, and a job in a sweatshop is a cherished dream, an escalator out of poverty, the kind of gauzy if probably unrealistic ambition that parents everywhere often have for their children.[331]

An important component of this argument, therefore, is the idea of cultural relativism—to what extent should actions in overseas countries be judged by the home country's moral, ethical, and religious standards, and to what extent should they be judged in terms of the historical and cultural context in which they occur? Western NGOs, in particular, are accused of actively campaigning against the opening of Western operations in developing countries based on Western notions of *acceptable* work conditions but are not able to provide alternative sources of investment if the company is forced to withdraw:

International NGOs in Guatemala train local leaders to "empower" minorities and indigenous groups and to denounce the mines as "neo-colonial" ventures. But the reality is that the very nature of the NGO saves it from having a real stake in the communities it affects through its activism. It can blow through town like a hurricane disrupting development and then be gone.[332]

In short, while there are instances of either extreme, it is not clear whether outsourcing and other foreign involvement in local communities overseas is an absolute *good* or *bad:*

When a corporation from an advanced economy does business in a developing country, it may . . . establish a level of corporate virtue consistent with the host country's civil foundation. Notoriously, Nike, by running its Southeast Asian athletic footwear plants and paying its workers in accordance with local customs and practices, opened itself to charges of operating sweatshops. In essence, it was accused of averaging down its level of corporate responsibility. Although the company protested that its conduct was virtuous by local standards, angry U.S. consumers made it clear that they expected Nike to conform to [the standards of] the U.S. civil foundation.[333]

Case Study   Nike

Nike has long been plagued by allegations that it oversees sweatshop conditions in its factories abroad. The allegation is made against the company whether the factories are Nike owned and operated or merely contractors producing shoes and clothing on behalf of the firm:

Even after ten years of campaigning against Nike over alleged abuse of workers in "sweatshops" of its developing

world subcontractors, NikeWatch and its cohorts are still going strong. This reinforces how much harder it is to restore a reputation than to lose it. Nike is still demonized by many despite impressive sustainability initiatives, including workplace monitoring.[334]

Once an image is established, it is difficult to dislodge from the minds of the public. Questions about Nike's sweatshops have even dogged the famous athletes that represent the company wherever they go. The goal has always been to balance diplomacy with capitalist instinct. Dan Le Batard calls it "sole-selling" and compliments Michael Jordan's ability to have walked the fine line ever since he joined forces with Nike:

> It's why [Jordan] famously recused himself from opining on controversial Jesse Helms in his home state of North Carolina because, in his words, "Republicans buy sneakers, too."[335]

In 2003, the issue of Nike's overseas operations rose to the level of the U.S. Supreme Court in a case brought against the company by a private citizen from California, Marc Kasky.[336] Kasky challenged Nike's claims that it does not operate sweatshops in Southeast Asia, that it pays its workers there competitive wages, and that they enjoy better-than-average working conditions. *Nike v. Kasky* originally emerged out of an exchange of opinions between the *New York Times* columnist Bob Herbert and Nike CEO Phil Knight in 1996 and 1997. Herbert had written two op-ed articles criticizing the conditions faced by Nike laborers in the company's Southeast Asian factories. He then contrasted these conditions with the huge salaries enjoyed by Knight and other Nike executives and also the company's stable of wealthy athletes who are paid to endorse Nike products. The contrast was all the greater due to the extreme poverty of Nike's factory laborers:

> More than 90 percent of the Nike workers in Vietnam are girls or young women, aged 15 to 28. . . . A meal consisting of rice, a few mouthfuls of a vegetable and maybe some tofu costs the equivalent of 70 cents. Three similarly meager meals a day would cost $2.10. But the workers only make $1.60 a day. And . . . they have other expenses. . . . To stretch the paycheck, something has to be sacrificed. Despite the persistent hunger, it's usually food.[337]

Herbert accused Nike of running the "boot camps" with military efficiency, and only "one bathroom break per eight-hour shift is allowed, and two drinks of water."[338] Herbert labeled this hierarchy a "pyramid of exploitation,"[339] with Nike executives at the top and the company's factory workers at the bottom.

Nike quickly responded to the provocation with a letter from Philip Knight to the *New York Times* defending the company's operations in Asia:

> Nike has been concerned with developing safe and healthy work environments wherever it has worked with contractors in emerging market societies.[340]

Mark Kasky was a consumer, completely unrelated to the issue, who happened to read this exchange. Under California law, anyone can sue a company for "false and misleading advertising." With the help of a large law firm (Milberg, Weiss, et al.), which has a reputation for suing large multinational corporations and collecting large settlement fees,[341] Kasky decided to intervene. He argued that Nike, using press releases, op-ed articles, letters to the editor, its own Web site, and other media,

(Continued)

(Continued)

has made false and misleading statements in describing the working conditions in its overseas factories where its athletic shoes are made.[342]

Putting aside the merits of the case, which were never conclusively decided, this confrontation shows the difficulty for a company in trying to shake a negative label. It also shows the potentially significant costs (both financial and in terms of negative publicity) that can result from operations deemed to be less than socially responsible. The initial ruling broadened these consequences to any company conducting business in California. It also had the effect of forcing many companies to review their public pronouncements on CSR-related issues and remain quiet on some issues of public interest, whereas they might previously have been encouraged to engage in public debate.[343] More worrying for businesses, perhaps, was the extent of the penalty that could have been imposed:

> Kasky seeks a court order requiring Nike to disgorge its California profits attributable to [the contested] statements. Under the California law, truth is not a defense to a charge of business fraud if the challenged statements are misleading in context.[344]

A press release announcing that the *Nike v. Kasky* case had been settled amicably was released by Nike on September 12, 2003:

> The two parties mutually agreed that investments designed to strengthen workplace monitoring and factory worker programs

are more desirable than prolonged litigation. As part of the settlement, Nike has agreed to make additional workplace-related program investments (augmenting the company's existing expenditures on monitoring, etc.) totaling $1.5 million. Nike's contribution will go to the Washington, D.C.-based Fair Labor Association (FLA) for program operations and worker development programs focused on education and economic opportunity.[345]

As a result,

> shares of Nike fell 11 cents, to $55.68, in trading Friday on the New York Stock Exchange.[346]

The case symbolized a growing desire among consumers that large corporations act, both overseas and at home, in ways that are transparent and acceptable in terms of standards applied by consumers in the companies' home markets. From the corporate perspective, however, it also highlights the difficulty for companies that are trying to implement effective CSR policies within their organizations. Many commentators argued that the litigation has already had negative consequences that are detrimental to the general good and public debate of issues of public interest. If the effect of any court decision is to leave companies feeling that it is better to say nothing than defend themselves in public and also to pull back from any effort to engage the communities within which they are based and improve corporate practices, then, arguably, the decision has done more harm than good:

The potential affect of the [California Supreme Court's] ruling is devastating. Nike has shelved any plans to produce social responsibility reports in the near future because any such statement can now be attacked on the basis of being an advert for the company.[347]

In responding to any accusations made against it, any company should be able to answer freely and honestly, to the best of its ability, without having to worry that if what it says is slightly wrong, taken out of context, or misunderstood in some way, that it is going to be prosecuted. It is also true, however, that the case has opened Nike's eyes to the danger of not ensuring all aspects of its operations are considered *responsible*. Following the decision, the company was much more sensitive to potential criticism, a position that is reflected in day-to-day decisions and policy implementation:

Because of intense criticism . . . over the past half-decade, companies like Gap, Reebok, and Nike are generally alert to labor issues. Many now monitor factories, and . . . physical working conditions have improved as a result. "After we started working with Nike, we had to change our philosophy," says Philip Lo, the [Yng Hsing tannery in Taiwan's] vice-general manager. "They have strict requests about how you treat safety, health, attitude, environment." Nike is so sensitive to potential criticism that when the company learned of Fortune's visit to Yng Hsing,

it immediately informed the tannery that unless it passed a hastily arranged inspection, it would be removed from Nike's supplier list.[348]

Since the Kasky case, Nike appears to have been genuine in its attempts to overhaul its supply chain practices. In particular, Nike has implemented a shift in its approach to its employees (whether direct employees or the employees of contract firms):

Nike, the world's biggest sports shoe and clothing brand, is to strengthen efforts to combat potential abuses of the 800,000 workers in its global supply chain with a push to promote labour rights, including the freedom to form and join trade unions.[349]

The shift seems to be more than cosmetic—an emphasis on promoting positive change, rather than simply avoiding potentially damaging crises:

Hannah Jones, Nike's vice-president for corporate responsibility, said the brand was now placing a greater effort on promoting "systemic" change in its supply chain, which would include strengthening the ability of factory workers to speak out on their own behalf about problems.[350]

The ongoing program of repositioning its brand on issues of social responsibility appears to be paying off for Nike. In many areas of CSR, the firm is now recognized as promoting best practice:[351]

(Continued)

(Continued)

Since facing criticism over workplace abuses in the mid-1990s, Nike has become a standard-setter for efforts to improve supply chain conditions and other companies have followed its lead on corporate responsibility.[352]

In general, factory audits conducted by independent, third parties are increasingly being used by firms. They are perceived as a solution whereby Western firms can continue to operate in low-cost environments, local employees can continue to benefit from their presence, and NGOs can receive some assurance that the local employees are not being abused.[354] Best practice, pushed by firms such as Nike and Gap, dictates that firms should work with contractors to improve conditions when violations occur and, in persistent cases, sever ties:

The decision to sever ties with Sialkot, Pakistan-based Saga sports follows a six month investigation by Nike and a local monitoring group that found Saga was illegally outsourcing manufacturing to local homes. . . . Nike also found multiple labor, environmental and health violations at Saga factories. . . . According to Nike, the company gave Saga a detailed plan for overhaul. . . . After several conversations, Nike said that while outsourcing diminished, other labor violations seemed to increase, prompting the termination.[355]

Others argue that binding international standards are the most effective means of securing improvements.[356] Although, such agreement among different nation-states is notoriously difficult to secure, a compliance-based regime is susceptible to avoidance,[357] and regulation can quickly become stifling.[358] A potential alternative is competition among firms. Once sufficient factories are established in local communities and a locally determined definition of work conditions that are acceptable to local workers becomes established, then a likely consequence of competition among factories to secure employees will lead to improved conditions for all:

In September, 2005, the Guangdong [China] Provincial Labour and Social Security Department published the first blacklist of 20 "bloody" companies that were defaulting on employees' wages. Besides receiving media attention, the blacklist was also distributed to local job fairs. Among the 20 companies, 12 paid their workers in full by December when the department publicized its second blacklist.[359]

What is clear is that outsourcing is not going away. Instead, the issue continues to evolve as CSR issues become ever more prominent in the strategic decisions firms take, seeking to locate operations in the geographic region offering the best mix of employee skills and costs. What is important from a CSR perspective is to ensure firms adhere to their legal and social obligations and that it is *best* practice, rather than *worst* practice, that is recognized and rewarded by consumers.

Online Resources

- Fair Labor Association, http://www.fairlabor.org/

  " . . . Fair Labor Association (FLA), a nonprofit organization dedicated to ending sweatshop conditions in factories worldwide."

- Institute for Supply Management, http://www.ism.ws/

  "Founded in 1915, the Institute for Supply Management™ (ISM) is the largest supply management association in the world."

- International Labour Organization, http://www.ilo.org/

  "The International Labour Organization (ILO) is the tripartite UN agency that brings together governments, employers and workers of its member states in common action to promote decent work throughout the world."

- Labour Behind the Label, http://www.labourbehindthelabel.org/

  "Labour Behind the Label supports garment workers' efforts worldwide to defend their rights."

- NikeWatch Campaign, http://www.oxfam.org.au/campaigns/labour-rights/nikewatch/

  "In 2006, Nike-branded products were made by more than 800,000 workers in almost 700 contract factories in 52 countries around the world. 80 per cent of these workers are women aged 18 to 24."

- Social Accountability International (SAI), http://www.sa-intl.org/

  "Social Accountability International (SAI)'s mission is to promote human rights for workers around the world."

- Sweatshop Watch, http://www.change.org/sweatshop_watch

  "Sweatshop Watch is a coalition of labor, community, civil rights, immigrant rights, women's, religious and student organizations, and individuals committed to eliminating the exploitation that occurs in sweatshops."

- Verité, http://www.verite.org/

  "Verité's mission is to ensure that people around the world work under safe, fair and legal conditions."

Questions for Discussion and Review

1. Is a firm responsible for its supply chain? If so, how far down the supply chain does this responsibility extend? Should a firm's operations abroad be judged by the standards (legal, economic, cultural, and moral) of the country in which it is operating or by the standards of its home market?

2. Do you wear Nike shoes? If so, why? If not, why not? Why is Nike so successful?

3. Is it *fair* to make the comparison between the amount Nike pays its factory workers in Vietnam and the salaries of its CEO and the athletes that endorse the company's products?

4. Why does Nike continue to source its production overseas? What advantages does this generate for the firm? What are the disadvantages that result from the decision? Should Nike have been able to see these threats ahead of time and avoid them? Overall, do the benefits of Nike's decision outweigh the costs?

5. Look at this video of Nike CEO Phil Knight and the documentary producer, Michael Moore: http://www.youtube.com/watch?v=cOI0V4kRCIQ. Is Nike a *good* company? Why or why not?

NOTES AND REFERENCES

1. The cost savings Walmart is able to secure by operating more sustainably, which we discussed in Chapter 3, is a good example of this.

2. The 2009 *Conscious Consumer Report* from the branding consultancy BBMG, for example, notes that 67% of Americans agree that "even in tough economic times, it is important to purchase products with social and environmental benefits" and also that 71% of consumers agree that they "avoid purchasing from companies whose practices they disagree with." Jack Loechner, "Consumers Want Proof It's Green," *Center for Media Research,* April 9, 2009, http://www.mediapost.com/publications/?fa=Articles.showArticle&art_aid=103504

3. The Fairtrade Foundation Web site, January 2003, http://www.fairtrade.org.uk/

4. Katy McLaughlin, "Is Your Grocery List Politically Correct?" *Wall Street Journal,* February 17, 2004, pp. D1 & D2.

5. Francis Percival, "No Bitter Aftertaste," *Financial Times, Life & Arts,* February 28/March 1, 2009, p. 5, http://www.ft.com/cms/s/2/3a99d2c8-045c-11de-845b-000077b07658.html

6. The Fairtrade Foundation Web site, April 2009, http://www.fairtrade.org.uk/what_is_fairtrade/faqs.aspx

7. Ibid.

8. "Equal Exchange Announces Its First Fair Trade Certified Sugar," Equal Exchange Press release, *CSRwire.com,* March 16, 2005.

9. "Fairtrade System Bears Fruit for Producers From Developing World," Financial Times, July 11, 2006, p. 4; "Naked Juice Teams Up With the Rainforest Alliance for Sustainable Fruit Procurement," Ethical Corporation, April 14, 2009, http://www.csrwire.com/News/15092.html

10. Alan Beattie, "Follow the Thread," *Financial Times,* July 22/23, 2006, p. WK1.

11. Fiona Harvey, "Industry Acts to Avert Damage," *Financial Times,* August 14, 2006, p. 6.

12. "Stuffed," *The Economist,* July 3, 2004, p. 31.

13. Michael Skapinker, "There Is a Good Trade in Ethical Retailing," *Financial Times,* September 11, 2007, p. 15, http://www.ft.com/cms/s/0/352205cc-5fc6-11dc-b0fe-0000779fd2ac.html

14. Quote from the 2005 *Green and Ethical Consumer* Report. In Poulomi Mrinal Saha, "Ethics Still Not Influencing UK Consumers," *Ethical Corporation,* March 15, 2005, http://www.ethicalcorp .com/content.asp?ContentID=3557

15. Alan Beattie, "Follow the Thread," *Financial Times,* July 22/23, 2006, p. WK1.

16. Ibid.

17. John Kay, "Justice in Trade Is Not Simply a Moral Question," *Financial Times* (U.S. edition), June 26, 2003, p. 13.

18. Adam Smith, quoted in "Economic Focus: Too Many Countries?" *The Economist,* July 17, 2004, p. 75.

19. Katy McLaughlin, "Is Your Grocery List Politically Correct?" *Wall Street Journal,* February 17, 2004, pp. D1 & D2.

20. Parminder Bahra, "Tea Workers Still Waiting to Reap Fairtrade Benefits," *The Times,* January 2, 2009, http://www.timesonline.co.uk/tol/news/uk/article5429888.ece

21. Stanley Homes & Geri Smith, "For Coffee Growers, Not Even a Whiff of Profits," *BusinessWeek,* September 9, 2002, p. 110.

22. John Vidal, "New Choc on the Bloc," *The Guardian,* June 2005, http://www.guardian.co.uk/world/2005/jun/03/outlook.development

23. Alan Beattie, "Follow the Thread," *Financial Times,* July 22/23, 2006, p. WK1.

24. Ibid.

25. Peter Heslam, "George and the Chocolate Factory," *The London Institute for Contemporary Christianity,* September 2005, http://www.licc.org.uk/engaging-with-culture/connecting-with-culture/business/george-and-the-chocolate-factory-203

26. John Vidal, "New Choc on the Bloc," *The Guardian,* June 2005, http://www.guardian.co.uk/world/2005/jun/03/outlook.development

27. James E. McWilliams, "Food That Travels Well," *New York Times,* August 6, 2007, http://www.nytimes.com/2007/08/06/opinion/06mcwilliams.html; Claudia H. Deutsch, "For Suppliers, the Pressure Is On," *New York Times, Special Section: Business of Green,* November 7, 2007, p. 1.

28. "Cadbury Dairy Milk Commits to Going Fairtrade," Cadbury Press Release, *CSRwire.com,* March 3, 2009, http://www.csrwire.com/News/14719.html

29. Michael Skapinker, "Fairtrade and a New Ingredient for Business," *Financial Times,* March 10, 2009, p. 11.

30. Bill Baue, "Chocolate and Social Responsibility," *CSRWire.com,* May 11, 2009, http://www.csrwire.com/press/press_release/15574-The-Latest-Corporate-Social-Responsibility-News-CSR-Chocolate-and-Social-Responsibility

31. Michael Skapinker, "Fairtrade and a New Ingredient for Business," *Financial Times,* March 10, 2009, p. 11.

32. For information about sustainable certification schemes that rival fair trade (e.g., Rainforest Alliance and Utz Certified), see John Russell, "Coffee Sourcing: Nespresso Points Nestlé Towards Sustainability," *Ethical Corporation,* June 29, 2009, http://www.ethicalcorp.com/content.asp?ContentID=6518

33. "Starbucks Corporation was the world's largest specialty coffee retailer, with $6.4 billion in annual revenue for the fiscal year ended October 2, 2005. . . . By the end of 2005, Starbucks . . . boasted more than 10,000 stores—up from 676 a decade earlier—and roasted 2.3 percent of the world's coffee. Each day it opened an average of four stores and hired 200 employees." In "Starbucks Corporate: Building a Sustainable Supply Chain," *Stanford Graduate School of Business,* Case: GS-54, May 2007, pp. 1–2.

34. Stanley Homes & Geri Smith, "For Coffee Growers, Not Even a Whiff of Profits," *BusinessWeek,* September 9, 2002, p. 110.

35. A Web site discussing Starbuck's policies regarding fair trade can be found at http://www.starbucks.com/sharedplanet/ethicalinternal.aspx?story=fairtrade. Other aspects of the company's fair trade program can be found at the firm's "Starbucks farmer stories" page of its Web site: http://www.starbucks.com/aboutus/farmstories.asp

36. Stanley Homes & Geri Smith, "For Coffee Growers, Not Even a Whiff of Profits," *BusinessWeek,* September 9, 2002, p. 110.

37. Ibid.

38. http://www.purefood.org/Starbucks/starbucks.html

39. http://www.organicconsumers.org/starbucks/

40. "100 Best Corporate Citizens 2007," *The CRO Magazine,* http://www.thecro.com/?q=node/304. Note: Due to a change in methodology, 2007 was the last year that Green Mountain was

eligible for inclusion in the rankings; "100 Best Corporate Citizens 2008," *The CRO Magazine,* http://www.thecro.com/node/615

41. Peter Asmus, "100 Best Corporate Citizens of 2003," *Business Ethics Magazine,* Spring 2003, pp. 6–10.

42. David Vetter, "UK Fairtrade—Shunted into a Siding," Ethical Corporation, December 14, 2007, http://www.ethicalcorp.com/content.asp?ContentID=5583

43. Lisa Roner, "US Coffee Roasters Say Expansion of Fair Trade Depends on Consumer Demand," *Ethical Corporation,* August 30, 2004, http://www.ethicalcorp.com/content.asp?ContentID=2623

44. Andrew Downie, "Fair Trade in Bloom," *New York Times,* October 2, 2007, p. C5.

45. Oliver Balch, "Peter Torrebiarte, Starbucks Coffee Agronomy Company," *Ethical Corporation,* June 24, 2004, http://www.ethicalcorp.com/content.asp?ContentID=2263

46. "Starbucks Corporate: Building a Sustainable Supply Chain," *Stanford Graduate School of Business,* Case: GS-54, May 2007, p. 4.

47. Oliver Balch, "Peter Torrebiarte, Starbucks Coffee Agronomy Company," *Ethical Corporation,* June 24, 2004, http://www.ethicalcorp.com/content.asp?ContentID=2263

48. "Starbucks Corporate: Building a Sustainable Supply Chain," *Stanford Graduate School of Business,* Case: GS-54, May 2007, p. 2.

49. Peter Torrebiarte, general manager of the Starbucks Coffee Agronomy Company, quoted in Oliver Balch, "Peter Torrebiarte, Starbucks Coffee Agronomy Company," *Ethical Corporation,* June 24, 2004, http://www.ethicalcorp.com/content.asp?ContentID=2263

50. Alex Blyth, "M&S to Switch All Served Coffee to Fairtrade," *Ethical Corporation,* September 10, 2004, http://www.ethicalcorp.com/content.asp?ContentID=2715

51. Javier Blas & Jenny Wiggins, "Coffee and Sugar Prices Stirred by Shortages," *Financial Times,* May 11, 2009, p. 13.

52. Brad Stone, "The Empire of Excess," *New York Times,* July 4, 2008, p. C1.

53. Andrew Downie, "Fair Trade in Bloom," *New York Times,* October 2, 2007, p. C1; "McDonald's to Sell Fair Trade Certified Coffee," Oxfam America Press Release, *CSRwire.com,* October 27, 2005, http://www.enn.com/top_stories/article/16249

54. Jenny Wiggins, "When the Coffee Goes Cold," *Financial Times, Life & Arts,* December 13/14, 2008, p. 2.

55. Jenny Wiggins, "McDonald's Lays the Ground to Mug Starbucks in Europe," *Financial Times,* May 27, 2009, p. 13.

56. For information about sustainable certification schemes that rival fair trade (e.g., Rainforest Alliance and Utz Certified), see John Russell, "Coffee Sourcing: Nespresso Points Nestlé Towards Sustainability," *Ethical Corporation,* June 29, 2009, http://www.ethicalcorp.com/content.asp?ContentID=6518

57. "Starbucks Serves up its First Fairtrade Lattes and Cappuccinos Across the UK and Ireland," *Fairtrade Foundation,* September 2, 2009, http://www.fairtrade.org.uk/press_office/press_releases_and_statements/september_2009/starbucks_serves_up_its_first_fairtrade_lattes_and_cappuccinos.aspx

58. Kuapa Kokoo ("with over 40,000 registered cocoa farmers across Ghana") is one of the fairtrade-certified cocoa producers that will supply Cadbury with the cocoa beans it needs to produce its fairtrade chocolate bars.

59. Katy McLaughlin, "Is Your Grocery List Politically Correct?" *Wall Street Journal,* February 17, 2004, pp. D1 & D2.

60. Andrew Newton, "NGOs Bringing Bank Scrutiny Back on Track," *Ethical Corporation,* May 2, 2004, http://www.ethicalcorp.com/content.asp?ContentID=1980

61. Sandy Weill, Memo to employees, June 4, 2003.

62. Marc Gunther, "The Mosquito in the Tent," *Fortune,* May 31, 2004, pp. 158–163.

63. Ibid.

64. Ibid.

65. Demetri Sevastopulo, "Revisions Raise Social Hurdles," *Financial Times,* Special Report: Sustainable Banking, June 12, 2006, p. 2.

66. http://www.equator-principles.com/

67. Citigroup Web site: http://www.citigroup.com/citigroup/citizen/socialresponsibility/index.htm

68. Alex Blyth, "NGOs Criticize Banks' Implementation of Equator Principles," *Ethical Corporation,* June 10, 2004, http://www.ethicalcorp.com/content.asp?ContentID=2188

69. Alan Murray, "Business: Scandals Leave Big Banks Vulnerable," *Wall Street Journal,* April 13, 2005, p. A2.

70. Mike Scott, "The Importance of an Ethical Approach to Project Finance," *Financial Times,* Special Report: Sustainable Banking, June 7, 2007, p. 2.

71. http://www.equator-principles.com/

72. Eoin Callan & Kimberly Wilson, "Expectations Are High But Often Exceeded," *Financial Times,* Special Report: Sustainable Banking, June 7, 2007, p. 2.

73. Demetri Sevastopulo, "Revisions Raise Social Hurdles," *Financial Times,* Special Report: Sustainable Banking, June 12, 2006, p. 2.

74. Mike Scott, "The Importance of an Ethical Approach to Project Finance," *Financial Times,* Special Report: Sustainable Banking, June 7, 2007, p. 2.

75. Eoin Callan & Kimberly Wilson, "Expectations Are High But Often Exceeded," *Financial Times,* Special Report: Sustainable Banking, June 7, 2007, p. 2.

76. Ibid.

77. Mike Scott, "The Importance of an Ethical Approach to Project Finance," *Financial Times,* Special Report: Sustainable Banking, June 7, 2007, p. 2.

78. Joe Leahy, "Citigroup Gives Indian Poor a Hand With Thumbprint ATMs," *Financial Times,* December 2, 2006, p. 15, http://www.ft.com/cms/s/0/3cedb2b0-81aa-11db-864e-0000779e2340.html

79. For information on the latest issues on this topic, see the *Financial Times'* "Sustainable Banking" reports: http://www.ft.com/reports/sustainablebanking2008 and http://media.ft.com/cms/68eb3bb2-502e-11de-9530-00144feabdc0.pdf

80. Francesco Guerrera, "Flawed Conception," *Financial Times,* January 17/18, 2009, p. 8.

81. A similar initiative, labeled the *Climate Principles,* was made by the banks Credit Agricole, HSBC, Munich Re, Standard Charter, and Swiss Re in February 2008. "Banks and Insurers Launch Climate Principles," *Ethical Corporation,* February 2, 2008, http://www.ethicalcorp.com/content.asp?ContentID=6232

82. "The principles were developed in partnership by Citi, JPMorgan, Chase, and Morgan Stanley and in consultation with power companies American Electric Power, CMS Energy, DTE Energy, NRG Energy, PSEG, Sempra and Southern Company. Environmental Defense and the Natural Resources Defense Council were also involved." In "Citigroup, JPMorgan, and Morgan Stanley Unveil 'Carbon Principles,'" *Environmental Leader,* February 4, 2008, http://www.environmentalleader.com/2008/02/04/citigroup-jpmorgan-and-morgan-stanley-unveil-carbon-principles/

83. http://www.carbonprinciples.com/

84. Some commentators have identified "June 12, 2007, when news broke that two Bear Stearns hedge funds speculating in mortgage-backed securities were melting down" as the starting point of the 2007–2009 economic crisis: Allan Sloan, "Unhappy Anniversary," *Fortune Magazine,* June 8, 2009, p. 14.

85. Lionel Barber, "How Gamblers Broker the Banks," *Financial Times Special Report: The FT Year in Finance, Financial Times,* December 16, 2008, p. 1.

86. Sarah O'Connor, "IMF Estimates Financial Sector's Loss at $4,100bn," *Financial Times,* April 22, 2009, p. 5.

87. See George A. Akerlof & Robert J. Shiller, *Animal Spirits: How Human Psychology Drives the Economy, and Why It Matters for Global Capitalism,* Princeton University Press, 2009, for an excellent description of the varied motivations driving human behavior with respect to economic behavior and the financial markets.

88. David Brooks, "An Economy of Faith and Trust," *The New York Times,* January 16, 2009, p. A27.

89. Luke Johnson, "A Tragedy for Champions of Free Markets," *Financial Times,* February 4, 2009, p. 10.

90. Thomas L. Friedman, "All Fall Down," *New York Times,* November 26, 2008, p. A31.

91. John Kay, "What a Carve up," *Financial Times,* August 1/2, 2009, Life & Arts, p. 12.

92. Editorial, "When the Music Stops," *The Guardian,* November 6, 2007, http://www.guardian .co.uk/commentisfree/2007/nov/06/comment.business

93. Philip Stephens, "Wanted: Global Politics to Rescue Global Capitalism," *Financial Times,* March 13, 2009, p. 11.

94. David Ignatius, "Obama's Vision of New Foundation Should Reassure Summiteers," *The Washington Post,* in *The Daily Yomiuri,* April 3, 2009, p. 17.

95. See Martin Wolf's excellent discussion of the causes and solutions of the economic crisis in the *Financial Times* at: http://blogs.ft.com/economistsforum/. A typical example: Martin Wolf, "Choices Made in 2009 Will Shape the Globe's Destiny," *Financial Times,* January 7, 2009, p. 9.

96. Seumas Milne, "Leaders Still Aren't Facing Up to Scale of Crisis," *The Guardian,* in *The Daily Yomiuri,* April 3, 2009, p. 17.

97. Ibid.

98. "Bashing the Rich Counterproductive," *The Economist* (April 4–10 issue) in *The Daily Yomiuri,* April 5, 2009, p. 8.

99. Bill Baue, "Questions Remain for CSR in 2009," *CSRwire.com,* January 12, 2009, http://www .csrwire.com/press/press_release/22696-CSRwire-Reports-Top-Corporate-Social-Responsibility-News-of-2008

100. Thomas L. Friedman, "The Inflection Is Near?" *New York Times,* March 8, 2009, p. WK12.

101. Bradley K. Googins, "Time for Capitalism to Adapt or Depart," *Boston College Center for Corporate Citizenship,* February 2009, http://blogs.bcccc.net/2009/02/time-for-capitalism-to-adapt-or-depart/

102. "A Question Revisited: Is Capitalism Working?" *Knowledge@Wharton,* March 4, 2009, http://knowledge.wharton.upenn.edu/article.cfm?articleid=2172

103. Michael Lewis, "The End," *Portfolio.com,* December 2008, http://www.portfolio.com/ news-markets/national-news/portfolio/2008/11/11/The-End-of-Wall-Streets-Boom

104. Michael Lewis & David Einhorn, "The End of the Financial World As We Know It," *New York Times,* January 4, 2009, p. WK9.

105. Martin Wolf, "Seeds of Its Own Destruction," *Financial Times,* March 9, 2009, p. 7.

106. Bill Gates, *Creative Capitalism: A Conversation with Bill Gates, Warren Buffett, and Other Economic Leaders,* Simon & Schuster, 2008. See also Text of Gates's speech at 2008 World Economic Forum at Davos, http://www.microsoft.com/Presspass/exec/billg/speeches/2008/01-24WEFDavos.mspx

107. Muhammad Yunus, *Creating a World Without Poverty: Social Business and the Future of Capitalism,* Public Affairs, 2009. See also Brad Buchholz, "You May Say He's a Dreamer . . . ," *Austin American-Statesman,* March 1, 2009, http://www.martinfrost.ws/htmlfiles/mar2009/yunus-maybe-dreamer.html

108. Thomas L. Friedman, "The Inflection Is Near?" *New York Times,* March 8, 2009, p. WK12.

109. Skeptics, on the other hand, advise caution and suggest that the talk of reform is premature: "'Capitalism with a conscience' promised on the sickbed may be quickly forgotten in recovery. Don't imagine the stake is through the neoliberal heart yet." Polly Toynbee, "Brown Should Spend More to Save Young People," *The Times,* in *The Daily Yomiuri,* April 6, 2009, p. 8.

110. George Soros, "The Worst Market Crisis in 60 Years," *Financial Times,* January 23, 2008, p. 9, http://www.ft.com/cms/s/0/1a7af090-c956-11dc-9807-000077b07658.html

111. Martin Wolf, "Why the Financial Turmoil Is an Elephant in a Dark Room," *Financial Times,* January 23, 2008, p. 9, http://www.ft.com/cms/s/0/11a6145e-c956-11dc-9807-000077b07658.html

112. Donald Cohen, "The Education of Alan Greenspan," *The Huffington Post,* October 31, 2008, http://www.alternet.org/workplace/105414/the_education_of_alan_greenspan/

113. See Justin Fox, *The Myth of the Rational Market,* Harper Business, 2009; Richard Thaler, "The Price Is Not Always Right and Markets Can Be Wrong," *Financial Times,* August 5, 2009, p. 7.

114. Editorial, "A Survival Plan for Capitalism," *Financial Times,* March 9, 2009, p. 8.

115. Eric Lipton, "Ex-Lenders Profit From Home Loans Gone Bad," *New York Times,* March 4, 2009, p. A1.

116. James R. Hagerty, "Marketing Into a Meltdown," *Wall Street Journal,* January 7, 2009, p. A11.

117. Ibid.

118. Quoting Michael Lewis, in Thomas L. Friedman, "All Fall Down," *New York Times,* November 26, 2008, p. A31.

119. Edward Luce, "Subprime Explosion: Who Isn't Guilty?"' *Financial Times,* May 6, 2009, p. 3.

120. James R. Hagerty, "Marketing Into a Meltdown," *Wall Street Journal,* January 7, 2009, p. A11.

121. Mallen Baker, "Financial Services: Will Banks Ever Treat Customers Fairly?" *Ethical Corporation,* April 1, 2008, http://www.ethicalcorp.com/content.asp?ContentID=5807

122. Ibid.

123. Karl Rove, "President Bush Tried to Rein in Fan and Fred," *Wall Street Journal,* January 8, 2009, p. A13.

124. Brian Gow, "Bank of America Works Out Countrywide Mortgages," *BusinessWeek,* February 19, 2009, http://www.businessweek.com/magazine/content/09_09/b4121022492701.htm

125. Karl Rove, "President Bush Tried to Rein in Fan and Fred," *Wall Street Journal,* January 8, 2009, p. A13.

126. Petter S. Goodman & Gretchen Morgenson, "Saying Yes to Anyone, WaMu Built Empire on Shaky Loans," *New York Times,* December 28, 2008, p. A1.

127. "Northern Rock To Be Nationalized," *BBC News,* February 17, 2008, http://news .bbc.co.uk/1/hi/business/7249575.stm

128. Chris Tighe, "Future Looks Brighter As The Rock Begins To Roll," *Financial Times, Special Report: Doing Business in North-East England,* February 27, 2009, p. 2.

129. Bill Baue, "CSRwire Reports Top Corporate Social Responsibility News of 2008," *CSRwire.com,* January 12, 2009, http://www.csrwire.com/press/press_release/22696-CSRwire-Reports-Top-Corporate-Social-Responsibility-News-of-2008

130. Mara Der Hovanesian, "Sex, Lies, and Mortgage Deals," *BusinessWeek,* November 24, 2008, p. 71.

131. Mark Goyder, "How We've Poisoned the Well of Wealth," *Financial Times,* February 15, 2009, http://www.ft.com/cms/s/da50a3ae-fa03-11dd-9daa-000077b07658.html

132. See *People v. Countrywide,* Los Angeles Superior Court case number LC081846. "Company Profile: Countrywide Financial (Subsidiary of Bank of America)," *Crocodyl.org,* http://www.crocodyl .org/wiki/countrywide_financial_subsidiary_of_bank_of_america

133. "Company Profile: Countrywide Financial (Subsidiary of Bank of America)," *Crocodyl.org,* http://www.crocodyl.org/wiki/countrywide_financial_subsidiary_of_bank_of_america

134. Marketplace, *National Public Radio,* January 16, 2009.

135. William Cohen, "The Tattered Strategy of the Banker of the Year," *Financial Times,* January 20, 2009, p. 13.

136. Saskia Scholtes, BofA Lays Countrywide Brand to Rest," *Financial Times,* April 27, 2009, p. 17.

137. Greg Farrell, "Mortgage Executives Charged by SEC," *Financial Times,* June 5, 2009, p. 1.

138. C. K. Prahalad & Allen Hammond, "Serving the World's Poor, Profitably," *Harvard Business Review,* September 2002, Vol. 80, No. 9, pp. 48–58.

139. A related term is *microfranchising*—"Microfranchising is an economic development tool currently being researched and tested at the BYU Center for Economic Self-Reliance. The impetus behind the idea is to provide sound business opportunities and services to the poor by introducing scaled-down business concepts found in successful franchise organizations." See "What Is MicroFranchising?" *Economic Self-Reliance Center, BYU,* http://marriottschool.byu.edu/selfreliance/microfranchise/

140. Rajesh Chhabara, "Microfinance—Banking on the Poor," *Ethical Corporation,* December 15, 2008: http://www.ethicalcorp.com/content.asp?ContentID=6263

141. Ibid.

142. Special Report, "Taking Tiny Loans to the Next Level," *BusinessWeek,* November 27, 2006, http://www.businessweek.com/magazine/content/06_48/b4011089.htm

143. "Microcredit Is Becoming Profitable, Which Means New Players and New Problems," *Knowledge@Wharton,* April 20, 2005, http://knowledge.wharton.upenn.edu/article/1177.cfm

144. Vikas Bajaj, "Out to Maximize Social Gains, Not Profit," *New York Times,* December 9, 2006, p. A4, http://www.nytimes.com/2006/12/09/business/worldbusiness/09yunus.html

145. Jo Johnson, "Tea With the FT: Muhammad Yunus," *Financial Times,* December 8, 2006, p. W3, http://www.ft.com/cms/8b54bcd4-85c7-11db-86d5-0000779e2340.html

146. Pete Engardio, "A Way to Help Africa Help Itself," *BusinessWeek,* July 21, 2003, p. 40.

147. Ibid.

148. http://www.yearofmicrocredit.org/

149. See a text and video of Yunus's acceptance Nobel Lecture at http://nobelprize.org/nobel_prizes/peace/laureates/2006/yunus-lecture.html

150. http://www.ftconferences.com/sustainablebanking/

151. Eric Bellman, "Entrepreneur Gets Big Banks to Back Very Small Loans," *Wall Street Journal,* May 15, 2006, p. A1.

152. http://www.accion.org/

153. William Baue, "ACCION Creates Self-Sufficiency by Providing Microfinance to Microenterprises," *SocialFunds.com,* July 24, 2003, http://www.socialfunds.com/news/article.cgi/1181.html

154. http://www.fastcompany.com/social/2006/statements/accion.html

155. Eric Bellman, "Entrepreneur Gets Big Banks to Back Very Small Loans," *Wall Street Journal,* May 15, 2006, p. A1.

156. William Baue, "ACCION Creates Self-Sufficiency by Providing Microfinance to Microenterprises," *SocialFunds.com,* July 24, 2003, http://www.socialfunds.com/news/article.cgi/1181.html

157. "Microcredit Is Becoming Profitable, Which Means New Players and New Problems," *Knowledge@Wharton,* April 20, 2005, http://knowledge.wharton.upenn.edu/article/1177.cfm

158. Rajesh Chhabara, "Microfinance—Banking on the Poor," *Ethical Corporation,* December 15, 2008: http://www.ethicalcorp.com/content.asp?ContentID=6263

159. March 2009, http://www.accion.org/Page.aspx?pid=492

160. "Community Investing Pays," http://www.socialfunds.com/news/article.cgi/article945.html

161. Larger banks and other financial institutions in the United States were introduced to the concept of extending loans to underserved communities via the Community Reinvestment Act of 1977. The Act was introduced to provide access to finance from private lending institutions for underprivileged borrowers and avoid the practice of "redlining," where large banks refused to serve particular geographic regions, largely "poor, and predominantly minority, urban areas." Robert E. Rubin & Michael Rubinger, "Don't Let Banks Turn Their Backs on the Poor," *New York Times,* December 4, 2004, p. A31.

162. Rona Fried & Marjorie Kelly, "Getting Started in Community Investing," *Business Ethics Magazine,* Summer 2003, pp. 21–22.

163. Ibid.

164. Emily Parker, "Subprime Lender," *Wall Street Journal,* March 1/2, 2008, p. A9.

165. Lee Gomes, "Silicon Valley Moguls Support Microlenders, Just Not in the U.S.," *Wall Street Journal,* December 6, 2006, p. B1.

166. Tim Harford, "Conflicts of Interest," *Financial Times,* Life & Arts, December 6/7, 2008, pp. 1–2.

167. Rachel Emma Silverman, "A New Way to Do Well by Doing Good," *Wall Street Journal,* January 5, 2006, p. D1.

168. See Fergal Byrne, "Matters of Faith, Hope and Charity," *Financial Times,* March 25/26, 2006, p. W3; Catherine Holahan, "Ebay: The Place for Microfinance," *BusinessWeek,* October 24, 2007, http://www.businessweek.com/technology/content/oct2007/tc20071023_930086.htm

169. David Wighton, "Citigroup Plans to Fund Microfinance Programme," *Financial Times,* September 22, 2006, p. 18.

170. Rajesh Chhabara, "Microfinance—Banking on the poor," *Ethical Corporation,* December 15, 2008, http://www.ethicalcorp.com/content.asp?ContentID=6263

171. Cris Prystay, "With Loans, Poor South Asian Women Turn Entrepreneurial," *Wall Street Journal,* May 25, 2005, p. B1.

172. "Sup-par But Not Subprime," *The Economist,* March 31, 2009, p. 82.

173. Ross Tieman, "Mobile Phone Operators Revolutionise Cash Transfers," *Financial Times,* June 3, 2008, p. 14.

174. Richard Lapper, "A Call to South Africa's Masses," *Financial Times,* January 7, 2009, p. 10.

175. Ross Tieman, "Mobile Phone Operators Revolutionise Cash Transfers," *Financial Times,* June 3, 2008, p. 14.

176. "Calling an End to Poverty," *The Economist,* July 9, 2005, p. 51.

177. David Wighton, "Citigroup Plans to Fund Microfinance Programme," *Financial Times,* September 22, 2006, p. 18.

178. Jonathan Wheatley, "Small Is Beautiful for Latin America's Pioneers," *Financial Times,* February 27, 2009, p. 18.

179. Ketaki Gokhale, "A Global Surge in Tiny Loans Spurs Credit Bubble in a Slum," *Wall Street Journal,* August 13, 2009, p. A1, http://online.wsj.com/article/SB125012112518027581.html

180. See also Clive Cookson, "Barnevik Lends a Hand," *Financial Times,* May 31, 2007, p. 12.

181. William Baue, "Community Investing Pays," October 10, 2002, http://www.socialfunds.com/news/article.cgi/article945.html

182. Kris Axtman & Ron Scherer, "Enron Lapses and Corporate Ethics," *Christian Science Monitor,* February 4, 2002, http://www.csmonitor.com/2002/0204/p01s01-ussc.html

183. Patti Waldmeir, "Supreme Court Tackles US Patent Pandemic LEGAL COUNSEL," *Financial Times,* November 16, 2006, p. 8, http://www.ft.com/cms/s/bdbdf770-74bb-11db-bc76-0000779e2340.html

184. Henry I. Miller, "Bookshelf: Fighting Disease Is Only Half the Battle," *Wall Street Journal,* August 25, 2004, p. D10.

185. Ibid.

186. Editorial, "Pre-empting Drug Innovation," *Wall Street Journal,* March 5, 2009, p. A16.

187. An interesting proposal to provide "Advance Market Commitments" for firms that develop medication for specific diseases (by, for example, guaranteeing that governmental and international agencies would buy a specific number of vaccines once developed) was discussed at the 2006 G8 summit in St. Petersburg, Russia. See Harvey Bale & Christopher Earl, "A Market Remedy That Can Bring Vaccines to the Poor," *Financial Times,* July 3, 2006, p. 17; Michael M. Phillips, "Politics & Economics: Global Vaccine Initiative Hits Snag U.S.-French Discord Hinders Plan to Give Drug Makers Incentive to Focus on Poor Countries," *Wall Street Journal,* July 7, 2006, p. A5.

188. Rikki Stancich, "EU Generic Drugs Exports Plan Raises Health-Risk and Market Concerns," *Ethical Corporation,* November 2, 2004, http://www.ethicalcorp.com/content.asp?ContentID=3091

189. Paul Gilding, "Making Market Magic," *Ecos Corporation Newsletter,* June 2001.

190. Editorial, "For the World's Poor," *Miami Herald,* August 11, 2003, p. 6B.

191. The United States is "home to 70 percent of all pharmaceutical research." In Editorial, "For the World's Poor," *Miami Herald,* August 11, 2003, p. 6B.

192. Ibid.

193. An agreement was delayed for 2 days by final haggling from the pharmaceutical industry, during which time African delegations noted "that 8,480 more people had died in Africa of HIV/AIDS and other diseases." Naomi Koppel, "Poor Countries Can Now Buy Generic Drugs," *Miami Herald,* August 31, 2003, p. 13A.

194. An additional issue is drugs that are produced in the West and exported only to developing countries, either because they have failed to secure regulatory approval in the West or because they were specifically designed for weaker regulatory environments: "An analysis published [in 2005] by Kenya's Medical Research Institute showed that more than 40 per cent of the most common anti-malaria drugs on sale in the country were sub-standard." Andrew Jack, "'Poor Drugs' Start to Come Under the European Microscope," *Financial Times,* September 26, 2006, p.15.

195. Ronald W. Buzzeo, "Counterfeit Pharmaceuticals and the Public Health," *Wall Street Journal,* October 4, 2005, p. A20.

196. Daniel Vasella, CEO of Novartis, quoted in John Gapper, "The Hidden Cost of Free Vaccines," *Financial Times,* June 18, 2009, p. 11.

197. Editorial, "For the World's Poor," *Miami Herald,* August 11, 2003, p. 6B.

198. John Russell, "Getting to Grips With HIV," *Ethical Corporation Magazine,* January 2006, p. 40.

199. Andrew Jack, "The Man Who Battled Big Pharma," *Financial Times,* March 29, 2008, p. 14, http://us.ft.com/ftgateway/superpage.ft?news_id=fto032820081826526065

200. Catherine Arnst, "Why Business Should Make AIDS Its Business," *BusinessWeek,* August 2, 2004, p. 78.

201. Silvia Sansoni, "Keeping Alive," *Forbes,* February 3, 2003, pp. 64–66.

202. Ibid.

203. Catherine Arnst, "Why Business Should Make AIDS Its Business," *BusinessWeek,* August 2, 2004, p. 78.

204. Richard Holbrooke & Mark Moody-Stuart, "Business Has a Vital Role to Play in Fighting AIDS," *Financial Times,* May 22, 2006, p. 15.

205. Alec Russell, "Answers to an AIDS Epidemic," *Financial Times,* October 4, 2007, p. 10.

206. "Making the Small Count," *The Economist,* July 23, 2005, p. 60.

207. Alec Russell, "Answers to an AIDS Epidemic," *Financial Times,* October 4, 2007, p. 10.

208. John Russell, "Getting to Grips With HIV," *Ethical Corporation Magazine,* January 2006, p. 40.

209. Naomi Koppel, "Poor Countries Can Now Buy Generic Drugs," *Miami Herald,* August 31, 2003, p. 13A.

210. http://hivaidsphilanthropy.pfizer.com/

211. "Firm Drops Drug Prices for AIDS in Poor Lands," *Miami Herald,* April 29, 2003, p. 14A.

212. John Dorschner, "Stage Is Set for a Struggle Over Generics," *Miami Herald,* November 9, 2004, pp. 1E & 2E.

213. Ibid.

214. It is interesting that food companies do not face the same pressures to distribute food to the hungry of the world!

215. Sarah Boseley, "Investors Urge Drug Firms to Do More for World's Poor," *The Guardian,* September 20, 2004, p. 6.

216. Andrew Jack, "A New Mood of Co-operation," *Financial Times,* December 1, 2006, p. 3, http://www.ft.com/cms/s/0bf3d478-7aed-11db-bf9b-0000779e2340.html. This article appeared in a special supplement of the *Financial Times* that was published in conjunction with World AIDS Day at the end of November.

217. Mienke Retief, "Generic Drugs—Licence to Cure," *Ethical Corporation,* December 1, 2008, http://www.ethicalcorp.com/content.asp?ContentID=6228

218. Leila Abboud, "Branded Drugs Settling More Generic Suits," *Wall Street Journal,* January 17, 2006, p. B1.

219. Andrew Jack, "A New Mood of Co-Operation," *Financial Times,* December 1, 2006, p. 3, http://www.ft.com/cms/s/0bf3d478-7aed-11db-bf9b-0000779e2340.html. This article appeared in a special supplement of the *Financial times* that was published in conjunction with World AIDS Day at the end of November.

220. "GlaxoSmithKline—A Shake-up for Big Pharma," *Ethical Corporation,* April 2, 2009, http://www.ethicalcorp.com/content.asp?contentid=6414

221. Natasha Singer, "Glaxo and Pfizer Join Forces to Develop HIV Drugs," *New York Times,* April 17, 2009, p. B3; Andrew Jack, "GSK and Pfizer Pool Resources for New Strategy on HIV Drugs," *Financial Times,* April 17, 2009, p. 1.

222. Oliver Balch, "How GSK's Access to Medicine Plans Will Shake Up Big Pharma," *Ethical Corporation,* March 31, 2009, http://www.ethicalcorp.com/content.asp?contentid=6408

223. Sarah Boseley, "Drug Firm Blocks Cheap Blindness Cure," *The Guardian,* June 17, 2006, http://www.guardian.co.uk/medicine/story/0,,1799772,00.html

224. Andrew Jack & Jo Johnson, "HIV/AIDS Victims in India Protest Over Drug Patent," *Financial Times*, May 11, 2006, p. 4.

225. "Got a Match?" *The Economist*, November 27, 2004, p. 64.

226. Roger Bate, "The Companies Everyone Loves to Hate," *Wall Street Journal*, September 16, 2005, p. W13.

227. John J. Miller, "*The Jungle*: Purveyor of Pessimism," *Wall Street Journal*, February 23, 2006, p. D8.

228. John Carey, "The Hundred Years' War at the FDA," *BusinessWeek,* July 28, 2003, p. 20. Review of the book *Protecting America's Health: The FDA, Business, and One Hundred Years of Regulation,* by Philip J. Hilts, Knopf, 2003.

229. http://www.nestle.com/

230. S. Prakash Sethi, "A Conceptual Framework for Environmental Analysis of Social Issues and Evaluation of Business Response Patterns," *Academy of Management Review,* Vol. 4, No. 1, 1979, pp. 63–74.

231. Ibid.

232. Ibid.

233. The ICIFI has since been replaced by the Association of Infant Food Manufacturers (IFM).

234. http://www.maketradefair.com/

235. Ibid.

236. David Case, "Warning: This Bottle May Contain Toxic Chemicals. Or Not." *Fast Company Magazine*, February 2009, p. 92.

237. Jeremy Rifkin, "A Precautionary Tale," *The Guardian,* May 12, 2004, p. 23.

238. Patrick Lin, "A Small But Important Dimension to Corporate Responsibility," *Ethical Corporation Magazine*, June 2006, p. 43.

239. Lyndsey Layton, "Europe: Chemical Law Has Global Impact," *The Washington Post*, June 12, 2008, http://www.corpwatch.org/article.php?id=15092

240. Ibid.

241. David Case, "Warning: This Bottle May Contain Toxic Chemicals. Or Not." *Fast Company Magazine*, February, 2009, p. 99.

242. Ibid.

243. "The List: The Price of Safety," *BusinessWeek,* September 15, 2003, p. 12.

244. Ibid.

245. Jeremy Rifkin, "A Precautionary Tale," *The Guardian,* May 12, 2004, p. 23.

246. Editorial, "Incredibly Shrinking Europe," *Wall Street Journal,* April 28, 2005, p. A18.

247. Jeremy Rifkin, "A Precautionary Tale," *The Guardian,* May 12, 2004, p. 23.

248. "EU Chemicals Regulation Workable, Study Says," *Wall Street Journal,* April 27, 2005, p. A12.

249. Mary Jacoby, "Companies Brace for EU Chemical Curbs," *Wall Street Journal*, December 13, 2006, p. A4.

250. Lyndsey Layton, "Europe: Chemical Law Has Global Impact," *Washington Post*, June 12, 2008, http://www.corpwatch.org/article.php?id=15092

251. Ibid.

252. Ibid.

253. David Case, "Warning: This Bottle May Contain Toxic Chemicals. Or Not." *Fast Company Magazine*, February 2009, p. 99.

254. Jenny Wiggins, "EC Prioritises Safety in Wake of Food Scares," *Financial Times*, August 3, 2006, p. 18.

255. David Barboza, "Development of Biotech Crops Is Booming in Asia," *The New York Times,* February 21, 2003, p. A3.

256. Frederic Golden, "Who's Afraid of Frankenfood?" Time, November 21, 1999, http://www.time.com/time/magazine/article/0,9171,34817,00.html

257. Julie Forster, "GM Foods: Why Fight Labeling?" *BusinessWeek,* November 11, 2002, p. 44.

258. Ibid.

259. "Oregon Rejects GM Food Labeling Initiative," *Food & Drink Weekly,* November 11, 2002, http://www.findarticles.com/p/articles/mi_m0EUY/is_43_8/ai_94461771

260. Scott Miller & Juliane von Reppert-Bismarck, "EU Seeks to Toughen Reviews of Genetically Modified Foods," *Wall Street Journal*, April 13, 2006, p. A10.

261. Paul Gilding, "Making Market Magic," Ecos Corporation Web site, June 2001.

262. Andrew Pollack, "Planting of Modified Crops Rose in 2002," *New York Times,* January 16, 2003, p. C6.

263. "Genetically Modified Food Items Are Common, but Little Noticed," *Wall Street Journal,* March 24, 2005, p. D4.

264. Javier Blas, "Warning of 'Food Crunch' With Prices Poised to Rise," *Financial Times*, January 26, 2009, p. 3.

265. Felicity Lawrence, "Flab Grab," *The Guardian*, September 15, 2007, http://www.guardian.co.uk/books/2007/sep/15/healthmindandbody.health

266. Mark Bittman, "Rethinking the Meat-Guzzler," *New York Times*, January 27, 2008, p. WK1.

267. Dan Barber, "Food Without Fear," *New York Times*, November 23, 2004, p. A27.

268. Pallavi Gogoi, "Wal-Mart's Organic Offensive," *BusinessWeek*, March 29, 2006, http://www.businessweek.com/bwdaily/dnflash/mar2006/nf20060329_6971.htm; Melanie Warner, "Wal-Mart Is Going Organic, and Brand Names Get in Line," *New York Times*, May 12, 2006, p. A1.

269. William Saffire, "Locavorism," *New York Times Magazine*, October 12, 2008, p. 18.

270. Michael Pollan, "Mass Natural," *New York Times*, June 4, 2006, p. 15.

271. Caroline Stacey, "Food Miles," *BBC online*, http://www.bbc.co.uk/food/food_matters/foodmiles.shtml

272. Sarah Murray, "Something to Chew Over," *Financial Times*, September 9/10, 2006, p. W7.

273. Brian Hindo, "Monsanto: Winning the Ground War," *BusinessWeek*, December 7, 2007, http://newsletters.businessweek.com/c.asp?685460&c55a2ee820194f0f&3

274. Ibid.

275. Mark Bittman, "Why Take Food Seriously? Because Your Life Depends on It," *New York Times Magazine*, October 12, 2008, p. 14, http://www.nytimes.com/2008/10/12/magazine/12wwln-lede-t.html

276. Monsanto was a manufacturer of Agent Orange, the "defoliant used by the US in the Vietnam war that caused thousands of deaths and disabilities." In Hal Weitzman, "Prepared to Wait for a Bigger Yield," *Financial Times*, June 15, 2009, p. 12.

277. Hal Weitzman, "Ambitious Plan Built on Hard Targets to Drive the Bottom Line," *Financial Times*, June 15, 2009, p. 12.

278. Charles Handy, "What's a Business For?" *Harvard Business Review*, Vol. 80, No. 12, December 2002, p. 55.

279. David Foster, "Intel's Amazon Ambitions," *Fast Company Magazine*, February 2008, p. 86, http://www.fastcompany.com/magazine/122/intels-amazon-ambitions.html

280. Chris Giles, "Half the World's Assets Held by 2% of Population," *Financial Times*, December 6, 2006, p. 6.

281. C. K. Prahalad & Allen Hammond, "Serving the World's Poor, Profitably," *Harvard Business Review,* Vol. 80, No. 9, September 2002, pp. 48–58.

282. Cait Murphy, "The Hunt for Globalization That Works," *Fortune,* October 28, 2002, p. 164.

283. David Ignatius, "World's Poor Represent Huge Potential Market," *Washington Post*, in *The Daily Yomiuri*, July 7, 2005, p. 11.

284. "Face Value: Profits and Poverty," *The Economist,* August 21, 2004, p. 54.

285. C. K. Prahalad & Allen Hammond, "Serving the World's Poor, Profitably," *Harvard Business Review,* Vol. 80, No. 9, September 2002, pp. 48–58.

286. Cait Murphy, "The Hunt for Globalization That Works," *Fortune,* October 28, 2002, p. 164.

287. For HP's e-Inclusion announcement, see http://www.hp.com/hpinfo/newsroom/press/2000/001012a.html. Note: "HP launched its e-inclusion initiative in 2000 and fulfilled its e-inclusion commitments in 2006, but we are still supporting many of the projects that evolved from this initiative" (http://h41111.www4.hp.com/globalcitizenship/uk/en/e-inclusion/project/index.html).

288. E-Inclusion "aims to deliver computer and Internet technology to the world's 4 billion poor people through sustainable microenterprises." *Fortune* writer David Kirkpatrick called e-Inclusion "the most visionary step I've ever seen a large tech company take." Marc Gunther, "Can One Person Change a Major Corporation," *Business Ethics Magazine,* Winter 2004, pp. 10–12.

289. C. K. Prahalad & Allen Hammond, "Serving the World's Poor, Profitably," *Harvard Business Review,* Vol. 80, No. 9, September 2002, pp. 48–58.

290. Cait Murphy, "The Hunt for Globalization That Works," *Fortune,* October 28, 2002, p. 164.

291. C. K. Prahalad outlines his work and ideas in this area in a *Wall Street Journal* article: "Aid Is Not the Answer," August 31, 2005, p. A8, and in his book: *The Fortune at the Bottom of the Pyramid: Eradicating Poverty Through Profits,* Wharton School Publishing, 2004.

292. C. K. Prahalad, quoted in "Face Value: Profits and Poverty," *The Economist,* August 21, 2004, p. 54.

293. C. K. Prahalad & Allen Hammond, "Serving the World's Poor, Profitably," *Harvard Business Review,* Vol. 80, No. 9, September 2002, pp. 48–58.

294. See "Will Corporations Really Help the World's Poor?" *Lifeworth* Press Release, *CSRwire.com,* January 31, 2005, http://www.csrwire.com/News/3483.html; Mallen Baker, "Is There REALLY a Fortune at the Bottom of the Pyramid," *Ethical Corporation,* September 3, 2006, http://www.ethicalcorp.com/content.asp?ContentID=4458

295. "2004 Lifeworth Annual Review of Corporate Responsibility," *Lifeworth,* 2005, p. 2.

296. "Business Prophet," *BusinessWeek Special Report,* January 23, 2006, http://www.businessweek.com/magazine/content/06_04/b3968089.htm

297. Sarah Ellison & Eric Bellman, "Clean Water, No Profit," *Wall Street Journal,* February 23, 2005, p. B1; Ellen Byron, "P&G Has Big Plans for the Shelves of Tiny Stores in Emerging Nations," *Wall Street Journal,* July 17, 2007, p. 16.

298. Jonathan Wheatley & Jenny Wiggins, 'Little by Little Nestlé Aims to Woo Brazil's Poor," *Financial Times,* February 20, 2007, p. 6.

299. Barney Jopson, "Unilever Looks to Clean up in Africa," *Financial Times,* November 15, 2007, p. 18.

300. Mark Jewell, "Laptop Project: A Leg up for Third World," *Miami Herald,* April 4, 2005, p. 5A.

301. A similar project is B24B (Business 2 the 4 Billion, http://www.cra.org/Activities/grand.challenges/slides/b24b.pdf), which was initiated by Thomas Kalil (President Bill Clinton's deputy assistant for science and technology) and presented to the Computing Research Association (CRA) on June 25, 2002. "Grand Challenge: Provide affordable, useful digital services to the 4 billion people on the planet earning less than $1,500."

302. Mark Jewell, "Laptop Project: A Leg up for Third World," *Miami Herald,* April 4, 2005, p. 5A.

303. Steve Stecklow, "The $100 Laptop Moves Closer to Reality," *Wall Street Journal,* November 14, 2005, p. B1.

304. Ibid.

305. Ibid.

306. Joe Nocera, "Computer CARE Packages," *New York Times,* April 29, 2006, p. B1.

307. Hal R. Varian, "A Plug for the Unplugged $100 Laptop Computer for Developing Nations," *New York Times,* February 9, 2006, p. C3.

308. Joe Nocera, "Computer CARE Packages," *New York Times,* April 29, 2006, p. B1.

309. Kathrin Hille, "The Race for the $100 Laptop," *Financial Times,* April 9, 2007, p. 6.

310. Steve Hamm, "The Face of the $100 Laptop," *BusinessWeek,* March 1, 2007, http://www.businessweek.com/innovate/content/mar2007/id20070301_063165.htm

311. David Pogue, "$100 Laptop a Bargain at $200," *New York Times*, October 4, 2007, p. C1.

312. Ibid.

313. Ibid.

314. John Markoff, "Intel Quits Effort to Get Computers to Children," *New York Times*, January 5, 2008, p. A3, http://www.nytimes.com/2008/01/05/technology/05laptop.html

315. James Lamont, "India Plans a $20 Laptop to Meet Education Challenge," *Financial Times*, February 2, 2009, p. 1.

316. See "New WRI Blog Launches With Sights on 'Next Billion' Consumers Dollars," May, 2005, http://archive.wri.org/news.cfm?id=328

317. Timothy Ogden, "Computer Error?" *Miller-McCune*, September–October, 2009, pp. 12–15, http://www.miller-mccune.com/business_economics/computer-error-1390

318. Jathon Sapsford & Norihiko Shirouzu, "Mom, Apple Pie and . . . Toyota?" *Wall Street Journal*, May 11, 2006, p. B1.

319. Glenn Hubbard, "Offshoring Can Benefit Workers of All Skill Levels," *Financial Times*, September 28, 2006, p. 19.

320. Jo Johnson, "India Extends Prohibitions on Employing Children," *Financial Times*, August 3, 2006, p. 4.

321. See: Andrea Tunarosa, "What Do NGOs Have Against Poor Guatemalans?" *Wall Street Journal*, July 21, 2006, p. A15; Glenn Hubbard, 'Offshoring Can Benefit Workers of All Skill Levels," *Financial Times*, September 28, 2006, p. 19.

322. See Sam Chambers, "China's Factories—Exploitation Ain't What It Used to Be," *Ethical Corporation*, August 30, 2006, http://www.ethicalcorp.com/content.asp?ContentID=4458; "Secrets, Lies, and Sweatshops," *BusinessWeek*, Cover Story, November 27, 2006, http://www.businessweek.com/magazine/content/06_48/b4011001.htm; Richard McGregor, 'We Must Count the True Cost of Cheap China," *Financial Times*, August 2, 2007, p. 7.

323. Tracey Taylor, "A Label of Pride That Pays," *New York Times*, April 23, 2009, p. B4.

324. Clare Ansberry, "Laid-Off Factory Workers Find Jobs Are Drying Up for Good," *Wall Street Journal*, July 21, 2003, pp. A1 & A8.

325. "Outsourcing Abroad," *Wall Street Journal*, July 14, 2003, p. A2.

326. Dale Neef, "Supply Chain Ethics: The Devil Is in the Details," *Ethical Corporation*, April 14, 2005, http://www.ethicalcorp.com/content.asp?ContentID=3629

327. For example, see: Kris Hudson & Wilawan Watcharasakwet, "The New Wal-Mart Effect: Cleaner Thai Shrimp Farms," *Wall Street Journal*, July 24, 2007, p. B1.

328. "Moral Maze for Retailers Reliant on Developing World Suppliers," *Financial Times*, July 2, 2008, p. 16, http://www.ft.com/cms/s/0/f5771c20-47d0-11dd-93ca-000077b07658.html

329. For example, see the controversy that surrounds the use of forced child labor in the harvesting of cotton: Toby Webb, "Special Report Cotton: Corporate Action on Uzbeki White Gold," *Ethical Corporation*, March 6, 2008, http://www.ethicalcorp.com/content.asp?ContentID=5760

330. Nicholas D. Kristof, "In Praise of the Maligned Sweatshop," *New York Times*, June 6, 2006, p. A21.

331. Nicholas D. Kristof, "Where Sweatshops Are a Dream," *New York Times*, January 15, 2009, p. A27.

332. Andrea Tunarosa, "What Do NGOs Have Against Poor Guatemalans?" *Wall Street Journal*, July 21, 2006, p. A15.

333. Roger Martin, "The Virtue Matrix," *Harvard Business Review,* Vol. 80, No. 3, March 2002, pp. 68–75.

334. Paul Gilding, "Making Market Magic," Ecos Corporation Web site, June 2001.

335. Dan Le Batard, "Michael Jordan's Asian Tour: Selling His Name, Not His Game," *Miami Herald,* June 29, 2004, p.1D.

336. *Nike, Inc. v. Kasky* (02–575, Supreme Court of the United States), 123 S. Ct. 817; 154 L. Ed. 2d 767; 2003 U.S. LEXIS 556; 71 U.S.L.W. 3470; 2003 Daily Journal DAR 403, January 10, 2003, Decided.

337. Bob Herbert, "In America: Nike's Boot Camps," *New York Times,* March 31, 1997, p. A15.

338. Ibid.

339. Ibid.

340. Philip H. Knight, "Letter to the Editor: Nike Pays Good Wages to Foreign Workers," *New York Times,* June 21, 1996, p. A26.

341. Peter Clarke, "California Supreme Court Decision Potentially Devastating for Corporate Responsibility Reporting and SRI Funds Worldwide," *Ethical Corporation,* October 17, 2002, http://www.ethicalcorp.com/content.asp?ContentID=242

342. Linda Greenhouse, "Supreme Court to Review Nike `Free Speech' Case," *New York Times,* January 11, 2003, pp. A1 & A12.

343. As a result of the case, "Nike has decided not to issue its corporate responsibility report externally for its fiscal year 2002 and will continue to limit its participation in public events and media engagement in California." Nikebiz Press Release, September 12, 2003.

344. Linda Greenhouse, "Supreme Court to Review Nike `Free Speech' Case," *New York Times,* January 11, 2003, pp. A1 & A12.

345. Nikebiz Press Release, "Nike, Inc. and Kasky Announce Settlement of Kasky v. Nike First Amendment Case," September 12, 2003.

346. William McCall, "Nike Settles Speech Lawsuit," *Miami Herald,* September 13, 2003, p. C1.

347. Mallen Baker, "Nike and Short-Sighted Victories in Free Speech," *Ethical Corporation,* November 13, 2002, http://www.ethicalcorp.com/content.asp?ContentID=261

348. Nicholas Stein, "Labor Trade: No Way Out," *Fortune,* January 8, 2003, http://www.nickstein.com/articles/no-way-out/

349. Jonathan Birchall, "Nike to Strengthen Efforts to Combat Worker Abuse," *Financial Times,* 31 May 2007, p. 9, http://www.ft.com/cms/s/59cf226e-0f13-11dc-b444-000b5df10621.html

350. Ibid.

351. See also Nicholas Casey, "New Nike Sneaker Targets Jocks, Greens, Wall Street," *Wall Street Journal,* February 15, 2008, p. B1, http://online.wsj.com/article/SB120303911940170393.html

352. Jonathan Birchall, "Nike to Strengthen Efforts to Combat Worker Abuse," *Financial Times,* 31 May 2007, p. 9, http://www.ft.com/cms/s/59cf226e-0f13-11dc-b444-000b5df10621.html

353. Amelia Gentleman, "Gap Vows to Combat Child Labor at Suppliers," *New York Times,* November 16, 2007, p. A6, http://www.nytimes.com/2007/11/16/business/worldbusiness/16gap.html

354. James Hyatt, "China Checkup," *CRO Magazine,* May 2008, http://thecro.com/node/672

355. Stephanie Kang, "Nike Cuts Ties With Pakistani Firm," *Wall Street Journal,* November 21, 2006, p. B5.

356. Christian Barry & Sanjay Reddy, "The False Dilemma of the Sweatshop," *Financial Times,* July 25, 2006, p. 13.

357. Peter Davis, "Supply Chain Hot Air," *Ethical Corporation,* March 16, 2005, http://www.ethicalcorp.com/content.asp?ContentID=3561

358. Alan Beattie, "Ethical Rules Impose Perverse Incentives," *Financial Times, Special Report: India and Globalization,* January 30, 2009, p. 2.

359. Sam Chambers, "China's Factories—Exploitation Ain't What It Used to Be," *Ethical Corporation,* August 30, 2006, http://www.ethicalcorp.com/content.asp?ContentID=4458

CHAPTER 8

Societal Issues and Case Studies

ACCOUNTABILITY

CSR CONNECTION: This issue tackles the problem of how best to measure CSR. It emphasizes the growing importance of accountability and transparency in a firm's relations with its various stakeholders, demonstrated by the increasingly common auditing and reporting of CSR performance.

Issue

Do you think of CSR in terms of a dichotomy (i.e., a firm is either socially responsible or not)? Or do you think of CSR in terms of a continuum (i.e., all firms are either more or less socially responsible, depending on a number of factors and the context in which they occur)? If it is the former, then CSR is relatively easy to measure, and there are plenty of options out there that claim to measure the CSR profile of firms. If it is the latter, however, then CSR is very difficult even to conceptualize fully (with many dimensions), let alone measure accurately.

In general, dichotomous measures of CSR are unhelpful to those who advocate for greater CSR for two reasons: First, because they contain the biases of the measuring organization (e.g., excluding specific industries, such as tobacco or firearms); and, second, because CSR is more complicated than a simple *yes* or *no*. All firms contain *good* and *bad;* the value is in being able to capture accurately the *net effect*—On balance, is a firm better or worse than other firms? The difficulty is equating these effects across the spectrum of different firm activities. As a result, any attempt to use dichotomous ratings to measure a causal relationship between CSR and overall firm performance (the underlying foundation of a business argument for CSR) is unlikely to generate reliable or valid results. The importance of thinking of CSR as a continuum, rather than a dichotomy, therefore, is essential for those who study CSR and seek to evaluate firms in this respect.

Once CSR is thought of in terms of a continuum, what is the best way to measure CSR? Is a tobacco firm that employs tens of thousands of people and pays significant taxes a *better* or *worse* firm (in terms of CSR performance) than a supermarket that sells food but pays its employees low wages? Is a firearms manufacturer, whose products are used to defend national security, *better* or *worse* than a pharmaceutical firm that produces life-saving drugs but refuses to make them affordable in developing countries? In adding up the *good* and the *bad,* it is firms that have a *net positive value added* that are effectively incorporating social responsibility into everyday operations. Capturing all of the different metrics in a way that is objective and makes them comparable across firms and industries, however, is incredibly complex. Given this, how can a company be held accountable for its CSR actions in a way that is objectively measurable, yet financially feasible? A *CSR report* by a firm provides some answers. A *CSR audit,* containing objective standards developed by an independent third party, provides much more information.

The evolution of environmental reporting from its beginnings in the 1970s and 1980s offers a model for CSR reports and audits. Today, an environmental report is increasingly considered a vital component of an organization's comprehensive annual report:

> Sony was . . . one of the first Japanese firms to take environmental issues seriously, setting up its Environmental Conservation Committee in 1990. It produces an in-house newsletter on environmental issues in both Japanese and English, as well as environmental reports for wider distributions, also in both languages. . . . Sony pays a great deal of attention to its environmental profile, producing separate environmental reports for each of its plants and setting up the Sony Eco Plaza at the entrance to its head office.[1]

CSR reports are also increasingly recognized as an important tool for firms to communicate with stakeholders. Important developments in this area include: Gap's 2003 Social Responsibility report, which disclosed vendor violations of the firm's Code of Conduct; Nike's 2004 Corporate Responsibility report, which identified its complete list of worldwide supplier factories; Timberland's 2006 *Our Footprint* labeling scheme, which clearly listed the environmental and social impact of the production process for each of its products; Stoneyfield Farm's 2008 partnership with Climate Counts to measure carbon emissions; and Patagonia's 2009 *Footprint Chronicles,* which combines elements of all of the above:[2]

> Auditing firm KPMG reported a 30 percent jump from 2005 to 2008 in the percentage of large companies generating CSR reports; four out of five (79%) of the world's largest companies now provide this information in a publicly available form.[3]

The benefit of transparency and honesty in all aspects of an organization's operations is that it allows external observers to evaluate the organization, its managers, and policies more effectively. The reporting of a corporation's activities in a misleading way, however, can have a negative impact on the perception of that organization among external stakeholders. Although CSR reporting has come a long way in recent years, it still suffers from the potential for *greenwashing* and the lack of authenticity that only an independent audit can provide.

As a result, CSR auditing is evolving rapidly. The field is moving beyond the foundation of the triple bottom line (which measures firm performance on various financial, environmental, and social metrics)[4] into the search for detailed, objective standards that allow stakeholders to compare different firms in different industries. In addition to presenting a more complete CSR perspective of a company's operations, establishing these standards represents an essential component for those seeking a holistic assessment of business risk:

"We are not social activists; we're independent risk assessors," says George Dallas of S&P. The information in non-financial reports "contributes to building up a company's risk profile." And although it has still not been convincingly demonstrated that good environmental and social practices create value for shareholders, it is clear, says Mr. Dallas, that bad ones can destroy it.[5]

Case Study	ISO 26000

Over the last two decades, a variety of CSR audit organizations have emerged to help develop more transparent relations among firms and their stakeholders via CSR reports and audits.

Global Reporting Initiative (http://www.globalreporting.org/) is the leading light in the field. Launched in 1997, GRI works with the United Nations to realize its vision "that disclosure on economic, environmental, and social performance is as commonplace and comparable as financial reporting, and important to organizational success."[6]

Since its inception, the GRI has become a worldwide, multi-stakeholder network which includes representatives from business, civil society, labour, investors, accountants and others. Revisions to the framework take place through an exhaustive set of committees and subcommittees, [which, GRI claims, ensures] the credibility and trust needed to make a global framework successful.[7]

GovernanceMetrics International (http://www.gmiratings.com/), formed in 2000, claims on its Web site to be "the world's first global corporate governance ratings agency."[8] GMI compiles its reports, which focus on corporate governance and transparency, by rating over 4,000 companies worldwide:

Our premise is straightforward: companies that emphasize corporate governance and transparency will, over time, generate superior returns and economic performance and lower their cost of capital. The opposite is also true: companies weak in corporate governance and transparency represent increased investment risks and result in a higher cost of capital.[9]

AccountAbility (http://www.accountability21.net/), a British organization founded in 1995, has been at the forefront of the push to establish a credible objective means by which the CSR performance of companies can be evaluated. In March 2003, the organization launched its assurance standard:

The AA1000 Assurance Standard is the world's first assurance standard developed to ensure the credibility and quality of reporting on social, environmental and economic performance.[10]

Social Accountability International (http://www.sa-intl.org/), founded in 1997, is another organization that has done pioneering work in this area. SAI was one of the eight founding members of the auditing and accreditation alliance ISEAL (International Social and Environmental Accreditation and Labeling). ISEAL is

(Continued)

(Continued)

important because of the international scope the organization's different members lend to the project and shows the willingness among accreditation organizations to move toward a set of internationally recognized standards:

> Social Accountability 8000 (SA8000) has been developed by SAI. . . . SA8000 is promoted as a voluntary, universal standard for companies interested in auditing and certifying labour practices in their facilities and those of their suppliers and vendors. It is designed for independent third party certification.[11]

Verité (http://www.verite.org/), founded in 1995, is also a major influence in the social auditing field as a nonprofit organization that works with firms, through factory inspections, to improve the working conditions throughout the supply chain:

> Verité works to empower companies, factories, NGOs, governments, and workers to create sustainable practices in the facilities and communities where our consumer goods are made. Verité's client companies come from the apparel, footwear, electronics, agriculture, food and beverage, toy, extractive and retail sectors.[12]

The organization does this, as well as working with other organizations (such as the Center for Reflection, Education and Action, http://www.crea-inc.org/) to introduce processes that "facilitate the development of standards for the knowledge, skills, and competencies of social auditors."[13]

The Fair Labor Association (http://www .fairlabor.org/), founded in 1999, is taking the industry one step further by encouraging multinational organizations to allow their overseas factories to be audited by FLA auditors. Significantly, the FLA pushes to allow the final reports to be made public, something often resisted by corporations in the past. This occurred for the first time in June 2003. In describing its work, the organization claims:

> The FLA [is] a unique multi-stakeholder initiative to end sweatshop labor and improve working conditions in factories worldwide. The FLA holds its participants—those involved in the manufacturing and marketing process—accountable to the FLA Workplace Code of Conduct.[14]

While allowing these companies to take the moral high ground in the sweatshop debate, this move by the FLA also places a great deal of pressure on other brands (which have been the subject of unwanted NGO attention in the past) to submit their factory operations to the same level of public scrutiny. In addition, the FLA reports are deemed to be genuine, simply because the depressing operating practices they reveal are still being continued in these factories. They note the steps companies are taking to attempt to redress the negative practices that still exist. This, as well as the reports themselves, offers a benchmark by which all companies can be measured moving forward.

As the field develops, new tools are constantly being introduced to help observers evaluate different firms' operations from a CSR perspective. In November 2004, SustainAbility, an independent think tank, strategy consultancy, and expert in corporate responsibility and sustainable development, released its sixth triple bottom line survey together with the UN Environment Program (UNEP) and, for the first time, Standard & Poor's ("the first time a credit-rating agency has been involved.")[15] In 2006, the British Standard BS 8900—Guidance for Managing Sustainable Development was released, emphasizing "stakeholder consultation" as central to the management of sustainability.[16] And, in January 2009, the Center for Sustainable Innovation (CSI) launched its *Corporate Water Gauge,* which allows a firm to compare its water use:

> to the carrying capacity of the local water supplies and the size of the population. . . . The Gauge complements CSI's Social Footprint and Global Warming Footprint, a suite of tools that similar[ly] measures an organization's social and environmental impacts compared to goals of sustainable impacts.[17]

One of the most important developments in recent years is the negotiation for a voluntary standard for CSR by the International Organization for Standardization (ISO). The consultation phase for the Corporate Social Responsibility standard, ISO 26000, was initiated in 2005, with the standard being "available for public use globally in 2010."[18] The standard is intended to act as a guide for *appropriate* behavior and will not be available as a certification process (unlike other ISO standards). In the process, however, the ISO 26000 Social Responsibility Working Group (SRWG) has become:

> the leading global multi-stakeholder forum for debate on what is meant by social responsibility and how it should be applied to organizations on a day-to-day basis.[19]

Additional detail about the ISO 26000 (which, in draft form, has grown to "80 pages, excluding annexes")[20] can be found at: http://www.iso.org/sr/.

Some commentators, while supporting ISO 26000, caution against it being held up as the gold standard of CSR behavior. They argue that CSR is not like *quality* or *environmental performance,* either of which is more easily broken down into quantitative metrics, but contains important qualitative components that are not easily captured in numbers. This is the primary reason why ISO 26000 was developed as a *guide,* rather than as a *standard:*

> Fundamentally, CSR is about relationships. Stakeholders change their minds. They can punish you today for doing what they demanded yesterday. Building those relationships—and resolving the dilemmas that present themselves along the way is really more of an art than a science. It's not something that easily lends itself to a standards-based approach.[21]

Other commentators and some governments, however, are concerned that, what is guidance on the surface can quickly become a socially accepted standard if widely adopted:

> ISO's brand recognition and credibility give it potential to make a positive contribution to social responsibility. ISO standards are voluntary, but they frequently become benchmarks for good practice among businesses. They are often referenced in supply chain requirements. And many are absorbed into national regulations and standards.[22]

(Continued)

(Continued)

As a result of this qualitative component of CSR, perhaps, and in spite of all this activity on measuring CSR, making meaningful progress on a universally accepted CSR standard remains difficult. Commentators complain that firms' CSR reports remain focused on the process, rather than focusing on the outcome. In general, CSR reports today

[talk] about whether the company sets targets. [They talk] about whether the report follows the GRI guidelines. [They talk] about whether the report is assured by an independent third party. The only thing [they do not] talk about is how that company is actually performing on a social, environmental or economic scale. . . . By and large, CSR reports—whether GRI, independently assured, or printed on hemp with biodegradable ink, are not being accepted as providing useful evidence.[23]

Equally, the 2009 *Amsterdam Declaration on Transparency and Reporting* issued by GRI announced that "the lack of transparency in the existing system for corporate reporting has failed its stakeholders."[24] It claimed that "the root causes of the [2007–2009] economic crisis would have been moderated"[25] by a more transparent and accountable international system of corporate environmental, social, and governance (ESG) reporting. As a result, the Declaration

calls on governments to take leadership in rebuilding a revitalized and resilient economic system through

- Introducing policy requiring companies to report on ESG factors or publicly explain why they have not done so.
- Requiring ESG reporting by their public bodies—in particular: state owned companies, government pension funds and public investment agencies.
- Integrating sustainability reporting within the emerging global financial regulatory framework being developed by leaders of the G20.[26]

Online Resources

- British Standard BS 8900, http://shop.bsigroup.com/en/ProductDetail/?pid=000000000030118956

  "BS 8900:2006 Guidance for managing sustainable development is designed to help organizations to develop an approach to sustainable development that will continue to evolve and adapt to meet new and continuing challenges and demands."

- Center for Sustainable Innovation (CSI), http://www.sustainableinnovation.org/

  "[CSI's] purpose is to conduct research, development, training and consulting for, and with, companies around the world interested in improving the sustainability performance of their operations."

- EU Eco-Management and Audit Scheme, http://www.iema.net/ems/emas

  "EMAS—the Eco-Management and Audit Scheme, is a voluntary initiative designed to improve companies' environmental performance."

- International Social and Environmental Accreditation and Labeling (ISEAL) Alliance, http://www.isealalliance.org/

  "The ISEAL Alliance is the global hub for social and environmental standards systems."

- International Organization for Standardization (ISO), http://www.iso.org/:

  ISO 14000, http://www.iso.org/iso/iso_14000_essentials

  ISO 26000, http://www.iso.org/sr/

- SustainAbility, http://www.sustainability.com/

  "SustainAbility is a strategy consultancy and think tank working with senior corporate decision makers to achieve transformative leadership on the sustainability agenda."

- United Nations Millennium Goals, http://www.un.org/millenniumgoals/

  "The eight Millennium Development Goals (MDGs)—which range from halving extreme poverty to halting the spread of HIV/AIDS and providing universal primary education, all by the target date of 2015—form a blueprint agreed to by all the world's countries and all the world's leading development institutions."

Questions for Discussion and Review

1. Do you think of CSR in terms of a dichotomy, or do you think of CSR in terms of a continuum? If it is the former, what advantages does this approach provide? If it is the latter, what implications does this have for those seeking to measure CSR?

2. Is a tobacco firm that employs tens of thousands of people and pays significant taxes a *better* or *worse* firm (in terms of CSR performance) than a supermarket that sells food but pays its employees low wages?

3. Who benefits most from the publication of a CSR report—the firm or its stakeholders? What are the dangers of *greenwash,* where a firm inflates or misrepresents its CSR achievements in the hope of reputation benefits?

4. Why is it important that an audit of any aspect of a company's operations be conducted by an independent organization? What benefits are there for a firm in working together with NGOs to conduct a social audit of operations? What are the dangers? Which approach would you use if a major client wanted you to demonstrate your CSR commitment?

5. Respond to the following quote concerning Nike's relationship with its global network of over 700 independent supplier factories:

The relationship is delicate. . . . NGOs have berated firms such as Nike for failing to ensure that workers are paid a "living wage." But that can be hard, even in America. . . . In developing countries, the dilemma may be even greater: "In Vietnam, [Nike's] workers are paid more than doctors. What's the social cost if a doctor leaves his practice and goes to work for [Nike]? That's starting to happen.[27]

COMPLIANCE

 CSR CONNECTION: This issue reflects an ongoing debate within CSR—the extent to which companies should be compelled, or encouraged to adhere voluntarily, to more socially responsible practices.

Issue

It is generally recognized that firms seek to pursue their best interests and that those interests are narrowly defined around profit maximization. What is debated, however, is the extent to which this focus on profit also maximizes the level of social value added by firms. Should firms be free to pursue their self-interest and let the market determine the nature of their actions (through interactions with consumers and competitors, for example), or should society impose specific actions on firms with the goal of achieving specific social outcomes (through government legislation and other forms of coercion)?

Those who support the *mandating* of specific actions argue that this is the only way to ensure firms will behave in a way that is socially acceptable:

Unfortunately, the evidence in support of the business case for corporate social responsibility is weak. . . . [and, as such] corporations do not have sufficient incentive to devote the resources needed to ameliorate the problems corporate social responsibility is intended to address.[28]

Those who support the opposite position, however, argue that additional regulation is a distraction and added cost to business—that firms are adept at avoiding laws they oppose and it is only when an organization genuinely believes that CSR is in its best interests that it will commit sufficient resources to achieving that goal. Working to encourage such *voluntary* action, therefore, is the most effective way of producing genuine and meaningful change:

Legislation is designed to enforce minimum standards. CSR is about best practice. . . . A government can no more legislate for best practice than it can repeal the laws of gravity.[29]

Voluntary Versus Mandatory

At one end of the spectrum is an argument in favor of legislation to control the worst excesses of firms:

Existing laws do not compel a high enough standard of social behavior. Companies will never do more than is required of them if the action is considered a cost to business. Therefore, new and stricter legislation is required to compel more responsible corporate behavior.

At the other end of the spectrum is an argument in favor of encouraging voluntary action by providing incentives and constructing an argument that demonstrates the value of compliance:

Companies will eventually come to realize that it is in their best interests to make sure the communities in which they do business accept them. It is those communities' expectations and shifting standards that will define what is and what is not acceptable behavior. Best practice cannot easily be defined or mandated. If CSR behavior is tied to corporate success, then the profit motive will provide the ideal incentive for the necessary innovation.

Needless to say, there are also several shades of gray between these two extreme points of view.

Compliance with external expectations goes to the heart of CSR because it largely dictates the degree to which a company is accepted by society. Those companies that add value will be welcomed, and those that are perceived to be detracting from the general well-being will be criticized and even rejected. As such, there is a strong case for the strict regulation of a company's actions when they come into (potentially negative) contact with society. Left to its own devices and if it felt it could get away with it, for example, a firm transporting nuclear waste might be tempted to avoid undertaking all the costly precautions necessary to ensure a completely safe journey. There is an equally strong case, however, that a company has to be genuinely committed to implementing CSR in order for it to be effective and that no amount of regulation can dictate such commitment:

Mandatory disclosure requirements would not help—especially if they were highly prescriptive. If requirements were too rigid, the result would be a bureaucratic compliance culture, where disclosure would relate not to any real commitment to good behavior but to a desire to tick the right boxes. . . . If corporate social responsibility means anything, it must involve some voluntary recognition by companies that they cannot thrive in isolation or opposition to the society in which they are trying to do business.[30]

Alan Greenspan, chairman of the Federal Reserve Board in the United States from 1987 to 2006, has long been an advocate of self-regulation, or voluntary compliance, within the finance industry:

"It is in the self-interest of every businessman to have a reputation for honest dealings and a quality product," he wrote . . . in 1963. Regulation, he said, undermines this "superlatively moral system" by replacing competition for reputation with force. . . . [Greenspan] still admires the laissez-faire capitalism of the mid-19th century. At that time, competition, not regulation, kept financial markets honest. Banks, for example, issued their own currency whose value fluctuated with the issuer's reputation.[31]

Government regulatory interventions—such as producing a national currency and guaranteeing individual savings deposits—Greenspan argues, reduced

the incentive for bankers and businessmen to act prudently . . . [and made] depositors less concerned about the reputation of the bank to which they entrusted their money.[32]

It is worth noting, however, that the 2007–2009 economic crisis has shaken Greenspan's unwavering faith in the self-correcting power of the market. Appearing before the House Committee on Oversight and Government Reform to give testimony on the crisis, Greenspan declared

Those of us who have looked to the self-interest of lending institutions to protect shareholders' equity, myself included, are in a state of shocked disbelief.[33]

In 2004, the European Multi Stakeholder Forum on Corporate Social Responsibility (CSR EMS Forum) indicated a growing awareness of the need to encourage voluntary change:

Participants agreed [on] a definition of corporate social responsibility. They reaffirmed that it is the voluntary integration of environmental and social considerations into core business operations over and above legal obligations, and is based on dialogue with stakeholders.[34]

It is also true, however, that many companies would prefer to determine operational costs based on self-interest (i.e., as low as possible), rather than on what an objective evaluation indicates would be best for society in general, if money were no object. Hence, the case for stricter legislation in specific areas as a safeguard:

Enron, for example, proudly presented its CSR credentials as a giant PR exercise while internally betraying them. Unless companies really own CSR it is only window-dressing, argue the voluntarists. . . . The best instrument is to show business that behaving well is good business, so that it adopts CSR willingly and internalizes it.[35]

As a general rule, people have argued for a place for regulation in areas of greatest interest to the largest number of people:

In France, since 2002 all public companies have been required to report social and environmental information as part of the annual report.[36]

While too much regulation stifles entrepreneurship and encourages inefficiency, firms' best interests require an understanding that consumer definitions of acceptable behavior are dynamic. If firms ignore consumer expectations, a potentially more damaging backlash of widespread, punitive regulation may stifle the business environment for all. Ironically, it is often those firms that have felt the brunt of the attention of CSR campaigners up until now that are the firms that are most proactive regarding CSR. These companies understand more completely the self-interest in reacting positively to prior stakeholder backlash and instigating CSR protection to try and avoid similar problems in the future:

> Shell's experience with Brent Spar and in Nigeria convinced it to take relations with its stakeholders more seriously, becoming an exemplar of best practice in its environmental and social reporting.[37]

It is always difficult to tell, of course, whether these incidents prompt a company genuinely to reevaluate its operations and strategic perspective to incorporate the importance of CSR or whether the company merely recognizes a need to *appear* concerned about issues that are potentially harmful. Shell's more recent CSR performance indicates there may be some truth to this. A 2009 study that looked at publicly available data in the oil industry to evaluate emissions reporting by six major oil companies on a scale of 1 = *bad* to 5 = *good* in terms of "the level of detail, frequency and coherency of emissions disclosures," for example,

> scored Shell at 1.15 out of 5 on its carbon disclosures. That compares with 3.05 for BP, 2.76 for Exxon, 2.64 for Conoco-Phillips, 2.4 for Chevron and 2.03 for Total.[38]

The voluntary versus mandatory debate continues. . . .

Case Study Paper Versus Plastic

What is the most effective way to encourage recycling? Is it better to appeal to people's self-interest, arguing the importance of creating a sustainable economic model that minimizes the impact on the world's resources so that their children and their children's children can have a planet to inherit? Or is it better to mandate specific actions that seek to alter behavior? Much of the argument presented in *Strategic CSR* is based on the assumption that it is only when firms become convinced of the self-interest inherent in socially responsible behavior that meaningful change will occur. In terms of individual consumer behavior in relation to recycling, however, there is evidence to suggest that mandated action is effective. There is also evidence to suggest that, if a shift in consumer behavior occurs, then firms will quickly adapt.

In the case of recycling by organizations, some understand the value of voluntary action—that they can reduce costs and, therefore, increase efficiency, by recycling raw materials. As highlighted in Chapter 3,

(Continued)

(Continued)

Walmart's work in this area is now considered best practice. This is partly to do with Walmart's size of operations, but it is also clear that the firm genuinely sees action on sustainability issues as a means of becoming more efficient and passing those efficiency savings on to customers as ever lower prices.

Anheuser-Busch is another firm that has long been recognized as promoting recycling best practice. In 2003, the firm "recycled more than 97 per cent of its solid waste . . . more than 5 billion pounds of material."[39] In 2005, it "decreased the amount of paperboard used to produce its packaging by almost 21 million pounds since 2002." In 2006, the firm announced it

> generated enough renewable fuel to heat more than 25,000 homes, recycled more than 27 billion cans, cut its employee injury rate by nearly half in the last five years and helped its employees lose 5,000 pounds—an amount equal to the weight of two-and-a-half Clydesdales.[40]

More recently, Coca-Cola announced plans

> to build the world's largest plastic bottle-to-bottle recycling plant in Spartanburg, S.C., and revealed its goal to recycle and reuse 100 percent of its plastic packaging in the United States.[41]

By establishing a separate company that is dedicated to recycling all Coca-Cola's plastic packaging in the United States (Coca-Cola Recycling), the firm is emphasizing solutions that generate revenue (or reduce costs) as much as they minimize environmental impact.[42]

But what about action on sustainability-related issues by individual consumers? Again, Walmart has made impressive inroads here in terms of encouraging a change in consumer behavior by prominently displaying products such as energy-efficient light bulbs in its stores. Again, simply because of its size, the firm is able to reach a large percentage of the population:

> The company is changing a lot more than its trucks. For instance: Replacing incandescent bulbs in all the ceiling fans on display in the company's stores reaped savings of $7 million a year. Now Wal-Mart is using in-store displays to promote compact fluorescent bulbs to consumers, and has sold over 100 million of them—more than one per customer—saving enough energy to run a city the size of Philadelphia.[43]

In spite of some progress, however, the statistics for the amount of waste consumers recycle make for depressing reading. In the United States, for example,

> While some 52% of paper, 36% of metals, and 22% of glass get recycled, only 7% of all plastics do, according to the Environmental Protection Agency.[44]

An interesting subsection of the recycling debate and the damaging environmental impact of current consumer behavior is the question of how best to reduce the use of plastic bags:

> After the plastic water bottle, you couldn't do much better than the plastic shopping bag as a symbol of American consumerism run amok. We

go through 380 billion a year. An estimated 5.2% get recycled; in landfills, they could last 1,000 years. Bags are made from oil, and our bag habit costs us 1.6 billion gallons each year.[45]

In an April 2009 study, "Marine Litter: A Global Challenge," UNEP reported that plastic bags made up 9.4 percent of the world's coastal litter.[46]

CSR Newsletters: Paper or Plastic?

A recent article[47] compares paper or plastic bags to see which imposes the greater environmental burden, in terms of both production, consumption, and disposal:

Paper or Plastic? . . . The reality is that both paper and plastic bags gobble up natural resources and cause significant pollution.

There are some surprising statistics, but the upshot is that neither is particularly good:

It takes more than four times as much energy to manufacture a paper bag as it does a plastic bag. The production of paper bags generates 70 percent more air and 50 times more water pollutants than production of plastic bags.

It can cost $4,000 to process and recycle 1 ton of plastic bags. This can then be sold on the commodities market for about $32.

More often than not, bags collected for recycling never get recycled. A growing trend is to ship them to countries such as India and China, where they are cheaply incinerated under more lax environmental laws.

Paper is degradable, but it cannot completely break down in modern landfills because of the lack of water, light, oxygen and other necessary elements.

An editorial at the *Washington Post*[48] makes a similar point in response to a proposal to ban plastic shopping bags in Maryland:

The problem, opponents of the idea counter, is that paper bags are harmful, too: They cost more to make, they gobble up more resources to transport, and recycling them causes more pollution than recycling plastic. The argument for depriving Annapolis residents of their plastic bags is far from made.

It seems there is only one thing on which most people can agree:

Disposable shopping bags of any type are wasteful, and the best outcome would be for customers to reuse bags instead.

(Continued)

(Continued)

The extent of the problem is forcing some U.S. municipalities, which have to clean up the bags after they are (often) discarded, to take action:

> The city of San Francisco, which spends $8 million a year on bag cleanup, will require grocery stores with net profits of more than $2 million a year and drugstores with more than five locations to use compostable bags. . . . The city will collect the bags from households, along with food scraps, and turn them into fertilizer.[49]

The bags have to be collected to be composted, but only 5% of the plastic bags we use currently are recycled. In addition, such schemes are subject to the fluctuating price for recycled materials, which go down[50] as readily as they go up.[51] The corresponding wild fluctuations in the market price for specific recycled materials mean that it is sometimes cheaper for firms to dispose of them (to avoid storage costs) than sell them on the market.[52]

The results of two interesting social experiments, however, indicate that legislation mandating specific action carries the potential to produce much greater change in consumer behavior in a much shorter time frame. First, IKEA introduced a policy of charging consumers for any bags they use and donating the money generated to a nonprofit organization:

> The policy [in six months] cut bag consumption in the United States by more than 50%, far more than executives had expected. . . . In the United Kingdom, the policy . . . cut bag use by 95%.[53]

In a press release, IKEA announced the U.S. results on the first-year anniversary of its plan to minimize the number of plastic bags used by its customers and, again, reported a marked change in consumer behavior:

> With the introduction of its leadership "bag the plastic bag" program . . . , IKEA set a goal of reducing its US stores' plastic bag consumption by 50%; from 70 million to 35 million plastic bags in the first year. . . . Now it is one year since the program began and . . . more than 92% of their customers said no more plastic bags![54]

As a result, the firm decided to extend its policy and "IKEA will no longer offer plastic bags, and paper bags are not available in IKEA stores either."[55]

The environmental impact of these policies has the potential to be very significant:

> According to the Environmental Protection Agency, the U.S. consumes over 380 billion plastic bags, sacks and wraps each year. Each year, Americans throw away some 100 billion polyethylene plastic bags, and less than one percent of them are recycled.[56]

The second social experiment occurred in 2002 when the Irish government passed a tax on plastic bags, requiring that customers had to pay the equivalent of 33 cents for every bag they used. In a result very similar to the one experienced by IKEA, the tax had a dramatic and immediate impact on consumer behavior:

> Within weeks, plastic bag use dropped 94 percent. Within a year, nearly everyone had bought reusable cloth bags, keeping them in offices and in the backs of cars. Plastic bags were not outlawed, but carrying them became socially unacceptable—on a par with wearing a fur coat or not cleaning up after one's dog.[57]

The Web site http://reusablebags.com/ reports that "In January [2008] almost 42 billion plastic bags were used worldwide"[58]—that is in only one month! The IKEA and Ireland experiments show that dramatic change is possible, given the political will and the ability to approach problems innovatively. Other firms are seeking to build on IKEA's early success:

> Wal-Mart, long the target of environmentalists, is teaming with the [Environmental Defense Fund] in a so-called Global Plastic Shopping Bag Waste Reduction Program, which it says will reduce the number of shopping bags by 9 million by 2013.[59]

City governments from New York[60] to New Delhi[61] also noted the rapid change in behavior and have announced similar schemes. Ireland is planning to build on the success of its scheme and extend similar taxes to influence other areas of consumer behavior:

> Ireland has moved on with the tax concept, proposing similar taxes on customers for A.T.M. receipts and chewing gum. . . . [In 2008], the government plans to ban conventional light bulbs, making only low-energy, long-life fluorescent bulbs available.[62]

While, as a general rule, knee-jerk government intervention should be avoided, the examples presented in this case indicate the potential for social policy to shift public behavior radically and quickly in a positive direction.

Online Resources

- EurActiv, http://www.euractiv.com/en/socialeurope/voluntary-vs-mandatory-remain-point-contention-csr/article-128568

  "Placing the emphasis on voluntary initiatives or mandatory measures is the hot debate as the EU's Multi Stakeholder Forum on CSR concludes its 20-month mandate and delivers its final conclusions."

- European Multi Stakeholder Forum on CSR (CSR EMS Forum) http://forum.europa.eu.int/irc/empl/csr_eu_multi_stakeholder_forum/info/data/en/csr%20ems%20forum.htm

  "The (CSR EMS Forum) . . . brings together European representative organisations of employers, business networks, trade unions, and NGOs, to promote innovation, convergence, and transparency in existing CSR practices and tools. The Forum's mandate was approved at the launch on 16th October 2002."

- IIED—International Institute for Environment and Development, http://www.iied.org/

"The International Institute for Environment and Development is a global leader in sustainable development."

- ICIS.com, http://www.icis.com/Articles/2002/04/15/161455/csr-mandatory-or-voluntary-approach.html

"CSR: mandatory or voluntary approach?"

- IKEA, the NEVER ENDING job, http://www.ikea.com/ms/en_US/about_ikea/our_responsibility/the_never_ending_list/about.html

"We have decided to help create a world where we take better care of the environment, the earth's resources, and each other. We know that sometimes we are part of the problem. So, we are working hard to become a part of the solution."

- MyDD, http://www.mydd.com/story/2008/4/20/22529/4708

"A Briefing Paper on Corporate Social Responsibility: Mandatory or Voluntary?"

- Royal Dutch/Shell Group, http://www.shell.com/

"Do you still think of Shell as an oil company? In fact we are a global group of energy and petrochemicals companies, operating in over 145 countries and employing more than 119,000 people."

- Shell's *Brent Spar* Dossier, http://www.shell.co.uk/home/content/gbr/aboutshell/shell_businesses/e_and_p/facts_figures/decommissioning/brent_spar/brent_spar.html

- Shell Nigeria, http://www.shell.com/home/content/nigeria/news_and_library/publications/dir_briefing_notes.html

- Whole Foods Market, http://www.wholefoodsmarket.com/abetterbag/index.php

"A Better Bag—80% Recycled, 100% Reusable."

Questions for Discussion and Review

1. Which argument do you favor—persuading a company to incorporate a CSR perspective voluntarily or forcing them to change using legislation? Why? Which of these two approaches is ideal? Which is more realistic?

2. Enter the search terms *csr, mandatory, voluntary* into Google. Have a brief look at some of the relevant documents this search produces. What is your sense of the argument that is playing out within the business world? Where would most corporations like the balance to fall? Is that the same as the nonprofit organizations or NGOs that are also participating in the debate?

3. Have a look at this Financial Times article (http://www.ft.com/cms/s/0/c6d8c8a2-5902-11de-80b3-00144feabdc0.html), which describes a law passed by the Norwegian

government to force "listed companies to have women as 40 per cent of their directors." Similar to the IKEA and Irish government social experiments outlined in the case, the results were dramatic:

> Politicians in egalitarian Norway, aware that by 2002 only 6 per cent of directors were female, legislated the following year to introduce the controversial quota, which came into full force [in 2008]. . . . [By 2009] the country now has the world's highest proportion of female board members. . . . 44 per cent of directors are women.[63]

How well do you feel women are represented in executive and board positions in firms in your country? Do you think a similar scheme would improve things?

4. Have a look at this video, which shows Coca-Cola's "World's Largest Bottle-to-Bottle Recycling Plant" (http://www.youtube.com/watch?v=0f4Sl804HPM). What are your thoughts? Does it change your perception of the firm? Would you ever choose the drinks you buy because of action such as this?

5. Have a look at the UK newspaper *The Daily Mail*'s "Banish the bags" campaign (http://www.dailymail.co.uk/news/article-519770). If you are not in the United Kingdom, can you imagine a similar campaign being waged by a newspaper in your country? If you are, did you know about the campaign? Was it a success? Why or why not?

ENVIRONMENTAL SUSTAINABILITY

 CSR CONNECTION: This issue rose to public prominence ahead of the broader issue of CSR. Environmental awareness, in the form of *sustainability,* however, remains a central component of the CSR debate.

Issue

The issue of *environmental sustainability* raises a number of important questions that business and society will need to address in the very near future:

* Do firms have a social responsibility to the environment?

* Beyond legal requirements, should they internalize the environmental costs of operations (e.g., clean up the pollution their operations produce)? Should governments help with these costs?

* Should firms be allowed to deplete the Earth's resources (i.e., remove more than they replenish) during production?

- Should firms support government-led efforts to place a minimum price (a tax) or a market price (a cap-and-trade scheme) on carbon?

- Should the price of a product (such as a car, for example) contain the costs to the environment incurred during consumption?

- *Should* consumers be expected to pay a premium to ensure products are produced in a way that protects the environment? *Will* they pay this premium or continue to reward firms that find ways to avoid the full costs of production?

In other words, what is sustainability?

CSR Newsletters: The Brundtland Report

An in-depth article[64] chronicles the impact of the 1987 Brundtland Report, which was named after its main author, Gro Harlem Brundtland—Norwegian prime minister and chair of the UN's World Commission on Environment and Development. One of the key contributions of the report was to define the term *sustainable development* and identify the importance of sustainability for firms:

"Sustainable development is development that meets the needs of the present without compromising the ability of future generations to meet their own needs," the report famously states in its oft-cited quote.

Beyond this, however, the report was also prescient in framing the importance of a business case for CSR-related practices. It formed an important step in the debate that has emerged around social responsibility and sustainability issues, and particularly regarding the role that society demands of its for-profit organizations:

The Brundtland Report, which inspired the 1992 Earth Summit in Rio de Janeiro that resulted in the Climate Change Convention and in turn the Kyoto Protocol, acknowledged that many "of the development paths of the industrialized nations are clearly unsustainable." However, it held fast to its embrace of development toward industrialized nation living standards as part of the solution, not part of the problem. "If large parts of countries of the global South are to avert economic, social, and environmental catastrophes, it is essential that global economic growth be revitalized," the report stated.

The second half of the article looks at how the report continues to influence the current and future debate concerning sustainability:

To celebrate the 20th anniversary of its founding (coinciding with the release of the Brundtland Report, which coined the term "sustainable development"), UK-based think tank and consultancy SustainAbility published a report projecting the future of sustainability over the next 20 years.

The Brundtland Report, published in April 1987, popularized the term *sustainability*[65] and its definition has become the essential definition:

Sustainability

Meeting the needs of the present without compromising the ability of future generations to meet their own needs.

One of the reasons this quote has become so widely accepted, however, is that it is extremely broad. This has the advantage of making it applicable to all organizations that are able to interpret it to suit their circumstances. Another interpretation of such versatility, however, is vagueness—because it can be interpreted to suit a firm's circumstances, *sustainability* is also subject to varying levels of implementation. In practice, therefore, what does *sustainability* mean and, equally important, why should businesses care?

The myth is that financial issues are "hard" while social issues are "soft"—meaning: unimportant and irrelevant, because they don't impact investor money. . . . When society forces companies to internalize social costs, via legal or other penalties, social issues *become* financial issues—which is the way to get companies to sit up and take notice.[66]

Reports increasingly suggest that there is a growing financial risk for any corporation not conducting business in what is considered an appropriate manner by contemporary society:

Munich Re, a large German insurance company, estimates that the effects of climate change could cost companies $300 billion annually by 2050 in weather damage, pollution, industrial and agricultural losses. . . . Companies may also face unexpected expenses resulting from future taxes, regulations, fines, and caps on products that produce greenhouse gases.[67]

Rather than wait for the government to impose restrictions on how they operate, however, many firms are voluntarily choosing to act now in an attempt to influence the debate. In particular, carbon emissions and the market for carbon have become an area of increased firm activity.[68] Pepsi's move, in association with Carbon Trust,[69] to measure the carbon footprint through the lifecycle of one half gallon of its Tropicana orange juice is one example of many:

PepsiCo finally came up with a number: the equivalent of 3.75 pounds of carbon dioxide is emitted to the atmosphere for each half-gallon carton of orange juice. . . . PepsiCo is among the first [in the United States] that will provide consumers with an absolute number for a product's carbon footprint, which many expect to be a trend.[70]

The results of Pepsi's attempt to measure the carbon footprint of its Tropicana orange juice, with the majority of emissions occurring during production (as opposed to distribution, packaging, and consumption), are presented in Figure 8.1.

Figure 8.1   The Carbon Footprint of Tropicana Orange Juice

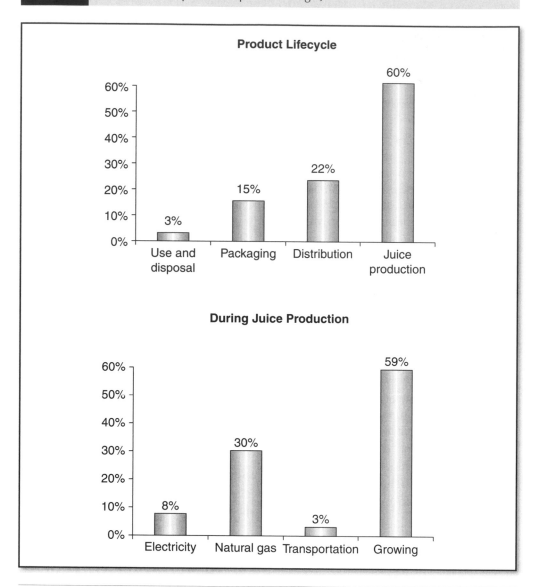

Source: Data from Tropicana. Adapted from Andrew Martin, "How Green Is My Orange," *New York Times*, January 22, 2009, p. B1.

Note: One half gallon = 3.75 lbs (1.7 kg) of CO_2.

These actions mirror earlier decisions by firms like Walkers and Cadbury in the United Kingdom,[71] which are demonstrating best practice in this area:

The famous glass and a half of milk that goes into a Cadbury milk chocolate bar is responsible for 60% of the product's greenhouse gas emissions.[72]

In addition, many firms see economic opportunity in the increasing environmental awareness and concern. In the United States, GE, in particular, has acted early to stake its claim to a significant share of the sustainability market. GE, which appointed its first vice president for corporate citizenship in 2002, launched its drive to capitalize on the shifting business context by launching its Ecomagination program in 2005:

"The world's changed," [GE CEO, Jeff] Immelt says. "Businesses today aren't admired. Size is not respected. There's a bigger gulf today between haves and have-nots than ever before. It's up to us to use our platform to be a good citizen. Because not only is it a nice thing to do, it's a business imperative."[73]

The results for GE from the introduction of Ecomagination have been impressive. In 2008,

Revenue at GE's three-year-old Ecomagination division, centered on renewable energy, water services, and clean tech, rose an estimated 21% to $17 billion. GE's annual investment in cleaner R&D doubled to $1.4 billion.[74]

Other firms, such as Nike,[75] Dr. Hauschka,[76] and many others, have also made sizeable bets that their future business model relies on sustainability becoming a central and necessary component of business in the 21st century. As Walmart[77] has successfully demonstrated, an effective sustainability program saves, rather than costs, money[78] and, in the most progressive firms, is "a key component of long-term strategy."[79] In the case of Unilever, for example, the firm sees little distinction between a sustainability business model and economic success:

As [Unilever CEO, Patrick] Cescau sees it, helping [developing] nations wrestle with poverty, water scarcity, and the effects of climate change is vital to staying competitive in coming decades. Some 40% of the company's sales and most of its growth now take place in developing nations. . . . As environmental regulations grow tighter around the world, Unilever must invest in green technologies or its leadership in packaged foods, soaps, and other goods could be imperiled. "You can't ignore the impact your company has on the community and the environment," Cescau says. CEOs used to frame thoughts like these in the context of moral responsibility, he adds. But now, "it's all about growth and innovation. In the future, it will be the only way to do business."[80]

A 2009 article in *Harvard Business Review* argued from an even stronger perspective that "sustainability is now the key driver of innovation" for firms:

Executives behave as though they have to choose between the largely social benefits of developing sustainable products or processes and the financial costs of doing so. But that's simply not true. . . . sustainability is a mother lode of organizational and technological innovations that yield bottom-line and top-line returns. . . . smart companies now treat sustainability as innovation's new frontier.[81]

Advocates also argue that there are a large number of "green-collar jobs" that will assist in retraining workers for the 21st century and revitalize inner-cities.[82] This claim is supported by President Obama, who pledged to create "5 million green-collar jobs" as part of his New Energy for America plan,[83] along with roughly $70 billion or more in grants, loans and loan guarantees . . . for high-tech research and commercial projects for renewable energy such as biofuels and wind, solar and geothermal power.[84]

To be effective, however, pledges of sustainability need to be supported by action. Unless firms are genuinely committed to a sustainable existence, the danger is that some firms will implement superficially. Such "little green lies"[85] can occur as a result of either intentional deception or ignorance; what is common to both forms, however, is that such activity is designed to take advantage of growing consumer interest and concern, while not investing the resources necessary to operate in a sustainable manner:

It's astonishing how suddenly and absolutely the motor industry has been converted to the green cause. The "environment" used to be regarded as that boring blurry thing that flashed past between Esso [Exxon] stations. Now, data about fuel economy and CO_2 emissions takes precedence over performance criteria, such as torque and acceleration. Reading press packs and auto manuals, you could almost mistake car manufacturers for environmental charities.[86]

CSR Newsletters: Greenwash

Green-wash (green'wash,' -wôsh')—verb: the act of misleading consumers regarding the environmental practices of a company or the environmental benefits of a product or service. (http://www.terrachoice.com/)

The article quoted here[87] summarizes a recent report that makes for interesting reading for anyone interested in the extent to which firms are willing to jump on the CSR bandwagon and mislead consumers in the hope of financial gain:

Not everything called "green" is going to do much for the environment, according to a report issued this week by a marketing firm, TerraChoice Environmental Marketing (terrachoice.com). Titled "The Six Sins of Greenwashing," the report is based on a study of 1,018 consumer products that make environmental claims. Of those, according to the report, "all but one made claims that are demonstrably false or that risk misleading intended audiences."

The report's "six sins" include the Sin of the Hidden Trade-off, the Sin of No Proof, the Sin of Vagueness, the Sin of Irrelevance, the Sin of Fibbing, and Sin of the Lesser of Two Evils that, taken together, indicate

both that the individual consumer has been misled and that the potential environmental benefit of his or her purchase has been squandered.

For the full report and definitions of each of the six sins (later extended to add the seventh sin, the Sin of Worshipping False Labels) go to: http://sinsofgreenwashing.org/

Whether greenwashing by firms is intentional (see the discussion in Chapter 4), what is clear is that, currently, too much legitimate business activity is causing too much environmental damage:

CSR Newsletters: Oil Sands

A recent article[88] presents the conundrum facing oil firms that seek to extract oil from the tar sands in Canada but have presented themselves as socially responsible. With oil prices rising, extracting the oil from these tar sands becomes profitable. Canada's oil reserves are second only to Saudi Arabia, and the country's friendly and stable business environment is rare in the oil industry. The article makes clear, however, that the processes used to extract the oil cause significant environmental damage:

Producing crude oil from the tar sands—a heavy mixture of bitumen, water, sand and clay . . . generates up to four times more carbon dioxide, the principal global warming gas, than conventional drilling. . . . The oil rush is also scarring a wilderness landscape: millions of tonnes of plant life and top soil is scooped away in vast open-pit mines and millions of litres of water are diverted from rivers—up to five barrels of water are needed to produce a single barrel of crude and the process requires huge amounts of natural gas. . . . it takes two tonnes of the raw sands to produce a single barrel of oil.

There are also tales of water pollution and increased medical consequences for nearby populations. Where does responsibility lie here? Greenpeace's claim that "in the era of climate change it should not be being developed at all" is too flippant. BP's reply that "These are resources that would have been developed anyway" seems equally unsatisfactory. What is clear is that the economic opportunity is generating

a £50bn [billion] "oil rush" as American, Chinese, and European investors rush to profit from high oil prices. Despite production costs per barrel of up to £15, compared to £1 per barrel in Saudi Arabia, the Canadian province expects to be pumping five million barrels of crude a day by 2030.

Surely, the Canadian government is responsible for generating and enforcing environmental legislation in Canada, although the politicians also seek the tax revenues and other benefits that come with a booming industry. Surely, the oil firms have a primary duty to remain in business and obey the law, but many of them also present a public image that implies a concern for the environment over and above merely "obeying the law."

Those economies that have developed the furthest, the fastest, have also been producing the most carbon emissions. Figure 8.2 presents the amount of carbon emissions, per country/region, from 1950–2007 (amounts in billions of tons):

Figure 8.2 Carbon Emissions by Country/Region (billions of tons, 1950–2007)

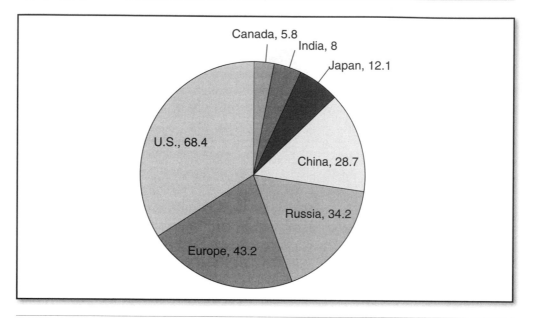

Source: Data from Fiona Harvey & Sheila McNulty, "Savings Potential Scales New Heights," *Financial Times,* August 21, 2009, p. 17.

Case Study   e-waste

Waste is a central component of the economic model that drives the global economy. For the majority of for-profit firms, the more you buy of their product, the better they perform, and the faster the economy grows. In other words, if you buy a product, the quicker you throw it away and buy another one, the better for all concerned. A huge assumption of this economic model, however, is that the world's resources are infinite. As a result, when a company extracts a resource and converts it into something that consumers want to buy, the consumer pays only for the cost the firm incurred during the extraction and conversion. For the most part, there is no charge associated with the replenishment of the resource (for example, the cost of replanting trees cut down to make paper), nor the environmental costs incurred during consumption (for example, the CO2 emitted when driving a car). Such costs are termed externalities—costs that are incurred, but not paid for, by either the firm or the consumer:

Over the past century, companies have been rewarded financially for maximizing externalities in order to minimize costs. . . . Not until we more broadly "price in" the external costs of investment decision across all sectors will we have a sustainable economy and society.[89]

In short, at present, our economy is founded on waste—the more the company and the consumer waste, the stronger the economy becomes. As one article asks, "Are we sinking under the weight of our disposable society?"[90]

There are not far off 7bn [billion] people in the world and between us we generate between 2.5bn and 4bn tonnes of waste a year. . . . Rich countries produce far more waste than the poor: about 700 kilograms per inhabitant is collected across the US in a year, but in India only about 150kg per person in urban areas [is collected].[91]

CSR Newsletters: Waste

It will come as no surprise to many that a huge amount of the daily food consumption in the United States is wasted. One article,[92] however, reports research that attempts to quantify just how much food this wastage represents:

In 1997, in one of the few studies of food waste, the Department of Agriculture estimated that two years before, 96.4 billion pounds of the 356 billion pounds of edible food in the United States was never eaten.

This amounts to "an estimated 27 percent of the food available for consumption" and is not only a U.S. phenomenon:

In England, a recent study revealed that Britons toss away a third of the food they purchase, including more than four million whole apples, 1.2 million sausages and 2.8 million tomatoes. In Sweden, families with small children threw out about a quarter of the food they bought, a recent study there found.

This article reports that a new study is being undertaken to update the figure, this time accounting for the recent growth in pre-prepared food produced by supermarkets. Optimistically, Jonathan Bloom, the creator of the Web site WasteFood.com (http://wastefood.com/) believes recent events suggest things might be improving:

"The fundamental thing that I'm fighting against is, 'why should I care? I paid for it,'" Mr. Bloom said. "The rising prices are really an answer to that."

A second article[93] shows that the amounts involved are truly staggering and depressing:

The food wasted each day in the UK and the US alone would be enough to alleviate the hunger of 1.5bn people—more than the global number of malnourished.

(Continued)

(Continued)

What happens to our waste when we no longer need it? A lot of it is shipped overseas to countries with less strict environmental regulations. Even as we upgrade our industrial infrastructure and production processes in the West, our old factories and equipment are exported to the developing world to continue polluting:

The global market for hand-me-down industrial machinery and vehicles has been valued at an estimated $150 billion a year by the German environmental think tank Adelphi Research. The U.S. feeds the market with products ranging from four-ton trucks to entire power plants. . . . A 1950s paper-making machine from Adams [Massachusetts], operates in Egypt; a rock-crushing machine from Vermont has been reassembled in Colombia; a five-story, coal-fired power plant in Turners Falls [Massachusetts] is being reassembled in Guatemala.[94]

e-waste is the waste associated with technology-related products, such as computers and cell phones.[95] In addition to the plastic casing that surrounds many of these products, various metals and soldering are used to make the electronic components inside. The amount of e-waste we produce as technology becomes an increasingly central component of our everyday lives is a particular problem in terms of disposal or recycling because of these plastics and metals; it also fully demonstrates the ecological consequences of a consumption-based economic model that treats all resources as

infinite and fails to fully account for the externalities created during the manufacture processes. As CBS's *60 Minutes* reported in August 2009[96]

- 130,000 computers thrown away every day in the United States
- 100 million cell phones thrown away every year in the United States

The total amount of e-waste in the United States keeps growing:

The [U.S. Environmental Protection Agency] estimates that 2.6 million tons of electronic waste were dropped into landfills in 2007. . . . Once buried, the waste leaches poisons like chlorinated solvents and heavy metals into soil and groundwater.[97]

The amount of heavy metals contained within all this waste adds up quickly and presents a serious problem in terms of disposal or recycling:

Discarded TVs and PCs can contain as much as eight pounds of lead, as well as mercury, cadmium and other substances that are harmless when part of a piece of equipment but a health risk when they reach a landfill.[98]

And, with new technological devices being introduced constantly, the problem of what to do with the old devices is not going to go away any time soon:

The [EPA] estimates that 99 million television sets sit unused in closets and basements across the [United States].[99]

Much of the West's recycling is outsourced to China, where it is often dismantled by hand by low-paid women and children. As a result, it is hard to know what the best disposal option for consumers is when they no longer need these products. In the case of plastics recycling, for example,

> employees in Chinese recycling facilities are exposed to toxic fumes from the materials they are recycling. Which means that my recycling options just got a whole lot more complicated. Some choice: noxious chemicals in the soil versus the health of Chinese workers. It really isn't easy being green.[100]

Specific areas in China, in particular, have become wastelands as workers save us the cost and effort of recycling our own e-waste. With little more than hand tools,

> they take apart old computers, monitors, printers, video and DVD players, photocopying machines, telephones and phone chargers, music speakers, car batteries and microwave ovens.[101]

What is being done to regulate the movement of e-waste from country to country? The United Nation's Basel Convention (http://www.basel.int/) and the EU legislation on Waste Electrical and Electronic Equipment (http://ec.europa.eu/environment/waste/weee/index_en.htm) are two important examples of initiatives at the intergovernmental level to regulate e-waste. Although these international regulatory efforts are extensive and would protect workers in developing countries if they were enforced, it appears that this does not occur in China:

> In [Guiyu, Guandong] China, recycling e-waste is apparently free of any environmental or health and safety regulation. . . . Chinese law forbids the importation of electronic waste and Beijing is also a signatory to the Basel agreement, an international treaty banning the shipment of e-waste from the developed to the developing world. But so far, official prohibitions have been about as effective as the official banners urging environmental protection that flap in the breeze above the trash-congested streets of Guiyu.[102]

As a result of the difficulties with enforcement in different cultures and legal systems, some commentators have argued that a reduction in waste is a more realistic goal than better recycling at the current rate of consumption.[103] In spite of all the doom and gloom, however, some firms are finding ways to recycle waste products and profit in the process:

Rubber Flooring[104]

Trash: More than 290 million tires are scrapped each year in the United States.

Salvage: Diamond Safety Concepts buys finely ground used tires and then makes and sells playground covers and athletic fields.

Cash: Crumb rubber sells for $700 per ton, and Diamond Safety Concepts experienced a 20% sales bump in 2008.

(Continued)

(Continued)

In addition, as landfills fill up and the dangers of e-waste become more apparent, local and state governments in the United States are pursuing innovative policies to try and change consumer behavior and limit the amount we throw away (or at least have it correctly recycled). In 2006, for example, Washington state passed a law

> mandating that electronics and computer companies pay for the recycling of old equipment, enacting the nation's most far-reaching electronic waste law to date. . . . [As a result] no manufacturer can sell an electronic product in the state unless the manufacturer is partici- pating in an approved electronic waste recycling plan.[105]

> Since 2004, 18 states and New York have approved laws that make manufacturers responsible for recycling electronics and similar statutes were introduced in 13 other states [in 2009].[106]

Some innovative local governments are experimenting with a radical recycling program called *Pay-As-You-Throw* (PAYT):

> With PAYT, residents are charged based on how much garbage they generate, often by being required to buy special bags, tags or cans for their trash. Separated recyclables like glass and cardboard are usually hauled away free or at minimal cost. . . . The EPA said that about 7,100 cities and towns were using PAYT in 2006, up from 5,200 in 2001.[107]

The obvious incentive is to minimize disposed waste by maximizing the amount of waste each household recycles. In spite of the plan's apparent common sense, however, implementing it is proving to be problematic. In particular, there is debate over whether pollution costs should be borne by the individual (based on the amount disposed) or society (based on the idea that comprehensive and efficient waste disposal is a public good):

> About three-quarters of the nation's households still have unlimited disposal service. In some communities, they pay a flat annual fee. In others, local property taxes cover the tab so residents aren't aware of the cost, making the service seem free.[108]

So, what is a possible solution to the abundance of waste we generate? Those who advocate change tend to fall into one of two camps. People in the first camp tend to be more idealistic. They argue that we should be striving for a particular lifestyle, given the state of current knowledge. Above all, they demand sacrifice:

> In this mindset saving the planet demands that people give up their foreign holidays, abandon their cars, turn down the heating and clean their teeth in the dark. Through this prism, pain is a virtue and the halting global warming metamorphoses into a much broader attack on consumerism, materialism and, at the extreme, anything that smacks of the market.[109]

People in the second camp, however, tend to be more pragmatic. They think it is fruitless to try and get people in the developed world to consume less and ask people in the developing world to grow at a much slower rate. There is some truth to this position, as even the most progressive firms that are committed to a sustainable business model, such as Tesco in the United Kingdom, find it difficult to expand their business and reduce their overall carbon footprint simultaneously.[110] As a result, in this view, the only solution is through technological innovation and the problem we face is

> an opportunity rather than a burden. Technological innovation—in automobile design, energy efficiency, renewable energy and the rest—is more than a useful adjunct to an austere low carbon lifestyle. It is a vital pillar of any plan to reduce the build-up of CO_2. Bluntly stated, unless we find a way to capture emissions from coal-fired power stations, the game will be lost.[111]

Strategic CSR argues for a compromise position between the two extremes. Such a position recognizes that the status quo is untenable, but also recognizes the power of the market to innovate and overcome the most intractable human problems. In short, we need a comprehensive reassessment of our capitalist model, but one in which we retain what is most effective about market forces to mobilize and allocate valuable and scarce resources in ways that encourage innovation and, therefore, maximize social value.

In general, this is best achieved by firms implementing a comprehensive CSR perspective throughout all aspects of operations and strategic planning. It is the inclusion of all aspects of firm operations that maximizes the strategic advantages of CSR. In terms of regulating waste disposal and recycling, it is important that firms work in tandem with government agencies to incentivize efforts where the market does not provide an acceptable solution.[112] It is this concept of *systemwide* sustainability that is essential—maintaining a focus on CSR in its broadest interpretation. It is only by focusing on the system as a whole that meaningful and lasting change can occur.

Online Resources

- Ceres, http://www.ceres.org/

  "Ceres (pronounced "series") is a national network of investors, environmental organizations and other public interest groups working with companies and investors to address sustainability challenges such as global climate change."

- Cool Earth, http://www.coolearth.org/

  "Cool Earth is a charity that protects endangered rainforest to combat global warming, protect ecosystems and provide sustainable jobs for local people."

- Eco-Portal, http://www.eco-portal.com/

  "Eco-Portal: An information gateway empowering the movement for environmental sustainability"

- Electronic Industry Citizenship Coalition, http://www.eicc.info/

  "EICC promotes an industry code of conduct for global electronics supply chains to improve working and environmental conditions."

- Freecycle, http://www.freecycle.org/

  "The Freecycle Network™ is made up of 4,801 groups with 7,214,000 members across the globe. It's a grassroots and entirely nonprofit movement of people who are giving (& getting) stuff for free in their own towns."

- GreenBiz.com, http://www.greenbiz.com/

  "GreenBiz.com™, Business Voice of the Green Economy, is the leading source for news, opinion, best practices, and other resources on the greening of mainstream business."

- International Standards Organization (ISO), http://www.iso.org/iso/iso_14000_essentials

  "The ISO 14000 family addresses various aspects of environmental management."

- SustainAbility, http://www.sustainability.com/

  "SustainAbility is a strategy consultancy and think tank working with senior corporate decision makers to achieve transformative leadership on the sustainability agenda."

- Sustainability Institute, http://sustainer.org/

  "We focus on understanding the root causes of unsustainable behavior in complex systems to help restructure systems and shift mindsets that will help move human society toward sustainability."

- UK Sustainable Development Commission, http://www.sd-commission.org.uk/

  "The Sustainable Development Commission is the Government's independent advisory body on sustainable development."

- United Nation's Basel Convention, http://www.basel.int/

  "The Basel Convention on the Control of Transboundary Movements of Hazardous Wastes and their Disposal is the most comprehensive global environmental agreement on hazardous and other wastes."

- World Business Council for Sustainable Development, http://www.wbcsd.org/

  "The World Business Council for Sustainable Development (WBCSD) is a CEO-led, global association of some 200 companies dealing exclusively with business and sustainable development."

Questions for Discussion and Review

1. Is environmental sustainability an issue you consider in your purchase decisions? Why or why not?

2. Have a look at this 20-minute video: http://www.storyofstuff.com/index.html. Does it change your answer to Question 1 in any way? How do you answer the main question posed in the video: How can we make a linear economic system more sustainable?

3. Go to Dell's *Plant a Tree for Me* Web site: http://content.dell.com/us/en/corp/d/corp-comm/PlantaTreeforMe.aspx. The program gives Dell's consumers the option to pay the cost of planting trees to offset the carbon footprint created in the manufacture of their computer. Is this just a public relations effort by the company, or is this really a new approach to sustainable business? Why isn't Dell focused on minimizing the carbon footprint created in the production process, rather than expecting customers to cover these costs for them? Why not make computers that last longer, thereby reducing markedly the CO_2 emissions per sale?[113] What connection does planting trees have with Dell's core business model? Does this matter? Would it be more effective to donate the same amount of money to an NGO that has an established environmental track record (such as the Sustainable Forestry Initiative, http://www.sfiprogram.org/)?

4. What is your image of the NGO Greenpeace? Do you trust the organization to provide accurate and objective assessments of the environmental impact of business? Visit the organization's Web site (http://www.greenpeace.org/). Is environmental sustainability given a high enough priority in business, politics, and society today? Why, or why not?

5. Have a look at this short video on e-waste processing in India: http://video.google.com/videoplay?docid=5944615355863607664 or this *60 Minutes* report on e-waste in China: http://www.cbsnews.com/video/watch/?id=5274959n. What can you do to minimize your carbon footprint and the amount of e-waste you produce? How often do you change your cell phone? What about your computer? Is it *fair* that poor workers in India or China (often including children) get to clean up our e-waste?

ETHICS

CSR CONNECTION: This issue investigates organizational ethics in light of the corporate scandals that occurred at the turn of the century. In particular, the role of ethics and compliance officers in creating an ethical environment within a firm is highlighted.

Issue

To what extent do people, who are able to distinguish right from wrong, make the *correct* decisions, especially when there is a significant personal incentive to do otherwise?

A 2006 survey by Duke University's Center for Academic Integrity (http://www .academicintegrity.org/) reveals that, although many students are concerned about the ethics of U.S. business leaders, they are unable to apply the same high standards to their own personal conduct:

> 56 percent of MBA students admitted cheating, compared with 47 per cent of graduate students in non-business programmes.[114]

Another 2008 survey of 400 MBA students at MIT's Sloan School of Business reports that

> the downturn in the economy has made a potential employer's record on sustainability less of a priority. . . . about 60 per cent say they were more concerned with securing a position.[115]

In other words, Is ethical capitalism possible?[116]

Many recognize the value of instilling ethics early as a key component of a student's education. This basic foundation then becomes a resource on which the individual can draw later in life. With the corporate scandals around the turn of this century bringing ethics to the newspaper front pages and TV headlines on a daily basis, calls for ethics to be a core component of the curricula in business schools, which are responsible for training the next generation of business leaders, have grown.[117] These calls intensified during the 2007–2009 economic crisis. A 2008 survey by the student organization Net Impact (http://www.netimpact.org) and the Aspen Institute Center for Business Education (http://aspencbe.org) of 1,850 students from 80 business schools, for example, reports that:

> Nine out of ten respondents say that a focus in business on short-term rather than long-term results has been one of the contributing factors to the global financial crisis. Just 24% of respondents strongly agree that they are learning how to make business decisions that will help avert similar crises.[118]

Others feel, however, that, particularly at the graduate education level, it is very difficult to influence the core of an individual's personality; that, in a one-semester class, you cannot instill an ethical predisposition, but only build on one if it already exists. In other words, the characters of young adults are already formed by the time they get to business school.

What does all this mean, therefore, for the ethics of the firms at which these students aspire to work? What drives a company to be *ethical,* to be a good *corporate citizen* and implement CSR throughout operations? How should external stakeholders discern the difference between a firm that implements CSR substantively and a firm that implements it symbolically, when many of the observable components of an ethical or CSR structure (a CSR/ethics officer, a code of conduct, a CSR report, ethics training, etc.) ostensibly can look and sound the same in both cases? How can they tell the difference between those firms that genuinely intend to be socially responsible, but fall short, and those firms that seek to mislead stakeholders with a sheen of social responsibility fluff that is intended to hide executives' real beliefs and intentions?

> Take a look at this list of corporate values: Communication. Respect. Integrity. Excellence. They sound pretty good don't they? Strong, concise, meaningful. Maybe they even resemble your own company's values, the ones you spent so much time writing, debating, and revising. If so, you should be nervous. These are the corporate values of Enron, as stated in the company's 2000 annual report. And as events have shown, they're not meaningful; they're meaningless.[119]

Enron is a good example of an organization that, on the surface, had excellent CSR credentials. It is also a good example of the danger presented by a firm's CSR policy that is ill-defined and superficially championed. Without leadership from the top, a company's CSR policy merely presents the organization with sufficient rope to hang itself (see Chapter 5):

> The underlying reasons for Enron's collapse can be traced to characteristics common to all corporations: obsession with profits and share prices, greed, lack of concern for others and a penchant for breaking legal rules. [It shows] what can happen when the characteristics we take for granted in a corporation are pushed to the extreme.[120]

To what extent are a company's efforts at social responsibility window dressing? To what extent is there a genuine intention to recognize and reflect the shifting consumer market globalization is producing, as well as a company's larger responsibility to all its stakeholders and the wider social context in which it operates? CSR advocates understand that it is very easy for a company to say one thing while intending to do another. To what extent is the CSR movement a façade, therefore, providing short-term relief to companies that are not willing to adopt a broader perspective? *Business Ethics Magazine* (now *CRO Magazine*) identified the core of the problem at Enron, a firm that serves as the poster child for the ethical scandals that occurred around the turn of this century:

> Enron rang all the bells of CSR. It won a spot for three years on the list of the 100 Best Companies to Work for in America. In 2000 it received six environmental awards. It issued a triple bottom line report. It had great policies on climate change, human rights and (yes indeed) anti-corruption. Its CEO gave speeches at ethics conferences and put together a

statement of values emphasizing "communication, respect, and integrity." The company's stock was in many social investing mutual funds when it went down. Enron fooled us.[121]

How can the stakeholders of an organization trust a firm's actions if its CSR pronouncements are intended to mislead people into believing the firm is something that it is not?

As officers and employees of Enron Corp., its subsidiaries, and its affiliated companies . . . we are responsible for conducting the business affairs of the Company in accordance with all applicable laws and in a moral and honest manner.[122]

Increasingly, firms are being held accountable for all aspects of operations by the societies in which they are located. Those firms that do not appreciate this, or attempt to circumvent responsibility with superficial commitments to CSR, run the risk of exposure in our always-on, media-driven world. Different firms and different industries have different CSR threshold levels (see Chapter 5). Firms that avoid crossing their threshold by adopting an effective CSR perspective stand a much better chance of long-term survival. Those firms that ignore the threshold, like Enron, eventually are held accountable for their actions.

Case Study   Ethics and Compliance Officers

Three events in the United States since the corporate scandals early this century illustrate a conscious determination to reassert the importance of socially responsible behavior and ethics in business:

- The passage of Sarbanes-Oxley (2002), which added stringent and costly requirements to final reporting by publicly traded firms.

- The requirements by the New York Stock Exchange (2002) and Securities and Exchange Commission (2003) that companies disclose whether or not they have implemented a code of ethics.

- The revised federal sentencing guidelines in the United States (2004), which "require companies to make stronger commitments to ethical standards and prove they are living up to those commitments."[126]

The impact of these changes is reflected in the rapid growth of the Ethics and Compliance Officers Association (ECOA, http://www.theecoa.org/), which, since its founding in 1992, has grown to more than 1,300 members (see Figure 8.3).[127] The ECOA estimates that, in 2008, 85% of the Fortune 500 firms had adopted the Ethics and Compliance Officer (ECO) position, with much of that expansion occurring since 2000.

Figure 8.3   The Growth in ECOA Membership (1992–2007)

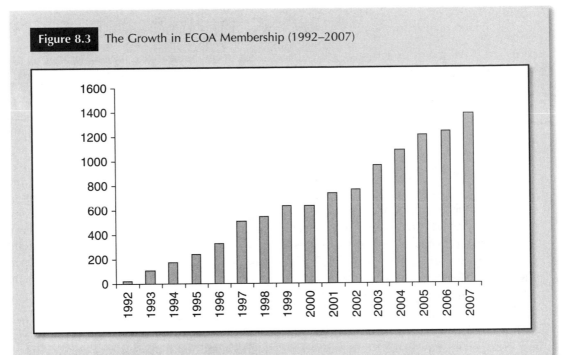

In response to allegations of corporate financial abuses, for example, the U.S. government limited the discretion of companies in reporting their financial information with Sarbanes-Oxley, which added specific responsibilities to management and board of directors. The goal of the Act is to guarantee the accuracy of information produced concerning operations, as well as ensure legal behavior. Compliance, in terms of ethics and corporate governance, is now legally mandated and has become an important—and expensive—measure of a company's effectiveness of operations:

A survey of board members conducted by RHR International for Directorship magazine found that big companies with $4 billion or more in revenues are spending an average of $35 million to comply with the act. Another survey by Financial Executives International found $3.1 million in added costs for companies with average revenues of $2.5 billion.[128]

In the United States, the evolution of corporate compliance programs—and the growth in the ECOs that enforce these

(Continued)

(Continued)

programs—has been driven largely by the desire to avoid the legal consequences of a failure to comply:

> The first corporate-ethics office was created in 1985 by General Dynamics, which was being investigated by the government for pricing scams.[129]

In 1991, this desire to avoid litigation was enhanced by an additional incentive provided by the 1991 Federal Sentencing Guidelines, which empowered judges to act leniently when penalizing those companies that had an established ethics program and accompanying implementation policies in place.

The position of an individual ECO, which first emerged in the 1970s[130] but expanded rapidly in response to the 1991 Federal Sentencing Guidelines, therefore, has its roots in the field of legal compliance. More specifically, the position can be traced back to Chapter 8 of the 1991 guidelines, which holds all organizations (firms, nonprofit organizations, and governmental agencies) liable for the criminal acts of their employees. As a result of the guidelines, for example, in 1996, both Archer Daniels Midland (price-fixing, $100 million) and the Japanese bank Daiwa (concealing information from federal authorities, $340 million) incurred fines for unethical behavior.[131] Importantly, however, the Chapter 8 guidelines also offer incentives that enable organizations to minimize their liability in the event of an ethical transgression:[132]

> 1) executives may face legal charges when an employee commits a crime, and; 2) the corporation may face mandatory fines up to $290 million

(a threshold long since pierced). However, the commissioners said firms could *reduce their risk* by developing an effective ethics program. A profession was born as more companies named chief ethics and compliance officers.[133] [Emphasis added]

This compliance incentive was further heightened with the passing of the Sarbanes-Oxley legislation in 2002 and again in November 2004 with the announcement of the updated federal sentencing guidelines:

> New amendments to the guidelines raise the bar on what it means to have an effective ethics program. The amendment requires boards and executives to assume responsibility for the oversight of ethics programs. At a minimum, the guidelines require organizations to identify areas of risk where criminal violations may occur, train employees in their obligations, and give ethics officers sufficient authority and resources.[134]

As a result of the shifting compliance landscape, a compliance industry within the United States has blossomed and a new career path has opened up for potential ethics officers.[135] In addition, the appointment of chief governance officers (CGOs) in large companies is seen as helping prevent negative publicity or legal action as well as promoting a more positive image of a company. Both factors encourage investor confidence in the company's management and strategic perspective:

Pharmaceutical company Pfizer Inc. is widely credited with hiring the first chief governance officer in 1992. . . . [As late as 2002], the number of chief governance officers could be counted on one hand. . . . CGOs currently number only about 60, [but] their ranks are expected to grow exponentially over the next year or so.

Disney . . . recently appointed . . . [a] CGO in the wake of heavy criticism for a board largely perceived as a rubber stamp for CEO Michael Eisner's decisions. Disney has twice topped *BusinessWeek's* list of companies with the worst boards of directors.[136]

These appointments are also being made in reaction to the increasing profile corporate governance has enjoyed in the wake of the Sarbanes-Oxley legislation. Institutional investors, as well as the credit-rating agencies—Moody's Investors Service and Standard & Poor's—are now demanding action in this area:

Deloitte Touche Tohmatsu, for example, recently appointed a chief ethics partner at about one-third of its 85 member firms, including one in each of the major countries where the firm operates. . . . The firm has also created a Web-based ethics course for employees in all 150 countries where it operates. It has the kind of 1-800 hotline mandated by Sarbanes-Oxley for the anonymous reporting of malfeasance.[137]

Some companies, however, are more reluctant to comply. Sometimes it takes unwelcome media attention before they are encouraged to implement significant reform in this area and create such compliance positions:

[Former CEO of Walmart, Lee] Scott complained about the criticism that has been heaped on [Walmart] in the last couple of years but said the glare of the spotlight has helped the company function better. Wal-Mart created a compliance office [in 2004] that has 140 people working to ensure the company follows the rules and procedures.[138]

A key part of compliance, and the Sarbanes-Oxley legislation, includes the responsibility to identify and publicize the wrongdoing of senior officers when it is found:

The Sarbanes-Oxley law . . . protects whistle-blowers from retaliation and requires lawyers and senior executives to report wrongdoing to their superiors. Outside lawyers and auditors who alert corporate executives or directors of suspected wrongdoing are required by law to quit if no action is taken. Many corporations now have internal rules requiring employees to bring concerns to a top corporate lawyer or the board—a trend encouraged by the U.S. Sentencing Commission, which oversees sentencing guidelines and looks kindly on companies with strong legal-compliance programs.[139]

An effective ethics officer, combined with the infrastructure of an independent compliance program, encourages a healthier work environment and the ability for employees to come forward in confidence.[140]

(Continued)

(Continued)

There is a danger, however, that even the most effective ECO will be unable to establish an effective ethics culture within a firm without sufficient support from senior executives' willingness to implement it throughout operations. Some commentators have argued, counterintuitively, that a strong focus on a culture of compliance undermines the installation of a culture of ethics:

Too many boards have outsourced the task of ethics to ethics officers, who have turned to consultants to define the company's values. Ethics have become something that "other people" in the organization worry about, leaving everyone else unfettered by such concerns.[141]

Ultimately, however, the value of instilling an effective ethics and compliance program throughout operations is increasingly recognized by large firms. And, a dedicated ECO is perceived to be the most effective means of realizing such a culture:

The most compelling case for business ethics is simply what happens without them. The cost of ethical shortfalls at Enron, WorldCom, Parmalat and others is there for all to see.[142]

Online Resources

- Association for Integrity in Accounting (Citizen Works), http://www.citizenworks.org/actions/aia.php

  "The mission of the Association for Integrity in Accounting is to provide an independent forum to present and advance positions on a wide range of critical accounting and auditing issues, standards and regulations affecting the accountability and integrity of the profession and the public interest in maintaining trust and confidence in accounting."

- *CRO Magazine (formerly Business Ethics Magazine)*, http://www.thecro.com/

- *Ethics & Enron* (ethics online bookstore) has a collection of books on ethics and Enron, as well as papers, SEC filings, and other documents about the company and its downfall at http://www.ethicsweb.ca/books/enron.htm

- Ethical Leadership Group, http://www.ethicalleadershipgroup.com/

  "We provide high quality, customized consulting in ethics, compliance, value and corporate responsibility."

- Ethics and Compliance Officers Association, http://www.theecoa.org/

  "As the only organization exclusively serving ethics and compliance practitioners, ECOA is the mission-driven leader and voice for the ethics and compliance community."

- Ethics Resource Center (ERC), http://www.ethics.org/

"ERC is a nonprofit, nonpartisan research organization, dedicated to independent research that advances high ethical standards and practices in public and private institutions."

- Graduation Pledge Alliance, http://www.graduationpledge.org/

"I pledge to explore and take into account the social and environmental consequences of any job that I consider and will try to improve these aspects of any organization for which I work."

- Society of Corporate Compliance and Ethics (SCCE), http://corporatecompliance.org/

"The Society of Corporate Compliance & Ethics (SCCE) is dedicated to improving the quality of corporate governance, compliance and ethics."

- The Ethics Classroom, http://www.ethicsclassroom.info/

"The Ethics Classroom was developed as an interactive forum for individuals interested in current issues involving values, morals, and ethics across American society."

- *The Smoking Gun* (TSG, Web site) presents a copy of Enron's in-house *Code of Ethics* at http://www.thesmokinggun.com/enron/enronethics1.shtml

"TSG is understandably proud to present a copy of a truly valuable artifact, Enron's in-house "Code of Ethics." The 64-page booklet was distributed to employees along with an introductory letter from Chairman Kenneth Lay noting the "moral and honest manner" in which the energy firm's business affairs should be conducted."

Questions for Discussion and Review

1. What makes one person more or less ethical than another? Where does that component of an individual's character come from? Can ethics be taught to university students (graduate or undergraduate)? Is that a job for which universities (business schools, in particular) should be held responsible?

2. What does it mean for an organization to be *ethical?* What is the difference between an *unethical* and an *illegal* act?

3. What do you imagine the day-to-day work of an ECO entails? Do you think it is viewed as a position of importance within companies today? Why, or why not?

4. An important component of implementing an ethical or CSR perspective organization wide is consistency across departments. Do you feel that the lessons you are learning in this class are supported by classes you take from other departments in the business school?

5. What is your reaction when you read about the survey of ECOs attending the Conference Board's ethics conference, which reported:

About 45 percent said that their ethics and compliance programs would reduce the likelihood of an ethics scandal at their companies only "a little" or "not at all."?[143]

MEDIA

> **CSR CONNECTION:** This issue analyzes the role of the media in an increasingly wired world that allows NGOs and nonprofit organizations to expose corporate actions they feel to be socially irresponsible. What is the role of the media in terms of CSR?[144] To what extent do the media have a responsibility to hold firms accountable for their actions?

Issue

The expansion of global media conglomerates and the spread of TV into every corner of the world are radically changing the way we consume news and information:

Before the second world war, radio reached a mere 10% of the population, the print media no more than 20%. Now papers and TV both reach 90% of adults, and radio around 98%. The power of the media has effected a sea change in the development of public attitudes. As the raw material of politics, public opinion has become a mere reflection of the messages put out by the system, the producers of which insist unconvincingly that they follow what, in fact, they are creating. . . . Without noticing it, we are abandoning representative democracy and marching towards opinion-led democracy.[145]

The Internet multiplies this trend, threatening traditional media (newspapers, in particular)[146] and decreasing the time it takes for information to reach us:

We watch 60-second television commercials that have been sped up to fit into 30-second spots, even as we multitask our way through e-mails, text messages and tweets. . . . Changes that used to take generations . . . now unfurl in a span of years. Since 2000, we have experienced three economic bubbles (dot-com, real estate, and credit), three market crashes, a devastating terrorist attack, two wars and a global influenza pandemic.[147]

Life is lived today at a hectic pace. And, when a newsworthy event occurs, we know about it almost instantly. When a US Airways plane crash-landed in the Hudson River in New York on January 15, 2009, for example, a passenger on the ferry that went to the rescue of the plane's passengers took a photo of the plane with a cell phone (http://twitpic.com/135xa) and uploaded it instantly with the following message to Twitter:

There's a plane in the Hudson. I'm on the ferry going to pick up the people. Crazy.[148]

This trend is important for news stations because the channel that breaks the story tends to hold the viewers. And for the media today, bad news is good news is entertainment:

This obsession with speed creates problems—we report rumors, with caveats, but mistakes are made. . . . It's a complicated world. The media have a lot to say and not much time to say it. They also have to win audiences, so they sensationalize and simplify. Stalin said that every death is a tragedy; the death of a million, a mere statistic. That's how the media, albeit with different motives, work as well.[149]

Not only is news spreading much quicker, but how it is interpreted depends on the context. Activities around the world are viewed and judged by the standards where the news is absorbed, not where it occurred. When Al-Jazeera reports on U.S. actions in the Middle East, it does so for an Arab audience. Although President Obama awarded his first presidential interview with a foreign media outlet to Al-Jazeera's English channel,[150] the United States has little control over the way the country and its foreign policy is portrayed and interpreted in the streets and cafes of Baghdad or Lebanon. An ad for the channel that appeared in the *New York Times* states:

Bold and fearless journalism that doesn't shy away from the truth. We put the human being at the center of our news agenda and take you to the heart of the story. Exploring events that are often years, decades and even centuries in the making. Located at the center of the most complicated region in the world—get the real picture, every angle, every side. Al Jazeera.[151]

The speed at which news travels today and how it is ultimately interpreted should also be a point of both interest and concern for global corporations, who are already portrayed in a negative light in the media.[152] Firms can no longer trust they can control the flow of information (see Figure 4.4). No actions can be hidden and if anything goes wrong, the whole world knows about it very quickly. When two employees from Domino's Pizza decided to film a prank video in the kitchen where they worked and upload it to YouTube, for example, the consequences were swift, both for the employees and Domino's:[153]

In a few days, thanks to the power of social media, [the two employees] ended up with felony charges, more than a million disgusted viewers, and a major company facing a public relations crisis. . . . By Wednesday afternoon, the video had been viewed more than a million times on YouTube. References to it were in five of the 12 results on the first page of Google search for "Dominos," and discussions about Domino's had spread throughout Twitter.[154]

Today, a firm needs to strive to maintain positive ties with a broad array of stakeholders, both internal and external. The Internet and global media conglomerates make it relatively easy for individuals or small NGOs to mobilize and spread their message to multiple audiences before firms even know a problem exists. The growth in importance of global brands in recent years, twinned with the rise of the media conglomerate, leaves companies exposed to any consumer backlash against activities perceived to be unacceptable or running counter to the image a company's brand portrays.

Case Study   CNN

Four hostile newspapers are more to be feared than 10,000 bayonets.

—Napoleon Bonaparte[155]

The media are an essential part of the democratic society in which we live. Their role is to inform the public and hold those in power accountable to those they are supposed to serve. In an age of information overload and advertising revenue driven by viewer numbers, however, what information to present to the public and how to present it is central to the integrity of the industry. The temptation to condense in order to capture people's attention soon leads to the need to entertain to keep them watching.

Today, the news of the world is conveyed in 30-minute segments, squeezed between the sports and personal finance programs. *CNN Headline News,* without blushing, manages to fit the day's major news from around the world into a segment that used to be called "The Global Minute"! The news media often simplify the message and repeat news that is handed to them by public relations departments. As Nick Davies writes in his book, *Flat Earth News,*[156]

In the end, the researchers found that only 12 percent of stories [in the five national UK newspapers—*The Times, the Guardian, The Independent,* the *Daily Telegraph,* and the *Daily Mail*] were based on material generated entirely by the papers' own reporters.[157]

The 24-hour news cycle today is a CNN world of voyeurism and reality TV, where a firm's difficulties or ethical transgressions are everyone else's fascinating tidbits:

Fear of embarrassment at the hands of NGOs and the media has given business ethics an even bigger push. Companies have learnt the hard way that they live in a CNN world, in which bad behavior in one country can be seized on by local campaigners and beamed on the evening television news to customers back home.[158]

CNN, launched in June 1980, came to prominence in the living rooms of the world and North America, in particular, during the first Gulf War. Their willingness to push the envelope in what is expected of a 24-hour cable news channel's frontline reporters enabled them to carry on presenting after the competition had evacuated to safety:

CNN had been a failing venture until the 1991 Gulf War, when it provided the only television coverage from inside Baghdad. That exclusive was possible only because every other network had pulled its correspondents to protect their lives. Tom Johnson, CNN's president at the time, wanted to do the same, but [Ted] Turner told him: "I will take on myself the responsibility for anybody who is killed. I'll take it off of you if it's on your conscience." No one was killed, but Mr. Turner's roll of the dice with other men's lives is no less jarring.[159]

The role CNN plays in conveying information to the public is now a legitimate consideration for the U.S. government when selecting military bombing targets during a war. This is particularly so when the targets are located in civilian or urban areas. As in all aspects of society today, rapidly developing technology allows more things to be done in a much shorter time frame. In a war, the information field commanders receive has multiplied exponentially, as has the speed in which they must decide what to do. When the wrong decision or a mistake is made, CNN is there to tell the world about it:

> When missiles do go awry, as happened when the United States accidentally struck the Chinese Embassy in Belgrade in May 1999 . . . there is alarm worldwide.[160]

The "CNN Test" is the test military commanders must consider when choosing potential targets for bombing during warfare today. This issue was the focus of a number of news items in the lead up to the second Iraq war, which began in March 2003:[161]

> Military commanders have long had legal advisers. But more than ever, attorneys are in the teams that choose the strategies, the targets and even the weapons to be used. . . . And legal issues aren't the only factors [to consider]. . . . Commanders must also worry about "the CNN test." Is the target worth all the loss of innocent life—and the inevitable outcry?[162]

Public opinion greatly influences a country's foreign policy (which, after all, is determined by politicians who need to be re-elected). And the media today play a central role in shaping that public opinion. People react much more strongly to pictures that they see than to words that they read. With words, they have to use their own imagination, which requires effort; pictures are spoon-fed to the public via TV and, increasingly, the Internet. And, when the pictures are riveting, they're played over and over again until they become ingrained in the public conscience. From Vietnam to Somalia to the World Trade Center towers in New York, TV footage personalizes the story, introduces emotions, and removes the larger context within which foreign policy decisions must be made:

> [The WTO protests in Seattle in 1999] revealed a new face of globalization: the rising influence of civil society in international relations. . . . Now, international crises are measured on the CNN scale, but the media always focus on extraordinary events, distorting reality.[163]

As such, the story that the news media convey is not always complete or accurate. In his book, *Flat Earth News,* Nick Davies quotes U.S. Army General Tom Metz in a 2006 Military Review:

> We must recognize that the current global media gravitate toward information that is packaged for ease of dissemination and consumption.[164]

(Continued)

(Continued)

Nevertheless, CNN's successes have caused their competitors to respond and improve the product they deliver. From BBC World News (http://www.bbcworldnews .com/) to Al-Jazeera (Web site: http://www .aljazeera.net/english and live online at: http://www.livestation.com/aje), cable news channels have reshaped the way we watch TV and receive our news. It is perhaps not surprising, therefore, that in the same way that the first Iraq war enabled CNN to establish itself in the ultracompetitive media market, the 2007–2009 financial crisis has enabled another cable network, CNBC, to find its identity:[165]

> Partisanship aside, this is CNBC's equivalent of a war. Just as the first cable news channel, CNN, rose to prominence during the gulf war in 1991, and another one, the Fox News Channel, became a ratings leader in the period before the Iraq war in 2002 and 2003, CNBC is on a war footing. . . . the network's home audience started to surge in August 2007

as the upheaval began in the credit markets. They peaked in March 2008 when Bear Stearns was sold to JP Morgan Chase . . . After hitting a plateau that spring, the ratings soared [in fall 2008] when other investment banks collapsed, setting records for the network.[166]

The increased viewers the channel attracted in the aftermath of the financial crisis also helped its parent company, NBC, dominate the network news ratings in the United States at the time.[167] The role played by the station in reporting the crisis (both before and after it occurred), however, was not without its critics:

> A showdown between a comedian who has become one of America's most challenging news commentators and a news commentator known for his comedic antics has shone the brightest spotlight on the media market's coverage since the financial crisis began.[168]

CSR Newsletters: CNBC

For those of you who missed Jon Stewart's lambasting of CNBC on *The Daily Show* in March 2009, his interview (in three parts) with Jim Cramer (host of *Mad Money*) is compelling TV:

http://www.thedailyshow.com/watch/thu-march-12-2009/jim-cramer-pt--1

As usual, Stewart employs comedy to great effect. In addition, however, he confronts Cramer with an honesty and directness that you rarely see on current affairs TV in the United States. Stewart articulates succinctly the behavior of Wall Street that got us into the mess of the 2007–2009 financial crisis but also skewers Cramer (and CNBC) for becoming part of the problem, rather than being the journalists they purport to be. As a result, the interview is both entertaining and uncomfortable to watch because Stewart so completely undermines what it is that must get Cramer out of bed every morning to do his show.

Stewart's analysis was all the more compelling because it challenged what it means to be a journalist in a democratic society today. Beyond merely castigating CNBC (and, by implication, the business media in general) for failing to perform their role of oversight more effectively, Stewart accuses CNBC of complicity—knowing what was going on, but being overly concerned with their status as *insiders,* rather than maintaining their journalistic integrity. To what extent is journalism part of the establishment and to what extent do journalists have a civic responsibility to hold the great social institutions (e.g., politics and businesses) accountable for their actions? It is hard to do both:

> The problem here is not individuals but attitudes, including a media culture that causes some people, particularly in the entertainment-driven medium of television, to blur the line between entertainment, good journalism and sound analysis. . . . As long as everyone was making money, nobody wanted to hear the bad news.[169]

As indicated by other commentators, the media, with all their flaws, are only capable of writing "a flawed first draft of history" as it unfolds.[170] This does not stop attention-demanding anchors such as Jim Cramer, however, from continuing to seek out the limelight:

> There is only one Jim Cramer, host of CNBC's popular finance show *Mad Money.* His latest notable outburst came [in April 2009]: "Right now, right here, on this show—I am announcing the depression [is] over!" He is going too far again.[171]

This discussion does not diminish the concern firms should have about their loss of control over the free flow of information. If anything, it should heighten it. As we become increasingly interconnected and words and images are shared more freely, the ability to assert control is lost, and it is not coming back. The Internet is anarchic at heart. As a result, firms need to do all they can to ensure their relations with their myriad of stakeholders are as positive as possible, to ensure they do not become the next victim of this communication medium.

Online Resources

- 10 × 10, http://tenbyten.org/10x10.html

  "10 × 10™ (ten by ten) is an interactive exploration of the words and pictures that define the time. . . . Every hour, 10x10 collects the 100 words and pictures that matter most on a global scale, and presents them as a single image, taken to encapsulate that moment in time."

- Accuracy in Media, http://www.aim.org/

  "Accuracy In Media is a non-profit, grassroots citizens watchdog of the news media that critiques botched and bungled news stories and sets the record straight on important issues that have received slanted coverage."

- BBC World News, http://www.bbcworldnews.com/

  "BBC World News is the BBC's commercially funded, international 24-hour news and information channel, broadcast in English in more than 200 countries and territories across the globe."

- Business & Media Institute, http://www.businessandmedia.org/

  "The mission of BMI is to audit the media's coverage of the free enterprise system. It is our goal to bring balance to economic reporting and to promote fair portrayal of the business community in the media."

- CNBC, http://www.cnbc.com/

  "CNBC is the recognized world leader in business news, providing real-time financial market coverage and business information to more than 340 million homes worldwide, including more than 95 million households in the United States and Canada."

- Mad Money, http://www.cnbc.com/id/15838459

  "Our mission is educational, to teach you how to analyze stocks and the market through the prism of events."

- CNN, http://www.cnn.com/

  "CNN is the original 24-hour cable television news service. In 2003, CNN/U.S. delivered its highest audience levels in a decade, maintaining a 20-percent-plus advantage vs. its two closest competitors in total unique viewers and all key demographics."

- Independent Media Center, http://www.indymedia.org/

  "The Independent Media Center is a network of collectively run media outlets for the creation of radical, accurate, and passionate tellings of the truth. We work out of a love and inspiration for people who continue to work for a better world, despite corporate media's distortions and unwillingness to cover the efforts to free humanity."

- mediachannel.org, http://www.mediachannel.org/

  "MediaChannel is concerned with the political, cultural and social impacts of the media, large and small. MediaChannel exists to provide information and diverse perspectives and inspire debate, collaboration, action and citizen engagement."

- Media CSR Forum, http://www.mediacsrforum.org/

  "The "Media corporate social responsibility (CSR) forum" is a group of media organisations developing CSR and sustainability practices and understanding for the UK media sector."

- The Daily Show with Jon Stewart, http://www.thedailyshow.com/

"One anchor, six correspondents, zero credibility. . . . *The Daily Show* with Jon Stewart, the nightly half-hour series unburdened by objectivity, journalistic integrity or even accuracy. . . . *The Daily Show* with Jon Stewart—it's even better than being informed."

Questions for Discussion and Review

1. Do the media today *report* the news or *distort* the news? Do we watch *news* or *entertainment?* What do you think CNN's role, or the BBC's, should be? What about Al-Jazeera?[172] Is news reporting objective or culturally biased?

2. Should the armed services have to answer to CNN or any other news organization? Isn't that the responsibility of the civilian planners and politicians that shape the strategies that the armed services implement? Should the media's powers be restricted during wartime? Have embedded journalists helped the reporting of war or just upped the entertainment level closer to Hollywood special-effects levels?

3. Is collateral damage or friendly fire an acceptable cost of war? Is it acceptable for innocent lives to be sacrificed in the name of national security?

4. What is the correct role of a media channel in a democratic society? Are the media there to police society's institutions and hold them accountable based on their own biases and political agendas? Or are they there to report the news objectively without taking sides? From what you know of CNBC, did they perform well or badly in terms of reporting before, during, and after the 2007–2009 financial crisis?

5. Watch the three parts of Jon Stewart's interview of Jim Cramer from CNBC's *Mad Money* (http://www.thedailyshow.com/watch/thu-march-12-2009/jim-cramer-pt-1). Do you think Stewart's questions are fair? What do you think about Cramer's answers? As a result of the interview, do you trust Cramer's stock advice more or less? Why?

NGOS

> **CSR CONNECTION:** This issue forms an important element of the CSR debate. Globalization and the growth of the Internet empower stakeholders, giving them the means to communicate and mobilize. They are equalizing powers that allow individuals or small groups to hold corporations more accountable. As such, there is a strategic advantage for companies and NGOs that maintain open lines of communication.

Issue

To what extent has globalization changed the nature of the debate surrounding CSR? How has globalization made CSR more relevant and more immediate for businesses, particularly global corporations? The Internet has provided businesses with a powerful tool to expand the global reach of operations while greatly increasing efficiencies. It has also, however, increased their exposure globally. The Internet provides a communications network to nonprofit organizations (NPOs), nongovernmental organizations (NGOs), and consumer activists, who use it to band together and convey their message to supporters worldwide. Thus, the Internet poses risks for firms; it also, however, presents numerous opportunities.

As discussed in Chapter 1 and Chapter 4, a major reason for the increased influence of NGOs and consumers in the corporate world today is the shift in control of the free flow of information. The abundance of information and the speed with which it can be disseminated dramatically alters the balance of power between individuals, NGOs, regulating authorities, and corporations. It is an enabling power that some feel, unless managed correctly, is in danger of spiraling out of control:

> A few facts, mixed with fear, speculation and rumor, amplified and relayed swiftly worldwide by modern information technologies, have affected national and international economies, politics and even security in ways that are utterly disproportionate with the root realities. . . . Managed and understood, however, the forces that fuel infodemics can . . . help us reduce the number of distortional and destabilizing outbreaks of the types we have recently seen.[173]

Another powerful reason for the increased influence of NGOs today is simply the rapid growth in their numbers, which took place during the last half of the 20th century. As a result,

> Collectively, nonprofit organizations . . . have a significant impact on the [U.S.] economy, controlling more than $1 trillion in assets and earning nearly $700 billion annually.[174]

The *Independent Sector,* a nonprofit-focused publication, reports,

> Nonprofit employment has doubled in the last 25 years and now represents 9.5% of the U.S. work force.[175]

Howard Rheingold believes this activist trend, enhanced by technology, extends beyond organized NGOs to the spontaneous actions of individuals. By using the Internet, individuals and small groups can quickly and easily band together to enact powerful change. These "Smart Mobs" are all the more powerful because of their tendency to form and disband spontaneously for single events, aligning with others who share their passion for the issue at hand. He terms this behavior a higher form of democracy, or "ad-hocracy." Rheingold focuses specifically on the power of mobile or wireless technology and text messaging, citing the overthrow of President Joseph Estrada in the Philippines in 2001, but he believes the power of wireless technology in the hands of individual citizens is beyond current comprehension:

> Imagine the impact of the Rodney King video multiplied by the people power of Napster.[176]

Mobile technology is particularly influential in areas of the world that don't yet have easy access to land telephone lines and therefore cannot access the Internet using computers, as in much of the developed world. Thus, mobile phones open up much of the developing world to the power of the Internet and help circumvent authorities that attempt to curtail people power. Their influence becomes even more apparent as camera phones become standard and Web sites evolve to allow people to display the photos they take.

CSR Newsletters: IT

A recent article[177] demonstrates the extent to which the revolution in communications technology, twinned with the increasingly wired, online world, is empowering individual stakeholders:

> The Hub (http://hub.witness.org/) [is] a video-sharing Web site launched by ex-rock star Peter Gabriel to empower people to document and publicize unseen atrocities. Now in beta, the Hub allows anyone around the world to submit clips to a central site where its target audience of activists can connect and take action.

Although still most evident in terms of political issues, it is easy to imagine how this technology can extrapolate to ever increasing vigilance of corporate activities in a way that drives CSR further up the agendas of corporate executives:

> "Once everyone has a camera inside a mobile phone, the issue is about creating a place where people can upload footage safely and make connections with people who might further their cause and their campaigns" [Gabriel says] . . . The site also lets users comment on the content and eventually will host discussion groups, online petitions, and interactive maps.

What is important is the education of individual stakeholders (in particular, consumers) so that firms are fully incentivized to change. This message is apparent in another article:[178]

> For some reason, though, retailers haven't figured out how to inspire customers to buy, say, organic cotton. It's bad marketing. If consumers knew how many chemicals it takes to grow and manufacture conventional cotton goods—how it affects our water, food, air, and our risk of cancer—maybe that would change. In a crowded marketplace, it is an unexploited competitive advantage.

Corporations, too, should use globalization to spot consumer and activist trends originating in one area of the world before it reaches them in their area of the world:

> If you're an American firm, listen to what your European divisions and partners say. . . . Europe is becoming an "incubator" of social issues for American firms. . . . Most European companies have a broader view of who their stakeholders are; American firms often concentrate solely on their stockholders.[179]

The power of the Internet (in all its manifestations) to spread information and to inform lies beyond the control of authoritarian governments, just as it lies beyond the control of individual corporations. As consumers, nonprofits, and NGOs realize the power they have been granted to combat institutions (governmental or corporate) that were previously thought to be unassailable, corporations face much greater scrutiny and public pressure to ensure they have a genuine and effective CSR policy in place. Firms, therefore, that embrace both the technology and the nonprofit and activist organizations that wield it will cope much better than those that resist their stakeholders' interests.[180] In reality, for firms in today's modern society, "the moral high ground goes to anyone with a Web site."[181] As a result,

Twitter is the canary in the coal mine of public opinion.[182]

Case Study   Product (RED)

Increasingly, corporations around the world are seeing an opportunity to work in partnership with nongovernmental organizations (NGOs) that previously might have campaigned against the company or its products. Perceptions of CSR stimulate consumer and other stakeholders' reactions that can either advance or hold back an organization's ability to succeed. Corporations have sought to create favorable relations with NGOs as the strategic value of such relationships has become increasingly apparent:

Corporations provided more than $9 billion in gifts to nonprofit organizations and charities in 2001. Corporate sponsors spent more than $700 million in the previous year to sponsor nonprofit organizations and social causes. . . . An increasing number of executives now point to collaborations with NPOs as an important component of their corporate social responsibility strategies.[183]

Getting the seal of approval from a highly visible NGO can be an effective selling point for a company trying to differentiate its products and help it gain a sustainable competitive advantage. Two important conditions are necessary, however, to ensure any cooperation between a firm and a NGO works for all involved. First, it is important for a corporation to separate the serious NGOs that want to engage in dialogue and reach a practical solution, from the radical NGOs who believe that "just talking to corporations is a sellout, and that only violent revolution will change the world."[184] As in business, selecting NGO partners wisely is vital for a successful outcome. And, second, it is important for the NGO to see the practical advantages that can be gained by engaging business on business's terms, while maintaining the integrity of core values and retaining the objectivity necessary to criticize the same companies when necessary. The attraction both for firms and their nonprofit partners, therefore, is clear. Both sides, however, are also aware of the downsides of publicly aligning themselves with each other:[185]

Even within a more meaningful relationship, companies risk wasting time and money, and possibly divulging sensitive information which could be misused. NGOs risk reputational damage if a partnership goes wrong and wasting scarce resources if the desired outcomes are not achieved. The risks can be worth it, of course. For businesses, an NGO can bring knowledge and expertise, but also credibility and reputational gains. . . . For an NGO, business brings money, but more substantially a chance to change the way that particular business, and possibly a whole industry, operates.[186]

One of the earliest examples of businesses and NGOs working together was Greenpeace's 1992 approval of an environmentally appropriate refrigerator containing a new technology, *Greenfreeze:*

Since 1992, Greenfreeze has become the dominant technology in North Western Europe, having taken over nearly 100% of the German market. . . . By the year 2000, over 40 million Greenfreeze refrigerators will have been built in Europe alone. . . . There are over 100 different Greenfreeze models on the market. . . . All of the major European companies, Bosch/Siemens, Electrolux, Liebherr, Miele, Quelle, Vestfrost, Whirlpool, Bauknecht, Foron, AEG are marketing Greenfreeze.[187]

Even with this relative success story, however, differences in strategic approach regarding the technology caused difficulties for Greenpeace's corporate partner, Foron Household Appliances of Germany:

As the technology could not be patented, Foron relied heavily on Greenpeace's public endorsement and grassroots campaign to generate sales. In the first three months of the campaign, 70,000 orders were received. In the meantime, however, Greenpeace was actively giving away the technology to other companies and entrepreneurs as part of its efforts to generate industrywide change. . . . Without Greenpeace's marketing support and without a competitive edge, the company lost its advantage and subsequently declared bankruptcy.[188]

The decision to work in partnership with certain corporations in developing this technology was a conscious move by Greenpeace. Many within the NGO saw the importance of accessing markets and consumer power, where possible, rather than merely relying on direct action alone. Paul Gilding,[189] a former executive director of Greenpeace International, saw the Greenfreeze project as a tactical deviation from direct action to

"solutions campaigning" . . . work[ing] privately with individual companies, while continuing to attack business publicly. . . . Civil disobedience apart, the most potent NGO tactics of the future will unquestionably revolve around redesigning and creating markets for more sustainable outcomes.[190]

Other examples of NGOs working together with multinational corporations to

(Continued)

(Continued)

achieve common goals include McDonald's alliance with the Environmental Defense Fund (EDF) to seek ways of minimizing waste throughout McDonald's operations, as well as Starbucks's partnerships with the Alliance for Environmental Innovation and Conservation International to explore how the coffee company can make its products and supply chains more sustainable.[191]

It is important to point out, however, that there are more examples of both individual and NGO activism working to shame corporations into changing their operating practices than there are examples of constructive relationships.[192] If corporations were looking for an incentive to begin communicating and cooperating with relevant NGOs, then the reputational damage inflicted on companies that ignored NGOs and their supporters can be motivating. Coca-Cola's run-in with the controversial group Adbusters, for example, saw the innovative NGO successfully turn Coke's multimillion-dollar advertising campaign back on itself, making a political point and directly affecting sales:

> Coca-Cola buckled within weeks after its precious brand and Olympic sponsorship were embroiled in a campaign against the company's use of greenhouse-polluting HFCs in refrigeration units. . . . Adbusters launched "culture jamming" attacks on the company's logos and slogans, demonstrating novel and creative approaches that can be a key feature of successful market campaigning.[193]

More recently, rather than relying on the operational expertise of for-profit firms to advance their agenda, activists have begun to design and implement their own business models and then invite firms to participate. While this provides the firms with an easier means of presenting themselves to their consumers as concerned citizens, the NGOs who orchestrate the campaigns benefit from the legitimacy offered by major corporations, as well as the access they provide to a broad market that is increasingly seeking ways to make socially responsible purchase decisions.

Bono's Product (RED)[194] is a good example of how activists are beginning to wrest control of project operations from corporations and dictate the terms under which they can participate in the enterprise.

CSR Newsletters: Product (RED)

A recent article[195] offers a detailed case study of the early successes and failures of Product (Red):

> Product Red, announced [in 2006] at the World Economic Forum at Davos, is seeking a commercial solution to the humanitarian disaster of Aids in Africa.

The idea is being led by Bono and is designed as cause-related marketing, with firms designing products that incorporate the brand (and red color), improving sales by associating with a worthy and high-profile cause, and donating a percentage of profits to support the treatment of AIDS in Africa:

Red works quite simply. Its trademark, a pair of red parentheses symbolising the embrace of solidarity, is licensed to "partner companies" which use it on specific products. In return, the partners donate some of the revenue or profits to the Geneva-based Global Fund to Fight Aids, Tuberculosis and Malaria—launched in 2002 to combat the diseases in the developing world—and pay a fee to Red itself to cover marketing and administration.

The ethos behind the brand is that there is a market solution to poverty, and many are encouraged by Red's progress. Within a year, Product (RED) "put 800,000 people in the developing world as a whole on antiretroviral drugs" and aimed to double that number in year two. It would be interesting to know, however, whether consumers are buying the products because they sympathize with the cause (ultimately, a limited market), or seek the value these differentiated products bring and are willing to pay the associated premium (potentially, a much larger, sustainable market).

It is interesting to contrast the cynicism towards the idea "that we can help poor victims of AIDS in Africa by going shopping" with the notable success of Product (RED):

$110 million. That's the amount of money that (Red) partners have generated for the Global Fund To Fight AIDS, Tuberculosis and Malaria to provide AIDS treatment in Ghana, Rwanda, Swaziland and Lesotho.[196]

Product (RED) was launched in January 2006[197] with the stated aim of commercial viability. Bono was clear that Product (RED) is not a charity but seeks to appeal to (and expand) "the market for conscious consumers."[198] Product (RED) started its campaign with firms largely from the apparel industry:

Partner companies include Gap, which is selling a number of Red-branded products including an African cotton T-shirt made in Lesotho; Converse,

which is offering a limited-edition sneaker made of African mud cloth; and Giorgio Armani, which plans to expand its Product Red line to include fragrances and jewelry this spring.[199]

The range of firms and industries involved in the project today and the different kinds of products included, however, is significantly more extensive:

Now you can buy (Red) phones from Motorola, (Red) iPods from Apple, (Red) greeting cards from Hallmark, (Red) laptops from Dell, (Red) shoes from Converse and (Red) watches from Emporio Armani.[200]

In spite of Product (RED)'s success, however, it has still been criticized on three main points that expose the limitations of such campaigns.[201] In spite of the project's claim of commercial viability, it is also clear that they draw heavily on ethical purchase decisions—the market for which is limited. The first criticism centers on the

(Continued)

(Continued)

the participating firms in terms of the amounts of money donated for each Product (RED) product purchased. Although Product (RED) donates "about 40% to 50%" of profits to the global AIDS fund to support its work in Africa[202] and claims on its Web site that a participating firm "give up to fifty-percent of its profit to buy and distribute antiretroviral medicine to our brothers and sisters dying of AIDS in Africa,"[203] when a consumer purchases a Product (RED) T-shirt from Gap, for example, it is not clear the actual amount of money that is being forwarded by Gap. This issue is related to the larger concern about the accountability of NGOs that adopt strong positions in advocating their cause without any indication that they represent a significant body of opinion. In response, Product (RED) claims the support of the market:

> Mr. Clinton praises the rock singer Bono's campaign to obtain debt forgiveness for African countries. Whether this is a wise move or not, who elected Bono to do it? The answer is, capitalism did.[204]

The second criticism questions whether the goal of the campaign, to encourage further consumption, represents a sustainable solution to any social problem. This is a harder point to rebut as many think our economic model at present is unsustainable. Product (RED), however, would no doubt argue that they are working within the framework that exists to bring about valuable social change:

> But Americans already consume way too much stuff. The message of Product

(Red) is that we can buy that new cell phone or wrist watch and feel good about it because we are helping victims of AIDS.[205]

The final (weaker) criticism raises the potential for Product (RED)'s success to result in an overall decrease in social engagement:

> But what if, after buying that Gap T-shirt, consumers feel they've done their part? What if Product (Red) becomes a substitute for either activism or charitable giving?[206]

It is important to note that all three of these criticisms are directed more at Product (RED) and less at the firms with which the organization partners. While a number of NGO partnerships cause more problems than they are worth for firms, Product (RED) appears to be more successful. One explanation for this success is the extent to which Product (RED) was founded on market principles and has avoided the labels *charity* or *philanthropy*. Philanthropy has a role to play within CSR, but strategic CSR, in its entirety, represents a much more comprehensive approach to business. Bono understands this distinction and is able to sell the idea of Product (RED) to firms from a perspective to which firms can relate. Product (RED)'s success, therefore, also demonstrates the hit-and-miss aspect of corporate philanthropy, which is often driven by the timing and "trendiness" of the issue at hand, rather than any objective calculation of the relative needs of the victims. Bono's focus, in contrast, is a sustainable operation.

Rather than short-term charity, it is much more important to secure meaningful, long-term commitment from the business community to help solve some of the largest social problems facing humanity today, often in the developing world. This means identifying instances of profit potential that can mobilize firms in areas where they are not currently active. To the extent that Product (RED) is able to meet the needs of the "conscious consumer," while also serving consumers who just want to buy a fashionable, well-designed, and effective T-shirt, computer, or credit card, it demonstrates a superior business model to existing alternatives. Of the three kinds of organizations operating within society (for-profit, non-profit, and governmental), only for-profit organizations have the resources combined with the efficiency and innovation to tackle these largest issues on a meaningful, societal scale. An effective partnership with a well-run NGO focusing on a specific issue provides a meaningful way to combine market gain and added social value.

Online Resources

- Adbusters, http://www.adbusters.org/

"We are a global network of artists, activists, writers, pranksters, students, educators and entrepreneurs who want to advance the new social activist movement of the information age. Our aim is to topple existing power structures and forge a major shift in the way we will live in the 21st century."

- Business for Social Responsibility, http://www.bsr.org/

"BSR works with its global network of more than 250 member companies to develop sustainable business strategies and solutions through consulting, research, and cross-sector collaboration."

- Guidestar, http://www2.guidestar.org/

"GuideStar's Mission: To revolutionize philanthropy and nonprofit practice by providing information that advances transparency, enables users to make better decisions, and encourages charitable giving."

- Independent Sector, http://www.independentsector.org/

"Independent Sector is the leadership forum for charities, foundations, and corporate giving programs committed to advancing the common good in America and around the world."

- Leader to Leader Institute (formerly The Peter F. Drucker Foundation), http://www.pfdf.org/

  "Mission Statement: To Strengthen the Leadership of the Social Sector."

- NGO Café, http://www.gdrc.org/ngo/

  "Realizing the growing importance and voice of NGOs in development in general, the NGO Café was set up on the internet as a meeting place for NGOs to discuss, debate and disseminate information on their work, strategies and results."

- NGO Global Network, http://www.ngo.org/

  "[Our] aim is to help promote collaborations between NGOs throughout the world, so that together we can more effectively partner with the United Nations and each other to create a more peaceful, just, equitable and sustainable world for this and future generations."

- NGO Worldline, http://www.sover.net/~paulven/ngo.html

  "A place on the Web for and about the international community of non-governmental organizations."

- Product (RED), http://www.joinred.com/

  "(RED) is not a charity. (RED) is not a cause. (RED) is not a theory. (RED) is a simple idea that transforms our incredible collective power as consumers into a financial force to help others in need. (RED) is where desire meets virtue."

Questions for Discussion and Review

1. NGOs and nonprofits, along with charities, form the *social sector*. What important functions do these organizations perform that cannot be performed by either governmental or for-profit organizations?

2. What potential problems do you see in the rapid growth of nonprofit or nongovernmental organizations? For whom do these groups speak? To whom are they accountable? Particularly in terms of accountability, how might their legitimacy be improved?

3. What advantages and/or disadvantages are there for corporations that work closely with NGOs or nonprofit organizations? Can you think of any examples of successful partnerships?

4. Do NGOs lose their legitimacy if they begin cooperating with the very companies whose actions they are trying to affect? Where should the line be drawn?

5. Many NGOs face a real issue of accountability and transparency. Any independently wealthy individual can set up a nonprofit or NGO and claim to be an expert on a particular issue. Using the Internet, it is relatively easy to mobilize support. How would you advise a company to deal with an NGO causing it problems if the company does not feel the NGO represents one of its significant stakeholder groups?

RELIGION

> **CSR CONNECTION:** This issue places *religion* in a CSR context. To what extent is religion a unifying concept? How can firms incorporate religion into their operating and strategic outlook? What does it mean to be socially responsible with respect to religion?

Issue

What does it mean to be socially responsible with respect to religion? Beyond tolerance, how can firms respond to stakeholders' religious needs and interests without changing the firm's position from issue to issue or seeming to favor one constituency over another? Where people disagree, how can firms respect that diversity to the advantage of all?

In the United States, it is hard to identify definitive statistics about the religious profile of the nation. Religion is a sensitive subject. Federal law, for example, prohibits the census from asking someone's religious affiliation on anything other than a voluntary basis.[207] There are some interesting statistics available from other sources, however. From these sources, a religious profile of the U.S. can be constructed using 2007 data, as illustrated in Figure 8.4.

Figure 8.4 Religion in the United States (2007)

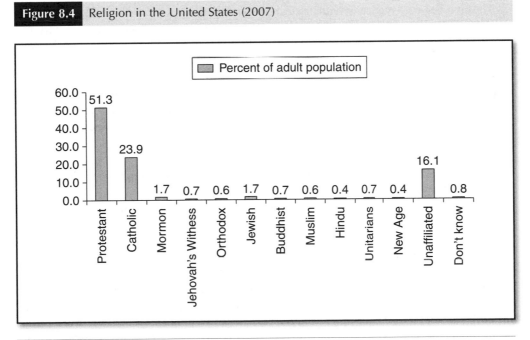

Source: "U.S. Religious Landscape Survey," The Pew Forum on Religion & Public Life, Washington, D.C., February 2008. Downloaded from: http://www.census.gov/compendia/statab/cats/population/religion.html

The data presented in Figure 8.4 can be compared against numbers published by John Green from the University of Akron:

> White Evangelicals alone—many of whom support the Christian Right and who voted overwhelmingly for President Bush in 2004—make up 26% of the population. . . . When you add in Catholics, mainline Protestants, black Evangelicals, and other Christians, Green figures that nearly 80% of Americans are affiliated with a Christian church.[208]

Some have interpreted these data as an indication that religion in the United States, while still stronger than in most developed countries, is not as strong as it used to be. According to the 2009 American Religious Identification Survey,

> the number of Americans who claim no religious affiliation has nearly doubled since 1990, rising from 8 to 15 percent. . . . the percentage of self-identified Christians has fallen 10 percentage points since 1990, from 86 to 76 percent. . . . A separate Pew Forum poll echoed the ARIS finding, reporting that the percentage of people who say they are unaffiliated with any particular faith has doubled in recent years, to 16 percent. . . . This is not to say that the Christian God is dead, but that he is less of a force in American politics and culture than at any other time in recent memory.[209]

It is also true, however, that

> The number of Americans with faith in a spiritual being—nearly nine in 10—has not changed much over the past two decades, according to historical polling. . . . Eighty-five percent said religion is "very important" or "fairly important" in their own lives—a number that hasn't changed much since 1992.[210]

Of course, the degree of importance of religion in a country is more interesting as a relative measure. In the United Kingdom, the census includes questions about religious affiliation. As such, an accurate profile of the religious affiliation of the population is more readily available:

> The 2001 Census identified 8.6 million people in Great Britain who said they had no religion. Christianity is the main religion, with 41 million people. Muslims were the largest non-Christian religious group—1.6 million—and their profile shows a young, tightly clustered, but often disadvantaged, community.[211]

As the data in Figure 8.5 indicate, a significant number of people in the United Kingdom identify themselves as having "no religion" (15.1%). This is a stronger label than the 16.1% of Americans who identify themselves as "unaffiliated," which includes those who are religious but not affiliated with a particular church or organized religion. In a *Newsweek* poll in the United States, for example, "Only 9 percent [of respondents] said they were neither religious nor spiritual."[212] Combining the "No religion" and the "Religion not stated" groups

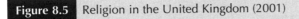

Figure 8.5   Religion in the United Kingdom (2001)

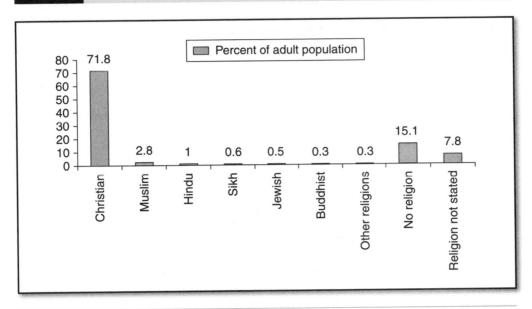

Source: UK Government's National Statistics, April 2009, http://www.statistics.gov.uk/cci/nugget.asp?id=954

from Figure 8.5 gives a total in the United Kingdom of 22.9%, much larger than the 16.9% of Americans in Figure 8.4 who are either "Unaffiliated" or "Don't know." This difference is reflected in everyday life, where religion plays a role in the United States to which many British find it hard to relate.[213] Ironically, it is the United States (with a constitutionally defined separation of Church and State) that is overtly religious, whereas the United Kingdom (where the head of State, the Queen, is also the head of the State Church of England) is more agnostic and atheist.[214]

In spite of this distinction, however, religion causes as many issues in the United Kingdom as the United States; they just tend to be of a different nature. While in the United States, for example, it is hard to imagine a candidate being elected president unless he/she is willing to state publicly (and often) his/her belief in God, in the United Kingdom, religion is detrimental to a successful political career. As Alistair Campbell, Tony Blair's press secretary, famously declared when the prime minister was asked a question about his Christianity, "We don't do religion!"

While in the United States, the overly sensitive nature of the religious debate means that even a minor slight can have major ramifications, in the United Kingdom, it is the lack of sensitivity to issues surrounding religion that tend to be the problem. In 2006, for example, British Airways found itself in the media spotlight for suspending an employee for wearing "a small crucifix." In defense of its actions, and in the face of strong public criticism and accusations of "religious discrimination," BA reverted to parroting its "uniform policy," looking somewhat ridiculous in the process:

> BA says that, under its uniform policy, employees may wear jewelry—including religious symbols—but it must be concealed underneath the uniform. However, the airline says that items such as turbans, hijabs, and bangles can be worn "as it is not practical for staff to conceal them beneath their uniforms."[215]

At around the same time, a government minister drew attention to himself for criticizing a Muslim teacher who wore a veil during school lessons. The minister, Jack Straw (then Leader of the House of Commons), suggested the veil helped create "parallel communities" within Britain[216] and that if he could choose, "he would prefer Muslim women not to wear veils which cover the face."[217] And, in 2009, the Atheist Bus Campaign (http://www.atheistbus .org.uk/) launched a series of advertisements on London's famous red buses to promote atheism in the country. The campaign was initially intended to counter overtly religious ads that had been displayed previously on the buses and present "a corrective to the religious [ads]."[218] The text of the ads read:

> There's probably no God. Now stop worrying and enjoy your life.[219]

Gaining the support of high-profile atheists, such as Richard Dawkins (famous for his book, *The God Delusion*),[220] however, the campaign was an overwhelming success and is expanding internationally:

> When the organizers announced the effort in October [2008], they said they hoped to raise a modest $8,000 or so. But something seized people's imagination. . . . the campaign raised $150,000 in four days. [In January 2009, the campaign] has more than $200,000, and . . . unveiled its advertisements on 800 buses across Britain.[221]

In contrast, in the United States, when issues arise, it tends to be because of the overbearing influence of too much religion, rather than a lack of sensitivity to the issue. The political influence of the Christian Right, for example, is well-reported. What is less well known is the influence this same lobby has over firm behavior in the United States:

> Wal-Mart and Land's End have been forced to apologize for slighting Christmas. And the [American Family Association] has boasted that its complaints led to Ford yanking ads for Jaguar and Land Rover from gay publications.[222]

A similar fight in 2005 over support for gay rights legislation in Washington state (protecting gays and lesbians against employment discrimination) saw Microsoft criticized by fundamentalist Christian groups. Microsoft eventually withdrew its support for the legislation under criticism from the gay and lesbian community.[223] The company also faced similar pressures over its support for legislation supporting employee benefits for same-sex partners in 2007/2008.[224]

In the United States, however, religion also has its lighter side, with commentators using humor to convey their message. The What Would Jesus Drive? (WWJDrive) campaign (http://www.whatwouldjesusdrive.info/intro.php), for example, is organized and sponsored by the Evangelical Environmental Network (EEN), a biblically orthodox Christian environmental organization. The campaign seeks to reduce the numbers of SUVs, vans, and pickups on U.S. roads because of the environmental damage these vehicles cause. In terms of critics, the controversial comedian Bill Maher, after drawing public ire by refusing to label the 9/11 terrorists *cowards,* decided to take on organized religion in a documentary titled *Religulous.* The film is effective because it

takes savagely funny pot-shots at three of the major religions (Christianity, Judaism and Islam) and the apparently deluded 3.7 billion people who practice them. "We're looking at the zillions of religious people in the world," he says. "These are nice people who happen to need their myths to live by. We ask: 'How does all this turn into suicide bombings, exorcisms and [molesting] children?'"[225]

In terms of the CSR debate, to what extent are religion and business compatible? In general,

Businesses should accept the diverse cultural traditions of their staff, provided they do not threaten their ability to succeed as businesses. Society should also accept that diversity, provided its expression does not threaten the core values of freedom, equality and the rule of law. . . . In the vast majority of cases [of conflict between a firm's pursuit of success and employee rights to religious expression], firms and employees should be able to find sensible compromises, without interference by government or the law.[226]

An appreciation of the world's religions helps firms implement tolerant and diverse policies that appeal to all stakeholders. As such, in addressing the question, "Is ethical capitalism possible?" Devin Stewart answers a resounding "yes":

Ethical principles that emphasize reciprocal rights and responsibilities have long characterized human societies. The Golden Rule is a feature of more than 100 world religious and cultural canons. . . . The ancient Egyptians and Greeks alike pointed to the moral worth of not doing to your neighbor "what you would take ill from him." The Golden Rule is found in both the Old and the New Testament, with the Great Commandment found in Leviticus: "Love thy neighbor as thyself." For Islam, the Golden Rule was offered in the last sermon of Muhammad: "Hurt no one so that no one may hurt you." Variations and extensions of the principle are also found in Buddhism, Hinduism, Taoism, and Jainism.[227]

Different groups recognize this common ground among all religions and seek to encourage it, rather than emphasize issues that demarcate religions. The Charter for Compassion is a good example of such an organization:

By recognizing that the Golden Rule is fundamental to all world religions, the Charter for Compassion can inspire people to think differently about religion. The Charter is a collaborative project and everyone is encouraged to participate.[228]

Tom Chappell, the CEO of Tom's of Maine, presents a good example of how to incorporate religion into everyday working life. In his case, the time he spent at Harvard Divinity School during a break from running his company provided him with

"a worldview that I could use everywhere in life." More important, he says, he no longer felt he had to apologize for wanting to incorporate values more thoroughly into his business. After Harvard, he says, "I could argue quite confidently that a holistic view of what's good for society or nature was also good for consumers and shareholders."[229]

While there is certainly no conflict between capitalism and religion, in general, however, specific areas of business raise difficult moral challenges for religious believers. Stefan Stern of the *Financial Times,* for example, argues that the finance industry is a particularly challenging forum in which to work, be successful, yet remain true to a strong moral and religious compass. He argues this has been particularly so recently and cites a book by a vice chairman of UBS bank, Ken Costa,[230] in support of his argument:

During the last 30 years, being a Christian at work has, if anything, become more difficult. . . . Financial markets have become more volatile, decisions more complex and few choices are clear-cut. . . . The work place is the coal-face where faith is tested and sharpened by day-to-day encounters with ambiguities and stresses of modern commerce.[231]

Rather than evidence that this makes religion and finance incompatible, however, Costa finds plenty of support for his career choice in the Bible:

He reminds us that in the Bible's parable of the talents (Luke 19:11–27) it is the two servants who put the master's money to work who are rewarded, while the one who preserved the capital and took no risks is punished. And he quotes the great Methodist John Wesley, who told his followers: "Gain all you can, without hurting either yourself or your neighbor."[232]

Books on Religion and Business

- Tom Chappell, *Managing Upside Down: The Seven Intentions of Values-centered Leadership,* William Morrow & Co., 1999.
- Laura Nash and Scotty McLennan, *Church on Sunday, Work on Monday: The Challenge of Fusing Christian Values With Business Life,* Jossey-Bass, 2001.
- Douglas A. Hicks, *Religion and the Workplace: Pluralism, Spirituality, Leadership,* Cambridge University Press, 2003.
- Ken Costa, *God at Work: Living Every Day With Purpose,* Continuum Books, 2007.

Case Study   Islamic Finance

Further evidence that the worlds of religion and finance are compatible (or, at least, that the market is capable of adapting to religious needs when there is sufficient potential profit at stake) can be seen in the rapid growth in Shari`a-compliant financial instruments.

CSR Newsletters: Religious SRI Funds

A recent article[233] presents a new subset of the socially responsible investing (SRI) community—"religiously themed mutual funds":

> There are around 50 of these funds, with assets topping $17 billion, according to investment researcher Morningstar Inc., up from $500 million 10 years ago.

As usual with stories about SRI, the article follows its early enthusiasm with debate questioning the *wisdom* or *value* of such themed mutual funds. The story reflects, however, the seeming rising profile of religion within the CSR realm.

Reinforcing this sense, another article[234] appeared on the front page of the *Financial Times* announcing the first leveraged buy-out in the West to be financed solely by bonds compliant with Shari`a (Islamic) law:

> Now West LB, the German bank, has been appointed to arrange £225m of quasi-debt finance to back the LBO—but only that which accords with the Koran's opposition to interest and speculation.

Religion and finance have not always happily co-existed. Usury (the charging of interest), which is the core issue that has resulted in the need for Shari`a-compliant financial instruments, has traditionally not been accepted by the major religions. The early Christian church, for example, banned the collection of interest on loans, on punishment of excommunication and condemnation to hell![235]

Based on biblical passages—fallen man must live "by the sweat of his brow" (Genesis 3:19), Jesus' appeal to his followers to "lend, expecting nothing in return" (Luke 6:35)—medieval theologians considered the lending of money at interest to be sinful. Thomas Aquinas, based on Aristotle, considered usury—like sodomy—to be contrary to nature because "it is in accordance with nature that money should increase from natural goods and not from money itself."[236]

Dante's third ring of hell reserves a special distaste for the work of usurers:

> The third ring—inside the first two—is a barren plain of sand ignited by flakes of fire that torment three separate groups of violent offenders against God: those who offend God directly (blasphemers: Inferno 14); those who violate nature, God's offspring

(Continued)

(Continued)

(sodomites: Inferno 15–16); and those who harm industry and the economy, offspring of nature and therefore grandchild of God (usurers: Inferno 17). . . . Dante's emotional reactions to the shades in the seventh circle range from neutral observation of the murderers and compassion for a suicide to respect for several Florentine sodomites and revulsion at the sight and behavior of the lewd usurers.[237]

The partner of *interest* is *credit*. Interest, today, is charged on loans that are made on the basis of credit, which is extended on the understanding that the borrower undertakes a future obligation to repay the loan. While Jesus might have appealed "to his followers to `lend, expecting nothing in return'" (Luke 6:35),[238] however, financiers today are not so altruistic. In addition to their commitment to repay the debt, borrowers agree to pay a fee to the lender for the service that reflects the level of risk the lender is accepting in agreeing to loan the money to the borrower. This risk fluctuates based on variables such as the size of the loan, the likelihood of repayment, and competing demands for the funds. In addition, however, there is an unspoken element of mutual *trust*—I lend money to you because I trust that you will pay it back; I pay you with this banknote because you trust that the Treasury will honor it to the extent of its face value:

The root of [the word] credit is *credo*, the Latin for "I believe."[239]

Without trust, our economic system breaks down, as the 2007–2009 financial crisis demonstrated only too clearly. Today, the global economic system is underpinned by an interlocking financial system founded on credit. While trust, fundamentally, underpins this model, however, it is also true that the profit incentive has distorted the relationship between lender and borrower.

Some commentators have argued that it was "the legalization of usury" that was the cause of the 2007–2009 financial crisis.[240] The root of the problem, according to these arguments, goes to a 1978 U.S. Supreme Court case[241] that prevented Minnesota from enforcing strict limits on the amount of interest charged on a credit card loan by an out-of-state bank. In response to the case, other states quickly repealed similar laws in an attempt to prevent national banks from relocating to other states, which led to the situation today where banks and credit card companies have an incentive to offer unlimited credit and charge high interest rates to customers who are unable to repay the loans plus interest:

[Following the U.S. Supreme Court's decision] no longer was a credit-worthy borrower the best customer. The bigger profits were made when credit card companies could charge 25 or 35 percent interest on an account that was only intermittently paid off. For payday lenders, interest rates could reach annual levels of 500 percent or higher, as long as the borrower was kept in a cycle of perpetual indebtedness.[242]

As Thomas Geoghegan,[243] who has advocated this argument, put it in a television interview

You know, if you are Mr. Potter in *It's a Wonderful Life* and can only get six percent, seven percent on your loan, you want the loan to be repaid. Moral character is important. You want to scrutinize everybody very carefully. But if you're able to charge 30 percent or, in a payday lender case, 200 or 300 percent, you don't care so much if the loan—in fact, you actually want the loan not to be repaid. You want people to go into debt. You want to accumulate this interest.[244]

In contrast to modern-day Western finance, Islamic (or Shari`a) law forbids the charging of interest (or *riba*). Money should be used only as a facilitator of business and the trade of goods; it cannot be used as a commodity to be traded or a tool for speculation. In other words, money should be used to create *things,* not just to create more *money:*

> The Prophet Mohammed said debts must be repaid in the amount that was loaned. Money proffered must be backed by collateral, and if financial instruments are traded, they generally have to sell for face value, which deters banks from repackaging debt.[245]

As a result, there is a significant market of devout Muslim investors who have previously either compromised their principles and felt guilty about it, or who traditionally avoided modern finance because of its conflict with their beliefs. This has not only had personal limitations; some also believe it has affected the Muslim world as a whole:

> While ignored by many secular Muslims and the conventional banks that operate in most Muslim nations today, this ban [on usury] has long denied the benefits of modern banking to strict believers—contributing, some way, to the Muslim's world's relative decline after interest-based bonds and loans powered the West's industrial revolution.[246]

Now, many Muslims see Islamic finance as a way to compete and catch up.[247] Banks do this by developing financial products that, although based on alternatives to interest, aim to deliver similar investment returns. These alternatives

> are technically based on profit-sharing, leasing or trading—all activities permissible in Islam because they involve entrepreneurial work rather than simply moneylending.[248]

To determine whether a particular investment or financial product is Shari`a-compliant, banks appoint boards of Shari`a scholars (Muslim clerics) to advise in the development of such products and certify them as compliant when they are issued. The trouble is that many Islamic scholars are not trained in finance and those who are are in short supply and highly sought-after:

> At present, devout Muslims will only buy such instruments if a recognized shari`a scholar, such as a mullah, has issued a *fatwa* to approve it. . . . However, there are very few Islamic scholars who command enough religious respect to issue *fatwas,* understand the complexities of global structured financial products—and speak good enough English to read the necessary market documentation.[249]

Like all financial instruments, Shari`a-compliant products run the spectrum from

(Continued)

(Continued)

mortgages, to bonds (*sukuk*), to mutual funds and stocks, each with its own set of rules that enable it to remain compliant with Islamic law. A common method for devout Muslims to take out a Shari`a-compliant mortgage, for example, is *ijara*. With *ijara,* instead of the bank lending the home buyer the money to buy the property and charging them a fee (interest) until they repay the loan, a bank buys the property on behalf of the home buyer, who then pays back the principal over time, while also paying a "lease payment" to use the property in the meantime.[250]

In order for Islamic bonds (*sukuk*) to be Shari`a-compliant, it is important they

> don't pay interest, but instead give investors profits from an underlying business that backs a bond, to comply with a Koranic ban on interest payments.[251]

There is also considerable overlap with the more mainstream financial community. Muslim investors seeking to invest in stocks, for example, need to buy the stocks of firms (directly or indirectly through mutual funds) that are considered to be Shari`a-compliant:

> To be Shari`a-compliant, companies can't run casinos or sell tobacco, alcohol, pork, or pornography, and debt can't exceed 30% of equity. Such rules leave more than half the companies in the Standard & Poor's 500-stock index— including Microsoft, Southwest Airlines, and Nike—in compliance.[252]

By 2007, the size of the Islamic finance market was estimated to range "from $250bn [billion] to $750bn."[253] While the total size is disputed and subject to different definitions of Shari`a-compliance, it is now recognized that the industry has moved into the mainstream:

> Though Islamic banking still represents only 1 per cent of global banking assets, most observers expect this heady pace of growth to continue for many years.[254]

The growth of the Islamic finance industry was initially fueled largely with money from the expanding oil countries of the Persian Gulf,[255] with Western banks (such as Citigroup, HSBC, and Deutsche Bank) becoming interested only once the potential became apparent and growing awareness prompted Muslim communities living in the West to push for change. Among Muslim countries, however, even though the Dubai Islamic Bank, "the world's first Islamic bank" was established in 1975,[256] it is Malaysia that is credited as the leading source of expansion and product innovation.[257] In 1983, the Malaysian government passed an Islamic banking law and established Bank Islam, "which gave out the nation's first Islamic loans. . . . more than a decade before Saudi clerics followed suit."[258] In the West, Britain has worked hard to market itself as a "global centre of Islamic finance,"[259] in spite of international competition,[260] with the UK government announcing its intention to become "the first western state to issue Islamic bonds."[261] There have also been calls for a U.S. dollar-denominated Shari`a-compliant Treasury bond[262] as a way of healing rifts between Islamic communities and the West following the September 2001 terrorist attacks in the United States.[263]

Along with a rapidly growing market for Islamic finance is a corresponding growth in organizations seeking to cater to an Islamic clientele. This growth extends from Citigroup (a subdivision of which, back in 2005, "operates what is effectively the world's largest Islamic bank in terms of transactions. Some $6 billion of Citibank deals now have been structured and marketed in conformance with Islamic laws since starting out in 1996.")[264] to the FTSE (which, in 2007, launched a series of Shari`a-compliant indices[265] that are "designed to meet the requirements of Islamic investors globally.")[266] to local "hometown" banks in Ann Arbor, Michigan, such as University Bank, and across the United States:

University Bank's boomlet forms only part of a national trend. Institutions like Devon Bank in Chicago and Guidance Residential in Reston, Va., also offer mortgage alternatives. The Amana Funds, based in Bellingham, Wash., has several mutual funds operating on Islamic principles.[267]

Similarly, in response to the growing demand for Shari`a-compliant financial products and a growth in firms willing to provide them, the demand for financiers who are trained in Islamic finance has also grown. Schools that offer MBA[268] and other master's[269] degrees that comply with Islamic teachings have arisen to fulfill this need.

CSR Newsletters: MBAs and Islamic Finance

A recent article[270] documents the growing interest in the business world surrounding the potential of Islamic finance and outlines the potential for an MBA incorporating training that revolves around Shari`a law:

> The need for MBA graduates armed with a knowledge of Islamic norms has become increasingly pressing. Bankers working to put together deals involving Islamic finance point towards a fundamental skill gap in finding professionals who combine the knowledge of Islamic Shari`a (jurisprudence) principles with knowledge of the marketplace.

The article provides insight into the forces driving this interest (oil revenues and potential profit), while also accounting for those who think there is either insufficient interest or need at present. It also discusses how Shari`a law forbids the use of interest-based financial transactions, but still allows investors to profit from specific kinds of investments:

> Islam seeks to promote the idea of partnership-type structures, where depositors provide money through a bank or other institution and borrowers use that money for investment purposes. Profit or loss from the investment is supposed to be shared between the provider and the borrower, with the bank charging a fee for managing the transaction.

In other ways, funds or investment vehicles based around Shari`a principles (*sukkuk*) sound very similar to the SRI funds that have grown in popularity among Western investors in recent years:

> Other obvious prohibitions include investments in anything considered a vice under Islamic law, such as pork, investments in hotels where alcohol is served and outlets for gambling, as well as businesses involved with the trade of arms.

(Continued)

(Continued)

In 2009, Islamic finance was being heralded by advocates as offering a way forward for those wishing to remodel a global financial system founded on credit and the collection of interest.[271] Others, however, contend that the Islamic finance industry is really no different from Western finance and is merely subverting the rules in search of profit.[272] The argument continues that what Muslim clerics are doing today in certifying these products as Shari`a-compliant is no different than steps taken throughout the ages to subvert the inherent tension that exists between religion and capitalism:

In about 1220 a canonist named Hispanus proposed that, although usury was prohibited, a lender could charge a fee if his borrower was late in making repayment. The period between the date on which the borrower should have repaid and the date on which he did repay, Hispanus termed *interesse*, literally that which "in between is."[273]

The accusation is leveled that the Islamic finance industry is merely the latest evolution of financial products that are designed to conform to strict limitations on the surface, but, in fact, generate "interest-bearing loan[s] in all but name":

The gestation of products within this very un-Islamic framework has resulted in the ultimate mutant, an Islamic personal loan at 7.9 per cent annual percentage rate courtesy of the Islamic Bank of Britain. How different this is from the original vision of Muslim economists.[274]

Online Resources

- Accounting and Auditing Organization for Islamic Financial Institutions, http://www.aaoifi.com/

  "AAOIFI is an Islamic international autonomous non-for-profit corporate body that prepares accounting, auditing, governance, ethics and Shari`a standards for Islamic financial institutions and the industry."

- American Family Association, http://www.afa.net/

  "The American Family Association represents and stands for traditional family values and exists to motivate and equip citizens to reform our culture to reflect Biblical truth on which it was founded."

- Atheist Bus Campaign, http://www.atheistbus.org.uk/

  "The official Web site of the Atheist Bus Campaign."

- Bank Islam (Malaysia), http://www.bankislam.com.my/

  "Bank Islam emerged as Malaysia's maiden Shari`a-based financial institution when it commenced operations in July 1983. Since then, Bank Islam has become the symbol of Islamic banking in Malaysia."

- Charter for Compassion, http://charterforcompassion.com/

"The Charter for Compassion is a collaborative effort to build a peaceful and harmonious global community. Bringing together the voices of people from all religions, the Charter seeks to remind the world that while all faiths are not the same, they all share the core principle of compassion and the Golden Rule."

- European Islamic Investment Bank, http://www.eiib.co.uk/html/

"EIIB is the first independent Shari`a compliant Islamic investment bank authorized by the FSA."

- FTSE Shariah Global Equity Index Series, http://www.ftse.com/Indices/FTSE_Shariah_Global_Equity_Index_Series/index.jsp

"FTSE Group has developed a range of Shari`a-compliant indices designed to meet the requirements of Islamic investors globally."

- Interfaith Center on Corporate Responsibility, http://www.iccr.org/

"For thirty-eight years the Interfaith Center on Corporate Responsibility (ICCR) has been a leader of the corporate social responsibility movement."

- Islamic Bank of Britain, http://www.islamic-bank.com/

"As the first stand-alone, Shari`a compliant, retail bank in the UK to be authorised by the Financial Services Authority we aim to provide a friendly, inclusive and personal service for all our customers."

- Islamic Finance Services Board, http://www.ifsb.org/

"The Islamic Financial Services Board (IFSB) is an international standard-setting organisation that promotes and enhances the soundness and stability of the Islamic financial services industry by issuing global prudential standards and guiding principles for the industry, broadly defined to include banking, capital markets and insurance sectors."

- National Religious Broadcasters, http://www.nrb.org/

"NRB is the preeminent association of Christian communicators working to keep the doors of electronic media open for the spread of the Gospel, which promotes standards of excellence, integrity, and accountability."

- What Would Jesus Drive? http://www.whatwouldjesusdrive.info/intro.php

"WWJDrive is organized and sponsored by the Evangelical Environmental Network (EEN), a biblically orthodox Christian environmental organization."

Questions for Discussion and Review

1. What role does religion play in your life? Do you feel the society in which you live is becoming more or less religious? Is this *good* or *bad*? Does it matter?

2. Have a look at photos of the Atheist Bus Campaign's advertisements on London buses at: http://www.atheistbus.org.uk/bus-photos/. What is your reaction? Are they provocative, or do you not understand what all the fuss is about?

3. Are you interested in a career in finance? Would you have any religious or moral concerns about working in the finance industry? Are there any jobs or industries that you would avoid based on your moral or religious values?

4. What is your reaction to the accusation that the Islamic finance industry is generating "interest-bearing loan[s] in all but name"? From what you have learned in the case, do you agree that Islamic financial products are Shari`a-compliant, or are banks just finding ways to make people feel comfortable when investing their money with them?

5. Have a look at the Web site of the campaign What Would Jesus Drive? (http://www.whatwouldjesusdrive.info/intro.php). If he were alive today, what car would Jesus drive? Why?

STAKEHOLDER RELATIONS

CSR CONNECTION: This issue builds on the Shareholder Activism issue (Chapter 6) and discusses the extent to which corporate managers incorporate the needs and concerns of a broad range of stakeholders within the strategic planning and day-to-day operations of the firm.

Issue

CSR, in various forms, has been around for a long time,

even prior to Thomas Clarkson kicking off the first major boycott over the UK slave trade in 1787. Continuing through the Quakers and Marx in 19th-century capitalism, early 20th-century antitrust and booms and busts, into 1950s American theory, the movement was resurgent in the late 1960s and throughout the social and economic unrest of the 1970s. The 1980s, with its junk bond-fuelled takeover frenzy and resulting scandals brought ethics sharply into focus once again. Soon after, in the midst of the 1990s boom, The Body Shop issued its first values report. And then . . . came Shell's planned disposal of the Brent Spar storage platform and the execution of Ken Saro-Wiwa in Nigeria. In 1995 these seminal events . . . can be said to be the beginning of the most recent stage in the evolution of stakeholder expectations of multi-national business.[275]

This historical framework of CSR and activism presents a compelling argument for firms to include stakeholders as an integral component of their strategic perspective. To what extent today, however, does this occur?

Some years ago, the world became convinced that shareholders were the most important stakeholders of business. The role of the business, it was agreed, was to maximize shareholder return. That wasn't always considered the case. Today, however, it is as immutable as the laws of gravity.[276]

Stakeholder relations involve a number of issues that reflect the wide variety of groups that can be defined as an organization's primary constituents in today's globalizing world (see Figure 2.2). Perceptions differ, however, from country to country and culture to culture:

> Indeed, one survey of managers in various countries has shown just how divergent opinions can be on the question of "whose company is it?" In Japan, 97% of those surveyed said a company exists for all stakeholders, compared with 83% in Germany, 78% in France, 76% in the United States and 71% in the United Kingdom.[277]

The size and complexity of this issue, therefore, indicates the importance of a stakeholder perspective as part of a comprehensive, strategic approach to CSR. Firms will differ on which of their stakeholders are the most important, and these priorities will also shift from issue to issue. What is important, however, is that firms are aware of their stakeholders' concerns, so they can take them into account in making decisions. By implementing an effective stakeholder relations policy, firms counter the prevailing perception, created in the wake of the corporate scandals in the United States, that organizations are as much a force for bad as for good. As the extent to which a company's stakeholders are being considered and consulted before making significant company decisions increases, so the benefits of such policies gain wider recognition. As Dieter Wissler, head of Novartis Communications, said during a speech at the World Bank Forum:

> The collaboration with other stakeholders provides stability and predictability for the peaceful resolution of conflicts. Establishing a level of mutual trust, respect and understanding of each one's needs is a requirement for any public-private partnership. We, at Novartis, believe that this is an important factor for a successful and sustainable development.[278]

It is important to note, however, that multi-stakeholder initiatives need to be genuine and they need to demonstrate progress. Otherwise, the potential for backlash increases. For example

> At the end of [2008], two global multistakeholder initiatives came under heavy fire from campaigning NGOs. The Roundtable on Sustainable Palm Oil (RSPO) found itself and some of its members being targeted by Greenpeace, dissatisfied with its slow progress in creating a sustainable palm oil supply chain to feed the growing demand for this commodity in a range of cosmetic and food products. At around the same time, the much older Forest Stewardship Council once again found itself under pressure. Friends of the Earth UK went so far as to stop recommending FSC to its members.[279]

Worse than trying and failing for a firm, however, is to ignore its stakeholders altogether. By definition, the interests and demands of different stakeholders will conflict. As such, firms will not be able to please all of their stakeholders all of the time. Installing a process that allows a firm to take its stakeholders' concerns into account in its strategic decision making, however, will help the firm make better decisions and insulate it from potential threats to its societal legitimacy.

One of the earliest corporate pioneers in the area of stakeholder relations was Ben & Jerry's, which opened its first shop in Vermont in 1981 and went public in 1984.[280] In building Ben & Jerry's into a global brand, the company's cofounders, Ben Cohen and Jerry Greenfield, set new standards in defining the concept of a concerned and responsive employer. Although the importance of addressing stakeholder needs and concerns was among the values on which the firm was established, it first began to codify these values as part of its groundbreaking social audit—first commissioned in 1989. Ben & Jerry's was the first major corporation to allow an independent social audit of its business operations:

> This social auditor recommended that the report be called a Stakeholders Report (the concept of stakeholders existed but this was possibly the first-ever report to stakeholders) and that it be divided into the major stakeholder categories: Communities (Community Outreach, Philanthropic Giving, Environmental Awareness, Global Awareness), Employees, Customers, Suppliers, Investors. After this first social audit in 1989, B&J continued to issue annual social reports, rotating to different social auditors as they sought to develop the concept.[281]

Ben & Jerry's has continued developing the concept of a business that places its stakeholder concerns at the core of its

business model ever since, a stance that is reflected in the firm's Mission Statement.

Ben & Jerry's Mission Statement

Ben & Jerry's is founded on and dedicated to a sustainable corporate concept of linked prosperity. Our mission consists of three inter-related parts. . . . Underlying the mission of Ben & Jerry's is the determination to seek new and creative ways of addressing all three parts, while holding a deep respect for individuals inside and outside the company and for the communities of which they are a part.

Social Mission: To operate the Company in a way that actively recognizes the central role that business plays in society by initiating innovative ways to improve the quality of life locally, nationally, and internationally.

Product Mission: To make, distribute, and sell the finest quality all natural ice cream and euphoric concoctions with a continued commitment to incorporating wholesome, natural ingredients and promoting business practices that respect the Earth and the Environment.

Economic Mission: To operate the Company on a sustainable financial basis of profitable growth, increasing value for our stakeholders and expanding opportunities for development and career growth for our employees.[282]

One practical example of Ben & Jerry's approach to business was the issue of executive pay, on which the firm took a dramatic stance: No employee could earn more than seven times the salary of the lowest paid worker in the company:

The gap between CEO salaries and those on the factory floor is widening. In 1973, for example, the typical CEO made 45 times the wage of the average worker. Today, it's as much as 500 times [in the United States]. . . . Japanese executives earn 20 to 30 times the lowest-paid worker while, in Europe, the ratio is about 40 times. Ben Cohen and Jerry Greenfield, the quirky entrepreneurs behind Ben & Jerry's ice cream, kept the [salary] ratio of top to bottom earners at 7:1—though that did not last after the two stepped down in 1995.[283]

As noted earlier, however, stakeholder interests often conflict and resolving these conflicts on this issue (and all issues) is not easy:

Costco Wholesale Corp. often is held up as a retailer that does it right, paying well and offering generous benefits. But Costco's kind-hearted philosophy toward its 100,000 cashiers, shelf-stockers and other workers is drawing criticism from Wall Street. Some analysts and investors contend that the Issaquah, Wash., warehouse-club operator actually is too good to employees, with Costco shareholders suffering as a result.[284]

In addition to the top-to-bottom pay ratio, other aspects of working for Ben & Jerry's, such as the firm's benefits (including an onsite day-care center) and its "no-layoff policy," ensured the commitment and loyalty of the firm's key stakeholder group—its employees:

If a position required revamping or removal, the employee holding the position would be transferred to another position, with attention given to matching responsibilities and qualifications.[285]

As Ben & Jerry's became more successful, it began to attract the attention of other firms. As people began to worry about the prospect of a merger or acquisition, calls increased to protect the firm's independence and its stakeholder-centric approach to business. The Vermont state government responded by passing legislation:

US federal law decrees that a company must accept a takeover bid if it is in the best interests of shareholders, but Vermont has introduced new law allowing a company's directors to reject a bid if "they deem it to be not in the best interests of employees, suppliers, and the economy of the state."[286]

In Vermont, the law became known as the "Ben & Jerry's law":

Thus, even when a company was offered a financial premium in a buyout situation, its directors were permitted to reject the offer based on the best interests of the State of Vermont.[287]

In spite of this legislation, Ben & Jerry's board agreed to a $326 million takeover by the corporate giant Unilever in August 2000.[288] Although Unilever's management gave assurances that Ben & Jerry's unique approach to business would be maintained,

(Continued)

(Continued)

the firm's cult status was tarnished by the takeover. One example: *Business Ethics* dropped Ben & Jerry's from its list of 100 Best Corporate Citizens in 2001 because of its unfavorable evaluation of Unilever, the new parent company. A second example: The top-to-bottom compensation ratio, referred to above, (including benefits and bonuses) jumped to an average of 16:1 in 1999, 2000, and 2001.

Today, at several points on the company's Web site, the firm's managers continue to reaffirm a strong activist message, while claiming to run Ben & Jerry's by "leading with progressive values across our business."[289] In addition, the following message is relayed by Ben & Jerry's CEO to visitors at "the world-famous Ben & Jerry's ice-cream factory" in Vermont:

> Our commitment to social and economic justice and the environment is as important to us as profitability. It's our heritage. . . . this isn't a short-term strategy to drive up sales. These are issues that are important for our society to address.[290]

Although it is also clear that some things have changed and the commitment to the cofounders' original values and social goals is not as strong as it once was. The accusation is made by some critics that the firm's activist message has become "just a slick Madison Avenue advertising gimmick to hike profits."[291] The following comment, for example, was posted on the company's Web site in March 2003:

> Ben & Jerry's continues to support the progressive principles on which the company was founded. Ben & Jerry's has a progressive, nonpartisan Social Mission that seeks to meet human needs and eliminate injustices in our local, national and international communities. We have long supported nonviolent initiatives that seek to achieve peace. In all of our dealings, we are guided by a mission statement which makes the community's quality of life integral to and inseparable from our product and financial goals.[292]

Today, however, the commitment to "support the progressive principles on which the company was founded" has been removed. Taken together with Unilever's steps to match Ben & Jerry's operating policies more closely with Unilever's corporate brand (such as the decision to prevent political campaigning that does not comply with being "Unilever legal"),[293] the sense is that Ben & Jerry's is not the same. Whether this shift is better or worse for all stakeholders, however, is not clear. While Ben & Jerry's is not as quirky as it once was, it is a more stable organization that has continued to expand and build on its initial success.

Online Resources

- AccountAbility's AA1000 Stakeholder Engagement Standard, http://www.accountability21.net/blogs.aspx?id=3944&blogid=42
- Ben & Jerry's, http://www.benjerry.com/

"Underlying the mission of Ben & Jerry's is the determination to seek new and creative ways of addressing all three parts [social, product, and economic], while holding a deep respect for individuals inside and outside the company and for the communities of which they are a part."

- Future500, http://www.future500.org/stakeholder-engagement/

"Excellent corporate citizenship and stakeholder engagement requires strong Performance, Trust, and Leadership. We provide focused services at all three levels of the Corporate Social Responsibility (CSR) Pyramid."

- Global Governance Watch, http://www.globalgovernancewatch.org/

"[GGW's] goal is to raise awareness about global governance, to monitor how international organizations influence domestic political outcomes, and to address issues of transparency and accountability within the United Nations, related intergovernmental organizations (IGOs), and other non-state actors."

- Multi-stakeholder Processes (UNED Forum), http://www.earthsummit2002.org/msp/

"The term multi-stakeholder processes (MSPs) describes *processes which aim to bring together all major stakeholders* in a new form of communication, decision-finding (and possibly decision-making) on a particular issue."

- SustainAbility, http://www.sustainability.com/

"SustainAbility is a strategy consultancy and think tank working with senior corporate decision makers to achieve transformative leadership on the sustainability agenda."

Questions for Discussion and Review

1. What is a stakeholder? Define the term in your own words.

2. Have a look at the wide variety of stakeholders that form a key component of Mallen Baker's definition of CSR, including the diagram at http://www.mallenbaker.net/csr/definition.php. How can an organization begin to balance such an array of competing stakeholder interests?

3. Do you think Ben & Jerry's does a good job of interacting with its stakeholders and presenting its stakeholder approach on its Web site? Did Unilever's assurances that this approach would not change after they bought the company in August 2000 do enough to safeguard this important element of Ben & Jerry's? Why, or why not?

4. Do you eat Ben & Jerry's ice-cream? If yes, why do you buy this brand? If no, are you now more likely to do so?

5. Look at some of the causes that Ben & Jerry's promotes at: http://www.benjerry.com/activism/inside-the-pint/. Do you agree with a firm adopting such blatant social causes? Do you agree with the stances they take? Do their positions make you more or less likely to buy their ice cream?

NOTES AND REFERENCES

1. "Taking Care of Shareholder Needs," *Focus Japan,* JETRO, March 2001, pp. 3–6.

2. "Patagonia Takes Next Step in Corporate Transparency and Accountability," *CSRwire.com,* March 25, 2008, http://www.csrwire.com/News/11480.html

3. Amy J. Hebard & Wendy S. Cobrda, "The Corporate Reality of Consumer Perceptions: Bringing the Consumer Perspective to CSR Reporting," *GreenBiz Reports,* February 2009, p. 2, http://neec.no/uploads/GreenBizReports-ConsumerPerceptions.pdf

4. See Chapter 5, Figure 5.2.

5. "Wood for the Trees," *The Economist,* November 26, 2004, http://www.cfo.com/article.cfm/3372352

6. http://www.globalreporting.org/AboutGRI/

7. Mallen Baker, "The Global Reporting Initiative (GRI)," http://www.mallenbaker.net/csr/gri.php

8. http://www.gmiratings.com/

9. September 2009, http://www.gmiratings.com/(rw0rtx45q1dsjdrokgkjzb55)/about.aspx#methodology

10. The Institute of Social and Ethical AccountAbility, http://www.accountability.org.uk/

11. Mallen Baker, http://www.mallenbaker.net/csr/CSRfiles/SA8000.html

12. http://www.socialauditor.org/about_us.html

13. http://www.socialauditor.org/

14. http://www.fairlabor.org/what_we_do.html

15. "Wood for the Trees," *The Economist,* November 26, 2004, http://www.cfo.com/article.cfm/3372352

16. Dave Knight, "Corporate Sustainability Management: Standards-Based Flexibility—The Way Forward," *Ethical Corporation,* July 26, 2006, http://www.ethicalcorp.com/content.asp?ContentID=4405

17. "Expanding CSR Toolbox Helps Achieve Sustainability," *CSRwire.com,* January 27, 2009, http://www.csrwire.com/News/14418.html

18. Paul Hohnen, "ISO Steps Towards Social Responsibility," *Ethical Corporation,* September 22, 2008, http://www.ethicalcorp.com/content.asp?ContentID=6094

19. Paul Hohnen, "ISO Moves Towards a Social Responsibility Standard," *Ethical Corporation,* October 5, 2005, http://www.ethicalcorp.com/content.asp?ContentID=3914

20. Paul Hohnen, "ISO Steps Towards Social Responsibility," *Ethical Corporation,* September 22, 2008, http://www.ethicalcorp.com/content.asp?ContentID=6094

21. Mallen Baker, "Labelling the Good Company," *Ethical Corporation,* July 5, 2005, http://www.ethicalcorp.com/content.asp?ContentID=3772

22. "ISO 26000: Social Responsibility Talks Tread on Government Toes," *Ethical Corporation,* May 15, 2009, http://www.ethicalcorp.com/content.asp?ContentID=6474

23. Mallen Baker, "Why CSR Reporting Is Broken—And How It Should Be Fixed," *Ethical Corporation,* November 28, 2008, http://www.ethicalcorp.com/content.asp?ContentID=6224

24. "The Amsterdam Declaration on Transparency and Reporting," Global Reporting Initiative, March 10, 2009, http://www.csrwire.com/News/14774.html

25. Ibid.

26. Ibid.

27. "Business Ethics: Doing Well by Doing Good," *The Economist,* April 22, 2000, pp. 65–68.

28. David Vogel, "The Limits of the Market for Virtue," *Ethical Corporation,* August 25, 2005, http://www.ethicalcorp.com/content.asp?ContentID=3855

29. Mallen Baker, "Time to Move on From the Endless Regulation Debate," *Ethical Corporation,* March 27, 2006, http://www.ethicalcorp.com/content.asp?ContentID=4170

30. Peter Montagnon, "Companies Need to Get a Social Life," *Financial Times* (insert), April 22, 2002, http://specials.ft.com/ftfm/FT3VAPKG80D.html

31. Greg Ip, "A Less-Visible Role for the Fed Chief: Freeing Up Markets," *Wall Street Journal,* November 19, 2004, pp. A1 & A8.

32. Ibid.

33. Chris Lester, "Alan, Like Atlas, Shrugged," *The Kansas City Star,* November 3, 2008, http://www.military.com/entertainment/books/book-news/alan-like-atlas-shruagged

34. Alex Blyth, "EU Multi-Stakeholder Forum Presents Final Report," *Ethical Corporation,* July 5, 2004, http://www.ethicalcorp.com/content.asp?ContentID=2327

35. Will Hutton, "Capitalism Must Put Its House in Order," *The Observer*, November 24, 2002, http://www.guardian.co.uk/politics/2002/nov/24/politicalcolumnists.guardiancolumnists

36. Deborah Doane, "Mandated Risk Reporting Begins in UK," *Business Ethics Magazine,* Spring 2005, p. 13.

37. Will Hutton, "Capitalism Must Put Its House in Order," *The Observer*, November 24, 2002, http://www.guardian.co.uk/politics/2002/nov/24/politicalcolumnists.guardiancolumnists

38. Carola Hoyos, "Emissions Disclosure Study Puts Shell Bottom of the Big Oil Class," *Financial Times,* March 16, 2009, http://www.ft.com/cms/s/0/d02d7252-11a1-11de-87b1-0000779fd2ac.html

39. Lisa Roner, "Anheuser-Busch Reports Recycling 97% of Solid Waste," *Ethical Corporation Magazine,* June 21, 2004, http://www.ethicalcorp.com/content.asp?ContentID=2228

40. "Anheuser-Busch Releases 2006 Environmental, Health and Safety Report," Anheuser-Busch Press Release, *CSRwire.com,* July 26, 2007, http://www.csrwire.com/News/9287.html

41. "Coca-Cola Enterprises Forms Coca-Cola Recycling LLC," Coca-Cola Enterprises Press Release, *CSRwire.com,* September 6, 2007, http://www.csrwire.com/press/press_release/17692-Coca-Cola-Enterprises-Forms-Coca-Cola-Recycling-LLC

42. This url contains an interesting blog comment on Coke's announcement if you are interested in further background and discussion around this issue: http://makower.typepad.com/joel_makower/2007/09/cokes-message-i.html

43. Ann Monroe, "Wal-Mart: Jolly *'Green'* Giant?" MSN Money, January 18, 2008, http://articles.moneycentral.msn.com/Investing/StockInvestingTrading/Wal-MartJollyGreenGiant.aspx

44. Melanie Warner, "Green Business: Plastic Potion No. 9," *Fast Company*, Issue 128, September 2008, p. 103, http://www.fastcompany.com/magazine/128/green-business-plastic-potion-no-9.html

45. Elizabeth Royte, "Moneybags: Citywide Plastic-Bag Bans Are Gaining Momentum. But Will Companies Be the Ones That Force Us to Change?,' *Fast Company*, Issue 119, October 2007, p. 64, http://www.fastcompany.com/magazine/119/moneybags.html

46. Jon Entine, "Battle of the Bags: Are Plastic Bags an Environmental Threat?" *Global Governance Watch*, September 2, 2009, http://www.globalgovernancewatch.org/in_the_news/battle-of-the-bags-are-plastic-bags-an-environmental-threat

47. Brenna Maloney & Laura Stanton, "More Than Meets the Eye: Paper or Plastic?" *Washington Post*, October 4, 2007, http://www.washingtonpost.com/wp dyn/content/graphic/2007/10/03/GR2007100301385.html

48. "Paper or Plastic?" *Washington Post*, July 6, 2007, http://www.washingtonpost.com/wp-dyn/content/article/2007/07/05/AR2007070501806.html

49. Elizabeth Royte, "Moneybags: Citywide Plastic-Bag Bans Are Gaining Momentum. But Will Companies Be the Ones That Force Us to Change?,' *Fast Company*, Issue 119, October 2007, p. 64, http://www.fastcompany.com/magazine/119/moneybags.html

50. Matt Richtel & Kate Galbraith, "Back at Junk Value, Recyclables Are Piling Up," *New York Times,* December 8, 2008, http://www.nytimes.com/2008/12/08/business/08recycle.html

51. Frederik Balfour, "China's Recycler: Is a Rebound Ahead?" *BusinessWeek*, January 26, 2009, http://www.businessweek.com/globalbiz/content/jan2009/gb20090126_576842.htm

52. For other perspectives on this debate, see Jeffrey Ball, "Paper or Plastic? A New Look at the Bag Scourge," *Wall Street Journal,* June 12, 2009, p. A11; Jon Entine, "Battle of the Bags: Are Plastic Bagsan Environmental Threat?" *Global Governance Watch*, September 2, 2009, http://www.globalgovernancewatch.org/in_the_news/battle-of-the-bags-are-plastic-bags-an-environmental-threat

53. Elizabeth Royte, "Moneybags: Citywide Plastic-Bag Bans Are Gaining Momentum. But Will Companies Be the Ones That Force Us to Change?,' *Fast Company*, Issue 119, October 2007, p. 64, http://www.fastcompany.com/magazine/119/moneybags.html

54. 'The Results Are in . . . Over 92% of IKEA Customers Bagged the Plastic Bag! As of October 2008, IKEA Will No Longer Offer Plastic or Paper Bags,' IKEA press release, *CSRwire.com*, April 2, 2008, http://www.csrwire.com/News/11588.html

55. Ibid. For additional results, see "The 'No More Plastic Bag' Movement Continues," IKEA press release, *CSRwire.com*, April 28, 2009, http://www.csrwire.com/press/press_release/16628--The-No-More-Plastic-Bag-Movement-Continues-

56. Ibid.

57. Elisabeth Rosenthal, "With Irish Tax, Plastic Bags Go the Way of the Snakes," *New York Times*, February 2, 2008, http://www.nytimes.com/2008/02/02/world/europe/02bags.html

58. Ibid.

59. Jon Entine, "Battle of the Bags: Are Plastic Bags an Environmental Threat?" *Global Governance Watch*, September 2, 2009, http://www.globalgovernancewatch.org/in_the_news/battle-of-the-bags-are-plastic-bags-an-environmental-threat

60. Mireya Navarro, "Seeing a Pitched Battle for Plastic Bags," *New York Times*, November 18, 2008, p. A20.

61. Heather Timmons, "Paper or Plastic? At a Trade Show, the Latter Wins Easily," *New York Times*, February 17, 2009, p. B3.

62. Elisabeth Rosenthal, "With Irish Tax, Plastic Bags Go the Way of the Snakes," *New York Times*, February 2, 2008, http://www.nytimes.com/2008/02/02/world/europe/02bags.html

63. Richard Milne, "Skirting the Boards," *Financial Times*, June 15, 2009, p. 2.

64. Bill Baue, "Brundtland Report Celebrates 20th Anniversary Since Coining Sustainable Development," *Ethical Corporation*, June 18, 2007, http://www.ethicalcorp.com/content.asp?ContentID=5175

65. Michael Hopkins, "Sustainable Development: From Word to Policy," *OpenDemocracy*, April 11, 2007, http://www.opendemocracy.net/globalization-institutions_government/sustainable_word_4515.jsp

66. *BizEthics Buzz,* December 2002. *BizEthics Buzz* is an online news report from *Business Ethics Magazine*.

67. Ibid.

68. For an in-depth discussion of this issue, see Oliver Balch, "Carbon Accounting—Emissions Disclosure Stacking Up," *Ethical Corporation*, July 21, 2009, http://www.ethicalcorp.com/content.asp?ContentID=6540

69. "PepsiCo and Carbon Trust Announce Groundbreaking Agreement and Certify Carbon Footprint of Tropicana," *CSRwire.com*, PepsiCo Press Release, January 22, 2009, http://www.csrwire.com/News/14362.html

70. Andrew Martin, "How Green Is My Orange?" *New York Times*, January 22, 2009, p. B1.

71. Fiona Harvey, "Food Footprints Coming Soon to a Label Near You," *Financial Times*, *Special Report: Sustainable Business*, October 12, 2007, p. 4.

72. "Environmental Leaders: Green Beacons Burning Bright," *Ethical Corporation*, September 3, 2009, http://www.ethicalcorp.com/content.asp?ContentID=6576

73. Marc Gunther, "Money and Morals at GE," *Fortune Magazine*, November 15, 2004, p. 178.

74. Anya Kamenetz, "GE's New Ecomagineer," *Fast Company*, February 2009, p. 71.

75. Sarah Murray, "The Products That Never Say Die," *Financial Times*, September 18, 2007, p. 12.

76. Carleen Hawn, "Can't Buy Me Love," *Fast Company*, December 2007/January 2008, pp. 60–62; Mark Landler, "Garden Is a Seedbed for Green Cosmetics," *New York Times*, June 28, 2008, p. B3.

77. See Chapter 3.

78. Alan G. Robinson & Dean M. Schroeder, "Greener and Cheaper," *Wall Street Journal*, March 23, 2009, p. R4.

79. Daniel Vermeer & Robert Clemen, "Why Sustainability Is Still Going Strong," *Financial Times*, *Managing in a Downturn Part IV: Sustainable Business*, February 13, 2009, p. 4.

80. "Beyond the Green Corporation," *BusinessWeek*, Cover Story, January 29, 2007, http://www.businessweek.com/magazine/content/07_05/b4019001.htm

81. Ram Nidumolu, C. K. Prahalad, & M. R. Rangaswami, "Why Sustainability Is Now the Key Driver of Innovation," *Harvard Business Review*, September 2009, p. 57.

82. Linda Baker, "I'm Bad! I'm Slick!" *Fast Company*, May 2008, pp. 103–106.

83. March 2009, http://www.barackobama.com/issues/newenergy/index.php

84. Steven Mufson, "Will Obama's Revolution Deliver Energy Independence?" *Washington Post*, in *The Daily Yomiuri*, April 8, 2009, p. 14.

85. Ben Elgin, "Little Green Lies," *BusinessWeek*, Cover Story, http://www.businessweek.com/magazine/content/07_44/b4056001.htm

86. Sathnam Sanghera, "Green Cars: Will Someone Hit the Accelerator?" *The Times*, March 30, 2009, http://www.timesonline.co.uk/tol/driving/article5998066.ece

87. Dan Mitchell, "Being Skeptical of Green," *New York Times*, November 24, 2007, p. A5, http://www.nytimes.com/2007/11/24/technology/24online.html

88. Cahal Milmo, "The Biggest Global Warming Crime in History," *CorpWatch,* December 13, 2007, http://www.corpwatch.org/article.php?id=14858

89. Al Gore & David Blood, "For People and Planet," *Wall Street Journal*, March 28, 2006, p. A20.

90. "Made to Break: Are We Sinking Under the Weight of Our Disposable Society?" *Knowledge@Wharton*, August 9, 2006, http://knowledge.wharton.upenn.edu/article.cfm?articleid=1536

91. Fiona Harvey, "Reduction Should Be the Target," *Financial Times*, *Special Report: Waste and the Environment*, April 18, 2007, p. 1.

92. Andrew Martin, "One Country's Table Scraps, Another Country's Meal," *New York Times,* May 18, 2008, p. A3, http://www.nytimes.com/2008/05/18/weekinreview/18martin.html. "Into the trash it goes: A federal study found that 96.4 billion pounds of edible food was wasted by U.S. retailers, food service businesses and consumers in 1995—about 1 pound of waste per day for every adult and child in the nation at that time. That doesn't count food lost on farms and by processors and wholesalers. For a family of four people, that amounted to about 122 pounds of food thrown out each month in grocery stores, restaurants, cafeterias and homes."

93. Fiona Harvey, "Our Guilty Secret," *Financial Times*, July 18/19, 2009, Life & Arts, p. 14.

94. Beth Daley, "Old Equipment Gets New Chance to Pollute," *Boston Globe*, August 19, 2007; reported in *Wall Street Journal*, August 20, 2007, p. B7.

95. See http://www.greenpeace.org/international/campaigns/toxics/electronics

96. "The Electronic Wasteland," CBS News, *60 Minutes,* August 30, 2009, http://www.cbsnews.com/video/watch/?id=5274959n

97. Leslie Kaufman, "New Laws Offer a Green Way to Dump Low-Tech Electronics," *New York Times*, June 30, 2009, p. A1. For additional data, see Ashley Chapman, "The Color of Recycling," *Wall Street Journal*, December 2, 2005, p. W12.

98. Laurie J. Flynn, "A State Says Makers Must Pay for Recycling PCs and TVs," *New York Times*, March 25, 2006, p. B2.

99. Leslie Kaufman, "New Laws Offer a Green Way to Dump Low-Tech Electronics," *New York Times*, June 30, 2009, p. A1.

100. Melanie Warner, "Green Business: Plastic Potion No. 9," *Fast Company*, Issue 128, September 2008, p. 103, http://www.fastcompany.com/magazine/128/green-business-plastic-potion-no-9.html

101. David Murphy, "Toxic Town," *South China Morning Post*, June 7, 2005, p. A16.

102. Ibid.

103. Fiona Harvey, "Reduction Should Be the Target," *Financial Times*, *Special Report: Waste and the Environment*, April 18, 2007, p. 1.

104. Kate Rockwood, "From Trash to Cash," *Fast Company*, February 2009, p. 44.

105. Laurie J. Flynn, "A State Says Makers Must Pay for Recycling PCs and TVs," *New York Times*, March 25, 2006, p. B2.

106. Leslie Kaufman, "New Laws Offer a Green Way To Dump Low-Tech Electronics," *New York Times*, June 30, 2009, p. A1.

107. Robert Tomsho, "Currents: Kicking the Cans: Plymouth, Mass., Wrestles With 'Pay-As-You-Throw' Trash Fees," *Wall Street Journal*, July 29, 2008, p. A12, http://www.wsj.com/article/SB121729506485991917.html

108. Ibid.

109. Philip Stevens, "Global Warming: The Way Not to Mobilize the Masses," *Financial Times*, December 12, 2008, p. 9.

110. Zara Maung, "Tesco's Low Carbon Supermarket: A New Way Forward?" *Ethical Corporation*, January 21, 2009, http://www.ethicalcorp.com/content.asp?ContentID=6296

111. Philip Stevens, "Global Warming: The Way Not to Mobilize the Masses," *Financial Times*, December 12, 2008, p. 9.

112. See Issue: CSR Compliance.

113. Maija Palmer & Kevin Allison, "Computer Makers Miss the Big Green Picture," *Financial Times*, June 7, 2007, p. 18.

114. Rebecca Knight, "Business Students Portrayed as Ethically Minded," *Financial Times,* October 25, 2006, p. 7.

115. Rebecca Knight, "Sustainability Not a Priority for Students," *Financial Times,* June 9, 2008, p. 11.

116. Devin Stewart, "Is Ethical Capitalism Possible?" *CSRWire.com*, January 29, 2009, http://www.csrwire.com/press/press_release/14072-Is-Ethical-Capitalism-Possible-

117. For example, "From Crimson to Green," *The Economist*, May 6, 2006, p. 31; "Haas Takes New Tack on Investing," *Wall Street Journal*, September 18, 2007, p. B8; Sarah Murray, "Lessons in Helping the World Develop," *Financial Times*, February 25, 2008, p. 10; Stuart Hart, "'Sustainability Must Be Integral to Schools' DNA,' *Financial Times*, October 13, 2008, p. 15.

118. "MBA Students Want Changes in Their Curriculum," *CSRwire.com,* March 11, 2009, http://www.csrwire.com/News/14781.html

119. Patrick M. Lencioni, "Make Your Values Mean Something," *Harvard Business Review,* Vol. 80, No. 7, July 2002, pp. 113–117.

120. Joel Bakan, *The Corporation: The Pathological Pursuit of Profit and Power,* Free Press, 2004. Quoted in *Business Ethics Magazine,* Spring 2004, p. 6.

121. "The Next Step for CSR: Economic Democracy," *Business Ethics Magazine,* Cover Story, Summer 2002, p. 10.

122. Memorandum from Kenneth Lay to all employees, Subject: Code of Ethics, July 1, 2000.

123. Enron Corp.'s Code of Ethics, p. 5.

124. Ibid.

125. Ibid., p.12.

126. Newsdesk, "Ethics Officers—A Growing Breed?," *Ethical Corporation,* February 7, 2005, http://www.ethicalcorp.com/content.asp?ContentID=3466

127. In March 2007, the ECOA had 1,388 individual members and approximately 750 organizational members. Individual members are defined by the ECOA as "ethics and compliance professionals."

128. David Henry & Amy Borrus, "Death, Taxes and Sarbanes-Oxley?" *BusinessWeek,* January 17, 2005, pp. 28–31.

129. "Business Ethics: Doing Well by Doing Good," *The Economist,* April 22, 2000, pp. 65–68.

130. James Weber & Dana Fortun, "Ethics and Compliance Officer Profile: Survey, Comparison, and Recommendations," *Business & Society Review*, Vol. 110, No. 2, 2005, pp. 97–115.

131. Debbie T. LeClair, O. C. Ferrell, & John P. Fraedrich, *Integrity Management: A Guide to Managing Legal and Ethical Issues in the Workplace,* University of Tampa Press, 1998.

132. Michael Metzger, Dan R. Dalton, & John W. Hill, "The Organization of Ethics and the Ethics of Organizations: The Case for Expanded Organizational Ethics Audits," *Business Ethics Quarterly*, Vol. 3, No. 1, 1993, pp. 27–43.

133. Keith Darcy, "Ethics Birth Certificate in Question," *Business Ethics Magazine*, Vol. 19, No. 3, 2005, p. 4.

134. Ibid.

135. See "Ethics Officers Double in Four Years," *Business Ethics Magazine,* Spring 2005, p. 9; Editorial, "Ethics Officers—A Growing Breed?" *Ethical Corporation,* February 7, 2005, http://www.ethicalcorp.com/content.asp?ContentID=3466

136. Tamara Loomis, "Scandals Spur New Kind of Corporate Exec," *New York Law Journal,* May 2, 2003, http://www.law.com/jsp/article.jsp?id=1051121819676

137. Kris Maher, "Global Companies Face Reality of Instituting Ethics Programs," *Wall Street Journal,* November 9, 2004, p. B8.

138. Chuck Bartels, "Wal-Mart to Alter Pay System," *Miami Herald,* June 5, 2004, p. 1C.

139. Kara Scannell & Almar Latour, "Raising a Red Flag Isn't Enough," *Wall Street Journal,* April 21, 2004, p. C1.

140. George R. Wratney & Patrick J. Gnazzo, "Are You Serious About Ethics? For Companies That Can't Guarantee Confidentiality, the Answer Is No," *Across the Board,* July/August 2003, http://www.conference-board.org/articles/atb_article.cfm?id=206

141. John Plender & Avinash Persaud, "When Compliance Is Not Enough,' *Financial Times*, August 22, 2006, p. 5.

142. Ibid.

143. Patrick McGeehan, "Most Corporate Ethics Officials Are Critical of Top Officers' Pay," *New York Times,* June 17, 2003, p. C8.

144. For example, see Kaevan Gazdar, "Special Report: Media Responsibility—Making Ethics Headline News," *Ethical Corporation,* October 14, 2007, http://www.ethicalcorp.com/content.asp?ContentID=5433

145. Michel Rocard, "Entente cordiale?" *Kent Bulletin,* The University of Kent at Canterbury, No. 35, Autumn 2000, pp. 10–11, http://www.kent.ac.uk/alumni/pdf/kent35.pdf

146. See Andrew Edgecliffe-Johnson, "When Papers Fold," *Financial Times*, March 17, 2009, p. 7; Leonard Pitts Jr., "As Newspapers Die, Expect No Mourning From the Crooks," *Chicago Tribune*, in *The Daily Yomiuri*, March 31, 2009, p. 17.

147. Tom Hayes & Michael S. Malone, "The Ten-Year Century," *Wall Street Journal*, August 11, 2009, p. A17.

148. http://twitter.com/jkrums/status/1121915133

149. Mark Laity, "The Media: Part of the Problem or Part of the Solution?" *Kent Bulletin,* The University of Kent at Canterbury, No. 42, Spring 2004, pp. 8–10, http://www.kent.ac.uk/alumni/pdf/kent42.pdf

150. Al Jazeera's English channel was launched in November 2006. See William Wallis, "Al-Jazeera Launches News Channel in English," *Financial Times*, November 15, 2006, p. 8, and Alessandra Stanley, "Not Coming Soon to a Channel Near You," *New York Times*, November 16, 2006, p. A22). It arrived on YouTube in April 2007. See Sara Ivry, "Now on YouTube: The Latest News From Al Jazeera, in English," *New York Times*, April 16, 2007, p. C5.

151. "Al Jazeera," *New York Times*, January 9, 2009, p. A7.

152. "According to a study published [in June, 2006] by the Business & Media Institute, in the world of TV entertainment, `businessmen [are] a greater threat to society than terrorists, gangs, or the mob.'" In Review & Outlook, "TV's Killer Capitalists," *Wall Street Journal,* July 14, 2006, p. W9.

153. For an additional dimension to this issue, see Mallen Baker, "Corporate Culture—Crisis Management With Extra Cheese," *Ethical Corporation*, May 11, 2009, http://www.ethicalcorp.com/content .asp?ContentID=6464

154. Stephanie Clifford, "Video Prank at Domino's Goes Sour," *New York Times*, April 16, 2009, p. B5.

155. Quoted in Mark Laity, "The Media: Part of the Problem or Part of the Solution?" *Kent Bulletin,* The University of Kent at Canterbury, No. 42, Spring 2004, pp. 8–10, http://www.kent.ac.uk/alumni/ pdf/kent42.pdf

156. Nick Davies, *Flat Earth News,* Random House UK, 2008, http://www.flatearthnews.net/

157. John Mecklin, "Over the Horizon," *Miller-McCune,* June-July 2008, p. 7.

158. "Business Ethics: Doing Well by Doing Good," *The Economist,* April 22, 2000, pp. 65–68.

159. Noah Oppenheim, "Bookshelf: From Network to Nowhere," *Wall Street Journal,* October 21, 2004, p. D8.

160. Steven Komarow, "U.S. Attorneys Dispatched to Advise Military," *USA Today,* March 10, 2003, http://www.usatoday.com/news/world/iraq/2003-03-10-jags_x.htm

161. National Public Radio, March 15, 2003.

162. Steven Komarow, "U.S. Attorneys Dispatched to Advise Military," *USA Today,* March 10, 2003, http://www.usatoday.com/news/world/iraq/2003-03-10-jags_x.htm

163. Shunji Yanai, former Japanese ambassador to the United States, quoted in "Diplomacy Under Scrutiny," *The Daily Yomiuri,* May 23, 2003, p. 13.

164. Quoted in John Mecklin, "Over the Horizon," *Miller-McCune*, June-July 2008, p. 7.

165. Bill Carter, "With Rivals Ahead, Doubts for CNN's Middle Road," *New York Times*, April 27, 2009, p. B1.

166. Brian Stelter & Tim Arango, "Business News With Attitude," *New York Times*, March 9, 2009, p. B6.

167. Bill Carter, "A Matrix of News Winners Buoys NBC," *New York Times*, March 9, 2009, pp. B1 & B6.

168. Andrew Edgecliffe-Johnson, "Wall St Riveted by Comedy Clash," *Financial Times*, March 14/15, 2009, p. 1.

169. Clarence Page, "A Mad Comic vs. 'Mad Money,'" *Chicago Tribune*, in *The Daily Yomiuri*, March 24, 2009, p. 17.

170. Lionel Barber, "A Flawed First Draft of History," *Financial Times*, April 22, 2009, p. 11.

171. Stefan Stern, "Snap out of It and Smile: Four Reasons to Be Cheerful," *Financial Times*, April 14, 2009, p. 12.

172. http://english.aljazeera.net/

173. David J. Rothkopf, "When the Buzz Bites Back," *Washington Post* in *The Daily Yomiuri,* May 14, 2003, pp. 19 & 23.

174. Gail A. Lasprogata & Marya N. Cotton, "Contemplating 'Enterprise': The Business and Legal Challenges of Social Entrepreneurship," *American Business Law Journal,* Vol. 41, 2003, pp. 67–113.

175. George Melloan, "Global View: As NGOs Multiply, They Expand a New 'Private Sector,'" *Wall Street Journal,* June 22, 2004, p. A19.

176. Howard Rheingold, quoted by Robert D. Hof, "Coming on the Net: People Power," *BusinessWeek,* November 18, 2002, p. 18.

177. David Kushner, "In Your Eyes," *Fast Company Magazine*, November 2008, pp. 80–82, http://www.fastcompany.com/magazine/130/in-your-eyes.html

178. Melanie Warner, "The Sad Life of the Eco-Shopper," *Fast Company Magazine*, November, 2008, p. 92, http://www.fastcompany.com/magazine/130/green-business-the-sad-life-of-the-eco-shopper.html

179. Michael Elliott, "Embracing the Enemy Is Good Business," *Time,* August 13, 2001, p. 29.

180. Jena McGregor, "Consumer Vigilantes," *BusinessWeek*, February 21, 2008, http://www.businessweek.com/magazine/content/08_09/b4073038437662.htm

181. Jo Johnson, "Giving the Goliaths a Good Kicking," *Financial Times*, August 12/13, 2006, p. W2.

182. Robert Scoble, "Brand New Day," *Fast Company Magazine*, May 2009, p. 52.

183. Dennis A. Rondinelli & Ted London, "How Corporations and Environmental Groups Cooperate: Assessing Cross-Sector Alliances and Collaborations, *Academy of Management Executive,* Vol. 17, No. 1, 2003, p. 61.

184. Michael Elliott, "Embracing the Enemy Is Good Business," *Time,* August 13, 2001, p. 29.

185. For an overview of the benefits and dangers of business/NGO partnerships, see Michael Skapinker, "Why Companies and Campaigners Collaborate," *Financial Times*, July 8, 2008, p. 13; Roger Cowe, "Analysis: Business/NGO partnerships–What's the Payback," *Ethical Corporation,* April 16, 2004, http://www.ethicalcorp.com/content.asp?ContentID=1921; Peter Asmus, "NGO Engagement and Partnerships—Ten Lessons for Corporations," *Ethical Corporation,* July 31, 2006, http://www.ethicalcorp.com/content.asp?ContentID=4412

186. Roger Cowe, "Analysis: Business/NGO partnerships–What's the Payback?" *Ethical Corporation Magazine,* April 16, 2004, http://www.ethicalcorp.com/content.asp?ContentID=1921

187. Greenpeace position paper, 1997, http://archive.greenpeace.org/~ozone/index.html

188. Ted London & Dennis Rondinelli, "Partnerships for Learning: Managing Tensions in Nonprofit Organizations' Alliances With Corporations," *Stanford Social Innovation Review,* Winter 2003, p. 35, http://www.ssireview.org/pdf/2003WI_features_london.pdf

189. For additional background on Gilding's transformation from activist to consultant, see Michael Freedman, "From Red to Green," *Forbes Magazine,* October 31, 2005, http://www.forbes.com/global/2005/1031/034A.html

190. Paul Gilding, "Making Market Magic," Ecos Corporation Web site, June 2001.

191. Dennis A. Rondinelli & Ted London, "How Corporations and Environmental Groups Cooperate: Assessing Cross-Sector Alliances and Collaborations, *Academy of Management Executive,* Vol. 17, No. 1, 2003, p. 65.

192. For example, Jena McGregor, "Consumer Vigilantes," *BusinessWeek,* February 21, 2008, http://www.businessweek.com/magazine/content/08_09/b4073038437662.htm, and Stephen Moore & Jonathon Burns, "Welcome to Indonesia," *Wall Street Journal,* March 15, 2006, p. A22.

193. Paul Gilding, "Making Market Magic," Ecos Corporation Web site, June 2001.

194. Product (RED) was started by Bono together with "Bobby Shriver, a nephew of former President John F. Kennedy. Mr. Shriver is chairman of a group called Debt, AIDS, Trade Africa, or DATA." In Eric Pfanner, "Cellphone Companies Join Bono's Efforts to Help Africa," *New York Times,* May 15, 2006, p. C12.

195. Alan Beattie, "Spend, Spend, Spend. Save, Save, Save," *Financial Times,* January 27, 2007, p. 18, http://www.ft.com/cms/s/e96ffa6e-aaa6-11db-b5db-0000779e2340.html

196. Marc Gunther, "Better (Red) Than Dead," *CSRwire.com,* August 5, 2008, http://www.csr-wire.com/csrlive/commentary_detail/110-Better-Red-Than-Dead

197. Tim Weber, "Bono Bets on Red to Battle Aids," *BBC News,* January 26, 2006, http://news.bbc.co.uk/2/hi/business/4650024.stm

198. Alan Beattie, "Product Red Must Be Commercially Sustainable, Not Charity, Says Bono," *Financial Times,* January 27, 2006, p. 4.

199. Kerry Miller, "Humanity Is Now in Fashion," *BusinessWeek,* January 12, 2007, http://images.businessweek.com/ss/07/01/0110_gradtees/source/1.htm

200. Marc Gunther, "Better (Red) Than Dead," *CSRwire.com,* August 5, 2008, http://www.csrwire.com/csrlive/commentary_detail/110-Better-Red-Than-Dead

201. Ibid.

202. Steve Stecklow, "Products Turn Red to Augment AIDS Fund," *Wall Street Journal,* April 13, 2006, p. B1.

203. http://www.joinred.com/Learn/AboutRed/Idea.aspx

204. Christopher Caldwell, "Unaccountable Generosity," *Financial Times,* September 8, 2007, p. 11, http://www.ft.com/cms/s/0/7fe5cc9a-5d75-11dc-8d22-0000779fd2ac.html

205. Marc Gunther, "Better (Red) Than Dead," *CSRwire.com,* August 5, 2008, http://www.csrwire.com/csrlive/commentary_detail/110-Better-Red-Than-Dead

206. Ibid.

207. March 2009, http://www.census.gov/prod/www/religion.htm

208. Bill Symonds, "The Media Hears the Sermon," *BusinessWeek,* December 14, 2005, http://www.businessweek.com/bwdaily/dnflash/dec2005/nf20051214_8338_db016.htm

209. Jon Meacham, "The End of Christian America," *Newsweek,* April 4, 2009, http://www.newsweek.com/id/192583

210. Daniel Stone, "One Nation Under God," *Newsweek* 2009, http://www.newsweek.com/id/192915

211. April 2009, http://www.statistics.gov.uk/focuson/religion/

212. Daniel Stone, "One Nation Under God," *Newsweek,* 2009, http://www.newsweek.com/id/192915

213. See also Hanna Rosin, "Religious Revival," *New York Times Book Review*, April 26, 2009, p. 14; Laurie Goodstein, "More Atheists Are Shouting It From Rooftops," *New York Times*, April 27, 2009, p. A1; Charles M. Blow, "Defecting to Faith," *New York Times*, May 2, 2009, p. A14.

214. See also the book by the British journalist Christopher Hitchins: *God Is Not Great: How Religion Poisons Everything*, Twelve Books, 2007.

215. James Blitz, "BA Under Fire Over Ban on Employee's Crucifix," *Financial Times*, October 16, 2006, p. 3.

216. Ibid.

217. "Veils Harm Equal Rights—Harman," *BBC News*, October 11, 2006, http://news.bbc.co.uk/2/hi/uk_news/politics/6040016.stm

218. Sarah Lyall, "Atheists Decide to Send Their Own Message, on 800 Buses," *New York Times*, January 7, 2009, p. A6.

219. Images of the bus ads can be seen at: http://www.atheistbus.org.uk/bus-photos/

220. Richard Dawkins, *The God Delusion*, Houghton Mifflin Harcourt, 2006.

221. Sarah Lyall, "Atheists Decide to Send Their Own Message, on 800 Buses," *New York Times*, January 7, 2009, p. A6.

222. Bill Symonds, "The Media Hears the Sermon," *BusinessWeek*, December 14, 2005, http://www.businessweek.com/bwdaily/dnflash/dec2005/nf20051214_8338_db016.htm

223. Sandeep Kaushik, "Microsoft Caves on Gay Rights," *The Stranger*, April 21–April 27, 2005, http://www.thestranger.com/seattle/Content?oid=21105

224. Andrea James, "Conservative Pastor Urges Buying Microsoft Stock to Fight Its Gay Rights Efforts," *Seattle Post-Intelligencer*, January 8, 2008, http://www.seattlepi.com/business/346431_antiochmsft08.html

225. Kevin Maher, "Ridiculous, Ridiculous, Don't Be So religulous!" *The Times*, in *The Daily Yomiuri*, April 5, 2009, p. 15.

226. Editorial, "Religion at Work," *Financial Times*, October 17, 2006, p. 12.

227. Devin Stewart, "Is Ethical Capitalism Possible?" *CSRwire.com*, January 29, 2009, http://www.csrwire.com/press/press_release/14072-Is-Ethical-Capitalism-Possible-

228. The full Charter is available at the organization's Web site: http://charterforcompassion.com/

229. Linda Tischler, "God and Mammon at Harvard," *Fast Company*, May 2005, p. 81.

230. Ken Costa, *God at Work: Living Every Day with Purpose*, Continuum Books, 2007.

231. Stefan Stern, "In the Market for a Messiah," *Financial Times*, September 6, 2007, p. 10.

232. Ibid.

233. Rob Wherry, "Putting Faith in Mutual Funds—Religious Investing Sometimes Offers Saintly Returns," *Wall Street Journal*, March 20, 2007, p. D2, http://online.wsj.com/public/article/SB117435124164642157-ELuRqW48rqhoT31fH_m6TSNXab4_20070329.html

234. Gillian Tett, "Islamic Bonds Recruited for Purchase of 007's Favourite Car," *Financial Times*, March 17, 2007, p. 1.

235. As a result of this ban, Christians turned to Jews for money-lending services "since they were presumed to be already excommunicated." Gillian Tett, "Make Money, Not War," *Financial Times*, September 23/24, 2006, p. WK2.

236. "Circle 7, cantos 12–17," *University of Texas at Austin*, http://danteworlds.laits.utexas.edu/circle7.html

237. Ibid.

238. Ibid.

239. Niall Ferguson, "The Ascent of Money," *BBC*, 2008.

240. Robyn Blumner, "Road to Ruin: Usury, Greed and the Paper Economy," *Chicago Tribune*, in *The Daily Yomiuri*, March 31, 2009, p. 16.

241. U.S. Supreme Court, *Marquette National Bank of Minneapolis v. First of Omaha Service Corp.*, 439 U.S. 299 (1978).

242. Robyn Blumner, "Road to Ruin: Usury, Greed and the Paper Economy," *Chicago Tribune*, in *The Daily Yomiuri*, March 31, 2009, p. 16.

243. See also Thomas Geoghegan, "How Unlimited Interest Rates Destroyed the Economy," *Harper's Magazine*, April, 2009, http://www.harpers.org/archive/2009/04/0082450

244. Amy Goodman, "Thomas Geoghegan on 'Infinite Debt: How Unlimited Interest Rates Destroyed the Economy'" *Democracy Now*, March 24, 2009, http://www.democracynow.org/2009/3/24/thomas_geoghegan_on_infinite_debt_how

245. Frederik Balfour, "Islamic Finance May Be on to Something," *BusinessWeek*, November 24, 2008, p. 88.

246. Yaroslav Trofimov, "Malaysia Transforms Rules for Finance Under Islam," *Wall Street Journal*, April 4, 2007, p. A1.

247. For examples of the range of issues covered under the umbrella term *Islamic finance* and to get a sense of how the industry has evolved, see the *Financial Times*'s series of *Special Report: Islamic Finance*: http://www.ft.com/reports/islamicfinance2008 and http://www.ft.com/reports/islamic-finance-2009

248. Yaroslav Trofimov, "Malaysia Transforms Rules for Finance Under Islam," *Wall Street Journal*, April 4, 2007, p. A1.

249. Gillian Tett, "Banks Seek Islamic Scholars Versed in World of Finance," *Financial Times*, May 20/21, 2006, p. 1.

250. Joanna Slater, "When Hedge Funds Meet Islamic Finance," *Wall Street Journal*, August 9, 2007, p. A1.

251. Gillian Tett, "Secondary Trading in Islamic Bonds Promises Earthly Riches," *Financial Times*, July 14, 2006, p. 20.

252. Frederik Balfour, "Islamic Finance May Be on to Something," *BusinessWeek*, November 24, 2008, p. 88.

253. Roula Khalaf, Gillian Tett, & David Oakley, "Eastern Promise Turns to Western Delight," *Financial Times*, January 18, 2007, p. 17.

254. Roula Khalaf & Gillian Tett, "Backwater Sector Moves Into Global Mainstream," *Financial Times, Special Report: Islamic Finance*, May 23, 2007, p. 1.

255. Farhan Bokhari, Roula Khalaf, & Gillian Tett, "Booming Gulf Gives Fillip To Islamic Bonds," *Financial Times*, July 11, 2006, p. 17.

256. Gillian Tett, "Make Money, Not War," *Financial Times*, September 23/24, 2006, p. WK2.

257. Chris Prystay, "Malaysia Seeks Role as Global Player After Nurturing Islamic Bond Market," *Wall Street Journal*, August 9, 2006, p. C1.

258. Yaroslav Trofimov, "Malaysia Transforms Rules for Finance Under Islam," *Wall Street Journal*, April 4, 2007, p. A1.

259. See David Oakley, "Shari'a-Compliant Institutions Buck Trend," *Financial Times, Special Report: Middle East Banking & Finance*, November 25, 2008, p. 6; David Oakley, "Britain Leads Secondary Market for Islamic Bonds," *Financial Times*, February 6, 2007, p. 4; Gillian Tett, "UK Aims to Be Global Centre of Islamic Finance," *Financial Times*, June 13, 2006, p. 3.

260. Shyamantha Asokan, "France and the US Vie for the UK's Crown," *Financial Times Special Report: Islamic Finance*, May 6, 2009, p. 5.

261. James Blitz, "UK Government to Issue West's First Islamic Bond," *Financial Times*, April 23, 2007, p. 4.

262. Marc Chandler, "An Islamic Bond Would Be a Golden Opportunity for the US," *Financial Times*, November 20, 2006, p. 13.

263. Gillian Tett, "Make Money, Not War," *Financial Times*, September 23/24, 2006, pp. WK1–2.

264. Hugh Pope, "Islamic Banking Grows, With All Sorts of Rules," *Wall Street Journal*, May 3, 2005, p. C1.

265. http://www.ftse.com/shariah

266. April 2009, http://www.ftse.com/shariah

267. Samuel G. Freedman, "A Hometown Bank Heeds a Call to Serve Its Islamic Clients," *New York Times*, March 7, 2009, p. A9.

268. Farhan Bokhari, "Dubai's Facility Keeps the Faith," *Financial Times*, April 16, 2007, p. 7.

269. Shyamantha Asokan, "New Class for Islamic Finance," *Financial Times*, January 19, 2009, p. 9.

270. Farhan Bokhari, "Oil Wealth Paves Way for Islamic MBA," *Financial Times*, December 18, 2006, p. 10, http://www.ft.com/cms/s/f3af2530-8c5c-11db-9684-0000779e2340.html

271. See Faiza Saleh Ambah, "Islamic Banking: Steady in Shaky Times," *Washington Post*, October 31, 2008, p. A16; John Aglionby, "Islamic Banks Urged to Show West the Shari`a Was Forward," *Financial Times*, March 3, 2009, p. 3.

272. For an example of how Islamic finance seeks to extend the range of Shari`a-compliant instruments, see Sophia Grene, "Moves Afoot to Plug Gap in Islamic Finance,' *Financial Times FTfm*, August 3, 2009, p. 3.

273. Tarek El Diwany, "How the Banks Are Subverting Islam's Ban on Usury," *Financial Times*, July 14, 2006, p. 11.

274. Ibid.

275. Editorial, "Corporate Responsibility in Modern Times," *Ethical Corporation Magazine*, December, 2005, p. 8.

276. Mallen Baker, "Remuneration—Value Society, Mr President," *Ethical Corporation*, March 11, 2009, http://www.ethicalcorp.com/content.asp?ContentID=6391

277. "'Whose Company Is It?' New Insights Into the Debate Over Shareholders vs. Stakeholders," *Knowledge@Wharton*, October 17, 2007, http://knowledge.wharton.upenn.edu/article.cfm?articleid=1826

278. Novartis Web site, January 2003.

279. Brendan May & Tony Juniper, "NGO Campaigns—Better the Devil You Know?" *Ethical Corporation*, February 2, 2009, http://www.ethicalcorp.com/content.asp?ContentID=6309

280. For a detailed history of Ben & Jerry's, see James E. Austin & James Quinn, "Ben & Jerry's: Preserving Mission and Brand Within Unilever," *Harvard Business School* [Case # 9–306–037], December 8, 2005.

281. Alice & John Tepper Marlin, "A Brief History of Social Reporting," Business Respect, March 9, 2003, http://www.businessrespect.net/page.php?Story_ID=857

282. September 2009, http://www.benjerry.com/activism/mission-statement/

283. Kris Axtman & Ron Scherer, "Enron Lapses and Corporate Ethics," *The Christian Science Monitor*, February 4, 2002, http://www.csmonitor.com/2002/0204/p01s01-ussc.html

284. Ann Zimmerman, "Costco's Dilemma: Be Kind to Its Workers, or Wall Street?" *Wall Street Journal*, March 26, 2004, p. B1.

285. James E. Austin & James Quinn, "Ben & Jerry's: Preserving Mission and Brand Within Unilever," *Harvard Business School* [Case # 9–306–037], December 8, 2005, p. 2.

286. "Ben & Jerry's Takes a Licking," *Eurofood*, February 3, 2000, http://findarticles.com/p/articles/mi_m0DQA/is_2000_Feb_3/ai_59544165/

287. James E. Austin & James Quinn, "Ben & Jerry's: Preserving Mission and Brand Within Unilever," *Harvard Business School* [Case # 9–306–037], December 8, 2005, p. 5.

288. "Unilever Scoops Up Ben & Jerry's," *BBC News*, April 12, 2000, http://news.bbc.co.uk/1/hi/business/710694.stm

289. September 2009, http://www.benjerry.com/activism/mission-statement/

290. Stephen Moore, "Ice Cream Hangover," *Wall Street Journal*, October 20, 2005, p. A15.

291. Ibid.

292. http://www.benjerry.com/activism/mission-statement/

293. James E. Austin & James Quinn, "Ben & Jerry's: Preserving Mission and Brand Within Unilever," *Harvard Business School* [Case # 9–306–037], December 8, 2005, p. 9.

Subject Index

COMPANY INDEX

ABOUT THE AUTHORS

William B. Werther, Jr. is a founding co-director of the Center for Nonprofit Management at the University of Miami. He is a fellow and former chair of the International Society for Productivity and Quality Research, a fellow in the World Academy of Productivity Science, and former chair for the Managerial Consultation Division of the Academy of Management. His teaching and research focus on strategy with its implications for human performance and corporate social responsibility.

Recognizing his 40 years of experience among nonprofit, government, and business organizations, *Fortune,* the *Wall Street Journal,* the *Washington Post,* and the *Nightly Business Report* (PBS) have sought his expertise. Public sector involvement includes work for the White House Conference on Productivity, the U.S. House of Representatives, NASA, and the Arizona State Senate. Private sector work includes Anheuser-Busch, Bell Canada, Citicorp, Fiat, IBM, State Farm, UPS, and scores of others.

He is an award-winning author and teacher. In addition to more than 100 professional articles, his publications include *Third Sector Management* (Georgetown University Press, 2001), *Human Resources and Personnel Management5/E* (McGraw-Hill, 1996), and other books translated into more than a half-dozen languages. He earned a PhD (University of Florida, 1971) in Economics and Business Administration (Phi Beta Kappa). Prior to joining the faculty at the University of Miami in 1985, he was a professor of management at Arizona State University for 14 years. In addition, he teaches at the Universidade do Porto (Portugal), where he serves as visiting professor each spring.

David Chandler is a PhD candidate in strategic management and organization theory at the University of Texas at Austin. His research interests lie at the intersection of the organization and its operating environment. Theoretically, he is interested in explaining why organizations respond in different ways to the same environmental forces, as well as understanding the consequences of these different actions. Empirically, he is interested in studying these questions within the context of corporate social responsibility, organizational ethics, and firm/stakeholder relations.

Since graduating with an undergraduate degree in American Studies: Politics and Government in 1991 (University of Kent, UK), David has divided his time between the United States, the United Kingdom, and Japan, working in the fields of business, politics, and education. In addition to his PhD, David has an MSc in East Asian Business from the University of Sheffield, United Kingdom; an MBA from the University of Miami, Florida; and an MS in Management from the University of Texas at Austin.

Supporting researchers for more than 40 years

Research methods have always been at the core of SAGE's publishing program. Founder Sara Miller McCune published SAGE's first methods book, *Public Policy Evaluation*, in 1970. Soon after, she launched the *Quantitative Applications in the Social Sciences* series—affectionately known as the "little green books."

Always at the forefront of developing and supporting new approaches in methods, SAGE published early groundbreaking texts and journals in the fields of qualitative methods and evaluation.

Today, more than 40 years and two million little green books later, SAGE continues to push the boundaries with a growing list of more than 1,200 research methods books, journals, and reference works across the social, behavioral, and health sciences. Its imprints—Pine Forge Press, home of innovative textbooks in sociology, and Corwin, publisher of PreK–12 resources for teachers and administrators—broaden SAGE's range of offerings in methods. SAGE further extended its impact in 2008 when it acquired CQ Press and its best-selling and highly respected political science research methods list.

From qualitative, quantitative, and mixed methods to evaluation, SAGE is the essential resource for academics and practitioners looking for the latest methods by leading scholars.

For more information, visit **www.sagepub.com**.